Human–Computer Interaction

Alan Dix, Janet Finlay
University of York

Gregory Abowd
Carnegie Mellon University, Pittsburgh

Russell Beale
University of Birmingham

PRENTICE HALL
New York   London   Toronto   Sydney   Tokyo   Singapore

First published 1993 by
Prentice Hall Europe
Campus 400, Maylands Avenue
Hemel Hempstead
Hertfordshire, HP2 7EZ
A division of
Simon & Schuster International Group

Printed and bound in Great Britain at
Redwood Books, Trowbridge, Wiltshire.

Library of Congress Cataloging-in-Publication Data

Human–computer interaction/Alan Dix ... [et al.].
    p. cm.
Includes bibliographical references and index.
ISBN 0-13-458266-7 (hbk.) — ISBN 0-13-437211-5 (pbk.)
1. Human–computer interaction. 2. System design. I. Dix, Alan.
QA76.9.H85H85 1993
004.2'1'019- -dc20

92-43148
CIP

British Library Cataloguing in Publication Data

A catalogue record for this book is available from
the British Library
ISBN 0-13-458266-7 (hbk)
ISBN 0-13-437211-5 (pbk)

5   97 96

Human–Computer Interaction

Contents

Foreword

Human–computer interaction is about devices that seem to exhibit a kind of magic. These devices respond with complex contingencies to actions visited upon them by people. They are used to build 'user illusions' (Alan Kay's term) of reactive paper or virtual worlds or artificial personae. They are used as computational mediators and media for individual and group work. This book is a text for how to engineer such devices.

Starting early in this century, there has been professional concern with how to match tools and machines to humans, their tasks, and their social aspirations. 'Industrial engineering', 'human factors', 'ergonomics', and 'man–machine systems' are all names of professional specialities which took on this task. In recent years, the speciality called 'human–computer interaction' has emerged as another of these, reflecting the twin developments that many machines are being transformed into versions of interactive digital computers and that personal computers have propagated by the million. As a result, the techniques used to build interactive computer systems can be used to build many kinds of machines for many machine users.

Human–computer interaction can be defined as 'the discipline concerned with the design, evaluation, and implementation of interactive computing systems for human use and with the study of major phenomena surrounding them' [3]. It is concerned with the joint performance of tasks by humans and machines; the structure of human–machine communication; the social and organizational interactions with machine design; human capabilities to use machines (including their learnability); algorithms and programming of the interface itself; engineering concerns that arise in designing and building interfaces; the process of specification, design and implementation of interfaces; and design tradeoffs. It is vertically more extensive than human factors, being concerned not just with the human–machine interface of interaction, but also with the technical design of the interacting machine itself. But it is horizontally less extensive than human factors, being limited to a much narrower class of machines.

As a professional community, human–computer interaction dates from about 1982, the date of the Gaithersburg conference on Human Factors in Computing and about the date of the commercial emergence of the personal computer. During the ensuing decade, there was an increase in research and development activities surrounding computer interfaces and the use of computers. The development of the area has reached the point where first steps are being taken to codify the field.

This textbook is one of these first steps and part of that process.

This text comes at an important historical juncture when there are enough scattered results to move the field to a new stage and when there is beginning to be a demand for courses and a process of academic institutionalization. Early texts in a field not only help the field be taught, but they also serve to crystallize the content of the field itself. They must work directly from the tangle and patchwork of literature, designed systems and informal practice to bring order and shape and definition that did not exist before. That codification is then transmitted to students, who further propagate it.

An important part of the development of a field is the development of abstractions that give insight into its phenomena and allow predictions of the consequences of actions or designs. Dix, Finlay, Abowd and Beale give considerable attention in this text to emerging models and other abstractions that provide practical insight and lay the foundations for further progress and thus help the field and its students rise above a mere collection of miscellaneous techniques. At this stage in the development of the human–computer interaction field, their text is likely to change the very field it explicates.

Stuart K. Card

Xerox Palo Alto Research Center

Preface

Human–computer interaction (or HCI) is, put simply, the study of people, computer technology and the ways these influence each other. We study HCI to determine how we can make this computer technology more usable by people. This requires an understanding of at least three things: the computer technology, the people who interact with it and what is meant by 'more usable.' However, there is a fourth aspect which is implicit in the simple definition: understanding the work that people are trying to perform by using the technology. These four strands provide the focus for this book. We discuss human cognitive and physical capabilities and how to incorporate knowledge of these into the design of technology. We consider the technology itself, both in terms of what is available and how we can specify its functionality. We introduce principles and paradigms which embody usability and present methods for evaluating our designs against these. We consider the user's activity, both in terms of the tasks to be performed and the context in which they occur.

But, if this book has four primary areas of interest, it is unified by one central theme: the design of computer technology. Human–computer interaction is a multi-disciplinary subject and we aim to demonstrate the importance of contributions from many disciplines. However, it is only when these contributions affect the actual design of interactive systems that we will see improvements in usability. We therefore stress a principled approach to interactive system design which will fit into a software engineering environment. We describe techniques and models for interaction which can be used within the requirements, specification and analysis stages of a design life cycle. This design process must of course be centred on the user and will therefore incorporate cognitive models, which assess or predict the usability of designs, and analytical or empirical techniques for evaluating whether the system meets the user's requirements.

The book is influenced by several disciplines, drawing particularly on the contributions of psychology, cognitive science and sociology. But it is focused primarily on human–computer interaction from the perspective of computer science. We do not apologize for this. In many instances, computer scientists are trained in systems design or software engineering yet are given no exposure to HCI. Little wonder they then build systems which are unusable. If we can encourage computer scientists and system designers to adopt a user-centred design strategy then we will have succeeded in our aims. This is not to say that the book has nothing to offer students and practitioners from other backgrounds. We hope that psychologists, cognitive scientists, and others with an interest in HCI will find it helpful to consider the user within the wider context of a user-centred design process.

In the book we provide a broad coverage of the important topics within HCI with an emphasis on design methods. We also include a sufficient level of detail and worked examples from everyday activity to allow readers to apply the techniques in practice. The computer science and psychology perspectives are taken to be the major complementary components of a user-centred design process. However, we do not assume that the reader has a deep knowledge of either discipline.

We aimed this book as an introductory text for HCI courses, but hope that its depth and breadth of coverage will also make it appropriate as a core text for more advanced courses and for those eager to begin a research career in HCI. Accordingly, the structure of the book is flexible for use in a variety of courses; the layout provides hints on how material can be selected to meet different needs (for example, a basic foundation course, or a course on models and methods of HCI design).

The book is structured in three parts. The first part covers the basic foundations of HCI in terms of human psychology, computer systems, and the implications of the interaction between them. In Chapter 1 we look at human perception, cognition and problem-solving as factors which influence the usability of a design. This gives us an understanding of what the user can and cannot do. Students with a background in psychology may wish to skip this chapter. We then take a parallel look at the computer in Chapter 2, discussing the technology that is available to the designer, and how it works. This material may be familiar to computer science majors. The final chapter in this part discusses the nature of the interaction between these two, how they communicate and how we can analyze the effectiveness of the interaction. The whole of this part can be used as an introduction to the second two parts, or on its own as the basis for a short introduction to HCI.

The second part concentrates on the design process and the integration of HCI into design practice. In Chapter 4 we look at the history of interactive system design and identify principles which support usability. We then, in Chapter 5, discuss the design process from a software engineering perspective and how this is influenced by insisting on user-centred design. Chapters 6 to 9 discuss modelling techniques which can be used to ensure usability principles are not violated. These include cognitive and user models, task analysis techniques, dialogue models, and mathematically-based software engineering models. In Chapter 10 we survey the support tools and environments that are available to programmers of interactive systems, and in Chapter 11 we look at analytic and empirical methods for evaluating the systems to see if they meet user requirements. Finally, in Chapter 12, we discuss the design of user support systems.

The third part of the book covers two more advanced topics which are currently central research issues in HCI, namely computer-supported cooperative work (CSCW) and multi-sensory interfaces. They are considered advanced topics in so far as they are less commonly found in undergraduate curricula. However, they are pivotal areas of current research interest, so they are included. These chapters serve as a suitable springboard into understanding and pursuing further HCI research and interactive system design.

Any textbook on HCI is necessarily limited: we are using a static, non-interactive medium to convey information about dynamic, interactive systems. HCI is about interactive technology and cannot be adequately learned without exposure to such technology. Many of the exercises in this book therefore encourage readers to experiment with interactive systems, and course organizers are urged to ensure that practical experience goes hand in hand with theoretical training. We hope that the combination of these two will lead to the design of interactive systems which put the user first.

Stylistic conventions

As with all books, we have had to make some global decisions regarding style and terminology. Specifically, in a book in which the central characters are 'the user' and 'the designer', it is difficult to avoid the singular pronoun. We therefore use the pronoun 'he' when discussing the user and 'she' when referring to the designer. In other cases we use 'she' as a generic term. This should not be taken to imply anything about the composition of any actual population.

Similarly, we have adopted the convention of referring to the field of 'Human–Computer Interaction' and the notion of 'human–computer interaction'. In many cases we will also use the abbreviation HCI.

Trademarks

Apple, HyperCard, Lisa, Macintosh, Powerbook and System 7 are trademarks of Apple Computer, Inc. registered in the U.S. and other countries.
Microsoft, MSDOS and Windows are trademarks of Microsoft Corporation.
VAX is a registered trademark of Digital Equipment Corporation.
Postscript is a trademark of Adobe.
UNIX is a trademark of AT&T Bell Laboratories.
SunView is a trademark of Sun Microsystems, Inc.
All other trademarks are acknowledged.

Acknowledgements

In a book of this size, written by four authors, there will always be a myriad of people behind the scenes who have aided, supported and abetted our efforts. We would like to thank all those who provided information, pictures and software which have enhanced the quality of the final product. In particular, we are indebted to Wendy Mackay for the photograph of EVA, Wendy Hall and her colleagues at the University of Southampton for the screen shot of Microcosm, Saul Greenberg for the reactive keyboard, Alistair Edwards for Soundtrack and Christina Engelbart for the photographs of Douglas Engelbart's early chord keyset and mouse. Special thanks also to Simon Shum whose doctoral thesis at the University of York provided invaluable information on design rationale and to Steve Brewster whose report on sound in the interface was also most helpful.

We are also grateful to the reviewers and survey respondents whose feedback helped us to select our subject matter and improve our coverage, and to our colleagues at York, Birmingham and CMU who gave insight, encouragement and tolerance in what has been a long project.

Personal thanks must go to Fiona, Esther, Ruth, Meghan, and Sue who all endured 'The Book' well beyond the call of duty, and Bruno who forewent long walks in the country and instead put up with long hours in the office without complaint.

The efforts of all of these has meant that the book is better than it would otherwise have been. Where it could still be better, we take full responsibility.

Alan Dix
Janet Finlay
Gregory Abowd
Russell Beale

December 1992

Introduction

Why Human–Computer Interaction?

This is the authors' second attempt at writing this introduction. Our first attempt fell victim to a design quirk coupled with an innocent though weary and less than attentive user. The word-processing package we originally used to write this introduction is menu based. Menu items are grouped to reflect their function. The 'save' and 'delete' options, both of which are correctly classified as file-level operations, are consequently adjacent items in the menu. With a cursor controlled by a trackball it is all too easy for the hand to slip, inadvertently selecting delete instead of save. Of course, the delete option, being well thought out, pops up a confirmation box allowing the user to cancel a mistaken command. Unfortunately, the save option produces a very similar confirmation box — it was only as we hit the 'Confirm' button that we noticed the word 'delete' at the top...

Unfortunately, this is an all too common occurrence. Errors such as these, resulting from poor design choices, happen every day. Perhaps they are not catastrophic: after all nobody's life is endangered nor is there environmental damage (unless the designer happens to be nearby or you break something in frustration!). However, when you lose several hours' work with no written notes or backup and a publisher's deadline a week away, 'catastrophe' is certainly the word that springs to mind.

Why is it then that in an age when computers are marketed as 'user friendly' and 'easy to use', simple mistakes like this can still occur? Did the designer of the word-processor actually try to use it with the trackball, or was it just that he or she was so expert with the system that the mistake never arose? We hazard a guess that no one tried to use it when tired and under pressure. But these criticisms are not levied only on the designers of traditional computer software. More and more, our everyday lives involve programmed devices which do not sit on our desk, and these devices are just as unusable. Exactly how many VCR designers understand the universal difficulty people have trying to set their machines to record a television program? Do car radio designers actually think it is safe to use so many knobs and displays that the driver has to divert their attention away from the road completely in order to tune the radio or adjust the volume?

Computers and related devices have to be designed with an understanding that people with specific tasks in mind will want to use them in a way that is seamless with respect to their everyday work. To do this, those who design these systems need to know how to think in terms of the eventual users' tasks and how to translate that knowledge into an executable system. But there is a problem with trying to teach the notion of designing computers for people. All designers *are* people and, most probably, they are users as well. Isn't it therefore intuitive to design for the user? Why does it need to be taught when we all know what a good interface looks like? As a result, the study of human–computer interaction (HCI) tends to come late in the designer's training, if at all. The scenario with which we started shows that this is a mistaken view; it is not at all intuitive or easy to design consistent, robust systems that will cope with all manner of user carelessness. The interface is not something that can be plugged in at the last minute; its design should be developed integrally with the rest of the system. It should not just present a 'pretty face', but should support the tasks that people actually want to do, and forgive the careless mistakes. We therefore need to consider how HCI fits into the design process.

Designing usable systems is not simply a matter of altruism towards the eventual user, or even marketing; it is increasingly a matter of law. National health and safety standards are going to constrain employers to provide their workforce with usable computer systems: not just safe but *usable*. The designers of the future cannot afford to ignore the user or to assume that the user is just like they are. HCI is about to become everyone's business.

What is HCI?

The term *human–computer interaction* has only been in widespread use for a little over a decade, but has its roots in more established disciplines. Systematic study of human performance began in earnest at the beginning of this century in factories, with an emphasis on manual tasks. The Second World War provided the impetus for studying the interaction between humans and machines, as each side strove to produce more effective weapons systems. This led to a wave of interest in the area among researchers and the formation of the Ergonomics Research Society in 1949. Traditionally, ergonomists have been concerned primarily with the physical characteristics of machines and systems, and how these affect user performance. Human Factors incorporates these issues, and more cognitive issues as well. The terms are often used interchangeably, with Ergonomics being the preferred term in the United Kingdom and Human Factors in the English-speaking parts of North America. Both of these disciplines are concerned with user performance in the context of any system, whether computer, mechanical, or manual. As computer use became more widespread, an increasing number of researchers specialized in studying the interaction between people and computers, concerning themselves with the physical, psychological and theoretical aspects of this process.

This research originally went under the name *man–machine interaction*, but this became *human–computer interaction* in recognition of the particular interest in computers and the composition of the user population!

Another strand of research which has influenced the development of HCI is information science and technology. Again the former is an old discipline, predating the introduction of technology, and is concerned with the management and manipulation of information within an organization. The introduction of technology has had a profound effect on the way that information can be stored, accessed and utilized and, consequently, a significant effect on the organization and work environment. Systems analysis has traditionally concerned itself with the influence of technology in the workplace, and fitting the technology to the requirements and constraints of the job. These issues are also the concern of HCI.

HCI draws on many disciplines, as we shall see, but it is in computer science and systems design that it must be accepted as a central concern. For all the other disciplines it can be a specialization, albeit one which provides crucial input; for systems design it is an essential part of the design process. From this perspective, HCI involves the design, implementation and evaluation of interactive systems in the context of the user's task and work.

However, when we talk about human–computer interaction, we do not necessarily envisage a single user with a desktop computer. By *user* we may mean an individual user, a group of users working together, or a sequence of users in an organization, each dealing with some part of the task or process. The user is whoever is trying to get the job done using the technology. By *computer* we mean any technology ranging from the general desktop computer, to a large scale computer system, a process control system or an embedded system. The system may include non-computerized parts, including other people. By *interaction* we mean any communication between a user and computer, be it direct or indirect. Direct interaction involves a dialogue with feedback and control throughout performance of the task. Indirect interaction may involve background or batch processing. The important thing is that the user is interacting with the computer in order to accomplish something.

Who is Involved in HCI?

HCI is undoubtedly a multi-disciplinary subject. The ideal designer of an interactive system would have expertise in a range of topics: psychology and cognitive science to give her knowledge of the user's perceptual, cognitive and problem-solving skills; ergonomics for the user's physical capabilities; sociology to help her understand the wider context of the interaction; computer science and engineering to be able to build the necessary technology; business to be able to market it; graphic design to produce an effective interface presentation; technical writing to produce the manuals, and so it goes on. There is obviously too much expertise here to be held by one person (or indeed four!), perhaps even too much for the average design team. Indeed, although HCI is recognized as an interdisciplinary subject, in practice people tend to take a strong stance on one side or another. However, it is not possible to design effective interactive systems from one discipline in isolation. Input is needed from all sides. For example, a beautifully designed graphic display may be unusable if it ignores dialogue constraints or the psychological limitations of the user.

In this book we want to encourage the multi-disciplinary view of HCI but we too have our 'stance', as computer scientists. We are interested in answering a particular question. How do principles and methods from each of these contributing disciplines in HCI help us to design better systems? In this we must be pragmatists rather than theorists: we want to know how to apply the theory to the problem rather than just acquire a deep understanding of the theory. Our goal, then, is to be multi-disciplinary but practical. We concentrate particularly on computer science, psychology and cognitive science as core subjects, and on their application to design; other disciplines are consulted to provide input where relevant.

Theory and HCI

Unfortunately for us, there is no general and unified theory of HCI that we can present. Indeed, it may be impossible ever to derive one; it is certainly out of our reach today. However, there is an underlying principle that forms the basis of our own views on HCI, and it is captured in our claim that people use computers to accomplish work. This outlines the three major issues of concern: the people, the computers and the tasks that are performed. The system must support the user's task, which gives us a fourth focus, usability: if the system forces the user to adopt an unacceptable mode of work then it is not usable.

There are, however, those who would dismiss our concentration on the task, saying that we do not even know enough about a theory of human tasks to support them in design. There is a good argument here (to which we return in Chapter 5). However, we can live with this confusion about what real tasks are because our understanding of tasks at the moment is sufficient to give us direction in design. The user's current tasks are studied and then supported by computers, which can in turn affect the nature of the original task and cause it to evolve. To illustrate, word processing has made it easy to manipulate paragraphs and reorder documents, allowing writers a completely new freedom that has affected writing styles. No longer is it vital to plan and construct text in an ordered fashion, since free-flowing prose can easily be restructured at a later date. This evolution of task in turn affects the design of the ideal system. However, we see this evolution as providing a motivating force behind the system development cycle, rather than a refutation of the whole idea of supportive design.

The question of whether HCI, or more importantly the design of interactive systems and the user interface in particular, is a science or a craft discipline is an interesting one. Does it involve artistic skill and fortuitous insight or reasoned methodical science? Here we can draw an analogy with architecture. The most impressive structures, the most beautiful buildings, the innovative and imaginative creations that provide aesthetic pleasure, all require inventive inspiration in design and a sense of artistry, and in this sense the discipline is a craft. However, these structures also have to be able to stand up, to fulfil their purpose successfully, and to be able to do this the architect has to use science. So it is for HCI: beautiful and/or novel interfaces are artistically pleasing *and* capable of fulfilling the tasks required; a marriage of art and science into a successful whole. We want to reuse lessons learned from the past about how to achieve good results and avoid bad ones. For this we require both craft and science. Innovative ideas lead to more usable systems, but in order to maximize the potential benefit from the ideas, we need to understand not only that they work, but how and why they work. This scientific rationalization allows us to reuse related concepts in similar situations, in much the same way that architects can produce a bridge and know that it will stand, since it is based upon tried and tested principles.

The craft–science tension becomes even more difficult when we consider novel systems. Their increasing complexity means that our personal ideas of good and bad are no longer enough; for a complex system to be well designed we need to rely on something more than simply our intuition. Designers may be able to think about how one user would want to act, but how about groups? And what about new media? Our ideas of how best to share workloads or present video information are open to debate and question even in non-computing situations, and the incorporation of one version of good design into a computer system is quite likely to be unlike anyone else's version. Different people work in different ways, whilst different media colour the nature of the interaction; both can dramatically change the very nature of the original task. In order to assist designers, it is unrealistic to assume that they can rely on artistic skill and perfect insight to develop usable systems. Instead we have to provide them with an understanding of the concepts involved, a scientific view of the reasons why certain things are successful whilst others are not, and then allow their creative nature to feed off this information. Creative flow, underpinned with science. Or maybe scientific method, accelerated by artistic insight. The truth is that HCI is required to be both a craft and a science in order to be successful.

HCI in the Curriculum

If HCI involves both craft and science then it must, in part at least, be taught. Imagination and skill may be qualities innate in the designer or developed through experience, but the underlying theory must be learned. In the past, when computers were used primarily by expert specialists, concentration on the interface was a luxury that was often relinquished. Now designers cannot afford to ignore the interface in favour of the functionality of their systems: the two are too closely intertwined. If the interface is poor, the functionality is obscured; if it is well designed, it will allow the system's functionality to support the user's task.

Increasingly, therefore, computer science educators cannot afford to ignore HCI. We would go as far as to claim that HCI should be integrated into every computer science or software engineering course, either as a recurring feature of other modules or, preferably, as a module itself. It should not be viewed as an 'optional extra' (although, of course, more advanced HCI options can complement a basic core course). This view is shared by the ACM SIGCHI curriculum development group, who propose a curriculum for such a core course [3]. The topics included in this book, although developed without reference to this curriculum, cover the main emphases of it, and include enough detail and coverage to support specialized options as well.

In courses other than computer science, HCI may well be an option specializing in a particular area, such as cognitive modelling or task analysis. Selected use of the relevant chapters of this book can also support such a course.

HCI must be taken seriously by designers and educators if the requirement for additional complexity in the system is to be matched by increased clarity and usability in the interface. In this book we demonstrate how this can be done in practice.

Part I

Foundations

This part is concerned with the fundamental components of an interactive system: the human user, the computer system itself and the nature of the interactive process. This breakdown is reflected in the chapters.

Chapter 1 discusses the psychological and physiological attributes of the user, providing us with a basic overview of the capabilities and limitations that affect our ability to use computer systems. It is only when we have an understanding of the user at this level that we can understand what makes for successful designs. Chapter 2 considers the computer in a similar way. Input and output devices are described and explained and the effect that their individual characteristics have on the interaction highlighted. The computational power and memory of the computer is another important component in determining what can be achieved in the interaction, whilst due attention is also paid to paper output since this forms one of the major uses of computers and user's tasks today. Having approached interaction from both the human and the computer's side, we then turn our attention to the dialogue between them in Chapter 3. Models of interaction are presented, and the different paradigms for interaction are discussed.

Chapter 1

The Human

Overview

- Humans are limited in their capacity to process information. This has important implications for design.

- Information is received and responses given via a number of input and output channels:

  - visual channel
  - auditory channel
  - haptic channel
  - movement

- Information is stored in memory:

  - sensory memory
  - short-term (working) memory
  - long-term memory

- Information is processed and applied:

  - reasoning
  - problem-solving
  - skill acquisition
  - error

- Users share common capabilities but are individuals with differences which should not be ignored.

1.1 Introduction

This chapter is the first of three in which we introduce some of the 'foundations' of HCI. We start with the human, the central character in any discussion of interactive systems. The human, the *user*, is, after all, the one whom computer systems are designed to assist. It is fitting, therefore, that the requirements of the user should be our first priority.

In this chapter we will look at areas of human psychology coming under the general banner of *cognitive psychology*. This may seem a far cry from designing and building interactive computer systems, but it is not. In order to design something for someone, we need to understand the capabilities and limitations of that person. We need to know if there are things that person will find difficult or, even, which they will not be able to do at all. It will also help us to know what people find easy and how we can help them by encouraging these things. We will look at aspects of cognitive psychology which have a bearing on the use of computer systems: how humans perceive the world around them, how they store and process information and solve problems, and how they physically manipulate objects.

We have already said that we will restrict our study to those aspects which are relevant to HCI. One way to structure our discussion of these areas is to view the user in a way which highlights the aspects in which we are most interested. In other words to think of a simplified *model* of what is actually going on. Many models have been proposed and it useful to consider one of the most influential in passing, to understand the context of the discussion that is to follow. In 1983, Card, Moran and Newell [28] described the *Model Human Processor*, which is a simplified view of the human processing involved in interacting with computer systems. The model comprises three subsystems: the perceptual system, handling sensory stimulus from the outside world, the motor system, which controls actions, and the cognitive system, which provides the necessary processing to connect the two. Each of these subsystems has its own processor and memory, although obviously the complexity of these in each case varies depending on the complexity of the tasks the subsystem has to perform. The model also includes a number of *principles of operation* which dictate the behaviour of the systems under certain conditions.

We will retain the analogy of the user as an information processing system, but in our model, make the analogy closer to that of a conventional computer system. Information comes in, is stored and processed, and information is passed out. We will therefore discuss three components of this system: input–output, memory and processing. In the human, we are dealing with an intelligent information processing system, and processing therefore encompasses problem-solving, learning, and, consequently, making mistakes. This model is obviously a simplification of the real situation, since memory and processing are required at all levels, as we have seen in the Model Human Processor. However, it is convenient as a way of grasping how information is handled by the human system. The human, unlike the computer, is also influenced by external factors such as the social and organizational environment, and we need to be aware of these influences as well. However, we will ignore such factors for now and concentrate on the human's information processing capabilities only. We will return to social and organizational influences in Chapter 3.

In this chapter, we will first look at the human's input–output channels, the senses and responders or effectors. This will involve some low-level processing. Secondly, we will consider human memory and how it works. We will then think about how humans perform complex problem-solving, how they learn and acquire skills, and why they make mistakes. Finally, we will discuss how these things can help us in the design of computer systems.

1.2 Input–Output Channels

A person's interaction with the outside world occurs through information being received and sent: input and output. In an interaction with a computer the user receives information that is output by the computer, and responds by providing input to the computer — the user's output becomes the computer's input and vice versa. Consequently the use of the terms input and output may lead to confusion so we shall blur the distinction somewhat and concentrate on the channels involved. This blurring is appropriate since, although a particular channel may have a primary role as input or output in the interaction, it is more than likely that it is also used in the other role. For example, sight may be used primarily in receiving information from the computer, but it can also be used to provide information to the computer, for example, by fixating on a particular screen point.

Input in the human occurs mainly through the senses and output through the motor control of the effectors. There are of course five major senses: sight, hearing, touch, taste and smell. Of these, the first three are the most important to HCI. Taste and smell do not currently play a significant role in HCI, and it is not clear whether they could be exploited at all in general computer systems, although they could have a role to play in more specialized systems (smells to give warning of malfunction, for example). However, vision, hearing and touch are central.

Similarly there are a number of effectors, including the limbs, fingers, eyes, head and vocal system. In the interaction with the computer, the fingers play the primary role, through typing or mouse control, with lesser use of speech, and eye and head position.

Imagine using a personal computer (PC) with a mouse and a keyboard. The application you are using has a graphical interface, with menus, icons and windows. (If you are unfamiliar with this technology, skip forward to Chapter 2 where it is described more fully.) In your interaction with this system you receive information primarily by sight, from what appears on the screen. However, you may also receive information by ear: for example, the computer may 'beep' at you if you make a mistake. Touch plays a part too in that you may feel a key depressing or the orientation of the mouse, which provides vital feedback about what you have done. You yourself send information to the computer mainly by hand, either by hitting keys or moving the mouse. Sight and hearing do not play a direct role in sending information in this example, although they may be used to receive information from a third source (for example, a book, or the words of another person) which is then transmitted to the computer.

In this section we will look at the main elements of such an interaction, first considering the role and limitations of the three primary senses and going on to consider motor control of the hands.

1.2.1 Vision

Human vision is a highly complex activity with a range of physical and perceptual limitations, yet it is the primary source of information for the average person. We can roughly divide visual perception into two stages: the physical reception of the stimulus from the outside world, and the processing and interpretation of that stimulus. On the one hand the physical properties of the eye and the visual system mean that there are certain things that cannot be seen by the human; on the other the interpretative capabilities of visual processing allow images to be constructed from incomplete information. We need to understand both stages as both influence what can and cannot be perceived visually by a human being, which in turn directly affects the way that we design computer systems. We will begin by looking at the eye as a physical receptor, and then go on to consider the processing involved in basic vision.

The human eye

Vision begins with light. The eye is a mechanism for receiving light and transforming it into electrical energy. Light is reflected from objects in the world and their image is focused upside-down on the back of the eye. The receptors in the eye transform it into electrical signals which are passed to the brain.

The eye has a number of important components (see Figure 1.1) which we will look at in more detail. The *cornea* and *lens* at the front of the eye focus the light into a sharp image on the back of the eye, the *retina*. The retina is light sensitive and contains two types of *photoreceptor*: *rods* and *cones*.

Rods are highly sensitive to light and therefore allow us to see under a low level of illumination. However, they are unable to resolve fine detail and are subject to light saturation. This is the reason for the temporary blindness we get when moving from a darkened room into sunlight: the rods have been active and are saturated by the sudden light. The cones do not operate either as they are suppressed by the rods. We are therefore temporarily unable to see at all. There are approximately 120 million rods per eye which are mainly situated towards the edges of the retina. Rods therefore dominate peripheral vision.

Cones are the second type of receptor in the eye. They are less sensitive to light than the rods and can therefore tolerate more light. There are three types of cone,

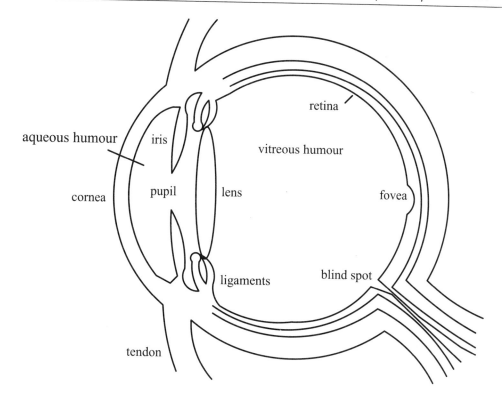

Figure 1.1   *The human eye*

each sensitive to a different wavelength of light. This allows colour vision. The eye has approximately 6 million cones, mainly concentrated on the *fovea*, a small area of the retina on which images are fixated.

Although the retina is mainly covered with photoreceptors there is one *blind spot* where the optic nerve enters the eye. The blind spot has no rods or cones, yet our visual system compensates for this so that in normal circumstances we are unaware of it.

The retina also has specialized nerve cells called *ganglion cells*. There are two types: X-cells, which are concentrated in the fovea and are responsible for the early detection of pattern; and Y-cells which are more widely distributed in the retina and are responsible for the early detection of movement. The distribution of these cells mean that, while we may not be able to detect changes in pattern in peripheral vision, we can perceive movement.

Visual perception

Understanding the basic construction of the eye goes some way to explaining the physical mechanisms of vision but visual perception is more than this. The information received by the visual apparatus must be filtered and passed to processing elements which allow us to recognize coherent scenes, disambiguate relative distances and differentiate colour. We will consider some of the capabilities and limitations of visual processing later, but first we will look a little more closely at how we perceive size and depth, brightness and colour, each of which is crucial to the design of effective visual interfaces.

Perceiving size and depth. Imagine you are standing on a mountain top. Beside you on the summit you can see rocks, sheep and a small tree. On the hillside is a farm house with outbuildings and farm vehicles. Someone is on the track, walking towards the summit. Below in the valley is a small market town.

Even in describing such a scene the notions of size and distance predominate. Our visual system is easily able to interpret the images which it receives to take account of these things. We can identify similar objects regardless of the fact that they appear to us to be of vastly different sizes. In fact, we can use this information to judge distances.

So how does the eye perceive size, depth and relative distances? To understand this we must consider how the image appears on the retina. As we noted in the previous section, reflected light from the object forms an upside-down image on the retina. The size of that image is specified as a *visual angle*. Figure 1.2 illustrates how the visual angle is calculated.

If we were to draw a line from the top of the object to a central point on the front of the eye and a second line from the bottom of the object to the same point, the visual angle of the object is the angle between these two lines. Visual angle is affected by both the size of the object and its distance from the eye. Therefore if two objects are at the same distance, the larger one will have the larger visual angle. Similarly, if two objects of the same size are placed at different distances from the eye, the furthest one will have the smaller visual angle. The visual angle indicates how much of the field of view is taken by the object. The visual angle measurement is given in either degrees or *minutes of arc*, where 1 degree is equivalent to 60 minutes of arc, and 1 minute of arc to 60 seconds of arc.

So how does an object's visual angle affect our perception of its size? Firstly, if the visual angle of an object is too small we will be unable to perceive it at all. *Visual acuity* is the ability of a person to perceive fine detail. A number of measurements have been established to test visual acuity, most of which are included in standard eye tests. For example, a person with normal vision can detect a single line if it has a visual angle of 0.5 seconds of arc. Spaces between lines can be detected at 30 seconds to 1 minute of visual arc. These represent the limits of human visual acuity.

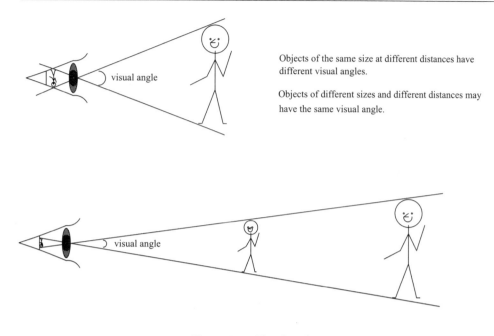

Objects of the same size at different distances have different visual angles.

Objects of different sizes and different distances may have the same visual angle.

Figure 1.2 *Visual angle*

However, assuming that we can perceive the object, does its visual angle affect our perception of its size? Given that the visual angle of an object is reduced as it gets further away, we might expect that we would perceive the object as smaller. In fact, our perception of an object's size remains constant even if its visual angle changes. So a person's height is perceived as constant even if he moves further from you. This is the *law of size constancy*, and it suggests that our perception of size relies on factors other than the visual angle.

One of these factors is our perception of depth. If we return to the hilltop scene there are a number of *cues* which we can use to determine the relative positions and distances of the objects which we see. If objects overlap, the object which is partially covered is perceived to be in the background, and therefore further away. Similarly, the size and height of the object in our field of view provides a cue to its distance. A third cue is familiarity; if we expect an object to be of a certain size then we can judge its distance accordingly. This has been exploited for humour in advertising: a recent drinks advertisement shows a man apparently walking away from a bottle in the foreground. As he walks, he bumps into the bottle, which is in fact a giant one in the background!

Perceiving brightness. A second aspect of visual perception is the perception of *brightness*. Brightness is in fact a subjective reaction to levels of light. It is affected by *luminance* which is the amount of light emitted by an object. The luminance of an object is dependent on the amount of light falling on the object's surface and its reflective properties. Luminance is a physical characteristic and can be measured using a *photometer*. *Contrast* is related to luminance: it is a function of the luminance of an object and the luminance of its background.

Although brightness is a subjective response, it can be described in terms of the amount of luminance that gives a *just noticeable difference* in brightness. However, the visual system itself also compensates for changes in brightness. In dim lighting, the rods predominate vision. Since there are fewer rods on the fovea, objects in low lighting can be seen less easily when fixated upon, and are more visible in peripheral vision. In normal lighting, the cones take over.

Visual acuity increases with increased luminance. This may be an argument for using high display luminance. However, as luminance increases, *flicker* also increases. The eye will perceive a light switched on and off rapidly as constantly on. However, if the speed of switching is less than 50 Hz then the light is perceived to flicker. In high luminance flicker can be perceived at over 50 Hz. Flicker is also more noticeable in peripheral vision. This means that the larger the display (and consequently the more peripheral vision that it occupies), the more it will appear to flicker.

Perceiving colour. A third factor that we need to consider is perception of colour. Colour is usually regarded as being made up of three components: *hue, intensity* and *saturation*. Hue is determined by the spectral wavelength of the light. Blues have short wavelengths, greens medium and reds long. Approximately 150 different hues can be discriminated by the average person. Intensity is the brightness of the colour, and saturation is the amount of whiteness in the colour. By varying these two, we can perceive in the region of 7 million different colours. However, the number of colours that can be identified by an individual without training is far fewer (in the region of 10).

The eye perceives colour because the cones are sensitive to lights of different wavelengths. There are three different types of cone, each sensitive to a different colour (blue, green and red). Colour vision is best in the fovea, and worst at the periphery where rods predominate. It should also be noted that only 3-4% of the fovea is occupied by cones which are sensitive to blue light. Therefore blue acuity is lower.

Finally, we should remember that around 8% of males and 1% of females suffer from colour blindness, most commonly being unable to discriminate between red and green.

Figure 1.3   *An ambiguous shape?*

The capabilities and limitations of visual processing

In considering the way in which we perceive images we have already encountered some of the capabilities and limitations of the human visual processing system. However, we have concentrated largely on low-level perception. Visual processing involves the transformation and interpretation of a complete image, from the light that is thrown onto the retina. As we have already noted, our expectations affect the way an image is perceived. For example, if we know that an object is a particular size, we will perceive it as that size no matter how far it is from us.

Visual processing compensates for the movement of the image on the retina, which occurs as we move around and as the object which we see moves. Although the retinal image is moving, the image that we perceive is stable. Similarly, colour and brightness of objects are perceived as constant, in spite of changes in luminance.

This ability to interpret and exploit our expectations can be used to resolve ambiguity. For example, consider the image shown in Figure 1.3. What do you perceive? Now consider Figure 1.4 and Figure 1.5. The context in which the object appears allows our expectations to clearly disambiguate the interpretation of the object, as either a B or a 13.

However, it can also create optical illusions. For example, consider Figure 1.6. Which line is longer? Most people when presented with this will claim that the top line is longer than the bottom. However, in fact, the two lines are the same length. This may be due to a false application of the law of size constancy: the top line appears like a concave edge, the bottom like a convex edge. The former therefore seems further away than the latter and is therefore scaled to appear larger. A similar illusion is the Ponzo illusion (Figure 1.7). Here the top line appears longer, due to the distance effect, although both lines are the same length. These illusions demonstrate that our perception of size is not completely reliable.

Another illusion created by our expectations compensating an image is the proof reading illusion. Read the text in Figure 1.8 quickly. Did you notice anything

Figure 1.4   *ABC*

Figure 1.5   *12 13 14*

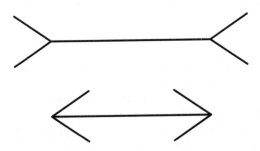

Figure 1.6   *The Muller Lyer illusion*

Figure 1.7   *The Ponzo illusion*

The quick brown

fox jumps over the

the lazy dog.

Figure 1.8   *Is this text correct?*

wrong with it? Most people reading this rapidly will read it correctly, although closer inspection shows that the word 'the' is repeated in lines 2 and 3.

These are just a few examples of how the visual system compensates, and sometimes overcompensates, to allow us to perceive the world around us.

Reading

So far we have concentrated on the perception of images in general. However, the perception and processing of text is a special case of this that it is important to consider in the context of interface design, which invariably requires some textual display. We will therefore end this section by looking at *reading*. There are several stages in the reading process. First, the visual pattern of the word on the page is perceived. It is then decoded with reference to an internal representation of language. The final stages of language processing include syntactic and semantic analysis and operate on phrases or sentences.

We are most concerned with the first two stages of this process and how they influence interface design. During reading, the eye makes jerky movements called *saccades* followed by fixations. Perception occurs during the fixation periods, which account for approximately 94% of the time elapsed. The eye moves backwards over the text as well as forwards, in what are known as *regressions*. If the text is complex there will be more regressions.

Adults read approximately 250 words a minute. It is unlikely that words are scanned serially, character by character, since experiments have shown that words can be recognized as quickly as single characters. Instead, familiar words are recognized using word shape. This means that removing the word shape clues (for example, by capitalizing words) is detrimental to reading speed and accuracy.

The speed at which text can be read is a measure of its legibility. Experiments have shown that standard font sizes of 9 to 12 points are equally legible, given proportional spacing between lines [175]. Similarly line lengths of between 2.3 and 5.2 inches are equally legible. However, there is evidence that reading from a computer screen is slower than from a book [118]. This is thought to be due to a number of factors including a longer line length, fewer words to a page, orientation and the familiarity of the medium of the page. These factors can of course be reduced by careful design of textual interfaces.

A final word about the use of contrast in visual display. A negative contrast (dark characters on a light screen) provides higher luminance and, therefore, increased acuity, than a positive contrast. This will in turn increase legibility. However, it will also be more prone to flicker. Experimental evidence suggests that in practice negative contrast displays are preferred and result in more accurate performance [15].

1.2.2   Hearing

The sense of hearing is viewed as secondary to that of sight, but we tend to underestimate the amount of information that we receive through our ears. Close your eyes for a moment and listen. What sounds can you hear? Where are they coming from? What is making them? As I sit at my desk I can hear cars passing on the road outside, machinery working on a site nearby, the drone of a plane overhead and bird song. But I can also tell *where* the sounds are coming from, and estimate how far away they are. So from the sounds I hear I can tell that a car is passing on a particular road near my house, and which direction it is travelling in. I know that building work is in progress in a particular location, and that a certain type of bird is perched in the tree in my garden.

The auditory system has a tremendous capacity for conveying information about our environment. But how does it work?

The human ear

Just as vision begins with light, hearing begins with vibrations in the air or *sound waves*. The ear receives these vibrations and transmits them, through various stages, to the auditory nerves. The ear comprises three sections, commonly known as the *outer ear, middle ear* and *inner ear*.

The outer ear is the visible part of the ear. It has two parts: the *pinna* which is the structure which is attached to the sides of the head, and the *auditory canal* along which sound waves are passed to the middle ear. The outer ear serves two purposes. Firstly, it protects the sensitive middle ear from damage. The auditory canal contains wax which prevents dust, dirt and over-inquisitive insects reaching the middle ear. It also maintains the middle ear at a constant temperature. Secondly, the pinna and auditory canal serve to amplify some sounds.

The middle ear is a small cavity, connected to the outer ear by the *tympanic membrane* or ear drum, and to the inner ear by the *cochlea*. Within the cavity are the *ossicles*, the smallest bones in the body. Sound waves pass along the auditory canal and vibrate the eardrum which in turn vibrates the ossicles, which transmit the vibrations to the cochlea, and so into the inner ear. This 'relay' is required because, unlike the air-filled outer and middle ears, the inner ear is filled with a denser cochlean liquid. If passed directly from the air to the liquid, the transmission of the sound waves would be poor. By transmitting them via the ossicles the sound waves are concentrated and amplified.

The waves are passed into the liquid-filled cochlea in the inner ear. Within the cochlea are delicate hair cells or *cilia* which bend because of the vibrations in the cochlean liquid and release a chemical transmitter which causes impulses in the auditory nerve.

Processing sound

As we have seen, sound is changes or vibrations in air pressure. It has a number of characteristics which we can differentiate. *Pitch* is the frequency of the sound. A low frequency produces a low pitch, a high frequency, a high pitch. *Loudness* is proportional to the amplitude of the sound; the frequency remains constant. *Timbre* relates to the type of the sound: sounds may have the same pitch and loudness but be made by different instruments and so vary in timbre. We can also identify a sound's location, since the two ears receive slightly different sounds, due to the time difference between the sound reaching the two ears and the reduction in intensity caused by the sound waves reflecting from the head.

The human ear can hear frequencies from about 20 Hz to 15 kHz. It can distinguish frequency changes of less than 1.5 Hz at low frequencies but is less accurate at high frequencies. Different frequencies trigger activity in neurons in different parts of the auditory system, and cause different rates of firing of nerve impulses.

The auditory system performs some filtering of the sounds received, allowing us to ignore background noise and concentrate on important information. We are selective in our hearing, as illustrated by the *cocktail party effect*, where we can hear our name spoken across a crowded noisy room. However, if sounds are too loud, or frequencies too similar, we are unable to differentiate sound.

As we have seen, sound can convey a remarkable amount of information. It is rarely used to its potential in interface design, usually being confined to warning sounds. However, the ear can differentiate quite subtle sound changes and can recognize familiar sounds without concentrating attention on the sound source. This suggests that sound could be used more extensively in interface design, to convey information about the system state for example. This is discussed in more detail in Chapter 15.

1.2.3 Touch

The third and last of the senses that we will consider is touch or *haptic perception*. Although this sense is viewed as less important than sight or hearing, imagine life without it. Touch provides us with vital information about our environment. It tells us when we touch something hot or cold, and can therefore act as a warning. It also provides us with feedback when we attempt to lift an object, for example. Consider the act of picking up a glass of water. If we could only see the glass and not feel when our hand made contact with it or feel its shape, the speed and accuracy of the action would be reduced. This is the experience of users of certain *virtual reality* games: they can see the computer-generated objects which they need to manipulate but they have no physical sensation of touching them. Watching such users can be an informative and amusing experience! Touch is therefore an important means of feedback, and this is no less so in using computer systems.

Feeling buttons depress is an important part of the task of pressing the button. Also, we should be aware that, although for the average person, haptic perception is a secondary source of information, for those whose other senses are impaired, it may be vitally important. For such users, interfaces such as Braille may be the primary source of information in the interaction. We should not therefore underestimate the importance of touch.

The apparatus of touch differs from that of sight and hearing in that it is not localized. We receive stimuli through the skin. The skin contains three types of sensory receptor: *thermoreceptors* respond to heat and cold, *nociceptors* respond to intense pressure, heat and pain, and *mechanoreceptors* respond to pressure. It is the last of these that we are concerned with in relation to human–computer interaction.

There are two kinds of mechanoreceptor, which respond to different types of pressure. *Rapidly adapting mechanoreceptors* respond to immediate pressure as the skin is indented. These receptors also react more quickly with increased pressure. However, they stop responding if continuous pressure is applied. *Slowly adapting mechanoreceptors* respond to continuously applied pressure.

Although the whole of the body contains such receptors, some areas have greater sensitivity or acuity than others. It is possible to measure the acuity of different areas of the body using the *two point threshold test*. Take two pencils, held so their tips are about 12 mm apart. Touch the points to your thumb and see if you can feel two points. If you cannot, move the points a little further apart. When you can feel two points, measure the distance between them. The greater the distance, the lower the sensitivity. You can repeat this test on different parts of your body. You should find that the measure on the forearm is around ten times that of the finger or thumb. The fingers and thumbs have the highest acuity.

A second aspect of haptic perception is *kinesthesis*: awareness of the position of the body and limbs. This is due to receptors in the joints. Again there are three types: rapidly adapting which respond when a limb is moved in a particular direction; slowly adapting which respond to both movement and static position; and positional receptors which only respond when a limb is in a static position. This perception affects both comfort and performance. For example, for a touch typist, awareness of the relative positions of the fingers and feedback from the keyboard are very important.

1.2.4 *Movement*

Before leaving this section on the human's input–output channels, we need to consider motor control and how the way we move affects our interaction with computers. A simple action such as hitting a button in response to a question involves a number of processing stages. The stimulus (of the question) is received through the sensory receptors and transmitted to the brain. The question is processed and a valid response generated. The brain then signals the appropriate muscles to respond. Each of these stages takes time: which can be roughly divided into reaction time and movement time.

Movement time is obviously dependent largely on the physical characteristics of the subjects: their age and fitness for example. Reaction time should not be underestimated, however. This is dependent on the sense through which the stimulus is received. A person can react to an auditory signal in approximately 150 ms, to a visual signal in 200 ms and to pain in 700 ms. However, a combined signal will result in the quickest response. Factors such as skill or practice can reduce reaction time, and fatigue can increase it.

A second measure of motor skill is accuracy. One question that we should ask is whether speed of reaction results in reduced accuracy. This is dependent on the task and the user. In some cases, requiring increased reaction time reduces accuracy. This is the premise behind many arcade and video games where less skilled users fail at levels of play that require faster responses. However, for skilled operators this is not necessarily the case. Studies of keyboard operators have shown that, although the faster operators were up to twice as fast as the others, the slower ones made ten times the errors.

Speed and accuracy of movement are important considerations in the design of interactive systems, primarily in terms of the time taken to move to a particular target on a screen. The target may be a button, a menu item or an icon, for example. The time taken to hit a target is a function of the size of the target and the distance that has to be moved. This is formalized in *Fitts' law* [66]. There are many variations of this formula, which have varying constants, but they are all very similar. One common form is

$$\text{Movement time} = a + b \log_2(\text{Distance}/\text{Size} + 1)$$

where a and b are empirically determined constants.

This affects the type of target we design. Since users will find it difficult to manipulate small objects, targets should generally be as large as possible and the distance to be moved as small as possible. This has led to suggestions that pie chart shaped menus are preferable to lists since all options are equidistant. However, if lists are used, the most frequently used options can be placed closest to the user's start point (for example, at the top of the menu).

1.3 Human Memory

Have you ever played the party game that goes along the lines of 'I went to the market and bought a lemon...'? Each player has to recount the shopping list so far and add another item. As the list gets longer the mistakes become more frequent until one person emerges the winner. Such games rely on our ability to store and retrieve information, even seemingly arbitrary items. This is the job of our memory system.

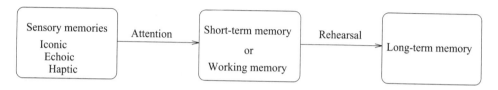

Figure 1.9 *A model of the structure of memory*

Indeed, much of our everyday activity relies on memory. As well as storing all our factual knowledge, our memory contains our knowledge of actions or procedures. It allows us to repeat actions, to use language, and to use new information received via our senses. It also gives gives us our sense of identity, by preserving information from our past experiences.

But how does our memory work? How do we remember arbitrary lists such as those generated in the memory game? Why do some people remember more easily than others? And what happens when we forget?

In order to answer questions such as these, we need to understand some of the capabilities and limitations of human memory. Memory is the second part of our model of the human as an information processing system. However, as we noted earlier, such a division is simplistic since, as we shall see, memory is associated with each level of processing. Bearing this in mind, we will consider the way in which memory is structured and the activities which take place within the system.

It is generally agreed that there are three types of memory or memory function: *sensory buffers, short-term memory* or *working memory*, and *long-term memory*. There is some disagreement as to whether these are three separate systems or different functions of the same system. We will not concern ourselves here with the details of this debate, which is discussed in detail by Baddeley [7], but will indicate the evidence used by both sides as we go along. For our purposes, it is sufficient to note three separate types of memory. These memories interact, with information being processed and passed between memory stores, as shown in Figure 1.9.

1.3.1 *Sensory memory*

The sensory memories act as buffers for stimuli received through the senses. A sensory memory exists for each sensory channel: *iconic memory* for visual stimuli, *echoic memory* for aural stimuli and *haptic memory* for touch. These memories are constantly overwritten by new information coming in on these channels.

We can demonstrate the existence of iconic memory by moving a finger in front of the eye. Can you see it in more than one place at once? This indicates a persistence of the image after the stimulus has been removed. A similar effect is noticed most vividly at firework displays where moving sparklers leave a persistent image. Information remains in iconic memory very briefly, in the order of 0.5 seconds.

Similarly, the existence of echoic memory is evidenced by our ability to ascertain the direction from which a sound originates. This is due to information being received by both ears. However, since this information is received at different times, we must store the stimulus in the mean time. Echoic memory allows brief 'play-back' of information. Have you ever had someone ask you a question when you are reading? You ask them to repeat the question, only to realize that you know what was asked after all. This experience, too, is evidence of the existence of echoic memory.

Information is passed from sensory memory into short-term memory by attention, thereby filtering the stimuli to only those which are of interest at a given time. Attention is the concentration of the mind on one out of a number of competing stimuli or thoughts. It is clear that we are able to focus our attention selectively, choosing to attend to one thing rather than another. This is due to the limited capacity of our sensory and mental processes. If we did not selectively attend to the stimuli coming into our senses, we would be overloaded. We can choose which stimuli to attend to, and this choice is governed to an extent by our *arousal*, our level of interest or need. This explains the cocktail party phenomenon mentioned earlier: we can attend to one conversation over the background noise, but we may choose to switch our attention to a conversation across the room if we hear our name mentioned. Information received by sensory memories is quickly passed into a more permanent memory store, or overwritten and lost.

1.3.2   Short-term memory

Short-term memory or working memory acts as a 'scratch-pad' for temporary recall of information. It is used to store information which is only required fleetingly. For example, calculate the multiplication 35x6 in your head. The chances are that you will have done this calculation in stages, perhaps 5x6 then 30x6 or 2x35 then 3x70. To perform calculations such as this we need to store the intermediate stages for use later. Or consider reading. In order to comprehend this sentence you need to hold in your mind the beginning of the sentence as you read the rest. Both of these tasks use short-term memory.

Short-term memory can be accessed rapidly, in the order of 70 ms. However, it also decays rapidly, meaning that information can only be held there temporarily, in the order of 200 ms.

Short-term memory also has a limited capacity. There are two basic methods for measuring memory capacity. The first involves determining the length of a sequence which can be remembered in order. The second allows items to be freely recalled in any order. Using the first measure, the average person can remember 7

+/- 2 digits. This was established in experiments by Miller [114]. Try it. Look at the following number sequence:

2653976208

Now write down as much of the sequence as you can remember. Did you get it all right? If not, how many digits could you remember? If you remembered between five and nine digits your *digit span* is average.

Now try the following sequence:

071 242 6378

Did you recall that more easily? Here the digits are grouped or *chunked*. A generalization of the 7+/-2 rule is that we can remember 7+/-2 *chunks* of information. Therefore chunking information can increase the short-term memory capacity. The limited capacity of short-term memory produces a subconscious desire to create chunks, and so optimize the use of the memory. The successful formation of a chunk is known as *closure*. This process can be generalized to account for the desire to complete or close tasks, held in short-term memory. If a subject fails to do this or is prevented from doing so by interference, the subject is liable to lose track of what he or she is doing and make consequent errors.

The sequence of chunks given above also makes use of pattern abstraction: it is written in the form of a telephone number which makes it easier to remember. Patterns can be useful as aids to memory. For example, most people would have difficulty remembering the following sequence of chunks:

HEC ATR ANU PTH ETR EET

However, if you notice that by moving the last character to the first position, you get the statement 'the cat ran up the tree', the sequence is easy to recall.

In experiments where subjects were able to recall words freely, evidence shows that recall of the last words presented was better than recall of those in the middle [143]. This is known as the *recency effect*. However, if the subject is asked to perform another task between presentation and recall (for example counting backwards) the recency effect is eliminated. The recall of the other words was unaffected. This suggests that short-term memory recall is damaged by interference of other information. However, the fact that this interference does not affect recall of earlier items, provides some evidence for the existence of separate long-term and short-term memories. The early items are held in a long-term store which is unaffected by the recency effect.

However, interference does not necessarily impair recall in short-term memory. Baddeley asked subjects to remember six-digit numbers and attend to sentence processing at the same time [7]. They were asked to answer questions on sentences, such as 'A proceeds B: AB is true or false?'. Surprisingly, this did not result in interference, suggesting that in fact short-term memory is not a unitary system but is made up of a number of components, including a visual channel and an articulatory channel. The task of sentence processing used the visual channel,

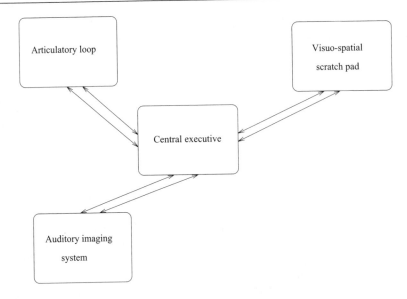

Figure 1.10 *A more detailed model of short-term memory*

while the task of remembering digits used the articulatory channel. Interference only occurs if tasks utilize the same channel.

These findings led Baddeley to propose a model of working memory which incorporated a number of elements together with a central processing executive. This is illustrated in Figure 1.10.

1.3.3 Long-term memory

If short-term memory is our working memory or 'scratch-pad', long-term memory is our main resource. Here we store factual information, experiential knowledge, procedural rules of behaviour, in fact, everything that we 'know'. It differs from short-term memory in a number of significant ways. Firstly, it has a huge, if not unlimited, capacity. Secondly, it has a relatively slow access time of approximately a tenth of a second. Thirdly, forgetting occurs more slowly in long-term memory, if at all. These distinctions provide further evidence of a memory structure with several parts.

Long-term memory is intended for the long-term storage of information. Information is placed there from working memory after a few seconds. Unlike working memory there is little decay: long-term recall after minutes is the same as that after hours or days.

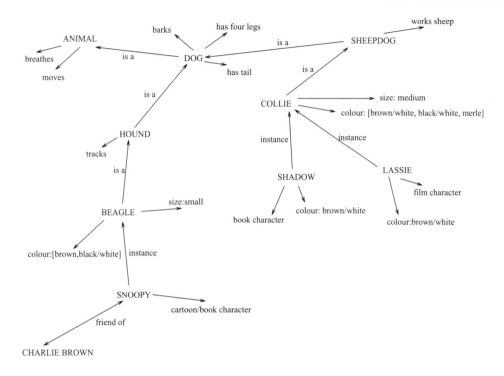

Figure 1.11   *Long-term memory may store information in a semantic network*

Long-term memory structure

There are two types of long-term memory: *episodic memory* and *semantic memory*. Episodic memory represents our memory of events and experiences in a serial form. It is from this memory that we can reconstruct the actual events that took place at a given point in our lives. Semantic memory, on the other hand, is a structured record of facts, concepts and skills that we have acquired. The information in semantic memory is derived from that in our episodic memory, such that we can learn new facts or concepts from our experiences.

Semantic memory is structured in some way to allow access to information, representation of relationships between pieces of information, and inference. One model for the way in which semantic memory is structured is as a network. Items are associated to each other in classes, and may inherit attributes from parent classes. This model is known as a *semantic network*. As an example, our knowledge about dogs may be stored in a network such as that shown in Figure 1.11.

Specific breed attributes may be stored with each given breed, yet general dog information is stored at a higher level. This allows us to generalize about specific cases. For instance, we may not have been told that the sheepdog Shadow has four legs and a tail, but we can infer this information from our general knowledge about sheepdogs and dogs in general. Note also that there are connections within the network which link into other domains of knowledge, for example, cartoon characters. This illustrates how our knowledge is organized by association.

The viability of semantic networks as a model of memory organization has been demonstrated by Collins and Quillian [39]. Subjects were asked questions about different properties of related objects and their reaction times were measured. The type of question asked (taking examples from our own network) were 'Can a collie breathe?', 'Is a beagle a hound?' and 'Does a hound track?'. In spite of the fact that the answers to such questions may seem obvious, subjects took longer to answer questions such as 'Can a collie breathe?' than ones such as 'Does a hound track?'. The reason for this, it is suggested, is that in the former case subjects had to search further through the memory hierarchy to find the answer, since information is stored at its most abstract level.

A number of other memory structures have been proposed to explain how we represent and store different types of knowledge. Each of these represents a different aspect of knowledge and, as such, the models can be viewed as complementary rather than mutually exclusive. Semantic networks represent the associations and relationships between single items in memory. However, they do not allow us to model the representation of more complex objects or events, which are perhaps composed of a number of items or activities. Structured representations such as *frames* and *scripts* organize information into data structures. *Slots* in these structures allow attribute values to be added. Frame slots may contain default, fixed or variable information. A frame is instantiated when the slots are filled with appropriate values. Frames and scripts can be linked together in networks to represent hierarchical structured knowledge.

Returning to the 'dog' domain, a frame-based representation of the knowledge may look something like Figure 1.12. The fixed slots are those for which the attribute value is set, default slots represent the usual attribute value, although this may be overridden in particular instantiations (for example, the Basenji does not bark), and variable slots can be filled with particular values in a given instance. Slots can also contain procedural knowledge. Actions or operations can be associated with a slot and performed, for example, whenever the value of the slot is changed.

Frames extend semantic nets to include structured, hierarchical information. They represent knowledge items in a way which makes explicit the relative importance of each piece of information.

Scripts attempt to model the representation of stereotypical knowledge about situations. Consider the following sentences:

John took his dog to the surgery. After seeing the vet, he left.

From our knowledge of the activities of dog owners and vets, we may fill in a substantial amount of detail. The animal was ill. The vet examined and treated the animal. John paid for the treatment before leaving. We are less likely to assume the alternative reading of the sentence, that John took an instant dislike to the vet on sight and did not stay long enough to talk to him!

```
┌─────────────────────────────────┐   ┌─────────────────────────────────┐
│              DOG                │   │             COLLIE              │
│  Fixed                         │   │  Fixed                          │
│      legs: 4                   │   │      breed of: DOG              │
│                                │   │      type: sheepdog             │
│  Default                       │   │                                 │
│      diet: carnivorous         │   │  Default                        │
│      sound: bark               │   │      size: 65 cm                │
│                                │   │                                 │
│  Variable                      │   │  Variable                       │
│      size:                     │   │      colour:                    │
│      colour:                   │   │                                 │
└─────────────────────────────────┘   └─────────────────────────────────┘
```

Figure 1.12 *A frame-based representation of knowledge*

A script represents this default or stereotypical information, allowing us to interpret partial descriptions or cues fully. A script comprises a number of elements, which, like slots, can be filled with appropriate information:

Entry conditions conditions that must be satisfied for the script to be activated.

Result conditions that will be true after the script is terminated.

Props objects involved in the events described in the script.

Roles actions performed by particular participants.

Scenes the sequences of events that occur.

Tracks a variation on the general pattern representing an alternative scenario.

An example script for going to the vet is shown in Figure 1.13.

A final type of knowledge representation which we hold in memory is the representation of procedural knowledge, our knowledge of how to do something. A common model for this is the production system. Condition–action rules are stored in long-term memory. Information coming into short-term memory can match a condition in one of these rules and result in the action being executed. For example, a pair of production rules might be

IF dog is wagging tail
THEN pat dog

IF dog is growling
THEN run away

Script for a visit to the vet

Entry conditions: *dog ill*
vet open
owner has money

Result: *dog better*
owner poorer
vet richer

Props: *examination table*
medicine
instruments

Roles: *vet examines*
diagnoses
treats

owner brings dog in
pays
takes dog out

Scenes: *arriving at reception*
waiting in room
examination
paying

Tracks: *dog needs medicine*
dog needs operation

Figure 1.13   *A script for visiting the vet*

If we then meet a growling dog, the condition in the second rule is matched, and we respond by turning tail and running. (Not to be recommended by the way!)

Long-term memory processes

So much for the structure of memory, but what about the processes which it uses? There are three main activities related to long-term memory: storage or remembering of information, forgetting and information retrieval. We shall consider each of these in turn.

Firstly, how does information get into long-term memory and how can we improve this process? Information from short-term memory is stored in long-term memory by rehearsal. The repeated exposure to a stimulus or the rehearsal of a piece of information transfers it into long-term memory.

This process can be optimized in a number of ways. Ebbinghaus performed numerous experiments on memory, using himself as a subject [53]. In these experiments he tested his ability to learn and repeat nonsense syllables, comparing his recall minutes, hours and days after the learning process. He discovered that the amount learned was directly proportional to the amount of time spent learning. This is known as the *total time hypothesis*. However, experiments by Baddeley and others suggest that learning time is most effective if it is distributed over time [8]. For example, in an experiment in which Post Office workers were taught to type, those whose training period was divided into weekly sessions of one hour performed better than those who spent two or four hours a week learning (although the former obviously took more weeks to complete their training). This is known as the *distribution of practice effect*.

However, repetition is not enough to learn information well. If information is not meaningful it is more difficult to remember. This is illustrated by the fact that it is more difficult to remember a set of words representing concepts than a set of words representing objects. Try it. First try to remember the words in list A and test yourself.

List A: Faith Age Cold Tenet Quiet Logic Idea Value Past Large

Now try list B.

List B: Boat Tree Cat Child Rug Plate Church Gun Flame Head

The second list was probably easier to remember than the first since you could visualize the objects in the second list.

Sentences are easier still to memorize. Bartlett performed experiments on remembering meaningful information (as opposed to meaningless such as Ebbinghaus used) [13]. In one such experiment he got subjects to learn a story about an unfamiliar culture and then retell it. He found that subjects would retell the story replacing unfamiliar words and concepts with words which were meaningful to them. Stories were effectively translated into the subject's own culture. This is related to the semantic structuring of long-term memory: if information is meaningful and familiar, it can be related to existing structures and more easily incorporated into memory.

So if learning information is aided by structure, familiarity and concreteness, what causes us to lose this information, to forget? There are two main theories of forgetting: *decay* and *interference*. The first theory suggests that the information held in long-term memory may eventually be forgotten. Ebbinghaus concluded from his experiments with nonsense syllables that information in memory decayed logarithmically, that is, that it was lost rapidly to begin with, and then more slowly. *Jost's law*, which follows from this, states that if two memory traces are equally strong at a given time the older one will be more durable.

The second theory is that information is lost from memory through interference. If we acquire new information it causes the loss of old information. This is termed *retroactive interference*. A common example of this is the fact that if you change telephone numbers, learning your new number makes it more difficult to remember your old number. This is because the new association masks the old. However, sometimes the old memory trace breaks through and interferes with new information. This is called *proactive inhibition*. An example of this is when you find yourself driving to your old house rather than your new one.

Forgetting is also affected by emotional factors. In experiments, subjects given emotive words and non-emotive words found the former harder to remember in the short-term but easier in the long-term. Indeed, this observation tallies with our experience of selective memory. We tend to remember positive information rather than negative (hence nostalgia for the 'good old days'), and highly emotive events rather than mundane.

It is debatable whether we ever actually forget anything or whether it becomes increasingly difficult to access certain items from memory. This question is in some ways meaningless since it is impossible to prove that we *do* forget: appearing to have forgotten something may just be caused by not being able to retrieve it! However, there is evidence to suggest that we may not lose information completely from long-term memory. Firstly, proactive inhibition demonstrates the recovery of old information even after it has been 'lost' by interference. Secondly, there is the 'tip of the tongue' experience, which indicates that some information is present but cannot be satisfactorily accessed. Thirdly, information may not be recalled but may be recognized, or may be recalled only with prompting.

This leads us to the third process of memory: information retrieval. Here we need to distinguish between two types of information retrieval, recall and recognition. In recall the information is reproduced from memory. In recognition, the presentation of the information provides the knowledge that the information has been seen before. Recognition is the less complex cognitive activity since the information is provided as a cue.

However, recall can be assisted by the provision of retrieval cues which enable the subject to quickly access the information in memory. One such cue is the use of categories. In an experiment subjects were asked to recall lists of words, some of which were organized into categories and some of which were randomly organized. The words which were related to a category were easier to recall than the others [19]. Recall is even more successful if subjects are allowed to categorize their own lists of words during learning. For example, consider the following list of words:

child red plane dog friend blood cold tree big angry

Now make up a story which links the words using as vivid imagery as possible. Now try to recall as many of the words as you can. Did you find this easier than the previous experiment where the words were unrelated?

The use of vivid imagery is a common cue to help people remember information. It is known that people often visualize a scene that is described to them. They can then answer questions based on their visualization. Indeed, subjects given a description of a scene often embellish it with additional information. Consider the following description and imagine the scene:

The engines roared above the noise of the crowd. Even in the blistering heat people rose to their feet and waved their hands in excitement. The flag fell and they were off. Within seconds the car had pulled away from the pack and was careering round the bend at a desperate pace. Its wheels momentarily left the ground as it cornered. Coming down the straight the sun glinted on its shimmering paint. The driver gripped the wheel with fierce concentration. Sweat lay in fine drops on his brow.

Without looking back to the passage, what colour is the car?

If you could answer that question you have visualized the scene, including the car's colour. In fact, the colour of the car is not mentioned in the description at all.

1.4 **Thinking: Reasoning and Problem-solving**

We have considered how information finds its way into and out of the human system and how it is stored. Finally, we come to look at how it processed and manipulated. This is perhaps the area which is most complex and which separates humans from other information processing systems, both artificial or natural. Although it is clear that animals receive and store information, there is little evidence to suggest that they can use it in quite the same way as humans. Similarly, artificial intelligence has produced machines which can see (albeit in a limited way) and store information. But their ability to use that information is limited to small domains.

Humans, on the other hand, are able to use information to reason and solve problems, and indeed do these activities when the information is partial or unavailable. Human thought is conscious and self-aware: while we may not always be able to identify the processes we use, we can identify the products of these processes, our thoughts. In addition, we are able to think about things of which we have no experience, and solve problems which we have never seen before. How is this done?

Thinking can require different amounts of knowledge. Some thinking activities are very directed and the knowledge required is constrained. Others require vast amounts of knowledge from different domains. For example, performing a subtraction calculation requires a relatively small amount of knowledge, from a constrained domain, whereas understanding newspaper headlines demands knowledge of politics, social structures, public figures and world events.

In this section we will consider two categories of thinking: reasoning and problem-solving. In practice these are not distinct since the activity of solving a problem may well involve reasoning and vice versa. However, the distinction is a common one and is helpful in clarifying the processes involved.

1.4.1 *Reasoning*

Reasoning is the process by which we use the knowledge we have to draw conclusions or infer something new about the domain of interest. There are a number of different types of reasoning: *deductive, inductive* and *abductive*. We use each of these types of reasoning in everyday life, but they differ in significant ways.

Deductive reasoning

Deductive reasoning derives the logically necessary conclusion from the given premises. For example,

> If it is Friday then she will go to work
> It is Friday
> Therefore she will go to work.

It is important to note that this is the *logical* conclusion from the premises; it does not necessarily have to correspond to our notion of truth. So for example,

> If it is raining then the ground is dry
> It is raining
> Therefore the ground is dry

is a perfectly valid deduction, even though it conflicts with our knowledge of what is true in the world.

Deductive reasoning is therefore often misapplied. Given the premises

> Some people are babies
> Some babies cry

many people will infer that 'Some people cry'. This is in fact an invalid deduction since we are not told that all babies are people. It is therefore logically possible that the babies who cry are those who are not people.

It is at this point, where truth and validity clash, that human deduction is poorest. One explanation for this is that people bring their world knowledge into the reasoning process. There is good reason for this. It allows us to take short cuts which make dialogue and interaction between people informative but efficient. We assume a certain amount of shared knowledge in our dealings with each other, which in turn allows us to interpret the inferences and deductions implied by others. If validity rather than truth was preferred, all premises would have to be made explicit.

Inductive reasoning

Induction is generalizing from cases we have seen to infer information about cases we have not seen. For example, if every elephant we have ever seen has a trunk, we infer that all elephants have trunks. Of course this inference is unreliable and cannot be proved to be true; it can only be proved to be false. We can disprove the inference simply by producing an elephant without a trunk. However, we can

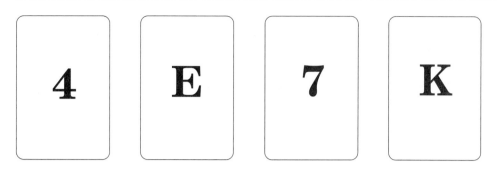

Figure 1.14   *Wason's cards*

never prove it true because, no matter how many elephants with trunks we have seen or known to exist, the next one we see may be trunkless. The best that we can do is gather evidence to support our inductive inference.

However, in spite of its unreliability, induction is a useful process, which we use constantly in learning about our environment. We can never see all the elephants that have ever lived or will ever live, but we have certain knowledge about elephants which we are prepared to trust for all practical purposes, which has largely been inferred by induction. Even if we saw an elephant without a trunk, we would be unlikely to move from our position that 'All elephants have trunks', since we are better at using positive than negative evidence. This is illustrated in an experiment first devised by Wason [182]. You are presented with four cards as in Figure 1.14. Each card has a number on one side and a letter on the other. Which cards would you need to pick up to test the truth of the statement 'If a card has a vowel on one side it has an even number on the other'?

A common response to this (was it yours?) is to check the E and the 4. However, this uses only positive evidence. In fact to test the truth of the statement we need to check negative evidence: if we can find a card which has an odd number on one side and a vowel on the other we have disproved the statement. We must therefore check E and 7. (It does not matter what is on the other side of the other cards: the statement does not say that all even numbers have vowels, just that all vowels have even numbers.)

Abductive reasoning

The third type of reasoning is abduction. Abduction reasons from a fact to the action or state that caused it. This is the method we use to derive explanations for the events we observe. For example, suppose we know that Sam always drives too fast when she has been drinking. If we see Sam driving too fast we may infer that she has been drinking. Of course, this too is unreliable since there may be another reason why she is driving fast: she may have been called to an emergency, for example.

However, in spite of its unreliability, it is clear that people do infer explanations in this way, and hold onto them until they have evidence to support an alternative theory or explanation. This can lead to problems in using interactive systems. If an event always follows an action, the user will infer that the event is caused by the action unless evidence to the contrary is made available. If, in fact, the event and the action are unrelated, confusion and even error often result.

1.4.2   Problem-solving

If reasoning is a means of inferring new information from what is already known, problem-solving is the process of finding a solution to an unfamiliar task, using the knowledge we have. Human problem-solving is characterized by the ability to adapt the information we have to deal with new situations. However, often solutions seem to be original and creative. There are a number of different views of how people solve problems. The earliest, dating back to the first half of this century, is the *Gestalt* view that problem-solving involves both reuse of knowledge and insight. This has been superseded but the questions it was trying to address remain and its influence can be seen in later research. A second major theory, proposed in the 1970s by Newell and Simon, was the *problem space theory*, which takes the view that the mind is a limited information processor. Later variations on this drew on the earlier theory and attempted to reinterpret Gestalt theory in terms of information processing theories. We will look briefly at each of these views.

Gestalt theory

Gestalt psychologists were answering the claim, made by behaviourists, that problem solving is a matter of reproducing known responses or trial and error. This explanation was considered by the Gestalt school to be insufficient to account for human problem solving behaviour. Instead, they claimed, problem-solving is both *productive* and *reproductive*. Reproductive problem-solving draws on previous experience as the behaviourists claimed, but productive problem-solving involves insight and restructuring of the problem. Indeed, reproductive problem-solving could be a hindrance to finding a solution, since a person may 'fixate' on the known aspects of the problem and so be unable to see novel interpretations that might lead to a solution.

Gestalt psychologists backed up their claims with experimental evidence. Kohler provided evidence of apparent insight being demonstrated by apes, which he observed joining sticks together in order to reach food outside their cages [98]. However, this was difficult to verify since the apes had once been wild and so could have been using previous knowledge.

Other experiments observed human problem-solving behaviour. One well-known example of this is Maier's *pendulum problem* [106]. The problem was this: the subjects were in a room with two pieces of string hanging from the ceiling. Also in the room were other objects including pliers, poles and extensions. The task set was to tie the pieces of string together. However, they were too far apart to catch hold of both at once. Although various solutions were proposed by subjects, few chose to use the weight of the pliers as a pendulum to 'swing' the strings together. However, when the experimenter brushed against the string, setting it in motion, this solution presented itself to subjects. Maier interpreted this as an example of productive restructuring. The movement of the string had given insight and allowed the subjects to see the problem in a new way. The experiment also illustrates fixation: subjects were initially unable to see beyond their view of the role or use of a pair of pliers.

Although Gestalt theory is attractive in terms of its description of human problem-solving, it does not provide sufficient evidence or structure to support its theories. It does not explain when restructuring occurs or what insight is, for example. However, the move away from behaviourist theories was helpful in paving the way for the information processing theory that was to follow.

Problem space theory

Newell and Simon proposed that problem-solving centres on the *problem space*. The problem space comprises *problem states*, and problem-solving involves generating these states using legal state transition operators. The problem has an initial state and a goal state and people use the operators to move from the former to the latter. However, such problem spaces may be huge, and so *heuristics* are employed to select appropriate operators to reach the goal. One such heuristic is *means–ends analysis*. In means–ends analysis the initial state is compared to the goal state and an operator chosen to reduce the difference between the two. For example, imagine you are reorganizing your office and you want to move your desk from the north wall of the room to the window. Your initial state is that the desk is at the north wall. The goal state is that the desk is by the window. The main difference between these two is the location of your desk. You have a number of operators which you can apply to moving things: you can carry them or push them or drag them, etc. However, you know that to carry something it must be light and that your desk is heavy. You therefore have a new sub-goal: to make the desk light. Your operators for this may involve removing drawers, and so on.

An important feature of Newell and Simon's model is that it operates within the constraints of the human processing system, and so searching the problem space is limited by the capacity of short-term memory, and the speed at which information can be retrieved. Within the problem space framework, experience allows us to solve problems more easily since we can structure the problem space appropriately and choose operators efficiently.

Newell and Simon's theory, and their *General Problem Solver* model which is based on it, have largely been applied to problem-solving in well-defined domains, for example, solving puzzles. These problems may be unfamiliar but the knowledge that is required to solve them is present in the statement of the problem and the expected solution is clear. In real-world problems finding the knowledge required to solve the problem may be part of the problem, or specifying the goal may be difficult. Problems such as these require significant domain knowledge: for example, to solve a programming problem you need knowledge of the language and the domain in which the program operates. In this instance specifying the goal clearly may be a significant part of solving the problem.

However, the problem space framework provides a clear theory of problem-solving, which can be extended, as we shall see when we look at skill acquisition in the next section, to deal with knowledge intensive problem-solving. First we will look briefly at the use of analogy in problem-solving.

Analogy in problem-solving

A third strand of problem-solving research is the consideration of analogy in problem-solving. Here we are interested in how people solve novel problems. One suggestion is that this is done by mapping knowledge relating to a similar known domain to the new problem — called *analogical mapping*. Similarities between the known domain and the new one are noted and operators from the known domain are transferred to the new one.

This process has been investigated using analogous stories. Gick and Holyoak [73] gave subjects the following problem:

A doctor is treating a malignant tumour. In order to destroy it he needs to blast it with high-intensity rays. However, these will also destroy the healthy tissue surrounding the tumour. If he lessens the rays' intensity the tumour will remain. How does he destroy the tumour?

The solution to this problem is to fire low-intensity rays from different directions converging on the tumour. That way, the healthy tissue receives harmless low-intensity rays while the tumour receives the rays combined, making a high-intensity dose. The investigators found that only 10% of subjects reached this solution without help.

However, this rose to 80% when they were given this analogous story and told that it may help them:

A general is attacking a fortress. He can't send all his men in together as the roads are mined to explode if large numbers of men cross them. He therefore splits his men into small groups and sends them in on separate roads.

In spite of this, it seems that people often miss analogous information, unless it is semantically close to the problem domain. When subjects were not told to use the story, many failed to see the analogy. However, the number spotting the analogy rose when the story was made semantically close to the problem, e.g a general using rays to destroy a castle.

The use of analogy is reminiscent of the Gestalt view of productive restructuring and insight. Old knowledge is used to solve a new problem.

1.4.3 *Skill acquisition*

All of the problem-solving that we have considered so far has concentrated on handling unfamiliar problems. However, for much of the time, the problems that we face are not completely new. Instead, we gradually acquire skill in a particular domain area. But how is such skill acquired and what difference does it make to our problem-solving performance? We can gain insight into how skilled behaviour works, and how skills are acquired, by considering the difference between novice and expert behaviour in given domains.

A commonly studied domain is chess playing. It is particularly suitable since it lends itself easily to representation in terms of problem space theory. The initial state is the opening board position; the goal state is one player check-mating the other; operators to move states are legal moves of chess. It is therefore possible to examine skilled behaviour within the context of the problem space theory of problem-solving.

Studies of chess players by DeGroot, Chase and Simon, among others, produced some interesting observations [34, 35, 47, 48]. In all the experiments the behaviour of chess masters was compared to less experienced chess players. The first observation was that players did not consider large numbers of moves in choosing their move, nor did they look ahead more than six moves (often far fewer). Masters considered no more alternatives than the less experienced, but they took less time to make a decision and produced better moves.

So what makes the difference between skilled and less skilled behaviour in chess? It appears that chess masters remember board configurations and good moves associated with them. When given actual board positions to remember, masters are much better at reconstructing the board than the less experienced. However, when given random configurations (which were unfamiliar), the groups of players were equally bad at reconstructing the positions. It seems therefore that expert players 'chunk' the board configuration in order to hold it in short-term memory. Expert players use larger chunks than less experienced and can therefore remember more detail.

This behaviour is also seen among skilled computer programmers. They can also reconstruct programs more effectively than novices since they have the structures available to build appropriate chunks. They acquire plans representing code to solve particular problems. When that problem is encountered in a new domain or new program they will recall that particular plan and reuse it.

Another observed difference between skilled and less skilled problem-solving is in the way that different problems are grouped. Novices tend to group problems according to superficial characteristics such as the objects or features common to both. Experts, on the other hand, demonstrate a deeper understanding of the problems and group them according to underlying conceptual similarities which may not be at all obvious from the problem descriptions.

Each of these differences stems from a better encoding of knowledge in the expert: information structures are fine-tuned at a deep level to enable efficient and accurate retrieval. But how does this happen? How is skill such as this acquired? One model of skill acquisition is Anderson's *ACT** model [5]. *ACT** identifies three basic levels of skill:

1. The learner uses general-purpose rules which interpret facts about a problem. This is slow and demanding on memory access.

2. The learner develops rules specific to the task.

3. The rules are tuned to speed up performance.

General mechanisms are provided to account for the transitions between these levels. For example, *proceduralization* is a mechanism to move from the first to the second. It removes the parts of the rule which demand memory access and replaces variables with specific values. *Generalization*, on the other hand, is a mechanism which moves from the second level to the third. It generalizes from the specific cases to general properties of those cases. Commonalities between rules are condensed to produce a general-purpose rule.

These are best illustrated by example. Imagine you are learning to cook. Initially you may have a general rule to tell you how long a dish needs to be in the oven, and a number of explicit representations of dishes in memory. You can instantiate the rule by retrieving information from memory.

```
IF cook[type, ingredients, time]
THEN
    cook for: time

cook[casserole, [chicken,carrots,potatoes], 2 hours]
cook[casserole, [beef, dumpling, carrots], 2 hours]
cook[cake, [flour, sugar,butter, egg], 45 mins]
```

Gradually your knowledge becomes proceduralized and you have specific rules for each case:

```
IF type is casserole
AND ingredients are [chicken,carrots,potatoes]
```

THEN
    cook for: 2 hours

IF type is casserole
AND ingredients are [beef,dumplings,carrots]
THEN
    cook for: 2 hours

IF type is cake
AND ingredients are [flour,sugar.butter,eggs]
THEN
    cook for: 45 mins

Finally, you may generalize from these rules to produce general-purpose rules, which exploit their commonalities:

IF type is casserole
AND ingredients are ANYTHING
THEN
    cook for: 2 hours

    The first stage uses knowledge extensively. The second stage relies upon known procedures. The third stage represents skilled behaviour. Such behaviour may in fact become automatic and as such be difficult to make explicit. For example, think of an activity at which you are skilled, perhaps driving a car or riding a bike. Try to describe to someone the exact procedure which you go through to do this. You will find this quite difficult. In fact experts tend to have to mentally rehearse their actions in order to identify exactly what they do. Such skilled behaviour is efficient but may cause errors when the context of the activity changes.

1.4.4 *Errors and mental models*

Human capability for interpreting and manipulating information is quite impressive. However, we do make mistakes. Some are trivial, resulting in no more than temporary inconvenience or annoyance. Others may be more serious, requiring substantial effort to correct. Occasionally an error may have catastrophic effects, as we see when 'human error' results in a plane crash or nuclear plant leak.

    Why do we make mistakes and can we avoid them? In order to answer the latter part of the question we must first identify what is going on when we make an error. There are in fact several different types of error. As we saw in the last section some errors result from changes in the context of skilled behaviour. These are known as *slips*. If a pattern of behaviour has become automatic and we change some aspect of it, the more familiar pattern may break through and cause an error. A familiar example of this is where we intend to stop at the shop on the way home from work but in fact drive past. Here, the activity of driving home is the more familiar and overrides the less familiar intention.

Other errors result from an incorrect understanding, or model, of a situation or system. People build their own theories to understand the causal behaviour of systems. These have been termed *mental models*. They have a number of characteristics. Mental models are often partial: the person does not have a full understanding of the working of the whole system. They are unstable and are subject to change. They can be internally inconsistent, since the person may not have worked through the logical consequences of their beliefs. They are often unscientific and may be based on superstition rather than evidence. However, often they are based on an incorrect interpretation of the evidence.

Assuming a person builds a mental model of the system being dealt with, errors may occur if the actual operation differs from the mental model. For example, on one occasion we were staying in a hotel in Germany, attending a conference. In the lobby of the hotel was a lift. Beside the lift door was a button. Our model of the system, based on previous experience of lifts, was that the button would call the lift. We pressed the button and the lobby light went out! In fact the button was a light switch and the lift button was on the inside rim of the lift, hidden from view.

This illustrates the importance of a correct mental model and the dangers of ignoring conventions. There are certain conventions which we use to interpret the world. If these are to be violated, explicit support must be given to enable us to form a correct mental model. A label on the button saying 'light switch' would have been sufficient.

1.5 Individual Differences

In this chapter we have been discussing humans in general. We have made the assumption that everyone has similar capabilities and limitations and that we can therefore make generalizations. To an extent this is true: the psychological principles and properties that we have discussed apply to the majority of people. Notwithstanding this, we should remember that, although we share processes in common, humans, and therefore users, are not all the same. We should be aware of individual differences so that we can account for them as far as possible within our designs. These differences may be long term, such as sex, physical capabilities, and intellectual capabilities. Others are shorter term and include the effect of stress or fatigue on the user. Still others change through time such as age.

These differences should be taken into account in our designs. It is useful to consider, for any design decision, if there are likely to be users within the target group who will be adversely affected by our decision. At the extremes a decision may exclude a section of the user population. For example, the current emphasis on visual interfaces excludes those who are visually impaired, unless the design also makes use of the other sensory channels. However, on a more mundane level, designs should allow for users who are under pressure, feeling ill or distracted by other concerns: they should not push users to their perceptual or cognitive limits.

1.6   Psychology and the Design of Interactive Systems

In this chapter we have looked briefly at the way in which humans receive, process and store information, solve problems and acquire skill. But how can we apply what we have learned to designing interactive systems? Sometimes, straightforward conclusions can be drawn. For example, we can deduce that blue should not be used for conveying important detail since it is most difficult for the user to perceive. However, in the majority of cases, application is not so obvious or simple. In fact, it may actually be dangerous, leading us to make generalizations which are not valid. In order to apply a psychological principle or result properly in design, we need to understand its context, both in terms of where it fits in the wider field of psychology and in terms of the details of the actual experiments, the measures used and the subjects involved, for example. This may appear daunting, particularly to the novice designer who wants to acknowledge the relevance of cognitive psychology but does not have the background to derive appropriate conclusions. Fortunately for such a designer, principles and results from research in psychology have been distilled into guidelines for design, models to support design and techniques for evaluating design. The second part of this book is concerned in part with how such guidelines, models and techniques can be used to support the design process.

1.6.1   Guidelines

Throughout this chapter we have discussed the strengths and weaknesses of human cognitive and perceptual processes but, for the most part, we have avoided attempting to apply these directly to design. This is because such an attempt could only be partial and simplistic, and may give the impression that this is all psychology has to offer.

However, general design principles and guidelines can and have been derived from the theories we have discussed. Some of these are relatively straightforward: people can hold only 7+/- 2 items in short-term memory, therefore interactive systems should not require users to remember more. Others are more complex and context-dependent. In Chapters 4 and 5 we discuss principles and guidelines further, many of which are derived from psychological theory. The interested reader is also referred to Gardiner and Christie (1987) in the recommended reading list which illustrates how guidelines can be derived from psychological theory.

1.6.2   Models to support design

As well as guidelines and principles, psychological theory has led to the development of analytic and predictive models of user behaviour. Some of these include a specific model of human problem-solving, others of physical activity, others attempt a more comprehensive view of cognition. Some predict how a typical computer user would behave in a given situation, others analyze why particular user behaviour occurred. All are based on cognitive theory. We discuss these models in detail in Chapter 6.

1.6.3   Techniques for evaluation

In addition to providing us with a wealth of theoretical understanding of the human user, psychology also provides a range of empirical techniques which we can employ to evaluate our designs and our systems. In order to use these effectively we need to understand the scope and benefits of each method. Chapter 11 provides an overview of these techniques and an indication of the circumstances under which each should be used.

1.7   Summary

In this chapter we have considered the human as an information processor, receiving inputs from the world, storing, manipulating and using information, and reacting to the information received. Information is received through the senses, particularly, in the case of computer use, through sight, hearing and touch. It is stored in memory: either temporarily in sensory or working memory, or permanently in long-term memory. It can then be used in reasoning and problem-solving. Recurrent familiar situations allow people to acquire skills in a particular domain, as their information structures become better defined. However, this can also lead to error, if the context changes.

Human perception and cognition are complex and sophisticated but they are not without their limitations. We have considered some of these limitations in this chapter. An understanding of the capabilities and limitations of the human as information processor can help us to design interactive systems which support the former and compensate for the latter. The principles, guidelines and models which can be derived from cognitive psychology and the techniques which it provides are invaluable tools for the designer of interactive systems.

Exercises

1.1 Suggest ideas for an interface which uses the properties of sound effectively.

1.2 Devise experiments to test the properties of (i) short-term memory (ii) long-term memory, using the experiments described in this chapter to help you. Try out your experiments on your friends. Are your results consistent with the properties described in this chapter?

1.3 Identify the goals and operators involved in the problem 'delete the second paragraph of the document' on a word-processor. Now use a word-processor to delete a paragraph and note your actions, goals and sub-goals. How well did they match your earlier description?

1.4 Observe skilled and novice operators in a familiar domain, for example, touch and 'hunt-and-peck' typists, expert and novice game players, or expert and novice users of a computer application. What differences can you discern between their behaviours?

1.5 Produce a semantic network of the main information in this chapter.

Recommended Reading

- E.B. Goldstein, *Sensation and Perception*, 3rd Edition, Wadsworth, 1989.

  A textbook covering human senses and perception in detail. Easy to read with many home experiments to illustrate the points made.

- Alan Baddeley, *Human Memory: Theory and Practice*, Lawrence Erlbaum Associates, 1990.

  The latest and most complete of Baddeley's texts on memory. Provides up to date discussion on the different views of memory structure as well as a detailed survey of experimental work on memory.

- Michael W. Eysenck and Mark T. Keane, *Cognitive Psychology: A Student's Handbook*, Lawrence Erlbaum Associates, 1990.

  A comprehensive and readable textbook giving more detail on cognitive psychology, including memory, problem-solving and skill acquisition.

- S. K. Card, T. P Moran and A. Newell, *The Psychology of Human–Computer Interaction*, Lawrence Erlbaum Associates, 1983.

  A classic text looking at the human as information processor interaction with the computer. Develops and describes the Model Human Processor in detail.

- A. Newell and H. Simon, *Human Problem Solving*, Prentice Hall, 1972.

  Describes the problem space view of problem-solving in more detail.

- Margaret M. Gardiner and Bruce Christie (eds.), *Applying Cognitive Psychology to User-Interface Design*, John Wiley and Son, 1987.

  A collection of essays on the implications of different aspects of cognitive psychology to interface design. Includes memory, thinking, language and skill acquisition. Provides detailed guidelines for applying psychological principles in design practice.

- Andrew Monk (ed.), *Fundamentals of Human Computer Interaction*, Academic Press, 1985.

  A good collection of articles giving brief coverage of aspects of human psychology including perception, memory, thinking and reading. Also contains articles on experimental design which are a useful introduction to the subject.

Chapter 2

The Computer

Overview

A computer system comprises various elements, each of which affects the user of the system.

- Input devices for interactive use, allowing text entry, drawing and selection from the screen:
    - text entry: keyboard, speech and handwriting
    - pointing: principally the mouse

- Output devices for interactive use, principally different forms of screen, but also audible outputs.

- Paper output and input: the paperless office and the less-paper office:
    - different types of printers and their characteristics, character styles and fonts
    - scanners and optical character recognition

- Memory:
    - short-term memory: RAM
    - long-term memory: magnetic and optical disks
    - capacity limitations related to document and video storage
    - access methods as they limit or help the user

- Processing:
    - the effects when systems run too slow or too fast, the myth of the infinitely fast machine
    - limitations on processing speed
    - networks and their impact on system performance

2.1 Introduction

In order to understand how humans interact with computers, we need to have an understanding of both parties in the interaction. The previous chapter explored aspects of human capabilities and behaviour of which we need to be aware in the context of human–computer interaction; this chapter considers the computer and associated input–output devices and investigates how the technology influences the nature of the interaction and style of the interface.

The computer can be defined as follows:

> The participant in the interaction that runs a program [174]

This general definition can be applied to a vast number of devices with which we interact. A light switch can be seen as a computer running a simple program: 'turn light on when pressed down, turn light off when pressed up'. We can learn a lot from studying such simple examples. Another example in a similar vein is a car — here the program is much more complex since the range of situations in which a car is used are much wider than those of a light switch. Our interaction with the car is similarly complex, and we develop complex approaches to understanding such a system. However, having shown that the general definition is broad, and indicated that we can learn from studying even everyday situations, we will now concentrate on the electronic computer.

When we interact with computers, what are we trying to achieve? Consider what happens when we interact with each other — we are either passing information to other people, or receiving information from them. Often, the information we receive is in response to the information that we have recently imparted to them, and we may then respond to that. Interaction is therefore a process of information transfer. Relating this to the electronic computer, the same principles hold: interaction is a process of information transfer, from the user to the computer and from the computer to the user.

The first part of this chapter concentrates on the transference of information from the user to the computer and back. We begin by considering a current typical computer interface and the devices it employs (the keyboard and mouse), showing that the design is constrained by and related to the technology used. Since the devices influence the style of interaction, we move on to see the effects of different devices, considering their strong and weak points, and how they might alter the interface and interaction. Then we move on to consider devices that are not in common use, and suggest how they may affect future interfaces.

In addition to direct input and output, information is passed to and fro via paper documents. This is dealt with in Section 2.6, which describes printers and scanners. Although not requiring the same degree of user interaction as a mouse or keyboard, these are an important means of input and output for many current applications.

We then consider the computer itself, its processor and memory devices, noting how the technology drives and empowers the interface. The details of computer

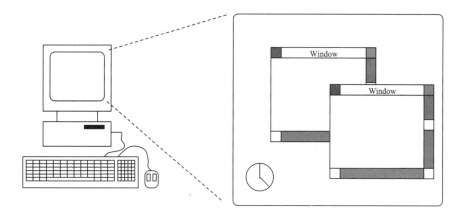

Figure 2.1 *A typical computer system*

processing should largely be irrelevant to the end-user. However, the interface designer needs to be aware of the limitations of storage capacity and computational power; it is no good designing on paper a marvellous new interface, only to find it needs a Cray to run. Software designers often have high-end machines on which to develop applications, and it is easy to forget what a more typical configuration feels like.

2.1.1 *A typical computer system*

Consider a typical computer setup as shown in Figure 2.1. There is the computer 'box' itself, a keyboard, a mouse and a colour screen. The screen layout is shown alongside it. If we examine the interface, we can see how its various characteristics are related to the devices used. The details of the interface itself, its underlying principles and design, are discussed in more depth in Chapter 3; we will simply consider the sorts of things that it allows us to do, and the device that facilitates the required actions. Each is discussed in turn, in conjunction with alternatives that offer a different approach to the same situation. The diversity of devices reflects the fact that there are many different types of data that may have to be entered into and obtained from a system, and there are also many different types of user, each with their own unique requirements.

2.1.2 *Batch and interactive input*

Information input can be performed in two ways: batch data entry and interactive use. Batch data entry is used when there is a large quantity of data to be entered into the system, in a well-defined format, so that the user is concerned primarily with getting the data into the machine as quickly as possible. Interactive use involves the entry of data by a user who is sitting at the screen, entering data when prompted to by the machine. More generally, the computer is used as a tool to manipulate and retrieve information; no new information is being added to the machine store but information is entered in the form of commands in order to get the computer to carry out a specific task or set of tasks. The field of Human–Computer Interaction has grown up as the interactive use of computers has increased. For batch data entry, there is very little interaction with the machine — the user may simply dump a pile of punched cards onto a reader, press the start button, and then return a few hours later. However, the changing role of the computer away from the back room and onto the desktop has meant that more and more people are interacting with the machine, with an ever-increasing amount of use being made of the computer as a tool to be controlled. As we are primarily concerned with *interaction*, we will not discuss batch input but will concentrate on interactive devices.

Interactive input devices can themselves be split into two broad categories: those that allow text entry, and those that allow pointing, selection of particular items on the screen, and movement. The first category consists of things such as keyboards and speech recognition systems, whilst the second category comprises devices like mice, joysticks and touchscreens. We will deal with each of these categories in turn.

2.2   Text Entry Devices

The different rectangular regions on our archetypical screen known as windows allow text to be entered, which is done in our system via the keyboard, which is discussed below, followed by an examination of some alternatives.

2.2.1   *The keyboard*

The different rectangular regions on our archetypical screen allow text to be entered, which is done in our system via the keyboard.

The keyboard is one of the most common input devices in use today. It is used for entering textual data and commands. The vast majority of keyboards have a standardized layout, and are known by the first six letters of the top row of alphabetical keys, QWERTY There are alternative designs, which have some advantages over the QWERTY layout, but these have not been able to overcome the vast technological inertia of the QWERTY keyboard. These alternatives are of two forms: 26 key layouts and chord keyboards. A 26 key layout rearranges the order of the alphabetic keys, putting the most commonly used letters under the strongest fingers, or adopting simpler practices. In addition to QWERTY, we will discuss two 26 key layouts, alphabetic and Dvorak, and chord keyboards.

How keyboards work

Current keyboards work by a keypress closing a connection, causing a character code to be sent to the computer. The connection is usually via a lead, but wireless systems are also in existence. One aspect of keyboards that is important to users is the 'feel' of the keys. Some keyboards require a very hard press to operate the key, much like a manual typewriter, whilst others are featherlight. The distance that the keys travel also affects the tactile nature of the keyboard. The keyboards that are used on most of the notebook computers currently are 'half-travel' keyboards, where the keys travel only a small distance before activating their connection; such a keyboard can feel dead to begin with, but such qualitative judgements are often changed as people become more used to it. By making the actual keys thinner, and allowing them a much reduced travel, a lot of vertical space can be saved on the keyboard, therefore making the machine thinner than would otherwise be possible. Some keyboards are even made of touch-sensitive buttons, which require a light touch and practically no travel; they often appear as a sheet of plastic with the buttons printed on them. Such keyboards are often found on shop tills, though the keys are not QWERTY, but specific to the task. Being fully sealed, they have the advantage of being easily cleaned and resistant to dirty environments, but have little feel, and are not popular with trained touch-typists. Feedback is important even at this level of human–computer interaction! With the recent increase of repetitive strain injuries (RSI) to users' fingers, and the increased responsibilities of the employers in these circumstances, it may be that such designs will enjoy a resurgence in the near future. RSI in fingers is caused by the tendons that control the movement of the fingers becoming inflamed due to over-use and making repeated unnatural movements.

The QWERTY keyboard

The layout of the digits and letters on a QWERTY keyboard is fixed (see Figure 2.2), but non-alphanumeric keys vary between keyboards. For example, there is a difference between key assignments on British and American keyboards (in particular, above the 3 on the U.K. keyboard is the pound sign £, whilst on the U.S. keyboard there is a dollar sign $). The standard layout is also subject to variation in the placement of brackets, backslashes and suchlike.

The QWERTY arrangement of keys is not optimal for typing, however. The reason for the layout of the keyboard in this fashion can be traced back to the days of mechanical typewriters. Hitting a key caused an arm to shoot towards the carriage, imprinting the letter on the head on the ribbon and hence onto the paper. If two arms flew towards the paper in quick succession from nearly the same angle, they would often jam — the solution to this was to set out the keys

Figure 2.2   *The standard QWERTY keyboard*

so that common combinations of consecutive letters were placed at different ends of the keyboard, which meant that the arms would usually move from alternate sides. One appealing story relating to the key layout is that it was also important for a salesman to be able to type the word 'typewriter' quickly in order to impress potential customers: the letters are all on the top row!

The electric typewriter and now the computer keyboard are not subject to the original mechanical constraints, but the QWERTY keyboard remains the dominant layout. The reason for this is social — the vast base of trained typists would be reluctant to relearn their craft, whilst the management are not prepared to accept an initial lowering of performance whilst the new skills were gained. There is also a large investment in current keyboards, which would either all have to be replaced at great cost, or phased out, with the subsequent requirement for people to be proficient on both keyboards.

The alphabetic keyboard

One of the most obvious layouts to be produced is the alphabetic keyboard, in which the letters are arranged alphabetically across the keyboard. It might be expected that such a layout would make it quicker for untrained typists to use, but this is not the case. Studies have shown that this keyboard is not faster for properly trained typists, as we may expect, since there is no inherent advantage to this layout. However, even for novice or occasional users, the alphabetic layout appears to make very little difference to the speed of typing. These keyboards are finding a niche market in pocket electronic personal organisers, however. The reason for this is difficult to determine, but it could well be that such a layout looks simpler to use than the QWERTY one. Also, it dissuades people from attempting to use their touch-typing skills on a very small keyboard and hence avoids criticisms of difficulty of use!

The DVORAK keyboard

The DVORAK keyboard uses a similar layout of keys to the QWERTY system, but assigns the letters to different keys. Based upon an analysis of typing, the keyboard is designed to aid people reach faster typing speeds. It is biased towards right-handed people, in that 56% of keystrokes are made with the right hand. The layout of the keys also attempts to ensure that the majority of keystrokes alternate between hands, thereby increasing the potential speed. By keeping the most commonly used keys on the home, or middle, row, 70% of keystrokes are made without the typist having to stretch far, thereby reducing fatigue and increasing keying speed. The layout also aims to minimize the number of keystrokes made with the weak fingers. Many of these requirements are in conflict, and the DVORAK keyboard represents one possible solution. Experiments have shown that there is a speed improvement of between 10 and 15%, coupled with a reduction in user fatigue due to the increased ergonomic layout of the keyboard [110].

Other aspects of keyboard design have been altered apart from the layout of the keys. A number of more ergonomic designs have appeared, in which the basic tilted planar base of the keyboard is altered. Moderate designs curve the plane of the keyboard, making it concave, whilst more extreme ones split the keys into those for the left and right hand and curve both halves separately. Often in these the keys are also moved to bring them all within easy reach, to minimize movement between keys. Such designs are supposed to aid comfort and reduce RSI by minimizing effort, but have had practically no impact on the majority of systems sold.

Chord keyboards

Chord keyboards are significantly different keyboards. In these designs, only a few keys, four or five, are used (see Figure 2.3). Letters are produced by pressing one or more of the keys at once. In the *Microwriter*, the pattern of multiple keypresses is chosen to reflect the actual letter shape.

Such keyboards have a number of advantages, often reflected in the computer system in which they are employed. They are extremely compact, and so may find a place in the portable computing and electronic organizer market, since the smaller the machine the more portable it becomes. Simply reducing the size of a conventional keyboard makes the keys too small and close together, with a correspondingly large increase in the difficulty of using it. The learning time for the keyboard is supposed to fairly short — of the order of a few hours — but social resistance is still high. Moreover, they are capable of fast typing speeds in the hands (or rather hand!) of a competent user. Chord keyboards can be used where only one-handed operation is possible, in cramped and confined conditions. A major problem with them is the tiring nature of their operation, in that human hands are incapable of pressing repeated key combinations without getting fatigued. Figure 2.4 shows comparative typing speeds using each of these keyboards.

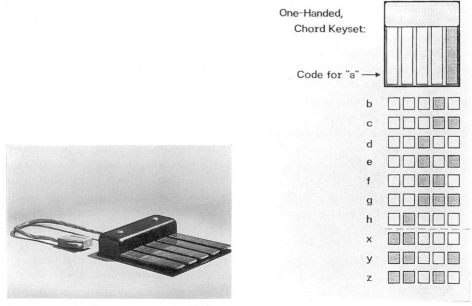

Figure 2.3   *An early chord keyboard (left) and its lettercodes (right). Courtesy Douglas Engelbart*

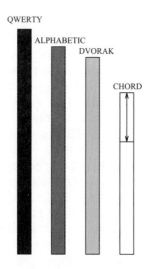

Figure 2.4   *Graph of relative keyboard speeds*

2.2.2   *Other text entry devices*

When we are considering text entry, there are alternative approaches to the keyboard. These will affect the nature of the interface, sometimes in minor ways as adaptations are made to a standard system to cope with the slightly different medium, and sometimes in major ways when the interface is completely redesigned to take full advantage of the different characteristics of the devices.

Handwriting recognition

Handwriting is a common and familiar activity, and is therefore attractive as a method of text entry. If we were able to write as we would when we use paper, but with the computer taking this form of input and converting it to text, we can see that it is an intuitive and simple way of interacting with the computer. However, there are a number of disadvantages with handwriting recognition. Current technology is still fairly inaccurate and so makes a significant number of mistakes in recognizing letters. Moreover, individual differences in handwriting are enormous, and make the recognition process even more difficult. The most significant information in handwriting is not in the letter shape itself but in the stroke information, which determines the way in which the letter is drawn. This means that devices which support handwriting recognition ought to be able to capture the stroke information as well as the final character shape. Further complications arise because letters within words are shaped and often drawn very differently depending on the actual word; the context can help determine the letter's identity, but often is unable to provide enough information. Handwriting recognition is covered in more detail later in the book, in Chapter 15. More serious in many ways is the limitation on speed; it is difficult to write at more than 25 words a minute, which is no more than half the speed of a decent typist.

We can envisage pen-based systems that use handwriting to replace the keyboard in our typical computer system, and then instead of typing we would have to write. However, the different nature of handwriting means that we may find it is more use in different situations, having features that overcome the disadvantages of a keyboard-based approach to the same problem. Such situations will invariably result in completely new systems being designed around the handwriting recognizer as the predominant mode of textual input, and may bear very little resemblance to the typical system. Consider the case for using handwriting in a small pocket organizer. Such a machine would typically be used for taking notes, for jotting down ideas, sketching ideas, as well as acting as a diary, address book and organizer. Using handwriting recognition has many advantages over using a keyboard. Firstly, a pen-based system can be small and yet still accurate and easy to use, whereas small keys become very tiring, or even impossible, to use accurately. The pen-based approach does not have to be altered when we move from jotting down text to sketching diagrams; pen-based input is highly appropriate for this also. If we were to design an organizer from scratch we may well decide to do away with the keyboard altogether, which means that we can consider all sorts of other ways to interact with the system that are not character based. For example, we may decide to use drawings to tell the system what to do rather than commands. The important point is that the different input device that was initially considered simply as an alternative to the keyboard opens up a whole host of alternative interface designs and different possibilities for interaction. Pen-based systems that use handwriting recognition are now being actively marketed in the notebook and portable computing market, where the advantage of using a familiar input device outweighs any disadvantages. These tend to utilize a pen-based operating system, which attempts to tackle some of the problems of using a pen-based approach to what is otherwise a standard keyboard and mouse-oriented system, in much the same way as we suggested above.

Speech recognition

Speech recognition is a promising area of text entry, but it has been promising for a number of years without actually delivering usable systems! It is forecast that the market for a successful system runs into billions of pounds and therefore a lot of development work is being put into this area. There is a natural enthusiasm for being able to talk to the machine and have it respond to commands, since this form of interaction is one with which we are very familiar. Successful recognition rates of over 97% have been reported, but since this represents a letter in error in approximately every 30, or one spelling mistake every six or so words, this is stoll unacceptible (*sic*)! Note also that this performance is usually quoted only for a restricted vocabulary of command words. Trying to extend such systems to the level of understanding natural language, with its inherent vagueness, imprecision and pauses, opens up many more problems that have not been satisfactorily solved even for keyboard-entered natural language. Moreover, since every person speaks differently, the system has to be trained and tuned to each new speaker, or its performance decreases. Strong accents, a cold or emotion can also cause recognition problems, as can background noise. This leads us on to the question of practicality within an office environment: not only may the background level of noise cause errors, but if everyone in an open-plan office were to talk to their machine, the level of noise would dramatically increase, with associated difficulties. Confidentiality would also be harder to maintain. Speech recognition is discussed in greater detail in Chapter 15, but again we can see that it offers two possibilities. The first is an alternative text entry device to replace the keyboard, whilst the second is a different approach to the whole problem, which produces a redesigned system, able to take full advantage of the benefits of the technique whilst minimizing the potential problems.

2.3   Positioning and Pointing Devices

Central to most modern computing systems is the ability to point at something on the screen and thereby manipulate it, or perform some function. There has been a long history of such devices, in particular in *computer aided design* (CAD), where positioning and drawing are the major activities. Pointing devices allow the user to point, position and select items, either directly or by manipulating a pointer on the screen. Of these devices, the mouse is most common, if not ubiquitous.

2.3.1   *The mouse*

The mouse has become a major component of the majority of personal computer systems and general-purpose workstations sold today, and is the little box with the tail connecting it to the machine in our basic computer system picture (Figure 2.1). It is a small, palm-sized box housing a weighted ball — as the box is moved over the tabletop, the ball is rolled by the table and so rotates inside the housing. This rotation is detected by small rollers that are in contact with the ball, and these adjust the values of potentiometers. The changing values of these potentiometers can be directly related to changes in position of the ball. The potentiometers are aligned in different directions so that they can detect both horizontal and vertical motion. The relative motion information is passed to the computer via a wire attached to the box, and moves a pointer on the screen, called the *cursor*. The whole arrangement tends to look rodent-like, with the box acting as the body and the wire as the tail, hence the term 'mouse'. In addition to detecting motion, the mouse has typically one, two or three buttons on top. These are used to indicate selection or to initiate action. Single-button mice tend to have similar functionality to multi-button mice, and achieve this by instituting different operations for a single and a double button click. A 'double-click' is when the button is pressed twice in rapid succession. Multi-button mice tend to allocate one operation to each particular button.

The mouse operates in a planar fashion, moving around the desktop, and is an indirect input device, since a transformation is required to map from the horizontal nature of the desktop to the vertical alignment of the screen. Left–right motion is directly mapped, whilst up–down on the screen is achieved by moving the mouse away–towards the user. The mouse only provides information on the relative movement of the ball within the housing: it can be physically lifted up from the desktop and replaced in a different position without moving the cursor. This offers the advantage that less physical space is required for the mouse, but suffers from being less intuitive for novice users. Since the mouse sits on the desk, moving it about is easy and users suffer little arm fatigue, although the indirect nature of the medium can lead to problems with hand–eye coordination. However, a major advantage of the mouse is that the cursor itself is small, and it can be easily

Figure 2.5 *The first mouse. Courtesy Douglas Engelbart*

manipulated without obscuring the display.

The mouse was developed around 1964 by Douglas C. Engelbart, and a photograph of the first prototype is shown in Figure 2.5. This used two wheels that slide across the desktop and transmit x–y coordinates to the computer. The housing was carved in wood, and has been damaged, exposing one of the wheels. The original design actually offers a few advantages of today's more sleek versions: by tilting it so that only one wheel is in contact with the desk, pure vertical or horizontal motion can be obtained. Also, the problem of getting the cursor across the large screens that are often used today can be solved by flicking your wrist to get the horizontal wheel spinning. The mouse pointer then races across the screen with no further effort on your behalf, until you stop it at its destination by dropping the mouse down onto the desktop.

Optical mice work differently from mechanical mice. A light-emitting diode emits a weak red light from the base of the mouse. This is reflected off a special pad with a grid-like pattern upon which the mouse has to sit, and the fluctuations in reflected intensity as the mouse is moved over the gridlines are recorded by a sensor in the base of the mouse and translated into relative x,z motion. The optical mouse is less susceptible to dust and dirt than the mechanical one, in that its mechanism is less likely to become gunged up.

Although most mice are hand operated, not all are — there is a device called the *footmouse*. As the name implies, it is a foot-operated device, although it is more akin to an isometric joystick than a mouse. The cursor is moved by foot pressure on one side or the other of a pad. A rare device, the footmouse has not found common acceptance for obvious reasons.

2.3.2   *Other positioning devices*

There are a number of alternatives to the mouse. Some of these devices offer a similar method of interaction, whilst others still provide positioning and pointing capabilities but in a completely different manner. Some of these alternatives are discussed in the following sections.

Trackball

The trackball is a little like an upside-down mouse. The weighted ball is rotated inside a static housing, the motion being detected in the same way as for a mechanical mouse, and the relative motion of the ball moves the cursor. Because of this, the trackball requires no additional space in which to operate, and is therefore a very compact device. It is an indirect device, and requires separate buttons for selection. It is fairly accurate, but is difficult to draw with, as long movements are difficult. Trackballs now appear in a wide variety of sizes; the most usual size of ball being about the same as a golf ball, with a number of larger and smaller devices available. Some of the smaller devices are becoming increasing popular for use with notebook and portable computers, with more enlightened designs having them actually built in, either above or below the keyboard, rather than clipping on to the side of the machine. The size and 'feel' of the trackball itself affords significant differences in the usability of the device: its weight, rolling resistance and texture all contribute to the overall effect.

Joystick

The joystick is an indirect input device, taking up very little space. Consisting of a small palm-sized box with a stick or shaped grip sticking up from it, the joystick is a simple device with which movements of the stick cause a corresponding movement of the screen cursor. There are two types of joystick, the *absolute* and the *isometric*. In the absolute joystick, movement is the important characteristic, since the position of the joystick in the base corresponds to the position of the cursor on the screen. In the isometric joystick, the pressure on the stick corresponds to the velocity of the cursor, and when released, the stick returns to its usual upright centred position. This type of joystick is also called the velocity-controlled joystick, for obvious reasons. The buttons are usually placed on the top of the stick, or on the front like a trigger. Joysticks are inexpensive and fairly robust, and for this reason they are often found in computer games. Another reason for their dominance of the games market is their relative familiarity to users, and their likeness to aircraft joysticks: aircraft are a favourite basis for games, leading to familiarity with the joystick that can be used for more obscure entertainment ideas.

Touch-sensitive screens (touchscreens)

Touchscreens are another method of allowing the user to point and select objects on the screen, but they are much more direct than the mouse, as they detect the presence of the user's finger, or a stylus, on the screen itself. They work in one of a number of different ways: by the finger (or stylus) interrupting a matrix of light beams, or by capacitance changes on a grid overlaying the screen, or by ultrasonic reflections. Because the user indicates exactly which item is required by pointing to it, no mapping is required and therefore this is a direct device.

The touchscreen is very fast, and requires no specialized pointing device. It is especially good for selecting items from menus displayed on the screen. Because the screen acts as an input device as well as an output device, there is no separate hardware to become damaged or destroyed by dirt; this makes them suitable for use in hostile environments. They are also relatively intuitive to use and have been used successfully as an interface to information systems for the general public.

They suffer from a number of disadvantages, however. Using the finger to point is not always suitable, as it can leave greasy marks on the screen, and, being a fairly blunt instrument, it is quite inaccurate. This means that the selection of small regions is very difficult, as is accurate drawing. Moreover, lifting the arm to point to a vertical screen is very tiring, and also means that the screen has to be within about a metre of the user to enable it to be reached, and this can make it too close for comfort. Recent research has shown that the optimal angle for the screen is about 15 degrees up from the horizontal.

Light pen

The light pen is similar in principle to the touchscreen, in that the user points directly to items on the screen rather than manipulating a device to move the screen cursor; again it is a direct input device. It differs from the touchscreen in that a particular pointing device is used — the light pen. The pen is connected to the screen by a cable and, in operation, is held to the screen and detects a burst of light from the screen phosphor during the display scan. The light pen can therefore address individual pixels and so is much more accurate than the touchscreen. It can be used for fine selection and drawing in a way that the touchscreen cannot. Problems with the light pen are that it too is tiring on the arm, and is a fragile device, easily broken, or lost on a busy desk. Both the light pen and touchscreen also suffer from the problem that, in use, the act of pointing actually obscures the display, making it harder to use, especially if complex detailed selections or movements are required in rapid succession. For this reason, and one of increased cost, neither device is as popular as any of the ball or joystick input devices.

Digitizing tablet

The digitizing tablet provides positional information by measuring the position of some device on a special pad, or *tablet*, and can work in a number of ways.

The *resistive tablet* detects point contact between two separated conducting sheets. It has advantages in that it can be operated without a specialized stylus — a pen or the user's finger is sufficient.

The *magnetic tablet* detects current pulses in a magnetic field using a small loop coil housed in a special pen. There are also capacitive and electrostatic tablets that work in a similar way.

The *sonic tablet* is similar to the above but requires no special surface. An ultrasonic pulse is emitted by a special pen which is detected by two or more microphones which then triangulate the pen position. This device can be adapted to provide 3D input, if required.

All digitizing tablets are capable of high resolution, and are available in a range of sizes from A5 to 60x60 in. Their sampling rate can vary between 50 and 200 Hz, affecting the resolution of cursor movement, which gets progressively finer as the sampling rate increases. The digitizing tablet can be used to detect relative motion *or* absolute motion, but is an indirect device since there is a mapping from the plane of operation of the tablet to the screen. It can also be used for text input; if supported by character recognition software, handwriting can be interpreted. Problems with digitizing tablets are that they require a large amount of desk space, and may be awkward to use if displaced to one side by the keyboard.

Dataglove

One of the mainstays of the new *virtual reality* systems (see Chapter 15), the dataglove is a three-dimensional input device. Consisting of a Lycra glove with optical fibres laid along the fingers, it detects the joint angles of the fingers and thumb. As the fingers are bent, the fibre optic cable bends too; increasing bend causes more light to leak from the fibre, and the reduction in intensity is detected by the glove and related to the degree of bend in the joint. Attached to the top of the glove are two sensors which use ultrasound to determine 3D positional information as well as the angle of roll, that is, the degree of wrist rotation. Such rich multi-dimensional input is currently a solution in search of a problem, in that most of the applications in use do not require such a comprehensive form of data input, whilst those that do cannot afford it. However, the availability of cheaper versions of the dataglove ($50 rather than the $10,000 required for the full dataglove) will encourage the development of more complex systems that are able to utilize the full power of the dataglove as an input device. There are a number of potential uses for this technology to assist disabled people, but cost remains the limiting factor at present.

The dataglove has the advantage that it is very easy to use, and is potentially very powerful and expressive (it can provide ten joint angles, plus the 3D spatial information and degree of wrist rotation, 50 times a second). It suffers from extreme expense, and the fact that it is difficult to use in conjunction with a keyboard. However, such a limitation is shortsighted; one can imagine a keyboard drawn onto a desk, with software detecting hand positions and interpreting whether the virtual keys had been hit or not. The potential for the dataglove is vast; gesture recognition and sign language interpretation are two obvious areas that are the focus of active research, whilst less obvious applications are evolving all the time.

Eyegaze

The eyegaze system consists of a small matchbox-sized unit mounted on a head-band that is worn over the user's head. Sitting in front of the eye, a low-power laser is shone into the eye and is reflected off the retina. The reflection changes as the angle of the eye alters, and by tracking the reflected beam the eyegaze system can determine the direction in which the eye is looking. This can then be used to move the screen cursor. The eyegaze is a very fast and accurate device, but is also expensive. It is fine for selection but not for drawing since the eye does not move in smooth lines. Such systems have been used in military applications, notably for guiding air-to-air missiles to their targets, but are starting to find more peaceable uses, again for disabled users and for workers in environments where it is impossible for them to use their hands. The rarity of the eyegaze is due partly to its novelty and partly to its expense, and it is usually found only in certain domain-specific applications.

2.3.3   *Keyboard-based positioning devices*

The number of ways of controlling a pointer on the screen are numerous, as shown by the examples discussed. There are many others as well. We are not attempting to provide a full categorization and list all the available devices, but to give a flavour of the range of devices available and the effect that the device chosen has on the form of the interaction. A number of devices that have specific characteristics can be grouped under the heading of keyboard based input, in that they are either special keys placed on the keyboard, or they are usually placed on it but do not use keys.

Cursor keys are available on most keyboards. Four keys on the keyboard are used to control the cursor, one each for up, down, left and right. Such a system is extremely cheap, but slow for general positioning tasks. The usefulness of such a system is limited to not much more than the basic requirements for text editing tasks. There is no standardized layout for the keys; arranging them in a line, a square, a 'T' or and inverted 'T', or a diamond shape are all common. Some common layouts are shown in Figure 2.6. Note that for text editing, the most common operation is down-and-to-the-right, which is ideal for cursor keys to cope

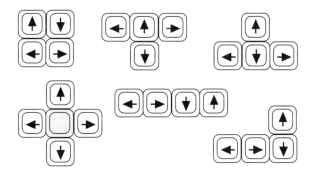

Figure 2.6 *Various cursor key layouts*

with, especially if they are laid out in the inverted 'T'. If the most common task is to be text editing, the cursor keys offer a better alternative than relying on, say, the mouse.

Instead of having four separate keys to control the motion of the cursor, we could have one key that can rock from side to side and forwards and backwards — this is known as a keymouse. The keymouse behaves in the same manner as an isometric joystick and is very compact, but provides little tactile feedback and its reliability is unproven. First introduced on notebook computers, the keymouse has yet to find wider acceptance.

Thumb-wheels are different in that they have two orthogonal dials to control the cursor position. Such a device is very cheap, but slow, and it is difficult to manipulate the cursor in any way other than horizontally or vertically. This limitation can sometimes be a useful constraint in the right application. For instance, in computer aided design the designer is almost always concerned with exact verticals and horizontals, and a device that provides such constraints is very useful, which accounts for the appearance of thumb-wheels in CAD systems. Another successful application for such a device has been in a drawing game such as Etch-a-Sketch in which straight lines can be created on a simple screen, since the predominance of straight lines in simple drawings means that the motion restrictions are an advantage rather than a handicap. However, if you were to try to write your signature using it, the limitations are all too apparent. The appropriateness of the device depends on the task to be performed.

Classifying pointing devices

There is obviously a vast range of pointing devices. Many different attempts have been made to categorize these devices, and each has its merits. Table 2.1 is one simple view.

Simple mappings are just transformations of user motion to screen motion;

Table 2.1   *A classification of pointing devices*

Device	Mapping	Selection	Dragging
Mouse	simple	button press	button hold
Trackball	simple	button press	button hold
Joystick	simple	button press	button hold
Touchscreen	direct	direct	screen contact
Light pen	direct	direct	screen contact
Digitizing tablet	simple	button press	button hold
Thumb-wheels	complex	button press	button hold
Cursor keys	complex	button press	button hold
Keymouse	simple	button press	button hold
Footmouse	simple	foot button press	foot button press
Isopoint	simple/complex	button press	button hold

complex mappings are those where the action taken to move in a particular direction is not obviously related to movement in the direction, whilst direct mappings are those where the motion on screen is dictated by user indication on the screen. Selection refers to the process of actually selecting an icon, whilst dragging refers to the method for moving such icons.

2.4   Output Devices

There is one predominant output device in use today: the computer screen, usually the cathode ray tube. This is highly expressive, relatively cheap and visually oriented. The vast majority of interactive computer systems would be unthinkable without screens, but many such systems do exist, though usually in specialized applications only. Considering the more general definition of the computer, systems such as cars, hi-fis, and light switches all have different outputs from those expressible on a screen, but in the personal computer and workstation market, screens are pervasive.

In this section, we discuss the computer screen in detail, looking at the different types of cathode ray tube as well as the more recent screen technologies, and then move on to look at some less obvious output devices and the different nature of the interaction that they support.

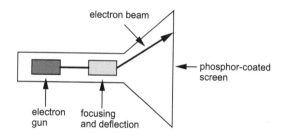

Figure 2.7   *CRT screen*

2.4.1   *Cathode ray tube*

The cathode ray tube (CRT) is the predominant display device. A stream of electrons is emitted from an electron gun, which is then focused and directed by magnetic fields. As the beam hits the phosphor-coated screen, the phosphor is excited by the electrons and glows (see Figure 2.7).

The basic description of how the cathode ray tube works holds for all types of display; however, there are three major types which have significant differences in the way in which they create an image. These are the *raster scan*, the *random scan* and *direct view* devices. Each of these will be discussed in turn.

Raster scan

This is the most common type, similar in operation to a standard television screen. The electron beam is scanned from left to right, then flicked back to rescan the next line, from top to bottom. This is repeated, at about 30 Hz (that is, 30 times a second), per frame, although higher scan rates are sometimes used to reduce the flicker on the screen. Another way of reducing flicker is to use *interlacing*, in which the odd lines on the screen are all scanned first, followed by the even lines. Using high-persistence phosphor, which glows for a longer time when excited, also reduces flicker, but causes image smearing especially if there is significant animation.

The resolution of screens using raster scanning is typically 512x512 pixels, although higher resolutions are increasingly popular. High-quality screens are available at up to approximately 1600x1200 pixels, which offer both excellent resolution *and* large screen estate allowing many windows to be open at once.

Black and white screens are able to display grayscale by varying the intensity of the electron beam; colour is achieved using more complex means. Three electron guns are used, one each to hit red, green and blue phosphors. Combining these colours can produce many others, including white, when they are all fully on. These three phosphor dots are focused to make a single point using a *shadow mask*, which is imprecise and gives colour screens a lower resolution than equivalent monochrome screens.

An alternative approach to producing colour on the screen is to use *beam penetration*. A special phosphor glows a different colour depending on the intensity of the beam hitting it.

The colour or, for monochrome screens, the intensity, at each pixel is held by the computer's video card. One bit per pixel can store on/off information, hence only black and white. More bits per pixel give rise to more colour or intensity possibilities. For example, eight bits/pixel gives rise to $2^8 = 256$ possible colours *at any one time*. The set of colours make up what is called the *colourmap*, and the colourmap can be altered at any time to produce a different set of colours. The system is therefore capable of actually displaying many more than the number of colours in the colourmap, but not simultaneously.

The cathode ray tube is a cheap display device, has fast enough response times for rapid animation coupled with a high colour capability. Note that animation does not necessarily mean little creatures and figures running about on the screen, but refers in a more general sense to the use of motion in displays; moving the cursor, opening windows, indicating processor-intensive calculations, or whatever. As screen resolution increases, however, the price rises. Because of the electron gun and focusing components behind the screen, cathode ray tubes are fairly bulky, though recent innovations have lead to less bulky displays in which the electron gun is not placed so that it fires directly at the screen, but fires parallel to the screen plane with the resulting beam bent through 90 degrees to hit the screen.

Considering the actual characteristics of the display, rather than the technology behind the screen, one of the problems with the raster scan display are 'jaggies'. Jaggies are diagonal lines that have discontinuities due to the horizontal nature of the raster scan process (see Figure 2.8).

The problem of jaggies is reduced by using high-resolution screens, or by a technique known as *anti-aliasing*. Anti-aliasing softens the edges of line segments, blurring the discontinuity and making the jaggie less obvious (see Figure 2.8).

Random scan display

The random scan display, also known as the *directed beam refresh*, or *vector display*, works differently from the raster scan. Instead of scanning the whole screen sequentially and horizontally, the random scan draws the lines to be displayed directly. Updating the screen at at least 30 Hz to reduce flicker, the direct drawing of lines at any angle means that jaggies are not created, and higher resolutions are possible, up to 4096x4096 pixels. Colour on such displays is achieved using beam penetration technology, and is generally of a poorer quality. Eyestrain and fatigue are still a problem, and these displays are more expensive than raster scan ones.

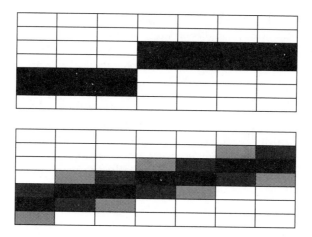

Figure 2.8 *Jaggies and anti-aliasing*

Direct view storage tube (DVST)

The DVST is used extensively as the display for an analog storage oscilloscope, which is probably the only place that these displays are used in any great numbers. They are similar in operation to the random scan CRT but the image is maintained by flood guns which have the advantage of producing a stable display with no flicker. The screen image can be incrementally updated but not selectively erased; removing items has to be done by redrawing the new image on a completely erased screen. The screens have a high resolution, typically about 4096x3120 pixels, but suffer from low contrast, low brightness and a difficulty in displaying colour.

Health hazards of CRT displays

Most people who habitually use computers are aware that screens can often cause eyestrain and fatigue; this is usually due to flicker, poor legibility or low contrast. However, there have also been many concerns relating to the emission of radiation from screens. These can be categorized as follows:

- X-rays which are largely absorbed by the screen (but not at the rear!)

- UV- and IR-radiation from phosphors in insignificant levels

- Radio frequency emissions, plus ultrasound (approximately 16 kHz)

- Electrostatic field which leaks out through tube to the user. The intensity is dependent on distance and humidity. This can cause rashes in the user.

- Electromagnetic fields (50 Hz–0.5 MHz) which create induction currents in conductive materials, including the human body. Two types of effects are attributed to this: in the visual system, a high incidence of cataracts in VDU operators, and concern over reproductive disorders (miscarriages and birth defects).

Research into the potentially harmful effect of these emissions is generally inconclusive, in that it is difficult to determine precisely what the causes of illness are, and many health scares have been the result of misinformed media opinion rather than scientific fact. However, users who are pregnant ought to take especial care and observe simple precautions. Generally, there are a number of common-sense things that can be done to relieve strain and minimize any risk. These include

- not sitting too close to the screen

- not using very small fonts

- not looking at the screen for a long time without a break

- working in well-lit surroundings

- not placing the screen directly in front of a bright window

2.4.2 *Other screen technology*

The cathode ray tube is not the only screen technology in existence. Recent innovations and advances have seen the introduction of smaller, lighter displays utilizing liquid crystal technology in ever more advanced forms. These are discussed in the following section, and are commonly referred to as flat panel displays. They have no radiation problems associated with them, and are matrix addressable, which means that individual pixels can be accessed without the need for scanning.

Liquid crystal display (LCD)

Similar in principle to the digital watch, a thin layer of liquid crystal is sandwiched between two glass plates. The top plate is transparent and polarized, whilst the bottom plate is reflective. External light passes through the top plate and is polarized, which means that it only oscillates in one direction. This then passes through the crystal, reflects off the bottom plate and back to the eye, and so that cell looks white. When a voltage is applied to the crystal, via the conducting glass plates, the crystal twists. This causes it to turn the plane of polarization of the incoming light, rotating it so that it cannot return through the top plate, making the activated cell look black. The LCD requires refreshing at the usual rates, but the relatively slow response of the crystal means that flicker is not usually noticeable. The low intensity of the light emitted from the screen, coupled with the reduced flicker, means that the LCD display is less tiring to use than standard CRT ones, with reduced eyestrain.

This different technology can be used to replace the standard screen on a desktop computer, and this is beginning to happen to a small extent. However, the particular characteristics of compactness, light weight and low power consumption have meant that these screens have created a large niche in the computer market by monopolizing the notebook and portable computer systems side. The advent of these screens allowed small, light computers to be built, and these have created a large market that did not previously exist. Such computers, riding on the back of the technological wave, have opened up a different way of working for a number of people, who now have access to computers when away from the office, whether out on business or at home. The different manner of working has given rise to different forms of software; one example is an integrated package comprising the basics of the systems used at work, coupled with a communications module. Working in a different location on a smaller machine with different software obviously represents a different style of interaction and so once again we can see that differences in devices may alter the human–computer interaction considerably. The upsurge in interest in the notebook computer market has fed back an investment in developing LCD screen technology, with super-twisted crystals increasing the viewing angle dramatically. Response times are also improving, which is necessary for even simple animation success such as blur-free cursor tracking. Colour LCD screens have now been developed and are becomingly increasingly available in any notebook computer range. This will have an impact on the appearance of screens, since notebook computing software will be required to look good in colour as well as black and white. Previously this was not an issue unless the software designer wanted to retain some compatibility with the appearance of the desktop machine which would usually be in colour.

2.5 Alternatives

There are other output devices that deserve a mention, although when one considers standard computer systems they are often overlooked. These range from modes of communication designed to supplement the screen, as well as those targeted as principal output devices.

They can be split into broad categories based on the nature of the communication channel they use: visual and auditory.

Apart from the CRT screen there are a number of visual outputs utilized in complex systems, especially in embedded systems. These can take the form of analog representations of numerical values, such as dials, gauges or lights to signify a certain system state. Flashing light-emitting diodes (LEDs) are used on the back of some computers to signify the processor state, whilst gauges and dials are found in process control systems. Once one starts in this mode of thinking, there are numerous visual outputs that can be thought of that are unrelated to the screen. One visual display that has found a specialized niche is the head-up display that is used in aircraft. The pilot is fully occupied looking forward and finds it difficult to look around the cockpit to get information. There are many different things that need to be known, ranging from data from tactical systems to navigational information and aircraft status indicators. The head-up display projects a subset of this information into the pilot's line of vision so that the information is directly in front of her eyes. This obviates the need for large banks of information to be scanned with the corresponding lack of attention to what is happening outside, and makes the pilot's job easier. Less important information is usually presented on a smaller number of dials and gauges in the cockpit to avoid cluttering the head-up display, and these can be monitored less often, during times of low stress.

The other mode of output that we should consider is that of auditory signals. Often designed to be used in conjunction with screen displays, auditory outputs are poorly understood: we do not yet know how to utilize sound in a sensible way to achieve maximum effect and information transference. We have discussed speech previously, but other sounds such as beeps, bongs, clanks, whistles and whirrs are all used to varying effect. As well as conveying system output, sounds offer an important level of feedback in interactive systems. Keyboards can be set to emit a click each time the key is pressed, and this appears to speed up interactive performance. Telephone keypads often sound different tones when the keys are pressed; a noise occurring signifies that the key has been successfully pressed, whilst the actual tone provides some information about the particular key that was pressed. The advantage of auditory feedback is evident when we consider a simple device such as a doorbell. If we press it and hear nothing, we are left undecided. Should we press it again, in case we did not do it right the first time, or did it ring but we did not hear it? And if we press it again but it actually did ring, will the people in the house think we are very rude, ringing insistently? We feel awkward and a little stressed. If we were using a computer system instead of a doorbell and were faced with a similar problem, we would not enjoy the interaction and would not perform as well. Yet it is a simple problem that could be easily rectified by a better initial design, using sound. Chapter 15 on multi-media discusses the use of the auditory channel in more detail.

2.6 Paper: Printing and Scanning

Some years ago, a recurrent theme of information technology was the *paperless office*. In the paperless office, documents would be produced, despatched, read and filed on-line. The only time electronic information would be committed to paper is when it went out of the office to ordinary customers, or to other firms who were laggards in this technological race. This vision was fueled by rocketing property prices, and the realization that the floor space for a wastepaper basket could cost thousands in rent each year. Some years on, many traditional paper files are now on-line, but the desire for the completely paperless office has faded. Offices still have wastepaper baskets, and extra floor space is even needed for the special computer tables to house 14 inch colour monitors.

In this section, we will look at some of the available technology which exists to get information to and from paper. We will look first at printing, the basic technology, and issues raised by it. We will then go on to discuss the movement from paper, back into electronic media. Although the paperless office is no longer seen as the goal, the less-paper office is perhaps closer, now that the technologies for moving between media are better.

2.6.1 *Printing*

If anything, computer systems have made it easier to produce paper documents. It is so easy to run off many copies of a letter (or book), in order to get it looking 'just right'. Older printers had a fixed set of characters available on a printhead. These varied from the traditional line-printer, to golf-ball and daisy-wheel printers. To change a typeface or the size of type meant changing the printhead, and was an awkward, and frequently messy, job, but for many years the daisy-wheel printer was the only means of producing high-quality output at an affordable price. However, the drop in the price of laser printers coupled with other cheap high-quality printers means that daisy-wheels are fast becoming a rarity.   All of the popular printing technologies, like screens, build the image on the paper as a series of dots. This enables, in theory, any character set or graphic to be printed, limited only by the resolution of the dots. This resolution is measured in *dots per inch* (dpi). Imagine a sheet of graph paper, and building up an image by putting dots at the intersection of each line. The number of lines per inch in each direction is the resolution in dpi. For some mechanical printers this is slightly confused: the dots printed may be bigger than the gaps, neighbouring printheads may not be able to print simultaneously and may be offset relative to one another (a diamond shaped rather than rectangular grid). These differences do not make too much difference to the user, but mean that, given two printers at the same nominal resolution, the output of one looks better than that of the other, because it has managed the physical constraints better.

The most common types of dot-based printers are listed below:

dot-matrix printers These use an inked ribbon, like a typewriter, but instead of a single character-shaped head striking the paper, a line of *pins* is used, each of which can strike the ribbon and hence dot the paper. Horizontal resolution can be varied by altering the speed of the head across the paper, and vertical resolution can be improved by sending the head twice across the paper at a slightly different position. So, dot-matrix printers can produce fast, draft quality output or slower 'letter' quality output. They are cheap, but noisy (although quieter than the old daisy-wheels). The typical resolution of a dot-matrix printer is about 80–120 dpi.

ink-jet and bubble-jet printers   These operate by sending tiny blobs of ink from the print head to the paper. The ink is squirted at pressure from an ink-jet, whereas bubble-jets use heat to create a bubble. Both are quite quiet in operation. The ink from the bubble-jet (being a bubble rather than a droplet) dries more quickly than the ink-jet and the latter can occasionally smear. Resolution is similar to dot-matrix, but can approach laser quality at 300 dpi. However, the dots tend to be more accurately positioned and of a less broken shape.

thermal printers   Special thermal-sensitive paper is used which changes colour when heated. The print head simply heats the paper where it wants a dot. Often only one line of dots is produced per pass, compared with the previous printers which have several pins or jets in parallel. Thermal paper is not particularly nice to look at, but thermal printers are mechanically simple and require little maintenance (no ink or toner splashing about). Thermal printers have their niche in special applications, for example, industrial equipment and some portable printers, and more commonly in fax machines. Resolution is similar to dot-matrix.

laser printer   This uses similar technology to a photocopier: 'dots' of electrostatic charge are deposited on a drum, which then picks up toner (black powder). This is then rolled onto the paper and cured by heat. The curing is why laser printed documents come out warm, and the electrostatic charge is why they smell of ozone! In addition, some toner can be highly toxic if inhaled, but this is more a problem for full-time maintenance workers than end-users changing the occasional toner cartridge. Laser printers give nearly document quality output. Typical printers operate at 300 dpi, but top-end printers used by desktop publishing firms may be as high as 1200 dpi. Indeed, many books are nowadays produced using laser printers. The camera-ready copy for the authors' previous books have been produced on 300 dpi laser printers, and this book is typeset on a 1200 dpi printer.

As well as resolution, printers vary in speed and cost. Typically, office quality laser printers produce between four and eight pages per minute. Dot-matrix printers are more often rated in *characters per second* (cps), and typical speeds may be 200 cps for draft and 50 cps for letter quality print. In practice, this means no more than a page or so per minute. Ink-jet and bubble-jets are similar, and thermal printers often much slower if based on a single print head. However, these are maximum speeds for simple text, and for graphics printers may operate much more slowly. It is not unusual for a dot-matrix printer to take 5–15 minutes to print a full page of graphics.

The initial costs of office printers is roughly in the order: dot-matrix, jet, laser. However, the recurrent costs of consumables may easily dominate this initial cost. Both jet and laser printers have special-purpose parts (printheads, toner cartridges, print drums) which need to be replaced every few thousand sheets and must also use high-grade paper. In addition, it may be more difficult to find suitable grades of recycled paper for laser printers. Despite the economic and ecological advantages of the dot-matrix, it is likely that jet and laser printers will take over as the principal office printers in the coming years, due primarily to their high-quality output. Small thermal printers are often cheap to produce in volume, and although the heat-sensitive paper is relatively expensive, in the principal application areas the volumes of output are comparatively low. They have a niche market and are therefore not really comparable with the other printers.

Colour dot-matrix and ink-jet printers are available, and are used extensively for producing over-head foils: pie-charts, histograms and so on. Laser-quality colour printing is currently prohibitively expensive, but no more so than monochrome laser printing was in the early eighties.

2.6.2   *Fonts and page description languages*

Most printers can act in a mode whereby any characters sent at it (encoded in ASCII, see Section 2.7) are printed, typewriter style, in a single font. Another case, simple in theory, is when you have a bitmap picture and want to print it. The dots to print are sent to the printer, and no further interpretation is needed. However, in practice, it is rarely so simple.

Many printed documents are far more complex — they incorporate text in many different fonts and many sizes, italicized, emboldened and underlined. Within the text you will find line drawings, digitized photographs and pictures generated from 'paint' packages, including the ubiquitous 'clip art'. Sometimes the computer does all the work, converting the page image into a bitmap of the right size to be sent to the printer. Alternatively, a description of the page may be sent to the printer. At the simplest level, this will include commands to set the print position on the page, and change the font size.

More sophisticated printers can accept a *page description language*, the most common of which is PostScript. This is a form of programming language for printing. It includes some standard programming constructs, but also some special ones: paths for drawing lines and curves, sophisticated character and font handling and scaled bitmaps. The idea is that the description of a page is far smaller than the associated bitmap, reducing the time taken to send the page to the printer. An A4 laser printer page at 300 dpi takes 8 Mbytes; to send this down a standard serial printer cable would take ten minutes! However, a computer in the printer has to interpret the Postscript program to print the page; this is typically faster than ten minutes, but is still the limiting factor for many print jobs.

Text is printed in a font with a particular size and shape. The size of a font is measured in points (pt). The point is a printer's measure and is about 1/72 of an inch. The *point size* of the font is related to its height: a 12 point font has about 6 lines per inch (12/72). The shape of a font is determined by its *font name*, for example, Times-Roman, Courier or Helvetica. Times-Roman font is similar to the

Courier is a fixed-pitch font
Times-Roman is a variable-pitch serif font
Palatino is also a variable-pitch serif font
Helvetica is a variable-pitch sans-serif font
A mathematics font: $\alpha\beta\xi\pm\pi\in\forall\infty\perp\neq\aleph\partial\sqrt{}\exists$

Figure 2.9   *Examples of different fonts*

type of many newspapers, such as the 'Times', whereas Courier has a typewritten shape. Some fonts, such as Courier, are *fixed-pitch*, that is, each character has the same width. The alternative is a variable-pitched font, such as Times-Roman or Helvetica, where some characters, such as the 'm', are wider than others, such as the 'i'. Another characteristic of fonts is whether they are *serif* or *sans-serif*. A serif font has splayed ends to the lines, imitating those found on cut stone lettering. A sans-serif font has square ended strokes. In addition, there are special fonts looking like Gothic lettering or cursive script, and fonts of Greek letters and special mathematical symbols.

This book is set in 10 point *Palatino* font using Postscript. Palatino is a variable-pitched serif font. Figure 2.9 shows examples of different fonts.

2.6.3 *Screen and page*

A common requirement of word-processors and desktop publishing software is that *'what you see is what you get'* (see also Chapters 4 and 9), which is often called by its acronym *WYSIWYG* (pronounced whizz-ee-wig). This means that the appearance of the document on the screen should be the same as its eventual appearance on the printed page. Insofar as this means that, for example, centred text is displayed centred on the screen, this is reasonable. However, this should not cloud the fact that screen and paper are very different media.

A typical screen resolution is about 50 dpi compared with a laser printer at 300 dpi. Some packages can show magnified versions of the document in order to help in this. On the other hand, even monochrome screens can show several levels of greyness or brightness, and many screens are in colour. Good colour printers are rare and at best printers show greyness by half-tones: black dots intermingled with white ones. In addition, the sizes and aspect ratios are very different. An A4 page is about 11 inches tall by 8 wide, whereas a screen is often of similar dimensions, but wider than it is tall.

These differences cause problems when designing software. Should you try to make the screen image as close to the paper as possible, or should you try to make the best of each? One approach to this would be only to print what could be displayed, but that would waste the extra resolution of the printer. On the other hand, one can try to make the screen as much like paper as possible, which is the intention behind the paper-white A4 (or double A4) display. This is a laudable aim, but cannot get rid of all the problems.

A particular problem is with fonts. Imagine we have a line of 'm's, each having a width of 0.15 inch. If we print them on a 50 dpi screen, then we can make the screen character 7 or 8 dots wide, in which case the screen version will be narrower or wider than the printed version. Alternatively, we can print the screen version as near as possible to where the printed characters would lie, in which case the 'm's on the screen would have different spaces between them 'mm mm mm mm m'. The latter looks horrible on the screen, so most software chooses the former approach. This means that text which aligns on screen may not do so on printing. Some systems use a uniform representation for screen and printer, using the same font descriptions and even, in the case of the Next machine, Postscript for screen display as well as printer output. However, this simply exports the problem from the application program to the operating system.

The differences between screen and printer mean that different forms of graphic design are needed for each. For example, headings and changes in emphasis are made using font style and size on paper, but using colour, brightness and line boxes on screen. This is not usually a problem for the display of the user's own documents as the aim is to give the user as good an impression of the printed page as possible, given the limitations. However, if one is designing parallel paper and screen forms, then one has to trade-off consistency between the two representations with clarity in each. An overall similar layout, but with different forms of presentation for details may be appropriate.

2.6.4 *Scanners and optical character recognition*

Printers take electronic documents and put them on paper — *scanners* reverse this process. They start by turning the image into a bitmap, but with the aid of *optical character recognition*, can convert the page right back into text. The image to be converted may be printed, but may also be a photograph or hand drawn picture.

There are two main kinds of scanner: flat-bed and hand-held. With a flat-bed scanner, the page is placed on a flat glass plate and the whole page is converted into a bitmap. Hand-held scanners are pulled over the image by hand. As the head passes over an area it is read in, yielding a bitmap strip. A roller at the ends ensures that the scanner knows how fast it is being pulled and thus how big the image is. The scanner is typically only 3 or 4 inches wide, so two or three strips must be 'glued' together by software to make a whole page image. This is quite a difficult process as the strips will overlap and perhaps be not completely parallel to one another, as well as suffering from problems of different brightness and contrast. However, for desktop publishing, small images such as photographs are quite common, and as long as one direction is less than the width of the scanner, they can be read in one pass. Many flat-bed scanners allow a small pile of sheets to be placed in a feed tray so that they can all be scanned without user intervention.

Scanners work by shining a beam of light at the page and then recording the intensity (and possibly colour) of the reflection. Like photocopiers, the colour of the light which is shone means that some colours may appear darker than others on a monochrome scanner. For example, if the light is pure red, then a red image will reflect the light completely and thus not appear on the scanned image.

Like printers, scanners differ in resolution. Typically they operate in the range 100–300 dpi, but more expensive ones may be as high as 1500 dpi. Monochrome scanners will usually yield 16 or 256 levels of grey. If a pure monochrome image is required (for instance, from a printed page), then one can *threshold* the greyscale image, that is, turn all pixels darker than some particular value black, and the rest white. Colour scanners are also common, and, unlike printers, not much more expensive than monochrome scanners.

Scanners have two principal applications at present. They are used extensively in *desktop publishing* (*DTP*) for reading in hand-drawn pictures and photographs. This means that cut-and-paste can be performed electronically rather than with real glue. In addition, the images can be rotated, scaled and otherwise transformed, using a variety of image manipulation software tools. Such tools are becoming increasingly powerful, allowing complex image transformations to be easily achieved ranging from colour correction, through the merging of multiple images to the application of edge-detection and special effects filters.

The other application area is in document storage and retrieval systems, where paper documents are scanned and stored on computer rather than (or sometimes as well as) in a filing cabinet. The costs of maintaining paper records are enormous, and electronic storage can be cheaper, more reliable and more flexible. Storing a bitmap image is neither most useful (in terms of access methods), nor space efficient (as we will see later), so scanning may be combined with *optical character recognition* to obtain the text rather than the page image of the document.

Optical character recognition (*OCR*) is the process whereby the computer can 'read' the characters on the page. It is only comparatively recently that print could be reliably read, since the wide variety of typefaces and print sizes makes this more difficult than one would imagine — it is *not* simply a matter of matching a character shape to the image on the page. In fact, OCR is rather a misnomer nowadays as, although the document is optically scanned, the OCR software itself operates on the bitmap image. Current software can recognize 'unseen' fonts and can even produce output in word-processing formats preserving super- and sub-scripts, centring, italics and so on.

2.7   **Memory**

Like the human memory, we can think of the computer memory as operating at different levels, with those that have the faster access typically having less capacity. By analogy with the human memory, we can group these into short-term and long-term memories (STM and LTM), but the analogy is rather weak — the capacity of the computer's STM is a lot more than seven items! These are more commonly called primary and secondary storage.

The details of computer memory are not in themselves of direct interest to the user interface designer. However, the limitations in capacity and access methods are important constraints on the sort of interface which can be designed. After some fairly basic information, we will put the raw memory capacity into perspective with the sort of information which can be stored, as well as again seeing how advances in technology offer more scope for the designer to produce more effective interfaces. In particular, we will see how the capacity of typical memory copes with video images as these are becoming important as part of multi-media applications (see Chapter 15).

2.7.1   Short-term memory

At the lowest level of computer memory are the registers on the computer chip, but these have little impact on the user except insofar as they affect the general speed of the computer. Most currently active information is held in *random access memory (RAM)*. Different forms of RAM differ as to their precise access times, power consumption and characteristics. Typical access times are of the order of 100 nano-seconds, that is a ten millionth of a second, and information can be accessed at a rate of around 10 Mbytes (million bytes) per second. Typical storage in modern personal computers is between 1/2 and 8 Mbytes.

Most RAM is *volatile*, that is, its memory is lost when the power is turned off. However, many computers have small amount of *non-volatile RAM*, which retains its contents, perhaps with the aid of a small battery. This may be used to store set-up information in a large computer, but in a pocket organizer will be the whole memory. Non-volatile RAM is more expensive so is only used where necessary, but with many notebook computers using very low-power static RAM, the divide is shrinking. By strict analogy, non-volatile RAM ought to be classed as long-term memory, but the important thing we want to emphasize is the gulf between STM and LTM in a computer system. Here non-volatile RAM sits squarely with other RAM as STM.

2.7.2   *Long-term memory*

For most computer users the LTM consists of disks[1], possibly with tapes for *backup*. The existence of backups and appropriate software to generate and retrieve backups is an important area for user security. However, we will deal mainly with those forms of storage which impact the interactive computer user.

There are two main kinds of technology used in disks: *magnetic disks* and *optical disks*. The most common storage medium, floppy disks and hard (or fixed) disks, are coated with magnetic material, like that found on an audio tape, on which the information is stored. Typical capacities of floppy disks lie between 300 kbytes and 1.4 Mbytes, but as they are removable, you can have as many as you have room for on your desk. Hard disks may store from under 40 Mbytes to over 400 Mbytes. With disks there are two access times to consider, the time taken to find the right track on the disk, and the time to read the track. The former dominates random reads, and is typically of the order of 10 ms for hard disks. The transfer rate once the track is found is then very high, perhaps several hundred kbytes per second.

Optical disks use laser light to read and (sometimes) write the information on the disk. The *CD-ROM* is the simplest device, using the same technology as audio compact discs. CD-ROMs have a very large capacity of many giga-bytes (Gbytes), that is, several thousand million bytes, but cannot be written to at all. They are useful for published material such as on-line reference books, or even large software libraries. *WORM* drives (write-once read-many) are more flexible in that information can be written, but (as the name suggests) only once at any location — more like a piece of paper than a blackboard. They are obviously very useful for backups and for producing very secure audit information. Finally, there are fully re-writable optical disks, but at the cost of reduced storage capacity. Optical media are more robust than magnetic disks and so it is easier to use a *jukebox* arrangement, whereby many optical disks can be brought on-line automatically as required. This can give an on-line capacity of hundreds of Gbytes. Optical disks are growing in popularity and dropping in price. However, they are still slower than their magnetic counterparts, so will not oust them for some time to come.

2.7.3   *Understanding speed and capacity*

So what effect do the various capacities and speeds have on the user? Thinking of our typical personal computer system, we can summarize some typical capacities in Table 2.2.

We think first of documents. This book is about 250 thousand words, or about 1.5 Mbytes. So we could conceivably read it all into the 4 Mbytes of RAM. To

---

[1] A disk (with a 'k') is a disc (with a 'c') shaped piece of material used in a computer. Like computer program (with one 'm'), it has now become a word in its own right rather than being a misspelling of disc.

Table 2.2 *Capacities of different storage media*

	STM small/fast	LTM large/slow
media	RAM	hard disk
capacity	4 Mbytes	100 Mbytes
access time	200 ns	10 ms
transfer rate	10 Mbytes/s	100 kbytes/s

take a more popular work, the Bible would take about 4.5 Mbytes, flooding main memory, but easily fitting on disk. This makes the memory look not too bad, so long as you do not intend to put your entire library on-line. However, many word-processors come with a dictionary and thesaurus, and there is no standard way to use the same one with several products. Together with help files and the program itself, it is not unusual to find each application consuming 5–10 Mbytes of disk space, making 100 Mbytes look not too great.

Similarly, although 4 Mbytes of RAM is enough to hold most (but not all) single programs, windowed systems will run several applications simultaneously, soon using up many mega-bytes. Operating systems handle this by *paging* unused bits of programs out of RAM onto disk, or even *swapping* the entire program onto disk. This make little difference to the logical functioning of the program, but has a significant effect on interaction. If you select a window, and the relevant application happens to be currently swapped out onto the disk, it has to be swapped back in. The delay this causes can be considerable, and is both noticeable and annoying on many systems.

The delays due to swapping are a symptom of the *von Neumann bottleneck* between disk and main memory. There is plenty of information in the memory, but it is not where it is wanted, in the machine's RAM. The path between them is limited by the transfer rate of the disk and is too slow. Swapping due to the operating system may be difficult to avoid, but as an interactive system designer some of these problems can be avoided by thinking carefully about where information is stored and when it is transferred. For example, the program can be *lazy* about information transfer. Imagine the user wants to look at a document. Rather than reading in the whole thing before letting the user continue, just enough is read in for the first page to be displayed, and the rest is read during idle moments.

Returning to documents, if they are scanned as bitmaps (and not read using OCR), then the capacity of our system looks even less impressive. Say an 11×8 inch page is scanned at 150 dpi, and then thresholded to give a pure monochrome bitmap. The image contains about 2 million bits, that is, about 1/4 Mbyte. So, our 100 Mbyte disk could store 400 pages, and this book would not fit on to it.

If we turn to video, things are even worse. Imagine we want to store moving video using 12 bits for each pixel (4 bits for each primary colour giving 16 levels of brightness), each frame is 512 × 512 pixels, and we store at 25 frames per second. This is by no means a high-quality image, but each frame requires approximately 400 kbytes, and our disk will overflow after 10 seconds. Even a jukebox of optical disks would only manage an hour or so (even assuming we could transfer it fast enough). Lowering our sights to video stills or simple screen snapshots, we see that main memory is soon swamped, although we could manage a fair few frames on disk.

2.7.4 *Compression*

In fact, things are not quite so bad, since *compression* techniques can be used to reduce the amount of storage required for text, bitmaps and video. All of these things are highly redundant. Consider text for a moment. In English, we know that if we use the letter 'q' then 'u' is almost bound to follow. At the level of words, some words like 'the' and 'and' appear frequently in text in general, and for any particular work one can find other common terms (this book mentions 'user' and 'computer' rather frequently). Similarly, in a bitmap, if one bit is white, there is a good chance the next will be as well. Compression algorithms take advantage of this redundancy. For example, *Huffman encoding* gives short codes to frequent words [89], and *run-length encoding* represents long runs of the same value by length-value pairs. Text can easily be reduced by a factor of 5 and bitmaps often compress to 1% of their original size.

For video, in addition to compressing each frame, one can take advantage of the fact that successive frames are often similar. One can compute the *difference* between successive frames and then store only this — compressed, of course. More sophisticated algorithms detect when the camera pans and uses this information also. These differencing methods fail when the scene changes, and so the process periodically has to restart and a new complete (but compressed) image sent. For storage purposes this is not a problem, but when used for transmission over telephone lines or networks it can mean glitches in the video as the system catches up.

With these reductions it is certainly possible to store low-quality video at 64 kbytes/second; that is, we can store half an hour of highly compressed video on our 100 Mbyte hard disk. However, it still makes the humble video-cassette look very good value.

Probably the leading edge of video still and photographic compression is *fractal compression*. Fractals have been popularized by the images of the *Mandelbrot set*. Fractals refer to any image which contains parts which, when suitably scaled, are similar to the whole. If we look at an image, it is possible to find parts which are approximately self-similar, and these parts can be stored as a fractal with only a few numeric parameters. Fractal compression is especially good for textured features which cause problems for other compression techniques. The *decompression* of the image can be performed to any degree of accuracy, from a very rough soft focus image, to one *more* detailed than the original. The former is very useful as one can produce poor quality output quickly, and better quality given more time. The latter is rather remarkable — the fractal compression actually fills in details which are not in the original. These details are not accurate, but look convincing!

2.7.5 *Storage format and standards*

The most common data stored by interactive programs are text and bitmap images (soon to be followed by video), and this sub-section looks at the ridiculous range of file storage standards. We will consider database retrieval in the next sub-section.

The basic standard for text storage is the *ASCII* character codes, which assign to each standard printable character and several control characters an internationally recognized seven-bit code (decimal values 0–127), which can therefore be stored in an eight-bit byte, or be transmitted as eight bits including parity. Many systems extend the codes to the values 128–255, including line drawing characters, mathematical symbols and international letters such as 'æ'. There is now an extended 16-bit ASCII standard, which has enough room for a much larger range of characters including the Japanese Kanji character set.

As we have already discussed, modern documents consist of more than just characters. The text is in different fonts and includes formatting information such as centring, page headers and footers. On the whole, the storage of formatted text is vendor specific, since virtually every application has its own file format. This is not helped by the fact that many suppliers attempt to keep their file formats secret, or update them frequently to stop other's products being compatible. With the exception of bare ASCII, the most common shared format is *rich text format* (*RTF*), which encodes formatting information including style sheets. However, even where an application will import or export RTF, it may represent a cut down version of the full document style.

RTF regards the document as formatted text, that is, it concentrates on the appearance. Documents can also be regarded as structured objects: this book has chapters containing sections, sub-sections ... paragraphs, sentences, words and characters. There are *OSI standards* for document structure and interchange, which in theory could be used for transfer between packages and sites, but these are rarely used in practice. Just as the Postscript language is used to describe the printed page, *standardized markup language* (*SML*) can be used to store structured text in a reasonably extensible way. You can define your own structures (the definition itself in SML), and produce documents according to them.

For bitmap storage the range of formats is seemingly unending. The stored image needs to record the size of the image, the number of bits per pixel, possibly a colour map, as well as the bits of the image itself. In addition, an icon may have a 'hot-spot' for use as a cursor. If you think of all the ways of encoding these features, or leaving them implicit, and then consider all the combinations of these different encodings, you can see why there are problems. And all this before we have even considered the effects of compression! There is, in fact, a whole software industry producing packages which convert from one format to another.

Given the range of storage standards (or rather lack of standards), there is no easy advice as to which is best, but if you are writing a new word-processor and are about to decide how to store the document on disk, think, just for a moment, before defining yet another format.

2.7.6   *Methods of access*

Standard database access is by special key fields with an associated index. The user has to know the key before the system can find the information. A telephone directory is a good example of this. You can find out someone's telephone number if you know their name (the key), but you cannot find the name given the number. This is evident in the interface of many computer systems. So often, when you contact an organization, they can only help you if you give your customer number, or last order number. The usability of the system is seriously impaired by a short-sighted reliance on a single key and index. In fact, most database systems will allow multiple keys and indices, allowing you to find a record given partial information. So these problems are avoidable with only slight foresight.

There are valid reasons for not indexing on too many items. Adding extra indices adds to the size of the database, so one has to balance ease of use against storage cost. However, with ever increasing disk sizes, this is not a good excuse for all but extreme examples. Unfortunately, brought up on lectures about algorithmic efficiency, it is easy for computer scientists to be *stingy* with storage. Another, more valid, reason for restricting the fields you index is privacy and security. For example, telephone companies will typically hold an on-line index which given a telephone number would return the name and address of the subscriber, but to protect the privacy of their customers, this information is not divulged to the general public.

It is often said that dictionaries are only useful for people who can spell. Bad spellers do not know what a word looks like so cannot look it up to find out. Not only in spelling packages, but in general, an application can help the user by matching badly spelt versions of keywords. One example of this is '*do what I mean*' (*DWIM*) used in several of Xerox Parc's experimental programming environments. If a command name is misspelt the system prompts the user with a close correct name. Menu-based systems make this less of an issue, but one can easily imagine doing the same with, say, file selection. Another important instance of this principle is *Soundex*, a way of indexing words, especially names. Given a key, Soundex finds those words which *sound* similar. For example, given McCloud, it would find MacCleod. These are all examples of *forgiving systems*, and in general one should aim to accommodate user's mistakes. Again, there are exceptions to this: you do not want a bank's automated teller machine (ATM) to give money when the PIN number is *almost* correct!

Not all databases allow long passages of text to be stored in records, perhaps setting a maximum length for text strings, or demanding the length be fixed in advance. Where this is the case, the database seriously restricts interface applications where text forms an important part. At the other extreme, *free text retrieval* systems are centred on unformatted, unstructured text. These systems work by keeping an index of *every* word in every document, and so you can ask 'give me all documents with the words "human" and "computer" in them'. Programs, such as versions of the UNIX 'grep' command give some of the same facilities by quickly scanning a list of files for a certain word, but are *much* slower.

2.8   Processing

Computers which run interactive programs will process of the order of 10 million instructions per second. It sounds a lot and yet, like memory, it can soon be used up. Indeed, the first program written by one of the authors (some while ago) 'hung' and all attempts to debug it failed. Later calculation showed that the program would have taken more than the known age of the universe to complete! Failures need not be as spectacular as all that to render a system unusable. Consider, for example, one drawing system known to the authors. To draw a line you press down the mouse button at one end, drag the mouse and then release the mouse button at the other end of the line — but not too quickly. You have to press down the button and then actually hold your hand steady for a moment, otherwise the line starts half way! For activities involving the user's hand–eye coordination, delays of even a fraction of a second can be disastrous.

2.8.1   *Effects of finite processor speed*

As we can see, speed of processing can seriously affect the user interface. These effects must be taken into account when designing an interactive system. There are two sorts of faults due to processing speed: those when it is too slow, and those when it is too fast!

We have seen one example of the former above. This was a *functional fault*, in that the program did the wrong thing. The system is supposed to draw lines from where the mouse button is depressed to where it is released. However, the program gets it wrong — after realizing the button is down, it does not check the position of the mouse fast enough, and so the user has moved the mouse before the start position is registered. This is a fault at the implementation stage of the system rather than of the design. However, to be fair, the programmer may not be given the right sort of information from lower levels of system software.

A second fault due to slow processing is where, in a sense, the program does the right thing, but the feedback is too slow, leading to strange effects at the interface. In order to avoid faults of the first kind, the system *buffers* the user input, that is, it remembers key-presses and mouse buttons and movement. Unfortunately, this leads to problems of its own. One example of this sort of problem is *cursor tracking*, which happens in character-based text editors. The user is trying to move backwards on the same line to correct an error, and so presses the cursor-left key. The cursor moves and when it is over the correct position, the user releases the key. Unfortunately, the system is behind in responding to the user, and so has a few more cursor-left keys to process — the cursor then overshoots. The user tries to correct this by pressing the cursor-right key, and again overshoots. There is typically *no way* for the user to tell whether the buffer is empty or not, except by interacting very slowly with the system and observing that the cursor has moved after every keypress.

A similar problem, *icon wars*, occurs on window systems. The user clicks the mouse on a menu or icon, and nothing happens; for some reason the machine is busy or slow. So the user clicks again, tries something else — then, suddenly, all the buffered mouse clicks are interpreted and the screen becomes a blur of flashing windows and menus. This time, it is not so much that the response is too slow — it is fast enough when it happens — but that the response is variable. The delays due to swapping programs in and out of main memory typically cause these problems.

Furthermore, a style of interaction which is optimal on one machine may not be on a slower machine. In particular, mouse-based interfaces cannot tolerate delays between actions and feedback of more than a fraction of a second otherwise the immediacy required for successful interaction is lost. If these responses cannot be met then a more old fashioned, command-based interface may be required.

The adverse effects of slow processing are made worse because the designers labour under the *myth of the infinitely fast machine*. That is, they design and document their systems as if response will be immediate. Rather than blithely hoping that the eventual machine will be 'fast enough', the designer ought to plan explicitly for slow responses where these are possible. A good example, where buffering is clear and audible (if not visible) to the user, is telephones. Even if the user gets ahead of the telephone when entering a number, the tones can be heard as they are sent over the line. Now this is probably an accident of the design rather than deliberate policy, as there are so many other problems with telephones as interfaces. However, this type of serendipitous feedback should be emulated in other areas.

Whereas it is immediately obvious that slow reponses can cause problems for the user, it is not so obvious why one should not always aim for a system to be as fast as possible. However, there are exceptions to this — the user must be able to read and understand the output of the system. For example, one of the authors was once given a demonstration disk for a spreadsheet. Unfortunately, the machine the demo was written on was clearly slower then the author's machine; not much, at worst half the speed, but different enough. The demo passed in a blur over the screen with nothing remaining on the screen long enough to read. Many high-resolution monitors suffer from a similar problem when they display text. Whereas older character based terminals scrolled new text from the bottom of the screen or redrew from the top, bitmap screens often 'flash' up the new page, giving no indication of direction of movement. A final example is the rate of cursor flashing: the rate is often at a fixed frequency, so varying the speed of the processor does not change the screen display. However, a rate which is acceptable for a CRT screen is too fast for an LCD screen which is more persistent, and the cursor may become invisible or a slight grey colour.

In some ways the solution to these problems is easier, the designer can demand fixed delays (dependent on media and user preference) rather than just going as fast as the machine allows. To plan for the first problem, that of insufficient speed, the designer needs to understand the limitations of the computer system and take account of these at all stages in the design process.

2.8.2 Limitations on interactive performance

There are several factors which can limit the speed of an interactive system:

computation bound This is rare for an interactive program, but possible, for example, when using find/replace in a large document. The system should be designed so that long delays are not in the middle of interaction and so that user gets some idea of how the job is progressing. For a very long processes try to give an indication of duration *before* it starts, and during processing an indication of the stage that the process has reached is helpful. This can be achieved by having a counter or slowly-filling bar on the screen that indicates the amount done, or by changing the cursor to indicate that processing is occurring. Many systems notice after they have been computing for some time and then say 'this may take some time: continue (Y/N)?'. Of course, by the time it says this the process may be nearly finished anyway!

storage channel bound As we discussed in the previous section, the speed of memory access can interfere with interactive performance. We discussed one technique, laziness, for reducing this effect. In addition, if there is plenty of raw computation power and the system is held up solely by memory, it is possible to trade-off memory against processing speed. For example, compressed data take less space to store, and are faster to read in and out, but must be compressed before storage and decompressed when retrieved. Thus faster memory access leads to increased processing time. If data are written more often than they are read, one can choose a technique which is expensive to compress but fairly simple to decompress. For many interactive systems the ability to browse quickly is very important, but users will accept delays when saving updated information.

graphics bound For many modern interfaces, this is the most common bottleneck. It is easy to underestimate the time taken to perform what appear to be simple interface operations. Sometimes clever coding can reduce the time taken by common graphics operations, and there is tremendous variability in performance between programs running on the same hardware. A special-purpose *graphics coprocessor* can be added to a computer system to handle many of the most common graphics operations. This will be both optimized for graphics and allow the main processor to do other work such as manipulating documents and other user data.

network capacity More and more computers are linked by networks. At the simplest this can mean using shared files on a remote machine. When accessing such files it can be the speed of the network rather than that of the memory which limits performance. This is discussed in greater detail below.

2.8.3 *Networked computing*

Computer systems in use today are much more powerful than they were a few years ago, which means that the standard computer on the desktop is quite capable of high-performance interaction without recourse to outside help. However, it is often the case that we use computers not in their stand-alone mode of operation, but linked together in networks. This brings added benefits in allowing communication between different parties, provided they are connected into the same network, as well as allowing the desktop computer to access resources remote from itself. Such networks are inherently much more powerful than the individual computers that make up the network: increased computing power and memory are only part of the story, since the effects of allowing people much more extensive, faster and easier access to information are highly significant to individuals, groups and institutions.

Such networked systems have an effect on interactivity, over and above any additional access to distant peripherals or information sources. Networks sometimes operate over large distances, and the transmission of information may take some appreciable time, which affects the response time of the system and hence the nature of the interactivity. There may be a noticeable delay in response, and if the user is not informed of what is going on, he may assume that his command has been ignored, or lost, and may then repeat it. This lack of feedback is an important factor in the poor performance and frustration users feel when using such systems, and can be alleviated by more sensible use of the capabilities of the desktop machine to inform users of what is happening over the network.

Another effect is that the interaction between human and machine becomes an open loop, rather than a closed one. Many people may be interacting with the machine at once, and their actions may affect the response to your own. Many users accessing a single central machine will slow its response; database updates carried out by one user may mean that the same query by another user at slightly different times may produce different results. The computer system, by the very nature of its dispersal, distribution and multi-access, has been transformed from a fully predictable, deterministic system under the total control of the user into a non-deterministic one, with an individual user being unaware of many important things that are happening to the system as a whole. Such systems pose a particular problem since ideals of consistency, informative feedback and predictable response are violated (see Chapter 4 for more on these principles). However, the additional power and flexibility offered by networked systems means that they are likely to be with us for a long time, and these issues need to be carefully addressed in their design.

2.9 Summary

In Sections 2.2 and 2.3, we described a range of input devices. These performed two main functions: text entry and pointing. The principal text entry device is the QWERTY keyboard, but we also discussed alternative keyboards, chord keyboards and speech input. Pointing devices included the mouse, trackerball and joystick, as well as a large array of less common alternatives. We also mentioned novel devices for manipulation and pointing: the dataglove, as used in many virtual reality systems, and eyegaze systems.

Section 2.4 dealt mainly with the screen as a direct output device. We discussed several different technologies, in particular CRT and LCD screens. Auditory output is still comparatively rare, and this will be discussed in detail in Chapter 15.

Section 2.6 discussed various forms of printer and scanner. Typical office printers include dot-matrix, ink-jet, bubble-jet and laser printers. In addition, thermal printers are used in specialized equipment. We also discussed font styles and page description languages. Scanners are used to convert printed images and documents into electronic form. They are particularly valuable in desktop publishing and for electronic document storage systems.

In Section 2.7, we considered the typical capacities of computer memory, both of main RAM memory, likened to human short-term memory, and long-term memory stored on magnetic and optical disks. The storage capacities were compared with document sizes and video images. We saw that a typical hard disk could only hold about 10 seconds of moving video, but that compression techniques can increase the capacity dramatically. We also discussed storage standards — or rather the lack of them — including the ASCII character set and mark-up languages. The user ought to be able to access information in ways which are natural and tolerant of small slips. Techniques which can help this included multiple indices, free-text databases, DWIM (do what I mean) and Soundex.

Section 2.8 showed how processing speed, whether too slow or too fast, can affect the user interface. In particular, we discussed the effects of buffering: cursor tracking and icon wars. Processing speed is limited by various factors: computation, memory access, graphics and network delays.

The lesson from this chapter is that the interface designer needs to be aware of the properties of the devices with which a system is built. This includes not only input and output devices, but all the factors which influence the behaviour of the interface, since all of these influence the nature and style of the interaction.

Exercises

2.1   What is the basic architecture of a computer system?

2.2   How do you think new, fast, high-density memory devices and quick processors have influenced recent developments in HCI? Do they make systems any easier to us? Do they expand the range of applications of computer systems?

2.3   What input and output devices would you use for the following systems? For each, compare and contrast alternatives, and if appropriate indicate why the conventional keyboard, mouse and c.r.t screen may be less suitable.

   a) portable word processor

   b) tourist information system

   c) tractor-mounted crop-spraying controller

   d) air traffic control system

   e) worldwide personal communications system

   f) digital cartographic system

Recommended Reading

- W. Buxton, There's More to Interaction Than Meets the Eye: Some Issues in Manual Input, in R. Baecker and W. Buxton, editors, *Readings in Human-Computer Interaction: A Multidisciplinary Approach*, Morgan Kaufmann, 1987.

- Deborah J. Mayhew, *Principles and Guidelines in Software User Interface Design*, Chapter 12, Prentice-Hall, 1992.

  A look at input and output devices, complete with guidelines for using different devices.

Chapter 3

The Interaction

Overview

- Interaction models help us to understand what is going on in the interaction between user and system. They address the translations between what the user wants and what the system does.

- Ergonomics looks at the physical characteristics of the interaction and how these influence its effectiveness.

- The dialogue between user and system is influenced by the style of the interface.

- The interaction takes place within a social and organizational context which affects both user and system.

3.1 Introduction

In the last two chapters we have looked at the human and the computer respectively. However, in the context of this book, we are not concerned with them in isolation. We are interested in how the human user uses the computer as a tool to perform, simplify or support a task. In order to do this the user must communicate his requirements to the computer.

There are a number of ways in which the user can communicate with the system. At one extreme is batch input, in which the user provides all the information to the computer at once and leaves the machine to perform the task. This approach does involve an interaction between the user and computer but does not support many tasks well. At the other extreme are highly interactive input devices and paradigms, such as *direct manipulation* (see Chapter 4) and the applications of *virtual reality* (Chapter 15). Here the user is constantly providing instruction and receiving feedback. These are the types of interactive system of which we are particularly thinking.

In this chapter, we consider the communication between user and system: the *interaction*. We will look at some models of interaction which enable us to identify and evaluate components of the interaction, as well as physical, social and organizational issues which provide the context for it. We will also survey some of the different styles of interaction that are used and consider whether or not they are effective in supporting the user.

3.2   Models of Interaction

In previous chapters we have seen the usefulness of models to help us to understand complex behaviour and complex systems. Interaction involves at least two participants: the user and the system. Both are complex, as we have seen, and are very different from each other in the way that they communicate and view the domain and the task. The interface must therefore effectively translate between them to allow the interaction to be successful. This translation can fail at a number of points and for a number of reasons. The use of models of interaction help us to understand exactly what is going on in the interaction and identify the likely root of difficulties. They also provide us with a framework to compare different interaction styles and to consider interaction problems.

We begin by considering the most influential model of interaction, Norman's *execution–evaluation cycle*, then we look at another model which extends the ideas of Norman's cycle. Both of these models describe the interaction in terms of the goals and actions of the user. We will therefore briefly discuss the terminology used and the assumptions inherent in the models, before describing the models themselves.

3.2.1   The terms of interaction

The purpose of an interactive system is to aid a user in accomplishing *goals* from some application *domain*. A domain defines an area of expertise and knowledge in some real-world activity. Some examples of domains are graphic design, authoring and process control in a factory. A domain consists of concepts which highlight its important aspects. In a graphic design domain, some of the important concepts are geometric shapes, a drawing surface and a drawing utensil. *Tasks* are operations to manipulate the concepts of a domain. A goal is the desired output from a performed task. For example, one task within the graphic design domain is the construction of a specific geometric shape with particular attributes on the drawing surface. A related goal would be to produce a solid red triangle centred on the canvas. An *intention* is a specific action required to meet the goal.

Task analysis involves the identification of the problem space (which we discussed in Chapter 1) for the user of an interactive system in terms of the domain, goals, intentions and tasks. We can use our knowledge of tasks and goals to assess the interactive system that is designed to support them. We discuss task analysis in detail in Chapter 7. The concepts used in the design of the system and the description of the user are separate, and so we can refer to them as distinct components, called the *System* and the *User*, respectively. The *System* and *User* are each described by means of a language which can express concepts relevant in the domain of the application. The *System*'s language we will refer to as the *core language* and the *User*'s language we will refer to as the *task language*. The core language describes computational attributes of the domain relevant to the *System* state, whereas the task language describes psychological attributes of the domain relevant to the *User* state.

The system is assumed to be some computerized application, in the context of this book, but the models apply equally to non-computer applications. It is also a common assumption that by distinguishing between user and system we are restricted to single-user applications. This is not the case either. However, the emphasis is on the view of the interaction from a single user's perspective. From this point of view, other users, such as those in a multi-party conferencing system, form part of the system.

3.2.2   *The execution–evaluation cycle*

Norman's model of interaction is perhaps the most influential in Human–Computer Interaction, possibly because of its closeness to our intuitive understanding of the interaction between human user and computer [129]. The user formulates a plan of action which is then executed at the computer interface. When the plan, or part of the plan, has been executed, the user observes the computer interface to evaluate the result of the executed plan, and to determine further actions.

The interactive cycle can be divided into two major phases: execution and evaluation. These can then be subdivided into further stages, seven in all. The stages in Norman's model of interaction are as follows:

- establishing the goal

- forming the intention

- specifying the action sequence

- executing the action

- perceiving the system state

- interpreting the system state

- evaluating the system state with respect to the goals and intentions

Each stage is of course an activity of the user. First the user forms a goal. This is the user's notion of what needs to be done and is framed in terms of the domain, in the task language. It is liable to be imprecise and therefore needs to be translated into the more specific intention, and the actual actions that will reach the goal, before it can be executed by the user. The user perceives the new state of the system, after execution of the action sequence, and interprets it in terms of his expectations. If the system state reflects the user's goal then the computer has done what he wanted and the interaction has been successful; otherwise the user must formulate a new goal and repeat the cycle.

Norman uses this model of interaction to demonstrate why some interfaces cause problems to their users. He describes these in terms of the *gulfs of execution* and the *gulfs of evaluation*. As we noted earlier, the user and the system do not use the same terms to describe the domain and goals — remember that we called the language of the system the *core language* and the language of the user the *task language*. The gulf of execution is the difference between the user's formulation of the actions to reach the goal, and the actions allowed by the system. If the actions allowed by the system correspond to those intended by the user, the interaction will be effective. The interface should therefore aim to reduce this gulf.

The gulf of evaluation is the distance between the physical presentation of the system state and the expectation of the user. If the user can readily evaluate the presentation in terms of his goal, the gulf of evaluation is small. The more effort that is required on the part of the user to interpret the presentation, the less effective the interaction.

Norman's model is a useful means of understanding the interaction, in a way which is clear and intuitive. It allows other, more detailed, empirical and analytic work to be placed within a common framework. However, it only considers the system as far as the interface. It concentrates wholly on the user's view of the interaction. It does not attempt to deal with the system's communication through the interface. An extension of Norman's model, proposed by Abowd and Beale, addresses this problem [2]. This is described in the next section.

3.2.3   The interaction framework

The interaction framework attempts a more realistic description of interaction by including the system explicitly, and breaks it into four main components, as shown in Figure 3.1. The nodes represent the four major components in an interactive system—the *System*, the *User*, the *Input* and the *Output*. Each component has its own language. In addition to the *User*'s task language and the *System*'s core language which we have already introduced, there are languages for both the *Input* and *Output* components to represent those separate, though possibly overlapping, components. *Input* and *Output* together form the *Interface*.

As the interface sits between the *User* and the *System*, there are four steps in the interactive cycle, each corresponding to a translation from one component to

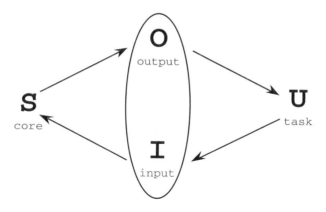

Figure 3.1   *The general interaction framework*

another, as shown by the labelled arcs in Figure 3.2. The *User* begins the interactive cycle with the formulation of a goal and task to achieve that goal. The only way the user can manipulate the machine is through the *Input*, and so the task must be articulated within the input language. The input language is translated into the core language as operations to be performed by the *System*. The *System* then transforms itself as described by the operation translated from the *Input*; the execution phase of the cycle is complete and the evaluation phase now begins. The *System* is in a new state, which must now be communicated to the *User*. The current values of system attributes are rendered as concepts or features of the *Output*. It is then up to the *User* to observe the *Output* and assess the results of the interaction relative to the original goal, ending the evaluation phase and, hence, the interactive cycle. There are four main translations involved in the interaction: articulation, performance, presentation and observation.

The *User*'s formulation of the desired task to achieve some goal needs to be *articulated* in the input language. The tasks are responses of the *User* and they need to be translated to stimuli for the *Input*. As pointed out above, this articulation is judged in terms of the coverage from tasks to input and the relative ease with which the translation can be accomplished. The task is phrased in terms of certain psychological attributes that highlight the important features of the domain for the *User*. If these psychological attributes map clearly on to the input language, then articulation of the task will be made much simpler. An example of a poor mapping that is common in our everyday lives, as pointed out by Norman, occurs in a large room with overhead lighting controlled by a bank of switches. Many times it is desirable to control the lighting so that only a certain section of the room is lit. We are then faced with the puzzle of determining which switches control which lights. The consternation resulting from repeated experimentations with the switches to achieve the desired lighting effect can be traced to the difficulty of articulating a

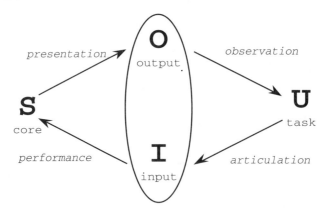

Figure 3.2   *Translations between components*

goal such as 'Turn on the lights in the front of the room' in the input language, which consists of a linear row of switches which may or may not be oriented in a manner suggestive of their operation.

Conversely, an example of a good mapping is in virtual reality systems, where novel input devices such as a dataglove are specifically geared toward easing articulation by making the user's psychological notion of gesturing an act that can be directly realized at the interface. Direct manipulation interfaces, such as those found on common desktop operating systems like the Macintosh, make the articulation of some file handling commands easier. On the other hand, some tasks, such as repetitive file renaming or launching a program whose icon is not visible, are not at all easy to articulate with such an interface.

At the next stage, the responses of the *Input* are translated to stimuli for the *System*. Of interest in assessing this translation is whether the translated input language can reach as many states of the *System* as is possible using the *System* stimuli directly. For example, the remote control units for some compact disc players do not allow the user to turn the power off on the player unit, hence the off state of the player cannot be reached using the remote control's input language. On the panel of the compact disc player, however, there is usually a button which controls the power. The ease with which this translation from *Input* to *System* takes place is of less importance because the effort is not expended by the user. However, there can be a real effort expended by the designer and programmer. In this case, the ease of the translation is viewed in terms of the cost of implementation.

Once a state transition has occurred within the *System*, the execution phase of the interaction is complete and the evaluation phase begins. The new state of the *System* must be communicated to the *User*, and this begins by translating the *System* responses to the transition into stimuli for the *Output* component. This presentation translation must preserve the relevant system attributes from the domain in the limited expressiveness of the output devices. The ability to capture the domain concepts of the *System* within the *Output* is a question of expressiveness for this translation.

For example, while writing a paper with some word-processing package, it is necessary at times to see both the immediate surrounding text where one is currently composing, say the current paragraph, and a wider context within the whole paper that cannot be easily displayed on one screen (say the current chapter).

Ultimately, the user must interpret the output to evaluate what has happened. The response from the *Output* is translated to stimuli for the *User* which trigger assessment. The observation translation will address the ease and coverage of this final translation. For example, it is difficult to tell the time accurately on an unmarked analog clock, especially if it is not oriented properly. It is diffi- cult in a command line interface to determine the result of copying and moving files in a hierarchical file system. Typesetting a report using one of the popular typesetting programs available today is made virtually impossible without some previewing facility which allows rapid (and tree-saving) feedback to assess pro- gress.

Assessing overall interaction

The interaction framework is presented as a means to judge the overall usability of an entire interactive system. In reality, all of the analysis that is suggested by the framework is dependent on the current task (or set of tasks) in which the *User* is engaged. This is not surprising since it is only in attempting to perform a particular task within some domain that we are able to determine if the tools we use are adequate. For example, different text editors are better at different things. For a particular editing task, one can choose the text editor best suited for interaction relative to the task. The best editor, if forced to choose only one, is the one that best suits the tasks that most frequently performed. Therefore, it is not too disappointing that we cannot extend the interaction analysis beyond the scope of a particular task.

A simple example of programming a VCR from a remote control shows that all four translations in the interaction cycle can affect the overall interaction. Inef- fective interaction is indicated by the user not being sure the VCR is set to record properly. This could be because the user has pressed the keys on the remote control unit in the wrong order; this can be classified as an articulatory problem. Or maybe the VCR is able to record on any channel but the remote control lacks the ability to select channels, indicating a coverage problem for the performance translation. It may be the case that the VCR display panel does not indicate that the program has been set, a presentation problem. Or maybe the user does not interpret the indication properly, an observational error. Any one or more of these deficiencies would give rise to ineffective interaction.

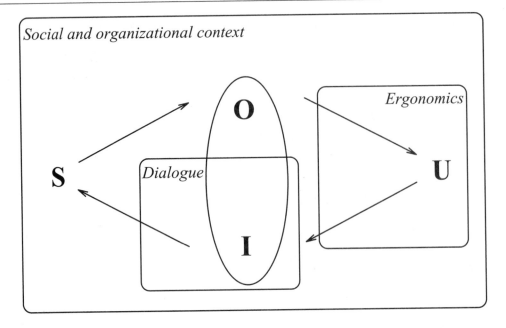

Figure 3.3   *A framework for human–computer interaction (after ACM SIGCHI Curriculum Development Group* [3])

3.3   **Frameworks and HCI**

As well as providing a means of discussing the details of a particular interaction, frameworks provide a basis for discussing other issues which relate to the interaction. The ACM SIGCHI Curriculum Development Group presents a framework similar to that presented here, and uses it to place different areas which relate to HCI [3]. In particular, the field of *ergonomics* addresses issues on the the user side of the interface, covering both input and output, as well as the user's immediate context. Dialogue design and interface styles can be placed particularly along the input branch of the framework, addressing both articulation and performance. However, it is most usually associated with the computer and so is biased to that side of the framework. The entire framework can in turn be placed within a social and organizational context which also affects the interaction (see Figure 3.3). Each of these areas has important implications to the design of interactive systems and the performance of the user. We will introduce them here briefly.

3.4 **Ergonomics**

Ergonomics (or human factors) is traditionally the study of the physical characteristics of the interaction: how the controls are designed, the physical environment
in which the interaction takes place, and the layout and physical qualities of the
screen. A primary focus is on user performance and how the interface enhances or
detracts from this. In seeking to evaluate these aspects of the interaction, ergonomics will certainly also touch upon human psychology and system constraints. It is
a large and established field which is closely related to but distinct from HCI, and
full coverage would demand a book in its own right. Here we consider a few of
the issues addressed by ergonomics as an introduction to the field. We will briefly
look at the arrangement of controls and displays, the physical environment, health
issues and the use of colour. These are by no means exhaustive and are intended
only to give an indication of the types of issues and problems addressed by ergonomics We do not have room here to do justice to the field; for more information
on ergonomic issues the reader is referred to the recommended reading list at the
end of the chapter.

3.4.1 *Arrangement of controls and displays*

In Chapter 1 we considered perceptual and cognitive issues which would affect
the way we present information on a screen and provide control mechanisms
to the user. However, in addition to these cognitive aspects of design, physical
aspects are important. Sets of controls and parts of the display should be grouped
logically to allow rapid access by the user. This may not seem so important when
we are considering a single user of a spreadsheet on a PC, but it becomes vital
when we turn to safety critical applications such as plant control, aviation and air
traffic control. In each of these contexts users are under pressure and are faced
which a huge range of displays and controls. Here it is crucial that the physical
layout of these be appropriate. Indeed, returning to the less critical PC application,
inappropriate placement of controls and displays can lead to inefficiency and
frustration. For example, on one particular electronic newsreader, used by one of
the authors, the command key to read articles from a newsgroup (y) is directly
beside the command key to unsubscribe from a newsgroup (u) on the keyboard.
This poor design frequently leads to inadvertent removal of newsgroups. Although
this is recoverable it wastes time and is annoying to the user. We can therefore see
that appropriate layout is important in all applications.

We have already touched on the importance of grouping controls together
logically (and keeping opposing controls separate). The exact organization which
this will suggest will depend on the domain and the application, but possible
organizations include:

functional controls and displays are organized so that those which are functionally related are placed together;

sequential controls and displays are organized to reflect the order of their use in a typical interaction (this may be particularly appropriate in domains where a particular task sequence is enforced such as aviation);

frequency controls and displays are organized according to how frequently they are used, with the most commonly used controls being the most easily accessible.

In addition to the organization of the controls and displays in relation to each other, the entire system interface must be arranged appropriately in relation to the user's position. So, for example, the user should be able to reach all controls necessary and view all displays without excessive body movement. Critical displays should be at eye level. Lighting should be arranged to avoid glare and reflection distorting displays. Controls should be spaced to provide adequate room for the user to manoeuvre.

3.4.2 The physical environment of the interaction

As well as addressing physical issues in the layout and arrangement of the machine interface, ergonomics is concerned with the design of the work environment itself. Where will the system be used? By whom will it be used? Will users be sitting, standing or moving about? Again this will depend largely on the domain and will be more critical in specific control and operational settings than in general computer use. However, the physical environment in which the system is used may influence how well it is accepted and even the health and safety of its users. It should therefore be considered in all design.

The first consideration here is the size of the users. Obviously this is going to vary considerably. However, in any system the smallest user should be able to reach all the controls (this may include a user in a wheelchair), and the largest user should not be cramped in the environment.

In particular, all users should be comfortably able to see critical displays. For long periods of use, the user should be seated for comfort and stability. Seating should provide back support. If required to stand, the user should have room to move around in order to reach all the controls.

3.4.3 Health issues

Perhaps we do not immediately think of computer use as a hazardous activity but we should bear in mind possible consequences of our designs on the health and safety of users. Leaving aside the obvious safety risks of poorly designed safety critical systems (aeroplanes crashing, nuclear plant leaks and the like), there are a number of factors which may affect the use of more general computers. Again these are factors in the physical environment which directly affect the quality of the interaction and the user's performance:

Physical position As we noted in the previous section users should be able to reach all controls comfortably and see all displays. Users should not be expected to stand for long periods and if sitting, should be provided with back support. If a particular position for a part of the body is to be adopted for long periods (for example, in typing) support should be provided to allow rest.

Temperature Although most users can adapt to slight changes in temperature without adverse effect, extremes of hot or cold will affect performance and, in excessive cases, health. Experimental studies show that performance deteriorates at high or low temperatures, with users being unable to concentrate efficiently.

Lighting The lighting level will again depend on the work environment. However, adequate lighting should be provided to allow users to see the computer screen without discomfort or eyestrain. The light source should also be positioned to avoid glare affecting the display.

Noise Excessive noise can be harmful to health, causing the user pain, and in acute cases, loss of hearing. Noise levels should be maintained at a comfortable level in the work environment. This does not necessarily mean no noise at all. Noise can be a stimulus to users and can provide needed confirmation of system activity.

Time The time users spend using the system should also be controlled. As we saw in the previous chapter, it has been suggested that excessive use of CRT displays can be harmful to users, particularly pregnant women.

3.4.4 *The use of colour*

In this section we have concentrated on the ergonomics of physical characteristics of systems, including the physical environment in which they are used. However, ergonomics has a close relationship to human psychology in that it is also concerned with the perceptual limitations of humans. For example, the use of colour in displays is an ergonomics issue. As we saw in Chapter 1, the visual system has some limitations with regard to colour, including the number of colours that are distinguishable and the difficulty with perceiving blue. We also saw that a relatively high proportion of the population suffer from a deficiency in colour vision. Each of these psychological phenomena lead to ergonomic guidelines; some examples are discussed below.

Colours used in the display should be as distinct as possible and the distinction should not be affected by changes in contrast. Blue should not be used to display critical information. If colour is used as an indicator it should not be the only cue: additional coding information should be included.

The colours used should also correspond to common conventions and user expectations. Red, green and yellow are colours frequently associated with stop, go and standby respectively. Therefore red is used to indicate emergency and alarms; green, normal activity; and yellow, standby and auxiliary function. These conventions should not be violated without very good cause.

3.4.5   *Ergonomics and HCI*

Ergonomics is a huge area which is distinct from HCI but sits alongside it. Its contribution to HCI is in determining constraints on the way we design systems and suggesting detailed and specific guidelines and standards. Ergonomic factors are in general more established and better understood than cognition and are therefore used as the basis for standardizing hardware designs. This issue is discussed further in Chapter 5.

3.5   Interaction Styles

Interaction can be seen as a dialogue between the computer and the user. The choice of interface style can have a profound effect on the nature of this dialogue. Dialogue design is discussed in detail in Chapter 8. Here we introduce the most common interface styles and note the different effects these have on the interaction. There are a number of common interface styles including

- command line interface
- menus
- natural language
- question/answer and query dialogue
- form-fills and spreadsheets
- WIMP

3.5.1   *Command line interface*

The command line interface was the first interactive dialogue style to be commonly used and, in spite of the availability of menu-driven interfaces, it is still widely used. It provides a means of expressing instructions to the computer directly, using function keys, single characters, abbreviations or whole word commands. In some systems the command line is the only way of communicating with the system; more commonly today it is supplementary to menu-based interfaces, providing accelerated access to the system's functionality for experienced users.

Command line interfaces are powerful in that they offer direct access to system functionality (as opposed to the hierarchical nature of menus), and can be combined to apply a number of tools to the same data. They are also flexible: the command often has a number of options or parameters which will vary its behaviour in some way, and it can be applied to many objects at once, making it useful for repetitive tasks. However, this flexibility and power brings with it difficulty in use and learning. Commands must be remembered as no cue is provided in the command line to indicate which command is needed. They are therefore better for expert users than for novices. However, this problem can be alleviated a little by using consistent and meaningful commands and abbreviations. The commands used should be terms within the vocabulary of the user rather than the technician. Unfortunately, commands are often obscure and vary across systems, causing confusion to the user and increasing the overhead of learning.

3.5.2   *Menus*

In a menu-driven interface, the set of options available to the user is displayed on the screen, and selected either using the mouse, or numeric or alphabetic keys. Since the options are visible they are less demanding on the user, relying on recognition rather than recall. However, menu options still need to be meaningful and logically grouped to aid recognition. Often menus are hierarchically ordered and the option required is not available at the top layer of the hierarchy. The grouping and naming of menu options then provides the only cue for the user to find the required option. Such systems can either be purely text based, with the menu options being presented as numbered choices, or may have a graphical component in which the menu appears within a rectangular box and choices are made, perhaps by typing the initial letter of the desired selection, or by entering the associated number, or by moving around the menu with the arrow keys. This is a restricted form of a full WIMP system, described in more detail shortly.

3.5.3   *Natural language*

Perhaps the most attractive means of communicating with computers, at least at first glance, is by natural language. Users, unable to remember a command or lost in a hierarchy of menus, may long for the computer which is able to understand instructions expressed in everyday words! Natural language understanding, both of speech and written input, is the subject of much interest and research. Unfortunately, however, the ambiguity of natural language makes it very difficult for a machine to understand. Language is ambiguous at a number of levels. Firstly, the

Figure 3.4   *A man with a stick or a boy with a stick?*

syntax, or structure, of a phrase may not be clear. If we are given the sentence

the man hit the boy with the stick

we cannot be sure whether the stick is the instrument with which the boy was hit, or whether it is the boy's possession (see Figure 3.4).

Even if a sentence's structure is clear, we may find ambiguity in the meaning of the words used. For example, the word 'pitch' may refer to a sport's field, a throw, a waterproofing substance or even, colloquially, a territory. We often rely on the context and our general knowledge to sort out these ambiguities. This information is difficult to provide to the machine. To complicate matters further, the use of pronouns and relative terms adds further ambiguity.

Given these problems, it seems unlikely that a general natural language interface will be available for some time, if at all. However, systems can be built to understand restricted subsets of a language. For a known and constrained domain, the system can be provided with sufficient information to disambiguate terms. It is important in interfaces which use natural language in this restricted form that the user is aware of the limitations of the system and does not expect too much understanding.

The use of natural language in restricted domains is relatively successful, but it is debatable as to whether this can still be called natural language. The user must learn which phrases the computer understands and may become frustrated if too much is expected. However, it is also not clear how useful a general natural language interface would be. Language is by nature vague and imprecise: this gives it its flexibility and allows creativity in expression. Computers on the other hand require precise instructions. Given a free rein, would we be able to describe our requirements precisely enough to guarantee a particular response? And if so, would the language we used turn out to be a restricted subset of natural language anyway?

3.5.4   *Question/answer and query dialogue*

Question and answer dialogue is a simple mechanism for providing input to an application in a specific domain. The user is asked a series of questions (mainly with yes/no responses, multiple choice, or codes) and so is led through the interaction step by step.

These interfaces are easy to learn and use, but are limited in functionality and power. As such, they are appropriate for restricted domains (particularly information systems) and for novice or casual users.

Query languages on the other hand are used to construct queries to retrieve information from a database. They use natural language style phrases, but in fact require specific syntax, as well as knowledge of the database structure. Queries usually require the user to specify an attribute or attributes for which to search the database, as well as the attributes of interest to be displayed. This is straightforward where there is a single attribute, but becomes complex when multiple attributes are involved, particularly if the user is interested in attribute A or attribute B, or attribute A and not attribute B, or where values of attributes are to be compared. Most query languages do not provide direct confirmation of what was requested, so that the only validation the user has is the result of the search. The effective use of query languages therefore requires some experience.

3.5.5 *Form-fills and spreadsheets*

Form-filling interfaces are used primarily for data entry but can also be useful in data retrieval applications. The user is presented with a display resembling a paper form, with slots to fill in (see Figure 3.5). Often the form display is based upon an actual form with which the user is familiar, which makes the interface easier to use. The user works through the form filling in appropriate values. The data are then entered into the application in the correct place. Most form-filling interfaces allow easy movement around the form and allow some fields to be left blank. They also require correction facilities as users may change their minds or make a mistake about the value that belongs in each field. The dialogue style is useful primarily for data entry applications and, as it is easy to learn and use, for novice users. However, assuming a design which allows flexible entry, form filling is also appropriate for expert users.

Spreadsheets are a sophisticated variation of form filling. The spreadsheet comprises a grid of cells, each of which can contain a value or a formula (see Figure 3.6). The formula can involve the values of other cells (for example, the total of all cells in this column). The user can enter and alter values and formulae in any order and the system will maintain consistency amongst the values displayed, ensuring that all formulae are obeyed. The user can therefore manipulate values to see the effects of changing different parameters. Spreadsheets are an attractive medium for interaction: the user is free to manipulate values at will and the distinction between input and output is blurred, making the interface more flexible and natural.

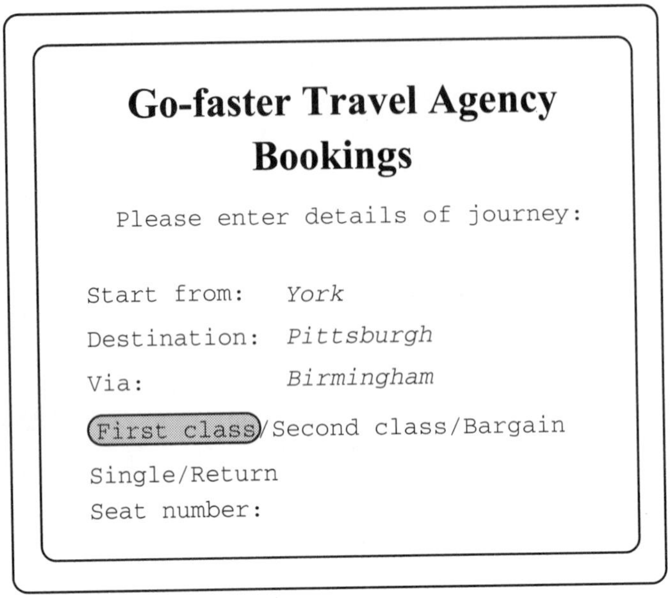

Figure 3.5   *A typical form-filling interface*

Pooches Pet Emporium					
Date	*Description*	*Dog*	*Income*	*Outgoings*	*Balance*
9/2/92	Fees - Mr C. Brown	Snoopy	96.37		96.37
10/2/92	Rubber bones			36.26	60.11
10/2/92	Fees - Mrs E.R. Windsor	7 corgis	1006.45		1066.56
12/2/92	Special order: 7 red carpets			74.28	992.28
16/2/92	Fees - Master T. Tin	Snowy	32.98		1025.26
17/2/92	Beefy Bruno's Bonemeal			243.47	781.79
21/2/92	Fees - Mr F. Flintstone	Dino	21.95		803.74
21/2/92	Special order: 1 Brontosaurus bone			6.47	797.27
28/2/92	Wages - Mr S.H. Ovelit			489.46	307.81

Figure 3.6   *A typical spreadsheet*

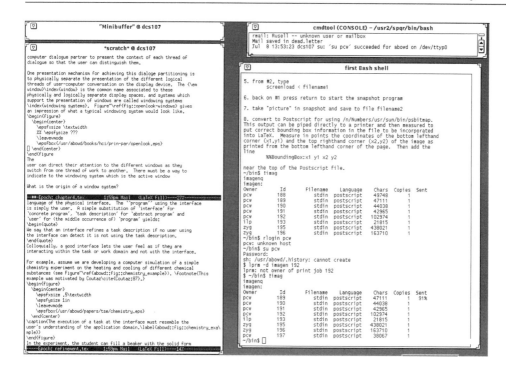

Figure 3.7 *A typical windowing system—the OpenLook system courtesy of Sun Microsystems*

3.5.6 *The WIMP interface*

This sub-section is devoted to a description of the most common environment for interactive computing, known as the WIMP environment. Systems which support the presentation of windows are called windowing systems. Figure 3.7 gives an impression of what a typical windowing system looks like.

WIMP stands for *windows, icons, menus* and *pointers*, (sometimes *windows, icons, mice* and *pull-down menus*), and is the default interface style for the majority of interactive computer systems in use today, especially in the PC and desktop workstation arena.

Windows

Windows are areas of the screen that behave as if they were independent terminals in their own right. A window can usually contain text or graphics, and can be moved or resized. More than one window can be on a screen at once, allowing separate tasks to be visible at the same time. Users can direct their attention to

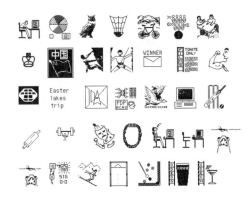

Figure 3.8   *A variety of icons*

the different windows as they switch from one thread of work to another. If one window overlaps the other, then the back window is partially obscured, and then refreshed when exposed again. Overlapping windows can cause problems in that they may obscure vital information, and so windows may also be *tiled*, when they are butted up next to but not overlapping each other.

Usually, windows have various things associated with them that increase their usefulness. *Scrollbars* are one such attachment, allowing the user to move the contents of the window up and down, or from side to side. This makes the window behave as if it were a real window onto a much larger world, where new information is brought into view by manipulating the scrollbars.

There is usually a title bar attached to the top of a window, identifying it to the user, and there may be special boxes in the corners of the window to aid resizing, closing, or making as large as possible. Each of these can be seen in Figure 3.7.

Icons

Windows can be closed and lost forever, or they can be shrunk to some very reduced representation. A small picture is used to represent a closed window, and this representation is known as an *icon*. By allowing icons, many windows can be available on the screen at the same time, ready to be expanded to their full size by clicking on the icon. Shrinking a window to the icon is known as *iconifying* the window. When a user temporarily does not want to follow a particular thread of dialogue, he can suspend that dialogue by iconifying the window containing the dialogue. The icon saves space on the screen and serves as a reminder to the user that he can subsequently resume the dialogue by opening up the window. Figure 3.8 shows a few examples of some icons used in a typical windowing system.

Icons can also be used to represent other aspects of the system, such as a wastebasket for throwing unwanted files into, or various disks and programs

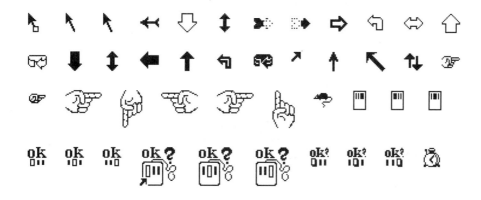

Figure 3.9   *A variety of pointer cursors. Courtesy of Sun Microsystems*

that are accessible to the user. Icons can take many forms; they can be realistic representations of the objects that they represent, or they can be highly stylized. They can even be arbitrary symbols, but these can be difficult for users to interpret.

3.5.7   *Pointers*

The pointer is an important component of the WIMP interface, since the interaction style required by WIMP relies very much on pointing and selecting things such as icons. The mouse provides an input device capable of such tasks, although joysticks and trackballs are other alternatives, as we have previously seen in Chapter 2. The user is presented with a cursor on the screen that is controlled by the input device. A variety of pointer cursors are shown in Figure 3.9.

Menus

The last main feature of window system is the *menu*, an interaction technique which is common across many non-windowing systems as well. A menu presents a choice of operations or services that can be performed by the system at a given time. In Chapter 1, we pointed out that our ability to recall information is inferior to our ability to recognize it from some visual cue. Menus provide information cues in the form of an ordered list of operations which can be scanned. This implies that the names used for the commands in the menu should be meaningful and informative.

The pointing device is used to indicate the desired option. As the pointer moves to the position of a menu item, the item is usually highlighted (by inverse

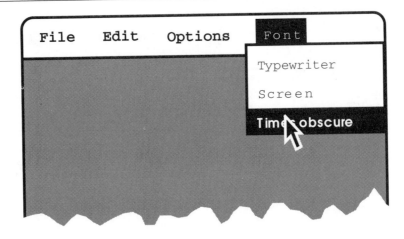

Figure 3.10 *Pull-down menu*

video, or some similar strategy) to indicate that it is the potential candidate for selection. Selection usually requires some additional user action, such as pressing a button on the mouse which controls the pointer cursor on the screen or pressing some special key on the keyboard. Menus are inefficient when they have too many items, and so cascading menus are utilized, in which item selection opens up another menu adjacent to it, allowing refinement of the selection. Several layers of cascading menus can be used. The main menu can be always visible to the user and sub-menus can be pulled down or across from it upon request. Alternatively, the main menu can be hidden and upon request it will pop-up onto the screen. Figure 3.10 shows an example of a pull-down menu.

Pull-down menus are dragged down from the title at the top of the screen, by moving the mouse pointer into the title bar area and pressing the button. Fall-down menus are similar, except the menu automatically appears when the mouse pointer enters the title bar without the user having to press the button. Some menus are pin-up menus, in that they can be 'pinned' to the screen, staying in place until explicitly asked to go away. Pop-up menus appear when a particular region of the screen, maybe designated by an icon, is selected, but only stay as long as the mouse button is depressed.

Another approach to menu selection is to arrange the options in a circular fashion. The pointer appears in the centre of the circle, and so there is the same distance to travel to any of the selections. This has the advantages that it is easier to select items, since they each can have a larger target area, and that the selection time for each item is the same at it is the same distance to any selection. Compare this to a standard menu; remembering Fitts' law from Chapter 1, we can see that it will take longer to select items near the bottom of the menu than at the top. However, pie menus, as they are known, take up more screen space and are less common in interfaces.

Menus often offer *keyboard accelerators*; key combinations that have the same effect as selecting the menu item. This allows more expert users, familiar with the system, to manipulate things without moving off the keyboard and is often faster. The accelerators are often displayed alongside the menu items so that frequent use makes them familiar.

The major problems with menus in general are what to include in the menus and how to group the items. Including too many items makes menus too long or creates too many of them, whereas grouping causes problems in that items all relating to the same topic need to come under the same heading, but many items could be grouped under more than one heading. In pull-down menus the menu label should be chosen to reflect the function of the menu items, and items grouped within menus by function. These groupings should be consistent across applications so that the user can transfer learning to new applications. Menu items should be ordered in the menu according to importance and frequency of use, and opposite functionalities (such as 'save' and 'delete') should be kept apart to prevent accidental selection of the wrong function, with potentially disastrous consequences.

There are many other interaction techniques which are commonly associated to WIMP interfaces that are not windows, icons, menus nor pointers. These include:

Buttons These are individual and isolated regions within a display which can be selected by the user to invoke specific operations. These regions are referred to as buttons because they are purposely made to resemble the push buttons you would find on a control panel. 'Pushing' the button invokes a command, the meaning of which is usually indicated by a textual label. Buttons can also be used to toggle between two states, displaying status information such as whether the current font is italicized or not in a word processor. Such toggle buttons can be grouped together to allow a user to select one feature from a set of mutually exclusive options, such as the size in points of the current font. These are called *radio buttons*, since the collection functions much like the old-fashioned mechanical control buttons on car radios. If a set of options is not mutually exclusive, such as font characteristics like bold, italics and underlining, then a set of toggle buttons can be used to indicate the on/off status of the options. This type of collection of buttons is sometimes referred to as *check boxes*.

Palettes In many application programs, interaction can enter one of several *modes*. The defining characteristic of modes is that the interpretation of actions, such as keystrokes or gestures with the mouse, changes as the mode changes. For example, using the standard UNIX text editor **vi**, keystrokes can be interpreted either as operations to insert characters in the document (insert mode) or as operations to perform file manipulation (command mode). Problems occur if the user is not aware of the current mode. Palettes are a mechanism for making the set of possible modes and the active mode visible to the user. A palette is usually a collection of icons which are reminiscent of the purpose of the various modes. An example in a drawing package would be a collection of icons to indicate the pixel colour or pattern which is used to fill in objects, much like an artist's palette for paint.

Dialogue boxes These information windows are used by the system to bring the user's attention to some important information, possibly an error or a warning used to prevent a possible error. Alternatively, dialogue boxes are used to invoke a sub-dialogue between user and system for a very specific task that will normally be embedded within some larger task. For example, most interactive applications result in the user creating some file that will have to be named and stored within the filing system. When the user or system wants to save the file, a dialogue box can be used to allow the user to name the file and indicate where it is to be located within the filing system. When the save sub-dialogue is complete, the dialogue box will disappear. Just as windows are used to separate the different threads of user–system dialogue, so too are dialogue boxes used to factor out auxiliary task threads from the main task dialogue.

Together, these elements of the WIMP interfaces are called *widgets*, and they comprise the toolkit for interaction between user and system. In Chapter 10 we will describe windowing systems and interaction widgets more from the programmer's perspective. There we will discover that though most modern windowing systems provide the same set of basic widgets, the 'look and feel'—how widgets are physically displayed and how users can interact with them to access their functionality—of different windowing systems and toolkits can differ drastically.

3.6 The Context of the Interaction

We have been considering the interaction between a user and a system, and how this is affected by interface design. However, this interaction does not occur within a vacuum. We have already noted some of the physical factors in the environment which can directly affect the quality of the interaction. This is part of the context in which the interaction takes place. However, this still assumes a single user operating a single, albeit complex, machine. In reality, users work with a wider social and organizational context. This context provides the wider context for the interaction, and may influence the activity and motivation of the user. In Chapter 14 we consider in more detail the issues involved when more than one user attempts to work together on a system. Here we will confine our discussion to the influence social and organizational factors may have on the user's interaction with the system. These may not be factors over which the designer has control. However, it is important to be aware of such influences to understand the user and the work domain fully.

The presence of other people in a work environment affects the performance of the worker in any task. In the case of peers, competition increases performance, at least of known tasks. Similarly the desire to impress management and superiors improves performance on these tasks. However, when it comes to acquisition of new skills, the presence of these groups can inhibit performance, due to the fear of failure. Consequently, privacy is important to allow users the opportunity to experiment.

In order to perform well users must be motivated. There are a number of possible sources of motivation, as well as those we have already mentioned, including fear, allegiance, ambition and self-satisfaction. The latter is influenced by the user's perception of the quality of the work done which leads to job satisfaction. If a system makes it difficult for the user to perform necessary tasks, or is frustrating to use, the user's job satisfaction, and consequently performance, will be reduced.

The user may also lose motivation if a system is introduced which does not match the actual requirements of the job to be done. Often systems are chosen and introduced by managers rather than the users themselves. In some cases the manager's perception of the job may be based upon observation of results and not on actual activity. The system introduced may therefore impose a way of working which is unsatisfactory to the users. If this happens there may be three results: the system will be rejected, the users will be resentful and unmotivated, or the user will adapt the intended interaction to his own requirements. This indicates the importance of involving actual users in the design process.

On the other hand the introduction of new technology may prove to be a motivation to users, particularly if it is well designed, integrated with the user's current work, and challenging. Providing adequate feedback is an important source of motivation for users. If no feedback is given during a session, the user may become bored, unmotivated, or worse, unsure of whether the actions performed have been successful. In general, an action should have an obvious effect to prevent this confusion and to allow early recovery in the case of error. Similarly, if system delays occur, feedback can be used to prevent frustration on the part of the user — the user is then aware of what is happening and is not left wondering if the system is still working.

3.7 Summary

In this chapter, we have looked at the interaction between human and computer, and in particular, how we can ensure that the interaction is effective in allowing the user to get the required job done. We have seen how we can use Norman's execution–evaluation model, and the interaction framework which extends it, to analyze the interaction in terms of how easy or difficult it is for the user to express what he wants and determine whether it has been done.

We have also looked at the role of ergonomics in interface design, in analyzing the physical characteristics of the interaction, and we have discussed a number of interface styles. We have considered how each of these factors can influence the effectiveness of the interaction.

Interaction between user and computer does not take place in a vacuum but is affected by numerous social and organizational factors. These may be beyond the designer's control but awareness of them can help to limit any negative effects on the interaction.

Exercises

3.1 Choose two of the interaction styles (described in Section 3.5) that you have experience of using. Use the interaction framework to analyze the interaction involved in using these interface styles for a database selection task. Which of the distances is greatest in each case?

3.2 Find out all that you can about natural language interfaces. Are there any successful systems? For what applications are these most appropriate?

3.3 What influence does the social environment in which you work have on your interaction with the computer? What effect does the organization (commercial or academic) to which you belong have on the interaction?

Recommended Reading

- Donald A. Norman, *The Psychology of Everyday Things*, Basic Books, 1988. (Republished as *The Design of Everyday Things* by Penguin 1991)

  A classic text which discusses psychological issues in designing everyday objects and addresses why such objects are often so difficult to use. Discusses the execution–evaluation cycle. Very readable and entertaining.

- Robert W. Bailey, *Human Performance Engineering: A Guide for System Designers*, Prentice Hall, 1982.

  Detailed coverage of human factors and ergonomics issues, with plenty of examples.

- M. Helander (ed.), *Handbook of Human–Computer Interaction*. Part II: User interface design. North-Holland, 1988.

  Comprehensive coverage of interface styles.

Part II

Design Practice

In this part, we concentrate on how design practice addresses the critical feature of an interactive system—usability from the human perspective. The chapters in this part promote the purposeful design of more usable interactive systems. We begin in Chapter 4 with a historical perspective on the evolution of interactive systems and how they have increased the usability of computers in general. We conclude that chapter with a catalogue of more abstract principles of interactive systems which support usability. The remaining chapters in this part are all focused on describing design activities which promote and demonstrate usability characteristics.

Chapter 5 defines the design process within a software engineering framework and how that process suits a user-centred approach to design. Chapters 6–9 are concerned with abstract modelling techniques which can be used at earlier stages of a user-centred design process in order to support specific usability principles. Chapter 6 discusses models with psychological or cognitive origins, where the emphasis is on formulating aspects of user behaviour such as goal formation and problem solving. Chapter 7 describes task analysis techniques for determining the relevant actions a user performs in some work domain. Chapter 8 describes dialogue description techniques used to specify and analyze the communication between user and system. Chapter 9 describes the use of general mathematical notations used in software engineering notations to specify and analyze abstract descriptions of interactive systems.

Chapters 10–12 address usability issues which occur later in the user-centred design process. In Chapter 10, we provide an overview of implementation support for the programmer of an interactive system. In Chapter 11 we describe techniques for evaluation of an interactive system to see if it satisfies the users' needs. In Chapter 12 we discuss the provision of user support in the form of help systems and documentation.

Chapter 4

Usability Paradigms and Principles

Overview

- Designing for maximum usability is the goal of interactive systems design.

- Examples of effective strategies for building interactive systems provide paradigms for designing usable interactive systems. The evolution of these usability paradigms also provide a good perspective on the history of computing.

- Abstract principles offer a way of understanding usability in a more general sense, especially if we can express them within some coherent catalogue.

4.1 Introduction

As we noted in Chapter 3, the primary objective of an interactive system is to allow the user to achieve particular goals in some application domain, that is, the interactive system must be usable. The designer of an interactive system, then, is posed with two open questions:

- How can an interactive system be developed to ensure its usability?

- How can the usability of an interactive system be demonstrated or measured?

There are two approaches to answering these questions. The first is by means of example, in which successful interactive systems are commonly believed to enhance usability and, therefore, serve as *paradigms* for the development of future products. The second approach is more theoretically driven, deriving abstract *principles* for effective interaction from knowledge of the psychological, computational and sociological aspects of the problem domains. These principles direct the design and evaluation of a product from its onset.

This distinction between paradigms and principles is an important reflection on the history of HCI as a discipline. We believe that we now build interactive systems which are more usable than those built in the past. We also believe that there is considerable room for improvement in designing more usable systems in the future. As discussed in Chapter 2, the great advances in computer technology have increased the power of machines and enhanced the bandwidth of communication between humans and computers. The impact of technology alone, however, is not sufficient to enhance its usability. As our machines have become more powerful, the key to increased usability has come from the creative and considered application of the technology to accommodate and augment the power of the human. Paradigms for interaction have for the most part been dependent upon technological advances and their creative application to enhance interaction. Principles for interaction are independent of the technology; they depend to a much greater extent on a deeper understanding of the human element in the interaction.

The creative development of paradigms for interaction, which we discuss in Section 4.2, is the main reason we are able today to build more usable systems. The problem with those paradigms is that they are rarely well defined. It is not clear how they support a user in accomplishing some tasks. As a result, it is entirely possible that repeated use of some paradigm will not result in the design of a more usable system. Derivation of principles for interaction, discussed in Section 4.3, have usually arisen out of a need to explain why a paradigm is successful and when it might not be. Principles can provide the repeatability which paradigms in themselves cannot provide. However, in defining these principles it is all too easy to provide general and abstract definitions which are not very helpful to the designer. Therefore, the future of interactive system design relies on a complementary approach. The creativity giving rise to new paradigms should be strengthened by the development of a theory which provides principles to support the paradigm in its repeated application.

4.2 Paradigms for Interaction

As we have said, the greatest advances in HCI have come by way of exploratory and creative design. In this section, we investigate some of the principal advances in interactive designs. What is important to notice here is that the techniques and designs mentioned are recognized as major improvements in interaction, though it is sometimes hard to find a consensus for the reason behind the success.

We will discuss 11 different paradigms in this section. They do not provide mutually exclusive categories, as particular systems will often incorporate ideas from more than one of the following paradigms. In a way, this section serves as a history of interactive system development, though our emphasis is not so much on historical accuracy as on interactive innovation. We are concerned with the advances in interaction provided by each paradigm.

4.2.1   *Time-sharing*

In the 1940s and 1950s, the significant advances in computing consisted of new hardware technologies. Mechanical relays were replaced by vacuum electron tubes. Tubes were replaced by transistors, and transistors by integrated chips, all of which meant that the amount of sheer computing power was increasing by orders of magnitude. By the 1960s it was becoming apparent that the explosion of growth in computing power would be wasted if there was not an equivalent explosion of ideas about how to channel that power. One of the leading advocates of research into human-centred applications of computer technology was J. C. R. Licklider, who became the director of the Information Processing Techniques Office of the United States Defense Department's Advanced Research Projects Agency (ARPA). It was Licklider's goal to finance various research centres across the United States in order to encourage new ideas about how best to apply the burgeoning computing technology.

One of the major contributions to come out of this new emphasis in research was the concept of *time-sharing*, in which a single computer could support multiple users. Previously, the human (or more accurately, the programmer) was restricted to batch sessions, in which complete jobs were submitted on punched cards or paper tape to an operator who would then run them individually on the computer. Time-sharing systems of the sixties made programming a truly interactive venture and brought about a sub-culture of programmers known as 'hackers'—single-minded masters of detail who took pleasure in understanding complexity. Though the purpose of the first interactive time-sharing systems was simply to augment the programming capabilities of the early hackers, it marked a significant stage in computer applications for human use. Rather than rely on a model of interaction as a pre-planned activity that resulted in a complete set of instructions being laid out for the computer to follow, truly interactive exchange between programmer and computer was possible. The computer could now project itself as a dedicated partner with each individual user and the increased throughput of information between user and computer allowed the human to become a more reactive and spontaneous collaborator. Indeed, with the advent of time-sharing, real human–computer interaction was now possible.

4.2.2   *Video display units*

As early as the mid-1950s researchers were experimenting with the possibility of presenting and manipulating information from a computer in the form of images on a video display unit (VDU). These display screens could provide a more suitable medium than a paper printout for presenting vast quantities of strategic information for rapid assimilation. The earliest applications of display screen images were developed in military applications, most notably the Semi-Automatic

Ground Environment (SAGE) project of the U. S. Air Force. It was not until 1962, however, when a young graduate student at the Massachussetts Institute of Technology, Ivan Sutherland, astonished the established computer science community with his *Sketchpad* program, that the capabilities of visual images was realized. As described in Howard Rheingold's history of computing *Tools for Thought* [147]:

> Sketchpad allowed a computer operator to use the computer to create, very rapidly, sophisticated visual models on a display screen that resembled a television set. The visual patterns could be stored in the computer's memory like any other data, and could be manipulated by the computer's processor... But Sketchpad was much more than a tool for creating visual displays. It was a kind of simulation language that enabled computers to translate abstractions into perceptually concrete forms. And it was a model for totally new ways of operating computers; by changing something on the display screen, it was possible, via Sketchpad, to change something in the computer's memory.

Sketchpad demonstrated two important ideas. Firstly, computers could be used for more than just data processing. They could extend the user's ability to abstract away from some levels of detail, visualizing and manipulating different representations of the same information. Those abstractions did not have to be limited to representations in terms of bit sequences deep within the recesses of computer memory. Rather, the abstractions could be made truly visual. To enhance human interaction, the information within the computer was made more amenable to human consumption. The computer was made to speak a more human language, instead of the human being forced to speak a more computerized tongue. Secondly, Sutherland's efforts demonstrated how important the contribution of one creative mind (coupled with a dogged determination to see the idea through) could be to the entire history of computing.

4.2.3 *Programming toolkits*

Douglas Engelbart's ambition since the early 1950s was to use computer technology as a means of complementing human problem-solving activity. Engelbart's idea as a graduate student at the University of California at Berkeley was to use the computer to teach humans. This dream of naive human users actually learning from a computer was a stark contrast to the prevailing attitude of his contemporaries that computers were a purposely complex technology that only the intellectually privileged were capable of manipulating. Engelbart's dedicated research team at the Stanford Research Institute in the 1960s worked toward achieving the manifesto set forth in an article published in 1963 [60]:

> By 'augmenting man's intellect' we mean increasing the capability of a man to approach a complex problem situation, gain comprehension to suit his particular needs, and to derive solutions to problems.... We refer to

a way of life in an integrated domain where hunches, cut-and-try, intangibles, and the human 'feel for the situation' usefully coexist with powerful concepts, streamlined terminology and notation, sophisticated methods, and high-powered electronic aids.

Many of the ideas that Engelbart's team developed at the Augmentation Research Centre—such as word-processing and the mouse—only attained mass commercial success decades after their invention. A live demonstration of his oNLine System (NLS—also later known as NLS/Augment) was given in the Autumn of 1968 at the Fall Joint Computer Conference in San Francisco before a captivated audience of computer skeptics. We are not so concerned here with the interaction techniques which were present in NLS, as many of those will be discussed later. What is important here is the method that Engelbart's team adopted in creating their very innovative and powerful interactive systems with the relatively impoverished technology of the 1960s.

Engelbart wrote of how humans attack complex intellectual problems like a carpenter who produces beautifully complicated pieces of woodwork with a good set of tools. The secret to producing computing equipment which aided human problem-solving ability was in providing the right *toolkit*. Taking this message to heart, his team of programmers concentrated on developing the set of programming tools they would require in order to build more complex interactive systems. The idea of building components of a computer system which will allow you to rebuild a more complex system is called bootstrapping and has been used to a great extent in all of computing. The power of programming toolkits is that small, well-understood components can be composed in fixed ways in order to create larger tools. Once these larger tools become understood, they can continue to be composed with other tools, and the process continues.

4.2.4 *Personal computing*

Programming toolkits provide a means for those with substantial computing skills to greatly increase their productivity. But Engelbart's vision was not exclusive to the computer literate. The decade of the 1970s saw the emergence of computing power aimed at the masses, computer literate or not. One of the first demonstrations that the powerful tools of the hacker could be made accessible to the computer novice was a graphics programming language for children called LOGO. The inventor, Seymour Papert, wanted to develop a language that was easy for children to use. He and his colleagues from MIT and elsewhere designed a computer-controlled mechanical turtle that dragged a pen along a surface to trace its path. A child could quite easily pretend they were 'inside' the turtle and direct it to trace out simple geometric shapes, such as a square or a circle. By typing in English phrases, such as `Go forward` or `Turn left`, the child/programmer could teach the turtle to draw more and more complicated figures. By adapting the graphical programming language to a model which children could understand and use,

Papert demonstrated a valuable maxim for interactive system development—no matter how powerful a system may be, it will always be more powerful the easier it is to use.

Alan Kay was profoundly influenced by the work of both Engelbart and Papert. He realized that the power of a system such as NLS was only going to be successful if it was as accessible to novice users as was LOGO. In the early 1970s his view of the future of computing was embodied in small, powerful machines which were dedicated to single users, that is *personal computers*. Together with the founding team of researchers at the Xerox Palo Alto Research Center (PARC), Kay worked on incorporating a powerful and simple visually based programming environment, Smalltalk, for the personal computing hardware that was just becoming feasible. As technology progresses, it is now becoming more difficult to distinguish between what constitutes a personal computer, or workstation, and what constitutes a mainframe. Kay's vision in the mid-1970s of the ultimate hand-held personal computer—he called it the Dynabook—outstrips even the technology we have available in the nineties [95].

4.2.5 *Window systems and the WIMP interface*

With the advent and immense commercial success of personal computing, the emphasis for increasing the usability of computing technology focused on addressing the single user who engaged in a dialogue with the computer in order to perform some work. Humans are able to think about more than one thing at a time, and in accomplishing some piece of work, they frequently interrupt their current train of thought to pursue some other related piece of work. A personal computer system which forces the user to progress in order through all of the tasks needed to achieve some objective, from beginning to end without any diversions, does not correspond to that standard working pattern. If the personal computer is to be an effective dialogue partner, it must as flexible in its ability to 'change the topic' as the human is.

But the ability to address the needs of a different user task is not the only requirement. Computer systems for the most part react to stimuli provided by the user, so they are quite amenable to a wandering dialogue which is initiated by the user. As the user engages in more than one plan of activity over a stretch of time, it becomes difficult for him to maintain the status of the overlapping threads of activity. It is therefore necessary for the computer dialogue partner to present the context of each thread of dialogue so that the user can distinguish them.

One presentation mechanism for achieving this dialogue partitioning is to separate physically the presentation of the different logical threads of user–computer conversation on the display device. The *window* is the common mechanism associated with these physically and logically separate display spaces. We discussed windowing systems in detail in Chapter 2.

More and more computer users are becoming familiar with interaction based on windows, icons, menus and pointers—the WIMP interface. These interaction devices first appeared in the commercial marketplace in April, 1981, when Xerox Corporation introduced the 8010 Star Information System. But many of the interaction techniques underlying a windowing system were used in Engelbart's group in NLS and at Xerox PARC in the experimental precursor to Star, the Alto.

4.2.6 *The metaphor*

In developing the LOGO language to teach children, Papert used the metaphor of a turtle dragging its tail in the dirt. Children could quickly identify with the real-world phenomenon and that instant familiarity gave them an understanding of how they could create pictures. Metaphors are used quite successfully to teach new concepts in terms of ones which are already understood, as we saw when looking at analogy in Chapter 1. It is no surprise that this general teaching mechanism has been successful in introducing computer novices to relatively foreign interaction techniques. We have already seen how metaphors are used to describe the functionality of many interaction widgets, such as windows, menus, buttons and palettes. Tremendous commercial successes in computing have arisen directly from a judicious choice of metaphor. The Xerox Alto and Star were the first workstations based on the metaphor of the office desktop. The majority of the management tasks on a workstation have to do with file manipulation. Linking the set of tasks associated to file manipulation to the filing tasks in a typical office environment makes the actual computerized tasks easier to understand at first. And the success of the desktop metaphor is unquestionable. Another good example in the personal computing domain is the widespread use of the spreadsheet metaphor for accounting and financial modelling.

Very few will debate the value of a good metaphor for increasing the initial familiarity between user and computer application. The danger of a metaphor is usually realized after the initial honeymoon period. When word processors were first introduced, they relied heavily on the typewriter metaphor. The keyboard of a computer closely resembles that of a standard typewriter, so it seems like a good metaphor from which to start. However, the behaviour of a word processor is different from any typewriter. For example, the space key on a typewriter is passive, producing nothing on the piece of paper and just moving the guide further along the current line. For a typewriter, a space is not a character. However, for a word processor, the blank space *is* a character which must be inserted within a text just as any other character is inserted. So an experienced typist is not going to be able to predict correctly the behaviour of pressing the spacebar on the keyboard by appealing to her experience with a typewriter. Whereas the typewriter metaphor is beneficial for providing a preliminary understanding of a word processor, the analogy is inadequate for promoting a full understanding of how the word processor works. In fact, the metaphor gets in the way of the user understanding the computer.

A similar problem arises with most metaphors. Although the desktop metaphor is initially appealing, it falls short in the computing world because there are no office equivalents for ejecting a floppy disk or printing a document. When designers try too hard to make the metaphor stick, the resulting system can be more confusing. Who thinks it is intuitive to drag the icon of a floppy disk to the wastebasket in order to eject it from the system? Ordinarily, the wastebasket is used to dispose of things that we never want to use again, which is why it works for deleting files. We must accept that some of the tasks we perform with a computer do not have real-world equivalents. Or if they do, we cannot expect a single metaphor to account for all of them.

Another problem with a metaphor is the cultural bias that it portrays. With the growing internationalization of software, it should not be assumed that a metaphor will apply across national boundaries. A meaningless metaphor will only add another layer of complexity between the user and the system.

A more extreme example of metaphor occurs with *virtual reality* systems. In a virtual reality system, the metaphor is not simply captured on a display screen. Rather, the user is also portrayed within the metaphor, literally creating an alternative, or virtual, reality. Any actions that the user performs are supposed to become more natural and so more movements of the user are interpreted, instead of just key presses, button clicks and movments of an external pointing device. A virtual reality system also needs to know the location and orientation of the user. Consequently, the user is often 'rigged' with special tracking devices so that the system can locate them and interpret their motion correctly.

4.2.7   Direct manipulation

In the early 1980s as the price of fast and high-quality graphics hardware was steadily decreasing, designers were beginning to see that their products were gaining popularity as their visual content increased. As long as the user–system dialogue remained largely unidirectional—from user command to system command-line prompt—computing was going to stay within the minority population of the hackers who revelled in the challenge of complexity. In a standard command-line interface, the only way to get any feedback on the results of previous interaction is to know that you have to ask for it and to know how to ask for it. In terms of the interaction framework discussed in Chapter 3, not every articulated input expression from the user is accompanied by some output expression which reveals an underlying change in the internal state of the system. Rapid visual and audio *feedback* on a high-resolution display screen or through a high-quality sound system makes it possible to provide evaluative information for every executed user action.

Rapid feedback is just one feature of the interaction technique known as *direct manipulation*. Ben Shneiderman [156, 157] is attributed with coining this phrase in 1982 to describe the appeal of graphics based interactive systems such as Sketchpad and the Xerox Alto and Star. He highlights the following features of a direct manipulation interface:

- visibility of the objects of interest

- incremental action at the interface with rapid feedback on all actions

- reversibility of all actions, so that users are encouraged to explore without severe penalties

- syntactic correctness of all actions, so that every user action is a legal operation

- replacement of complex command languages with actions to manipulate directly the visible objects (and, hence, the name direct manipulation)

The first real commercial success which demonstrated the inherent usability of direct manipulation interfaces for the general public was the Macintosh personal computer, introduced by Apple Computer, Inc. in 1984 after the relatively unsuccessful marketing attempt in the business community of the similar but more pricey Lisa computer. We discussed earlier how the desktop metaphor makes the computer domain of file management, usually described in terms of files and directories, easier to grasp by likening it to filing in the typical office environment, usually described in terms of documents and folders. The direct manipulation interface for the desktop metaphor requires that the documents and folders are made visible to the user as icons which represent the underlying files and directories. An operation such as moving a file from one directory to another is mirrored as an action on the visible document which is 'picked up and dragged' along the desktop from one folder to the next. In a command-line interface to a filing system, it is normal that typographical errors in constructing the command line for a move operation would result in a syntactically incorrect command (for example, mistyping the file's name results in an error if you are fortunate enough not to accidentally spell another file in the process). It is impossible to formulate a syntactically incorrect move operation with the pick up and drag style of command. It is still possible for errors to occur at a deeper level, as the user might move a document to the wrong place. But it is relatively easy to detect and recover from those errors. While the document is dragged, continual visual feedback is provided, creating the illusion that the user is actually working in the world of the desktop and not just using the metaphor to help them understand.

Ed Hutchins, Jim Hollan and Donald Norman [90] provide a more psychological justification in terms of the *model-world metaphor* for the directness that the above example suggests. In Norman and Draper's collection of papers on *User-Centered Design* [130] they write:

> In a system built on the model-world metaphor, the interface is itself a world where the user can act, and which changes state in response to user actions. The world of interest is explicitly represented and there is no intermediary between user and world. Appropriate use of the model-world metaphor can create the sensation in the user of acting upon the

objects of the task domain themselves. We call this aspect of directness *direct engagement*.

In the model-world metaphor, the role of the interface is not so much one of mediating between the user and the underlying system. From the user's perspective, the interface *is* the system.

A consequence of the direct manipulation paradigm is that there is no longer a clear distinction between input and output. In the interaction framework, in Chapter 3 we talked about a user articulating input expressions in some input language and observing the system-generated output expressions in some output language. In a direct manipulation system, the output expressions are used to formulate subsequent input expressions. The document icon is an output expression in the desktop metaphor, but that icon is used by the user to articulate the move operation. This aggregation of input and output is reflected in the programming toolkits, as widgets are not considered as input or output objects exclusively. Rather, widgets embody both input and output languages, so we consider them as *interaction objects*.

Somewhat related to the visualization provided by direct manipulation is the *WYSIWYG* paradigm, which stands for 'What you see is what you get'. What you see on a display screen, for example, when you are using a word-processor, is not the actual document that you will be producing in the end. Rather, it is a representation or rendering of what that final document will look like. The implication with a WYSIWYG interface is that the difference between the representation and the final product is minimal, and the user is easily able to visualize the final product from the computer's representation. So, in the word-processing example, you would be able to see what the overall layout of your document would be from its image on screen, minimizing any guesswork on your part to format the final printed copy.

With WYSIWYG interfaces, it is the simplicity and immediacy of the mapping between representation and final product that matters. In terms of the interaction framework, the observation of an output expression is made simple so that assessment of goal achievement is straightforward. But WYSIWYG is not a panacea for usability. What you see is all you get! In the case of a word-processor, it is difficult to achieve more sophisticated page design if you must always see the results of the layout on screen. For example, suppose you want to include a picture in a document you are writing. You design the picture and then place it in the current draft of your document, positioning it at the top of the page on which it is first referenced. As you make changes to the paper, the position of the picture will change. If you still want it to appear at the top of a page, you will no doubt have to make adjustments to the document. It would be easier if you only had to include the picture once, with a directive that it should be positioned at the top of the printed page, whether or not it appears that way on screen. You might sacrifice the WYSIWYG principle in order to make it easier to incorporate such floatable objects in your documents.

4.2.8 *Language versus action*

Whereas it is true that direct manipulation interfaces make some tasks easier to perform correctly, it is equally true that some tasks are more difficult, if not impossible. Contrary to popular wisdom, it is not generally true that actions speak louder than words. The image we projected for direct manipulation was of the interface as a replacement of the underlying system as the world of interest to the user. Actions performed at the interface replace any need to understand their meaning at any deeper, system level. Another image is of the interface as the interlocutor or mediator between the user and the system. The user gives the interface instructions and it is then the responsibility of the interface to see that those instructions are carried out. The user–system communication is by means of indirect language instead of direct actions.

We can attach two meaningful interpretations to this language paradigm. The first requires that the user understands how the underlying system functions and the interface as interlocutor need not perform much translation. In fact, this interpretation of the language paradigm is similar to the kind of interaction which existed before direct manipulation interfaces were around. In a way, we have come full circle!

The second interpretation does not require the user to understand the underlying system's structure. The interface serves a more active role, as it must interpret between the intended operation as requested by the user and the possible system operations that must be invoked to satisfy that intent. Because it is more active, some people refer to the interface as an *agent* in these circumstances. We can see this kind of language paradigm at work in an information retrieval system. You may know what kind of information is in some internal system database, such as the British highway code, but you would not know how that information is organized. If you had a question about speed limits on various roads, how would you ask? The answer in this case would be that you would ask the question in whatever way it comes to mind, typing in a question such as, 'What are the speed limits on different roads?'. You then leave it up to the interface agent to reinterpret your request as a legal query to the highway code database.

Whatever interpretation we attach to the language paradigm, it is clear that it has advantages and disadvantages when compared to the action paradigm implied by direct manipulation interfaces. In the action paradigm, it is often much easier to perform simple tasks without risk of certain classes of error. For example, recognizing and pointing to an object reduces the difficulty of identification and the possibility of misidentification. On the other hand, more complicated tasks are often rather tedious to perform in the action paradigm, as they require repeated execution of the same procedure with only minor modification. In the language paradigm, there is the possibility of describing a generic procedure once (for example, a looping construct which will perform a routine manipulation on all files in a directory) and then leaving it to be executed without further user intervention.

The action and language paradigms need not be completely separate. In the above example, we distinguished between the two paradigms by saying that we can describe generic and repeatable procedures in the language paradigm and not in the action paradigm. An interesting combination of the two occurs in *programming by example* when a user can perform some routine tasks in the action paradigm and the system records this as a generic procedure. In a sense, the system is interpreting the user's actions as a language script which it can then follow.

4.2.9   *Hypertext*

In 1945, Vannevar Bush, then the highest ranking scientific administrator in the United States war effort, published an article entitled 'As We May Think' in *The Atlantic Monthly*. Bush was in charge of over 6000 scientists who had greatly pushed the frontiers of scientific knowledge during the Second World War. He recognized that a major drawback of these prolific research efforts was that it was becoming increasingly difficult to keep in touch with the growing body of scientific knowledge in the literature. In his opinion, the greatest advantages of this scientific revolution were to be gained by those individuals who were able to keep abreast of an ever-increasing flow of information. To that end, he described an innovative and futuristic information storage and retrieval apparatus—the *memex*—which was constructed with technology wholly existing in 1945 and aimed at increasing the human capacity to store and retrieve connected pieces of knowledge by mimicking our ability to create random associative links.

The memex was essentially a desk with the ability to produce and store a massive quantity of photographic copies of documented information. In addition to its huge storage capacity, the memex could keep track of links between parts of different documents. In this way, the stored information would resemble a vast interconnected mesh of data, similar to how many perceive information is stored in the human brain. In the context of scientific literature, where it is often very difficult to keep track of the origins and interrelations of the ever-growing body of research, a device which explicitly stored that information would be an invaluable asset.

We have already discussed some of the contributions of 'disciples' of Bush's vision—Douglas Engelbart and Alan Kay. One other follower was equally influenced by the ideas behind the memex, though his dreams have not yet materialized to the extent of Engelbart's and Kay's. Ted Nelson was another graduate student/dropout whose research agenda was forever transformed by the advent of the computer. An unsuccessful attempt to create a machine language equivalent of the memex on early 1960s computer hardware led Nelson on a life-long quest to produce *Xanadu*, a potentially revolutionary worldwide publishing and information retrieval system based on the idea of interconnected, non-linear text and other media forms. A traditional paper is read from beginning to end, in a linear fashion. But within that text, there are often ideas or footnotes that urge the reader to digress into a richer topic. The linear format for information does not provide much support for this random and associated browsing task. What Bush's memex suggested was to preserve the non-linear browsing structure in the actual documentation. Nelson coined the phrase *hypertext* in the mid-1960s to reflect this non-linear text structure.

It was nearly two decades after Nelson coined the term hypertext before the first hypertext systems came into commercial use. In order to reflect the use of such non-linear and associative linking schemes for more than just the storage and retrieval of textual information, the terms *hypermedia* and *multi-media* are used for non-linear storage of all forms of electronic media. We will discuss these systems in Part 3 of this book (see Chapter 15). Most of the riches won with the success of hypertext and hypermedia were not gained by Nelson, though his project Xanadu survives to this day.

4.2.10 *Multi-modality*

The vast majority of interactive systems use the traditional keyboard and possibly a pointing device such as a mouse for input and are restricted to one (possibly colour) display screen with limited sound capabilities for output. Each of these input and output devices can be considered as communication channels for the system and they correspond to certain human communication channels, as we saw in Chapter 1. A *multi-modal* interactive system is a system that relies on the use of multiple human communication channels. Each different channel for the user is referred to as a modality of interaction. In this sense, all interactive systems can be considered multi-modal, for humans have always used their visual and haptic (touch) channels in manipulating a computer. In fact, we often use our audio channel to hear whether the computer is actually running properly.

Modern multi-modal systems have come to rely to a greater extent on simultaneous use of multiple communication channels for both input and output. Humans quite naturally process information by simultaneous use of different channels. We point to someone and refer to them as 'you', and it is only by interpreting the simultaneous use of voice and touch that our directions are easily articulated and understood. Designers have wanted to mimic this flexibility in both articulation and observation by extending the input and output expressions an interactive system will support. So, for example, we can modify a gesture made with a pointing device by speaking, indicating what operation is to be performed on the selected object.

Multi-modal, multi-media and virtual reality systems form a large core of current research in interactive system design which we categorize under the heading *multi-sensory systems*. These are discussed in more detail in Chapter 15.

4.2.11   *Computer-supported cooperative work*

Another development in computing in the 1960s was the establishment of the first computer networks which allowed communication between separate machines. Personal computing was all about providing the individual with enough computing power so that they were liberated from dumb terminals which operated on a timesharing system. It is interesting to note that as computer networks have become more prevalent, individuals have retained their powerful workstations but now want to reconnect themselves to the rest of the workstations in their immediate working environment, and even throughout the world! A result of this reconnection is the emergence of collaboration between individuals via the computer—called computer-supported cooperative work, or CSCW.

The main distinction between CSCW systems and interactive systems designed for a single user is that designers can no longer neglect the society within which any single user operates. CSCW systems are built to allow interaction between humans via the computer and so the needs of the many must be represented in the one product. A fine example of a CSCW system is electronic mail—or *email*—yet another metaphor by which individuals at physically separate locations can communicate via electronic messages which work in a similar way to convential postal systems. One user can compose a message and 'post' it to another user (specified by his electronic mail address). When the message arrives at the remote user's site, he is informed that a new message has arrived in his 'mailbox'. He can then read the message and respond as desired. Although email is modelled after conventional postal systems, its major advantage is that it is often much faster than the traditional system (jokingly referred to by email devotees as 'snail mail'). Communication turnarounds between sites across the world can be in the order of minutes, as opposed to weeks.

Electronic mail is an instance of an asynchronous CSCW system because the participants in the electronic exchange do not have to be working at the same time in order for the mail to be delivered. The reason we use mail is precisely because of its asynchronous characteristics. All we need to know is that the recipient will eventually receive the message. In contrast, it might be desirable for synchronous communication, which would require the simultaneous participation of sender and recipient, as in a phone conversation.

CSCW is a major emerging topic in current HCI research, and so we devote much more attention to it in Part 3 of this book. CSCW systems built to support users working in groups are referred to as *groupware*. Chapter 13 discusses groupware systems in depth. In Chapter 14 the more general issues and theories arising from CSCW are discussed.

4.3 Principles to Support Usability

In this section, we focus on general principles which can be applied to the design of an interactive system in order to promote its usability. It is too bold an objective to produce a comprehensive catalogue of usability principles. Instead, our emphasis will be on structuring the presentation of usability principles in such a way that the catalogue can be easily extended as our knowledge increases.

The principles we present are first divided into three main categories:

Learnability the ease with which new users can begin effective interaction and achieve maximal performance.

Flexibility the multiplicity of ways the user and system exchange information.

Robustness the level of support provided the user in determining successful achievement and assessment of goals.

In the following sub-sections, we will sub-divide these main categories into more specific principles which support them. In most cases, we have been able to situate these more specific principles within a single category, but we have made explicit those cases when a principle falls into two of the above categories.

4.3.1 Learnability

Learnability concerns the features of the interactive system that allow novice users to understand how to use it initially and then how to attain a maximal level of performance. The specific principles which support learnability are described in this sub-section. Table 4.1 contains a summary of the principles to support learnability.

Predictability

Except when interacting with some video games, a user does not take very well to surprises. Predictability of an interactive system means that the user's knowledge of the interaction history is sufficient to determine the result of his future interaction with it. There are many degrees to which predictability can be satisfied. The knowledge can be restricted to the presently perceivable information, so that the user need not remember anything other than what is currently observable. The knowledge requirement can be increased to the limit where the user is actually forced to remember what every previous keystroke was and what every previous screen display contained (and the order of each!) in order to determine the consequences of the next input action.

Predictability of an interactive system is distinguished from deterministic behaviour of the computer system alone. Most computer systems are ultimately

Table 4.1   *Summary of principles affecting learnability*

Principle	Definition	Related principles
Predictability	Support for the user to determine the effect of future action based on past interaction history.	Operation visibility
Synthesizability	Support for the user to assess the effect of past operations on the current state.	Immediate/Eventual honesty
Familiarity	The extent to which a user's knowledge and experience in other real-world or computer-based domains can be applied when interacting with a new system.	Guessability, Affordance
Generalizability	Support for the user to extend knowledge of specific interaction within and across applications to other similar situations.	
Consistency	Likeness in input/output behaviour arising from similar situations or similar task objectives.	

deterministic machines, so that given the state at any one point in time and the operation which is to be performed at that time, there is only one possible state that can result. Predictability is a user-centred concept; it is deterministic behaviour from the perspective of the user. It is not enough for the behaviour of the computer system to be determined completely from its state, as the user must be able to take advantage of the determinism.

For example, a common mathematical puzzle would be to present you with a sequence of three or more numbers and ask you what would be the next number in the sequence. The assumption in this puzzle (and one that can often be incorrect) is that there is a unique function or algorithm which produces the entire sequence of numbers and it is up you to figure it out. We know the function, but all you know are the results it provides from the first three calculations. The function is certainly deterministic; the test for you is a test of its predictability given the first three numbers in the sequence.

As another possibly more pertinent example, imagine you have created a complex picture using a mouse-driven graphical drawing package. You leave the picture for a few days and then go back to change it around a bit. You are allowed to select certain objects for editing by positioning the mouse over the object and clicking a mouse button to highlight it. Can you tell what the set of selectable objects is? Can you determine which area of the screen belongs to which of these objects, especially if some objects overlap? Does the visual image on the screen indicate what objects form a compound object which can only be selected as a group? Predictability of selection in this example depends on how much of the history of the creation of the visual image is necessary in order for you to determine what happens when you click on the mouse button.

This notion of predictability deals with the user's ability to determine the effect of operations on the system. Another form of predictability has to do with the user's ability to know which operations can be performed. *Operation visibility* refers to how the availability of operations which can next be performed is shown to the user. If an operation can be performed, then there may be some perceivable indication of this to the user. This principle supports the performance in humans of recognition over recall. If not, then the user will have to remember when they can perform the operation and when they cannot. Likewise, the user should understand from the interface if an operation they might like to invoke cannot be performed.

Synthesizability

Predictability focuses on the user's ability to determine the effect of future interactions. This assumes that the user has some mental model (see Chapter 1) of how the system behaves. Predictability says nothing about the way the user forms a model of the system's behaviour. In building up some sort of predictive model of the system's behaviour, it is important for the user to assess the consequences of previous interactions in order to formulate a model of the behaviour of the system. Synthesis, therefore, is the ability of the user to assess the effect of past operations on the current state.

When an operation changes some aspect of the internal state, it is important that the change is seen by the user. The principle of honesty relates to the ability of the user interface to provide an observable and informative account of such change. In the best of circumstances, this notification can come immediately, requiring no further interaction initiated by the user. Or at the very least, the notification should appear eventually, after explicit user directives to make the change observable. A good example of the distinction between immediacy and eventuality can be seen in the comparison between command language interfaces and visual desktop interfaces for a file management system. You have moved a file from one directory to another. The principle of honesty implies that after moving the file to its new location in the file system you are then able to determine its new whereabouts. In a command language system, you would typically have to remember the destination directory and then ask to see the contents of that directory in order to verify that the file has been moved (in fact, you would also have to check that the file is no longer in its original directory to determine that it has been moved and not copied). In a visual desktop interface, a visual representation (or icon) of the file to be moved is dragged from its containing directory and placed in its destination directory where it remains visible (assuming the destination folder is selected to reveal its contents). In this case, the user need not expend any more effort to assess the result of the move operation. In this case, the visual desktop is immediately honest.

The problem with eventual honesty is that the user must know to look for the change. In a situation in which the user is learning a new interactive system, it is likely that he will not know to look for change. In earlier versions of the Apple Macintosh Finder, performing the operation to create a new folder in another folder did not necessarily result in that new folder's icon being visible in the original folder. New users (and even some experienced users) would often think that they had not issued the new folder operations correctly and would ask for another new folder (and another, and another, ...). They would not know to search through the entire open folder in search of the latest addition. Then several minutes (hours, days) later, they would notice that there were a number of empty and untitled folders lying around. The eventual (accidental) discovery of the change brought about by the new folder operation was then difficult to associate to that operation. Fortunately, this problem was addressed in Version 7 of the Finder.

As another example of the benefit of immediate over eventual honesty, let us examine a typical global search and replace function in a word processor. Imagine you have noticed in the past a tendency to repeat words in a document (e.g. you type "the the" without noticing the error). In an attempt to automate your proofreading, you decide to globally replace all occurrences of "the the" with "the". The typical global search and replace function performs this substitution without revealing the changes made to you. Suddenly, a careless typing error is transformed into unacceptable grammar as the sentence

We will prove <u>the the</u>orem holds as a corollary of the following lemma.

is transformed to

We will prove <u>the</u>orem holds as a corollary of the following lemma.

Familiarity

New users of a system bring with them a wealth of experience across a wide number of application domains. This experience is obtained both through interaction in the real world and also through interaction with other computer systems. For a new user, the familiarity of an interactive system measures the correlation between the user's existing knowledge and the knowledge required for effective interaction. For example, when word-processors were originally introduced, the analogy between the word-processor and a typewriter was intended to make the new technology more immediately accessible to those who had little experience with the former but quite a bit of experience with the latter. Familiarity has to do with a user's first impression of the system. In this case, we are interested in how the system is first perceived and whether the user can determine how to initiate any interaction. An advantage of a metaphor, such as the typewriter metaphor for word-processing described above, is precisely captured by familiarity. Jordan *et al.* refer to this familiarity as the *guessability* of the system [94].

Some psychologists argue that there are intrinsic properties, or affordances, of any visual object that suggest to us how they can be manipulated. The appearance of the object stimulates a familiarity with its behaviour. For example, the shape of a door handle can suggest how it should be manipulated to open a door, and a key on a keyboard suggests to us that it can be pushed. In the design of a graphical user interface, it is implied that a soft button used in a form's interface suggests it should be pushed (though it does not suggest how it is to be pushed via the mouse). Effective use of the affordances which exist for interface objects can enhance the familiarity of the interactive system.

Generalizability

Users often try to extend their knowledge of specific interaction behaviour to situations which are similar but previously unencountered. The generalizability of an interactive system supports this activity, leading to a more complete predictive model of the system for the user. We can apply generalization to situations in which the user wants to apply knowledge which helps achieve a particular goal, to another situation in which the goal is in some way similar. Generalizability can be seen as a form of consistency.

Generalization can occur within a single application or across a variety of applications. For example, in a graphical drawing package which draws a circle as a constrained form of ellipse, we would want the user to generalize that a square can be drawn as a constrained rectangle. A good example of generalizability across a variety of applications can be seen in multi-windowing systems which attempt to provide cut/paste/copy operations to all applications in the same way (with varying degrees of success). Generalizability within an application can be maximized by any conscientious designer. One of the main advantages of standards and programming style guides, which we will discuss in Section 5.3, is that they increase generalizability across a wide variety of applications within the same environment.

Consistency

Consistency relates to the likeness in behaviour arising from similar situations or similar task objectives. Consistency is probably the most widely mentioned principle in the literature on user interface design. "Be consistent!" we are constantly urged. The user relies on a consistent interface. However, the difficulty of dealing with consistency is that it can take many forms. Consistency is not a single property of an interactive system that is either satisfied or not satisfied. Instead, consistency must be applied relative to something. Thus we have consistency in command naming, or consistency in command/argument invocation.

Another consequence of consistency having to be defined with respect to some other feature of the interaction is that many other principles can be 'reduced' to qualified instances of consistency. Hence, familiarity can be considered as consistency with respect to past real-world experience and generalizability as consistency with respect to experience with the same system or set of applications on the same platform. Because of this pervasive quality of consistency, it might be argued that consistency should be a separate category of usability principles, on the same level as learnability, flexibility and robustness. Rather than do that, we will here discuss different ways in which consistency can be manifested.

Consistency can be expressed in terms of the form of input expressions or output responses with respect to the meaning of actions in some conceptual model of the system. For example, before the introduction of explicit arrow keys, some word-processors used the relative position of keys on the keyboard to indicate directionality for operations (e.g. to move one character to the left, right, up or down). The conceptual model for display based editing is a two-dimensional plane, so the user would think of certain classes of operations in terms of movements up, down, left or right in the plane of the display. Operations which required directional information, such as moving within the text or deleting some unit of text, could be articulated by using some set of keys on the keyboard which form a pattern consistent with up, down, left and right (e.g. the keys e, x, s and d, respectively). For output responses, a good example of consistency can be found in a warnings system for an aircraft. Warnings to the pilot are classified into three categories, depending on whether the situation with the aircraft requires immediate recovery action, eventual but not immediate action or no action at all (advisory) on the part of the crew. These warnings are signalled to the crew by means of a centralized warnings panel in which the categories are consistently colour-coded (red for immediate, amber for eventual and green for advisory).

Grudin has argued that because of the relative nature of consistency, it can be a dangerous principle to follow [78]. A good example he gives is with the development and evolution of the standard typewriter keyboard. When keyboards for typewriters were first made, the designers laid out the keys in alphabetical order. Then it was discovered that such an arrangement of keys was both inefficient from the machine's perspective (adjacent typewriter keys pressed in succession caused jams in the mechanism, so the likelihood of this occurrence had to be designed out) and tiring for the typist (a touch typist would not have equal stress distributed over all fingers). The resulting QWERTY and Dvorak keyboards have since been adopted to combat the problems of the 'consistent' keyboard layout[1].

---

[1]See Chapter 2 for a discussion of different keyboards.

Table 4.2   *Summary of principles affecting flexibility*

Principle	Definition	Related principles
Dialogue initiative	Allowing the user freedom from artificial constraints on the input dialogue imposed by the system.	System/User pre-emptiveness
Multi-threading	Ability of the system to support user interaction pertaining to more than one task at a time.	Concurrent vs. Interleaving, Multi-modality
Task migratability	The ability to pass control for the execution of a given task so that it becomes either internalized by user or system or shared between them	
Substitutivity	Allowing equivalent values of input and output to be arbitrarily substituted for each other.	Representation multiplicity, Equal opportunity
Customizability	Modifiability of the user interface by the user or the system.	Adaptivity, Adaptability

4.3.2   *Flexibility*

Flexibility refers to the multiplicity of ways the end-user and the system exchange information. We identify several principles that contribute to the flexibility of interaction, and these are summarized in Table 4.2.

Dialogue initiative

When considering the interaction between user and system as a dialogue between partners (see Chapter 8), it is important to consider which partner has the initiative in the conversation. The system can initiate all dialogue, in which case the user simply responds to requests for information. We call this type of dialogue *system pre-emptive*. For example, a modal dialogue box prohibits the user from interacting with the system in any way that does not direct input to the box. Alternatively, the user may be entirely free to initiate any action toward the system, in which case the dialogue is *user pre-emptive*. The system may control the dialogue to the extent that it prohibits the user from initiating any other desired communication concerning the current task or some other task the user would like to perform. From the user's perspective, a system-driven interaction hinders flexibility whereas a user-driven interaction favours it.

In general, we want to maximize the user's ability to pre-empt the system and minimize the system's ability to pre-empt the user. Although a system pre-emptive dialogue is not desirable in general, some situations may require it. In a cooperative editor (in which two people edit a document at the same time) it would be impolite for you erase a paragraph of text which your partner is currently editing. For safety reasons, it may be necessary to prohibit the user from the 'freedom' to do potentially serious damage. A pilot about to land an aircraft in which the flaps have asymmetrically failed in their extended position[2], should not be allowed to abort the landing, as this failure will almost certainly result in a catastrophic accident.

On the other hand, a completely user pre-emptive dialogue allows the user to offer any input action at any time for maximum flexibility. This is not an entirely desirable situation, since it increases the likelihood that the user will lose track of the tasks that have been initiated and not yet completed. However, if the designers have a good understanding of the sets of tasks the user is likely to perform with a system and how those tasks are related, they can minimize the likelihood that the user will be prevented from initiating some task at a time when they wish to do so.

Multi-threading

A thread of a dialogue is a coherent subset of that dialogue. In the user–system dialogue, we can consider a thread to be that part of the dialogue that relates to a given user task. *Multi-threading* of the user–system dialogue allows for interaction to support more than one task at a time. *Concurrent* multi-threading allows simultaneous communication of information pertaining to separate tasks. *Interleaved* multi-threading permits a temporal overlap between separate tasks but stipulates that at any given instant, the dialogue is restricted to a single task.

Multi-modality of a dialogue is related to multi-threading. Coutaz has characterized two dimensions of multi-modal systems [45]. First, we can consider how the separate modalities (or channels of communication) are combined to form a single input or output expression. Multiple channels may be available, but any one expression may be restricted to just one channel (keyboard or audio, for example). As an example, to open a window the user can choose between a double-click on an icon, a keyboard shortcut, or saying "open window". Alternatively, a single expression can be formed by a mixing of channels. Examples of such fused modality are error warnings which usually contain a textual message accompanied by an audible beep. On the input side, we could consider chord sequences of input with a keyboard and mouse (pressing the SHIFT key while a mouse button is pressed,

---

[2]Flaps increase the surface area and curvature of the aircraft's wing, providing the extra lift necessary for, among other things, a smooth touchdown. An asymmetric failure results in extreme instability and the aircraft will not fly level.

or saying "drop" as you drag a file over the trash icon. We can also characterize a multi-modality dialogue depending on whether it allows concurrent or interleaved use of multiple modes.

A windowing system naturally supports a multi-threaded dialogue which is interleaved amongst a number of overlapping tasks. Each window can represent a different task, for example, text editing in one window, file management in another, a telephone directory in another and electronic mail in yet another. A multi-modal dialogue can allow for concurrent multi-threading. A very simple example can occur in the windowing system with an audible bell. You are editing a program when a beep indicates that a new electronic mail message has arrived. Even though at the level of the system the audible beep has been interleaved with your requests from the keyboard to perform edits, the overlap between the editing task and the mail message from your perspective is simultaneous.

Task migratability

Task migratability concerns the transfer of control for execution of tasks between system and user. It should be possible for the user or system to pass the control of a task over to the other or promote the task from a completely internalized one to a shared and cooperative venture. Hence, a task that is internal to one can become internal to the other or shared between the two partners.

Spell-checking a paper is a good example of the need for task migratability. Equipped with a dictionary, you are perfectly able to check your spelling by reading through the entire paper and correcting mistakes as you spot them. This mundane task is perfectly suited to automation, as the computer can check words against its own list of acceptable spellings. It is not desirable, however, to leave this task completely to the discretion of the computer, as most computerized dictionaries do not handle proper names correctly, nor can they distinguish between correct and unintentional duplications of words. In those cases, the user task is handed over to the user. The spell-check is best performed in such a cooperative way.

In safety-critical applications, task migratability can decrease the likelihood of an accident. For example, on the flight deck of an aircraft, there are so many control tasks that must be performed that a pilot would be overwhelmed if she had to perform them all as well. Mundane control of the aircraft's position within its flight envelope is greatly automated. However, in the event of emergency, it must be possible to transfer flying controls easily and seamlessly from the system to the pilot.

Substitutivity

Substitutivity requires that equivalent values can be substituted for each other. For example, in considering the form of an input expression to determine the margin for a letter, you may want to enter the value in either inches or centimetres. You may also want to input the value explicitly (say 1.5 inches) or you may want to enter a calculation which produces the right input value (you know the width of the text is 6.5 inches and the width of the paper is 8.5 inches and you want the left margin to be twice as large as the right margin, so you enter $\frac{2}{3}(8.5 - 6.5)$ inches). This input substitutivity contributes toward flexibility by allowing the user to choose whichever form best suits the needs of the moment. By avoiding unnecessary calculations in the user's head, substitutivity can minimize user errors and cognitive effort.

We can also consider substitutivity with respect to output, or the system's rendering of state information. *Representation multiplicity* illustrates flexibility for state rendering. For example, the temperature of a physical object over a period of time can be presented as a digital thermometer if the actual numerical value is important or as a graph if it is only important to notice trends. It might even be desirable to make these representations simultaneously available to the user. Each representation provides a perspective on the internal state of the system. At a given time, the user is free to consider the representations that are most suitable for the current task.

Equal opportunity blurs the distinction between input and output at the interface. The user has the choice of what is input and what is output; in addition, output can be reused as input. Thimbleby describes this principle as, 'If you can see it, you can use it!' It is a common belief that input and output are separate. Many have stressed the significance of the link between input and output. Equal opportunity pushes that view to the extreme. For example, in spreadsheet programs, the user fills in some cells and the system automatically determines the values attributed to some other cells. Conversely, if the user enters values for those other cells, the system would compute the values for the first ones. In this example, it is not clear which cells are the inputs and which are the outputs. Furthermore, this distinction might not be clear or useful to the user. In a drawing package, the user may draw a line by direct manipulation and the system would compute the length of the line; or conversely, the user may specify the line coordinates and the system would draw the line. Both means of manipulating the line are equally important and must be made equally available. Note that equal opportunity implies that the system is not pre-emptive toward the user.

Customizability

Customizability is the modifiability of the user interface by the user or the system. From the system side, we are not concerned with modifications that would be attended to by a programmer actually changing the system and its interface during system maintenance. Rather, we are concerned with the automatic modification that the system would make based on its knowledge of the user. We distinguish between the user-initiated and system-initiated modification, referring to the former as *adaptability* and the latter as *adaptivity*.

Adaptability refers to the user's ability to adjust the form of input and output. This customization could be very limited, with the user only allowed to adjust the position of soft buttons on the screen or redefine command names. This type of modifiability, which is restricted to the surface of the interface, is referred to as lexical customization. The overall structure of the interaction is kept unchanged. The power given to the user can be increased by allowing the definition of macros to speed up the articulation of certain common tasks. In the extreme, the interface can provide the user with programming language capabilities, such as the UNIX shell or the script language Hypertalk in HyperCard. In these cases, Thimbleby points out that it would be suitable to apply well-known principles of programming languages to the user's interface programming language.

Adaptivity is automatic customization of the user interface by the system. Decisions for adaptation can be based on user expertise or observed repetition of certain task sequences. The distinction between adaptivity and adaptability is that the user plays an explicit role in adaptability, whereas his role in an adaptive interface is more implicit. A system can be trained to recognize the behaviour of an expert or novice and accordingly adjust its dialogue control or help system automatically to match the needs of the current user. This is in contrast with a system which would require the user to classify themselves as novice or expert at the beginning of a session. We discuss adaptive systems further in Chapter 12. Automatic macro construction is a form of programming by example, combining adaptability with adaptivity in a simple and useful way. Repetitive tasks can be detected by observing user behaviour and macros can be automatically (or with user consent) constructed from this observation to perform repetitive tasks automatically.

4.3.3 *Robustness*

A user is engaged with a computer in order to achieve some set of goals in the work or task domain. The robustness of that interaction covers features which support the successful achievement and assessment of the goals. In this sub-section, we describe principles which support robustness. A summary of these principles is presented in Table 4.3.

Observability

Observability allows the user to evaluate the internal state of the system by means of its perceivable representation at the interface. As we described in Chapter 3, evaluation allows the user to compare the current observed state with their intention within the task–action plan, possibly leading to a plan revision. Observability is can be discussed through five other principles—browsability, defaults, reachability, persistence and operation visibility. Operation visibility was covered in Section 4.3.1 in relation to predictability. The remaining four are discussed next.

Browsability allows the user to explore the current internal state of the system via the limited view provided at the interface. Usually the complexity of the

Table 4.3 *Summary of principles affecting robustness*

Principle	Definition	Related principles
Observability	Ability of the user to evaluate the internal state of the system from its perceivable representation.	Browsability, Static/Dynamic defaults, Reachability, Persistence, Operation visibility
Recoverability	Ability of the user to take corrective action once an error has been recognized.	Reachability, Forward/Backward recovery, Commensurate effort
Responsiveness	How the user perceives the rate of communication with the system.	Stability
Task conformance	The degree to which the system services support all of the tasks the user wishes to perform and in the way that the user understands them.	Task completeness, Task adequacy

domain does not allow the interface to show all of the relevant domain concepts at once. Indeed, this is one reason why the notion of task is used, in order to constrain the domain information needed at one time to a subset connected with the user's current activity. While you may not be able to view an entire document's contents, if you are only interested in its overall structure, you may be able to see all of an outline view of the document. Even with a restriction of concepts relevant to the current task, it is probable that all of the information a user needs to continue work on that task is not immediately perceivable. Or perhaps the user is engaged in a multi-threaded dialogue covering several tasks. There needs to be a way for the user to investigate, or browse, the internal state. This browsing itself should not have any side-effects on that state, that is, the browsing commands should be passive with respect to the domain-specific parts of the internal state.

The availability of *defaults* can assist the user by passive recall (for example, a suggested response to a question can be recognized as correct instead of recalled). It also reduces the number of physical actions necessary to input a value. Thus, providing default values is a kind of error prevention mechanism. There are two kinds of default values—static and dynamic. Static defaults do not evolve with the session. They are either defined within the system or are acquired at initialization. On the other hand, dynamic defaults evolve during the session. They are computed by the system from previous user inputs; the system is then adapting default values.

Reachability refers to the possibility of navigation through the observable system states. There are various levels of reachability that can be given precise mathematical definitions (see Chapter 9), but the main notion is whether the user can navigate from any given state to any other state. Reachability in an interactive system affects the recoverability of the system, as we will discuss later. In addition, different levels of reachability can reflect the amount of flexibility in the system as well, though we did not make that explicit in the discussion on flexibility.

Persistence deals with the duration of the effect of a communication act and the ability of the user to make use of that effect. The effect of vocal communication does not persist except in the memory of the receiver. Visual communication, on the other hand, can remain as an object which the user can subsequently manipulate long after the act of presentation. If you are informed of a new mail message by a beep at your terminal, you may know at that moment and for a short while later that you have received a new message. If you do not attend to that message immediately, you may forget about it. If, however, some persistent visual information informs you of the incoming message (say, the flag goes up on your electronic mailbox), then that will serve as a reminder that an unread message remains long after its initial receipt[3].

Recoverability

Users make mistakes from which they want to recover. *Recoverability* is the ability to reach a desired goal after recognition of some error in previous interaction. There are two directions in which recovery can occur, forward or backward. Forward error recovery involves the acceptance of the current state and negotiation from that state toward the desired state. *Forward error recovery* may be the only possibility for recovery if the effects of interaction are not revokable (for example, in building a house of cards, you might sneeze whilst placing a card on the seventh level, but you cannot undo the effect of your misfortune except by rebuilding). *Backward error recovery* is an attempt to undo the effects of previous interaction in order to return to a prior state before proceeding. In a text editor, a mistyped keystroke might wipe out a large section of text which you would want to retrieve by an equally simple undo button.

Recovery can be initiated by the system or by the user. When performed by the system, recoverability is connected to the notions of fault-tolerance, safety, reliability and dependability, all topics covered in software engineering. But in software engineering, this recoverability is considered only with respect to system functionality; it is not tied to user intent. When recovery is initiated by the user, it is important that it determines the intent of the user's recovery actions, i.e. whether they desire forward (negotiation) or backward (using undo/redo actions)

---

[3]Chapter 9 discusses notification mechanisms for email in more detail.

corrective action.

Recoverability is linked to reachability because we want to avoid blocking the user from getting to a desired state from some other undesired state (going down a blind alley).

In addition to providing the ability to recover, the procedure for recovery should reflect the work being done (or undone, as the case may be). The principle of *commensurate effort* states that if it is difficult to undo a given effect on the state, then it should have been difficult to do in the first place. Conversely, easily undone actions should be easily doable. For example, if it is difficult to recover files which have been deleted in an operating system, then it should be difficult to remove them, or at least it should require more effort by the user to delete the file than to, say, rename it.

Responsiveness

Responsiveness measures the rate of communication between the system and the user. Response time is generally defined as the duration of time needed by the system to express state changes to the user. In general, short durations and instant-aneous response times are desirable. Instantaneous means that the user perceives system reactions as immediate. But even in situations in which an instantaneous response cannot be obtained, there must be some indication to the user that the system has received the request for action and is working on a response.

As significant as absolute response time is response time *stability*. Response time stability covers the invariance of the duration for identical or similar computational resources. For example, pull-down menus are expected to pop up instantaneously as soon as a mouse button is pressed. Variations in response time will impede anticipation exploited by motor skill.

Task conformance

Since the purpose of an interactive system is to allow a user to perform various tasks in achieving certain goals within a specific application domain, we can ask whether the system supports all of the tasks of interest and whether it supports these as the user wants. *Task completeness* addresses the coverage issue and *task adequacy* addresses the user's understanding of the tasks.

It is not sufficient that the computer system fully implements some set of computational services that were identified at early specification stages. It is essential that the system allows the user to achieve any of the desired tasks in a particular work domain as identified by a task analysis that precedes system specification (see Chapter 7 for a more complete discussion of task analysis techniques). Task completeness refers to the level to which the system services can be mapped onto all of the user tasks. However, it is quite possible that the provision of a new computer based tool will suggest to a user some tasks that were not even conceivable before the tool. Therefore, it is also desirable that the system services be suitably general so that the user can define new tasks.

Discussion of task conformance has its roots in an attempt to understand the success of direct manipulation interfaces. We can view the direct manipulation interface as a separate world from that inside the system. Task completeness covers only one part of the conformance. This separate world is understood and operated upon by the user. With the intuition of the Hutchins, Hollan and Norman model-world metaphor mentioned earlier we require that the task, as represented by the world of the interface, matches the task as understood by the user and supported by the system. If the model-world metaphor satisfies the principle of task adequacy, then the user will be directly on their task plan, minimizing the effort required in the articulation and observation translations discussed in the interaction framework of Chapter 3.

4.4 **Summary**

In this chapter, we have discussed paradigms and principles to promote the usability of interactive systems. We have seen that the history of computing is full of examples of creative insight into how the interaction between humans and computers can be enhanced. While we expect never to replace the input of creativity in interactive system design, we still want to maximize the benefit of one good idea by repeating its benefit in many other designs. Achieving this goal relies less on creativity and more on purposeful and principled design. The second half of this chapter provided an outline of the principles of an interactive system which supports its usability.

Exercises

4.1 Look up and report back guidelines for the use of colour. Be able to state the empirical psychological evidence which supports the guidelines. Which principles of interaction do they support?

4.2 What was the problem with the synthesis example comparing a command language interface with a visual interface? Can you suggest a fix to make a visual interface really immediately honest?

4.3 It has been suggested in this chapter that consistency could be considered a major category of interactive principles, on the same level as learnability, flexibility and robustness. If this had been the case, which principles discussed in this chapter would appear in support of consistency?

4.4   Discuss the ways in which a full-page word-processor is or is not a direct manipulation interface for editing a document using Shneiderman's criteria. What features of a modern word processor break the metaphor of composition with pen (or typewriter) and paper?

Recommended Reading

- Howard Rheingold, *Tools for Thought*, Prentice Hall, 1985.

  An easy to read history of computing, with particular emphasis on developments in interactive systems. Much of the historical perspective of this chapter was influenced by this book.

- Harold Thimbleby, Design of interactive systems. In John A. McDermid, editor, *The Software Engineer's Reference Book*, chapter 57. Butterworth-Heinemann, 1991.

  Thimbleby provides a very insightful list of general principles which apply to interactive systems. Some of the principles we have described in this chapter come from Thimbleby's work, though we have concentrated more on providing an overall organizational framework for the principles.

Chapter 5

The Design Process

Objectives

- Software engineering provides a means of understanding the structure of the design process, and that process can be assessed for its effectiveness in interactive system design.

- Design rules in the form of standards and guidelines provide direction for design, in both general and more concrete terms, in order to enhance the interactive properties of the system.

- Usability engineering promotes the use of explicit criteria to judge the success of a product in terms of its usability.

- Iterative design practices work to incorporate crucial customer feedback early in the design process to inform critical decisions which affect usability.

- Design involves making many decisions among numerous alternatives. Design rationale provides an explicit means of recording those design decisions and the context in which the decisions were made.

5.1 Introduction

In the previous chapter, we concentrated on identifying aspects of usable interactive systems by means of both concrete examples of successful paradigms and by more abstract principles. The design goal is to provide reliable techniques for the repeated design of successful and usable interactive systems. It is therefore necessary that we go beyond the exercise of identifying paradigms and principles and examine the process of interactive system design.

Within Computer Science there is already a large sub-discipline which addresses the management and technical issues of the development of software systems—called *software engineering*. One of the cornerstones of software engineering is the *software life cycle* which describes the activities that take place from the initial concept formation for a software system up until its eventual phasing out and replacement. This is not intended to be a software engineering textbook, so it is not our major concern here to discuss in depth all of the issues associated with software engineering and the myriad of life cycle models.

The important point that we would like to draw out is that issues from HCI affecting the usability of interactive systems are relevant within all the activities of the software life cycle. Therefore, software engineering for interactive system design is not simply a matter of adding one more activity that slots in nicely with the existing activities in the life cycle. Rather, it involves techniques which span the entire life cycle.

We will begin this chapter by providing an introduction to some of the important concepts of software engineering in Section 5.2. Specifically, we will describe the major activities within the traditional software life cycle and discuss issues raised by the special needs of interactive systems. We will then describe three particular approaches to interactive system design which are used to promote product usability throughout the life cycle. In Section 5.3, we will describe the use of design rules in the form of standards and guidelines. In Section 5.4, we will describe a particular methodology called *usability engineering* in which explicit usability requirements are used as goals for the design process. In Section 5.5, iterative design practices which involve prototyping and participative evaluation are described. We conclude this chapter with a discussion of *design rationale*. Design is a decision-making activity and it is important to keep track of the decisions that have been made and the context in which those decisions were made. Various design rationale techniques, presented in Section 5.6, are used to support this critical activity.

5.2   The Software Life Cycle

One of the claims for software development is that it should be considered as an engineering discipline, in a way similar to how electrical engineering is considered for hardware development. One of the distinguishing characteristics of any engineering discipline is that it entails the structured application of scientific techniques to the development of some product. A fundamental feature of software engineering, therefore, is that it provides the structure for applying techniques to develop software systems. The software life cycle is an attempt to identify the activities which occur in software development. These activities must then be ordered in time in any development project and appropriate techniques must be adopted to carry them through.

In the development of a software product, we consider two main parties—the customer who requires the use of the product and the designer who must provide the product. Typically, the customer and the designer are groups of people and some people can be both customer and designer. It is often important to distinguish between the customer who is the client of the designing company and the customer

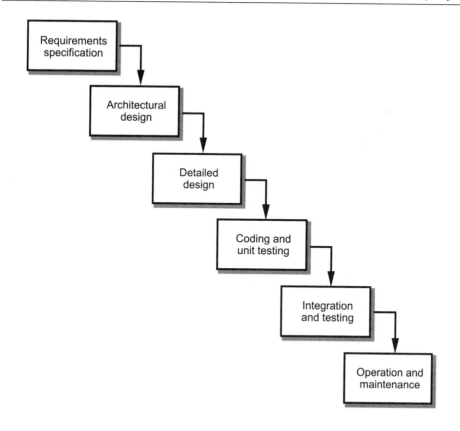

Figure 5.1 *The activities in the waterfall model of the software life cycle*

who is the eventual user of the system. These two roles of the customer as generally described above can be played by different people. The group of people who negotiate the features of the intended system with the designer may never be actual users of the system. In this chapter, we will use the term customer to refer to the group of people who interact with the design team and we will refer to those who will interact with the designed system as the user or end-user.

5.2.1 *Activities in the life cycle*

A more detailed description of the life cycle activities is depicted in Figure 5.1. The graphical representation is reminiscent of a waterfall, in which each activity naturally leads into the next. The analogy of the waterfall is not completely faithful to the real relationship between these activities, but it provides a good starting point for discussing the logical flow of activity. We describe the activities of this waterfall model of the software life cycle next[1].

Requirements specification

In requirements specification, the designer and customer try to capture a description of *what* the eventual system will be expected to provide. This is in contrast to determining *how* the system will provide the expected services, which is the concern of later activities. This activity involves eliciting information from the customer about the work environment. or domain, in which the final product will function. Aspects of the work domain include not only the particular functions that the software product must perform but also details about the environment in which it must operate, such as the people whom it will potentially affect and the new product's relationship to any other products which it is updating or replacing.

Requirements specification begins at the start of product development. Though the requirements are from the customer's perspective, if they are to be met by the software product they must be formulated in a language suitable for implementation. Requirements are usually initially expressed in the native language of the customer. The executable languages for software are less natural and are more closely related to a mathematical language in which each term in the language has a precise interpretation, or semantics. The transformation from the expressive but relatively ambiguous natural language of requirements to the more precise but less expressive executable languages is one key to successful development. In Chapter 7 we discuss task analysis techniques which are used to express work domain requirements in a form that is both expressive and precise.

Architectural design

As we mentioned, the requirements specification concentrates on what the the system is supposed to do. The next activities concentrate on *how* the system provides the services expected from it. The first activity is a high-level decomposition of the system into components that can either be brought in from existing software products or can be developed from scratch independently. It is the purpose of an architectural design to perform this decomposition. An architectural design is not only concerned with the functional decomposition of the system, determining which components provide which services. It must also describe the interdependencies between separate components and the sharing of resources that will arise between components.

There are many structured techniques which are used to assist a designer in deriving an architectural description from information in the requirements specification (such as CORE, MASCOT and HOOD). Details of these techniques are

---

[1]Some authors distinguish between the software development process and the software life cycle, the waterfall model being used to describe the former and not the latter. The main distinction for our purposes is that operation and maintenance of the product is not part of the development process.

outside the scope of this book, but can be found in any software engineering text-book. What we will mention here is that the majority of these techniques are adequate for capturing the *functional requirements* of the system—the services the system must provide in the work domain—but do not provide an immediate way to capture other *non-functional requirements*—features of the system which are not directly related to the actual services provided but relate to the manner in which those services must be provided. Some classic examples of non-functional re-quirements are the efficiency, reliability, timing and safety features of the system. Interactive features of the system, such as those described by the principles in Chapter 4, also form a large class of non-functional requirements.

Detailed design

The architectural design provided a decomposition of the system description that allows for isolated development of separate components which will later be in-tegrated. For those components which are not already available for immediate integration, the designer must provide a sufficiently detailed description so that they may be implemented in some programming language. The detailed design is a *refinement* of the component description provided by the architectural design. The behaviour implied by the higher level description must be preserved in the more detailed description.

Typically, there will be more than one possible refinement of the architectural component which will satisfy the behavioural constraints. Choosing the best refinement is often a matter of trying to satisfy as many of the non-functional requirements of the system as possible. Thus the language used for the detailed design must allow some analysis of the design in order to assess its properties. It is also important to keep track of the design options considered, the eventual decisions that were made and the reasons why, as we will discuss in Section 5.6 on design rationale.

Coding and unit testing

The detailed design for a component of the system should be in such a form that it is possible to implement it in some executable programming language. After coding, the component can be tested to verify that it performs correctly, ac-cording to some test criteria that were determined in earlier activities. Research on this activity within the life cycle has concentrated on two areas. There is plenty of research which is geared towards the automation of this coding activ-ity directly from a low-level detailed design. Most of the work in *formal methods* operates under the hypothesis that, in theory, the transformation from the de-tailed design to the implementation is from one mathematical representation to another and so should be able to be entirely automated. Other more practical work concentrates on the automatic generation of tests from output of earlier activities which can be performed on a piece of code to verify that it behaves correctly.

Integration and testing

Once enough components have been implemented and individually tested, they must be integrated as described in the architectural design. Further testing is done to ensure correct behaviour and acceptable use of any shared resources. It is also possible at this time to perform some acceptance testing with the customers to ensure that the system meets their requirements. It is only after acceptance of the integrated system that the product is finally released to the customer.

It may also be necessary to certify the final system according to requirements imposed by some outside authority, such as an aircraft certification board. As of 1993, a European health and safety act requires that all employers provide their staff with usable systems. The international standards authority, ISO, are currently drafting a standard (ISO 9241) to define the usability of office environment workstations. Coupled together, the health and safety regulations and ISO 9241 provide impetus for designers to take seriously the HCI implications of their design.

Maintenance

After product release, all work on the system is considered under the category of maintenance, until such time as a new version of the product demands a total re-design or the product is phased out entirely. Consequently, the majority of the lifetime of a product is spent in the maintenance activity. Maintenance involves the correction of errors in the system which are discovered after release and the revision of the system services to satisfy requirements that were not realized during previous development. Therefore, maintenance provides feedback to all of the other activities in the life cycle, as shown in Figure 5.2.

5.2.2   *Validation and verification*

Throughout the life cycle, the design must be checked to ensure that it both satisfies the high-level requirements agreed with the customer and is also complete and internally consistent. These checks are referred to as *validation* and *verification*, respectively. Boehm provides a useful distinction between the two, characterizing validation as designing 'the right thing' and verification as designing 'the thing right'. Various languages are used throughout design, ranging from informal natural language to very precise and formal mathematical languages. Validation and verification exercises are difficult enough when carried out within one language; they become much more difficult, if not impossible, when attempted between languages.

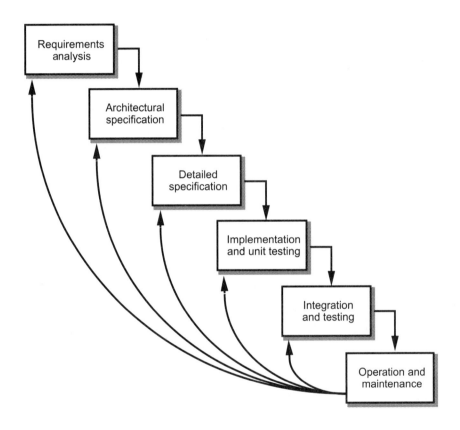

Figure 5.2 *Feedback from maintenance activity to other design activities*

Verification of a design will most often occur within a single life cycle activity or between two adjacent activities. For example, in the detailed design of a component of a payroll accounting system, the designer will be concerned with the correctness of the algorithm to compute taxes deducted from an employee's gross income. The architectural design will have provided a general specification of the information input to this component and the information it should output. The detailed description will introduce more information in refining the general specification. The detailed design may also have to change the representations for the information and will almost certainly break up a single high-level operation into several low-level operations that can eventually be implemented. In introducing these changes to information and operations, the designer must show that the refined description is a legal one within its language (internal consistency) and that it describes all of the *specified* behaviour of the high-level description (completeness) in a provably correct way (relative consistency).

Validation of a design demonstrates that within the various activities the customer's requirements are satisfied. Validation is a much more subjective exercise than verification, mainly because the disparity between the language of the requirements and the language of the design forbids any objective form of proof. In interactive system design, the validation against HCI requirements is often referred to as evaluation and can be performed by the designer in isolation or in cooperation with the customer. We discuss evaluation in depth in Chapter 11.

An important question, which applies to both verification and validation, asks exactly what constitutes a proof. We have repeatedly mentioned the language used in any design activity and the basis for the semantics of that language. Languages with a mathematical foundation allow reasoning and proof in the objective sense. An argument based entirely within some mathematical language can be accepted or refuted based upon universally accepted measures. A proof can be entirely justified by the rules of the mathematical language, in which case it is considered a formal proof. More common is a rigorous proof, which is represented within some mathematical language but which relies on the understanding of the reader to accept its correctness without appeal to the full details of the argument, which could be provided but usually are not. The difference between formality and rigour is in the amount of detail the prover leaves out while still maintaining acceptance of the proof.

Proofs which are for verification of a design can frequently occur within one language or between two languages which both have a precise mathematical semantics. Time constraints for a design project and the perceived economic implications of the separate components usually dictate which proofs are carried out in full formality and which are done only rigorously (if at all). As research in this area matures and automated tools provide assistance for the mechanical aspects of proof, the cost of proof should decrease.

Validation proofs are much trickier, as they almost always involve a transformation between languages. Furthermore, the origin of customer requirements arises in the inherent ambiguity of the real world and not the mathematical world. This precludes the possibility of objective proof, rigorous or formal. Instead, there

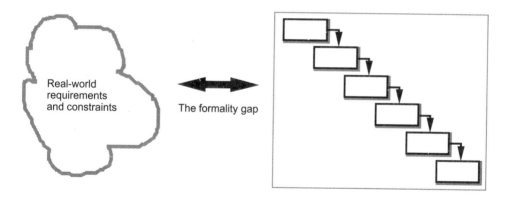

Figure 5.3 *The formality gap between the real world and structured design*

will always be a leap from the informal situations of the real world to any formal and structured development process. We refer to this inevitable disparity as the *formality gap*, depicted in Figure 5.3.

The formality gap means that validation will always rely to some extent on subjective means of proof. We can increase our confidence in the subjective proof by effective use of real-world experts in performing certain validation chores. These experts will not necessarily have design expertise, so they may not understand the design notations used. Therefore, it is important that the design notations used narrow the formality gap, making clear the claims which the expert can then validate. For interactive systems, the expert will have knowledge from a cognitive or psychological domain, so the design specification must be readily interpretable from a psychological perspective in order to validate it against interactive requirements of the system. We will discuss design techniques and notations in Chapters 6–9 which narrow the formality gap for validation of interactive properties of systems.

5.2.3 *Management and contractual issues*

The life cycle described above concentrated on the more technical features of software development. In a technical discussion, managerial issues of design, such as time constraints and economic forces, are not as important. The different activities of the life cycle are logically related to each other. We can see that requirements for a system precede the high-level architectural design which precedes the detailed design, and so on. In reality, it is quite possible that some detailed design is attempted before all of the architectural design. In management, a much wider perspective must be adopted which takes into account the marketability of a system, its training needs, the availability of skilled personnel or possible subcontractors, and other topics outside of the activities for the development of the isolated system.

As an example, we will take the development of a new aircraft on which there will be many software subsystems. The aircraft company will usually go through a concept evaluation period of up to ten years before making any decision about actual product development. Once it has been decided to build a certain type of aircraft, loosely specified in the case of commercial aircraft in terms of passenger capacity and flight range, more explicit design activity follows. This includes joint analysis for both the specification of the aircraft and determination of training needs. It is only after the architectural specification of the aircraft is complete that the separate systems to be developed are identified. Some of these systems will be software systems, such as the flight management system or the training simulator, and these will be designed according to the life cycle described earlier. Typically, this will take four to five years. The separate aircraft systems are then integrated for ground and flight testing and certification before the aircraft is delivered to any customer airlines. The operating lifetime of an aircraft model is expected to be in the range of 20–40 years, during which time maintenance must be provided. The total lifetime of an aircraft from conception to phasing out is up to 55 years, only 4–5 years (excluding maintenance) of which contains the software life cycle which we are discussing in this chapter.

In managing the development process, the temporal relationship between the various activities is more important as are the intermediate deliverables which represent the technical content, as the designer must demonstrate to the customer that progress is being made. A useful distinction, again taken from McDermid, is that the technical perspective of the life cycle is described in *stages* of activity, whereas the managerial perspective is described in temporally bound *phases*. A phase is usually defined in terms of the documentation taken as input to the phase and the documentation delivered as output from the phase. So the requirements phase will take any marketing or conceptual development information, identifying potential customers, as input and produce a requirements specification which must be agreed upon between customer and designer.

This brings up another important issue from the management perspective. As the design activity proceeds, the customer and the designer must sign off on various documents, indicating their satisfaction with progress to date. These signed documents can carry a varying degree of contractual obligation between customer and designer. A signed requirements specification indicates both that the customer agrees to limit demands of the eventual product to those listed in the specification and also that the designer agrees to meet all of the requirements listed. From a technical perspective, it is easy to acknowledge that it is difficult, if not impossible, to determine all of the requirements before embarking on any other design activity. A satisfactory requirements specification may not be known until after the product has been in operation! From a management perspective, it is unacceptable to both designer and customer to delay the requirements specification that long.

So contractual obligation is a necessary consequence of managing software development, but it has negative implications on the design process as well. It is very difficult in the design of an interactive system to determine *a priori* what requirements to impose on the system to maximize its usability. Having to fix on some requirements too early will result either in general requirements that are very little guide for the designer or in specific requirements that compromise the flexibility of design without guaranteeing any benefits.

5.2.4 *Interactive systems and the software life cycle*

The traditional software engineering life cycles arose out of a need in the 1960s and 1970s to provide structure to the development of large software systems. In those days, the majority of large systems produced were concerned with data processing applications in business. These systems were not highly interactive; rather, they were batch-processing systems. Consequently, issues concerning usability from an end-user's perspective were not all that important. With the advent of personal computing in the late 1970s and its huge commercial success and acceptance, most modern systems developed today are much more interactive, and it is vital to the success of any product that it be easy to operate for someone who is not expected to know much about how the system was designed. The modern user has a great amount of skill in the work that they perform without necessarily having that much skill in software development.

The life cycle for development we described above presents the process of design in a somewhat pipeline order. In reality, even for batch processing systems, the actual design process is *iterative*, work in one design activity affecting work in any other activity both before or after it in the life cycle. We can represent this iterative relationship as in Figure 5.4, but that does not greatly enhance any understanding of the design process for interactive systems. You may ask whether it is worth the intellectual effort to understand the interactive system design process. Is there really much design effort spent on the interactive aspects of a system to warrant our attention? A classic survey in 1978 by Sutton and Sprague at IBM resulted in an estimate that 50% of the designer's time was spent on designing code for the user interface [171]. A more recent and convincing survey by Myers and Rosson has confirmed that that finding holds true for the 1990s [121]. It is definitely worth the effort to provide structure and techniques to understand, structure and improve the interactive design process! In this section, we will address features of interactive system design which are not treated properly by the traditional software life cycle.

The traditional software life cycle suits a principled approach to design, that is, if we know what it is we want to produce from the beginning, then we can structure our approach to design in order to attain the goal. We have already mentioned how, in practice, designers do not find out all of the requirements for a system before they begin. Figure 5.4 depicts how discovery in later activities can be reflected in iterations back to earlier stages. This is an admission that the requirements capture activity is not executed properly. The more serious claim we are making here is that all of the requirements for an interactive system *cannot* be

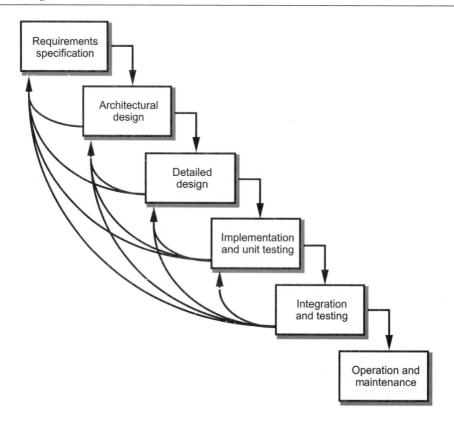

Figure 5.4   *Representing iteration in the waterfall model*

determined from the start, and there are many convincing arguments to support this position. The result is that systems must be built and the interaction with users observed and evaluated in order to determine how to make them more usable.

Our models of the psychology and sociology of the human and human cognition, whether in isolation or in a group, are incomplete and do not allow us to predict how to design for maximum usability. There is much research on models of human users which allow prediction of their performance with interactive systems, which we will discuss in Chapter 6. Those models, however, either rely on too much detail of the system to be useful at very early and abstract stages of design (see the section in Chapter 6 on the keystroke level model) or they only apply to goal-oriented planned activity and not highly interactive modern WIMP systems (refer to the discussion at the end of Chapter 6).

This dearth of predictive psychological theory means that in order to test certain usability properties of their designs, designers must observe how actual users interact with the developed product and measure their performance. In order for the results of those observations to be worthwhile, the experiments must be as close to a real interaction situation as possible. That means the experimental system must be very much like it would be in the final product whose requirements the designer is trying to establish! As John Carroll has pointed out, the very detail of the actual system can crucially affect its usability, so it is not worthwhile to experiment on crude estimates of it, as that will provide observations whose conclusions will not necessarily apply to the real system [31].

One principled approach to interactive system design which will be important in later chapters relies on a clear understanding early on in the design of the tasks that the user wishes to perform. One problem with this assumption is that the tasks a user will perform are often only known by the user after he is familiar with the system on which he performs them. The chicken-and-egg puzzle applies to tasks and the artefacts on which he perform those tasks. For example, before the advent of word-processors, an author would not have considered the use of a contracting and expanding outlining facility to experiment easily and quickly with the structure of a paper while it was being typed. A typewriter simply did not provide the ability to perform such a task, so how would a designer know to support such a task in designing the first word-processor?

Also, some of the tasks a user performs with a system were never explicitly intended as tasks by its designer. Take the example of a graphics drawing package which separates the constructed picture into separate layers. One layer is used to build graphical pictures which are entire objects—a circle or a square, for instance— and can be manipulated as those objects and retain their object identity. The other layer is used to paint pictures which are just a collection of pixels. The user can switch between the layers in order to create very complex pictures which are part object, part painted scene. But because of the complex interplay between overlapping images between the two layers, it is also possible to hide certain parts of the picture when in one layer and reveal it in the other layer. Such a facility will allow the user to do simple simulations, showing the effect of shadowing when switching a light on and off. It is very doubtful that the designers were thinking explicitly of supporting such simulation or animation tasks when they were designing such a graphics systems meant to build complex but static pictures.

A final point about the traditional software life cycle is that it does not promote the use of notations and techniques which support the user's perspective of the interactive system. We discussed earlier the purpose of validation and the formality gap. It is very difficult for an expert on human cognition to predict the cognitive demands that an abstract design would require of the intended user if the notation for the design does not reflect the kind of information the user must recall in order to interact. The same holds for assessing the timing behaviour of an abstract design which does not explicitly mention the timing characteristics of the operations to be invoked or their relative ordering. Though no structured development process will entirely eliminate the formality gap, the particular notations used can go a long way towards making validation of non-functional requirements feasible with expert assistance.

In the remaining sections of this chapter, we will describe various approaches

Figure 5.5   *Characterizing the authority and generality of standards and guidelines as design rules*

to augment the design process to better suit the design of interactive systems. These approaches are categorized under the banner of *user-centred design*.

5.3   Using Design Rules

One of the central problems which must be solved in a user-centred design process is how to provide designers with the ability to determine the usability consequences of their design decisions. We require *design rules* which are rules a designer can follow in order to increase the usability of the eventual software product. We can classify these rules along two dimensions, based on the rule's authority and generality. By authority, we mean an indication of whether or not the rule must be followed in design or whether it is only suggested. By generality, we mean whether the rule can be applied to many design situations or whether it is focused on a more limited application situation. It is also important to determine the origins of a design rule. The two kinds of design rules we are concerned with are *standards* and *guidelines*. Roughly speaking, standards are high in authority and limited in application, whereas guidelines tend to be lower in authority and more general in application (see Figure 5.5).

Design rules for interactive systems can be supported by psychological, cognitive, ergonomic, sociological, economic or computational theory which may or may not have roots in empirical evidence. Designers do not always have the relevant background in Psychology, Cognitive Science, Ergonomics, Sociology, Business or Computer Science necessary to understand the consequences of those theories in the instance of the design they are creating. The design rules are used to apply the theory in practice. Often a set of design rules will be in conflict with each other, meaning that strict adherence to all of them is impossible. The theory underlying the separate design rules can help the designer understand the trade-off for the design that would result in following or disregarding some of the rules. Usually, the more general a design rule is, the greater the likelihood that it will conflict with other rules and the greater the need is for the designer to understand the theory behind it.

Therefore, we can make another rough distinction between standards and guidelines. Since guidelines tend to be more general, it will be more important for a designer to know what theoretical evidence there is to support them. A designer will have less of a need to know the underlying theory for applying a standard. However, since standards carry a much higher level of authority, it is more important that the theory underlying them be correct or sound.

This chapter is about the process of design, and so we are concerned with when in that process design rules can be of use. Design rules are mechanisms for restricting the space of design options, preventing a designer from pursuing design options which would be likely to lead to an unusable system. Thus, design rules would be most effective if they could be adopted in the earliest stages of the life cycle, such as in requirements specification and architectural design, when the space of possible designs is still very large. However, if the assumptions underlying a design rule are not understood by the designer, it is quite possible that early application can prevent the best design choice. For example, a set of design rules might be specific to a particular hardware platform and inappropriate for other platforms (for example, colour vs. monochrome screens, one- vs. two- or three-button mouse). Such bias in design rules causes them to be applicable only in later stages of the life cycle.

We will now describe in more depth some examples of standards and guidelines for user-centred design.

5.3.1 *Standards*

Standards for interactive system design are usually set by national or international bodies to ensure compliance to a set of design rules by a large community. Standards can apply specifically to either the hardware or the software used to build the interactive system. Smith [161] points out the differing characteristics between hardware and software which affect the utility of design standards applied to them:

Underlying theory Standards for hardware are based on an understanding of physiology or ergonomics/human factors, the results of which are relatively well known, fixed and readily adaptable to design of the hardware. On the other hand, software standards are based on theories from psychology or cognitive science, which are less well formed, still evolving and not very easy to interpret in the language of software design. Consequently, standards for hardware can directly relate to a hardware specification and still reflect the underlying theory, whereas software standards would have to be more vaguely worded.

Change Hardware is more difficult and expensive to change than software, which is usually designed to be very flexible. Consequently, requirements changes for hardware do not occur as frequently as for software. Since standards are also relatively stable, they are more suitable for hardware than software.

Historically, for these reasons, a given standards institution, such as the British Standards Institute (BSI) or the International Standards Organization (ISO) or a national military agency, has had standards for hardware in place before any for software. For example, the U.K. Ministry of Defence has published an Interim Defence Standard 00–25 on *Human Factors for Designers of Equipment*, produced in 12 parts:

Part 1   Introduction
Part 2   Body Size
Part 3   Body Strength and Stamina
Part 4   Workplace Design
Part 6   Vision and Lighting
Part 7   Visual Displays
Part 8   Auditory Information
Part 9   Voice Communication
Part 10   Controls
Part 11   Design for Maintainability
Part 12   Systems

Only the last of these is concerned with the software design process. The international standard ISO 9241, entitled *Ergonomic requirements for office work with visual display terminals (VDT)s*, has 17 parts, varying from completed to planned. Seven of the parts are concerned with hardware issues—requirements for visual display, keyboard layout, workstation layout, environment, display with reflections, display colours and non-keyboard input devices. All but the last are at least in draft form. Seven parts are devoted to software issues—general dialogue principles, menu dialogues, presentation of information, user guidance, command dialogues, direct manipulation dialogues and form-filling dialogues. Only the first two are at draft stages.

Figure 5.6 provides examples of the language of standards for displays. Note the increasing generality and vagueness of the language as we progress from the hardware issues in a U.K. Defence standard for pilot cockpit controls and instrumentation through a German standard for user interface design of display workstations to a U.S. military standard for display contents.

One component of the ISO standard 9241, pertaining to usability specification applies equally to both hardware and software design. In the beginning of that document, the following definition of usability is given:

11.3 *Arrangement of displays*

11.3.1 Vertical Grouping. The engine display parameters shall be arranged so that the primary or most important display for a particular engine and aeroplane (thrust, torque, RPM, etc.) be located at the top of the display group if a vertical grouping is provided. The next most important display parameter shall be positioned under the primary display progressing down the panel with the least important at the bottom.

(a) A typical example of a military standard

5.1 *Subdivision of the display area*

In consideration of a simple, fast and accurate visual acquisition, the display area shall be divided into different sub-areas.

Such a division could be:

- Input area

- Output area

- Area for operational indications (such as status and alarms)

(b) From German standard DIN 66 234 Part 3 (1984), adapted from Smith [161]

5.15.3.2.1 *Standardization.*

The content of displays within a system shall be presented in a consistent manner.

(c) From U.S. Military standard MIL-STD-1472C, revised (1983), adapted from Smith [161]

Figure 5.6   *Sample design standards for displays*

Usability: The effectiveness, efficiency and satisfaction with which specified users achieve specified goals in particular environments.

Effectiveness: The accuracy and completeness with which specified users can achieve specified goals in particular environments.

Efficiency: The resources expended in relation to the accuracy and completeness of goals achieved.

Satisfaction: The comfort and acceptability of the work system to its users and other people affected by its use.

The importance of such a definition in the standard is as a means of describing explicit measurements for usability. We will discuss the implications of applying such a definition of usability when we discuss usability engineering later in this chapter.

The strength of a standard lies in its ability to force large communities to abide—the so-called authority we have referred to earlier. It should be noted that such authority does not necessarily follow from the publication of a standard by a national or international body. In fact, many standards applying to software design are put forth as suggestive measures, rather than obligatory. The authority of a standard (or a guideline, for that matter) can only be determined from its use in practice. Some software products become *de facto* standards long before any formal standards document is published (e.g. the X windowing system).

There is a much longer history of standards in safety-critical domains, such as nuclear power plants or aircraft design, where the consequences of poor design outweigh the expense of principled design. Only when the perceived costs of unusable software in less safety- critical domains become intolerable will there be a greater effort in standards for promoting usability.

5.3.2 Guidelines

We have observed that the incompleteness of theories underlying the design of interactive software makes it difficult to produce authoritative and specific standards. As a result, the majority of design rules for interactive systems are suggestive and more general guidelines. Our concern in examining the wealth of available guidelines is in determining their applicability to the various stages of design. The more abstract the guideline, the more it resembles the principles which we outlined in Chapter 4, which would be most suited to requirements specification. The more specific the guideline, the more suited it is to detailed design. The guidelines can also be automated to some extent, providing a direct means for translating detailed design specifications into actual implementation. There are a vast amount of published guidelines for interactive system design (they are frequently referred to as guidelines for user interface design). We will present only a few examples here to demonstrate the content of guidelines in that vast literature.

Several books and technical reports contain huge catalogues of guidelines. A classic example was a very general list compiled by Smith and Mosier in 1986 at the MITRE Corporation and sponsored by the Electronic Systems Division of the U.S. Air Force [163]. Mayhew has produced an equally comprehensive and more recent catalogue. The basic categories of the Smith and Mosier guidelines are:

1. Data Entry

2. Data Display

3. Sequence Control

4. User Guidance

5. Data Transmission

6. Data Protection

---

1. **Data Entry**

1.1. *Position Designation*

1.1–1 **Distinctive Cursor**
For position designation on an electronic display, provide a movable cursor with distinctive visual features (shape, blink, etc.).

Exception When position designation involves only selection among displayed alternatives, highlighting selected items might be used instead of a separately displayed cursor.

Comment When choosing a cursor shape, consider the general content of the display. For instance, an underscore cursor would be difficult to see on a display of underscored text, or on a graphical display containing many other lines.

Comment If the cursor is changed to denote different functions (e.g. to signal deletion rather than entry), then each different cursor should be distinguishable from the others.

Comment If multiple cursors are used on the same display (e.g. one for alphanumeric entry and one for line drawing), then each cursor should be distinguishable from the others.

Reference Whitfield, Ball and Bird, 1983

See also   1.1–17   Distinctive multiple cursors
4.0–9   Distinctive cursor

Figure 5.7   *Sample guideline from Smith and Mosier* [163]

Each of these categories is further broken down into more specific sub-categories which contain the particular guidelines. Figure 5.7 provides an example of the information contained in the Smith and Mosier guidelines. One striking feature of this compendium of guidelines is the extensive cross-referencing within the catalogue and citation to published work which supports each guideline. The MITRE Corporation has taken advantage of this structure and implemented the Smith and Mosier guidelines on a hypertext system which provides rapid traversal of the network of guidelines to investigate the cross-references and citations.

A more recent catalogue of general guidelines has been compiled by Mayhew [110]. Though this catalogue is only in book form, and so limits the possibility of quick cross-referencing, this is one of the best sources for the experimental results which back the specific guidelines.

A major concern for all of the general guidelines is the subject of *dialogue styles*, which in the context of these guidelines pertains to the means by which

Table 5.1   *Comparison of dialogue styles mentioned in guidelines*

Dialogue Styles	
Smith and Mosier	Mayhew
Question and answer	Question and answer
Form-filling	Fill-in forms
Menu selection	Menus
Function keys	Function keys
Command language	Command language
Query language	
Natural language	Natural language
Graphic selection	Direct manipulation

the user communicates input to the system, including how the system presents the communication device. Smith and Mosier identify eight different dialogue styles and Mayhew identifies seven (see Table 5.1 for a comparison). The only real difference is the absence of query languages in Mayhew's list, but we can consider a query language as a special case of a command language. These interface styles have been described in more detail in Chapter 3.

Most guidelines are applicable for the implementation of any one of these dialogue styles in isolation. It is also important to consider the possibility of mixing dialogue styles in one application. In contrasting the action and language paradigms in Chapter 4, we concluded that it is not always the case that one paradigm wins over the other for all tasks in an application and, therefore, an application may want to mix the two paradigms. This equates to a mixing of dialogue styles—a direct manipulation dialogue being suitable for the action paradigm and a command language being suitable for the language paradigm. Mayhew provides guidelines and a technique for deciding how to mix dialogue styles.

In moving from abstract guidelines to more specific and automated ones, it is necessary to introduce assumptions about the computer platform on which the interactive system is designed. So, for example, in Apple's *Human Interface Guidelines: the Apple Desktop Interface*, there is a clear distinction between the abstract guidelines (or principles), independent of the specific Macintosh hardware and software, and the concrete guidelines, which assume them. The abstract guidelines provide the so-called philosophy of programming that Apple would like designers to adopt in programming applications for the Macintosh. The more concrete guidelines are then seen as more concrete manifestations of that philosophy.

As an example, one abstract principle espoused in the Apple guidelines is *consistency*:

Effective applications are both consistent within themselves and consistent with one another.

We discussed consistency in Chapter 4 under the larger usability category of learnability, and the meaning in this context is similar. A more concrete directive that Apple provides is the 'noun–verb' ordering guideline—the user first selects an object (the noun) from the visible set on the desktop and then selects an operation (the verb) to be applied to the object. For the sake of consistency, this ordering guideline is to be followed for all operation invocation involving the explicit and separate indication of an operation and the object or arguments of that operation.

Another less straightforward example from the Apple guidelines refers to user control:

The user, not the computer, initiates and controls all actions.

We considered issues of dialogue initiative in Chapter 4 under the general usability category of flexibility. As we mentioned there, the issue of dialogue initiative involves a trade-off between user freedom and system protection. In general, single-user computer systems operate in strict abidance of this guideline for user control; the user is allowed to initiate any dialogue at all with the computer, whether or not it will have the intended result. Part of the success of direct manipulation interfaces lies in their ability to constrain user interaction to actions which are both syntactically correct (for example, preventing errors due to slips in typing) and will probably correspond to the intended user tasks.

Other popular graphical user interface (GUI) systems have published guidelines which describe how to adhere to abstract principles for usability in the narrower context of a specific programming environment. These guidelines are often referred to as *style guides* to reflect that they are not hard and fast rules, but suggested conventions for programming in that environment. Some examples are the OPEN LOOK and the Open Software Foundation (OSF) Motif graphical user interfaces, both of which have published style guides [170, 134]. Programming in the style of these GUIs involves the use of toolkits which provide high-level widgets, as we have mentioned earlier in this book and will discuss in more detail in Chapter 10. More importantly, each of these GUIs has their own *look and feel* which describes their expected behaviour. The style guides are intended to help a programmer capture the elements of the look and feel of a GUI in their own programming. Therefore, style guides for the look and feel of a GUI promote the consistency within and between applications on the same computer platform.

We discussed menus in Chapter 3 as one of the major elements of the WIMP interface. As one example of a guideline for the design of menus, the OPEN LOOK style guide suggests the following for grouping items in the same menu:

Use white space between long groups of controls on menus or in short groups when screen real estate is not an issue.

The justification for such a guideline is that the more options (or controls, as the term is used in the quoted guideline) on a menu, the longer it will take a user to locate and point to a desired item. As we discussed in Chapter 1, humans chunk related information in the learning process and this can be used to increase the efficiency of searching. Grouping of related items in a menu can supplement this chunking procedure. But be warned! Remember the scenario described in the Introduction to this book, in which we fell victim to closely grouped menu items which had drastically different effects in our word-processor. Saving and deleting files might be considered logically similar since they both deal with operations on the file level. But simple slips done in pointing (which are all too easy with tracker ball devices) can change an intended save operation into an unintended and dangerous delete.

5.4 Usability Engineering

Another approach to user-centred design has been the introduction of explicit *usability engineering* goals into the design process, as suggested by Whiteside and colleagues at IBM and Digital Equipment Corporation [184] and by Nielsen at Bellcore [127, 128]. Engineering depends on interpretation against a shared background of meaning, agreed goals and an understanding of how satisfactory completion will be judged. The emphasis for usability engineering is in knowing exactly what criteria will be used to judge a product for its usability.

The ultimate test of a product's usability is based on measurements of users' experience with it. Therefore, since a user's direct experience with an interactive system is at the physical interface, focus on the actual user interface is understandable. The danger with this limited focus is that much of the work that is accomplished in interaction involves more than just the surface features of the systems used to perform that work. In reality, the whole functional architecture of the system and the cognitive capacity of the users should be observed in order to arrive at meaningful measures. But it is not at all simple to derive measurements of activity beyond the physical actions in the world, and so usability engineering is limited in its application.

In relation to the software life cycle, one of the important features of usability engineering is the inclusion of a usability specification, forming part of the requirements specification, that concentrates on features of the user–system interaction which contribute to the usability of the product. Various attributes of the system are suggested as gauges for testing the usability. For each attribute, six items are defined to form the usability specification of that attribute. Table 5.2 provides an example of a usability specification for the design of a control panel for a video cassette recorder (VCR), based on the technique presented by Whiteside, Bennett and Holtzblatt [184].

In this example, we choose the principle of recoverability described in Chapter 4 as the particular usability attribute of interest. Recall that recoverability refers to the ability to reach a desired goal after recognition of some error in previous interaction, and that the recovery procedure can be in either a backward or forward

Table 5.2 *Sample usability specification for undo with a VCR*

Attribute:	Backward recoverability
Measuring Concept:	Undo an erroneous programming sequence
Measuring Method:	Number of explicit user actions to undo current program
Now Level:	No current product allows such an undo
Worst Case:	As many actions as it takes to program in mistake
Planned Level:	A maximum of two explicit user actions
Best Case:	One explicit cancel action

sense. Current VCR design has resulted in interactive systems which are notoriously difficult to use; the redesign of a VCR provides a good case study for usability engineering. In designing a new VCR control panel, the designer wants to take into account how a user might recover from a mistake they discover while trying to program the VCR to record some television program in their absence. One approach that the designer decides to follow is to allow the user the ability to undo the programming sequence, reverting the state of the VCR to what it was before the programming task began.

The backward recoverability attribute is defined in terms of a *measuring concept*, which makes the abstract attribute more concrete by describing it in terms of the actual product. So in this case, we realize backward recoverability as the ability to undo an erroneous programming sequence. The *measuring method* states how the attribute will be measured, in this case by the number of explicit user actions required to perform the undo, regardless of where in the programming sequence the user is.

The remaining four entries in the usability specification then provide the agreed criteria for judging the success of the product based on the measuring method. The *now level* indicates the value for the measurement with the existing system, whether it is computer-based or not. The *worst case value* is the lowest acceptable measurement for the task, providing a clear distinction between what will be acceptable and what will be unacceptable in the final product. The *planned level* is the target for the design and the *best case* is the level which is agreed to be the best possible measurement given the current state of development tools and technology.

In the example, the designers can look at their previous VCR products and those of their competitors to determine a suitable now level. In this case, it is determined that no current model allows such an undo which preserves the state of the VCR to what it was before the programming task. For example, if a VCR allows you three separate recording programs, once you begin entering a new program in the number 1 program slot, the VCR forgets the previous contents of that slot and so you cannot recover it unless you remember what it was and then reprogram it.

Determining the worst case value depends on a number of things. Usually, it should be no lower than the now level. The new product should provide some improvement on the current state of affairs, and so it seems that at least some of the usability attributes should provide worst case values that are better than the now level. Otherwise, why would the customer bother with the new system (unless it can be shown to provide the same usability at a fraction of the cost)? The designers in the example have determined that the minimal acceptable undo facility would require the user to perform as many actions as they had done to program in the mistake. This is a clear improvement over the now level, since it at least provides for the possibility of undo. One way to provide such a capability would be by including an undo button on the control panel which would effectively reverse the previous non-undo action. The designers figure that they should allow for the user to do a complete restoration of the VCR state in a maximum of two explicit user actions, though they recognize that the best case, at least in terms of the number of explicit actions, would require only one.

Tables 5.3 and 5.4, adapted from Whiteside *et al.*, provide a list of measurement criteria which can be used to determine the measuring method for a usability attribute and the possible ways to set the worst/best case and planned/now level targets. Measurements such as those promoted by usability engineering are also called *usability metrics*.

The ISO standard 9241, described earlier, also recommends the use of usability specifications as a means of requirements specification. Table 5.5 gives examples of usability metrics categorized by their contribution towards the three categories of usability—effectiveness, efficiency and satisfaction. Notice the particularly poor measures given for satisfaction measures. Measuring satisfaction appears to be a rather dubious venture.

5.4.1   Problems with usability engineering

The major feature of usability engineering is the assertion of explicit usability metrics early on in the design process which can be used to judge a system once it is delivered. There is a very solid argument which points out that it is only through empirical approaches such as the use of usability metrics that we can reliably build more usable systems. Although the ultimate yardstick for determining usability may be by observing user performance, but that does not mean that these measurements are the best way to produce a predictive design process for usability.

The problem with usability metrics is that they rely on measurements of very specific user actions in very specific situations. When the designer knows what the actions and situation will be, then she can set goals for measured observations. However, at early stages of design, the designers do not have this information. Take our example usability specification for the VCR. In setting the acceptable and unacceptable levels for backward recovery, there is an assumption that a button will be available to invoke the undo. In fact, the designer was already making an

Table 5.3 *Criteria by which measuring method can be determined, adapted from Whiteside* et al. [184]

1. time to complete a task
2. percent of task completed
3. percent of task completed per unit time
4. ratio of successes to failures
5. time spent in errors
6. percent or number of errors
7. percent or number of competitors better than it
8. number of commands used
9. frequency of help and documentation use
10. percent of favourable/unfavourable user comments
11. number of repetitions of failed commands
12. number of runs of successes and of failures
13. number of times interface misleads the user
14. number of good and bad features recalled by users
15. number of available commands not invoked
16. number of regressive behaviours
17. number of users preferring your system
18. number of times users need to work around a problem
19. number of times the user is disrupted from a work task
20. number of times user loses control of the system
21. number of times user expresses frustration or satisfaction

Table 5.4 *Possible ways to set measurement levels in a usability specification, adapted from Whiteside et al. [184]*

Set levels with respect to information on

1. an existing system or previous version
2. competitive systems
3. carrying out the task without use of a computer system
4. an absolute scale
5. your own prototype
6. user's own earlier performance
7. each component of a system separately
8. a successive split of the difference between best and worst values observed in user tests.

Table 5.5 *Examples of usability metrics from ISO 9241 (Committee Draft 9241–11.2)*

Usability objective	Effectiveness measures	Efficiency measures	Satisfaction measures
Suitability for the task	Percentage of goals achieved	Time to complete a task	Rating scale for satisfaction
Appropriate for trained users	Number of power features used	Relative efficiency compared with an expert user	Rating scale for satisfaction with power features
Learnability	Percentage of functions learned	Time to learn criterion	Rating scale for ease of learning
Error tolerance	Percentage of errors corrected successfully	Time spent on correcting errors	Rating scale for error handling

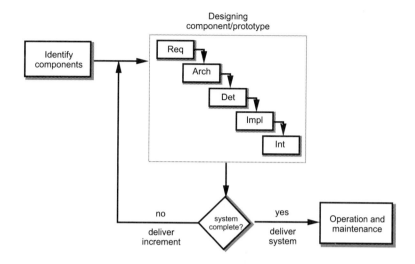

Figure 5.8 *Incremental prototyping within the life cycle*

implicit assumption that the user would be making errors in the programming of the VCR. Why not address the origin of the programming errors and maybe undo would not be necessary?

   We should recognize another inherent limitation for usability engineering, that is, it provides a means of satisfying usability specifications and not necessarily usability. The designer is still forced to understand why a particular usability metric enhances usability for real people. Again, in the VCR example, the designer assumed that fewer explicit actions make the undo operation easier. Is that kind of assumption warranted?

5.5   Iterative Design and Prototyping

A point we raised earlier is that requirements for an interactive system cannot be completely specified from the beginning of the life cycle. The only way to be sure about some features of the potential design is to build them and test them out on real users. The design can then be modified to correct any false assumptions that were revealed in the testing. This is the essence of *iterative design*, a purposeful design process which tries to overcome the inherent problems of incomplete requirements specification by cycling through several designs, incrementally improving upon the final product with each pass.

   The problems with the design process which lead to an iterative design philosophy are not unique to the usability features of the intended system. The problem holds for requirements specification in general, and so it is a general software

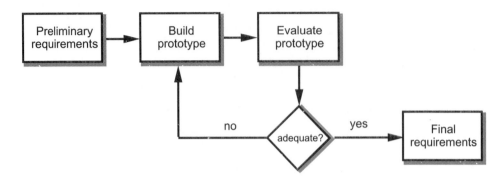

Figure 5.9   *Throw-away prototyping within requirements specification*

engineering problem, together with technical and managerial issues.

On the technical side, iterative design is described by the use of *prototypes*, artefacts that simulate or animate some but not all features of the intended system. There are three main approaches to prototyping:

Throw-away The prototype is built and tested. The design knowledge gained from this exercise is used to build the final product, but the actual prototype is discarded. Figure 5.9 depicts the procedure in using throw-away prototypes to arrive at a final requirements specification in order for the rest of the design process to proceed.

Incremental The final product is built as separate components, one at a time. There is one overall design for the final system, but it is partitioned into independent and smaller components. The final product is then released as a series of products, each subsequent release including one more component. This is depicted in Figure 5.8.

Evolutionary Here the prototype is not discarded and serves as the basis for the next iteration of design. In this case, the actual system is seen as evolving from a very limited initial version to its final release, as depicted in Figure 5.10. Evolutionary prototyping also fits in well with the modifications which must be made to the system that arise during the operation and maintenance activity in the life cycle.

Prototypes differ according to the amount of functionality and performance they provide relative to the final product. An *animation* of requirements can involve no real functionality, or limited functionality to simulate only a small aspect of the interactive behaviour for evaluative purposes. At the other extreme, full functionality can be provided at the expense of other performance characteristics, such as speed or error tolerance. Regardless of the level of functionality, the importance of a prototype lies in its projected realism. The prototype of an interactive

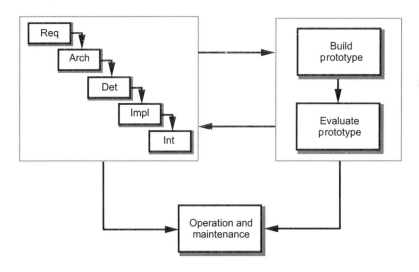

Figure 5.10   *Evolutionary prototyping throughout the life cycle*

system is used to test requirements by evaluating their impact with real users. An honest appraisal of the requirements of the final system can only be trusted if the evaluation conditions are similar to those anticipated for the actual operation. But providing realism is costly, so there must be support for a designer/programmer to create a realistic prototype quickly and efficiently.

On the management side, there are several potential problems, as pointed out by Sommerville [164]:

Time Building prototypes takes time and, if it is a throw-away prototype, it can be seen as precious time taken away from the real design task. Hence, the value of prototyping is only appreciated if it is fast, hence the use of the term *rapid prototyping*. However, rapid development and manipulation of a prototype should not be mistaken for rushed evaluation which might lead to erroneous results and invalidate the only advantage of using a prototype in the first place.

Planning Most project managers do not have the experience necessary for adequately planning and costing a design process which involves prototyping.

Non-functional features Often the most important features of a system will be non-functional ones, such as safety and reliability, and these are precisely the kinds of features which are sacrificed in developing a prototype. For evaluating usability features of a prototype, response time, yet another feature often compromised in a prototype, could be critical to product acceptance. This problem is similar to the technical issue of prototype realism.

Contracts The design process is often governed by contractual agreements between customer and designer which are affected by many of these managerial and technical issues. Prototypes and other implementations cannot form the basis for a legal contract, and so an iterative design process will still require documentation which serves as the binding agreement. There must be an effective way of translating the results derived from prototyping into adequate documentation. A rapid prototyping process might be amenable to quick changes, but that does not also apply to the design process.

5.5.1   Techniques for prototyping

Here we will describe some of the techniques that are available for producing rapid prototypes.

Storyboards

Probably the simplest notion of a prototype is the *storyboard*, which is a graphical depiction of the outward appearance of the intended system, without any accompanying system functionality. Storyboards do not require much in terms of computing power to construct; in fact, they can be mocked up without the aid of any computing resource. The origins of storyboards are in the film industry, where a series of panels roughly depicts snapshots from an intended film sequence in order to get the idea across about the eventual scene. Similarly, for interactive system design, the storyboards provide snapshots of the interface at particular points in the interaction. Evaluating customer or user impressions of the storyboards can determine relatively quickly if the design is heading in the right direction.

Modern graphical drawing packages now make it possible to create storyboards with the aid of a computer instead of by hand. Though the graphic design achievable on screen may not be as sophisticated as that possible by a professional graphic designer, it is more realistic because the final system will have to be displayed on a screen. Also, it is possible to provide crude but effective *animation* by automated sequencing through a series of snapshots. Animation illustrates the dynamic aspects of the intended user–system interaction which may not be possible with traditional paper-based storyboards.

How a non-functional storyboard prototype is evaluated depends on the way it is presented to potential users. In the design of a messaging system for the athletes attending the 1984 Olympics in Los Angeles, IBM sampled several variants on the kiosk design of the telephone based system using what it called the hallway and storefront methodology [75]. The final system was intended to be a walk-up-and-use system, so it was important to get comments from people without any knowledge of the system. Early versions of the kiosk were displayed as storyboards on a mock kiosk design in the front hallway of the Yorktown Research Lab. Passers-by were encouraged to browse at the display much as they would a storefront in the window. As casual comments were made and the kiosk was modified according to those comments, more and more active evaluation was elicited. This procedure helped to determine the final positioning of display screens and telephones for the final design.

Limited functionality simulations

More functionality must be built into the prototype to demonstrate the work that the application will accomplish. Storyboards and animation techniques are not sufficient for this purpose, as they cannot portray adequately the interactive aspects of the system. To do this, some portion of the functionality must be *simulated* by the design team.

Programming support for simulations means a designer can rapidly build graphical and textual interaction objects and attach some behaviour to those objects which mimics the system's functionality. Once this simulation is built, it can be evaluated and changed rapidly to reflect the results of the evaluation study with various users. For example, we might want to build a prototype for the VCR with undo described earlier using only a workstation display, keyboard and mouse. We could draw a picture of the VCR with its control panel using a graphical drawing package, but then we would want to allow a subject to use the mouse to position a finger cursor over one of the buttons to 'press' it and actuate some behaviour of the VCR. In this way, we could simulate the programming task and experiment with different options for undoing.

There are now plenty of prototyping tools available which allow the rapid development of such simulation prototypes. These simulation tools are meant to provide a quick development process for a very wide range of small but highly interactive applications. One of the most well-known and successful prototyping tool is *HyperCard*, a simulation environment for the Macintosh line of Apple computers. HyperCard is similar to the animation tools described in the previous section in that the user can create a graphical depiction of some system, say the VCR, with common graphical tools. The graphical images are placed on cards and links between cards can be created which control the sequencing from one card to the next for animation effects. What HyperCard provides beyond this type of animation is the ability to describe more sophisticated interactive behaviour by attaching a *script*, written in the HyperTalk programming language, to any object. So for the VCR, we could attach a script to any control panel button to highlight it or make an audible noise when the user clicks the mouse cursor over it. Then some functionality could be associated to that button by reflecting some change in the VCR display window.

Most of the simulations produced are intended to be throw-away prototypes because of their relatively inefficient implementation. They are not intended to support full-blown systems development and they are unsatisfactory in that role. However, as more designers recognize the utility of prototyping and iterative design, they are beginning to demand ways of incorporating the prototypes into the final delivered systems—more along the lines of evolutionary prototyping.

A good example of this is in the design of avionics industry, where it has long been recognized that iterative development via rapid prototyping and evaluation is essential for the design of flight deck instrumentation and controls. Workstation technology provides sufficient graphics capabilities to enable a designer to produce very realistic gauges which can be assessed and critiqued by actual pilots. With the advent of the glass cockpit—in which traditional mechanical gauges are replaced by gauges represented on video displays—there is no longer a technology gap between the prototype designs of flight deck instruments and the actual instruments in flight. Therefore, it is a reasonable request by these designers that they be able to re-use the functionality of the prototypes in the actual flight simulators and cockpits, and this demand is starting to be met by commercial prototyping systems which produce efficient code for use in such safety-critical applications.

One technique for simulation which does not require very much computer-supported functionality is the *Wizard of Oz* technique. With this technique, the designers can develop a limited functionality prototype and enhance its functionality in evaluation by providing the missing functionality through human intervention. A subject for evaluation for a new accounting system may not have any computer training but is familiar with accounting procedures. He is asked to sit down in front of the prototype accounting system and asked to perform some task, say to check the accounts receivable against some newly arrived payments. The naive computer user will not know the specific language of the system, but you do not want him to worry about that. Instead, he is given instructions to type in whatever seems the most natural commands to the system. One of the designers—the wizard in this scenario—is situated in another room, out of sight of the subject, but she is able to receive the subject's input commands and translate them into commands that will work on the prototype. By intervening between the user and system, the wizard is able to increase the perceived functionality of the system so that evaluation can concentrate on how the subject would react to the complete system. Examination of how the wizard had to interpret the subject's input can provide advice as to how the prototype must be enhanced in its later versions.

High-level programming support

HyperTalk was an example of a special-purpose high-level programming language which makes it easy for the designer to program certain features of an interactive system at the expense of other system features like speed of response or space efficiency. HyperTalk and many other languages similar to it allow the programmer to attach functional behaviour to the specific interactions that the user will be able to do, such as position and click on the mouse over a button on the screen. Previously, the difficulty of interactive programming was that it was so implementation dependent that the programmer would have to know quite a bit of intimate detail of the hardware system in order to control even the simplest of interactive behaviour. These high-level programming languages allow the programmer to abstract away from the hardware specifics and think in terms that are closer to the way the input and output devices are perceived as interaction devices.

Though not usually considered together with such simulation environments as HyperCard, a *user interface management system*—or UIMS (pronounced 'YOU-imz')—can be understood as providing such high-level programming support. The frequent conceptual model put forth for interactive system design is to separate the application functionality from its presentation. It then is possible to program the underlying functionality of the system and to program the behaviour of the user interface separately. The job of a UIMS, then, is to allow the programmer to connect the behaviour at the interface with the underlying functionality. In Chapter 10 we will discuss in more detail the advantages and disadvantages of such a conceptual model and concentrate on the programming implementation support provided by a UIMS. Of interest here is that the separation implied by a UIMS allows the independent development of the features of the interface apart from the underlying functionality. If the underlying system is already developed, then various prototypes of its interface can be quickly constructed and evaluated to determine the optimal one.

5.5.2 *Warning about iterative design*

Though we have put forth the process of iterative design as not only beneficial but necessary for good interactive system design, it is important to recognize some of its drawbacks, in addition to the very real management issues we have already raised. The ideal model of iterative design, in which a rapid prototype is designed, evaluated and modified until the best possible design is achieved in the given project time, is appealing. But there are two problems.

First, it is often the case that design decisions made at the very beginning of the prototyping process are wrong and, in practice, design inertia can be so great as never to overcome an initial bad decision. So, whereas iterative design is, in theory, amenable to great changes through iterations, it can be the case that the initial prototype has bad features that will not be amended. We will examine this problem through a real example of a clock on a microwave oven[2]. The clock has a numeric display of four digits. Thus, the display is capable of showing values in the range from 00:00 to 99:99. The functional model of time for the actual clock is only 12 hour, so quite a few of the possible clock displays do not correspond to possible times (e.g. 63:00, 85:49), even though some of them are legal four digit time designations. That poses no problem, as long as both the designer and the ultimate users of the clock both share the knowledge of the discrepancy between possible clock displays and legal times. Such would not be the case for someone assuming a 24 hour time format, in which case the displays 00:30 and 13:45 would represent valid times in their model but not in the microwave's model. In this particular example, the subjects tested during the evaluation must have all shared the 12 hour time model, and the mismatch with the other users (with a

---

[2]This example has been provided by Harold Thimbleby.

24 hour model) was only discovered after the product was being shipped. At this point the only impact of iterative design was a change to the documentation alerting the reader to the 12 hour format, as it was too late to perform any hardware change.

The second problem is slightly more subtle, and serious. If, in the process of evaluation, a potential usability problem is diagnosed, it is important to understand the reason for the problem and not just detect the symptom. In the clock example, the designers could have noticed that some subjects with a 24 hour time model were having difficulty setting the time. Say they were trying to set the time for 14:45, but they were not being allowed to do that. If the designers did not know the subject's goals, they might not detect the 24/12 hour discrepancy. They would instead notice that the users were having trouble setting the time and so they might change the buttons used to set the time instead of other possible changes, such as an analog time dial, or displaying AM or PM on the clock dial to make the 12 hour model more obvious, or to change to a 24 hour clock.

The moral for iterative design is that it should be used in conjunction with other more principled approaches to interactive system design. These principled approaches are the subject of the next four chapters of this book.

5.6 Design Rationale

In designing any computer system, many decisions are made as the product goes from a set of vague customer requirements to a deliverable entity. Often it is difficult to recreate the reasons, or rationale, behind various design decisions. *Design rationale* is the information that explains why a computer system is the way it is, including its structural or architectural description and its functional or behavioural description. In this sense, design rationale does not fit squarely into the software life cycle described in this chapter as just another phase or box. Rather, design rationale relates to an activity of both reflection (doing design rationale) and documentation (creating a design rationale) that occurs throughout the entire life cycle.

It is beneficial to have access to the design rationale for several reasons:

- In an explicit form, a design rationale provides a communication mechanism among the members of a design team so that during later stages of design and/or maintenance it is possible to understand what critical decisions were made, what alternatives were investigated (and, possibly, in what order) and the reason why one alternative was chosen over the others.

- Accumulated knowledge in the form of design rationales for a set of products can be reused to transfer what has worked in one situation to another situation which has similar needs. The design rationale can capture the context of a design decision in order that a different design team can determine if a similar rationale is appropriate for their product.

- The effort required to produce a design rationale forces the designer to deliberate more carefully about design decisions. The process of deliberation can be assisted by the design rationale technique by suggesting how arguments justifying or discarding a particular design option are formed.

In the area of HCI, design rationale has been particularly important, again for several reasons:

- There is usually no single best design alternative. More often, the designer is faced with a set of trade-offs between different alternatives. For example, a graphical interface may involve a set of actions that the user can invoke by use of the mouse and the designer must decide whether to present each action as a 'button' on the screen, which is always visible, or hide all of the actions in a menu which must be explicitly invoked before an action can be chosen. The former option maximizes the operation visibility (as discussed in Chapter 4) but the latter option takes up less screen space. It would be up to the designer to determine which criterion for evaluating the options was more important and then communicating that information in a design rationale.

- Even if an optimal solution did exist for a given design decision, the space of alternatives is so vast that it is unlikely a designer would discover it. In this case, it is important that the designer indicates all alternatives that have been investigated. Then later on it can be determined if she has not considered the best solution or had thought about it and discarded it for some reason. In project management, this kind of accountability for design is good.

- The usability of an interactive system is very dependent on the context of its use. The flashiest graphical interface is of no use if the end-user does not have access to a high-quality graphics display or a pointing device. Capturing the context in which a design decision is made will help later when new products are designed. If the context remains the same, then the old rationale can be adopted without revision. If the context has changed somehow, the old rationale can be re-examined to see if any rejected alternatives are now more favourable or if any new alternatives are now possible.

Lee and Lai [101] explain that various proponents of design rationale have different interpretations of what it actually is. We will make use of their classification to describe various design rationale techniques in this section. The first set of techniques concentrates on providing a historical record of design decisions and is very much tailored for use during actual design discussions. These techniques are referred to as process-oriented design rationale because they are meant to be integrated in the actual design process itself. The next category is not so concerned with historical or process-oriented information but rather with the structure of the space of all design alternatives, which can be reconstructed by *post hoc* consideration of the design activity. The structure-oriented approach does not capture historical information. Instead, it captures the complete story of the moment, as an analysis of the design space which has been considered so far. The final category of design rationale concentrates on capturing the claims about the psychology of the user which are implied by an interactive system and the tasks that are performed on them.

There are some issues which distinguish the various techniques in terms of their usability within design itself. We can use these issues to sketch an informal rationale for design rationale. One issue is the degree to which the technique impinges on the design process. Does the use of a particular design rationale technique alter the decision process, or does it just passively serve to document it? Another issue is the cost of using the technique, both in terms of creating the design rationale and in terms of accessing it once created. A related issue is the amount of computational power the design rationale provides and the level to which this is supported by automated tools. A design rationale for a complex system can be very large and the exploration of the design space changes over time. The kind of information stored in a given design rationale technique will affect how that vast amount of information can be effectively managed and browsed.

5.6.1 *Process-oriented design rationale*

Much of the work on design rationale is based on Rittel's *issue-based information system*, or *IBIS*, a style for representing design and planning dialogue developed in the 1970s [149]. In IBIS (pronounced 'ibbiss'), a hierarchical structure to a design rationale is created. A root *issue* is identified which represents the main problem or question that the argument is addressing. Various *positions* are put forth as potential resolutions for the root issue, and these are depicted as descendants in the IBIS hierarchy directly connected to the root issue. Each position is then supported or refuted by *arguments* which modify the relationship between issue and position. The hierarchy grows as secondary issues are raised which modify the root issue in some way. Each of these secondary issues is in turn expanded by positions and arguments, further sub-issues, and so on.

A graphical version of IBIS has been defined by Conklin and Yakemovic [42], called *gIBIS* (pronounced 'gibbiss'), which makes the structure of the design rationale more apparent visually in the form of a directed graph which can be directly edited by the creator of the design rationale. Figure 5.11 gives a representation of the gIBIS vocabulary. Issues, positions and arguments are nodes in the graph and the connections between them are labelled to clarify the relationship between adjacent nodes. So, for example, an issue can suggest further sub-issues, or a position can respond to an issue or an argument can support a position. The gIBIS structure can be supported by a hypertext tool to allow a designer to create and browse various parts of the design rationale.

There have been other versions of the IBIS notation, both graphical and textual, besides gIBIS. Most versions retain the distinction between issues, positions and arguments. Some add further nodes, such as Potts and Bruns's [144] addition of design artefacts which represent the intermediate products of a design that lead

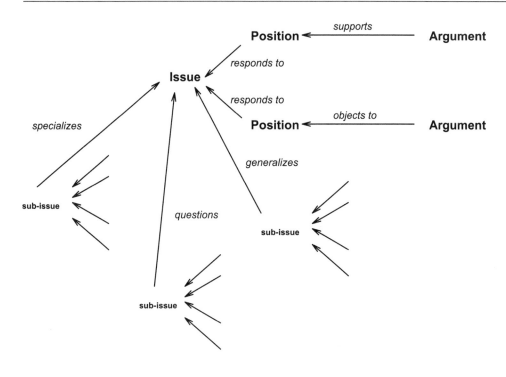

Figure 5.11   *The structure of a gIBIS design rationale*

to the final product and are associated with the various alternatives discussed in the design rationale. Some add a richer vocabulary to modify the relationships between the node elements, such as McCall's Procedural Hierarchy of Issues (PHI) [111] which expands the variety of inter-issue relationships. Interesting work at the University of Colorado has attempted to link PHI argumentation to computer aided design (CAD) tools to allow critique of design (in their example, the design of a kitchen) as it occurs. When the CAD design violates some known design rule, the designer is warned and can then browse a PHI argument to see the rationale for the design rule.

The use of IBIS and any of its descendants is process-oriented, as we described above. It is intended for use during design meetings as a means of recording and structuring the issues deliberated and the decisions made. It is also intended to preserve the order of deliberation and decision-making for a particular product, placing less stress on the generalization of design knowledge for use between different products. This can be contrasted with the structure-oriented technique described next.

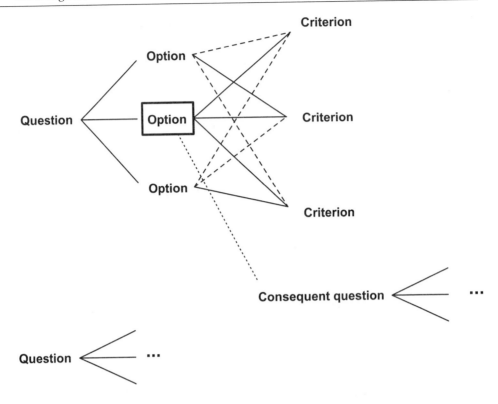

Figure 5.12   *The QOC notation*

5.6.2   *Design space analysis*

MacLean and colleagues [105] have proposed a more deliberative approach to design rationale which emphasizes a *post hoc* structuring of the space of design alternatives that have been considered in a design project. Their approach, embodied in the Questions, Options and Criteria (QOC) notation, is characterized as *design space analysis* (see Figure 5.12).

The design space is initially structured by a set of questions representing the major issues of the design. Since design space analysis is structure-oriented, it is not so important that the questions recorded are the actual questions asked during design meetings. Rather, these questions represent an agreed characterization of the issues raised based on reflection and understanding of the actual design activities. Questions in a design space analysis are therefore similar to issues in IBIS except in the way they are captured. Options provide alternative solutions to the question. They are assessed according to some criteria in order to determine the most favourable option. In Figure 5.12 an option which is favourably assessed in terms of a criterion is linked with a solid line, whereas negative links have a dashed line. The most favourable option is boxed in the diagram.

The key to an effective design space analysis using the QOC notation is deciding the right questions to use to structure the space and the correct criteria to judge the options. The initial questions raised must be sufficiently general that they cover a large enough portion of the possible design space, but specific enough that a range of options can be clearly identified. It can be difficult to decide the right set of criteria with which to assess the options. The QOC technique advocates the use of general criteria, like the usability principles discussed in the second half of Chapter 4, which are expressed more explicitly in a given analysis. In the example of the action buttons versus the menu of actions described earlier, we could contextualize the general principle of operation visibility as the criterion that all possible actions are displayed at all times. It can be very difficult to decide from a design space analysis which option is most favourable. The positive and negative links in the QOC notation do not provide all of the context for a trade-off decision. There is no provision for indicating, for example, that one criterion is more important than any of the others and the most favourable option must be positively linked.

Another structure-oriented technique, called Decision Representation Language (DRL), developed by Lee and Lai, structures the design space in a similar fashion to QOC, though its language is somewhat larger and it has a formal semantics. The questions, options and criteria in DRL are given the names decision problem, alternatives and goals. QOC assessments are also represented in DRL by a more complex language for relating goals to alternatives. The sparse language in QOC used to assess an option relative to a criterion (positive or negative assessment only) is probably insufficient, but there is a trade-off involved in adopting a more complex vocabulary which may prove too difficult to use in practice. The advantage of the formal semantics of DRL is that the design rationale can be used as a computational mechanism to help manage the large volume of information. For example, DRL can track the dependencies between different decision problems, so that subsequent changes to the design rationale for one decision problem can be automatically propagated to other dependent problems.

Design space analysis directly addresses the claim that no design activity can hope to uncover all design possibilities, so the best we can hope to achieve is to document the small part of the design space that has been investigated. An advantage of the *post hoc* technique is that it can abstract away from the particulars of a design meeting and therefore represent the design knowledge in such a way that it can be of use in the design of other products. The major disadvantage is the increased overhead such an analysis warrants. More time must be taken away from the design activity to do this separate documentation task. When time is scarce, these kinds of overhead costs are the first to be trimmed.

5.6.3   *Psychological design rationale*

The final category of design rationale tries to make explicit the psychological claims of usability inherent in any interactive system in order to better suit a product for the tasks users have. This psychological design rationale has been introduced by Carroll and Rosson [32], and before we can describe the application of the technique it is important to understand some of its theoretical background.

People use computers to accomplish some tasks in their particular work domain, as we have seen before. When designing a new interactive system, the designers take into account the tasks that users currently perform and any new ones that they may want to perform. This task identification serves as part of the requirements for the new system, and can be done through empirical observation of how people perform their work currently and presented through informal language or a more formal task analysis language (see Chapter 7). When the new system is implemented, or becomes an *artefact*, further observation reveals that in addition to the required tasks it was built to support, it also supports users in tasks that the designer never intended. Once designers understand these new tasks, and the associated problems that arise between them and the previously known tasks, the new task definitions can serve as requirements for future artefacts.

Carroll refers to this real-life phenomenon as the *task–artefact cycle*. He provides a good example of the task–artefact cycle through the evolution of the electronic spreadsheet. When the first electronic spreadsheet, *VisiCalc*, was marketed in the late 1970s, it was presented simply as an automated means of supporting tabular calculation, a task commonly used in the accounting world. Within little over a decade of its introduction, the application of spreadsheets has far outstripped its original intent within accounting. Spreadsheets are now used for all kinds of financial analysis, 'what-if' simulations, report formatting and even as a general programming language paradigm! As the set of tasks expanded, new spreadsheet products have flooded the marketplace trying to satisfy the growing customer base. Another good example of the task–artefact cycle in action is with word-processing, which was originally introduced to provide more automated support for tasks previously achieved with a typewriter and now provides users with the ability to carry out various authoring tasks that they never dreamed possible with a conventional typewriter. And today, the tasks for the spreadsheet and the word-processor are intermingled in the same artefact.

The purpose of psychological design rationale is to support this natural task-artefact cycle of design activity. The main emphasis is not to capture the designer's intention in building the artefact. Rather, psychological design rationale aims to make explicit the consequences of a design for the user, given an understanding of what tasks he intends to perform. Previously, these psychological consequences were left implicit in the design, though designers would make informal claims about their systems (for example, that it is more 'natural' for the user, or easier to learn).

The first step in the psychological design rationale is to identify the tasks that the proposed system will address and to characterize those tasks by questions that the user tries to answer in accomplishing them. For instance, Carroll gives an example of designing a system to help programmers learn the Smalltalk programming language environment. Smalltalk is an object-oriented programming language which requires a different approach to programming from a standard imperative language like Basic, C or Pascal. The main task the system is to support is learning how Smalltalk works. In learning about the new programming environment, the programmer will perform tasks that help her answer the questions:

- What can I do, that is, what are the possible operations or functions that this programming environment allows?

- How does it work, that is, what do the various functions do?

- How can I do this, that is, once I know a particular operation I want to perform, how do I go about programming it?

For each question, a set of *scenarios* of user–system behaviour is suggested to support the user in addressing the question. For example, to address the 'What can I do?' question, the designers can described a scenario whereby the novice programmer is first confronted with the learning environment and sees that she can invoke some demo programs to investigate how Smalltalk programs work. The initial system can then be implemented to provide the functionality suggested by the scenarios (e.g. some demos would be made accessible and obvious to the user/programmer from the very beginning). Once this system is running, observation of its use and some designer reflection is used to produce the actual psychological design rationale for that version of the system. This is where the psychological claims are made explicit. For example, there is an assumption that the programmer knows that what she can see on the screen relates to what she can do (if she sees the list of programs under a heading 'Demos', she can click on one program name to see the associated demo). The psychological claim of this demo system is that the user learns by doing, which is a good thing. However, there may also be negative aspects which are equally important to mention. The demos may not be very interactive, in which case the user clicks on it to initiate it and then just sits back and watches a graphic display, never really learning how the demo application is constructed in Smalltalk. These negative aspects can be used to modify later versions of the system to allow more interactive demos which represent realistic yet simple applications whose behaviour and structure the programmer can appreciate.

By forcing the designer to document the psychological design rationale, it is hoped that she will become more aware of the natural evolution of user tasks and the artefact, taking advantage of how consequences of one design can be used to improve later designs.

5.7   Summary

In this chapter, we have showed how software engineering and the design process relates to interactive system design. The software engineering life cycle aims to structure design in order to increase the reliability of the design process. For interactive system design, this would equate to a reliable and reproducible means of designing predictably usable systems. Because of the special needs of interactive systems, it is essential to augment the standard life cycle in order to address issues of HCI.

We have seen how design rules can be used to provide direction for the design process, though the more general and interesting the design rule is for promoting usability, the further away it is from the actual language of design. Usability engineering encourages incorporating explicit usability goals within the design process, providing a means by which the product's usability can be judged. Iterative design practices admit that principled design of interactive systems alone cannot maximize product usability, so the designer must be able to evaluate early prototypes and rapidly correct features of the prototype which detract from the product usability.

The design process is composed of a series of decisions which pare down the vast set of potential systems to the one that is actually delivered to the customer. Design rationale, in its many forms, is aimed at allowing the designer to manage the information about the decision-making process, in terms of when and why design decisions were made and what consequences those decisions had for the user in accomplishing their work.

Exercises

5.1   Starting with some of the principles outlined in Chapter 4, provide a usability specification for an electronic meetings diary or calendar. First identify some of the tasks that would be performed by a user trying to keep track of future meetings, and then complete the usability specification assuming that the electronic system will be replacing a paper-based system. What assumptions do you have to make about the user and the electronic diary in order to create a reasonable usability specification?

5.2   Can you think of any instances in which the 'noun–verb' guideline for operations, as suggested in the Apple human interface guidelines for the Desktop Interface, would be violated? Suggest other abstract guidelines or principles besides consistency which support your example. (**Hint:** Think about moving files around on the Desktop.)

5.3   Can you think of any instances in which the user control guideline suggested by Apple is not followed? (**Hint:** Think about the use of dialogue boxes.)

5.4   Find a book on guidelines. List the guidelines that are provided and classify them in terms of the activity in the software life cycle to which they would most likely apply.

5.5   What is the distinction between a process-oriented and a structure-oriented design rationale technique? Would you classify psychological design rationale as process- or structure-oriented? Why?

Recommended Reading

- John A. McDermid, editor, *The Software Engineer's Reference Book*. Butterworth-Heinemann, 1991.

  A very good general reference book for all topics in software engineering. We have already mentioned Thimbleby's chapter as recommended reading for Chapter 4 of this book. For this chapter, we refer you to Chapter 15 on software life cycles and Chapter 40 on prototyping.

- Ian Sommerville, *Software Engineering*, fourth edition. Addison-Wesley, 1992.

  This textbook is one of the few texts in software engineering which treats issues of HCI, with two chapters dedicated to the topic.

- John Whiteside, John Bennett, and Karen Holtzblatt, Usability engineering: our experience and evolution. In Martin Helander, editor, *Handbook for Human–Computer Interaction*. North-Holland Press, 1988.

  The seminal work on usability engineering. More recent work on usability engineering has also been published by Jakob Nielsen [127, 128].

- Deborah J. Mayhew, *Principles and Guidelines in Software User Interface Design*. Prentice Hall, 1992.

  A comprehensive and very up-to-date catalogue of general interactive system guidelines which provides much of the experimental evidence to support specific guidelines.

- The HCI Service, *HCI Tools & Methods Handbook*, 1991.

  This booklet has been produced under the United Kingdom Department of Trade and Industry (DTI) *Usability Now!* programme. It contains a list of books on guidelines as well as a more complete summary of the available user-centred design techniques as they can be applied to the software life cycle. The booklet and other information about the program is available from the HCI Service, P.O. Box 31, Loughborough, Leicestershire LE11 1QU, United Kingdom.

- John M. Carroll and Thomas P. Moran, editors, *Human–Computer Interaction*, special double issue on Design Rationale, Volume 6, Numbers 3 & 4, 1991.

This double issue of the journal is the origin of the review on design rationale provided in this chapter. It contains many references to relevant work in the field. All of the authors referenced in Section 5.6 have articles in this journal, and an expanded version of this journal, edited by Carroll and Moran, is expected to be published in book form.

Chapter 6

Models of the User in Design

Overview

- Cognitive models represent users of interactive systems.

- Hierarchical models represent a user's task and goal structure.

- Linguistic models represent the user–system grammar.

- Physical and device models represent human motor skills.

- Cognitive architectures underlie all of these cognitive models.

6.1 Introduction

In all engineering disciplines, the designer recruits a selection of models to contribute to the design process. If we were building a new office block, for example, then we would use models of air circulation to design the ventilation system, structural models for the fabric and possibly social models for the detailed design of the office layout.

Some models are *evaluative*, that is, they tell us, after the fact, whether a given design has appropriate properties. For instance, we could use a structural analysis program to tell us whether a blueprint for a bridge will stand up to 40 tonne trucks driving over it. Other models are *generative*, that is, they contribute during the design process itself, rather than merely commenting afterwards. In practice, all models are used to some extent in this generative manner. The engineer will have used less precise structural models in the design of the bridge before submitting it to the detailed analysis program. Also the program would be expected not only to say whether the bridge will fall down or not, but also where the weak spots are, thus contributing to the next stage of design.

Models are used in other disciplines too. We may analyze the structure of a piece of music and decide that it is a rondo, or say that a poem is in sonnet form. Further, we may deliberately set out to write a sonnet, thus imposing the model upon the creative process. Craft is the art of design within constraint, and models help to formulate the constraints.

This chapter and the next three describe a range of models that can be used during the interface design process. Just as in the design of the office block several different types of model are required for different aspects of the building, so in interface design we would expect to use a whole selection of complementary methods.

6.2   Cognitive Models

The techniques and models in this chapter all claim to have some representation of users as they interact with an interface; that is, they model some aspect of the user's understanding, knowledge, intentions or processing. The level of representation differs from technique to technique — from models of high-level goals and the results of problem-solving activities, to descriptions of motor-level activity, such as keystrokes and mouse clicks. The formalisms have largely been developed by psychologists, or computer scientists whose interest is in understanding user behaviour.

One way to classify them is in respect to how well they describe features of the *competence* and *performance* of the user. Quoting from Simon [160]:

> Competence models tend to be ones that can predict legal behaviour sequences but generally do this without reference to whether they could actually be executed by users. In contrast, performance models not only describe what the necessary behaviour sequences are but usually describe both what the user needs to know and how this is employed in actual task execution.

Competence models, therefore, represent the kinds of behaviour expected of a user but they provide little help in analyzing that behaviour to determine its demands on the user. Performance models provide analytical power mainly by focusing on routine behaviour in very limited applications.

Another useful distinction between these models is whether they address the acquisition or formulation of a plan of activity or the execution of that plan. Referring back to the interaction framework presented in Chapter 3, this classification would mean that some models are concerned with understanding the *User* and his associated task language while others are concerned with the articulation translation between that task language and the *Input* language. The presentation of the cognitive models in this chapter follows this classification scheme, divided into the following categories:

- Hierarchical representation of the user's task and goal structure

- Linguistic and grammatical models

- Physical and device level models

The first category deals directly with the issue of formulation of goals and tasks. The second category deals with the grammar of the articulation translation and how it is understood by the user. The third category again deals with articulation, but at the human motor level instead of at a higher level of human understanding.

Architectural assumptions about the user are needed in any of the cognitive models discussed here. Some of the more basic architectural assumptions were covered in Chapter 1, such as the distinction between long- and short-term memory. After discussing models in the three categories above, we will describe two additional cognitive architectures and how they are relevant for analyzing interactive system design.

Many of these nominally cognitive models have a rather computational flavour. This reflects the way that computational analogies are currently used in cognitive psychology. The similarity between the language describing the user and that describing the computer has some advantages and some dangers. On the positive side it makes communication and analysis of the combined human–computer system easier. For instance, cognitive complexity theory (described later) produces models of both user goals and the system grammar, and can reason about their interaction. On the other hand, there is a danger that this will encourage a mechanistic view of the user.

6.3   Goal and Task Hierarchies

Many models make use of a model of mental processing in which the user achieves goals by solving sub-goals in a divide-and-conquer fashion. We will consider two models, *GOMS* and *CCT*, where this is a central feature. However, we will see similar features in other models, such as *TAG* (Section 6.4.2) and when we consider task analysis techniques (Chapter 7).

Imagine we want to produce a report on sales of introductory HCI textbooks. To achieve this goal we divide it into several sub-goals, say gathering the data together, producing the tables and histograms, and writing the descriptive material. Concentrating on the data gathering, we decide to split this into further sub-goals: find the names of all introductory HCI textbooks and then search the book sales database for these books. Similarly each of the other sub-goals is divided up into further sub-goals, until some level of detail is found at which we decide to stop. We thus end up with a hierarchy of goals and sub-goals. The example can be laid out to expose this structure:

```
produce report
    gather data
      .    find book names
      .    .    do keywords search of names database
                  << further sub-goals >>
      .    .    sift through names and abstracts by hand
                  << further sub-goals >>
```

```
   .    search sales database
             << further sub-goals >>
       layout tables and histograms
             << further sub-goals >>
       write description
             << further sub-goals >>
```

Various issues arise as one attempts such analyses of computer use.

Where do we stop? We can go on decomposing tasks until we get down to the individual hand and eye movements of the user, or we can stop at a more abstract level. Where do we start? In a similar way, we can start our analyses at different points in the hierarchy of goals. At the extreme we could extend our analysis to larger and larger goals: 'light oven' is a sub-goal of 'boil peas' and so on to goals such as 'have my dinner', 'feed' and 'stay alive'.

These two questions are issues of *granularity*, and both of the methods described below leave this to some extent in the hands of the designer. Different design issues demand different levels of analysis. However, both methods operate at a relatively low level; neither would attempt to start with such an abstract goal as 'produce a report' which will involve real creativity and difficult problem-solving. Instead they confine themselves to more routine learned behaviour. This most abstract task is referred to as the *unit task*. The unit task does not require any problem-solving skills on the part of the user, though it frequently demands quite sophisticated problem-solving skills on the part of the designer to determine them.

What do we do when there are several ways of solving a problem, or if the solutions to two sub-goals interact? Users will often have more than one way to achieve a goal and there must be some way of representing how they select between competing solutions.

Another important issue has to do with the treatment of error. Users are not perfect. A goal hierarchy may show how the perfect user would achieve a goal, but what can it say about difficulties the user may have along the way? In general, prediction of error behaviour is poor amongst these hierarchical modelling techniques, though some (cognitive complexity theory (CCT), for example) can represent error behaviour.

6.3.1 GOMS

The *GOMS* model of Card, Moran and Newell is an acronym for: Goals, Operators, Methods and Selection [28]. A GOMS description consists of these four elements:

Goals These are the user's goals, describing what the user wants to achieve. Further, in GOMS the goals are taken to represent a 'memory point' for the user, from which he can evaluate what should be done and to which he may return should any errors occur.

Operators These are the lowest level of analysis. They are the basic actions that the user must perform in order to use the system. They may affect the system (e.g. press the 'X' key) or only the user's mental state (e.g. read the dialogue box). There is still a degree of flexibility about the granularity of operators; we may take the command level 'issue the SELECT command' or be more primitive 'move mouse to menu bar, press centre mouse button . . .'.

Methods   As we have already noted, there are typically several ways in which a goal can be split into sub-goals. For instance, in a certain window manager a currently selected window can be closed to an icon either by selecting the 'CLOSE' option from a pop-up menu, or by hitting the 'L7' function key. In GOMS these two goal decompositions are referred to as methods, so we have the CLOSE-METHOD and the L7-METHOD:

```
GOAL: ICONIZE-WINDOW
.  [select GOAL: USE-CLOSE-METHOD
.            .  MOVE-MOUSE-TO-WINDOW-HEADER
.            .  POP-UP-MENU
.            .  CLICK-OVER-CLOSE-OPTION
           GOAL: USE-L7-METHOD
.            .  PRESS-L7-KEY]
```

The dots are used to indicate the hierarchical level of goals.

Selection   From the above snippet we see the use of the word 'select' where the choice of methods arises. GOMS does not leave this as a random choice, but attempts to predict which methods will be used. This typically depends both on the particular user and on the state of the system and details about the goals. For instance, a user, Sam, never uses the L7-METHOD, except for one game, 'blocks', where the mouse needs to be used in the game until the very moment the key is pressed. GOMS captures this in a selection rule for Sam:

User Sam:
        Rule 1: Use the CLOSE-METHOD unless another rule applies.
        Rule 2: If the application is 'blocks' use the L7-METHOD.

The goal hierarchies described in a GOMS analysis are almost wholly below the level of the unit task defined earlier. A typical GOMS analysis would therefore consist of a single high-level goal which is then decomposed into a sequence of unit tasks, all of which can be further decomposed down to the level of basic operators:

```
GOAL: EDIT-MANUSCRIPT
.  GOAL: EDIT-UNIT-TASK repeat until no more unit tasks
```

The goal decomposition between the overall task and the unit tasks would involve detailed understanding of the user's problem-solving strategies and of the application domain. These are side-stepped entirely by the method as originally proposed. It would be possible to use the general notation in order to describe this sub-goal structure (as for instance in the book report example above). This form of high-level goal description is adopted during *task analysis* which will be discussed in Chapter 7. In particular, the aim of *hierarchical task analysis* is to produce task decompositions, which would be similar (but in a different notation) to that in the book report example.

Analysis of the GOMS goal structure can yield measures of performance. The stacking depth of a goal structure can be used to estimate short-term memory requirements. The model of the users' mental processes implied by this is, of course, very idealized. Also, the selection rules can be tested for accuracy against user traces, and changed in response to discrepancies. In early experiments on the technique, the inventors were able to achieve on average 90% correct prediction rate of user commands. Further, a very simple method of predicting times (basically assuming that each operator takes a constant time) was able to predict actual times with an error of 33%.

The original GOMS model has served as the basis for much of the cognitive modelling research in HCI. It was good for describing how experts perform routine tasks. Coupled with the physical device models discussed later, it can be used to predict the performance of these users in terms of execution times. It was never intended to provide the kind of information about the user's knowledge that could be compared across different tasks in order to predict things like training or transfer times.

6.3.2   Cognitive complexity theory

Cognitive complexity theory (CCT), introduced by Kieras and Polson [96] begins with the basic premises of goal decomposition from GOMS and enriches the model to provide more predictive power. CCT has two parallel descriptions: one of the user's goals and the other of the computer system (called the *device* in CCT). The description of the user's goals is based on a GOMS-like goal hierarchy, but is expressed primarily using *production rules*. We introduced production rules in Chapter 1 and we further describe their use in CCT below. For the system grammar, CCT uses *generalized transition networks*, a form of *state transition network*. This will not be described here, but state transition networks will be discussed in detail in Chapter 8.

The production rules are a sequence of rules:

if *condition* then *action*

where *condition* is a statement about the contents of working memory. If the condition is true then the production rule is said to fire. An *action* may consist of one or more elementary actions, which may either be changes to the working memory, or external actions such as keystrokes. The production rule 'program' is written in a LISP-like language.

As an example, we consider an editing task using the UNIX 'vi' editor. The task is to insert a space where one has been missed out in the text, for instance, if we noticed that in the above paragraph we had written 'cognitivecomplexity theory'. This is a reasonably frequent typing error and so we assume that we have developed good procedures to perform the task. We consider a fragment of the associated CCT production rules.

```
(SELECT-INSERT-SPACE
IF (AND (TEST-GOAL perform unit task)
        (TEST-TEXT task is insert space)
        (NOT (TEST-GOAL insert space))
        (NOT (TEST-NOTE executing insert space)) )
   THEN (  (ADD-GOAL insert space)
           (ADD-NOTE executing insert space)
           (LOOK-TEXT task is at %LINE %COL) ))


(INSERT-SPACE-DONE
IF (AND (TEST-GOAL perform unit task)
        (TEST-NOTE executing insert space)
        (NOT (TEST-GOAL insert space)) )
   THEN (  (DELETE-NOTE executing insert space)
           (DELETE-GOAL perform unit task)
           (UNBIND %LINE %COL) ))

(INSERT-SPACE-1
IF (AND (TEST-GOAL insert space)
        (NOT (TEST-GOAL move cursor))
        (NOT (TEST-CURSOR %LINE %COL)) )
   THEN (  (ADD-GOAL move cursor to %LINE %COL) ))

(INSERT-SPACE-2
IF (AND (TEST-GOAL insert space)
        (TEST-CURSOR %LINE %COL) )
   THEN (  (DO-KEYSTROKE 'I')
           (DO-KEYSTROKE SPACE)
           (DO-KEYSTROKE ESC)
           (DELETE-GOAL insert space) ))
```

To see how these rules work, imagine that the user has just seen the typing mistake and thus the contents of working memory (w.m.) are:

```
(GOAL perform unit task)
(TEXT task is insert space)
(TEXT task is at 5 23)
(CURSOR 8 7)
```

TEXT refers to the text of the manuscript that is being edited and CURSOR refers to the insertion cursor on the screen. Of course, these items are not actually located in working memory—they are external to the user—but we assume that knowledge from observing them is stored in the user's working memory.

The location (5,23) is the line and column of the typing mistake where the space is required. However, the current cursor position is at line 8 and column 7. This is of course acquired into the user's working memory by looking at the screen. Looking at the four rules above (SELECT-INSERT-SPACE, INSERT-SPACE-DONE, INSERT-SPACE-1 and INSERT-SPACE-2), only the first can fire. The condition for SELECT-INSERT-SPACE is:

```
(AND (TEST-GOAL perform unit task)
          true because (GOAL perform unit task) is in w.m.
     (TEST-TEXT task is insert space)
          true because (TEXT task is insert space) is in w.m.
     (NOT (TEST-GOAL insert space))
          true because (GOAL insert space) is not in w.m.
     (NOT (TEST-NOTE executing insert space)) )
          true because (NOTE executing insert space) is not in w.m.
```

So, the rule fires and its action is performed. This action has no external effect in terms of keystrokes, but adds extra information to working memory. The (LOOK-TEXT task is at %LINE %COL) looks for a corresponding entry and *binds* LINE and COL to 5 and 23 respectively. These are variables, somewhat as in a normal programming language, which are referred to again in other rules.

The contents of working memory after the firing of rule SELECT-INSERT-SPACE is follows (note that the order of elements of working memory is arbitrary):

```
(GOAL perform unit task)
(TEXT task is insert space)
(TEXT task is at 5 23)
(NOTE executing insert space)
(GOAL insert space)
(LINE 5)
(COL 23)
(CURSOR 8 7)
```

At this point neither rule SELECT-INSERT-SPACE nor INSERT-SPACE-DONE will fire as the entry (GOAL insert space) will make their conditions false. As LINE is bound to 5 and COL is bound to 23, the condition (TEST-CURSOR %LINE %COL) will be false also, hence only rule INSERT-SPACE-1 can fire.

After this rule's actions have been performed, the working memory will include the entry (GOAL move cursor to 5 23). The rules for moving the cursor are not included here, but would be quite extensive, moving up/down and right/left depending on the relative positions of the cursor and the target location. Eventually, assuming the cursor movement is successful, the cursor would be at (5,23) whence rule INSERT-SPACE-2 would be able to fire. This would perform the keystrokes: 'I', SPACE and ESC, which in 'vi' puts the editor into insert mode, types the space and then leaves insert mode. The actions also removes the `insert space` goal from working memory as this goal has been achieved.

Now, the goal has been removed, the second rule `INSERT-SPACE-DONE` is free to fire, which 'tidies up' working memory. In particular, it 'unbinds' the variables `LINE` and `COL`, that is, removes the bindings for them from working memory.

Notice that the rules did not fire in the order they were written. Although they look somewhat like the `if-then-else` commands one would get in a standard programming language, they behave very differently. The rules are all active and at each moment any rule that has its conditions true may fire. Some rules may never fire, for instance if the cursor is at the correct position the third rule would not fire. Furthermore, the same rule may fire repeatedly, for example, if we were to write out the production rules for moving the cursor, one rule may well be:

```
(MOVE-UP
IF (AND (TEST-GOAL move-up)
        (TEST-CURSOR-BELOW %LINE) )
THEN (   (DO-KEYSTROKE 'K') ))
```

This rule is to type 'K' (the vi command to move the cursor up one line) while the cursor is below the desired line. It will, of course, be constantly refired until the cursor is at the correct line.

Notice that the keystrokes for actually inserting the space, once you are at the right position, have been *proceduralized*. That is, the user does not go through the sub-goals 'enter insert mode', 'type space', 'leave insert mode'. For a complex insertion, it is quite likely that the user will perform exactly these goals. However, the act of inserting a single space is assumed to be so well rehearsed that it is stored as a single chunk. That is, the rules above represent *expert* knowledge of the vi editor.

Of course, novices may well do exactly the same keystrokes as the experts, but the way they store the knowledge will be different. To cope with this CCT has a set of 'style' rules for novices. These limit the form of the conditions and actions in the production rules. Basically, novices are expected to constantly test all the rules in their working memory and to check for feedback from the system after every keystroke. Thus a set of 'novice' rules would not include the proceduralized form of insert space. Bovair, Kieras and Polson provide a list of many style rules which can be used to embody certain psychological assumptions about the user (novice/expert distinction is only one) in a CCT description [20].

The rules in CCT need not represent error-free performance. They can be used to explain error phenomena, though they cannot predict it. For instance, the rules above for inserting a space are 'buggy'—they do not check the editor's mode. Imagine, you had just been typing the 'cognitive' in 'cognitivecomplexity theory' (with the space missing), you think for a few minutes and then look again at the screen and notice that the space is missing. The cursor is at the correct position for the space, so rule `INSERT-SPACE-1` never gets fired and we go directly through the sequence: `SELECT-INSERT-SPACE`, `INSERT-SPACE-2` then `INSERT-SPACE-DONE`. You type 'i', a space and then escape. However, the 'i' assumes that you are in vi's command mode, and is the command to move the editor into insert mode. If, however, after typing 'cognitive' you had not typed escape, to get you back into command mode, the whole sequence would be done in insert mode. The text would read: 'cognitiveI complexity theory'.

The CCT rules are closely related to GOMS-like goal hierarchies, the rules may be generated from such a hierarchy, or alternatively, we may analyze the production rules to obtain the goal tree:

```
GOAL: insert space
.       GOAL: move cursor    -  if not at right position
.       PRESS-KEY-I
.       PRESS-SPACE
.       PRESS-ESCAPE
```

The stacking depth of this goal hierarchy (as described for GOMS) is directly related to the number of (GOAL ...) terms in working memory.

In fact, the CCT rules can represent more complex plans than the simple sequential hierarchies of GOMS. The continuous activity of all production rules makes it possible to represent concurrent plans. For example, one could have one set of production rules representing the goal of writing a book, and another set representing the goal of drinking tea. These rules could both be active simultaneously, thus allowing an author to drink tea whilst typing. Despite this apparent flexibility, CCT is not normally used in this way. It is not clear why this is, except that CCT, like GOMS, is aimed at low-level, *proceduralized* goals — that is, the *unit task*. It is reasonable that successive unit tasks be chosen from different activities: the author may delete a word, have a drink, do a word search, but each time a complete unit task would be performed: the author does not take a drink of tea in the middle of deleting a word.

We have seen how CCT rules may be informally analyzed to discuss issues of proceduralization and error behaviour, and how we can relate them to GOMS-like goal hierarchies. However, the main aim of CCT is (as its name suggests) to be able to measure the complexity of an interface.

Basically, the more production rules in the CCT description the more difficult the interface is to learn. This claim rests on the assumption that the production rules represent reasonably accurately the way knowledge is stored and therefore that the time taken to learn an interface is roughly proportional to the number of rules you have to learn.

We have only discussed the user side of CCT here. If the cognitive user description is complemented by a description of the system, it is claimed that one can predict the difficulty of the mapping between the user's goals and the system model. The generalized transition networks which describe the system grammar themselves have a hierarchical structure. Thus both the description of the user and that of the system can be represented as hierarchies. These can then be compared to find mismatches and to produce a measure of dissonance.

There are various problems with CCT. As with many 'rich' description methods, the size of description for even a part of an interface can be enormous. Furthermore, there may be several ways of representing the same user behaviour and interface behaviour, yielding different measures of dissonance. To some extent this is catered for by the novice style rules, but there is no such set of rules for the system description.

Another problem is the particular choice of notations. Production rules are often suggested as a good model of the way people remember procedural knowledge, but there are obvious 'cludges' in the CCT description given above. In particular, the working memory entry (NOTE executing insert space) is there purely to allow the INSERT-SPACE-DONE rule to fire at the appropriate time. It is not at all clear that it has any real cognitive significance. One may also question whether the particular notation chosen for the system is critical to the method. One might choose to represent the system using any one of the dialogue description notations in Chapter 8. Different notations would probably yield slightly different measures of dissonance.

However, one should regard CCT as an engineering tool giving one a rough measure of learnability and difficulty combined with a detailed description of user behaviour. This can then be used by analysts employing their professional expertise. Arguably, the strength of the central idea of CCT lies beyond the particular notations used.

6.3.3 *Problems and extensions of goal hierarchies*

The formation of a goal hierarchy is largely a post-hoc technique and runs a very real risk of being defined by the computer dialogue rather than the user. One way to rectify this is to produce a goal structure based on pre-existing manual procedures and thus obtain a natural hierarchy [97]. To be fair, GOMS defines its domain to be that of expert use, and thus the goal structures which are important are those which users develop out of their use of the system. However, such a natural hierarchy may be particularly useful as part of a CCT analysis, representing a very early state of knowledge.

On the positive side, the conceptual framework of goal hierarchies and user goal stacks can be used to express interface issues, not directly addressed by the notations above. For instance, early bank teller machines gave the customers the money before returning their cards. Unfortunately, this led to many customers leaving their cards behind. This was despite on-screen messages telling them to wait. This is referred to as a problem of *closure*. The user's principal goal is to get money; when that goal is satisfied, the user does not complete or close the various sub-tasks which still remain open:

```
GOAL: GET-MONEY
.   GOAL: USE-ATM
.   .   INSERT-CARD
.   .   ENTER-PIN
.   .   ENTER-AMOUNT
```

```
.   .   COLLECT-MONEY
            <<  outer goal now satisfied goal stack popped >>
.   .   COLLECT-CARD    --    sub-goal operators missed
```

Banks (at least some of them) soon changed the dialogue order so that the card was always retrieved before the money was dispensed. A general rule that can be applied to any goal hierarchy from this is that no higher level goal should be satisfied until all sub-goals have been satisfied. However, it is not always easy to predict when the user will consider a goal to have been satisfied. For instance, one of the authors has been known to collect his card and forget the money!

6.4   Linguistic Models

The user's interaction with a computer is often viewed in terms of a language, so it is not surprising that several modelling formalisms have developed centred around this concept. Several of the dialogue notations described in Chapter 8 are also based on linguistic ideas. Indeed, BNF grammars are frequently used to specify dialogues. The models here, although similar in form to dialogue design notations have been proposed with the intention of understanding the user's behaviour and analyzing the cognitive difficulty of the interface.

6.4.1 *BNF*

Representative of the *linguistic approach* is Reisner's use of Backus–Naur Form (*BNF*) rules to describe the dialogue grammar [146]. This views the dialogue at a purely syntactic level, ignoring the semantics of the language. BNF has been used widely to specify the syntax of computer programming languages, and many system dialogues can be described easily using BNF rules. For example, imagine a graphics system which has a line drawing function. To select the function the user must select the 'line' menu option. The line drawing function allows the user to draw a polyline, that is a sequence of line arcs between points. The user selects the points by clicking the mouse button in the drawing area. The user double clicks to indicate the last point of the polyline.

```
draw-line       ::=   select-line + choose-points
                                  + last-point
select-line     ::=   position-mouse + CLICK-MOUSE
choose-points   ::=   choose-one
                    | choose-one + choose-points
choose-one      ::=   position-mouse + CLICK-MOUSE
last-point      ::=   position-mouse + DOUBLE-CLICK-MOUSE
position-mouse  ::=   empty | MOVE-MOUSE + position-mouse
```

The names in the description are of two types: *non-terminals*, shown in lower case, and *terminals*, shown in upper case. Terminals represent the lowest level of user behaviour, such as pressing a key, clicking a mouse button or moving the mouse. Non-terminals are higher level abstractions. The non-terminals are defined in terms of other non-terminals and terminals by a definition of the form:

```
name      ::=    expression
```

The '::=' symbol is read as 'is defined as'. Only non-terminals may appear on the left of a definition. The right hand side is built up using two operators '+' (sequence) and | (choice). For example the first rule says that the non-terminal draw-line is defined to be select-line followed by choose-points followed by last-point. All of these are non-terminals, that is, they do not tell us what the basic user actions are. The second rule says that select-line is defined to be position-mouse (intended to be over the 'line' menu entry) followed by MOUSE-CLICK. This is our first terminal and represents the actual clicking of a mouse.

To see what position-mouse is, we look at the last rule. This tells us that there are two possibilities for position-mouse (separated by the '|' symbol). One option is that position-mouse is empty — a special symbol representing no action. That is, one option is not to move the mouse at all. The other option is to do a MOVE-MOUSE action followed by position-mouse. This rule is recursive, and this second position-mouse may itself either be empty or be a MOVE-MOUSE action followed by position-mouse, and so on. That is, position-mouse may be any number of MOVE-MOUSE actions whatsoever.

Similarly, choose-points is defined recursively, but this time it does not have the option of being empty. It may be *one or more* of the non-terminal choose-one which is itself defined to be (like select-line) position-mouse followed by MOUSE-CLICK.

The BNF description of an interface can be analyzed in various ways. One measure is to count the number of rules. The more rules an interface requires to use it, the more complicated it is. This measure is rather sensitive to the exact way the interface is described. For example, we could have replaced the rules for choose-points and choose-one with the single definition:

```
choose-points  ::=    position-mouse + CLICK-MOUSE
              | position-mouse + CLICK-MOUSE + choose-points
```

A more robust measure also counts the number of '+' and '|' operators. This would, in effect, penalize the more complex single rule. Another problem arises with the rule for select-line. This is identical to the choose-one rule. However, the acts of selecting a menu option and choosing a point on a drawing surface are obviously so different that they must surely be separated. Decisions like this about the structure of a BNF description are less of a problem in practice than the corresponding problems we had with CCT.

In addition to these complexity measures for the language as a whole, we can use the BNF definition to work out how many basic actions are required for a particular task, and thus obtain a crude estimate of the difficulty of that task.

The BNF description above only represented the user's actions, not the user's perception of the system's responses. This input bias is surprisingly common amongst cognitive models, as we will discuss in Section 6.5. Reisner has developed extensions to the basic BNF descriptions which attempt to deal with this by adding 'information seeking actions' to the grammar.

6.4.2 Task-action grammar

Measures based upon BNF have been criticized as not 'cognitive' enough. They ignore the advantages of consistency both in the language's structure and in its use of command names and letters. *Task–action grammar (TAG)* [136] attempts to deal with some of these problems by including elements such as parametrized grammar rules to emphasize consistency and encoding the user's world knowledge (e.g. up is the opposite of down).

To illustrate consistency, we consider the three UNIX commands: cp (for copying files), mv (for moving files) and ln (for linking files). Each of these has two possible forms. They either have two arguments: a source and destination filename, or they have any number of source filenames followed by a destination directory:

```
copy    ::=    'cp' + filename + filename
            |  'cp' + filenames + directory
move    ::=    'mv' + filename + filename
            |  'mv' + filenames + directory
link    ::=    'ln' + filename + filename
            |  'ln' + filenames + directory
```

Measures based upon BNF could not distinguish between these consistent commands and an inconsistent alternative — say if ln took its directory argument first. Task–action grammar was designed to reveal just this sort of consistency. Its description of the UNIX commands would be:

```
file-op[Op]        :=    command[Op] + filename + filename
                     |  command[Op] + filenames + directory
command[Op=copy] :=    'cp'
command[Op=move] :=    'mv'
command[Op=link] :=    'ln'
```

This captures the consistency of the commands and closely resembles the original textual description. One would imagine that a measure of the complexity of the language based on the TAG description would be better at predicting actual learning and performance than a simple BNF one.

As well as handling consistency well, TAG has features for talking about 'world knowledge'. For example, imagine we have two command line interfaces for moving a mechanical turtle around the floor.

Command interface 1

```
movement[Direction]
              :=  command[Direction] + distance + RETURN
command[Direction=forward]    := 'go 395'
command[Direction=backward]   := 'go 013'
command[Direction=left]       := 'go 712'
command[Direction=right]      := 'go 956'
```

Command interface 2

```
movement[Direction]
              :=  command[Direction] + distance + RETURN
command[Direction=forward]    := 'FORWARD'
command[Direction=backward]   := 'BACKWARD'
command[Direction=left]       := 'LEFT'
command[Direction=right]      := 'RIGHT'
```

The first interface may not be as silly as it seems, the commands 'go 395' could be addresses of the machine code routines which perform the various movements. However, it is absolutely clear that the second interface is preferable to the first. TAG includes a special form known-item which is used to denote information that the user will already know, and thus not need to learn in order to use the system. Using this form, the TAG rules for the second interface are re-written:

Command interface 2

```
movement[Direction]
              :=  command[Direction] + distance + RETURN
command[Direction]   :=  known-item[Type=word,Direction]
*   command[Direction=forward]    := 'FORWARD'
*   command[Direction=backward]   := 'BACKWARD'
*   command[Direction=left]       := 'LEFT'
*   command[Direction=right]      := 'RIGHT'
```

The starred rules can be generated from the second rule using the user's world knowledge. They are included in any TAG description for completeness, but are not counted in any measure of complexity.

Sometimes it may not be clear what the appropriate command is, but once we know one, the rest become obvious. For example, consider a simple database displaying a list of records. We are expecting two commands, one to move up the list to the previous record, and another to move down the list to the next record. There are several options for the commands, for instance, UP/DOWN, PREVIOUS/NEXT, possibly in upper or lower case, possibly also just the first letter of the relevant word. In addition, one might have mixed up command sets such as UP/NEXT or N/previous. The fact that any of the former set of commands is easier to learn than the mixed up commands is called *congruence*. TAG has a notation

to describe the congruence of an interface. The notation F('next') is used to
denote the feature set related to the word 'next'. That is, next/previous. With this
notation a congruent grammar requires only one 'real' rule, such as:

```
browse[Direction]      :=  F('next') + return
*   browse[Direction=up]      :=  'previous' + return
*   browse[Direction=down]    :=  'next' + return
```

We have seen that the notation allows one to say that the commands RIGHT
and LEFT are consistent for opposite actions. How do we know that the user
regards the opposite of RIGHT to be LEFT rather than WRONG? Obviously, the
inclusion of worldknowledge depends upon the user of the system — the above
certainly assumes that the user's language is English. The designer is obviously
responsible for inputting this world knowledge into the TAG description and its
validity will depend on the professional judgement of the designer. However, TAG
will make these assumptions clear and thus, by highlighting them, hold them up
for inspection.

6.5   The Challenge of Display Based Systems

Both goal hierarchical and grammar based techniques were initially developed
when most interactive systems were command line or at most keyboard and cursor
based. There are significant worries as to how well these approaches can therefore
generalize to deal with more modern windowed and mouse-driven interfaces.

Both families of techniques largely ignore system output—what the user sees.
The implicit assumption is that the users know exactly what they want to do and
execute the appropriate command sequences blindly. There are minor exceptions to
this. We have already mentioned how Reisner's BNF has been extended to include
assertions about output. TAG has also been extended to include information about
how the display can affect the grammar rules.

Another problem for grammars is the lowest level lexical structure. Pressing
a cursor key is a reasonable *lexeme*, but moving a mouse one pixel is less sensible.
In addition, pointer based dialogues are more display-oriented. Clicking a cursor
at a particular point on the screen has a meaning dependent on the current screen
contents. This problem can be partially resolved by regarding operations such as
'select region of text' or 'click on quit button' as the terminals of the grammar.
If this approach is taken, the detailed mouse movements and parsing of mouse
events in the context of display information (menus, etc.) are abstracted away.

Goal hierarchy methods have different problems, as more display-oriented
systems encourage less structured methods for goal achievement. Instead of well-
defined plans, the user is seen as performing a more exploratory task, recognizing
fruitful directions and backing out of others. Typically, even when this exploratory
style is used at one level, we can see within it and around it more goal-oriented
methods. So for example, we might consider the high-level goal structure:

```
WRITE_LETTER
   .       FIND_SIMILAR_LETTER
   .       COPY_IT
   .       EDIT_COPY
```

However, the task of finding a similar letter would be exploratory, searching through folders, etc. Such recognition based searching is extremely difficult to represent as a goal structure. Similarly the actual editing would depend very much on non-planned activities: 'ah yes, I want to re-use that bit, but I'll have to change that'. If we then drop to a lower level again, goal hierarchies become more applicable. For instance, during the editing stage we might have the 'delete a word' sub-dialogue:

```
DELETE_WORD
   .       SELECT_WORD
   .       .       MOVE_MOUSE_TO_WORD_START
   .       .       DEPRESS_MOUSE_BUTTON
   .       .       MOVE_MOUSE_TO_WORD_END
   .       .       RELEASE_MOUSE_BUTTON
   .       CLICK_ON_DELETE
   .       .       MOVE_MOUSE_TO_DELETE_ICON
   .       .       CLICK_MOUSE_BUTTON
```

Thus goal hierarchies can partially cope with display-oriented systems by an appropriate choice of level, but the problems do emphasize the rather prescriptive nature of the cognitive models underlying them.

6.6 Physical and Device Models

6.6.1 Keystroke level model

Compared with the deep cognitive understanding required to describe problem-solving activities, the human motor system is well understood. The *KLM* (keystroke level model [27]) uses this understanding as a basis for detailed predictions about user performance. It is aimed at unit tasks within interaction — the execution of simple command sequences, typically taking no more than 20 seconds. Examples of this would be using a search/replace feature, or changing the font of a word. It does not extend to complex actions such as producing a diagram. The assumption is that these more complex tasks would be split into sub-tasks (as in *GOMS*) before the user attempts to map these into physical actions. The task is split into two phases:

acquisition of the task, when the user builds a mental representation of the task.

execution of the task using the system's facilities.

KLM only gives predictions for the latter stage of activity. During the acquisition phase the user will have decided how to accomplish the task using the primitives of the system, and thus, during the execution phase, there is no high-level mental activity — the user is effectively expert. KLM is related to the GOMS model, and can be thought of as a very low-level GOMS model where the method is given.

The model decomposes the execution phase into five different physical-motor operators, a mental operator and a system response operator.

K keystroking, actually striking keys, including shifts and other modifier keys.

B pressing a mouse button.

P pointing, moving the mouse (or similar device) at a target.

H homing, switching the hand between mouse and keyboard.

D drawing lines using the mouse.

M mentally preparing for a physical action.

R system response which may be ignored if the user does not have to wait for it, as in copy typing.

The execution of a task will involve interleaved occurrences of the various operators. For instance, imagine we are using a mouse based editor. If we notice a single character error we will point at the error, delete the character and retype it, then return to our previous typing point. This is decomposed as:

1	move hand to mouse	**H**[mouse]
2	position mouse after bad character	**PB**[LEFT]
3	return to keyboard	**H**[keyboard]
4	delete character	**MK**[DELETE]
5	type correction	**K**[char]
6	reposition insertion point	**H**[mouse]**MPB**[LEFT]

Notice that some operators have descriptions added to them, representing which device the hand homes to (e.g. [mouse]) and what keys are hit (e.g. LEFT — the left mouse button).

The model predicts the total time taken during the execution phase by adding the component times for each of the above activities. For example, if the time taken for one keystroke is t_K, then the total time doing keystrokes is

$$T_K = 2t_K$$

Similar calculations for the rest of the operators give a total time of:

$$\begin{aligned} T_{execute} &= T_K + T_B + T_P + T_H + T_D + T_M + T_R \\ &= 2t_K + 2t_B + t_P + 3t_H + 0 + 2t_M + 0 \end{aligned}$$

Table 6.1   *Times for various operators in KLM (adapted from Card, Moran and Newell [28])*

Operator	Remarks	Time (sec)
K	Press key	
	good typist (90 wpm)	0.12
	poor typist (40 wpm)	0.28
	non-typist	1.20
B	Mouse button press	
	down or up	0.10
	click	0.20
P	Point with mouse	
	Fitts' law	$0.1 \, log_2(D/S + 0.5)$
	average movement	1.10
H	Home hands to and from keyboard	0.40
D	Drawing — domain-dependent	—
M	Mentally prepare	1.35
R	Response from system — measure	—

In this example, the system response time was zero. However, if the user had to wait for the system then the appropriate time would be added. In many typing tasks, the user can type ahead anyway and thus there is no need to add response times. Where needed, the response time can be measured by observing the system.

The times for the other operators are obtained from empirical data. The keying time obviously depends on the typing skill of the user and different times are thus used for different users. Pressing a mouse button is usually quicker than typing (especially for two finger typists), and a more accurate time prediction can be made by separating out the button presses **B** from the rest of the keystrokes **K**. The pointing time can be calculated using Fitts' law (see Chapter 1), and thus depends on the size and position of the target[1]. Alternatively, a fixed time based on average within screen pointing can be used. Drawing time depends on the number and length of the lines drawn, and is fairly domain-specific, but one can easily use empirical data for more general drawing tasks. Finally, homing time and mental preparation time are assumed constant. Typical times are summarized in Table 6.1.

The mental operator is probably the most complex part of KLM. Remember that the user is assumed to have decided what to do, and how to do it. The mental preparation is thus just the slight pauses made as the user recalls what to do next.

---

[1]The form of Fitts' law used with the original KLM is $K \, log_2(D/S + 0.5)$, where D is the distance to the target and S is the target size. We will use this form for calculations in this sub-section, but revert to the form $a + b \, log_2(D/S + 1)$ in the next sub-section when we consider Buxton's three-state model as this form was used for these experiments.

There are complicated heuristics for deciding where to put M operators, but they all boil down to the level of chunking (see Chapter 1 for a discussion of chunking). If the user types a word, or a well-known command name, this will be one chunk, and hence only require one mental operator. However, if a command name were an acronym which the user was recalling letter by letter, then we would place one M operator per letter.

The physical operator times all depend on the skills of the user. Also the mental operator depends on the level of chunking, and hence the expertise of the user. One must therefore decide before using KLM predictions just what sort of user you are thinking about. You cannot even work out the operators and then fill in the times later, as different users may choose different methods and have different placings of M operators due to chunking. This sounds rather onerous, but the predictions made by KLM are only meant to be an approximation, and thus reasonable guesses about levels of expertise are enough.

Individual predictions may be interesting, but the power of KLM lies in comparison. Given several systems, we can work out the methods to perform key tasks, and then use KLM to tell us which system is fastest. This is considerably cheaper than conducting lengthy experiments (levels of individual variation would demand vast numbers of trials—see Chapter 11). Furthermore, the systems need not even exist. From a description of a proposed system, we can predict the times taken for tasks. As well as comparing systems, we can compare methods within a system. This can be useful in preparing training materials, as we can choose to teach the faster methods.

As an example, we compare the two methods for iconizing a window given in Section 6.3.1. One used the 'L7' function key, and the other the 'CLOSE' option from the window's pop-up menu. The later is obtained by moving to the window's title bar, depressing the left mouse button, dragging the mouse down the pop-up menu to the 'CLOSE' option, and then releasing the mouse button. We assume that the user's hand is on the mouse to begin with, hence only the L7_METHOD will require a homing operator. The operators for the two methods are as follows:

L7_METHOD   H[to keyboard] M K[L7 function key]
CLOSE_METHOD   P[to menu bar] B[LEFT down] M P[to option] B[LEFT up]

The total times are thus:

L7_METHOD   = 0.4 + 1.35 + 0.28
              = 2.03 seconds
CLOSE_METHOD = 1.1 + 0.1 + 1.35 + 1.1 + 0.1
              = 3.75 seconds

The first calculation is quite straightforward, but the second needs a little unpacking. The button presses are separate down and then up actions and thus each is only timed at 0.1 of a second, rather than 0.2 for a click, or 0.28 for typing. We have also used the simplified average 1.1 second time for the pointing task. From these predictions, we can see that the L7_METHOD is far faster. In Section 6.3.1, Sam's selection rule was to use L7_METHOD when playing blocks. To do so, he can go on playing the game using the mouse in his right hand whilst moving his left hand over the key. Thus the real time for Sam, from when he takes his attention from the game, to when the command is given, is less, 2.03 seconds minus the homing time, that is 1.63 seconds. Given the method is so fast, why does Sam not use it all the time?

Perhaps the average estimates for pointing times have biased our estimate. We can be a little more precise about the CLOSE_METHOD timing if we use Fitts' law instead of the average 1.1 seconds. The mouse will typically be in the middle of a 25 line high window. The title bar is 1.25 lines high. Thus the distance to target ratio for the first pointing task is 10:1. The 'CLOSE' option is four items down on the pop-up menu, hence the ratio for the second pointing task is 4:1. Thus we can calculate the pointing times:

$$
\begin{array}{lclcl}
\text{P[to menu bar]} & = & 0.1\log_2(10.5) & = & 0.339 \\
\text{P[to option]} & = & 0.1\log_2(4.5) & = & 0.217
\end{array}
$$

With these revised timings, KLM predicts the CLOSE_METHOD will take 2.1 seconds. So, Sam's selection rule is not quite as bad as it initially seemed!

Card, Moran and Newell empirically validated the keystroke level model against a range of systems, both keyboard and mouse based, and a wide selection of tasks. The predictions were found to be remarkably accurate (an error of about 20%). KLM is thus one of the few models capable of giving accurate quantitative predictions about performance. However, the range of applications is correspondingly small. It tells us a lot about the micro-interaction, but not about the larger scale dialogue.

However, we have seen that one has to be quite careful, as the approximations one makes can radically change the results—KLM is a guide not an oracle. One should also add a word of caution about the assumption that fastest is best. There are certainly situations where this is so, for example, highly repetitive tasks such as telephony or data entry. However, even expert users will often not use the fastest method. For example, the expert may have a set of general-purpose, non-optimal methods, rather than a few task-specific methods.

6.6.2 Three-state model

In Chapter 2, we saw that a range of pointing devices exists in addition to the mouse. Often these devices are considered logically equivalent, if the same inputs are available *to the application*. That is, so long as you can select a point on the screen, they are all the same. However, these different devices, mouse, trackball, light pen, feel very different. Although the devices are similar from the application's viewpoint, they have very different sensory-motor characteristics.

Buxton has developed a simple model of input devices [25], the *three state model*, which captures some of these crucial distinctions. He begins by looking at a mouse. If you move it with no buttons pushed, it normally moves the mouse

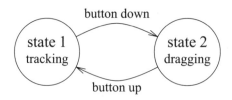

Figure 6.1   *Mouse transitions: states 1 and 2*

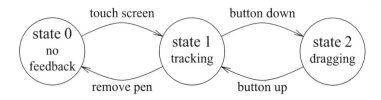

Figure 6.2   *Light pen transitions: three states*

cursor about. This tracking behaviour is termed state 1. Depressing a button over an icon and then moving the mouse will often result in an object being dragged about. This he calls state 2 (see Figure 6.1).

If instead we consider a light pen with a button, it behaves just like a mouse when it is touching the screen. When its button is not depressed, it is in state 1, and when its button is down, state 2. However, the light pen has a third state, when the light pen is not touching the screen. In this state the system cannot track the light pen's position. This state is called state 0 (see Figure 6.2).

A touch screen is like the light pen with no button. While the user is not touching the screen, the system cannot track the finger—that is state 0 again. When the user touches the screen, the system can begin to track—state 1. So a touch screen is a state 0-1 device whereas a mouse is a state 1-2 device. As there is no difference between a state 0-2 and a state 0-1 device, there are only the three possibilities we have seen. The only additional complexity is if the device has several buttons, in which case we would have one state for each button: 2_{left}, 2_{middle}, 2_{right}.

One use of this classification is to look at different pointing tasks, such as icon selection or line drawing, and see what state 0-1-2 behaviour they require. We can then see whether a particular device can support the required task. If we have to use an inadequate device, it is possible to use keyboard keys to add device states. For example, with a touch screen, we may nominate the escape key to be the 'virtual' mouse button whilst the user's finger is on the screen. Although the mixing of keyboard and mouse keys is normally a bad habit, it is obviously necessary on occasions.

At first, the model appears to characterize the states of the device by the inputs available to the system. So, from this perspective, state 0 is clearly different from states 1 and 2. However, if we look at the state 1-2 transaction, we see that it is symmetric with respect to the two states. In principle there is no reason why a program should not decide to do simple mouse tracking whilst in state 2 and drag things about in state 1. That is, there is no reason until you want to type something! The way we can tell state 1 from state 2 is by the activity of the *user*. State 2 requires a button to be pressed, whereas state 1 is one of relative relaxation (whilst still requiring hand–eye coordination for mouse movement). There is a similar difference in tension between state 0 and state 1.

It is well known that Fitts' law has different timing constants for different devices. Recall that Fitts' law says that the time taken to move to a target of size S at a distance D is:

$$a + b \log_2(D/S + 1)$$

The constants a and b depend on the particular pointing device used and the skill of the user with that device. However, the insight given by the three-state model is that these constants also depend on the device state. In addition to the timing, the final accuracy may be affected.

These observations are fairly obvious for state 0-1 devices. With a touch screen, or light pen, a cursor will often appear under the finger or pen when it comes in contact with the screen. The accuracy with which you can move the cursor around will be far greater than the accuracy with which you can point in the first place. Also it is reasonable to expect that the Fitts' law constant will be different, although not so obvious which will be faster.

There is a similar difference between states 1 and 2. Because the user is holding a button down, the hand is in a state of tension and thus pointing accuracy and speed may be different. Experiments to calculate Fitts' law constants in states 1 and 2 have shown that these differences do exist [104]. Table 6.2 shows the results obtained for a mouse and trackball.

We can recalculate the *KLM* prediction for the CLOSE_METHOD using these data. Recall that the method had two pointing operators, one to point to the window's title bar (with a distance to target size ratio of 10:1), the second to drag the selection down to 'CLOSE' on the pop-up menu (4:1). Thus the first pointing operator is state 1 and the second is state 2. The times are thus:

Mouse

P[to menu bar]	$=$	$-107 + 223\,log_2(11)$	$=$	664 ms
P[to option]	$=$	$135 + 249\,log_2(5)$	$=$	713 ms

Trackerball

P[to menu bar]	$=$	$75 + 300\,log_2(11)$	$=$	1113 ms
P[to option]	$=$	$-349 + 688\,log_2(5)$	$=$	1248 ms

Table 6.2   *Fitts' law coefficients (after MacKenzie, Sellen and Buxton* [104]*).*

Device	a (ms)	b (ms/bit)
Pointing (state 1)		
Mouse	−107	223
Trackball	75	300
Dragging (state 2)		
Mouse	135	249
Trackball	−349	688

Giving a further revised time for the CLOSE_METHOD of 2.93 seconds using a mouse and 3.91 seconds using a trackball.

6.7   Cognitive Architectures

The formalisms we have seen so far have some implicit or explicit model of how the user performs the cognitive processing involved in carrying out a task. For instance, the concept of taking a problem and solving it by divide-and-conquer using sub-goals is central to GOMS. CCT assumes the distinction between long- and short-term memory, with production rules being stored in long-term memory and 'matched' against the contents of short-term (or working) memory to determine which 'fire'. The values for various motor and mental operators in KLM were based on the Model Human Processor (*MHP*) architecture of Card, Moran and Newell [28]. Another common assumption which we have not discussed in this chapter is the distinction between linguistic levels—semantic, syntactic and lexical—as an architectural model of the user's understanding.

In Chapter 1, we discussed some of these architectural descriptions of the user as an information processing machine. Our emphasis in this section will be to describe a couple more architectural models that are quite distinct from those described in Chapter 1 and assumed in the earlier parts of this chapter. Here we will see that the architectural assumptions are central to the description of the cognitive modelling that these approaches offer.

There are interesting differences of emphasis between these architectural models and the previous models. The hierarchical and linguistic notations tend to assume perfect dialogue on the user's part. They may measure the complexity of that perfect dialogue, but tend not to consider diversions from the optimal command sequences. However, for the architectural models in this section the prediction and understanding of error is central to their analyses.

6.7.1   *The problem space model*

Rational behaviour is characterized as behaviour which is intended to achieve a specific goal. This element of rationality is often used to distinguish between intelligent and machine-like behaviour. In the field of artificial intelligence (AI), a system exhibiting rational behaviour is referred to as a *knowledge level* system. A knowledge level system contains an *agent* behaving in an environment. The agent has knowledge about itself and its environment, includings its own goals. It can perform certain actions and sense information about its changing environment. As the agent behaves in its environment, it changes the environment and its own knowledge. We can view the overall behaviour of the knowledge level system as a sequence of environment and agent states as they progress in time. The goal of the agent is characterized as a preference over all possible sequences of agent/environment states.

Contrast this rational behaviour with another general computational model for a machine, which is not rational. In computer science it is common to describe a problem as the search through a set of possible states from some initial state to a desired state. The search proceeds by moving from one state to another possible state by means of operations or actions, the ultimate goal of which is to arrive at one of the desired states. This very general model of computation is used in the ordinary task of the programmer. Once she has identified a problem and a means of arriving at the solution to the problem (the algorithm), the programmer then represents the problem and algorithm in a programming language which can be executed on a machine to reach the desired state. The architecture of the machine only allows the definition of the search or *problem space* and the actions which can occur to traverse that space. Termination is also assumed to happen once the desired state is reached. Notice that the machine does not have the ability to formulate the problem space and its solution, mainly because it has no idea of the goal. It is the job of the programmer to understand the goal and so define the machine to achieve it.

We can adapt the state based computational model of a machine in order to realize the architecture of a knowledge level system. The new computational model is the *problem spaces* model, based on the problem-solving work of Newell and Simon at Carnegie Mellon University (see Chapter 1). A problem space consists of a set of states and a set of operations that can be performed on the states. Behaviour in a problem space is a two-step process. First, the current operator is chosen based on the current state and then it is applied to the current state to achieve the new state. The problem space must represent rational behaviour, and so it must characterize the goal of the agent. A problem space represents a goal by defining the desired states as a subset of all possible states. Once the initial state is set, the task within the problem space is to find a sequence of operations that form a path within the state space from the initial state to one of the desired states, whereupon successful termination occurs.

From the above description, we can highlight four different activities that occur within a problem space—goal formulation, operation selection, operation application and goal completion. The relationship between these problem space processes and knowledge level activity is key. Perception which occurs at the knowledge level is performed by the goal formulation process, which creates the initial state based on observations of the external environment. Actions at the knowledge level are operations in the problem space which are selected and applied. The real knowledge about the agent and its environment and goals is derived from the state/operator information in the problem space. Because of the goal formulation process, the set of desired states indicates the knowledge level goal within the problem space. The operation selection process selects the appropriate operation at a given point in time because it is deemed the most likely to transform the state in the problem space to one of the desired states; hence rational behaviour is implied.

The cycle of activity within the problem space is as follows. Some change in the external environment which is relevant to the goal of the agent is sensed by the goal formulation process, which in turn defines the set of desired states for the agent and its initial state for the following task. The operation selection process suggests an operation which can act on that state and transform it 'closer' to a desired state. The operation application process executes the operation, changing the current state and surrounding environment. If the new state is a desired state, then the goal has been achieved and the goal completion process reverts the agent to inactive.

The real power of the problem space architecture is in recursion. The activity of any of the processes occurs only when the knowledge it needs to complete its chore is immediately available. For example, to decide which operation is most likely to lead to a desired state, the problem space will need to know things about its current state and that of the environment. If that information is not immediately available, then activity cannot continue. In that case, another problem space is invoked with the goal of finding out the information that was needed by the parent problem space. In this way, we can see the evolution of problems spaces as a stack-like structure, new spaces being invoked and placed on the problem space stack only to be popped off the stack once they achieve their goal.

Though the problem spaces model described briefly above is not directly implementable, it is the basis for at least one executable cognitive architecture, called Soar. We do not discuss the details of Soar's implementation; the interested reader is referred to Laird, Newell and Rosenbloom [100]. An interesting application of the Soar implementation of problem spaces has been done by Young and colleagues on *programmable user models* (or *PUMs*) [189]. Given a designer's description of an intended procedure or task that is to be carried out with an interactive system, an analysis of that procedure produces the knowledge that would be necessary and available for any user attempting the task. That knowledge is encoded in the problem spaces architecture of Soar, producing a 'programmed' user model (the PUM) to accomplish the goal of performing the task. By executing the PUM, the stacking and unstacking of problem spaces needed to accomplish the goal can be analyzed to measure the cognitive load of the intended procedure. More importantly, if the PUM cannot achieve the goal because it cannot find some knowledge necessary to complete the task, this indicates to the designer that there was a problem with the intended design. In this way, erroneous behaviour can be predicted before implementation.

6.7.2   *Interacting cognitive sub-systems*

Barnard has proposed a very different cognitive architecture, called *interacting cognitive sub-systems* (ICS) [10, 11, 12]. ICS provides a model of perception, cognition and action, but unlike other cognitive architectures, it is not intended to produce a description of the user in terms of sequences of actions that he performs. ICS provides a more holistic view of the user as an information processing machine. The emphasis is on determining how easy particular procedures of action sequences become as they are made more automatic within the user.

ICS attempts to incorporate two separate psychological traditions within one cognitive architecture. On the one hand is the architectural and general-purpose information processing approach of short-term memory research. On the other hand is the computational and representational approach characteristic of psycho-linguistic research and AI problem-solving literature.

The architecture of ICS is built up by the coordinated activity of nine smaller sub-systems: five peripheral sub-systems are in contact with the physical world and four are central, dealing with mental processes. Each sub-system has the same generic structure. A sub-system is described in terms of its typed inputs and outputs along with a memory store for holding typed information. It has transformation functions for processing the input and producing the output and permanently stored information. Each of the nine sub-systems is specialized for handling some aspect of external or internal processing. For example, one peripheral sub-system is the visual system for describing what is seen in the world. An example of a central sub-system is one for the processing of propositional information, capturing the attributes and identities of entities and their relationships with each other (a particular example is that propositional information represents ' "knowing" that a particular word has four syllables, begins with "P" and refers to an area in central London' [11]).

ICS is another example of a general cognitive architecture which can be applied to interactive design. One of the features of ICS is its ability to explain how a user proceduralizes action. Remember in the discussion of CCT we distinguished between novice and expert use of an interactive system. Experts can perform complicated sequences of actions as if without a thought, whereas a novice user must contemplate each and every move (if you do not believe this distinction is accurate, observe users at an automatic teller machine and see if you can tell the expert from the novice). The expert recognizes the task situation and recalls a 'canned' procedure of actions which, from experience, results in the desired goal being achieved. They do not have to think beyond the recognition of the task and consequent invocation of the correct procedure. Such proceduralized behaviour is much less prone to error. A good designer will aid the user in proceduralizing his interaction with the system and will attempt to design an interface which suggests to the user a task for which he already has a proceduralized response. It is for this reason that ICS has been suggested as a design tool which can act as an expert system to advise a designer in developing an interface.

6.8 Summary

In this chapter, we have discussed a wide selection of models of the users of interactive systems, or cognitive models. Cognitive models attempt to represent the users as they interact with a system, modelling aspects of their understanding, knowledge, intentions or processing. We divided cognitive models into three categories. The first described the hierarchical structuring of the user's task and goal structures. The GOMS model and CCT were examples of cognitive models in this category. The second category was concerned with linguistic and grammatical models which emphasized the user's understanding of the user–system dialogue. BNF and TAG were described as examples in this category. Most of these cognitive models have focused on the execution activity of the user, neglecting their perceptive ability and how that might affect less-planned and natural interaction strategies. The third category of cognitive models was based on the more solid understanding of the human motor system, applicable in situations where the user does no planning of behaviour and executes actions automatically. KLM was used to provide rough measures of user performance in terms of execution times for basic sequences of actions. Buxton's three-state model for pointing devices allowed for a finer distinction between execution times than with KLM. We concluded this chapter with a discussion of cognitive architectures, the assumptions of which form the foundation for any cognitive models. In addition to the basic architectural distinction between long- and short-term memory, we discussed two other cognitive architectures—the problem spaces model and ICS—which apply different assumptions to the analysis of interactive system.

Exercises

6.1   Create a GOMS description of the task of photocopying a paper from a journal. Discuss the issue of closure in terms of your GOMS description.

6.2   Recall the CCT description of the rule INSERT-SPACE-2 discussed in Section 6.3.2:

```
(INSERT-SPACE-2
IF (AND (TEST-GOAL insert space)
        (TEST-CURSOR %LINE %COL) )
THEN (  (DO-KEYSTROKE 'I')
        (DO-KEYSTROKE SPACE)
        (DO-KEYSTROKE ESC)
        (DELETE-GOAL insert space) ))
```

As we discussed, this is already proceduralized, that is, the rule is an expert rule. Write new 'novice' rules where the three keystrokes are not proceduralized. That is, you should have separate rules for each keystroke and suitable goals (such as GET-INTO-INSERT-MODE) to fire them.

6.3 Do a keystroke level analysis for opening up an application in a visual desktop interface using a mouse as the pointing device, comparing at least two different methods for performing the task. Repeat the exercise using a trackball. Discuss how the analysis would differ for various positions of the trackball relative to the keyboard and for other pointing devices.

6.4 One of the assumptions underlying the programmable user model approach is that it is possible to provide an algorithm to describe the user's behaviour in interacting with a system. Taking this position to the extreme, choose some common task with a familiar interactive system (e.g. creating a column of numbers in a spreadsheet and calculating their sum, or any other task you can think of) and describe the algorithm needed by the user to accomplish this task. Write the description in pseudocode. Does this exercise suggest any improvements in the system?

Recommended Reading

- S. K. Card, T. P. Moran and A. Newell, *The Psychology of Human Computer Interaction*, Lawrence Erlbaum, 1983.

  A classic text in this field of cognitive models, in which the basic architectural assumptions of the model human processor architecture are explained as well as the GOMS model and KLM.

- S. Bovair, D. E. Kieras and P. G. Polson, The acquisition and performance of text-editing skill: a cognitive complexity analysis. *Human–Computer Interaction*, Vol. 5, No. 1, pp. 1–48, 1990.

  This article provides a definitive description of CCT by means of an extended example. The authors also provide the definition of various style rules for writing CCT descriptions to distinguish, for example, between novice and expert users.

- F. Schiele and T. Green, HCI formalisms and cognitive psychology: the case of task–action grammars. In M. D. Harrison and H. W. Thimbleby, editors, *Formal methods in Human–Computer Interaction*, chapter 2, Cambridge University Press, 1990.

  A good description of TAG with several extended examples based on the Macintosh interface. The authors provide a good comparative analysis of TAG versus other cognitive modelling techniques.

- A. Newell, G. Yost, J. E. Laird, P. S. Rosenbloom and E. Altmann, Formulating the problem-space computational model. In Richard F. Rashid, editor, *CMU Computer Science: a 25th Anniversary Commemorative*, Chapter 11, ACM Press, 1991.

  The description of the problem spaces cognitive architecture was informed by this article, which also contains references to essential work on the Soar platform.

Chapter 7

Task Analysis

Overview

Task analysis is the study of the way people perform tasks with existing systems.

- Techniques for task analysis

    - decomposition of tasks into sub-tasks

    - taxonomic classification of task knowledge

    - listing things used and actions performed

- Sources of information

    - existing documentation

    - observation

    - interviews

- Using task analysis to design

    - manuals and documentation

    - new systems

7.1 Introduction

Task analysis is the process of analyzing the way people perform their jobs: the things they do, the things they act on and the things they need to know. For example, if we were considering the job of housekeeping, we would want to say things like:

in order to clean the house
    get the vacuum cleaner out
    fix the appropriate attachment
    clean the rooms
    when the dust bag gets full, empty it
    put the vacuum cleaner and tools away

To perform such a task, we need to know about vacuum cleaners, their attachments, dust bags, cupboards (in which the vacuum cleaner is kept), rooms (to be cleaned) and so on.

We will consider three different approaches to task analysis, which overlap, but which lay their emphases on slightly different areas. These are:

Task decomposition which looks at the way a task is split into sub-tasks, and the order in which these are performed.

Knowledge based techniques which look at what users need to know about the objects and actions involved in a task, and how that knowledge is organized.

Entity–relation based analysis an object based approach, where the emphasis is on identifying the actors and objects, the relationships between them and the actions they perform.

Task analysis is about existing systems and procedures, its main tools are those of observation in various forms. We will discuss these sources of information later. One of the purposes of task analysis is to help in the production of training materials and documentation. For this purpose, analysis of existing systems is sufficient.

However, where a new computer system is required, the task analysis also contributes to the statement of requirements of this system. We will see how it can be applied in a fairly straightforward way to menu design. However, the process of designing a new system based on an analysis of an existing system will involve a considerable amount of professional insight. The contribution of task analysis to this is principally one of clarifying and organizing one's knowledge about the current situation.

7.2   Differences between Task Analysis and Other Techniques

The scope of task analysis is quite wide. In addition to those tasks which directly involve a computer, the task analyst will typically model aspects of the world that are not, and are not expected to be, part of a computer system. So a task analysis of word-processing would include activities such as fetching documents from the filing cabinet, changing the printer ribbon and putting floppy disks in and out of the computer as well as the more obvious interaction with the machine.

So, like traditional systems analysis, task analysis is not limited to activities including a computer, although (again like systems analysis) the intention is usually

that a computer system will be installed. In fact, it is often hard to differentiate many modern task analysis techniques from their older cousins. The main
difference is one of emphasis; task analysis is there specifically to recognize the
importance of the user.

Some aspects of task analysis will look very like the goal-oriented cognitive
models discussed in Chapter 6. Indeed, there would be little to prevent one
using a GOMS-like notation to represent a task decomposition such as the vacuum
cleaning above. The difference between the two lies in the intention of the models.
The purpose of the goal-oriented models is to understand the internal cognitive
processes as a person performs a task — the granularity is thus usually rather
small. The emphasis of task analysis is more one of observing the user from the
outside and will include actions, such as retrieval of a document from a filing
cabinet, which would never be included in a GOMS analysis.

Task analysis therefore tends to look more at the observable behaviour of users
than their internal mental state. Some practitioners would say that task analysis
should be restricted to precisely this objective observable behaviour — you should
be interested in what, not why. However, even the most objective analysis will
include some inferences about the user's internal goals, and this will often be
evident in the names used in task decomposition. Furthermore, other practitioners
explicitly state that their intention is to build a *conceptual model* — the way the user
views the system and the task. This latter approach will be particularly evident in
the knowledge based approaches.

Sometimes task analysis will produce quite low-level task decompositions
which are identical to those one would expect from a goal-oriented analysis.
However, for task analysis this would tend to be the end of the process, to be
used, for instance, by the interface designer in structuring the dialogue. For goal-
oriented cognitive models, such a goal hierarchy is the central feature, to be further
analyzed for complexity, learnability and the like.

In terms of the design life cycle (Chapter 5) task analysis belongs at the beginning in requirements capture, whereas the cognitive models are normally used
towards the end of the process during evaluation.

7.3 Task Decomposition

The example above of vacuum cleaning showed how a task, 'clean the house', was
decomposed into several sub-tasks: 'get the vacuum cleaner out' and so on. Most
task analysis techniques involve some form of task decomposition to express this
sort of behaviour. *Hierarchical task analysis (HTA)* is typical of such an approach
[6, 155]. The outputs of HTA are a *hierarchy* of tasks and sub-tasks and also *plans*
describing in what order and under what conditions sub-tasks are performed.

For example, we could express the house cleaning example as in Figure 7.1,
further decomposing the sub-task 'clean rooms'. Indentation is used to denote the
levels in the task hierarchy, and the tasks are also numbered to emphasize this

0.   in order to clean the house
    1.   get the vacuum cleaner out
    2.   fix the appropriate attachment
    3.   clean the rooms
        3.1.   clean the hall
        3.2.   clean the living rooms
        3.3.   clean the bedrooms
    4.   empty the dust bag
    5.   put the vacuum cleaner and attachments away

Plan 0:   do 1 – 2 – 3 – 5 in that order.
            when the dust bag gets full do 4

Plan 3:   do any of 3.1, 3.2 or 3.3 in any order
            depending on which rooms need cleaning

Figure 7.1   *How to clean a house*

hierarchy. The plans are labelled by the task to which they correspond. So plan 0 refers to the way in which we perform the sub-tasks 1–5 of task 0. Similarly plan 3 refers to the way in which we perform 3.1–3.3. There are no plans for sub-tasks 1, 2, 4 and 5 as these have not been decomposed.

Reading the plans, we see that not all the sub-tasks need be performed, and not necessarily in the order presented. Looking first at plan 0, sub-task 4 'empty the dust bag' need only be performed when the dustbag is found to be full. As this is put in plan 0, we assume that we may empty the dust bag at any stage including when we first get the vacuum cleaner out or when we put it away. If we know that we only ever notice the bag is full when we are actively using the machine, we might choose to put this sub-task within 3. 'clean the rooms'. This sort of restructuring, finding the appropriate and meaningful hierarchy, is part of the process of HTA.

Looking now at plan 3, how to clean the rooms, we see that we are allowed to clean the rooms in any order. If the task had been varnishing the floors rather than cleaning them, we would presumably do the hall after the rest of the rooms! Furthermore, we only clean those rooms which need vacuuming. The bedrooms will not get dirty as fast as the hall, so we need not clean them so often. If we wanted to be more precise about when the rooms are cleaned, we could produce a more specific plan:

Plan 3:   do 3.1 every day
            3.2 once a week
            when visitors are due 3.3

How does one produce such a hierarchy with attendant rules? The process is iterative. Assume for the moment that we have some overall task in mind, such as house cleaning. We then ask, what sub-tasks must be accomplished in order to perform the main task? To answer this question we refer to various sources: direct observation, expert opinion, documentation and so on. These sources will be discussed later in Section 7.6. We then look at each sub-task and seek to sub-divide it, and so on.

One could go on with this process indefinitely, so one applies some form of *stopping rule* in order to decide when the tasks are basic enough. The level at which we do this will, of course, depend on the purpose of the task analysis. For example, imagine we were looking at a chemical plant and had produced a first level decomposition of what to do in an emergency:

0.   in an emergency
    1.   read the alarms
    2.   work out appropriate corrective action
    3.   perform corrective action

If our ultimate aim is to install computer monitoring of the plant, we would be interested in expanding tasks 1 and 3. On the other hand, if the aim is to produce on-line operations manuals, then it is task 2 which would require expansion. In fact, at this high level of task description the analyst would probably expand all the sub-tasks as the analyst ought to take a somewhat larger view. However, one would obviously put more effort into those sub-tasks which are directly relevant to the intended purpose.

A rule, which is particularly appropriate when the aim is to design training materials, is the $P \times C$ rule. This says that if the probability of making a mistake in the task (P) multiplied by the cost of the mistake (C) is below a threshold, then stop expanding. That is, simple tasks need not be expanded (because no one needs training), unless they are critical.

Another obvious stopping point is where the task contains complex motor responses (like mouse movement) or where it involves internal decision-making. In the first case, decomposition would not be productive, explaining how such actions are performed is unlikely to be either accurate or useful. In the second case, we would expand if the decision-making were related to external actions, such as looking up documentation or reading instruments, but not where the activity is purely cognitive. A possible exception to this would be if we were planning to build a decision support system, in which case we may want to understand the way someone thought about a problem in order to build tools to help. However, it is debatable whether hierarchical task analysis is the appropriate technique in this case.

The task hierarchy can be represented diagrammatically as well as textually. Figure 7.2 shows a task hierarchy for making a cup of tea. The main task 'make a cup of tea' is decomposed into six sub-tasks. Of these only the first 'boil water' is expanded further. The remaining tasks 2–6 and the sub-tasks of 1.1–1.4 are underlined showing that the analysis has been deliberately stopped at that point. This obviously denotes the same information as the textual form, but may be more accessible at a glance.

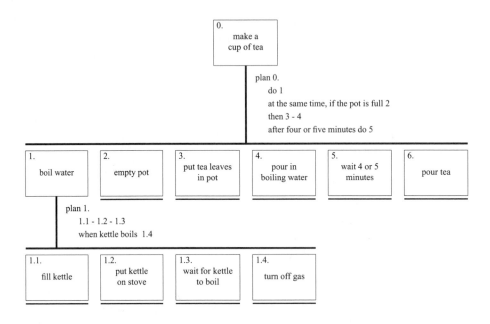

Figure 7.2 *Hierarchical task analysis: making a cup of tea*

Having produced a first stab at a task hierarchy, one would examine it for errors or omissions. One way of approaching this would be to describe the steps in the task hierarchy to a domain expert. This would quickly show that the plan for making tea has a significant error — it forgets to warm the pot. This has to be added between tasks 3 and 4.

It is the nature of expert knowledge that obvious things get missed for a task description. One way the analyst can search for such omissions is by examining the form of the sub-tasks. For example, 1.4 says 'turn off gas', but nowhere does it say to turn the gas on! Probably, this was implicit in 'put kettle on stove', but it should be added between tasks 1.2 and 1.3. At this point we might notice that the task hierarchy is a little unbalanced. This might be right, but we may have included too many detailed tasks at the highest level. We choose to add a new top level node 'make pot' which would encompass the tasks 3 and 4 and also the new 'warm pot' task.

The top level tasks would now be:

    0.   make a cup of tea
          1.   boil water
          2.   empty pot
          3.   make pot

    4.   wait 4 or 5 minutes

    5.   pour tea

Plan 0.   do 1
            at the same time, if the pot is full 2
            then 3 – 4
            after four or five minutes 5

This is almost there: the actions 'empty pot' and 'wait 4 or 5 minutes' are pretty basic and clearly do not need expansion. Neither do they need to be included within one of the other tasks. We might think that 'empty pot' should be in with 'make pot', but we can empty the pot whilst the kettle is boiling whereas we have to wait for the kettle to boil to do any of the other tea-making tasks. Similarly, the 'wait' node belongs at the top as the pouring of the tea depends on it.

The 'pour tea' node is a bit of anomaly. Is it really so much simpler than, say, making the pot? Perhaps we should expand this node too. We could decompose it into three parts:

    5.   pour tea
          5.1.   put milk in cup
          5.2.   fill cup with tea
          5.3.   add sugar to taste

Plan 5.   5.1 – 5.2
            if desired 5.3

However, the mention of cups, makes us wonder, do we really only want to describe the making of a single cup of tea. Perhaps we ought to allow several cups of tea to be made. To do this we modify the plan to allow repetitions of steps 1–3 for each cup. We could describe this plan in words, or use a simple diagram as in Figure 7.3.

The analyst can choose to use a more formal method of describing the plans, such as one of the dialogue notations described in Chapter 8, a simple self-explanatory diagram, or plain text. The choice is very much a matter of taste, except that it would be unwise to use too formal a representation until late in the process.

The modified HTA after all this analysis is given in Figure 7.4. In addition, adding the sugar has been expanded to include asking the guests whether or not sugar is required. Also note that the main goal has been altered from 'make *a* cup of tea' to 'make cup*s* of tea'.

We have now seen all the types of plan that are commonly found, most of them in Figure 7.4:

fixed sequence In plan 3, we always do the same sequence of sub-tasks.

optional tasks In plan 0 'empty pot' and in plan 5.3 'add sugar' may or may not be performed depending on circumstances. Sometimes, there will be a choice between several options.

Plan 5.

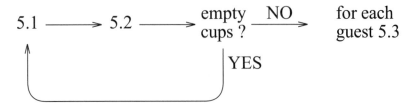

Figure 7.3   *Plan for pouring tea*

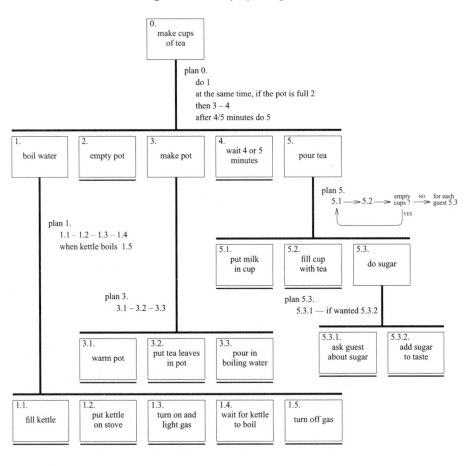

Figure 7.4   *Modified task hierarchy for making lots of cups of tea*

waiting for events In plan 1, we had to wait for the kettle to boil, and in plan 0 we waited four or five minutes. The latter, waiting a certain time, is probably more common in 'real-world' tasks, such as process control or office procedures, than in the use of computer software.

cycles As in plan 5, where we repeatedly perform tasks 5.1 and 5.2 until a condition was reached (no more empty cups).

time-sharing Tasks 1 and 2 could be done at the same time (or at the very least they can be intermingled).

discretionary For this we have to go back to the vacuum cleaning example in Figure 7.1. The person is allowed to clean the rooms (plan 3), in any order and whether or not they need it. Basically, you can keep your house as clean or as dirty as you like!

mixtures Most plans are a mixture of these elements. For instance, plan 1 for 'boiling water' is largely a fixed sequence but split by a wait.

As we can see the process is far from straightforward. In common with other task analysis techniques, the quality and form of the final output depends very much on the skill of the analyst. Furthermore, different analysts are likely to produce different results, especially as regards the level of detail. Remember also that there is no single 'right' answer — the output of the task analysis should reflect the purpose to which the analysis will be put.

7.4 Knowledge Based Analysis

Knowledge based task analysis begins by listing all the objects and actions involved in the task, and then building taxonomies of these. These are similar to the sort of hierarchical descriptions one often finds in biology: animals are invertebrates or vertebrates, vertebrates are fish, birds, reptiles, amphibians or mammals, etc. The aim is to understand the knowledge needed to perform a task and thus to help in the production of teaching materials and in assessing the amount of common knowledge between different tasks.

We will begin by looking at simple hierarchies of objects. Consider first the controls in a (non-automatic) motor-car. An example taxonomic structure is given in Figure 7.5; every control has exactly one place in the hierarchy.

Look at it for a moment: do you think it is a good one? We will discuss this in a moment. Consider how we might have produced such a hierarchy, and how to use it. The car controls are particularly simple, as we can simply get in and look for them all. If we extended our analysis to driving a car in general, we would have to consider more objects: the instruments (speedometer, etc.), the car keys, seat-belts, road signs, other cars, etc. Just as with HTA it can be hard to know when to stop. However, with any such procedure it is best to start by listing everything you can,

```
motor controls
    steering      steering wheel, indicators
    engine/speed
            direct      ignition, accelerator, foot brake
            gearing     clutch, gear stick
    lights
            external    headlights, hazard lights
            internal    courtesy light
    wash/wipe
            wipers      front wipers, rear wipers
            washers     front washers, rear washers
    heating       temperature control, air direction, fan, rear screen heater
    parking       hand brake, door lock
    radio
            numerous!
```

Figure 7.5   *First attempt at taxonomy of car controls*

later removing items which are felt to be unnecessary. Other sources for forming a list of objects include manuals, transcripts and observation and will be discussed in Section 7.6.

Having got an exhaustive list of objects, how does one go about forming the taxonomy? The analyst could ask a domain expert directly — often a classification may already exist for some of the domain objects. Another approach is to use a sorting task. Give a user cards with the objects listed on them and ask the user to sort the cards into piles of 'similar' objects. The user can then be asked to name the piles, or further sort the piles. This sort of sorting gives you the user's view of the structure.

Depending on the expected use of the task analysis, one may require different structures. If we were aiming to produce a car repair manual, we would almost certainly use a radically different taxonomy. For example, from a driver's viewpoint the accelerator and the brake perform related functions, but they have no connection mechanically.

Let us assume that our purpose is to produce an owner's manual for the car. It is likely that having produced a first attempt at an object taxonomy, we will examine it and find faults. Let us look again at Figure 7.5. The hand brake has been put with the door locks as an aspect of parking, but it should also be used as part of ordinary driving. Perhaps it would be better to put it in a separate 'braking' category with the foot brake. This shift might suggest a whole new superordinate classification into those controls needed for driving: steering, speed, brakes, most lights, as against those purely for comfort and security. With this classification, the courtesy lamp would get separated from the rest of the external lighting.

These decisions could be justified based on particular purposes, but others are purely arbitrary. We could just have easily classified the washer/wipers into front and rear first:

wash/wipe
      front
            front wipers, front washers
      rear
            rear wipers, rear washers

This better reflects the way they are positioned on most cars, but has no more logic to it than the classification in Figure 7.5. Really, there are two attributes 'function' (wash or wipe) and 'position' (front or rear). One technique *task analysis for knowledge description (TAKD)* uses a special form of taxonomy called *task descriptive hierarchy (TDH)*. TAKD is discussed in detail by Diaper [50] in the recommended reading list at the end of this chapter. The branches in the simple taxonomy are either/or branches — a car control is either a steering control or an engine/speed control or a lighting control. As well as these XOR branches TDH also uses AND and OR branches. The AND branches are used where an object must have a place in several categories. For instance, the washer/wiper example could be shown as:

wash/wipe **AND**
      function **XOR**
          wipe
               front wipers, rear wipers
          wash
               front washers, rear washers
      position **XOR**
          front
               front wipers, front washers
          rear
               rear wipers, rear washers

Notice that each control in the category 'wash/wipe' is mentioned *both* under 'function' and under 'position'.

The OR branches arise where the object could fall into more than one of the categories, but not necessarily all. For example, if we were considering kitchen objects, we might want to say that they were for either preparing food, cooking or dining. However, a plate may be used both for eating off (dining) and for chopping food on (preparation). Thus we have an OR branch:

kitchen item **OR**
      preparation
            mixing bowl, plate, chopping board
      cooking
            frying pan, casserole, saucepan
      dining
            plate, soup bowl, casserole, glass

Note that plate occurs under preparation and dining, but not under cooking (although one may cook a pie on a plate). The casserole is under cooking and under dining as a stew is often served in the casserole it was cooked in.

TAKD has a uniqueness rule, which demands that a completed TDH can distinguish any two specific objects. The kitchen hierarchy above fails this test. We can distinguish, say, the plate from the soup bowl, because the plate is in categories preparation and dining, whereas the bowl is only under dining. However, we cannot distinguish the soup bowl from the glass. TAKD would demand that we further refine this hierarchy until all pairs can be distinguished from one another:

```
kitchen item AND
/___ shape XOR
/    |___   dished
/    |             mixing bowl, casserole, saucepan, soup bowl, glass
/    |___   flat
/                  plate, chopping board, frying pan
/___ function OR
     {___   preparation
     {             mixing bowl, plate, chopping board
     {___   cooking
     {             frying pan, casserole, saucepan
     {___   dining XOR
            |___   for food
            |             plate, soup bowl, casserole
            |___   for drink
                          glass
```

Notice that the tree has been drawn using the characters: '/ | {'. These are a characteristic of TDH and represent AND, XOR and OR branches respectively. The explicit labels AND, etc. are not used in a normal TDH as these are implied by the way the tree is drawn.

At this point, each object can be represented by a unique path(s) in the hierarchy and thus by a term in the *knowledge representation grammar* (*KRG*). The KRG term is built up using '/' for AND branches, '()' for XOR branches and '{}' for OR branches, similar to the diagram. For example, we could refer to the plate as:

kitchen item/shape(flat)/function{preparation,dining(for food)}/

Translating, this says: a kitchen item whose shape is flat AND its function is preparation OR dining for food.

Strict application of the uniqueness rule is not always necessary. Other similar techniques cope quite happily without it, but they normally adopt simple hierarchies, rather than the more complex AND/OR/XOR TDH trees.

The test is perhaps most important when a tree has a lot of AND or OR branches rather than for simple hierarchies. In these cases it is often difficult to see whether the classification scheme is suitably precise. Finding two simple objects which are not differentiated can be a good way of generating new classifiers. The lack of distinction between glasses and soup bowls in the original kitchen item classification is a case in point. These are so clearly different, and one can ask the question 'how can I tell the difference between a soup bowl and a glass?' yielding the obvious food/drink distinction.

However, there are other examples where attempting to follow the rule is less useful. In a more extensive list of items, with a more complex classification tree, it was found that a corkscrew and a tin opener were not distinguished. Although it is possible to distinguish these, the categories introduced were not of 'general' use, that is, they did not help one to differentiate anything else. In general, then, the uniqueness rule is perhaps best viewed as an informative check, rather than adopted slavishly.

The production of a simple taxonomy, or a TDH, for actions is similar to that for objects. Imagine we have a list of specific actions which may occur in a kitchen: beating, mixing, pouring, frying, boiling, baking, eating and drinking. We may look at these and start to build a hierarchy. For example, we may use the same classes: preparation, cooking and dining as we did for the objects:

```
kitchen job OR
|__   preparation
|          beating, mixing
|__   cooking
|          frying, boiling, baking
|__   dining
           pouring, eating, drinking
```

We may subject this to the same analysis that we used for objects. For example, pouring has been put under dining, for example, pouring wine. However, we might also pour milk into a bowl to beat up with eggs for an omelette. This would mean putting pouring into both categories, or possibly a second look at the specific actions called pouring. Perhaps we should distinguish those of pouring drinks and pouring ingredients?

Note the difference between this taxonomy of actions and an HTA task hierarchy. The hierarchy above is one of genericity, whereas the HTA hierarchy was a 'how to do it' decomposition. HTA is about the sequencing of simple tasks to perform a single high-level task, whereas a taxonomy is about the similarity of simple tasks to one another. However, there will often be a relationship between the taxonomy of actions and the HTA descriptions of tasks. For example, having an omelette would consist of beating, frying and then eating, or having a cake would consist of mixing, baking and eating. In general, these tasks consist of one or more preparation and/or cooking action followed by dining actions. It is precisely when we can begin to make these general task statements that the power and usefulness of object and action taxonomies becomes apparent.

Looking back and forth between the objects and the actions will suggest omissions or restructuring on one side or another: What action do we do with a chopping board? Clearly we should add chopping as an action. The action of baking may suggest that we include baking trays and bread tins under the objects. This cross checking is particularly important for capturing all actions as it is often easier to see what people are *using* for their job than to work out what they are *doing*. Furthermore objects are often grouped naturally under their function, so the object groupings may suggest action groupings and vice versa. In addition, we can apply the TAKD uniqueness rule to the action TDH, which would mean performing some more sub-divisions, perhaps adding distinctions between those actions concerned with liquids and those with solids.

Having produced object and action taxonomies, one can use these in order to produce generic descriptions of simple tasks. For an example, we are considering particular kitchen tasks, and we shall assume that we have extended the object taxonomy to include foods. Consider the task of eating a fried egg off a plate. This can be regarded as doing a 'kitchen job(dining)' using a 'kitchen item/shape(flat)/function{dining,preparation}/' to a 'food(dairy)'. If we observed a kitchen for a day, we could describe each simple task as it is performed using similar terms. In TAKD this is called a sentence in the *KRG* grammar.

Notice that the KRG terms do not use the complete KRG description of each action and object, but instead opt for a generic description. Choosing the appropriate generic description is an art, but there are guidelines to help. One way is to take the TDH tree and to annotate it with the number of times each object or action is mentioned by an expert, or used or performed during our day's observation. If the number of occurrences of objects below a node is small then one does not bother to use the lower level distinctions. So, for example, in the above we have not bothered with the 'for food/for drink' distinction among dining items. This process is called *generification*.

The choice of an appropriate level to 'cut' the tree is also influenced by the number of different KRG sentences one gets for simple tasks. If there are an unmanageable number of different sentences, then it suggests that more generification is required. If, on the other hand, one found that all the observed tasks were represented by only two or three sentences, then this would suggest that the level of abstraction is too great. Of course, what constitutes an appropriate number of different sentences depends on the circumstances, the complexity of the job one is analyzing and (again) the purpose of the analysis.

In addition, the appropriate generic categories chosen for actions and objects are linked. If we consider the task of beating an egg in a mixing bowl (to make an omelette?), we could describe it as:

> kitchen job(preparation)
> > *using a* kitchen item/shape(dished)/function{preparation}/

However, the levels of detail of the action and object are not well matched. The detail about the mixing bowl — that it is dished — is needed for beating, but not for preparation in general. We should either be more specific about the action:

> kitchen job(preparation(beating))
> > *using a* kitchen item/shape(dished)/function{preparation}/

or more generic in the description of the object:

kitchen job(preparation)
> *using a* kitchen item/function{preparation}/

Possibly, if we observe the cook beating eggs in a soup bowl, we might generalize in a different direction to:

kitchen job(preparation(beating))
> *using a* kitchen item/shape(dished)/

It is possible to go further, looking at *generic task sequences*, that is, looking at frequently occurring sequences of simple tasks and their representation in KRG sentences. The sequences may be derived from independent observations or from an HTA type task analysis. We have already had an example of this when we described a general kitchen task as consisting of one or more preparation and/or cooking actions followed by a dining action.

The utility of both KRG sentences and sequences is not proven, but they add to our tools for analysis. However, even when the more complex parts of TAKD are inappropriate, the process of producing taxonomies and generification can be employed. In particular, they are especially useful for teaching purposes, where the taxonomy can be used to structure the presentation and description of the objects and actions to the student.

7.5 Entity–Relationship Based Techniques

Entity–relationship modelling is an analysis technique usually associated with database design and more recently object-oriented programming. When adopted for task analysis the major differences are in the kinds of entities modelled. In database and object-oriented design, the entities chosen for analysis will be those which are expected to be represented in the resulting computer system. However, in task analysis, we are interested in a wide range of non-computer entities including physical objects, the actions performed on them and the people who perform them.

Like knowledge based approaches, the cataloguing and examination of *objects* and *actions* is central to the analysis, but the emphasis is on the relationships between actions and objects, rather than on the similarity between different objects and the resulting taxonomic structure. For example, we might look at the three objects 'gardener', 'soil' and 'spade', and the action 'dig' and see how they are related. We would record that it is the gardener who *performs* the digging *acting upon* the soil *using* the spade. Particular importance is attached to the linking of actions with the objects which perform them, and thus the technique can rightly be seen as an *object based methodology*.

As an example, we will consider a task analysis of the market gardening firm 'Vera's Veggies'. Imagine we have talked to Vera Bradshaw, the owner/manager of 'Vera's Veggies' and have walked around the premises.

We begin by listing all the objects in the domain of interest. In the tool shed, we see a spade, a garden fork, a hoe and a small Ferguson tractor (called 'Fergie') with implements, plough and spring-tine harrow. There are two employees, Sam Gummage and Tony Peagreen, and Vera herself works the land as well as acting as manager. From our conversation with her, we have found that there are two main growing fields, 'One Hundred Acre' and 'Parker's Patch', and also a large glasshouse. She also, rather proudly, demonstrated the new computer controlled irrigation system she has just had installed; this has pumps for each field and the glasshouse, and, in addition, has a humidity sensor in the glasshouse. During the interview, we notice that Vera often refers to 'the kit', meaning all contents of the tool shed, and 'the men' meaning Sam and Tony. However, Vera has recently been on a management training course and so (when she remembers) she also uses the term 'the team' referring to the complete staff including herself.

We can classify the objects into three basic types: *concrete objects*, *actors* and *composite objects*. First of all there are simple concrete objects such as the spade, plough and glasshouse, that is, all the 'things'. The human actors are obvious: Vera, Sam and Tony, but we may need to exercise some caution where things, such as Fergie, have been given names. One frequently finds that computers, cars and vegetable varieties are named after people. On the other hand, human actors may be named impersonally, indirectly or not at all, for example, 'the seed merchant', 'the contractor's digger' or 'we sell a lot at the farm shop' (to whom?).

We may also want to discuss non-human actors, concrete objects which in some sense act autonomously, which can 'do' something. In the case of 'Vera's Veggies', we would place the irrigation computer in this category. It may not be clear whether or not to regard an object as an actor; we will see that consideration of the actions (below) helps to make this distinction clear.

Finally, we have composite objects such as 'the team', which consists of three other objects (Sam, Tony and Vera), and 'the kit'. These are both examples of a *'set'* composite object; we may also come across *'tuple'* composite objects. For example, during the interview, we may notice that a lot of times when 'the tractor' is mentioned Vera does not mean Fergie alone, but Fergie together with one or other implement, that is <Fergie, plough> or <Fergie, harrow>.

Composite objects need not always be named; for example, Vera may often say simply 'Sam and Tony' rather than 'the men'. Furthermore, it may sometimes be useful to regard an entity such as 'the team' as an abstract object in its own right, and link it to the (unnamed) composite object {Vera, Sam, Tony} by a relationship such as *consists_of*('the team', {Vera, Sam, Tony}).

We may wish to list some of the *attributes* of each object, for instance:

> **Object** Pump3 **simple** — *irrigation pump*
>> **Attributes:**
>>> status: on/off/faulty
>>> capacity:100 litres/minute

We need not strive to be as complete in the listing of attributes as we would for object-oriented programming. Remember. the intention is not to produce machine representations of the objects, but to describe their participation in human and computer tasks. For example, it is likely we will want to discuss the turning on and off of irrigation pumps, so it is natural to record the status as an attribute. The relevance of the pump's capacity is less obvious, and we may decide to drop it as we proceed with the analysis. As with all the task analysis techniques it is often best to be slightly over-inclusive during early phases, as it is easier to drop unwanted items than to add them later.

We now move on to *actions*. Typically actions change the state of something, called the *patient*, and are performed by someone or something, the *agent*, for example, 'Sam (*agent*) planted (*action*) the leeks (*patient*)'. There may be other attributes associated with an action, for example, if there is an *instrument* used to perform the action, as in our earlier example: 'the gardener dug the soil *with* the spade'. Frequently, accounts of activities are written in an impersonal manner: 'Parker's Patch was ploughed' which really means 'Sam ploughed Parker's Patch'. Taking such an account and uncovering the agent responsible is an important job for the analyst as one of the goals of this analysis is to produce, for each object, a comprehensive list of the actions it can perform.

Tracing the agent performing an action is a good way of classifying the actors. Normally, the agent will be an actor. For example, consider 'the glasshouse irrigation is turned on when humidity drops below 25%'. The agent doing this action is the irrigation controller. This verifies our original statement that the controller is a non-human agent. Sometimes the agency is indirect. For instance, it is often better to water at night to reduce evaporation, so Vera may program the irrigation controller to come on at midnight. Is the controller an agent turning on the water, or an instrument being used by Vera to turn it on (although she is asleep when it happens!)? There is an element of judgement here, but the condition is not that much different from Vera telling Sam to dig the carrots. In the latter case, we would definitely regard Sam as the agent of the digging.

One special sort of action is a message. The last example is better thought of as two actions, the first a message: Vera tells Sam (to dig), the second the digging itself (assuming Sam complies). In any situation involving several people, messages and communication will be a major part of their jobs. This communication is of particular interest in the field of *computer-supported cooperative work* which will be discussed in detail in Chapter 14.

As we analyze the actions people (or even non-human actors) perform, we will often find that they can be listed under several *roles*. For example, when Vera plants marrow seed, she is acting as *worker*, but when she tells Sam to dig the carrots, she is acting as *manager*. Identifying roles can be very important in a large organization as the result of introducing new systems may be to shift whole roles (not just specific tasks) between individuals or from humans to the computer.

At this stage of analysis, having identified the principal objects and actions, we can begin to build object/action descriptions of the form:

Object Sam **human actor**
    Actions:
        S1:   drive tractor
        S2:   dig the carrots

Object Vera **human actor** — the proprietor
    Actions: as worker
        V1:   plant marrow seed
        V2:   program irrigation controller
    Actions: as manager
        V3:   tell Sam to dig the carrots
Object the men **composite**
    Comprises: {Sam, Tony}

Object glasshouse **simple**
    Attribute:
        humidity: 0–100%

Object Irrigation Controller **non-human actor**
    Actions:
        IC1:   turn on Pump1
        IC2:   turn on Pump2
        IC3:   turn on Pump3

Closely allied to actions is the idea of an *event*. Events are anything which *happens*. The performing of an action is an event, but we may also encounter spontaneous events such as the germination of a marrow seed. There is no agent performing the germination and it should be listed as a spontaneous action of the marrow itself, but not implying that the marrow is in any sense an actor. Some spontaneous events, such as 'the humidity drops below 25%', have no associated object at all. A third type of event is timed, such as 'at midnight'.

Finally, we consider the *relationships* between objects, actions and events. The simplest relationships are object–object ones, such as the fact that Sam is subordinate to Vera, or that irrigation pump 3 is situated in the glasshouse. There are also action–object relationships. The relationship between the *agent* performing and action and the action itself is implicit, as the actions are listed under the object responsible. However, we may want to record explicitly the *patient* and *instrument* of an action. In addition, we may want to record relationships between actions and events, such as temporal order and causality:

Object Marrow **simple**
    Actions:
        M1:   germinate
        M2:   grow

Events

     Ev1: humidity drops below 25%

     Ev2: midnight

Relations: object–object

     location (Pump3, glasshouse)

     location (Pump1, Parker's Patch)

Relations: action–object

     patient (V3, Sam)

        –   Vera tells *Sam* to dig

     patient (S2, the carrots)

        –   Sam digs the *carrots* . . .

     instrument (S2, spade)

        –   . . . *with* the spade

Relations: action–event

     before (V1, M1)

        –   the marrow must be sown before it can germinate

     before (M1, M2)

        –   the marrow must germinate before it can grow

     triggers (Ev1, IC3)

        –   *when* humidity drops below 25%,
             the controller turns on pump 3

     triggers (Ev2, IC1)

        –   *when* it is midnight, the controller turns on pump 1

     causes (V2, IC1)

        –   the controller turns on the pump
             because Vera programmed it

     causes (V3, S2)

        –   Sam digs the carrots *because* Vera told him to

Rather than express all the ordering of events and actions using relationships, this form of analysis would normally be combined with some representation of the sequence between actions. For example, the *ATOM* method (*Analysis for Task Object Modelling*) [180], upon which much of the above description is based, uses JSD structure diagrams to represent this (JSD diagrams are described in Chapter 8). Alternatively, one might use HTA diagrams, or one of the other dialogue notations in Chapter 8.

This form of analysis can be applied in two ways. For a specific task, say growing marrows, we may analyze the order of sub-tasks and actions annotated by the objects involved. Using HTA we might have:

> 0.   in order to grow marrows
>   1.   Vera sows the marrow seed
>   2.   marrow germinates
>   3.   Vera programs controller
>   4.   controller waters field
>   5.   marrow grows
>   6.   Sam hoes
>   7.   Tony harvests marrows
>
> Plan: 1 – 2 – 5 – when crop is mature 7
>   when rainfall is low 3 – 4
>   when weeds grow 6

Notice that even though this task is centred on the marrow, there are several actions (for example, 3) which do not include the marrow, in any capacity.

Alternatively, we can produce for any particular object a 'life cycle' diagram representing all the actions in which it participates. Typically, this would cross over several tasks. For example, the irrigation controller would water the fields and glasshouse in any order determined by its program and humidity. This is obviously more in keeping with an object based approach, but both types of action sequence are important. Figure 7.6 shows an HTA diagram for the actions in which the tractor is involved. One is perhaps typically more interested in the life cycles of the agents, but in this example they are rather unstructured.

This form of analysis also fits very well with the sort of taxonomic analysis discussed previously — object-oriented methods usually include some notion of *class* or *inheritance* hierarchy. Indeed, looking at the commonality of actions and relationships can help us to find useful generic categories. For example, we may see that the two fields are treated very similarly, or that Sam, Tony and Vera perform many tasks in common.

7.6 Sources of Information and Data Collection

The different task analysis methods allow you to structure data about tasks. However, the resulting task analysis can only be as good as the original data.

The process of task analysis is not a simple one of collect data, analyze and organize and present results. Instead, the process of analysis will often throw you back to your original sources with new questions and insights. Ideally, the process then should be iterative with periods of data collection interspersed with analysis. In practice, limitations of time and cost will cut this short making the skill of the analyst in foreseeing possible problems in analysis and obtaining relevant data as quickly and economically as possible. The extreme cost of direct observation suggests that, where possible, the analyst ought to make maximum use of cheap sources of information such as manuals or pilot studies before embarking on more costly collection exercises.

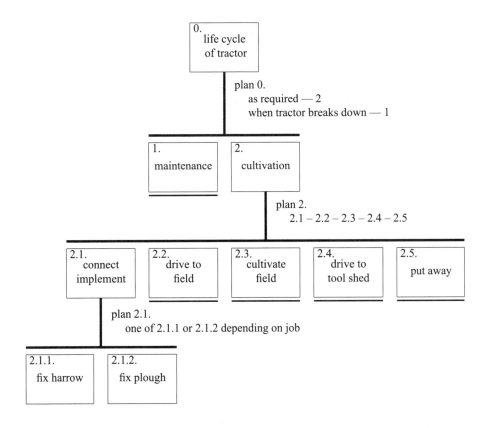

Figure 7.6   *Life cycle of tractor*

7.6.1   *Documentation*

The easiest source of data for the analyst is the existing manuals, instruction booklets, training materials, etc. for the task. These are most likely to be focused on specific items of equipment or computer software, but this is often the focus anyway. Furthermore, there may be corporate rule books and job descriptions which may be used to obtain information about tasks in a wider context. It should be remembered that these sources typically tell you how people are *supposed* to perform tasks, not what they actually do. In addition, equipment-specific manuals are likely to tell you about the *functions* of the device rather than the way it is used to perform a specific task. For example, a word-processor may describe a centring menu option, but this would be used as part of specific tasks such as writing a chapter title or producing a figure caption.

Although the *structure* of material in these sources may be misleading, they are a useful source of basic actions and objects involved in a task. These lists may be incomplete, as they will often ignore non-device actions. For example, the word-processor manual may not mention the use of physical filing cabinets. However, manuals form a starting point for future analysis, and may be used to structure experimental studies, or interviews; one can ask questions such as 'when do you use the centring option?'. Also the lists obtained from manuals may be compared with those of direct observation — unused facilities or objects may indicate either that the facility is redundant, or that it is part of a rare procedure. It is, of course, just these rare procedures which may be missed entirely by direct observation.

Rule books and job descriptions can be used as part of an interviewing process — 'your job description says ... is that right?', or may be compared against observation and then reflected back to the subject — 'according to the instructions you do ... but actually you did ...'. Of course, for such questions to be useful it is essential that the subjects are not put on the defensive or believe that their bending of the rules will be reported back to management. This sort of issue is central to analyses for *computer-supported cooperative work* and we will return to it in Chapter 14.

7.6.2 *Observation*

Some form of direct observation, whether formal or informal, is essential if the analyst is to get an understanding of the task situation. At the simplest level the analyst can simply spend time watching people and chatting, just to get the 'feel' of the task. Together with the reading of existing documentation this can form a good first stage before going on to more extensive and formal observation.

Formal observation can occur in the field or in the laboratory. The advantages and disadvantages of each approach are discussed in detail in Chapter 11 (Section 11.3). Arguably observation in the field is the ideal as this is the 'real' task. However, there may be better recording facilities in the laboratory (video, two-way mirrors, and so on) and we may want more control of the environment. Our observation can be passive (simply listening and watching) or active (asking questions). Especially where the observation is passive, we may want to perform a *post-task walkthrough*, that is, discuss the observations with the subject. This allows us to find out the reasons why the subject performed certain actions. Different recording methods and post-task walkthroughs are discussed further in Chapter 11 (Section 11.5).

7.6.3 *Interviews*

Questioning domain experts is often a direct and quick way to get information about a task. Remember that the expert is not necessarily the manager or foreman who knows *about* the job, but the worker who actually does it. Although there may be advantages to interviewing both sorts of expert, as the views of the manager or professional instructor are based on years of experience even if they are likely to be 'idealized' versions of the task.

It may be particularly appropriate to interview the 'professional' experts after doing some formal or informal direct observation. It is then possible to ask them to reflect on the various expected and unexpected behaviours; this can become a form of third-party walkthrough.

More normally, one would begin with a general set of questions, possibly asking the expert to describe a typical day, or task. This can then be followed with more leading questions such as 'Why do you do that?' or 'What if this develops a fault?'. The aim is both to uncover detail and to increase the range of behaviour discussed.

Where appropriate the expert can be asked to produce lists of objects/actions associated with the task; although it may be unwise to demand too structured information during a first interview, as this may limit the range of material discussed. The exception to this would be HTA where one often starts with a top-down decomposition. In this case one can begin by asking the expert 'What do you do to make a cup of tea?' and then successively expand the explanation.

7.6.4 Initial analysis

We assume we have got some sort of written transcript, whether from manuals, observation or interviews. The detailed analysis, of course, depends on the analysis method employed, but most start by trying to build up lists of elementary objects and actions. A simple device is to go through the transcript highlighting the nouns (which will be objects) and the verbs (which will be associated with actions). If the transcript is on-line this process can even be automated with the help of an on-line dictionary.

However, this simple association is rarely enough on its own. Some words may be either a verb or a noun, for instance, in chess 'castle' is both a noun (the piece) and also a verb (a particular move). Technical language is often full of 'verbed' nouns and even 'nouned' verbs, although the latter are often names for processes, so are not as great a problem. In addition, the objects or actions may be implicit. However, this problem may be better dealt with by checking consistency between lists, within the particular task analysis method employed.

Context is often important in interpreting words. For instance, we may have the two verb phrases:

'beat the eggs in the *bowl*'
'ate the porridge from the *bowl*'

It is only by looking at the context that we see the former is a mixing bowl and that the latter is a soup bowl. Similar problems arise with verbs:

'the rain *poured*'
'she *poured* the mixture into the pan'
'I *poured* the tea'

The first is clearly a different sort of pouring from the rest. Also the second sort of pouring may well be considered different from the last, as the pouring of mixture is an action during the preparation of food. Clearly, this second distinction is somewhat debatable and hence one should attempt to leave such decisions till later in the analysis process. To do this the object and action lists can be annotated, for example, 'pour (the tea)'.

7.6.5   Sorting and classification

Several of the techniques include the production of hierarchies and sorting of entries by various attributes. Some of this is carried out by the analyst, but some requires subjective assessments by domain experts.

Several techniques can be used to obtain the relevant information. This has been discussed briefly before in Section 7.4.

One way is to take the list of, say, task objects, and write each one on a slip of paper or card. The expert is then asked to sort them into piles of similar objects. Depending on the size of the piles the expert can be asked to further sub-divide the piles, or to group the piles into larger ones. If desired, the piles and groups of piles can be tied together with elastic bands or put in envelopes and labelled by the expert by the common characteristic. This process can be repeated several times, each time asking the expert to perform a different grouping. Also different experts can be asked and their groupings compared.

Alternatively, one can ask the expert to arrange the cards on a table top. This allows the expert to cluster the cards (showing similarity) and to use the spatial arrangement in order to give a classification by two attributes. Again, the expert can be questioned after the event as to why the particular arrangement was used.

A range of similar techniques can be used to elicit the user's or expert's knowledge about a task. Each object/action can be ranked against each task depending on how important the expert thinks they are for that task. Perhaps on a scale 0 — never used — to 10 — essential. So, for example, if the task were 'making an omelette' eggs would be scored 10, but the fork to beat the egg may only be scored 5. Alternatively, the expert can simply be asked to rank the objects as this may be easier than an absolute judgement.

However the classification and production of hierarchies is performed, the job of producing possibly large taxonomies and hierarchy diagrams is not trivial. This can be done by hand on paper or using a standard word-processor, but is easier if an outliner is used. There are several commercial outlining tools which can be used, and most word-processors and many spreadsheets have outlining facilities. These outliners make it easy to shift partially sorted groups as we refine the classification. They also allow us to hide unwanted information, say when we want to look at the top levels of decomposition of a task hierarchy, or of we want to 'cut' a TDH taxonomy to look at generic objects or actions.

7.7   Uses of Task Analysis

The output of task analysis is some breakdown of the tasks people perform and, depending on the techniques used, the things that are used and the plans and sequences of actions used to perform the tasks. The way this information is used depends very much on the use to which it is put. Three such uses will be described briefly, the production of manuals and tuition material, requirements capture and high-level systems design, and detailed interface design. Of these uses, only the first is aimed at the actual system analyzed; the latter two use the analysis of the existing system in order to suggest the design of a new one.

7.7.1   *Manuals and tuition*

Some of the earliest techniques in task analysis are aimed at teaching novices how to perform a task. In particular, this was important for military training, for example, how to disassemble and clean a rifle. Training had to be quick and efficient as conscripts in peace time may only serve a few years before returning to civilian life or in war time may only survive a few months.

The use of task analysis as part of the discipline of HCI is somewhat different, but training is still an important application. The hierarchical structure of HTA can be used to structure manuals or course material. For example, we want to write a beginner's manual on tea-making based on the hierarchical task analysis in Figure 7.4. We base each page on one level of task decomposition and its associated plan (Figure 7.7).

This kind of 'how to do it' manual is often useful for initial training, but for structuring a course, or for more advanced training material, a more conceptual structure is better. This is precisely where the knowledge based techniques are strong. The taxonomic structure can be used directly; for example, our course on cars may start with a lecture on steering controls, then have a lecture on controlling the engine speed and gears, etc. This is most likely to be useful when the taxonomy is a strict either/or tree. More generally, we can produce the shortened list of generic objects and actions by 'cutting' the taxonomic tree, and use these as the structuring principle. Given such a 'cut' of the taxonomy of kitchen tools and jobs in Section 7.4, we may structure a cookery course as follows:

```
┌─────────────────────────────┐  ┌─────────────────────────────┐
│     To make cups of tea     │  │        Make pot of tea      │
│                             │  │     once water has boiled   │
│                             │  │                             │
│  boil water — see page 2    │  │  warm pot                   │
│  empty pot                  │  │  put tea leaves in pot      │
│  make pot — see page 3      │  │  pour in boiling water      │
│  wait 4 or 5 minutes        │  │                             │
│  pour tea — see page 4      │  │                             │
│                             │  │                             │
│                             │  │                             │
│                             │  │                             │
│        — page 1 —           │  │        — page 3 —           │
│                             │  │                             │
└─────────────────────────────┘  └─────────────────────────────┘
```

Figure 7.7 *Instruction manual for tea-making*

Cookery in 8 easy lessons

lecture 1.	preparation — dished utensils
lecture 2.	preparation — flat utensils
lecture 3.	jobs for food preparation
lecture 4.	cooking — dished utensils
	. . .
lecture 8.	dining — graceful eating and drinking (followed by course dinner)

In addition to teaching totally new material, task analysis can be used to help a user transfer from one system to another. Assuming we have performed a task analysis of both systems, a comparison of these will highlight areas for training. A simple comparison of functionality is *not* sufficient as the crucial differences may be in procedures. On the other hand, two systems may seem completely different in terms of detailed commands and presentation, but have similar high-level concepts or similar patterns of use. These common features should be brought out and can be used to help the user transfer knowledge from one system to another.

7.7.2 *Requirements capture and systems design*

Task analysis can be used to guide the design of new (although possibly not novel) systems. Recall (from Chapter 5) that requirements capture is the process of eliciting what a new system should do. Task analysis in itself is not a form of requirements capture as it refers to the existing system, not the planned system, and it includes many elements which are not part of the system. However, it makes a strong contribution towards the complete statement of requirements. Typically, the original statement of requirements given by a client, will mention the new elements required and possibly refer to the existing *system* and its functionality. Further information elicited by a system developer may well concentrate on what the system should *do* but may forget how it will be *used*.

The task analysis of an existing system can help in two ways. Firstly, the analyst can ask 'Which of the existing objects, tasks, etc. should be in the new system?'. Secondly, the formalized presentation of the existing state of affairs may help the client to clarify what the novel features are to be. It may be decided to automate whole tasks or roles, or simply specific sub-tasks.

As the high-level design of the system progresses, task analysis continues to play a role. The structuring provided by, for instance, TDH taxonomies can help the designer to choose an internal model for the system which matches the existing expectations of the users. This may, of course, be modified to accommodate novel features, but gives a reasonable first structure.

We may also make some predictions about the use of the new system. Given the parts that are to be included and the planned behaviour of the system, we may see how this will interact with existing procedures, including how information will move in and out of the new system. Some of the procedures may be able to continue as before, especially if the system has been designed to mimic the old, possibly non-automated, system, but some may need to be retaught completely.

7.7.3   *Detailed interface design*

In a similar manner to the manual design, taxonomies of tasks or objects may be used in the design of menus. The TDH trees are obviously most useful in this respect. Top-level menus can be labelled after the top level decomposition and sub-menus after the next level, etc. For this, the tree may be first reduced to a simple either/or tree, thus guaranteeing that each object/action is under exactly one menu. Alternatively, more complex trees allowing AND and OR as well as XOR branches can be used. In this case, an object/action may be found by several paths through the menus.

An alternative menu layout could be based around roles and then tasks in roles. Again for such a layout, it is likely that a particular action is found under several roles/tasks. There is a tendency for users to find new tasks to perform with new systems, and, for such a new task, the required actions on the system may be difficult to find and be widely dispersed. So, this sort of layout is only sensible if the possible set of tasks is very well defined, but where this is true, such a layout and system design can be highly efficient.

If an object-oriented paradigm is being used in the interface, then the association of objects with actions may be particularly useful. For each object, a menu of possible actions, based on those for which it is the agent or patient, can be displayed. Default actions for each object may be chosen based on the frequency of actions (for efficiency) but informed by the generic classification scheme (for learnability). In most systems the generic action associated with a double click is to 'open' the object for editing. However, in specialist domains a different choice may be more appropriate.

Task sequences obtained from a task decomposition can be used when designing the system's dialogue (see Chapter 8). The order in which sub-tasks are performed in the system can be made to mirror that of the original job. Even where the interface style is more user directed, and hence the dialogue sequence is not defined by the designer, the task decomposition and plans are useful. If we know that a certain task is frequently performed, then we want it to be easy for the user to perform the sub-tasks in the appropriate order. If, for example, it involves constantly swapping modes, or moving between widely different parts of a menu based interface, this would be unacceptable.

Task analysis is never complete and hence it should not be the sole arbiter of the style and structure of an interface. However, the insights from a well-executed task analysis can make an interface that easily supports the way people want to work.

7.8 Summary

We have seen several task analysis methods. Hierarchical task analysis decomposes a task into sub-tasks. These can either be recorded in a textual outline format or in a tree diagram. Knowledge based techniques build taxonomies of the objects used during a task and the actions performed upon them. Cutting the taxonomy at some level gives one a set of generic objects and actions. Finally, one can again look at objects and actions, but concentrate on different kinds of object: passive object and active human and non-human agents, and the relationships between the objects and actions.

Information for task analysis can be drawn from existing documentation, observation of workers doing the tasks, or from interviews with workers and domain experts. Observations can be recorded in a variety of forms, from handwritten notes to video recording and computer logging. The early analysis may involve the subjects, asking them to 'relive' the task in a post-task walkthrough, or sort lists of task objects and actions for knowledge elicitation.

Analysis can be used to structure manuals and training courses. In this case the system studied will be the 'target' system for the documentation. Alternatively, an existing system (or systems) can be studied and the task analysis used to structure a new design. This can guide the choice of functionality and the objects and actions implemented within the system. It can also be used to guide the detailed design of dialogue so that frequent tasks are easy to perform.

Exercises

7.1 The following is a list of objects found in one of the authors' kitchens.

> teapot, mug, soup bowl, plate, spoon, table knife, cook's knife, fork, saucepan, frying pan, kettle, casserole, fish slice, tin opener, baking tray, scales, miking bowl, glasses, jugs, corkscrew, rolling pin, ladle, egg cup, chopping board

Produce a taxonomy using the TDH notation of these objects. Does it obey the TAKD uniqueness rule? Compare your answer with someone else's. (Note, the authors had great difficulty with items like the corkscrew, which did not fit easily into any generic category — perhaps you did better.)

7.2 Complete the tea-making manual in Figure 7.7. Do you think it would be useful? Think of situations where such a manual would be helpful and where a more conceptual manual would be better.

7.3 Figure 7.1 shows a textual representation of an HTA description of vacuum cleaning. Present the same information in a diagrammatic form.

7.4 (Converse to above) Figure 7.6 uses an HTA diagram to show the actions in which a tractor is involved; show the same information textually.

7.5 Observe an office, note the actions performed and the objects used depending on the available equipment, use different recording techniques as described in Chapter 11. Then use the different task analysis techniques to structure your findings. (Note, this could be a group project.)

7.6 Consider the activity of making a telephone call. Record the actions in an HTA diagram or textually. Start off simply, assuming you know the number to dial, but then add more complicated situations: finding the number in an address book, or what to do when the number is engaged.

7.7 The act of looking up a person in an address book or telephone directory is itself quite complicated. Get several friends to look up words in a dictionary. Observe closely their methods. You will probably have to develop shorthand notations to keep track of what pages they visit. Compare the strategies used by the different people. If they differ, try to abstract out the common parts of the task and the variable parts. Those with sufficient computing background can attempt to classify their methods in relation to known search algorithms: binary chop, linear search, etc.

Recommended Reading

- Dan Diaper (ed.), *Task Analysis for Human–Computer Interaction*, Ellis Horwood, 1989.

  This is a collection containing articles by experts in specific task analysis techniques which covers the complete range of this chapter. It includes detailed discussion of HTA (Section 7.3), TAKD (Section 7.4) and ATOM (Section 7.5). It also includes another knowledge based technique *task knowledge structures* (TKS) together with an associated methodology *knowledge analysis for tasks* (KAT). As well as explanation and examples, case studies are included for several methods, and an account of task observation methods.

- P. Johnson, *Human–Computer Interaction: psychology, task analysis and software engineering*, McGraw Hill, 1992.

  This is a short introductory HCI text, oriented towards task analysis and in particular Johnson's own KAT methodology (above).

Chapter 8

Dialogue Notations and Design

Overview

Dialogue is the syntactic level of human–computer interaction; it is rather like the script of a play, except the user, and sometimes the computer, has more choices.

- Notations used for dialogue description can be

  - diagrammatic: easy to read at a glance
  - textual: easier for formal analysis

- The dialogue is linked

  - to the semantics of the system, what it does
  - to the presentation of the system, how it looks

- Formal descriptions can be analyzed

  - for inconsistent actions
  - for difficult to reverse actions
  - for missing items
  - for potential miskeying errors

8.1 What is Dialogue?

Dialogue, as opposed to a monologue, is a conversation between two or more parties. It has also come to imply a level of cooperation or at least intent to resolve conflict. In the design of user interfaces, the *dialogue* has a more specific meaning, namely the *structure* of the conversation between the user and the computer system.

We can look at computer language at three levels:

lexical The lowest level: the shape of icons on the screen and the actual keys pressed. In human language, the sounds and spellings of words.

syntactic The order and structure of inputs and outputs. In human language, the grammar of sentence construction.

semantic The meaning of the conversation in terms of its effect on the computer's internal data structures and/or the external world. In human language, the meaning ascribed by the different participants to the conversation.

In user interfaces, the term dialogue is often taken to be almost synonymous with the syntactic level. However, the lexical/syntactic barrier is somewhat fuzzy and actual use of dialogue description often includes some lexical features.

In Sections 8.2–8.4 we will see why specific notations are required for dialogue design, and review a range of diagrammatic and textual dialogue notations. Having got a formal representation of the dialogue, what do we do with it? Section 8.5 discusses the links between these dialogue notations acting at the syntactic level and the detailed semantics of the system. Finally, in Section 8.6, we will see how a description of the dialogue can be analyzed to discover potential faults and problems.

In the rest of this section, we will look at structured human–human dialogues which will demonstrate several features which we will later see in human–computer dialogue.

8.1.1 *Structured human dialogues*

In contrast to most human conversation, dialogue with computers is relatively structured and constrained. It is only on Star Trek that one can freely chat to the computer and expect a response (although not as far from the truth as all that, see Chapter 15). So, whereas in human conversation, the grammar rules often stop once we get to the level of a sentence (and allow a lot of latitude even in sentence construction), those for computer dialogues may encompass the whole of the interaction.

There are of course more structured forms of human conversation. Consider the following fragment from a marriage service:

Minister: Do you *man's name*, take this woman . . .

Man: I do.

Minister: Do you *woman's name*, take this man . . .

Woman: I do.

Man: With this ring, I thee wed . . . (*places ring on woman's finger*)

Woman: With this ring, I thee wed . . . (*places ring on man's finger*)

Minister: I now pronounce you husband and wife.

This is a sort of script for the three participants to follow. It demonstrates several important features which we will see in computer dialogues. The participants must say certain things in a specific order. Some of their contributions are entirely predetermined, for instance, the phrase 'I do'. However, the minister must vary his words, substituting in the names of the husband- and wife-to-be. The instructions concerning the ring can be regarded as an annotation to the dialogue, or part of the dialogue. Different notations for describing computer dialogue will similarly differ on precisely what actions are considered part of the dialogue. Assuming the placing of the ring is included, we note that this happens at the same time as the marriage partners speak the words 'with this ring'. That is, parts of the dialogue are performed *concurrently*. Again we shall see later that different notations differ in their ability to handle concurrent dialogue.

Although the minister must substitute the man and woman's names, this has no effect on the rest of the service. This dialogue description makes no provision for alternative responses — 'I don't'!

However, typically, the future course of a dialogue does depend on the responses of the participants, for example, in a criminal trial:

Judge: How do you plead, guilty or not guilty?

Defendant: *either* Guilty *or* Not guilty.

If the defendant pleads not guilty then the trial will proceed with evidence and cross examination. If, on the other hand, the defendant pleads guilty, the trial will move directly to the sentencing. Because of the formalized nature of judicial processes, we could develop these court scripts further. However, they would still be normative; there is always the chance that the judge may address the court with a chorus of 'Somewhere over the rainbow', or, like the Queen of Hearts, 'Off with her head!'. The verdict of such an improper trial is likely to be overturned by a higher court, but is not ruled out because the human participants do not always behave as expected. Similarly, descriptions of computer dialogues may not cover all eventualities. Hitting the save option on a word-processor's menu is expected to save the file and then give control back to the user. Occasionally, the computer may instead respond with a 'core dumped' or 'unrecoverable application error' message. Should the dialogue description include such improper system responses? The answer is unclear and depends very much on the intended use.

Returning to the marriage service, the script given refers only to the words spoken. It does not directly address the *meaning* of those words: the legal nature of the ceremony, the fidelity of the partners or even whether the minister gets the partners' names right! We have noted that computer dialogue descriptions are usually aimed at the syntactic level of language, not the semantics (meaning). Similarly, the marriage ceremony does not directly address the semantics of marriage; for instance, the marriage may be acted out as part of a television programme, and the actor and actress would not expect to be really married at the end of it. However, an important issue for computer dialogues is how the syntax links into the semantics of the application. For instance, if I type 'print fred', I expect the file fred to be printed, not deleted.

8.2   Dialogue Design Notations

In this section we shall look at some of the notations which have been used for describing human–computer dialogues. Some may be familiar to the computer scientist as they have their roots in other branches of computing and have been 'appropriated' by the user interface developer.

But why bother to use a special notation? We already have programming languages, why not use them? Let us look at a simple financial advice program to calculate mortgage repayments. (This is *not* supposed to be an example of good dialogue design.)

```
            rate = 10
            term = 25

            print "Our current interest rate is 10%"
            print "What is your annual salary?"
            input salary
            max_loan = 3 * salary
            print "How much do you want to borrow"
            input amount
            if   amount > max_loan
            then   print "That is too much money"
                   print "Please consult our financial advisor"
                   goto finish
            end if
            repeat forever
                   print "Our standard term is 25 years."
                   print "Do you want this (yes/no)?"
                   input answer
                   if   answer == "yes"   goto calc
                   if   answer == "no"    goto rd_trm
                   print "You must answer yes or no"
            end repeat
rd_trm: print "What term do you require (years)"
```

```
            input term
calc:       r = ( 100 + rate ) / 100
            payment = r^term * ( r - 1 )
                              * amount / ( r^(term-1) - 1 )
            print "Monthly repayment is ", payment
finish: stop
```

Notice how the dialogue with the user is mixed up with the rest of the program, calculations are interspersed with input/output. Some of the if then statements represent the system's choices (amount > max_loan), others represent choices of the user (answer == "yes"). If you are a programmer, you will also have noticed the poor program structure and the use of goto. This is not because the authors are bad programmers. It would be possible to rewrite it using only structured programming constructs. However, the resulting program would be equally obtuse, and, in general, programs which have to parse are full of nasty structures. In this program, the biggest complication is the check that the answer is either 'yes' or 'no'. Error checking and correction often dominate interactive programs.

Imagine now you have been asked to analyze the dialogue in some way: for instance, to list all the possible sequences of user inputs and system responses, or to tell the user how to get the repayments on a 15 year loan. The mixing of user and system choices and the convoluted nature of the program structure makes this surprisingly difficult.

Alternatively you may be asked to change the interface style or fit the program with a mouse and window based interface — is this difficult? Remember, this is a short program which is almost all interaction with the user and should be relatively easy. Imagine a program of 10,000 or 100,000 lines. Various commercial applications began their life on traditional text based terminals, but are now available on Windows or Macintosh platforms. The ancestry of such programs is often all too obvious — not really surprising.

This gives us two reasons for using a separate dialogue description notation: ease of analysis and separation of the interface elements of the program from the actual calculations (semantics). These reasons both presuppose the program exists already — a third reason for using a special notation is to write down the dialogue *before* a program is written. This allows the designer to analyze the proposed structure, or perhaps use a prototyping tool to execute the dialogue. A dialogue notation is also a way for members of a design team to talk about the design and eventually for the designer to pass on the intended dialogue to the programmer of the actual application. Thus dialogue notations often form an integral part of *prototyping* methodologies and tools (discussed further in Chapter 5).

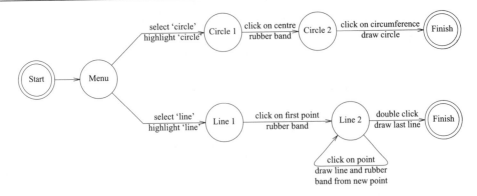

Figure 8.1   *State transition network for menu driven drawing tool*

8.3   Diagrammatic Notations

Diagrammatic notations are heavily used in dialogue design. At their best they allow the designer to see at a glance the structure of the dialogue. However, they often have trouble coping with more extensive or complex dialogue structures. Sub-sections 8.3.1–8.3.4 describe variants of state transition networks, which are the most heavily used diagrammatic notation. As part of this description several issues will be discussed which are shared by other diagrammatic and textual notations, in particular the treatment of concurrent dialogues and pre-emptive features. Sections 8.3.5–8.3.7 describe other diagrammatic notations: Harel's state charts, traditional flow diagrams and JSD diagrams.

8.3.1   State transition networks

State transition networks (*STN*) have long been used for dialogue description. Consider a simple mouse based drawing tool. It has a menu with two options 'circle' and 'line' and a drawing surface. If you select circle you are allowed to click on two further points on the drawing surface. The first of these is the circle's centre and the second any point on the circumference. After the first point is selected the system draws a 'rubber band' line between the centre and the current mouse position. After the second point is chosen the circle is drawn.

The 'line' option in the menu is to draw a polyline. That is, the user can select any number of points on the drawing surface which the system connects with straight lines. The last point is denoted by a double click on the mouse. Again the system 'rubber bands' between successive mouse positions.

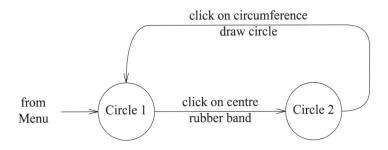

Figure 8.2 *Portion of STN allowing multiple circles to be drawn*

Figure 8.1 shows an STN describing the tool. Each circle denotes a 'state' the system can be in. For example, *Menu* is the state where the system is waiting for the user to select either 'circle' or 'line' from the menu, and *Circle 2* is the state after the user has entered the circle centre and is waiting for the point on the circumference.

Between the states are arrows, the *transitions*. These are labelled with the user actions that triggered the particular transition and the response the system makes. For instance, state *Circle 1* is where the system is waiting for the user to select the circle's centre. If the user clicks on a point, the system moves into state *Circle 2* and responds by drawing the rubber band between the point and the current mouse position. From this state, the user can click on another point, upon which the system draws the circle and then moves into the special *Finish* state. We can see from this that the STN is able to represent a *sequence* of user actions and system responses.

When in state *Circle 1*, the user had no other options: there was only one arc coming from it, corresponding to selecting a point. In other states, the user has several options. For example, from state *Menu* the user can select 'circle' from the menu, upon which the system moves into state *Circle 1* and highlights the 'circle' option on the menu, or alternatively, the user can select 'line' from where the system moves into state *Line 1*. That is, the STN is able to describe user *choice*.

There is a choice from state *Line 2* also: the user can double click on a point and finish the polyline, moving to the *Finish* state, or the user can single click, which adds a new point to the polyline. In the latter case, the transition points back into state *Line 2*. This represents *iteration* — the system stays in state *Line 2* accepting any number of points on the polyline, until the user double clicks on a point.

Iterations need not involve just one state. The dialogue as it stands only allows you to draw one circle. You presumably have to go through the menu selection again for each circle drawn. We could imagine altering the dialogue to allow any number of circles to be drawn. To do this we would make the arc from state

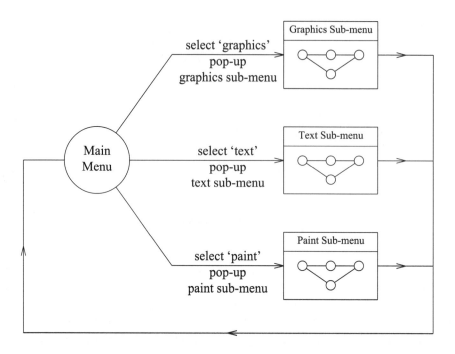

Figure 8.3   *Hierarchical state transition network for complete drawing tool*

Circle 2 loop back to state *Circle 1*. This is shown in Figure 8.2. There are some problems with this arrangement as it stands which we will discuss later. However, note that already we are using the STN to discuss different dialogue options.

8.3.2   *Hierarchical state transition nets*

The *Start* and *Finish* states are not real states, but are there merely to let us glue this bit of dialogue into a bigger dialogue. For example, the drawing tool may have a main menu, from which we can select one of three sub-menus: a graphics menu (as described for circles and lines), a text menu (for adding labels) and a paint menu (for freehand drawing). We could describe this complete system using the *hierarchical STN* in Figure 8.3. This is like the previous STNs, but has additional composite states represented as rectangles with a picture of a little STN in them. Each of these rectangles denotes the whole STN for the relevant sub-menu. We assume that the STN in Figure 8.1 is the *Graphics Sub-menu*. In a large specification this may be represented by a caption for the STN or by putting the label *Graphics Sub-menu* in the *Start* state.

To read this diagram we start in state *Main Menu* and follow the relevant transition from it as before. Imagine the user has selected 'graphics' from the main menu. The system responds by 'popping' the graphics sub-menu and then going into state *Graphics Sub-menu*. However, this is not really a single state, but corresponds to the STN described in Figure 8.1. We therefore enter this sub-dialogue at the state pointed to by its special *Start* state, that is the *Menu* state. We then follow through the graphics menu STN, either drawing a circle or a polyline. When we get to a *Finish* state we revert to the main diagram in Figure 8.3 and follow the (single) arrow from the *Graphics Sub-menu* state which leads us back to the *Main Menu*.

The use of hierarchical elements does not change the power of the basic notation as one can simply imagine gluing the sub-diagrams into the main diagram. However, it makes it far simpler to specify large systems; it would not be unreasonable to specify a whole system dialogue in this fashion, from the highest level down to individual keystrokes and mouse clicks.

There are other ways of making STNs hierarchical. Each variant has its own rules for tying the high-level STN with the detailed STNs. In addition, the conditions which enable a transition and the systems responses may be attached to a low-level STN. *Generalized transition networks* are probably the most well known of such variants as they are used to describe the computer system's behaviour in CCT (Chapter 6, Section 6.3.2).

8.3.3 *Concurrent dialogues and combinatorial explosion of states*

We have seen that STNs can be very good at representing the sequential, choice and iterative parts of a dialogue. Where they fail, quite dismally, is in describing a dialogue consisting of several *concurrent* parts. Take for example a simple dialogue box for describing text style as one might find in a word-processor (Figure 8.4). The box contains three toggles, one each for bold, italic and underline styles. A piece of text can be **emboldened**, *italicized*, <u>underlined</u> or any combination of these three. To select, say, emboldening, the user clicks over the *Bold* toggle. To deselect it, the user simply clicks again.

If we look at each toggle individually, we have simple two state STNs as in Figure 8.5. The arrows have been drawn with two heads, as the same user action moves you in either direction between the states. We have also omitted the system responses, which would be to invert the highlighting of the toggle, and possibly to change the style of any currently selected text in the document.

However, this does not tell us what happens if, say, the user clicks over the italic toggle and then the bold one. To do this we need to combine the diagrams. We'll do this first for just the bold and italic options. This is shown in Figure 8.6. This has four states: one with neither style selected, one for bold only, one for italic only and one for both. You may verify that each user action performs as expected,

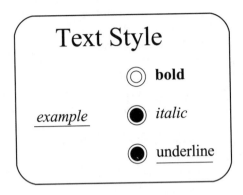

Figure 8.4   *Simple dialogue box with three toggles*

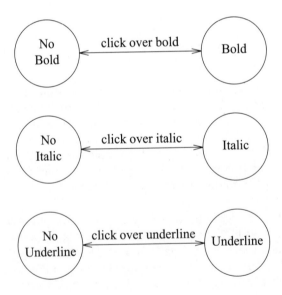

Figure 8.5   *Individual bold, italic and underline state transition diagrams*

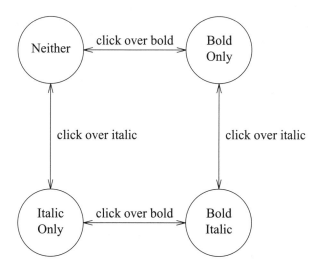

Figure 8.6   *Combined bold and italic state transition diagram*

for example, clicking over 'italic', whilst in *Bold Italic* would get you to the *Bold Only* state.

Finally, we add in the underline style in Figure 8.7. This time we have written the user actions simply as 'B' for 'click over "bold" ' and so on as the diagram has become cluttered enough as it is! Again, the reader can verify that the user actions perform as expected, for example, 'U' in state *Bold Italic* takes you to state *Underlined Bold Italic*.

The STN with two toggles had four states, the STN with three toggles had eight states and, in general, if we had had *n* toggles, we would have had a diagram with 2^n states in it. Not particularly easy to read! The problem is that the user is effectively operating the toggles concurrently; he can perform an action on any of them, and the actions on one are independent of the actions on the others. If we have two STNs with *m* and *n* states respectively, then the STN representing the two acting concurrently will have $m \times n$ states. Furthermore, the resulting diagram would hide the regularity of the interface.

This inability of STNs to handle concurrent dialogues is particularly a problem with modern direct manipulation interfaces. These are often full of toggles, option switches, style sheets, etc., all of which can be operated independently of one another. This seriously calls into question their usefulness under these circumstances

One suggestion, particularly associated with Jacob [92], is that STNs should be used to model the micro-dialogue of direct manipulation systems. That is, each

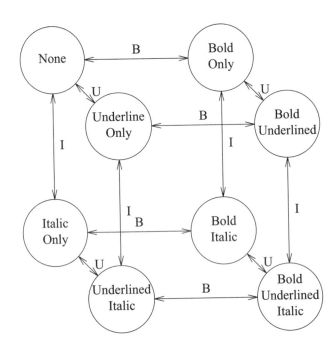

Figure 8.7   *Combined bold, italic and underline state transition diagram*

interface element (menu, toggle, dialogue box) would have an associated STN. However, the way that these are put together would use some alternative notation. Thus, for example, the above dialogue box would be represented as consisting of three STNs, as we originally had in Figure 8.5.

8.3.4 *Escapes and help*

Escapes and help systems pose problems that are similar to the combinatorial explosion from concurrent dialogues. Imagine that we have been observing the use of the drawing tool. We have noticed that users often find they have wrongly selected some option and want to get back to the menu. As the dialogue is currently specified, once they select, say, the circle option, they must select two points before they are allowed to continue. As the current system does not have any deletion at present, this was found to be particularly irksome.

As a solution to this problem, we want to add an escape key, which wherever you are, cancels what you are doing and returns you to the main menu. This seems quite a simple addition — it only took a sentence to say. However, to add it to

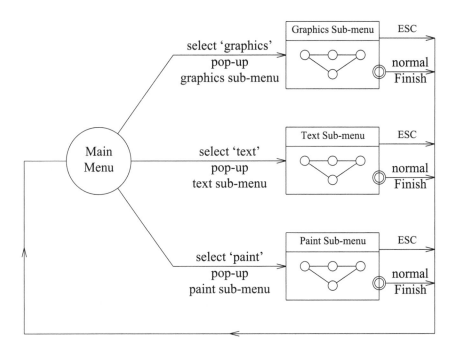

Figure 8.8   *STN for drawing tool with escapes*

the STN describing the system would require an arc from *every* state back to the main menu. Furthermore, this would make a complete mess of the hierarchical structure of the dialogue description.

Some forms of hierarchical STN explicitly cater for this by saying that if a composite state has a labelled arc coming from it, then this acts as an escape from the sub-dialogue. For example, we could redraw the overall system description as in Figure 8.8.

Each sub-menu state now has two arcs coming from it. One arc is labelled 'normal Finish' and represents the path taken when the sub-dialogue reaches its *Finish* state. This arc has a little state circle added to it in order to emphasize that it is tied to the finish state within the sub-dialogue. The other arc from the sub-menu state is labelled 'ESC' and this represents the user hitting the escape key. The difference is that this arc is 'active' at all times during the sub-dialogue. Even when the user is in the middle of drawing a circle or a line, if the escape key is pressed, the sub-dialogue is immediately aborted and the arc labelled 'ESC' is taken. In this case, both the 'ESC' and the 'normal Finish' arcs go to the same place. In general, this need not be so, and one may have several escapes activated by different user actions.

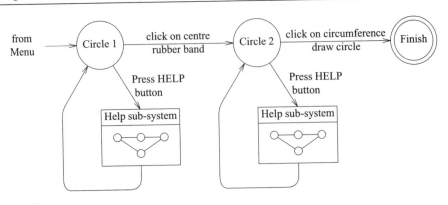

Figure 8.9   *Portion of STN with help system*

Help systems are similar to escapes in some ways, in that they may be invoked at any stage during the dialogue. However, unlike escapes, when you have finished using the help system, you expect to return to the same point in the dialogue that you left. That is, you can think of the help system as being a little sub-dialogue hanging off every state in the network. Figure 8.9 shows this for two states of the dialogue: as you can imagine, it would get a little tedious for the whole thing!

The case of a help system is very similar to concurrent dialogues (in fact it is an embedded dialogue), and the total number of states in the full diagram is again the product of the number of states in the help system times the number in the original system.

8.3.5   *State charts*

Harel's *state charts* can be seen as a form of STN. They were developed as a way of visually specifying complex reactive systems and address many of the problems described above, for example, concurrency and escapes, while still retaining a diagrammatic representation. They are characterized by a hierarchical structure, but not used as we have seen before to split a diagram up. The hierarchy in state charts is used within a single diagram to add structure, and to show which parts represent alternative states (like simple STNs) and which represent concurrent activity.

Figure 8.10 is a state chart of a television control panel. The controller has five buttons labelled 'ON', 'OFF', 'MUTE', 'SEL' and 'RESET'. The television can either be on, or in standby mode. Imagine we start at *Standby*. Pressing ON or RESET will turn the television on (TV_ON), then when it is on, pressing OFF puts it back into standby mode. When the television is on, the user can control the sound with the

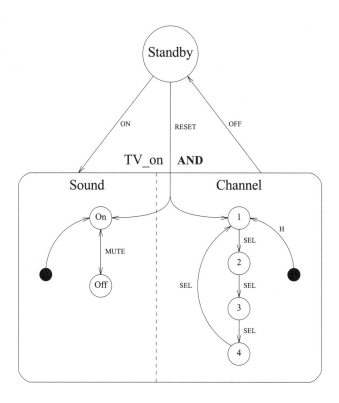

Figure 8.10   *State chart for television control panel*

MUTE button and the channel with the SEL button. Using MUTE turns the sound on or off, whereas SEL cycles between four channels (this is a rather cheap TV).

The SOUND and CHANNEL sub-dialogues each look somewhat like normal STNs. They are both part of the *TV_ON* composite state — this is an example of hierarchical grouping. However, the dashed line between them, together with the **AND** keyword says that the two sub-dialogues operate concurrently — that is, we can press MUTE or SEL in any order we like.

The *Sound* sub-dialogue has a black blob with an arc going to the *On* state. This corresponds to the *Start* node in the earlier STNs and represents the default start state. Each time the TV is turned on, the sound will be on. The channel's selection is slightly different: its start arc is marked with a 'H', short for history. This says that the channel sub-dialogue remembers where it last was — the first time you turn the TV on it will start in channel 1, but subsequently when you turn it on it will be set to the last channel you were watching. Unlike the ON arc the RESET arc overrides these default start states. Whereas ON is targeted at the *TV_on* box generally, RESET is directed to specific states within *TV_on*. Thus whenever the reset button is pressed from standby mode, the television is turned on with the channel set to 1 and the sound on.

Notice also that the OFF button acts as an escape to the *TV_on* dialogue. No matter where the SOUND and CHANNEL dialogues are, simply pressing OFF will put the TV in standby mode. A judicious use of the 'history' feature would allow one to specify a help system, but even with the expressiveness of state charts this would look clumsy.

8.3.6   Flow charts

Although somewhat out of fashion now, flow charts in various forms are perhaps the most widely used of any diagrammatic notation for programming. They can also be a simple, but useful, tool for dialogue design. In expressive power, they differ little from STNs and share the problems of concurrency, escapes and so on. However, within the area of simple dialogues, they have the advantage of simplicity and the added benefit that most programmers will know what they mean.

The boxes in a flow chart represent processes or decisions and are thus not equivalent to the states of an STN. For example, in an STN, the act of accepting a user's input is attached to an arc (and is often difficult to read), whereas in a flow chart it is in one of the boxes.

Flow charts employ a wide range of box shapes to represent different activities, but these reflect a programmer-centred rather than a user-centred view: for example, the use of a parallelogram for input/output, whether this is interaction with the user or with a database or file. If one uses flow charts for dialogue specification, it is probably best to employ a set of box types which reflect user-oriented actions.

Figure 8.11 shows a flow chart as used by one of the authors, some years ago, for specifying dialogues for forms based COBOL programs. The dialogue shown is a portion of a personnel database update system and is the sub-dialogue for deletion of records. The chart employs two main types of boxes — the rectangular boxes are 'screen images' of the forms used to communicate with the user. The angular boxes are the processes and decisions made by the system. In addition, there is an elliptical 'finish' box, where the user is returned to the main menu, and little 'tape' symbols which represent where the system reads or updates the database.

The dialogue starts with a form D1, which asks the user for an employee number. When this has been given the system reads in the relevant record, and displays it to the user for confirmation (form D2). If the user responds 'Y' to the question 'delete (Y/N)?' the record is deleted. If the user does not answer 'Y' or 'N', the record is redisplayed (form D3) with the error message 'Please enter Y or N'. Of course, in a real system there would be a similar loop around form D1 if the user entered a non-existent employee number.

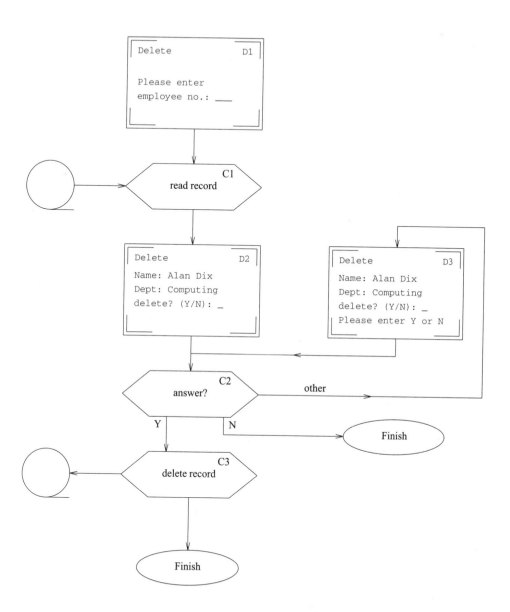

Figure 8.11   *Flow chart of deletion sub-dialogue*

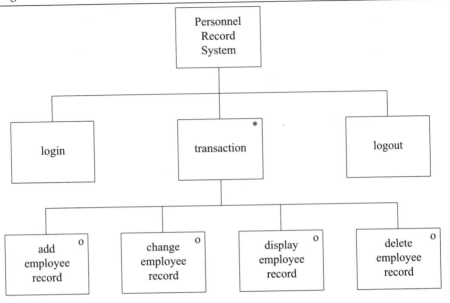

Figure 8.12 *JSD diagram for personnel system*

The big difference between using a flow chart for dialogue design and using it for program design is the level of detail on the program side. If, for example, reading the employee record involved a sequential search through the file to find the relevant record, a program flow chart would include this loop. For the dialogue, this would neither be necessary, nor appropriate. That is, that actual *program* flow chart would look nothing like this *dialogue* flow chart.

8.3.7 *JSD diagrams*

Of course, virtually any diagrammatic (or textual) notation employed in programming or system design can be recruited for dialogue design. *Jackson structured design* (JSD), while not as old as flow charts, has been around for many years. During that time it has developed significantly; however, it is one of the older parts of this methodology, the *JSD diagram*, which has been used for various aspects of task analysis and dialogue design. As with flow charts, there may be an advantage to using JSD diagrams if they are already familiar to the programmers who will implement the dialogue.

Figure 8.12 shows a JSD diagram for the top level structure of an employee personnel system. The system allows the user to update the personnel record in various ways: adding new employees, displaying, altering and removing existing ones.

The diagram looks rather like the hierarchical task analysis diagrams we saw in Section 7.3. However, the basic JSD diagram is somewhat more precise in its meaning. If we look at the top of the diagram, we see that the personnel system is decomposed into three parts, login, transactions and logout. These are implicitly in sequence left to right. That is, you are not allowed to do any transactions until you login!

The login and logout are assumed to be quite simple, so the diagram only expands the transaction node. Under this are listed the various transaction types: add, change, display and delete.

Some of the boxes have a little asterisk or 'o' in their top right hand corner. Without these decorations the diagram would represent a system which allowed you to login, then add, change, display and delete once each in that order and then logout. The decorations change this meaning. The asterisk represents iteration — any number of repetitions. That is, the dialogue can consist of a login followed by any number of transactions before the logout. The little 'o' represents optional elements. That is, a transaction may be any one of the four options.

Taking the decorations into account, the diagram describes what we would expect of such a system: a login followed by any number of add, change, display or delete transactions, and finally a logout.

The class of dialogues which can be represented by simple JSD diagrams is rather limited, but includes many basic menu-driven information systems. Arguably, the simple form of such dialogues could be regarded as a positive asset, especially if the diagram sticks to the higher levels of dialogue specification.

8.3.8 *An example about time*

Some diagrammatic notations may be clear enough to be used in user documentation as well as in design. Figure 8.13 shows a state transition diagram for the major modes of a digital watch, taken from the instruction booklet. The booklet goes on to use some similar diagrams and some tabular descriptions of each of the modes (using the other two buttons).

The watch only has three buttons, and only one of these, button 'A', is used to move between modes. As the diagram is being used in documentation, the states are denoted by representations of the watch in the appropriate mode. This is a useful approach for any stage in the design process, and is similar to the use of screen images in the flow diagram in Figure 8.11.

There are four modes, and pressing the button A moves between the modes. However, the most common modes are the time display and stop watch. The dialogue is designed to make it easy to switch between these modes and difficult to slip accidentally into the time or alarm setting modes. To achieve this aim, pressing 'A' usually toggles between the two main modes. However, the watch's

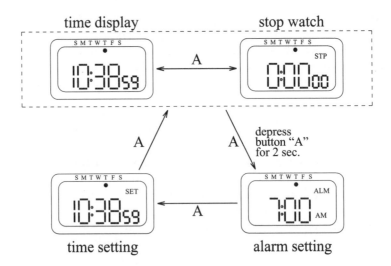

Figure 8.13 *Instructions for digital watch*

owner will want to set the time eventually, and the designer does not want another button to be used (buttons cost money and the watch only costs £2). Therefore, the setting modes are achieved by holding the button down for two or more seconds. So, a quick press does one thing, whereas a long one does something else. The semi-formal nature of a state transition diagram makes this *real-time* behaviour easy to denote. It is merely added as textual commentary.

However, this documentation diagram does not have all the information one would require for design purposes. If you are in the time setting mode and press 'A', what happens? Do you go to the time display or to the stop watch? Also, when going from time display to alarm setting, what do you see *during* the two seconds you hold down button 'A'?

After a little experimentation, one can generate the complete diagram, suitable for giving to the implementor of the watch electronics (Figure 8.14).

Notice that in order to deal adequately with the real-time behaviour, it is necessary to separate the depress and release events on button 'A'. This shows us that the toggle between time display and stop watch happens when the button is pressed down, but that each of these modes corresponds to two states, as the behaviour differs depending on the state of the button. From the diagram you can see that if you are in the time setting mode, then pressing 'A' will get you back to the time display, not to the stop watch. However, unexpectedly, if you do not release the button soon enough, you get back into the alarm setting mode.

Is this getting a little complicated? In fact it only represents about 10% of the instructions. This kind of time-dependent behaviour is rare in computer software,

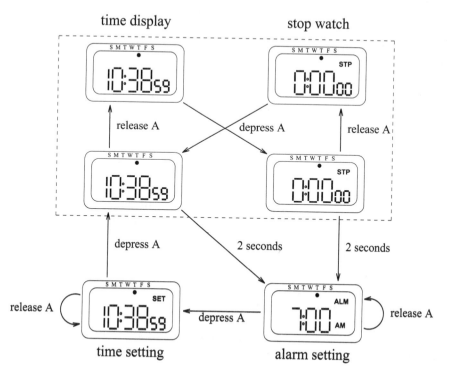

Figure 8.14 *Design diagram for digital watch*

but common in interfaces to consumer goods (watches, video controllers, control panels on white goods). This is because the number of buttons tends to be small compared to the number of functions. As we can see, in the presence of real-time behaviour even simple dialogues become complex. However, that is all the more reason for such dialogues to be *planned*. It is probably the case that the detailed design decisions above were taken as the watch was being programmed, not by the watch's designer. It is not surprising that many people cannot set the alarms or even change the time on their watch.

8.4 Textual Dialogue Notations

8.4.1 *Grammars*

As the images used for computer dialogue are linguistic, it is not surprising that formal grammars have been used as a dialogue notation.

BNF (Backus–Naur Form) is widely used to describe programming language syntax and we have already seen in Chapter 6 how descriptions of an interface can be used to measure its difficulty. The same description can be used to describe the dialogue for other purposes. In particular, there are several parser generators based upon BNF, such as the UNIX 'yacc' tool, which are suitable for producing crude prototypes.

As the BNF notation has been described in detail in Chapter 6, we will not repeat the description here. However, in order to compare it with other dialogue description notations, we recall that BNF has two connectives to denote *sequence* and *choice*. However, note that the use of '+' as a symbol for sequence in Chapter 6 is not standard — sequence is often simply represented by juxtaposition, and this convention will be followed in the examples below.

The definitions of named *non-terminals* gave a natural structure to the interface description. In addition, *recursive* definitions of non-terminals allowed the dialogue to represent *iteration*. However, BNF has no way of representing concurrent dialogues, nor can it easily deal with pervasive commands like escapes or help systems. Note, however, that both BNF and *regular expressions* (described below) are focused upon the user's actions, as opposed to the concentration upon the *state* in STNs.

Regular expressions are heavily used in editors to describe complex textual search criteria, and also in the *lexical analysis* of programming languages. They are similar to BNF but are slightly less powerful. However, their terseness and more easily computed behaviour make them very suitable for the above purposes. Unfortunately, the notation used within regular expressions differs from that used for similar concepts in BNF, and, to make matters worse, there are many different types of regular expression with many different notations. For example, when using the tools supplied with the UNIX operating system, there are at least three different notations. This may be particularly confusing, if, say, you are used to a particular editor's regular expression syntax, and then find a different syntax.

In text editors and lexical analyzers, the basic unit is the character. Often choice is only available at this level (e.g. [+-*/] represents any single arithmetic operator), and the whole notation is geared to rapid (for the expert), terse expression of relatively simple patterns. For example, 'Fred[.!?]' finds the name Fred when used at the end of a sentence. However, where regular expressions have been used in dialogue design, different criteria apply. The notation is less terse and tends to employ named sub-expressions (like non-terminals in BNF) for clarity. Unfortunately, this notation is slightly different again from both BNF and from other regular expressions.

As an example, we consider again the polyline drawing from Figure 8.1. This can be represented by the regular expression:

```
select-line click click* double-click
```

This says, that you must select the line option from the menu, click somewhere with the mouse, then click as many times as you like on intermediate points, and finally double click. It is assumed that the low-level terms `select-line`, `click` and `double-click` are either primitives, or have been defined elsewhere. The only other two notational forms that are used are sequencing, denoted by juxtaposition, and iteration, denoted by the *Kleene star* operator '*'. The former is similar to sequencing in BNF, it is the Kleene star operator which is characteristic of regular expressions.

In general, a regular expression of the form: *'thing*'*, means any number of *thing*, including none at all. To obtain the same effect in BNF, one would have to write:

```
some-things  ::=  thing + some-things
```

That is, BNF obtains the effect of iteration by using recursion. In regular expressions, iteration is primitive. However, this is the only way it can be obtained; even where regular expression-based notations allow named non-terminals, these are not allowed to be recursively defined. This means that there are some forms of pattern which it is possible to represent in BNF, but not in regular expressions, for instance, bracketing:

```
sentence  ::=  empty
            |  word sentence
            |  '(' sentence ')' sentence
```

No regular expression using Kleene star can express that the brackets must match. The best that you can do is say that the sentence is any number of words, open brackets or close brackets. In fact, regular expressions are as powerful in what they can express as state transition networks, it is just that BNF is more expressive. Whether that matters or not depends on whether the dialogues you want to represent include complex recursive elements such as bracket matching. Like STNs, neither BNF nor regular expressions can handle concurrent dialogues or escapes.

Where regular expressions have been used as a dialogue notation, they are confined to low levels of the dialogue, either the parsing of single lines of textual input, or the description of individual interface *widgets*. This is similar to the reflection that STNs are best used at this low level with different notation being used for high-level description.

One advantage of using BNF or regular expressions is that they are readily executed using existing tools. We have already mentioned the UNIX 'yacc' tool for BNF; there is also a tool 'lex' for compiling regular expressions. These tools are now also readily available on PCs. The tools are probably more suitable for parsing text commands than for graphical input. However, the execution techniques are so well understood that it is easy to write a prototyping tool if required.

8.4.2 *Production rules*

We have already encountered *production rules* as part of *CCT* in Chapter 6. They have also been used extensively to describe the dialogue component of *UIMS* (see Chapter 10). Recall that production rules are of the general form:

if *condition* then *action*

These rules are represented in various forms, for instance:

condition → *action*
condition: *action*

All rules are normally active and the system constantly matches the *condition* part of the rules against the user-initiated events which have occurred and its own memory. When the conditions of a rule becomes true, the rule is said to *fire* and the action part is executed. The action may take the form of a response to the user, or a change to the system's memory. Note especially that the order in which the rules are written is *not* important, any rule can fire at any time, so long as its condition part is true.

Production rule systems may be *event-* or *state*-oriented, or a mixture. We will consider first an event-oriented system, and describe again the polyline drawing part of Figure 8.1:

```
Sel-line            →   start-line <highlight 'line'>
C-point start-line  →   rest-line <rubber band on>
C-point rest-line   →   rest-line <draw line>
D-point rest-line   →   <draw line> <rubber band off>
```

Notice that in this example the condition and action parts of the production rules take the simple form of a set of event names (again, the order of events does not matter). These events are of three types:

user events which begin in upper case. These are Sel-line (user selects the 'line' option from the menu) C-point and D-point which represent the user single and double clicking on the drawing surface.

internal events which begin in lower case. These are used by the dialogue to keep track of the dialogue state, for example, rest-line is the state after the first point on the polyline has been selected.

system response events enclosed in angle brackets, such as <draw line>, These are the visible or audible effects of the system.

The dialogue manager which executes this form of production rule has a memory consisting of a set of events. A rule fires if the events named in its condition are all present in the memory. All interaction with the user is mediated by this event memory: user events, such as a mouse click, are added to the memory, and system responses, such as <draw line> are removed and acted upon by the display controller.

When a rule fires, all the events named in the condition are removed from the system's memory, and the events named in the action are added to it. For example, if the user has just selected the line option from the menu, the system's memory will contain Sel-line. This means that the first rule can fire. Sel-line is then removed from the memory and replaced by start-line and <highlight 'line'>. Finally, the display controller removes the <highlight 'line'> and performs the action. This leaves the system memory with only start-line in it, and so no more rules can fire until the user does something more.

The event-oriented nature of these production rules is evident in the way that events are removed from memory if they are used in the condition of a rule. The event has been 'dealt with' and can therefore be forgotten. This makes permanent status information difficult to represent. Notice in the third rule how the event rest-line is mentioned in both condition and action. It represents the state where additional points on the line are being selected after the first point. The rule is fired by a single click, which means that more points remain to be selected. The system must therefore continue in the same state. However, because the rest-line event has been mentioned in the condition it will be removed and therefore it must be re-established in the action part.

State-oriented production rules have a very different behaviour. The system's memory is again a set of named values, but these are not removed by default when a rule is fired; instead they must be removed explicitly by the action part of a rule. The production rules in *CCT* operate in this fashion, as evidenced by actions such as (DELETE-GOAL insert space). A specific example of a state-oriented production system, slightly different from CCT rules, is Olsen's *propositional production system* (PPS) [132]. In PPS, the system's state is divided into a finite set of attributes, each of which can take one of a set of values. Some of the attributes are set as the result of user actions, and others have an effect on the system's display.

In the polyline drawing example we could have five attributes:

Mouse:	{ mouse-off, select-line, click-point, double-click }
Line-state:	{ menu, start-line, rest-line }
Rubber-band:	{ rubber-band-off, rubber-band-on }
Menu:	{ highlight-off, highlight-line, highlight-circle }
Draw:	{ draw-nothing, draw-line }

The first attribute, **Mouse**, is set automatically whenever the user performs the relevant action; the second attribute is used by the dialogue to keep track of its state, and the last three are for controlling system responses. Again, we assume a display controller which acts appropriately upon these.

The PPS rules for polyline are somewhat similar to the previous event based rules:

select-line	$\rightarrow$	mouse-off start-line highlight-line
click-point start-line	$\rightarrow$	mouse-off rest-line rubber-band-on
click-point rest-line	$\rightarrow$	mouse-off draw-line
double-click rest-line	$\rightarrow$	mouse-off menu draw-line rubber-band-off

The rules are executed again, when the condition matches the state, but, this time, the attributes are not changed by this alone. Only when a new value is set for a particular attribute is the old value lost. For example, in the second rule, the action 'rest-line' sets the **Line-state** attribute, thus removing the previous value of 'start-line'. Notice, that in the third rule, the value 'rest-line' of the attribute **Line-state** need not be mentioned in the action as it was in the event based rules. This is because it persists by default.

The persistence of attributes has some rather odd effects on the user's input events. Each rule has to reset the **Mouse** attribute explicitly. Consider what would happen if this was not done. If the second rule fired, but did not have the 'mouse-off' action, then the system's memory would include the attribute binding **Mouse**=click-point (as it has not been reset) and **Line-state**=rest-line (set in the action of rule 2). This means that the third rule would be able to fire immediately, and, if it also did not reset **Mouse**, would continue to fire indefinitely without any further user actions whatsoever.

An appeal to formal simplicity would demand one used either purely event-oriented or purely state-oriented production rules, as it is always possible to get any effect with either. However, we can see from these two examples that some aspects of the dialogue are best described using events and others are best described using attributes. Hence a mixed notation involving both events and state is to be preferred. Several variants of production rules (and some STNs) allow both, for example, allowing rules of the form:

event: condition $\rightarrow$ *action*

The event (or possibly events) triggers the rule, but the rule does not fire unless the condition, which checks the state part of the system's memory, is also true. The event is reset by default, but the state attributes are unchanged, unless they are explicitly set by the action. As well as changing the memory state, the action may itself generate new events, which may then trigger further rules.

Concurrent dialogue elements may be represented easily using production systems as many rules may be active at the same time. For example, we can describe the bold/italic/underline dialogue box of Figure 8.4, using mixed event/state production rules. We have three attributes:

Bold:	{ off, on }
Italic:	{ off, on }
Underline:	{ off, on }

There are also three possible events, depending on which style the user clicks over: *select-bold, select-italic, select-under*. The six rules defining the dialogue box are then:

select-bold:	**Bold**=off	$\rightarrow$	**Bold**=on
select-bold:	**Bold**=on	$\rightarrow$	**Bold**=off
select-italic:	**Italic**=off	$\rightarrow$	**Italic**=on
select-italic:	**Italic**=on	$\rightarrow$	**Italic**=off
select-under:	**Underline**=off	$\rightarrow$	**Underline**=on
select-under:	**Underline**=on	$\rightarrow$	**Underline**=off

These are (although somewhat uninteresting) exactly what one would expect, and, unlike *state transition networks*, the number of rules only increases linearly with the number of toggles. If there are n toggles, then there will be $2n$ rules — substantially better than networks with 2^n states!

Also, escapes can be handled by having a rule of the form:

escape-key: $\rightarrow$ reset-action

where 'reset-action' involves setting all state attributes to some standard value. Because of the continuous activity of each rule, this escape rule can fire at any stage of the dialogue, whenever the user hits the escape key.

Although production rules are good at handling concurrency, they are not so good at sequential dialogues. The polyline drawing is a case in point. We want the user to perform actions in order: select 'line', click at first point, click at any number of intermediate points (including none) and then double click at the end point. However, to represent this simple sequence using a production system, we need to keep track of the current place in the sequence using some 'state' variable. In the examples this was the state attribute **Line-state** in the PPS description and the events 'start-line' and 'rest-line' in the event-oriented rules. This representation of sequence is both awkward to 'code' and difficult to analyze.

Where production rules are used as the dialogue description within a UIMS or other prototyping tool, various extensions to the simple forms described are used. Variables are added to the state to describe numeric values such as the mouse position. We saw this in CCT with the 'binding' of the variables %LINE and %COL. Different precedence rules are used to decide which of several production rules, which could potentially fire, will fire first. This enables help systems and pre-emptive dialogue boxes to be programmed. For example, in a word-processor, we may give rules for the help system higher priority than those for the normal system. Hence an event, such as a cursor movement, which would normally refer to the movement of the cursor in the document, would instead be 'caught' by the rules for the help system.

8.4.3 *CSP and event algebras*

We have seen notations such as *state transition networks* which are very good at handling sequential dialogue, but weak on concurrency, and *production rules* which are good at the opposite. The problem of dealing with both sequential and concurrent behaviour is common to many other areas of computing, such as telecommunications protocols and concurrent programming. We have already seen how one notation, Harel's *state charts*, which was designed with such complex systems in mind, has been used in interface design. *Process algebras* are a class of formal notations which have been developed to handle similar situations. One of these, *CSP* (*Communicating Sequential Processes*), has been adopted for dialogue specification as part of several formalisms, including Alexander's *SPI* [4] and Abowd's *Agents* [1].

The CSP notation is used because it is able to specify concurrency and sequence equally well, and because of its readability. We consider again the drawing tool from Figure 8.1, which demonstrates sequence and choice. The CSP description is as follows:

```
Draw-menu   =   ( select-circle?  → Do-circle
                [] select-line?   → Do-line )
Do-circle   =   click?  → set-centre → click?
                → draw-circle → skip
Do-line     =   Start-line ; Rest-line
Start-line  =   click?  → first-point → skip
Rest-line   =   ( click?   → next-point → Rest-line
                [] double-click?  → last-point → skip )
```

The events marked with a question mark are the user's mouse actions, the rest being internal system events. The description is built using four symbols '=' meaning definition, '→' event sequence (or guard), ';' process sequence and [] choice. The names in the dialogue denote *events* (all lower case) or *processes* (initial upper case). The processes roughly correspond to non-terminals in a grammar and are used both for structuring the dialogue description and also to give named points to go back to in recursion (for example, Rest-line).

The definition of Do-circle is a pure sequence. When the system executes Do-circle, it first takes a user mouse click, then does an internal event, set-centre, to record the mouse position, accepts a second click, draws the circle and is finished (shown by the special process symbol **skip**). Do-line is a sequence too, but has been written using the process sequencing symbol ';'. This is used between two processes, as opposed to '→' which is used after an event.

For an example of choice, look at the first line: Draw-menu is defined to be a choice of two options, a circle or a line. The choice is made by considering the events just after the choice ([]), select-circle? and select-line?. The first event to happen determines the choice. If the user does select-circle?, that is, selects the 'circle' option on the menu, then the `Do-circle` process is executed. Alternatively, if the user selects the line option (`select-line?`), the system executes `Do-line`.

The `Do-line` process begins by executing `Start-line`, which gets the initial point on the line, and then executes `Rest-line` getting one or more further points for the polyline. `Rest-line` is the only *recursive* definition. If we read through its definition, we have a choice. If the user double clicks, then the polyline is drawn and the process is finished. Alternatively, if the point is only single clicked, then it is processed (`next-point`) and the system repeats `Rest-line`.

So far this is pretty much like a BNF description, just with slightly different operator symbols and names for things. The new operator is | | indicating parallel composition. If we have two processes P and Q then P| |Q is the *interleaving* of P and Q. To see the use of this operator, we consider again the dialogue box example. We code the individual toggles:

```
Bold-toggle     =  select-bold?  → bold-on
                       → select-bold?  → bold-off
                       → Bold-toggle
Italic-toggle  =  select-italic?  → italic-on
                       → select-italic?  → italic-off
                       → Italic-toggle
Under-toggle   =  select-under?  → under-on
                       → select-under?  → under-off
                       → Under-toggle
```

The event `select-bold?` represents the user selecting the bold toggle with a mouse. So, the process `Bold-toggle` then turns the bold style on and off with alternate selections. The italic and underline options behave similarly. The dialogue box as a whole can then be represented as the parallel composition of the individual toggles:

```
Dialogue-box
     =  Bold-toggle || Italic-toggle || Under-toggle
```

Concurrent processes can also be used as a way of organizing the internal structure of the interface. For example, returning to the drawing tool, we may decide that we would like to allow keyboard short cuts activated by the 'ALT' key. As the line and circle options can be operated by the mouse or by the keyboard, we have a process for each. The mouse process simply waits for the user to select one or other menu option, and then performs an internal event depending on the choice. The keyboard process monitors the ALT key, and performs the same internal events depending on whether the user enters ALT-C or ALT-L:

```
Mouse      =  ( select-circle?  → int-sel-circle → Mouse
              [] select-line?   → int-sel-line → Mouse )
Keyboard   =  alt-key-down?  → ( Alt ; Keyboard )
Alt        =  ( alt-key-up?  → skip
              [] c-key?  → int-sel-circle → Alt
              [] l-key?  → int-sel-line → Alt )
```

So an `int-sel-circle` event may occur either because the circle option is selected from the menu or because the user typed ALT-C. The existing definition of `Draw-menu` expects to be activated by the user's mouse selections directly, so this must be modified to accept these new internal events.

```
Draw-menu   =  ( int-sel-circle → Do-circle
               [] int-sel-line → Do-line )
```

The three processes can now be run in parallel:

```
Mouse || Keyboard || Draw-menu
```

Note that the events `int-sel-circle` and `int-sel-line` are used to *communicate*, sending messages from the `Mouse` and `Keyboard` processes to the `Draw-menu` process. However, although this direction of causality is obvious from context, it is not immediately apparent from the notation. The only clue is that the events form the guards of the choice operator in the `Draw-menu` process, but that is not an infallible indication. The reason for this ambiguity is that CSP does not recognize causality, events are simply *synchronization* points. There are times when such an interpretation is useful, but in most dialogue descriptions the causality is important. One way to avoid this problem is to match events in pairs, as is done in some other process algebras writing, for instance, `int-sel-line!` for the sending of an event and `int-sel-line?` for the receiving of it. This loses us the special decoration for direct user input, but these may be listed separately. Alternatively, if the notation is to be typeset rather than in straight ASCII, one can use other pairs, such as x↑ and x↓ for send and receive.

8.4.4 *Parametrized and dynamic interleaved dialogue structure*

In many interfaces, the possible screen displays can be easily enumerated. The order in which such screens are produced, and the detailed contents of fields may differ, but the basic screen designs are finite. Other systems are more anarchic, especially multi-windowed interfaces where user interaction may dynamically cause the creation of new windows. Thus there is a clear difference between static and dynamic screen presentations.

A similar and related issue arises at the level of the dialogue structure. Some dialogues can be described by a finite set of dialogue states between which the user may move, whereas others are far more complex. Clearly, multi-windowed systems will have a correspondingly dynamic dialogue structure. Perhaps the dialogues within each window have a fairly static structure, but the number of such interleaved dialogues varies at run time.

The notations we have discussed can only address structurally static dialogues. Such notations would not (without modification) allow the expression of general multi-windowed dialogues. However, many *WIMP*-based systems do not require this level of generality. In addition, many run-time systems may only allow essentially static structures, for instance, prototypes programmed in HyperCard (except for very complex scripts) or under most forms based systems.

This issue of dynamic dialogue structure is often linked with that of parametrization. An instantiation of a parametrized dialogue often involves the creation of new screen resources. For example, we could imagine extending eventCSP to allow

```
Multi-window-editor
    =  new-name(name)  →
              ( Edit-window(name) [] Multi-window-editor )
```

The instantiation of `Edit_window(name)` implies that a new window and dialogue within that window would be initiated.

Both parametrization and dynamic dialogue structures make it more difficult to analyze the dialogue. A static notation has a sparser (and fundamentally less expressive) domain of application but allows a far greater degree of automatic or manual manipulation.

Thus, even where a notation allows parametrized or dynamic dialogues, they should be used sparingly. If there is a choice, the dialogue should be encoded using the more static forms of representation.

8.5 Dialogue Semantics

If the purpose of a dialogue description is simply to communicate between designers, or as a 'tool for thought' early in design it may be sufficient to annotate the formal dialogue with the intended meaning of the actions, or to leave it to the reader to infer the semantics. However, if the dialogue description is to serve as a formal specification, perhaps part of a contract, or for running as a prototype, there must be some way to describe formally the semantics of the dialogue. The dialogue notations we have seen, more or less clearly describe the structure of the dialogue. We must now move on to meaning.

There are two aspects to the dialogue semantics, inward towards the application, and outward towards the presentation. The semantic part of the dialogue should serve as a link between the two, performing as little as possible itself. Look back through the examples in this chapter and ask yourself how one knows that, for example, the lines drawn by the drawing tool are at the points indicated by the user's mouse location.

We will discuss three different approaches to linking dialogue and semantics:

notation-specific semantics special-purpose semantic forms designed as part of a dialogue notation.

links to programming languages attaching pieces of programming language code to the dialogue.

links to specification notations similar, but where a formal specification notation is used.

We will also discuss some issues which arise concerning the link between dialogue and semantics.

8.5.1 *Notation-specific semantics*

Augmented transition networks (ATN) are a form of *state transition network* (see Section 8.3.1). In the ATN, the system is assumed to hold a set of *registers*, storage locations which the transition network can set and test. Recall that the arcs in an STN may be labelled with the event that causes the transition and the system response. In an ATN this is extended. The arcs have a condition as well as the event; the condition can refer to the system's registers and the arc is only followed if the condition is true and the event occurs. The system response is augmented to include not only feedback and display, but also the setting of registers. These registers can be used simply to describe more complex dialogues, for example, a cash dispenser which retains your card after three wrong numbers. They may also be used to communicate with the application and to hold values from the mouse.

Production rules come in many variants and the link to the semantics is equally varied. Often the system's memory contains variables which can be used by the system to store input values such as the mouse position, and can then be examined by the conditions and actions of the rules. These variables may also be used to communicate with the underlying application, or the functions of this may be invoked directly by special forms of action. For instance, the following is a production rule which, when the user clicks within a target region, puts a dot at the mouse location and invokes the application routine 'another_point':

click_at(x, y) $\rightarrow$ dot_at(x, y), **call** another_point(x, y)

8.5.2   *Links to programming languages*

Often dialogue notations are 'attached' to a conventional programming language. For example, *input tools*, a regular expression based notation, uses C to express the dialogue semantics [179] The input tool description consists of 'tool' definitions, including regular expressions intermingled with normal C code. For example, the tool to read a number (from Plasmeijer [139]) begins as follows:

```
tool number
{   char buf[80];
    int index;
    int positive;

    input { ( digit* + sign; digit; digit*) ; return }

    tool digit
    {   input { key:| key_c>='0' && key_c<='9' | }

        if ( index < 79 )   /* append character to string */
        {    buf[index] = key_c;
             index = index + 1;
             echo(key_c);
        }
    }
    tool sign
    . . .
    tool return
    {   input { key:| key_c == '\n' | }
        . . .
    }
    . . .
}
```

Input tools uses its own regular expression syntax and has additional operators. Sequencing is denoted by semi-colon ';' rather than simple juxtaposition, and the '+' symbol is used for choice (like '|' in BNF). The expression 'key : |*condition*|' is a postfix guard: the expression only matches if the condition is true.

The specific input tools' expressions are as follows. The keyword tool introduces a new tool, which is similar to a non-terminal in a BNF grammar, and the regular expression which it denotes is enclosed in the input statement. The tools are arranged in a scoped hierarchy, so that the digit, sign and return tools are private to the number tool. The call to echo simply echoes the character back to the user. Finally, key is a primitive tool which matches a single character read from the keyboard, the actual character read is stored in the global variable key_c.

Notice how the sub-tool `digit` communicates its results back to the main tool using shared variable `buf`. This and the way it accepts values from the `key` tool are rather untidy. Such messiness is not just an aspect of this particular notation: alternative regular expression based notations are even worse!

8.5.3   *Links to formal specification*

Alexander's executable specification/prototyping language *SPI* (*Specifying and Prototyping Interaction*) is divided into two parts: *eventCSP*, a dialogue notation based closely on CSP, and *eventISL*, which describes the dialogue semantics.   The CSP part is as described in Section 8.4.3, but for each event there is a corresponding event definition in eventISL. EventISL, is partly standardized and partly dependent on the 'host' language chosen. The first host language was *me-too*, a formal specification notation based on VDM, but a 'C' variant is also available. The part which is independent of the host language consists of several elements: a clause giving the global variables used and updated by the event, a pre-condition expressing when the event can occur, and output and input parts. The host language part simply describes the updates, and the precise outputs.

Consider the following eventCSP description of a login sequence:

Login	=	login-mess → get-name → Passwd
Passwd	=	passwd-mess → (invalid → Login
		[] valid → Session)
Session	=	(logout → Login
		[] command → execute → Session)

A typical unsuccessful login sequence might be:

```
login:   fred
passwd:   b9fGk              (invisible)
Sorry bad user-id/password
```

We will not consider the detailed semantics for the commands during the session, but will give the eventISL descriptions of the other events. The two events login-mess and get-name handle the first line of the above dialogue:

event: login-mess =
      prompt: true
      out: "login:"

event: get-name =
uses: input
      set: user-id = input

The first event prints the prompt 'login:' (the **out:** clause) and says that user input is required (the **prompt:** clause). This user input is stored in a special variable called 'input'. The second event **uses** the input (which will be set to the name the user enters) and merely sets the variable 'user-id' to it. Note that 'user-id' is **set** to a new value by the event, but any previous value is not **used**.

The sequence for getting the password is similar except that there are two options depending on whether the user has typed a valid password or not:

```
event: passwd-mess =
        prompt: invis
        out: "passwd:"

event: valid =
uses: input, user-id, passwd-db =
        when: passwd-id = passwd-db(user-id)

event: invalid =
uses: input, user-id, passwd-db =
        when: passwd-id ≠ passwd-db(user-id)
        out: "Sorry bad user-id/password"
```

The password prompt is identical to the login prompt except that no echoing is required. However, the last two events demonstrate two additional features. As well as the user input variable, they also use the variable 'user-id', which was set by the `get-name` event, and the variable 'passwd-db'. This is assumed to be a database of passwords, so that 'passwd-db(user-id)' is the correct password for the user. The two events also have a '**when**' clause. This is a *precondition*, which specifies what must be true for the event to occur. So the 'valid' event can only occur when the user has typed a correct password and 'invalid' only occurs when it is incorrect.

Notice that, like input tools, eventISL is heavily dependent on the use of global variables to pass information between events. This reliance on global variables in many dialogue notations strikes against all good software engineering practice. At least in SPI the globals used and updated are made explicit and make tracing the effects of events somewhat easier, but still not straightforward. Dialogue notations often include effective structuring mechanisms (hierarchical networks, non-terminals in grammars, processes in CSP); it is a pity that these are not mirrored in their semantic effects.

8.5.4 *Distributed and centralized dialogue description*

If the dialogue is described by a pure grammar, with no semantic element, then it is easy to look at the dialogue syntax in isolation, and understand and evaluate it. At the other extreme, if we take a typical interactive program, aspects of the dialogue will be distributed throughout the code, making it difficult to trace the course of a typical interaction.

A notation that wishes to describe the semantics of dialogue as well as its syntax can try to retain the advantages of a simple syntactic description, by separating the semantic and syntactic parts, allowing the dialogue designer to examine the dialogue syntax in isolation. This is a *centralized dialogue description*. Alexander's SPI is exemplary of this approach to the extent that it has separate sub-languages for the two parts. This also demonstrates another advantage of this approach. The same form of the syntactic dialogue description may often be suitable both for high-level analysis and automatic coding (or run-time interpretation). The semantic description, on the other hand, is likely to have a different form when generated for specification or prototyping than for inclusion in a production system. Separating the two allows reuse of the dialogue description with different semantic parts, reflecting differing uses of the specification.

Alternatively, the notation can choose to put associated parts of the syntax and semantics together, as in *input-tools*. This has the advantage that parts of the interaction can be examined in detail, allowing the evaluation of the syntax and semantics in tandem. It also has advantages of abstraction; associated semantics and syntax can be packaged together. Its disadvantage is that, like the typical program, it has a *distributed dialogue description*. One has to examine diverse pieces of the specification in order to obtain an understanding of the large scale flow of the interaction.

The two approaches are not fundamentally incompatible. Given a notation of the former type, it would be quite easy to separate parts of the dialogue syntax and present them with the associated parts of the semantic description. Similarly, with some distributed notations it is possible to go through extracting the parts specifying the dialogue syntax and look at these together. For instance, with input-tools one could extract all the `input` clauses which contain the regular expression sub-tool syntax. These would then form the centralized dialogue for analysis.

8.5.5 *Maximizing syntactic description*

Extracting the dialogue structure is only possible with some notations. The reason why it is not always possible, and is not usually possible for general interactive programs, is itself an important issue. Usually it is possible to isolate the parts that are responsible for input and output (identifiable by `print`, `read`, etc.). However, how these fit together into a dialogue is masked by the surrounding code. In particular, what would be syntactic in a dedicated dialogue grammar description may be coded semantically. For instance, in eventCSP, one could write:

```
Text-editor   =   mouse-press → set-selection
               [] key-press → add-char-to-text
```

In a programming language one might have:

```
ev = read_event();
if ( ev.type == EV_mouse_press )
                  set_selection(ev.pos);
else              add_char_to_text(ev.char);
```

In the second version an analyzer would have to recognize that the boolean expression `ev.type == EV_mouse_press` corresponded to a simple dialogue decision rather than a deep semantic decision in the application.

Even more problems may arise in production systems, window managers or UIMS with *external control*, that is where the application is invoked on each event from the user (see Chapter 10). In these systems, the most obvious form of dialogue is completely user-controlled. If the designer wishes to provide any control over the input syntax then a 'program counter' must be explicitly coded. So, for instance, if we were operating under a window manager that calls a user routine `process_event`, we might have the following code for text editor selection (written in C):

```
enum { normal, selected }  mode;

process_event( event ev )
{
  switch ( ev.type ) {
    case  button_down:
        ...
        if ( in_text ( ev.pos ) ) {
            mode = selecting;
            mark_selection_start(ev.pos);
        }
        ...
    case  button_up:
        ...
        if ( in_text ( ev.pos ) && mode == selecting ) {
            mode = normal;
            mark_selection_end(ev.pos);
        }
        ...
    case  mouse_move:
        ...
        if ( mode == selecting ) {
            extend_selection(ev.pos);
        }
        ...
    }  /* end of switch */
}  /* end of process_event */
```

The dialogue for the selection is distributed widely over the event loop, and further it is only by keeping track of the `mode` variable that we can see that they are linked at all. The code is for a mythical but quite typical window manager.

In each case, the problem is that elements of the dialogue can be given either a syntactic or a semantic form. Obviously more complex elements of the dialogue will require complex computed decisions, but where possible, the more syntactic the dialogue description, the easier to analyze it will be. This concept underlies much of database normalization procedures which try to move the decision as to whether an update is acceptable from the semantic realm to the syntactic.

8.6   Dialogue Analysis and Design

In this section, we will look at several ways in which dialogues can be analyzed in order to discover potential usability problems, considering principles such as those described in Chapter 4. We will discuss these dialogue properties under three headings. The first focuses on user actions and whether they are adequately specified and consistent. The second concerns the dialogue states, including those you want to get to and those you do not. Finally, we will look at presentation and lexical issues, what things look like and what keys do what. Some of these properties have equivalents in Chapter 9, where we discuss models of interactive systems which include semantics.

8.6.1   *Action properties*

Look back to the STNs describing a graphics program (Figures 8.1–8.3) at the beginning of Section 8.3. There are four types of user action in these diagrams. Selecting from the main menu (graphics, text or paint), selecting a pop-up menu choice (circle or line), clicking on a point on the drawing surface and double clicking a point on the drawing surface.

If we look at the different dialogue states, we see that for any state only one or two actions are mentioned. Sometimes this is because some actions are impossible. For example, the pop-up menu choices can only happen while a pop-up menu is displayed. So, we do not need to worry about the user doing 'select "line" ' from the *Main menu* or while in state *Line 1*. But, what happens if we click on the drawing surface whilst at the Main menu, or try to select something from the main menu whilst in the middle of the drawing a circle, say in state *Circle 2*? The dialogue description is not *complete*.

If you take an actual system and try such odd combinations it is likely that the dialogue description starts to explode in complexity, just as in the example of the digital watch. It was reasonable to have a partial description for the purposes of instruction, and for discussing the general dialogue structure. But we need to make sure that these odd chains of events do not have disastrous consequences. Unfortunately, in practice, it is at best the implementor and, at worst, the user who discovers such behaviour. This is wrong. It is the responsibility of the designer to foresee just how the system behaves in unforeseen circumstances.

Surely it is a contradiction in terms to design for behaviour under *unforeseen* circumstances? Yes, but the presence of a dialogue description can make previously unforeseen events become apparent. Just as with the graphics STNs, we can, in general, list all the possible actions and then at each dialogue state look for 'forgotten events'. This can be done with any notation, but some are easier than others. In particular, it may be extremely difficult to perform such an analysis of a production rule system without automatic help. Furthermore, the structure of production rules may mean that you accidentally specify behaviour — what you say may not be what you mean.

For each unforeseen state/action pair, the designer ought to decide (or at least check during testing) what the behaviour will be. The simplest rule is to decide that all unspecified behaviour will have no effect (except possibly a warning) — when in doubt 'do nowt'. If this rule is not followed, more care is required. Imagine the user is drawing a polyline, but, before double clicking on the last point, selects a new option from the main menu. One option is to discard the partially completed line. If the user had only clicked on one point, this would be the only sensible option. However, if the user has just carefully selected 20 points and simply forgotten to double click on the last one, tempers may get frayed. A better option would be to treat the new selection as confirming the partially completed shape whenever this is at all sensible.

As well as finding that some states have forgotten actions, we may discover that some states have several arcs labelled with the same action. That is, the specification is not *deterministic* for that action. This can happen in several ways. It may be an accident. For example, if we are using a hierarchical STN with escapes, as in Figure 8.8, we may find that we have used an action as an escape at a high level, and for some other purpose at a lower level. Similarly, when using production rules, one may accidentally find that two rules are active at the same time triggered by the same event. The formalism may have default rules to deal with such eventualities. For example, both production rules may fire, or there may be a precedence between rules, the one with the highest precedence being chosen. Similarly, the STN may take the innermost arc. However, this is precisely where you should check that this default behaviour is what you want.

Sometimes, this non-determinism reflects semantic decisions in the system. For example, a grammar for a bank automated teller machine (ATM) might look like:

```
atm          ::= put-in-card get-number
get-number ::= digit digit  digit digit
                      get-money return-card atm
             | digit digit digit digit return-card atm
             | digit digit digit digit atm
digit        ::= 0 | 1 | 2 | 3 | 4 | 5 | 6 | 7 | 8 | 9
get-money  ::=   ...
```

The two different options depend on whether the digits entered are the correct PIN number. In the first case they are and the user gets some money out. In the second, the number is wrong and the card is returned. In the last case, too many wriong numbers have been used and the card is retained. Deciding which of the branches to take is a *semantic* issue, not one of dialogue structure.

Both *completeness* and *determinism* can be automatically checked in a dialogue description. However, the designer must go through the warnings thrown up by such an analysis and decide whether they represent a problem or are deliberate.

A third property, which cannot be automatically checked as easily, is *consistency*. We expect the same action in different circumstances to do roughly the same thing. For example, a user may get used to the 'tab' key moving the cursor eight spaces to the right. However, in a text entry area of a dialogue box, most text editing keys may behave as normal, but 'tab' may move to the next dialogue box entry. Such examples of inconsistency can cause obvious problems for the user. It is not possible to automate checks for consistency on a dialogue description. Firstly, this is because consistency also involves the semantics: similar actions should *do similar things*. Secondly, the interpretation of *similar* involves an understanding of what the user regards as similar.

However, by listing all dialogue states and actions, a dialogue description can help the analyst to go through the various combinations. In particular, the analyst can divide the states into major *modes* where actions may have different effects or be inactive. For example, in a word-processor, the search/replace key may not be active in the 'print' dialogue box.

8.6.2   *State properties*

The states in a dialogue represent points where the user has obtained information or where the system has done something useful. So, the user wants at least to be able to get to a desired dialogue state and ideally to be able to get there easily. In general, we can think of properties of this sort as *reachability*.

A basic check of any dialogue is whether it is fully connected. That is, for any two states is there a sequence of actions which will take the user from the first state to the second. Looking once more at Figures 8.1 and 8.3, we can see that, insofar as it is defined, the dialogue is connected. For example, suppose we were in state *Circle 1*, but wished we were back at the graphics sub-menu (state *Menu*). We can click and then double click anywhere on the drawing surface, taking us to the end of graphics sub-menu STN and back to the *Main Menu*. From here, we can select the 'graphics' option and get to where we want.

However, one suggested 'improvement' was to alter the circle drawing to allow multiple circles. The amendment was shown in Figure 8.2. Unfortunately, this destroys the connectivity of the dialogue. There is no way out of the circle dialogue, one can only fill up the screen with zillions of circles. This is a fairly obvious problem, but it is easy for more complex cases to slip through. For example, one of the authors was once shown a form-based financial planning system. Some inconsistent information was entered on one page of the form, which was allowed by the system. But, because of this, a later page was repeatedly rejected. There was no valid user input for that page, but the system would not allow you to return to the incorrectly filled page until the later one was accepted — *impasse*.

Reachability checking can be entirely automatic, but care must be taken to distinguish which choices are user controlled and which are system controlled. This is one reason why we emphasized the importance of maximizing syntactic description in a dialogue notation. In general, we cannot assume that the system will take the paths that we wish. So, for example, given the ATM dialogue, we cannot assume that the user can get from the atm state to the get-money state, as this depends on the system accepting the PIN number. An automatic tool can show where such unreachable points are, but the designer must say whether or not these are acceptable.

A special case of reachability is *reversability*, a form of *undo*. That is, the user wants to get to the previous state. For various reasons, some evident in Chapter 9, a dedicated 'undo' button or command is probably best dealt with as a meta-dialogue feature. However, we can analyze the existing commands to see how easy it is to recover one's position in the dialogue using standard commands. In effect, this is what we described at the beginning of this sub-section. We were on the *Circle 1* state of Figure 8.1, and wanted to get *back* to the graphics pop-up menu. Indeed, this was possible, but rather long winded. Any fully reachable dialogue will be able to reverse actions, but it may not be easy to do so. One form of reversability analysis is to take each action, and label it with the number of arcs that must be traversed in order to get back. Actions with large reversing costs are worthy of closer scrutiny: perhaps the dialogue ought to be re-designed to allow easier return paths, or possibly we may rely on a generic undo mechanism.

Note that this dialogue level reversability is *not* a true undo. For example, when the user goes from the *Circle 1* state back to the graphics menu, this leaves a circle behind on the screen. Thus the dialogue state has been undone, but the full system state has not. Reasoning about undo at this level requires a model of the

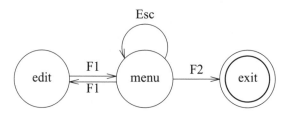

Figure 8.15   *Main modes of text editor*

system, and will be discussed in Chapter 9. There is also a corresponding more complete form of reachability in this setting.

So, there are some states that the user wants to be in, movement to which the dialogue ought to make easy. But, there are other states, such as that where the hard disk is being formatted, which should be deliberately difficult to reach. Again, knowing which states are 'dangerous' cannot be determined automatically, it depends on the system semantics and the designer's judgement. However, having labelled the dangerous states (coloured them red), we can perform analyses on the dialogue to determine how easy it is to get to these dangerous states. This labelling process may involve duplicating states which otherwise appear similar at the dialogue level.

For example, the text editor being used for this passage has two main modes, an editing screen where you type and edit the document, and a menu screen, obtained by pressing the 'F1' function key. The STN for these modes is shown in Figure 8.15. The menu screen has several options including 'F2' to exit (and save), and 'F1' to return to the editing screen. Exiting will automatically save the text if it has been changed. However, this can be overriden by pressing the escape key in the main menu. This makes the system pretend that the text has not been changed until the next alteration.

Pressing the escape key in the main menu has *no* effect on the dialogue, but the state of the system after this point can be thought of as dangerous. If the key has been pressed deliberately then all is well, but if there is any mistake, the user may lose the updated text. Figure 8.16 shows an STN with the dialogue states duplicated to show the dangerous states (hatched). We want the dangerous states to be reachable, but they should be difficult to get to by accident. In fact, the really dangerous state is when we go to the hatched exit: if we return to the hatched edit state, then we are most likely to type a further editing command and the system becomes 'safe' again. Therefore we can see that the particularly dangerous sequence is 'F1–Esc–F2'. The question then is: can this be typed by accident? It is very similar to the standard exit and save sequence 'F1–F2', but users are unlikely to hit the escape key by accident — or are they?

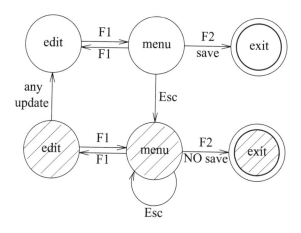

Figure 8.16   *Revised STN with dangerous states*

If we discover that a dangerous state is too easily reached, then we can attempt to prevent accidents. To do this, many systems initiate a dialogue with the user when a lot of information may be lost, for example:

```
C>del test\*.*
Are you sure (Y/N)?
```

This in itself is not enough to prevent mistakes as frequent requests for confirmation may make the user habitually type 'y' after every command. The moves to dangerous states must be different from other sequences — that is, *not* consistent! The moves between safe states and dangerous states really need detailed examination by the analyst, as one must decide whether a particular path can easily be taken by accident or not. We will see in remaining discussion that this is intimately connected to the presentation and lexical design of the system.

8.6.3   *Presentation and lexical properties*

It is often claimed that dialogue design should be independent of the detailed design of the presentation and lexical details of the interface. That is, one begins by deciding on the functionality of the system, then, possibly making use of cognitive models or task analysis, one designs the dialogue to perform those functions. Finally, one designs the visual presentation of the system and the lexical bindings between keypresses and mouse movement and the more abstract dialogue actions.

In fact, the dialogues described in this chapter have often involved detailed key bindings on their labels. For example, the STN for the graphics system in Figure 8.1 has arcs with labels such as 'click on point' or 'double click'. It could be argued that this is a fault in these descriptions. They should instead say things like 'enter a point', 'enter last point'. These actions could then be achieved with mouse clicks, or by typing coordinates.

For higher level descriptions, such as the JSD diagram in Figure 8.12, this form of argument is valid; it would be inappropriate, at least in early design, to decide what keys or menu selections will move you to the 'add employee record' sub-dialogue. However, later in design, and when we consider detailed dialogue, such a position becomes less tenable.

In sub-section 8.6.1, we discussed the labelling of *modes* in which user actions may have different interpretations. It is generally regarded as good practice to minimize the number of modes. However, where modes are used they should be visually distinct. That is, one ought to be able to tell which mode one is in from the computer display. So, the visual presentation, and the form of the dialogue are intimately connected. As well as major modes, one can compare any two dialogue states, and ask whether they can be distinguished from the display. If not, this may indicate a potential trouble spot where the user can get confused. These are both *visibility* requirements, and similar issues of *observability* and *predictability* will arise in Chapter 9.

The visibility issues are, in principle, one way the dialogue can be designed independently of the presentation, but can constrain the form of it. In practice, the two are more intermingled. However, there are further areas where the dialogue is even more intimately tied to presentation.

Different types of interfaces have very different dialogue styles. The normal dialogue form of a command based interface is verb–object, for example, 'print fred'. However, mouse based systems often have an object–verb syntax, for example, select a file icon and then select 'print' from a menu. Although it is possible to mingle these styles, it is inadvisable as users expect to find a certain interface style with a particular medium. So, detailed dialogue design must be dependent on the type of interface.

Furthermore, physical limitations may prohibit certain dialogue structures. For example, the dialogue for the digital watch (Figures 8.13 and 8.14) is designed with the restriction of only three buttons. A similar design for an on-screen alarm clock could make use of a full keyboard and thus have a completely different dialogue. Similarly, the range of outputs, visual and aural, will restrict the dialogue. If modes and states should be visually distinct then the device's display must be able to distinguish these modes. Unfortunately restricted input leads to a highly moded dialogue. For example, for three buttons to control all the functions of a digital watch with alarm and stop watch requires many modes, of which the four major modes are only the beginning. But it is precisely those interfaces which

Figure 8.17   *Dangerous function key layout*

have a limited input set which also have limited output, in particular consumer goods. It is thus no wonder that users often have trouble knowing what mode their video-controller is in.

Even knowing that you have a full keyboard and standard screen is not sufficient to design the dialogue. The precise positioning can affect the usability of a particular dialogue style. The text editor described above (Figures 8.15 and 8.16) was originally used on a computer with a separate function key pad on the left of the keyboard. No problems were encountered with the 'dangerous' states of the system. However, the editor was later used on a system with a different keyboard layout. The function keys are set out in a line along the top of the keyboard, as in Figure 8.17, with the escape key right next to function keys 'F1' and 'F2'! As we saw, the dangerous mistake is to hit the sequence 'F1–Esc–F2', which is similar to the exit and save sequence 'F1–F2'. With the original keyboard layout, this was an all but impossible mistake to make. However, on the new layout it is possible to hit the escape with the edge of your finger as you press down the function key 'F1'. If this happens as you type the sequence 'F1–F2' — disaster. This scenario is easily predictable from the dialogue structure and the physical layout — and it can happen — the authors know!

8.7 Summary

We saw, by example, how the dialogue of a user interface can become unmanageable, and impossible to analyze, if we do not have a separate description. We have looked at two main classes of description: diagrammatic and textual. Diagrammatic notations included various forms of state transition network, Harel state charts, flow charts and JSD diagrams. Under textual notations, we considered grammars (regular expressions and BNF), production rules (event based and state based) and CSP.

We found that some very different notations were essentially equivalent, for example, JSD diagrams and regular expressions can describe exactly the same dialogues. However, we also saw that there were major differences in expressive power between different formalisms. For example, BNF grammars are able to deal with recursively nested dialogues and are thus more powerful than regular expressions or state transition networks.

One important difference in expressive power is whether or not the formalism can handle concurrent dialogues. We found that some notations favour sequential dialogues (for example, STNs) and some concurrent (for example, production rules), but few could handle both (the exceptions being Harel state charts and CSP). However, increased expressive power is not always desirable as it may mean a more complex and less easily understood description. The important point is to match the notation to the form of the desired dialogue. Another important distinction was between state-oriented and event-oriented descriptions. This will be picked up in the next chapter.

Once we had a dialogue description, we considered the connection between the dialogue description and the description of the system semantics. We looked at examples where the dialogue description is linked closely to a programming language and where it is linked to a more formal description. Two issues arose in this discussion. One was whether we want a centralized or a distributed dialogue description, that is, should all the dialogue be in one place and the semantics separate, or should the dialogue be spread out with the associated semantics. The second issue concerned maximizing syntactic description. Where there is a choice, we should put things into the dialogue description, where they can be analyzed automatically, rather than in the semantic description.

Finally, we looked at properties of dialogues. Action properties focus on user actions, and under this heading we considered completeness — are there any missing actions?; determinism — do any actions appear twice?; and consistency — do similar actions do similar things? The first two of these are amenable to partial automatic checking. State properties concern the ability of the user to move between dialogue states. We considered reachability — whether we can reach any desired state — and reversability — a special case, whether we can get back to the last state. We noted that reversability at the dialogue level is *not* undo as this involves the whole semantics of the system. Finally under state properties, we considerd dangerous states, those we do not want to get into accidentally.

We found that presentation and lexical issues are *not* (as is commonly supposed) a separable issue from dialogue design. We need to consider the visibility of modes and the style of interaction. Even the layout of keys and menu items can influence the likelihood of making serious errors.

Exercises

8.1   Complete the drawing tool STN in Figures 8.1 and 8.3 by writing dialogue descriptions for the text and paint sub-menus. For the text sub-menu assume that there are three options: centred, left and right justified. The text is entered by clicking at a location in the drawing surface and then typing. You may initially assume that typing a line of text can be regarded as a single user action. But later try regarding each character typed as an action. The paint sub-menu has two options: a pencil for free hand drawing and a paint pot for flood filling. The former is performed by holding the mouse button down whilst moving the mouse about to draw the line. The paint pot is activated by simply clicking the mouse over the area to be filled.

8.2 Repeat the above exercise using different notations, grammars, production rules, JSD or CSP. You will need to specify the whole system from the main menu to the individual sub-menu selections such as circle drawing. Note the problems you have with each notation.

8.3 Develop the JSD diagram in Figure 8.12, expanding the various nodes until you get to basic operations such as 'prompt `"login"`' or 'user types in password'. Expand the 'delete employee' node using the dialogue style as described in Figure 8.11, and use your imagination for the rest.

8.4 Using CSP, construct a dialogue for one user with an application in one window of a multi-window system. Using this first general CSP description, provide a CSP description for a multi-window interaction using the parallel operator (| |). How does this approach handle interference and information sharing between windows?

8.5 In the example of the digital watch in Section 8.3.8, what would be the dangerous states? Relate the lexical issues of the buttons for a digital watch to these dangerous states and provide some design advice. Does your own digital watch satisfy these criteria?

Recommended Reading

- Heather Alexander. *Formally-based Tools and Techniques for Human–Computer Dialogues.* Ellis Horwood, 1987.

  This book is dedicated to the CSP-based notation, SPI (see Sections 8.4.3 and 8.5).

- Gilbert Cockton. Designing abstractions for communication control. In M. D. Harrison and H. W. Thimbleby, editors, *Formal Methods in Human–Computer Interaction*, chapter 10. Cambridge University Press, 1990.

  Describes *generative transition networks*, a form of state transition network which has many features of an event based production system. In particular, it attempts to solve some of the problems that STNs have with concurrent dialogues.

- Dan R. Olsen. Propositional production systems for dialogue description. In J.C. Chew and J. Whiteside, editors, *Empowering People — CHI'90 Conference Proceedings*, pages 57–63. Human factors in Computing Systems, ACM Press, 1990.

  Original paper on propositional production systems, including a examples and analysis.

- H. Rex Hartson, Antonio C. Siochi and Deborah Hix. The UAN: A user-oriented representation for direct manipulation. *ACM Transactions on Information Systems*, 8(3):181–203, July 1990.

  User Action Notation (UAN) is not a dialogue notation as such, but operates at the dialogue level. UAN is scenario based in the sense that it considers small snippets of user behaviour, for example, the deletion of a file. It describes the actions the user must perform *and* the system feedback.

- See also the reading list for Chapter 10 since the greatest use of dialogue description notations has been as the dialogue control portion of *user interface management systems*.

Chapter 9

Models of the System

Overview

We need to know what a system does in order to assess its usability.

- Standard software engineering formalisms can be used to specify an interactive system. These are of various types:

  - model based, such as Z, which describe the system's state and operations
  - algebraic formalisms, which describe the effects of sequences of actions
  - temporal and deontic logics, which describe when things happen and who is responsible

- Special interaction models are designed specifically to describe usability properties, including

  - predictabilty and observability, what you can tell about the system from looking at it
  - reachability and undo, what you can do with it

- A full interaction model may complicated to produce, so we consider an example of a semi-formal, easy to apply technique, which

  - classifies phenomena as event or status
  - embodies naïve psychology
  - highlights feedback problems in interfaces

9.1 Introduction

In the last chapter we looked at the specification of dialogue. In this chapter we will look at ways of modelling the semantics of an interactive system. The dialogue just tells us about what user actions are legal at any point, but here we will be interested in what the user's actions *do* to the system.

There is some overlap. In the last chapter we discussed some of the ways dialogue is linked to semantics. Also definitions of system semantics tend to define the acceptable dialogue. However, a system-oriented description will not describe the dialogue as well as a dedicated dialogue notation, and a dialogue notation may hardly define the system at all.

In Section 9.2, we will describe how standard formalisms can be used to specify interactive systems. Such formalisms are becoming part of software engineering practice and can be a way for interface designers to articulate their ideas and communicate them to system developers. These formal notations are used to specify the functionality and presentation of specific systems.

Section 9.3 looks at *interaction models*, formal models which describe general properties of systems. We will demonstrate how one such model, the *PIE model*, can be used to investigate generic principles such as *WYSIWYG* and undo.

Finally, in Section 9.4, we will demonstrate how a semi-formal technique, *status/event analysis*, can be used to match the required behaviour at an application level to the perceived behaviour of the user. It makes use of common concepts which can be applied at all levels, from the abstract application functionality, through the interface, to the user's perception. It is used to describe a 'slice' of system at all levels of abstraction, rather than the whole system at a specific level.

Each modelling technique takes the view that it is not enough to design the 'interface' as a thin layer between the user and the system. Usability is affected by the whole system functionality: what is there, what can be done to it, and how it is presented at the interface.

9.2 Standard Formalisms

In this section we will discuss 'off the shelf' formalisms which can be used to specify interactive systems. The purpose of a formal specification is twofold: communication and analysis. Sub-sections 9.2.1 and 9.2.2 will see how these influence their use for interface design.

We will then look at three brands of formalism. First we will look at model-oriented notations, Z in particular. We will use a graphics program as an example throughout this sub-section and also the next on algebraic specification. Finally sub-section 9.2.6 looks at temporal and other logics. Another major brand of notation is the process algebras, such as *CSP*. However, these are most suited to dialogue design and have been discussed in Chapter 8.

9.2.1   *Formal notations for communication*

A specification can be used as a common language within a design team, or between the designers and system developers. In the latter case it can also form a sort of contract between the parties. Ideas for screen layout can easily be visualized with the help of drawings or painting packages, but the dynamics and deeper behaviour of the system are more difficult to communicate. It is easy to discuss ideas with other developers or with a programmer without ever being sure you are talking about the same thing.

The claim is frequently made that a formal specification gets rid of ambiguity completely and provides a precise unambiguous description of the system. However, this claim is false. The symbols used and the manipulations of them have defined meanings within the formal systems, but the *interpretation* of those symbols can still vary from person to person. For example, if a specification of a screen defines the colour of pixels at any position (x, y), then one designer may think the coordinates have $(0,0)$ at the bottom left and another think that they start at the top left. The internal geometry of the screen is unambiguous, but the interpretation of one designer is upside down! These ambiguities tend to be of a different kind from those of the spoken and written word (and are often as silly as the above). This is why it is crucial that any formal specification is accompanied by extensive commentary and a parallel written description.

In a small group, where a specification is developed in cooperation, the needs for extensive documentation are less strong. The group can build up a shared interpretation of the symbols used. In such a setting, formal statements can be a succinct and precise mode of communication. However familiar the formalisms become, the group must remember that they are using an esoteric language which must be interpreted to outsiders.

9.2.2   *Formal notations for analysis*

Formal specifications can be analyzed in a variety of ways. First, they can be checked for internal consistency, that is, to see if any statement made in one part of it contradicts another. For example, we shall see in Section 9.3.3 that some of the requirements one might have for an undo command are in fact incompatible. It would, in theory and in practice, be impossible to build a system satisfying all the properties.

Second, a specification can be checked for external consistency with respect to the eventual program. This task of *verification*, previously discussed in Chapter 5 is one of the chief benefits of a formal specification, from a software engineering perspective. However, this is not the primary benefit for HCI.

Finally, a specification can be checked for external consistency with respect to requirements. Some of these requirements will be nothing to do with HCI (although still important), for example, security properties. Other requirements will be about the particular system, for example, that any function can be accessed within no more than three keystrokes. In addition, there are generic usability requirements which cover a range of systems, for example, the usability principles discussed in Chapter 4. The model in Section 9.3 is aimed at defining this last sort of generic requirement. As the requirements are themselves formally stated, they can be checked for internal consistency among themselves.

9.2.3   *Model-oriented notations*

Model-oriented notations were developed in the late 1970s and 1980s to provide software engineers with the ability to describe and reason about software components using precisely defined mathematical constructs, which mirror the kinds of constructs used in real programming languages. These mathematical notations provide a means of describing the behaviour of a software system in a way closely related to how they are programmed but in a more abstract language. This abstractness allows the designer to forget about machine or implementation bias at early stages of design and also allows the design, or specification, to be reasoned about rigorously.

The two major model-oriented specification notations in use today are Z and *VDM*. Both have been used for interface specifications. For example, Z has been used to specify editors [169], a window manager and a graphics toolkit called Presenter [176]. In the following description, we will follow the conventions defined in the Z notation. We do not assume any prior knowledge of Z; however, this chapter does not serve as a tutorial for the notation (interested readers should consult the Z reference manual for more details [165]).

Simple sets

Model-oriented notations are based on the use of sets and functions. The simplest sets correspond to standard types in programming languages, like reals $\mathcal{R}$, integers $\mathcal{Z}$ and the positive integers, or natural numbers $\mathcal{N}$. Non-standard types can be defined as new sets by explicitly listing the finite number of possible values in that set. For example, we can define a set which contains all possible types of geometric shapes used in a graphics package (line, ellipse and rectangle) and we can define another set of the possible keystrokes:

> *Shape_type* ::= *Line* | *Ellipse* | *Rectangle*
> *Keystroke* ::= a | b | $\cdots$ | z | A | $\cdots$ | 9 | *Cursor_left* | $\cdots$

In some instances, it is not necessary to give an exhaustive list of the members of a set; it simply suffices to know of the set's existence and worry about its detailed contents later. To signal the existence of such a set without providing a definition of its contents, we assert it as a *given set* and enclose it in square brackets. We could have introduced the set *Keystroke* in this manner:

[*Keystroke*]

From these base sets we can build more complex ones. These include ordered tuples, named and unordered tuples (like records in a programming language such as Pascal) called *schemas* in Z, sequences (or lists) and functions. For example, a point in space requires an *x* and a *y* coordinate. That is, it is a 2-tuple (or ordered pair) of real numbers, and we can define it using the cross product type constructor $\times$, as shown below:

Point ::= $\mathcal{R} \times \mathcal{R}$

A typical value of type *Point* would be written $(1.2, -3.0)$. A geometric shape might be defined by its width and height, a point (*Point*) for its centre and a tag describing what sort of shape it is (from *Shape_type*). This could either be defined as a 4-tuple *Shape_type* $\times \mathcal{R} \times \mathcal{R} \times$ *Point*, or using a Z schema, as we have done below. The schema type is named (*Shape*) and its constituent components are also identified by a name and their associated type.

Shape
type : *Shape_type*
wid : $\mathcal{R}$
ht : $\mathcal{R}$
centre : *Point*

If we use the schema declaration, then given a shape *s*, we can talk directly about the width or centre of *s* by writing *s.wid* or *s.centre*. The schema type corresponds to record types in Pascal or 'struct's in C.

A sequence type can be used to represent the history of a user's keystrokes:

History == seq *Keystroke*

This says that an object of type *History* consists of any number (including zero) of *Keystroke*s. A sequence may have a fixed length, in which case it is rather like a Pascal array type. The mathematical sequence is more flexible than the Pascal array type as it may have a varying length. Two sequences *a* and *b* can be tied together end to end to give a new sequence, written $a \frown b$. When used like this a sequence is most like a list type as found in the Lisp language.

Finally, we have *functions* which play the role of both standard calculation functions in a programming languages, such as sqrt or log, and also act like a 'lookup dictionary'. Depending on the context of its use, a function in a specification may be implemented (if it is implemented at all) by a program level function or a data structure. This is perhaps most strange to a programmer, but is an important abstraction.

We can demonstrate the use of a function in the graphics example. The schema type which defines any one shape does not allow us to single out any one shape or a collection of shapes, as we would need to do to represent the set of shapes that the user creates in any one session with the graphics editor. We can represent a group of identifiable shapes by naming a function which maps identifiers to particular shapes:

[*Id*]
Shape_dict == *Id* $\nrightarrow$ *Shape*

The set *Id* is some set of identifiers which will be used to label the shape. We are not particularly interested in what the identifiers are—they could be natural numbers, for instance—so we just assert *Id* as a given set for the moment. An object *shapes* of type *Shape$_D$ict* is a function mapping labels to shapes. If *id* were a particular label, then the shape dictionary *shapes* might map it to a rectangle with width 2.3, height 1.4 and centre (1.2, −3). We could write this formally as

shapes(*id*).*type* = *Rectangle*
shapes(*id*).*wid* = 2.3
shapes(*id*).*height* = 1.4
shapes(*id*).*centre* = (1.2, −3).

Shape_dict is only defined to be a set of *partial functions*. Functions map elements in one set to elements in another set. A partial function does not have to map every possible element in the source set to an element in the destination set. Therefore, not everything in *Id* is a valid argument for *shapes*. The set of values which are valid is called the *domain* of *shapes* and is written 'dom *shapes*'. For example, we might have:

dom *shapes* = { 5, 1, 7, 4 }.

So *shapes*(5), *shapes*(1), *shapes*(7) and *shapes*(4) would all be valid, but nothing else.

Zdraw – the state and invariants

Although it is not necessarily the case, model-oriented specifications tend to be written in an imperative fashion. One defines the *state* of the system, and then defines *operators* in terms of their effect on the state. In Z, this state and the operators are written using the schema notation. For example, the state of a simple graphics system, called Zdraw and depicted in Figure 9.1, would include a dictionary of shapes which have been created by the user and an indication of the currently selected shapes. The schema *State* below gives this definition:

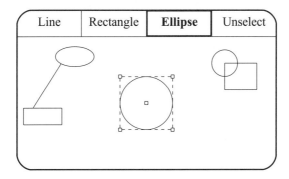

Figure 9.1   *Zdraw — ellipse option has just been selected*

┌─ *State* ──
│ *shapes* : *Shape_dict*
│ *selection* : $\mathcal{P}$ *Id*
│ ────────────────────
│ *selection* $\subseteq$ dom *shapes*
└──

The schema *State* is divided into two parts, above and below the middle line. Above the line we have the definition of components of the state of the graphics system. This part is similar to the component identification used to define the set *Shape*. Below the line is the state *invariant*, a condition which must always be satisfied by the components of the state. Predicates on separate lines are assumed to be joined by logical 'and' unless otherwise indicated. It says that the set of currently selected objects must always be contained in the set of created objects in the system. We will not allow a selected object to be one which has not been created by the user. Any operator which changes the state must ensure that it maintains this invariant.

What is the start state of the geometric modelling system? A reasonable assumption would be the state without any created or selected shapes. The initial state is defined by the schema *Init*:

┌─ *Init* ───
│ *State*
│ ────────────────────
│ dom *shapes* = { }
│ *selection* = { }
└──

Above the line we have included the previously defined schema *State*. Schema inclusion in Z is a mechanism to assist the gradual definition of a complex system in a series of simpler steps. Including the schema *State* above includes the declaration of all of its components (above the line in its original definition) and invariants (below the line). The additional invariants added in this initialization schema further restricts the initialized state, stipulating that the shape dictionary has no elements in its domain (there are no created shapes) and no currently selected shapes. The last predicate about the selected shapes was unnecessary, since it is already guaranteed by the invariant of *State*, namely that the set of selected shapes is a subset of the created ones. So an equivalent definition of the start state would remove that predicate and leave it to the reader to deduce from the state invariant.

```
┌─ Init ───────────────────────────────────────
│  State
│  ─────────────────────────────────
│  dom shapes = { }
└───────────────────────────────────────────────
```

Defining operations

Finally, we shall define two operations. The system is going to operate as follows. To create a new shape, say a circle, the user goes to the menu option 'ELLIPSE' and selects it. A fixed size circle appears in the middle of the screen. The user is then free to move and resize this to the desired position and shape. Figure 9.1 shows a screenshot just after the user has selected the ellipse option. The details of the menu are not presented here, but the basic functionality of the *NEW_ELLIPSE* and *UNSELECT* operation are defined as schemas below.

To define an operation, we need to describe the state of the graphics system before and after the operation is invoked. To do this in the schema language, we include two copies of the state description, called *State* (the 'before' copy) and *State'* (the 'after' copy). If an operation requires input or provides output, these are marked with a question mark for input (?) and an exclamation point for output (!). The *NewEllipse* operation is defined next:

```
┌─ NewEllipse ──────────────────────────────────
│  State
│  State'
│  newid? : Id
│  newshape? : Shape
│  ─────────────────────────────────
│     newid? ∉ dom shapes
│     newshape?.type = Ellipse
│     newshape?.wid = 1
│     newshape?.ht = 1
│     newshape?.centre = (0, 0)
│     shapes' = shapes ∪ { newid? ↦ newshape?}
│     selection' = { newid? }
└───────────────────────────────────────────────
```

This operation results in the creation of a new ellipse of a fixed size in the centre of the coordinate space (assumed to be the point $(0, 0)$). The result of the operation is that the shape dictionary is updated to include a mapping from some 'fresh' identifier (one that is not already used to point to an existing shape) to the new ellipse shape defined by *newshape?*. We do not indicate how this fresh identifier is provided to the operation, that is left as an issue for the implementor to settle. In addition, we have stipulated that the new object becomes the only selected object.

Note that the last part of the specification is quite an important interface choice and would *not* appear in a dialogue specification. One could just have easily left the selection as it was (*selection'* = *selection*). Possibly, we have made our choice because a (trivial) task analysis shows that users will normally want to move or resize a new object. This design decision may be wrong, but it is explicit and thus open to challenge. In an implementation such a decision would be deeply buried in the code.

The *Unselect* operation makes the set of currently selected objects empty. From this natural language description, we can derive an explicit formal description below:

$$
\begin{array}{|l}
\underline{\quad Unselect \quad\rule{6cm}{0pt}} \\
\quad State \\
\quad State' \\
\hline
\quad selection' = \{\ \} \\
\quad shapes' = shapes \\
\end{array}
$$

Notice that we chose to make explicit that the dictionary of shapes remained the same after the operation. This may seem obvious, but if the last predicate were removed from the definition of *Unselect*, then we would leave open the possibility that the shape dictionary could be anything at all after the operation, and that is certainly not intended. This becomes an even more important issue when the specification is used to judge the external consistency of the eventual program, as we discussed earlier.

9.2.4 *Issues for model-oriented notations*

The above is just a small sample of the method used to formally specify an interactive system with a model-oriented notation such as Z. But even this small example raises some important issues for interactive systems and formal specifications.

Recall in the definition *Init* of the initialized state that we did not have to mention explicitly that the set of selected shapes was empty. This fact is implied by the state invariant stipulating that the set of selected shapes is always a subset of the set of created shapes. However, in the definition of the *Unselect* operation, it was important that we explicitly state that the shape dictionary remains the same after the operation. This behaviour, though probably understood by the person who provides the natural language description of the operation, is not implied by the state invariant. If we do not make it explicit, then we have defined an operation far different from the one intended.

This issue is called the *framing problem* and comes up in a variety of areas both in interface design and elsewhere. As readers, we are quite good at inferring what should happen when things are not stated explicitly, but it is hard to formalize. One general rule is that if something is not mentioned, we assume it is unchanged. However, this simple rule cannot be used when we are dealing with a state with invariants. Imagine we were defining a delete operation and said that the *shapes* component stayed the same except for the selected object which was removed. If we do not explicitly mention what happens to the set of selected objects after the operation, what can we infer? Does it remain unchanged? No, because that would break the invariant that *selection* was in the domain of *shapes*. Normally such design decisions get missed until the implementor either deliberately or accidentally chooses one option or another.

Another issue which is generally ignored in such model-oriented specifications is the *separation* between system functionality and presentation. In the above specification, we identified a dictionary of shapes which have been created, but we have said nothing about how those shapes are presented on the user's display. It is quite possible that the user will want to create an image larger than the display coordinate space, so not all of the created objects will be visible at once. Furthermore, how do we indicate which objects are selected? Adding this kind of information to the above specification would make it more complete, but also more complicated. The presentation information is not necessary to define how the system works internally, but it is necessary to be just as precise about presentation issues as we have been about system functionality.

To address this issue of separation formally, we will need to provide more structure to the formal specification than the model-oriented approach provides. We will discuss this additional structure in Section 9.3.

9.2.5   *Algebraic notations*

There are a wide number of algebraic specification notations including *OBJ*, *Larch* and *ACT-ONE*. In particular, ACT-ONE has been used as the functional part of the ISO standard language *LOTOS*.

In principle, an algebraic specification does not try to build up a picture of the components of an object, but merely describes what the object is like *from the outside*. For an interface specification this sounds like a good thing, as we want to talk about the behaviour of a system from the user's viewpoint, not the way it is built. However, algebraic notations are more difficult to 'get in to'. They have a specific mind set which, once understood, is very clear, but takes some getting used to.

An algebraic version of Zdraw

If we continue the graphics example, we could imagine in Z having gone on to define the actions of resizing an object, and deleting it. In addition, we have an operation *select* which, given a point, makes the nearest object to it the current selection, and an operation *unselect* which clears the current selection. We will instead define these operations algebraically. As we have mentioned, an algebraic specification does not provide an explicit representation (or model) of the system. Rather, the types of interest in the state are declared along with the set of operations which manipulate those types. A set of axioms then implicitly defines the system state. An algebraic specification for the graphics system is given below:

Algebraic – draw =
types
      State, Pt
operations
        init : $\rightarrow$ *State*
        new_ellipse, new_rectangle, new_line : Pt $\times$ *State* $\rightarrow$ *State*
        move : Pt $\times$ *State* $\rightarrow$ *State*
        unselect : State $\rightarrow$ *State*
        delete : State $\rightarrow$ *State*
axioms
        for all *st* $\in$ *State; p, p'* $\in$ *Pt* •

1.	*delete(new_ellipse(st))*	*= unselect(st)*
2.	*delete(new_rectangle(st))*	*= unselect(st)*
3.	*delete(new_line(st))*	*= unselect(st)*
4.	*move(p, unselect(st))*	*= unselect(st)*
5.	*resize(p, unselect(st))*	*= unselect(st)*
6.	*move(p, move(p', st)*	*= move(p, st)*
7.	*resize(p, resize(p', st)*	*= resize(p, st)*
8.	*delete(delete(st))*	*= delete(st)*

    The specification is in a generic algebraic notation which captures the main features of most real notations. We first declare the types of interest in the specification—points which will serve as arguments for some of the operations, and the overall graphics system state. No further information is provided about the construction of these types. The operations are then listed and are defined in terms of their input and output. For example, the operation *new_ellipse* is defined to take a point and the current state as arguments and returns a new state. The operation *init* takes no argument and produces a state. The types and operations together form the *signature* of the specification *AlgebraicDraw*.

    After the individual operations have been declared, the algebraic specification describes the relationships between the various operations by means of *axioms*. Axioms indicate how the operations interact with one another. The first three axioms tell us that creating any object and then immediately deleting it has no net effect other than unselecting the current object. This is an important *safety property* for the user saying that there are no unexpected side-effects.

The next two axioms say that attempts to move or resize when there is no selected object do nothing at all. Axioms 6 and 7 say that both move and resize are 'forgetful' in the sense that if you do two resizes in a row the second overrides the first as if the first had never happened. This forgetful behaviour of the move operation is very different from the behaviour defined in the model-oriented specification. In the model-oriented approach, it would be easier to specify that a move operation is cumulative—two successive moves is the same as doing one move equal to the sum of the two moves. Finally, the last axiom says that the action of *delete* is even more forgetful, it is *idempotent*—doing a second delete achieves nothing.

Reading time order in algebraic formulae

Note that the algebraic notation reads from the inside out. So the first thing done is in the middle of the expression. For example, if an axiom reads

$$resize(p, move(p', new\_rectangle(st))),$$

then this corresponds to doing first a *new_rectangle*, then a *move* and then a *resize*. This becomes more clear if we put in the temporary results:

$$st_1 = new\_rectangle(st)$$
$$st_2 = move(p', st_1)$$
$$st_3 = resize(p, st_2)$$

Some algebraic notations are more imperative having an implicit state. In such a notation, the first and fifth axioms of *Algebraic − draw* would be written:

$$new\_ellipse ; \ delete \qquad = unselect$$
$$unselect ; \ resize(p) \qquad = unselect$$

Such a format is easier to read as 'time' goes from left to right, but is less flexible.

Completeness and observation

If we look back at the full set of axioms, we see that they are nowhere near enough to specify the behaviour of *Algebraic − draw*. That is, they are not *complete*. As far as the axioms are concerned there is no difference between *move* and *resize*, or between *new_ellipse* and *new_rectangle*. Now we could add some more axioms, for instance, adding an axiom to say that a move, resize or unselect after a delete has no effect.

There is a more fundamental problem, however. We are told nothing about the internal structure of *State* or *Point*. Presumably *Point* is generated from the mouse position, so we would really know something about it. We can put inputs into the system, but what do we get out? There are no *observation* operators. A system which cannot be observed can easily (and it is the simplest solution) do nothing at all. To be useful, this specification would have to be extended to include the presentation of a screen image or something similar. This screen image would be more concrete than the abstract internal state, and would be related to *State* by observation operators. This is a similar problem, concerning the relation between functionality and presentation, as was raised in the previous section with model-oriented notations.

9.2.6   *Temporal and other logics*

Many readers will be familiar with standard predicate logic, where letters are used to represent logical statements. For example, if one of the authors says:

$(p \wedge q) \vee r$
where p = 'my nose is green'
$\quad\quad q$ = 'I've got ears like a donkey'
$\quad\quad r$ = 'I'm called Alan'

then you can conclude that either the author in question is Alan, or he or she will stand out in a crowd.

In fact predicate logic and propositional logic (which allows parametrized logical formulae such as $P(x) \vee Q(x)$) are used as part of many other formalisms, for instance, in the model-oriented specification of the graphics drawing package.

However, predicate and propositional logic are only the simplest of vast families of logics developed as part of philosophy and mathematical logic. Of these specialized logics, several have been adopted and developed within computer science and have operators which are particularly useful for specifying properties of interactive systems.

Temporal logic

Temporal logics augment propositional logics with operators to reason about time. There are many different brands of temporal logic, but most share the basic symbols $\Box$ and $\Diamond$, which are read as 'always' and 'eventually'. These are the temporal equivalents of the quantifiers $\forall$ (universal quantification, read 'for all') and $\exists$ (existential quantification, read 'there exists'). So the statement

$\Box$ (rains on Tuesday)

says that it 'always rains on Tuesday.' The statement $\Box(\neg p)$ says that it is always *not* true that p. In other words, p never happens. So we can always read the combination $\Box\neg$ as 'never':

□¬ (computer explodes)

We can see that temporal operators are useful at specifying *safety properties*. More complex properties can also be given, for example,

□(user types 'print fred' ⇒ ◇the laser printer prints the file 'fred')

This statement says that at all times, if the user types the command 'print fred', then eventually the file 'fred' will be printed on the laser printer. Whereas it is easy with a model-oriented specification like Z to say what will happen immediately after a user action, this sort of delayed response property is very difficult indeed.

Further temporal operators

In fact, the above statement was quite weak; 'eventually' could mean in a thousand years' time. To cope with this, temporal logics introduce additional operators. These vary a bit more from logic to logic. Some reason over bounded time intervals, so that the meaning of 'eventually' becomes 'before the end of this interval'. A more popular approach is to use operators such as *until* and *before*.

p *until* q — p must remain true until q becomes true
p *before* q — p must be true at some time before q becomes true

We can think of *until* and *before* as bounded versions of □ and ◇ respectively, where the second argument q marks the end of the interval over which they act. Note that p *until* q is weaker than □p as the latter demands that p true remain true for ever, whereas the former only until q becomes true. On the other hand, p *before* q is stronger than ◇p as the former guarantees a time-scale in which p must occur.

As well as being used to specify systems in abstract, temporal and similar logics have been used to prototype interactive systems. To do this, special executable forms have to be used, as in general a temporal logic formula can look arbitrarily far into the future. Consider, for example:

(◇user types 'print fred') ⇒ the laser printer prints the file 'fred'

This formula says that if at any time in the future the user types 'print fred', then the system ought to print the file 'fred' *now*. Such clairvoyant systems are hard to produce, and thus the executable forms have to restrict the types of specification the user can enter.

Unfortunately, restricting oneself to executable formulae can also prevent the expression of useful requirements. Obviously all requirements should be consistent with being executed (we want to produce a system eventually), but they need not be sufficiently precise to be executable. This tension between executability and expressiveness is evident throughout the use of formal methods in computer science, but is especially pertinent to user interface design with its focus on a rapid prototyping cycle.

Real time

Temporal logics only deal with time in the sense that they represent the succession of events—one thing happens before another. They do not represent actual durations and times in hours, minutes and seconds. Clearly, there are important user interface aspects which require a real-time statement such as the following:

> When the ellipse option is selected it must be highlighted within100 ms and the new object must appear on the screen within 1 second.

Programming, specifying and reasoning about real-time behaviour is a very active research area, and a variety of notations have been developed, such as *real-time logic* and timed versions of the process algebras (CSP and CCS). However, as yet, none has been extensively used within HCI. One barrier to effective use is that general properties are difficult to state exactly—we usually want a response time of 'around' 100 ms. Also, the real-time notations have often been developed with time-critical applications in mind, whereas, for many human response time issues, there is a gradual degradation in performance as the time increases, rather than a critical time after which the system might as well not bother. On the other hand, there are some timing issues where critical bounds do occur, for example, in hand–eye coordination tasks, delays of even a few hundred milliseconds can destroy performance totally.

Whether or not we use a formalism to describe real-time properties of a design, we must always remember that these issues are important, and we are not using an 'infinitely fast machine' (see Chapter 2 and [51]).

Deontics—responsibility and freedom

Specifications say what the designer thinks should happen. Specifications of the system say what it should do, but real requirements are often about the world— 'the system should have a secure backup every week'. One could write a formal version of this statement using some form of temporal logic, but when we come to design a system to satisfy it we have trouble. We can design a 'backup' program which puts all the data onto tape, and which uses sophisticated error checking and redundancy to make sure the saved data are secure. We can even design a user interface which is resilient to mistakes on the operator's part, but which is so clear that such mistakes never happen. But all this is to no avail if the operator does not put the backup tape into the system! Traditional specifications say *what* happens, but do not mention who is responsible for making it happen.

Consider the following statements:

> *Hotel rules*:   the guests are to be in the Hotel by midnight
> *Prison rules*:   the inmates are to be locked in their cells from 9pm to 6am

The two statements are similar in form, and their propositional meanings are almost identical. If we swap a few words they transform into one another. However, *from context* we know that the first statement expresses a requirement on the Hotel guests, whereas the second expresses a requirement on the prison warders.

Deontic logics address these issues by including the concept of responsible agents (human, corporate and computer) and the mutual responsibilities between them. The most common deontic operators are *permission* (*per*) and *obligation* (*obl*). These both take two arguments; the first is who has the permission or obligation, and the second what it is they are permitted or obliged to make true. For example, we can refine the temporal logic statement about printing including these operators. The agents are the user 'Jane' and the laser printer 'lp3':

> *owns*(Jane, file 'fred') $\Rightarrow$ *per*(Jane, *request*(Jane, 'print fred'))
> *type*(Jane, 'print fred') $\Rightarrow$ *obl*(lp3, prints the file 'fred')

The first formula says that if Jane owns the file 'fred' then she is permitted to request the command 'print fred'. The second says that if she requests the command, then the printer is obliged to print 'fred'. The first statement is a little clumsy because it has to be phrased in terms of the proposition *request*(Jane, 'print fred'). If we also include the idea of actions, such as *request*('print fred'), which can be performed (*performs*) by agents, then the requirements can be rephrased using a modified obligation operator:

> *owns*(Jane, file 'fred') $\Rightarrow$ *per*(Jane, *request*('print fred'))
> *performs*(Jane, *request*('print fred')) $\Rightarrow$ *obl*(lp3, *print*(the file 'fred'))

Such a statement is not far different from the statement of the requirements in English, and they make quite clear the balance of responsibility.

Deontic logics are becoming popular in requirements engineering. It is thus possible that as an interface designer, you may be asked to produce a system which satisfies some (suitably explained) deontic specification. Even if this is not the case, it is worth noting, formally or informally, exactly what expectations you have of your users. In practice, one ought to work with several levels of expectation. For example, if you are designing an automatic bank teller, it may be true that customers are obliged to use only their own cards, and to use them in a particular fashion. However, you do not want the system to crash too terribly if a customer does not behave in this fashion. As interactive systems begin to involve more than a single user (see Chapters 13 and 14), it becomes more important to keep track of these responsibilities and freedoms, who must do what and who can do what. If the user of single-user system does not behave in the 'obliged' fashion then the impact is personal (although not necessarily acceptable). However, in a multi-user system, we want to restrict the bad effect on others—the system should still maintain its obligations to them and allow them to perform those things they are permitted to do.

9.3 Interaction Models

Interactive systems ought to be *'what you see is what you get'* (*WYSIWYG*), *consistent,* have a universal *undo* facility . . . the list goes on. But, if a supplier says that its word-processor 'Sludge-Word' is WYSIWYG, how do we test this? The screen fonts look very impressive, but are they the same as on the page? Perhaps the system appears WYSIWYG for simple jobs but this breaks down when things become more complex. What does WYSIWYG really *mean*?

It was to address these issues that the methodology described in this section was developed. Whereas the formal notations described in Section 9.2 describe specific systems, the aim in this section is to define *interaction models*, which are generic, formal models of interactive systems. Using such a generic model, one can define principles in a formal way which are then applicable to a range of systems. In particular, by regarding Sludge-Word as an instance of the general model we can verify (or refute) some of its supplier's claims.

The particular model we will describe, the *PIE model*, was designed to attack WYSIWYG-like properties. It would be nice to say that after reading this section, you will know exactly what WYSIWYG means. Unfortunately, it is too wide and varied a term to be formalized. However, we will describe several principles from Chapter 4, more limited in scope, which can be formalized. Of these some cover areas within the general area of WYSIWYG, namely *observability* — what you can tell about the current state of the system from the display — and *predictability* — what you can tell about its future behaviour. In addition, we will define principles concerning the control of the system by the user, such as *reachability* — can you get anywhere from anywhere — and *undo* — the ability to perform backwards error recovery.

As we mentioned in Chapter 4, we certainly cannot define 'usability' totally; we cannot say that if a system obeys a set of formal principles then it will be usable. Nevertheless, some of the formal principles are necessary for usability: any system which breaks them is bound to have problems. The formal principles form a 'safety net' to prevent some of the worst mistakes in an interactive system, but do not ensure a good design. That depends on a good designer.

This 'safety net', although valuable, is not the principal benefit of using interaction models. Their chief value lies in the insights gained by considering properties of interaction, away from the surface clutter of real or imagined systems. These insights become part of the background with which you approach new areas, whether or not a formal approach is explicitly taken there. Furthermore, some of these insights can be abstracted into informal principles, which, though derived by formal analyses, can, once stated, be justified in their own right. It is a strange paradox that some of the informal concepts which are obtained by such formal analysis are not themselves fully formalizable.

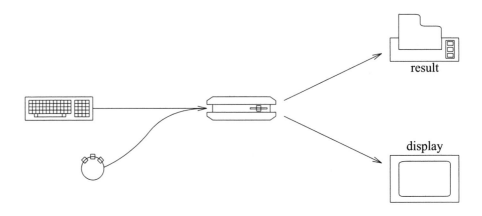

Figure 9.2   *Inputs and outputs of single-user system*

9.3.1   *The PIE model*

The PIE model is a *black-box model*. It does not try to represent the internal architecture and construction of a computer system, but instead describes it purely in terms of its inputs from the user and outputs to the user. For a simple single-user system typical inputs would be from keyboard and mouse, and outputs would be the computer's display screen and the eventual printed output (Figure 9.2).

The difference between the ephemeral *display* of a system, and the permanent *result* is central to the PIE model. We will call the set of possible displays D and the set of possible results R. In order to express principles of observability, we will want to talk about the relation between display and result. Basically, can we determine the result (what you will get) from the display (what you see)?

For a formal statement of predictability it helps (but is not essential) to talk about the internal state of the system. This does not counter our claim to have a black-box model. First, the state we define will be opaque, we will not look at its structure, merely postulate it is there. Second, the state we will be discussing is not the actual state of the system, but an idealization of it. It will be the minimal state required to account for the future *external behaviour*. We will call this the *effect* (E). Functions *display* and *result* obtain the current outputs from this minimal state:

$$display : E \rightarrow D$$
$$result : E \rightarrow R$$

The current display will be literally what is now visible. The current result is actually not what *is* available, but what the result would be if the interaction were finished. For example, with a word-processor, it is the pages that would be obtained if one printed the current state of the document.

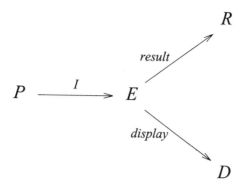

Figure 9.3   *The PIE model*

A single user action we will call a *command* (from a set C). The history of all the user's commands is called the *program* (P = seq C), and the current effect can be calculated from this history using an *interpretation function*:

$I : P \rightarrow E$

Arguably the input history would be better labelled H, but then the PIE model would lose its acronym! If we put together all the bits, we obtain a diagram of sets and functions (Figure 9.3), which looks rather like the original illustration.

In principle, one can express all the properties one wants in terms of the interpretation function, I. However, this often means expressing properties quantified over all possible past histories. To make some of the properties easier to express, we will also use a state transition function *doit*:

$doit : E \times P \rightarrow E$

The function *doit* takes the present state e and some user commands p, and gives the new state after the user has entered the commands *doit(e, p)*. It is related to the interpretation function I by the following axioms:

$$doit(I(p), q) \quad = \quad I(p \frown q)$$
$$doit(doit(e, p), q) \quad = \quad doit(e, p \frown q)$$

The PIE diagram can be read at different levels of abstraction. One can take a direct analogy with Figure 9.2. The commands set C is the keystrokes and mouse clicks, the display set D is the physical display, and the result R is the printed output:

$$
\begin{array}{rcl}
C & = & \{'a', 'b', \ldots, '0', '1', \ldots, '*', '\&', \ldots\} \\
D & = & \textit{Pixel\_coord} \rightarrow \textit{RGB\_value} \\
R & = & \text{ink on paper}
\end{array}
$$

This is a physical/lexical level of interpretation. One can produce a similar mapping for any system, in terms of the raw physical inputs and outputs. It is often more useful to apply the model at the logical level. Here the user commands are higher level actions such as 'select bold font' which may be invoked by several keystrokes and/or mouse actions. Similarly, we can describe the screen at a logical level in terms of windows, buttons, fields and so on. Also, for some purposes, rather than dealing with the final physical result, we may regard, say, the document on disk as the result.

The power of the PIE model is that it can be applied at many levels of abstraction. Some properties may only be valid at one level, but many should be true at all levels of system description. It is even possible to apply the PIE model just *within* the user, in the sense that the commands are the user's intended actions and the display, the perceived response.

When applying the PIE model at different levels it is possible to map between the levels. This leads to *level conformance* properties, which say, for example, that the changes one sees at the interface level should correspond to similar changes at the level of application objects.

9.3.2 *Predictability and observability*

WYSIWYG is clearly related to what can be inferred from the display (what you see). Harold Thimbleby has pointed out that WYSIWYG can be given two interpretations [174]. One is what you see is what you *will get* at the printer. This corresponds to how well you can determine the result from the display. The second interpretation is what you see is what you *have got* in the system. For this we will ask what the display can tell us about the effect. These can both be thought of as *observability* principles.

A related issue is *predictability*. Imagine you have been using a drawing package and in the middle you get thirsty and go to get a cup of tea. On returning, you are faced with the screen—do you know what to do next? If there are two shapes one on top of the other, the graphics package may interpret mouse clicks as operating on the 'top' shape. However, there may be no visual indication of which is topmost. The screen image does not tell you what the effect of your actions will be; you need to remember how you got there, your command history. This has been called the 'gone away for a cup of tea problem.' In fact, the state of the system determines the effects of any future commands, so if we have a system which is observable in the sense that the display determines the state, it is also predictable. Predictability is a special case of observability.

We will attempt to formalize these properties. To say that we can determine the result from the display is to say that there exists a function $transparent_R$ from displays to results:

$$\exists \, transparent_R : D \to R \, \bullet$$
$$\forall e \in E \, \bullet \, transparent_R(display(e)) = result(e)$$

It is no good having any old function from the display to the result, the second half of the above says that the function gives us exactly the result we would get from the system. We can call this property *result transparency*.

We can do a similar thing for the effect, that is the system state:

$$\exists \, transparent_E : D \to E \, \bullet$$
$$\forall e \in E \, \bullet \, transparent_E(display(e)) = e$$

We can call this property simply *transparency*.

What would it mean for a system to be transparent in one of these senses? If the system were result transparent, when we come back from our cup of tea, we can look at the display and then work out in our head (using $transparent_R$ exactly what the printed drawing would look like. Whether we could do this in our heads is another matter. For most drawing packages the function would be simply to ignore the menus and 'photocopy' the screen.

Simple transparency is stronger still. It would say that there is nothing in the state of the system that cannot be inferred from the display. If there are any modes, then these must have a visual indication; if there are any differences in behaviour between the displayed shapes, then there must be some corresponding visual difference. Even forgetting the formal principles, this is a strong and useful design heuristic.

Unfortunately, these principles are both rather too strong. If we imagine a word-processor rather than a drawing package, the contents of the display will be only a bit of the document. Clearly, we cannot infer the contents of the rest of the document (and hence the printed result) from the display. Similarly, to give a visual indication of, say, object grouping within a complex drawing package might be impossible (and this can cause the user problems).

When faced with a document on a word-processor, the user can simply scroll the display up and down to find out what is there. You cannot see from the current display everything about the system, but you can find out. The process by which the user explores the current state of the system is called a *strategy*. The formalization of a strategy is quite complex, even ignoring cognitive limitations. These strategies will differ from user to user, but the documentation of a system should tell the user how to get at pertinent information. For example, how to tell what objects in the drawing tools are grouped. This will map out a set of effective strategies with which the user can work.

Ideally, a strategy for observing the system should not disrupt the state of the application objects, that is, the strategy should be *passive*. For example, a strategy for looking at a document which involved deleting it would not be very useful.

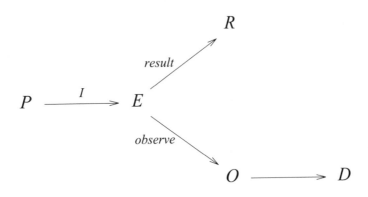

Figure 9.4   *The observable effect*

This seems almost too obvious, but consider again grouping in drawing tools. Often the only way to find out how a grouped object is composed is to ungroup it piece by piece. You then have to remember how to put it back together. The advantage of a passive strategy becomes apparent.

Using such a strategy then gives one a wider view of the system than the display. This is called the *observable effect* (O). In a word-processor this would be the complete view of the document obtained by scrolling plus any current mode indicators and a quick peek at the state of the cut/paste buffer. The observable effect contains strictly more information than the display, hence sits before it in a functional diagram (Figure 9.4).

We can now reformulate principles in terms of the observable effect. First of all the system is *result observable* if the result can be determined from the observable effect:

$$\exists \, predict_R : O \to R \bullet$$
$$\forall \, e \in E \bullet predict_R(observe(e)) = result(e)$$

This says that the observable effect contains at least as much information as the result. However, it will also contain additional information about the interactive state of the system. For example, you will observe the current cursor position, but this has no bearing on the printed document.

So you know what will happen if you hit the print button *now*. Refreshed from your cup of tea, you return to work. You press a function key which, unknown to you, is bound to a macro intended for an entirely different application. The screen rolls, the disk whirrs and, to your horror, your document and the entire disk contents are trashed. You leave the computer and go for another drink . . . not necessarily of tea.

A stronger condition is that the system be fully predictable:

$\exists\, transparent_E : O \rightarrow E \bullet$
$\quad\quad \forall\, e \in E \bullet predict(observe(e)) = e$

This says that you can observe the complete state of the system. You can then (in theory) predict anything the system will do. If the system were fully predictable, you would be able to tell what the bindings of the function keys were and hence (again in theory) would have been able to avoid your disaster.

This is as far as this bit of the formal story goes in this book. However, there are more sophisticated principles of observability and predictability which take into account aspects of user attention, and issues like keyboard buffers. Formalisms such as the PIE model have been used to portray other usability principles discussed in Chapter 4. Principles of predictability do not stand on their own; even if you had known what was bound to the function key, you might still have hit it by accident, or simply forgotten. Other protective principles like *commensurate effort* need to be applied. Also, although it is difficult to formalize completely, one prefers a system which behaves in most respects like the transparency principles, rather than requiring complicated searching to discover information. This is a sort of commensurate effort for observation.

9.3.3 *Reachability and undo*

In Chapter 8, we discussed connectivity issues for dialogues. We could check a dialogue description to see if there are any blind alleys, which once you had chosen them, would never let you back to the rest of the dialogue. Systems can have similar problems at a semantic level.

In a commercial program debugger used by one of the authors, there is a window listing all the variables. If a variable is a complex structure, then hitting the 'insert' key while the cursor is over the variable will expand the variable showing all its fields. If you only want a few of the fields to be displayed, you can move the cursor over the unwanted fields and type the 'delete' key and the field is removed. These operations can be repeated over complex hierarchical structures. If you remove a field and then wish you had not, you can always press 'insert' again over the main variable and all the fields will be re-displayed. Even this breaks somewhat the principle of *commensurate* effort, but worse is to come. The 'delete' key also works for top level variables, but once one of these is removed from the display there is *nothing* you can do to get it back, short of exiting the debugger and re-running it from scratch.

A principle which stops this type of behaviour is *reachability*. A system is reachable if from any state the system is in, you can get to any other state. The formal statement of this is as follows:

$\forall\, e, e' \in E \bullet (\exists\, p \in P \bullet doit(e, p) = e')$

Unlike the predictability principles, there are no awkward caveats. The only problem is that, if anything, it is too weak. For instance, a word-processor could have a delete key, but no way to move the cursor about, so you always type at the end of the document. Now you can, of course, get from any document state to any other, you simply delete the whole text and retype what you want. However, if you had just typed in a whole letter then noticed a mistake on the first line, you would not be pleased! So, ideally one wants an independent idea of 'distance' between states and make the difficulty of the path between them commensurate with the distance—small changes should be easy. Despite this, the principle on its own would have been strong enough to prevent the behaviour of the debugger!

One special case of reachability is when the state you want to get to is the one you have just been in, that is, *undo*. We expect undo to be easy, and ideally have a single undo button that will always undo the effect of the last command. We can state this requirement very easily:

$$\forall c \in C \bullet doit(e, c \frown undo) = e$$

This says exactly what we wanted. We start in a state e. We then do any command c and follow it by the special command *undo*. The state is then the same as we began in.

Stop! Before clapping ourselves on the back for so clearly defining undo, we should check that this requirement for undo is consistent. Indeed, it is consistent — so long as there are at most two states. That is, the above undo requirement is only possible for systems which *do* virtually nothing! The reason for this is that *undo* is itself a command and can undo itself. Take any state e and choose any command x. Let e_x be the state you get to after command x. That is $e_x = doit(e, x)$. Now we can apply the undo requirement to state e_x:

$$doit(e_x, undo) = doit(e, x \frown undo) = e$$

So, the *undo* command in state e_x gets us back to e. That is as expected. But what does *undo* do if we are in state e? Again we can employ the undo principle remembering that $e = doit(e_x, undo)$:

$$doit(e, undo) = doit(e_x, undo \frown undo) = e_x$$

This uses the undo principle when the command c is undo itself. However, our choice of command x was arbitrary, so if we had chosen another command, say y, we would have concluded that $doit(e, undo) = e_y$. This means that $e_x = e_y$, and in general anything we do from state e gets us to the same state. So at most we have two states, a toggle, with all the commands flipping back and forth between them. The only alternative is that the system does nothing.

We will not go on to describe the details of better undo requirements, the interested reader can find that elsewhere. The basis of most workable undo systems is that *undo* is not just any old command, but is treated differently. The simplest fix to the above undo principle is to restrict the commands to anything *except undo*!

The lesson from the above is clear. It is easy to say you want something which sounds quite reasonable. A formal description of the requirement may well reveal that, as in the case of undo, it is inconsistent — that is *no* system could be built which satisfies the requirement.

9.3.4 *Other interaction models*

The PIE model was the inspiration for a wide variety of different models. Some of these are similar, but take a slightly different standpoint. For example, one model has results only available at some states. This actually corresponds to the intuition that a printed document is only available when you invoke the print function, or that an updated file is only available in the file system when you ask the editor to save. However, that model also only had the display available at some states — less intuitive.

There is also a range of models focused at specific domain areas. The PIE model is very general model of deterministic single-user systems. Other models address areas including:

windowed systems A model describing the interference properties between windows. The distinctive feature is that the user is effectively regarded as having different personnae when interacting with different windows. This reflects the observation that when swapping between tasks (associated with windows), the user should not have to keep track of dependencies and is therefore acting like several users.

timing What happens when the system is not fast enough and the user's actions get ahead of the system's responses? The formal model describes the relationship between the steady state behaviour — what would happen if the machine was infinitely fast and there were no delays and the actual temporal behaviour. This analysis has highlighted deficiencies in the input–output model of window managers and operating systems.

attention This looks at ways of describing which parts of the display and result are used during any particular task. It uses *templates* for both, which model the selective attention during the task. The designer states what the expected templates are for any task, and then salience of the templates can be verified by experiment. These can then be tested using psychological experiments.

non-determinism If you are ignorant of certain information in a system, it may appear to behave non-deterministically. Many properties of different models, for example, the predictability of PIEs, map onto problems of non-determinism. Methods of handling this non-determinism from one domain can then suggest similar methods in what would otherwise appear disparate areas. The fact that supposedly deterministic interfaces often appear random, suggests that, where it is helpful for other purposes, the interface can be made deliberately non-deterministic.

dynamic pointers Interface objects often have special positions, such as the cursor or marked blocks. They also may have pointers into them, such as hypertext links. Dynamic pointers are a formalism which describe such positional information in a uniform manner. In particular, they help to manage the changes in pointers as the underlying object is updated. They also describe the mapping between positional information at different levels, for example, when mapping mouse positions on the screen to their appropriate positions in application objects.

These are all principally single-user models. However, there has been some recent work in applying these formal models to group systems (such as those in Chapter 13). In particular, this has led to significant new insight into the meaning of undo in a group context.

We will briefly describe one extension to the PIE model here as it gives a lead into the next section.

The PIE model is very asymmetric between input and output. Some sorts of output are difficult to deal with; for example, a beep used when something goes wrong. This is not clear in the formalism itself, but if we look at the principles, it is obvious that the display is expected to be persistent. If you go away and have a cup of tea, the display is still there when you get back. The beep is not. On the input side, mouse movement is not easy: one can regard each movement as being a command in C, but this is unnatural. Certainly, the user would not be conscious of each pixel movement!

A beep is similar to a keystroke: each is an *event*. The mouse's position is similar to the screen, they both have an observable value at any moment—we say each of them is a *status*. The PIE model is then an event-in/status-out model: the user does events (from C) and the system responds with a status (*display*). This suggests variations of the PIE which have different combinations of event and status.

One version has events and status for its input, but still a purely status output (any-in/status-out). The (single command) state transition function then depends on both the command and the current mouse position (M):

$$doit : E \times C \times M \rightarrow E$$

The display function is now not just a function of the state, but it too depends on the mouse position:

$$display : E \times M \rightarrow D$$

This allows for the display to include the mouse cursor, which moves with the mouse (pretty obvious really) and also allows for the change in the display when the mouse drags an object.

This model only describes a special sub-class of systems, those that are *trajectory-independent*. The mouse position only has a permanent effect at the moment a command (keystroke or mouse button) happens, the intermediate positions are forgotten. For example, the model cannot describe freehand drawing. It is possible to extend the model to include more general systems; however, the sub-class is interesting in itself. With the exception of drawing and similar tasks, such as 'air-brush' painting, most mouse based systems are trajectory-independent. Furthermore, the few that are not exhibit usability problems, suggesting that trajectory independence is itself a general usability principle for all but exceptional situations.

9.4 Status/Event Analysis

In Chapter 8, we saw that some dialogue notations were state-oriented, whereas others were event-oriented. Each type of notation had trouble describing some phenomena, but were good with others. Similarly, in Section 9.3.4 we found that formal models of interactive systems need to be able to deal with both *status* and *event* input and output.

Note that the word 'status' is used rather than 'state', as the term will be used to refer to any phenomenon with a persistent value. This includes the position of a mouse on a table and the current screen contents, as well as the internal state of the system. The word 'state' has connotations of the complete state of the system, rather than the selective particular views meant here by status. Note too that the plural of status is usually given as status! According to the *Oxford English Dictionary* these are pronounced differently: the 'u' in the singular is as the 'u' in dat*u*m, whereas the plural has an 'u' as in t*u*ne.

The distinction between status and event is between being and doing. Status phenomena always have a value one could consult. For example, you can ask the question 'what was the position of the mouse on the table top at 3:27pm?' An event, on the other hand, happens at a particular moment. Here the relevant question is 'at what time did the user press the mouse button?'

This section describes *status/event analysis*, an 'engineering' level technique which makes use of the status/event distinction. The label 'engineering' is used in a similar way to the way it is applied to the *keystroke level model* (Chapter 6). An engineering approach is built upon theoretical principles, but does not require a deep theoretical background on the part of the designer. Status/event analysis is built upon two theoretical foundations. On the one side, it is derived from work on formal models of interaction (as described briefly in Section 9.3.4). However, a designer using the method does not need to use, or even know about, these foundations. On the other side, status/event analysis makes use of fairly naïve psychological knowledge, to predict how particular interface features affect the user.

The strength of the method is that a single descriptive framework can be applied at a range of levels from the application, through the interface, to the user's perception. Indeed, the same descriptive framework can describe even the low-level electrical signals and logic in the microseconds from when a user hits a key to that key being 'noticed' by the system.

We will first consider an example of clocks and calendars, which demonstrates some of the important properties of events and status and how they interrelate. The design implications of this are discussed in Section 9.4.2. In particular, we will see that events generated by applications have an associated time-scale which tells us when we *want* them to be perceived by the user. Section 9.4.3 discusses a few simple psychological facts which help us to predict when interface events become salient for the user.

Event/status analysis looks at different layers of the system, such as user, screen (presentation), dialogue and application. It looks for the events perceived at each level and the status changes at each level. This, combined with the naïve psychological analysis of the presentation/user boundary, allows the designer to predict failures and more important suggest improvements. This approach is demonstrated in two examples: the 'mail has arrived' interface to an email system and the behaviour of an on-screen button.

9.4.1   *Properties of events: clocks and calendars*

Brian is due to meet Alison to go to the cinema at 20 to 8. He decides to stop work at 25 to, and keeps an eye on his watch. Every few minutes he looks at it, increasingly frequently as the time draw nigh. Eventually, he looks and it is 24 minutes to, so he quickly puts his coat on and leaves.

In fact Brian had an alarm on his watch. He could have set it for 7:35, and waited for it to ring. Unfortunately, he has never worked out how to set the alarm (nor how to stop it beeping every hour).

A few days later Alison is sitting in her office. In an idle moment she consults her calendar to see what is happening tomorrow. She sees that it is Brian's birthday, so decides to buy him the soundtrack of the film they recently saw.

From these scenarios, we can abstract many of the important properties of status and events.

status Brian's watch is a status — it always tells the time — so is Alison's calendar. Moreover, assuming Brian's watch is analog, this demonstrates that status phenomena may be both discrete (the calendar) or continuous (the watch face).

events The passing of the time 7:35, when Brian wanted to stop work, was an event. A different, but related, event was when Brian got up to go. The alarm on Brian's watch (if he could use it) would have caused an event, showing that Brian's watch is capable of both status and event outputs. Alison also experienced an event when she noticed it was Brian's birthday the next day, and of course, his birthday will also be an event.

polling Given Brian only had a status — the watch face — and he wanted an event — 7:35 — Brian looked periodically at his watch. In computing terms, Brian *polled* his watch. Polling is a normal activity that *people* do as well as machines. It is a standard way to turn a status into an event.

actual vs. perceived The event Brian was after was when the watch said 7:35. This event happened, but Brian obviously did not look at his watch at just the right moment. Instead, this *actual event* became a *perceived event* for Brian a minute later when Brian next looked at his watch. If one looks at a fine enough time-scale there are almost always gaps between actual and perceived events. Of course, there can be similar lags between actual and perceived status too.

granularity The watch showing 7:35 and Brian's birthday are both events, but they operate at completely different time-scales. The interpretation of events and status may differ depending on the time-scale one uses. In particular, the idea of immediacy changes.

These same properties all emerge during the analysis of interactive systems.

9.4.2   *Design implications*

Applications want to cause events for users and use various presentation techniques to do this. However, these techniques must be matched to the *time-scale* of the desired event. For example, if the stock of 6 mm bolts is running low, this requires reordering within days or weeks. On the other hand, a coolant failure in a nuclear power plant may require action within seconds.

The presented form of the event for the user must match these time-scales — both causing events too fast or too slow is wrong. It is fairly obvious that too slow an event is wrong. An email message to the power plant operator would be ineffectual, the operator and the computer would both be so much radioactive waste. However, the opposite fault can be equally damaging. Red flashing lights and alarm bells when the last box of 6 mm bolts is opened would be annoying, and could also distract the operator from more important tasks, such as dealing with that coolant.

A less extreme example would be an electronic alarm and calendar. Imagine we have an on-line alarm function, which can be set to sound a buzzer and put a message in the middle of the screen at any time we like. This would obviously have been useful for Brian who could have set it to say 'cinema with Alison' at 7:35. However, if Alison wanted to remind herself of Brian's birthday, she would be forced to set an alarm for a specific time, say noon on the day before. This would have been disruptive when it rang, and not in keeping with the time-scale of birthdays.

In order to cause a perceived event for the user at the appropriate time-scale, we must be able to predict the event time-scale of various interface techniques.

Simply presenting information on the screen, or causing an event at the interface, is no guarantee that that event will become a perceived event for the user.

9.4.3   *Naïve psychology*

In order to predict the effect of interface techniques, we need to employ some naïve psychology. This can tell us what sort of stimuli are salient and where the user's attention will be focused.

First, we can sometimes predict *where* the user will be looking.

mouse When the user is positioning the mouse pointer over a target, the user's attention will be focused on that target. This is guaranteed in all but a few situations by the feedback requirements of hand–eye coordination. However, this attention may not stay long after the target has been successfully 'hit'.

text insertion point While typing text, the user will intermittently look at the text just typed and hence the current insertion point. However, because of touch typing, this is less certain than the mouse except when moving the insertion point over large distances using cursor keys — another positioning task.

screen It is reasonably safe to assume that the user will look at the screen intermittently. However, there is no guarantee that any particular message or icon on the screen will be noticed, only that very large messages spread across a large part of the screen will probably be noticed.

If we know where the user is looking, then we can put information there (not in a status line at the top where noone ever looks). Also, changes at the user's visual focus will be salient and become a perceived event for the user. An example, where the mouse pointer itself is used for information, is the egg-timer or ticking watch icon used when a system is busy.

Second, immediate events can be caused even when we do not know where the user is looking. The most common are *audible events*: beeps, buzzers, bells and whistles. These cause perceived events even when the user is not looking at the screen. In addition, our *peripheral vision* is good at detecting *movement* (see Chapter 1). Whereas we might not notice a small *change* unless it is in our visual focus, we will notice something moving out of the corner of our eye. We will see an interesting example of this in the next section, but a common example of *large* change (rather than movement) is the use of a screen flash as a silent bell. Not only does this cause an event when you are looking anywhere on the screen, but even if you are looking at the keyboard or at a document beside the screen. The only proviso is that the duration of the flash must be timed suitably to avoid it being mistaken for normal screen flicker.

Finally, recall from Chapter 1, that when people complete some goal, they experience *closure*. This means that they have a feeling of completeness and go

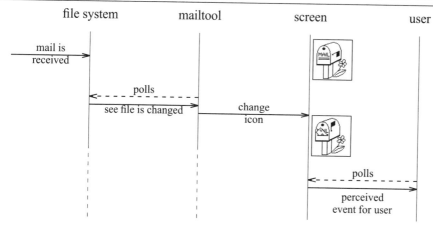

Figure 9.5   *Inputs and outputs of single-user system*

on to the next thing. Closure has implications both on perception and actions. It is why in the mouse positioning task, the user's eye may stray from the target as soon as the target is perceived as 'hit'. In addition, the user may begin some of the actions for the next task, while certain automatic actions terminating the last task are still going on. For example, it is easy to knock a glass from the table by beginning to turn round before fully letting go of the glass.

We will see examples of each of these three effects in the succeeding examples.

9.4.4   *Example — email interface*

Brian wants to thank Alison for his birthday present, which she left on his desk. He sends her a message by email. Consider the stages the message goes through, from when the message first arrives in Alison's system until Alison realizes it is there.

To make life easy we will assume that Brian is on the same network as Alison. When he hits the 'SEND' button on his machine, the message is sent — this is an event. The way that many systems handle internal mail is simply to append it to the recipient's mailbox file, for example, '/usr/spool/mail/Alison'. The *event* of receiving mail is therefore reflected in a change of *status* in the filesystem. You can see this event depicted as the first arrow in Figure 9.5. This figure shows timelines for various components in the interface, where time flows downwards. Events are denoted by arrows between the components' timelines.

On Alison's workstation runs a mailtool. When not in use, the mailtool is depicted by an 'empty mailbox' icon. The mailtool does not notice the change in the mailbox file immediately, but periodically it checks the file to see if it has changed — that is, it *polls*. So, after a while, the mailtool polls the file and sees that it has indeed changed. At this point the change in *status* of the file system has become a *perceived event* for the mailtool. Notice, that we are using the term perceived event of computer agents as well as of the user. Obviously, the final perceived event for the user is what is important, but we are also interested in similar phenomena at different levels.

Having noticed the event, the mailtool now knows that mail has arrived, and must try to make this event a perceived event for the user. To do this it changes its icon to denote a mailbox with a letter sticking out. That is, we again see an *event* giving rise to a change in *status*, this time on the screen.

Finally, we come to the user, Alison. She is sitting at her workstation busy on a report she must finish. She gets to the end of a difficult section and breaks in her typing for a moment. During such breaks, her eyes wander over the screen, and in particular she occasionally glances at the mailtool's icon to see if any mail has arrived — she *polls* it. This time when she looks up, she sees that mail has indeed arrived — the mail arrival has at last become a *perceived event* for Alison.

If we look at Figure 9.5, we see that a number of active agents (Brian, the mailtool and Alison) cause events for one another mediated by status elements (the filestore and screen). This is a very common scenario, especially if you look at fine details of interaction. However, it is also possible to have direct event based connections (which we will see in the next example), or even status–status connections. An example of the latter is the linkage between the mouse on the table and the mouse pointer on the screen. Even this is mediated by events in its implementation, but this is not apparent to the user.

Having analyzed the event/status dynamics of the system, we can ask whether it is functioning as it should. In fact, for this particular message and context it functioned well enough, but let us consider a few alternative scenarios.

If the message had been 'Fire! get out quick' Alison might now be dead. Forgetting the interface design, the mailtool probably does not poll the file system often enough to respond within the time-scale of such a message. If the system were required to support messages of such urgency, we would need to redesign the mail arrival mechanism so that the mailtool would receive a direct event, rather than wait to poll. Assuming this were done, would it have saved Alison? Probably not, because she would not have looked at the mailtool icon sufficiently often to see the crucial message.

On the other hand, the message may have been information about a forthcoming conference. Alison need not have read this message when she did. The perceived event is now at too fine a time-scale, and it is an unwanted interruption.

Finally, if at 12:30 Brian sent the message 'Thanks for the gift, see you for lunch at 1 o'clock?', then the time-scale may be appropriate, but the guarantee of delivery of the current system is too weak. Alison usually glances at the icon every few minutes, but occasionally, when engrossed in a task, she may miss it for hours. Alison has at least survived, but is getting hungry.

Split second requests are not normally sent by email and so the last form of message is the most urgent encountered in typical email traffic. The time-scale required is of the order of a few minutes. But we saw that the current interface, although of the appropriate time-scale, does not carry sufficient guarantees. There are other interfaces available, so we shall see how they fare.

explicit examination The traditional email interface required the user to examine the mailbox explicitly, say in the morning and evening. This was a form of polling, but at a much reduced time-scale. This would obviously be useless for Brian's message, but would have been much more appropriate for the conference announcement.

audible bell The existing mailtool can be set to sound a bell when mail arrives. This would cause an instant perceived event for Alison — if she was there. To avoid being missed entirely when Alison is out of the room, the bell has to be combined with a *status* indicator, such as the icon. However, even if Alison were there, the interruption caused to her work would not merit the normal time-scales of email messages — unless it said 'Fire!', that is.

moving faces Finally, there is a second mail-watcher available, which when mail arrives sees who it is from and slowly moves a bitmap picture of the sender into a sort of 'hall of fame' at the bottom of the screen. Whereas normally the mailtool icon is not noticed as it *suddenly* changes, this *movement* is noticed at once as it is in Alison's peripheral vision. Furthermore, it leaves a status indicator behind (the sender's face). It thus does the job of the buzzer and icon combined. However, the guaranteed event is still too quick.

What is really wanted is a guaranteed event at a time-scale of minutes. None of the available options supplies this. However, knowing what is wanted one can suggest designs to supply the need. For example, we could automatically notice gaps in typing, and notify the user (aurally or visually) during a gap on the assumption that this will be less obtrusive. Alternatively, we can use a non-guaranteed technique of the appropriate time-scale, such as the existing mailtool icon, but if the mail is not examined within a certain time use a more salient alarm.

Ideally, such mechanisms should be tuned to the particular time-scale of the application and, if anything, email is one of the most difficult examples as the time-scale depends on the message. Other applications, particularly command and control tasks, will have more well-defined time-scales making the matching job easier.

9.4.5   Example — screen button feedback

The last example used status/event analysis to suggest an improved interface to email. However, email is, as we admitted, a complex example, so it is not

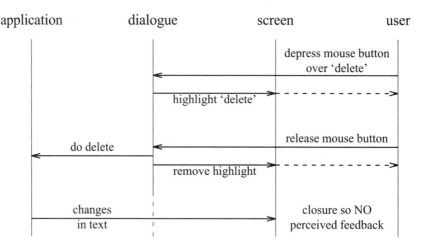

Figure 9.6   *Screen button — hit*

surprising that improvements can be found. In the following example, we find that status/event analysis is even able to suggest improvements in something as simple and heavily used as an on-screen button.

Screen buttons activated by clicking the mouse over them, are a standard *widget* in any interface toolkit and are found in most modern application interfaces. The application developer has little control over the detailed user interaction as this is fixed by the toolkit. So, the specific results of this example are most relevant to the toolkit designer, but the general techniques are more widely applicable.

A common problem with many on-screen buttons is that the user thinks the button has been pressed, but in fact it has not been. As an example, imagine Alison at work again on her word-processor. The report is too long and so when she notices a superfluous paragraph, she selects it and then moves her button up to the 'delete' button. She clicks over the button and thinks it has had an effect, but actually as she lifted her finger from the button, the mouse slipped from the button and the click was ignored (the button is activated by the mouse *up* event). Unfortunately, she does not notice until having, with difficulty, pared the report down to 1000 words, she notices that the unwanted paragraph remains.

We have two questions: why is this mistake so frequent, and why didn't she notice? To answer these we use status/event analysis to look two scenarios, the first where she successfully selects 'delete', and the one where she did not. There are four elements in the analysis: the application (word-processor), the button's dialogue (in the toolkit), the screen image and the user (Alison). Figures 9.6 and 9.7 depict the two scenarios, the first when successful — a hit — and the second when not — a miss.

Consider first the successful case in Figure 9.6, the hit. The first significant

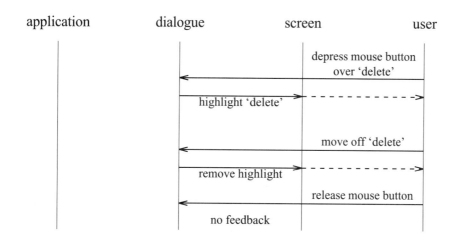

Figure 9.7   *Screen button — miss*

event is Alison's depression of the mouse button over the on-screen 'delete' button. This event goes directly to the toolkit dialogue, which responds by highlighting the 'delete' button. The next event is as Alison lifts her finger from the button. Again this is received by the dialogue which this time does two things. It removes the highlight from the 'delete' button, and also causes an event 'delete' for the application. The application then performs the action, deleting the paragraph. The effects of this change in the text are reflected in the screen content.

The unsuccessful case (Figure 9.7, the miss) starts similarly. Alison depresses the mouse button and receives feedback. However, this time before releasing the mouse button, she accidentally moves the mouse off the button. The toolkit dialogue responds to this by removing the highlight from 'delete' — the same feedback as in the first scenario. Alison's release of the mouse button has no further effect.

The two scenarios are very different in their effect: in one the application deletes some text, in the other it does not. However, Alison does not notice the difference. Her feedback from the toolkit dialogue is *identical*. In theory, she could have seen that the text did not change as she expected. However, after hitting the 'delete' button, she reaches *closure* on that operation and moves on to the next task. Her attention is not focused on the text to be deleted and so there is *no perceived event* for the user corresponding to the application event of the text being deleted.

Furthermore, this closure makes the mistake not just a possibility, but highly likely. Consider the moment when Alison has just pressed down the mouse button and the on-screen 'delete' button has been highlighted. She has done what she wanted and attains closure, and the remaining release of the mouse button is initiated. She now starts to look for the next action and begins to move the mouse to the location of next interaction. However, the two actions, releasing the mouse and moving it, are not synchronized with one another. There is no particular reason why one should happen before the other. It is, of course, a particularly dangerous point in a dialogue where the order of two unsynchronized user actions makes a crucial difference to behaviour.

It is quite difficult to see how to avoid the problem occurring. It is not that the current feedback is not salient, it is at the focus of the pointing task. However, all the feedback concerns events at the dialogue level. The most important event, the 'delete' to the application, has *no* corresponding perceived event. The toolkit assumes that the user will see some feedback from the application and therefore does not supply any feedback of its own. But, as we saw, the application's feedback is very likely to be missed.

The solution is fairly obvious, the dialogue should itself supply an event, which will be perceived by the user, corresponding to the application level event. This could be visual, but would have to be very salient as the user's eyes are beginning to move towards the next task. Alternatively, it could be aural, either with a keyboard-like 'click' as the button is successfully pressed, or with a beep if the mouse slips off. This improved feedback could be combined with some dynamic mechanism, such as making the screen button 'magnetic' and difficult to move out of.

It is interesting to note that, if Alison were a novice user, she would be more likely to check her actions and thus notice the mistake — an unnoticed button miss is an *expert slip*. As all but the most extensive user testing of a new device must, by definition, be with novices, there is no way this would be detected. Which is perhaps why most on-screen buttons have this problem. We hope this demonstrates how, on occasions, semi-fomal hand analysis may even be more effective than real user testing.

Exercises

9.1   Using the model-oriented approach with the example graphics program described in Section 9.2.3, specify the move operation as a schema which acts on the currently selected objects. Is the operation you have defined cumulative (two successive moves can be done as one move which is the sum of the other two) or is it 'forgetful?' Discuss the implications of the framing problem in your definition.

9.2   Write a similar schema for *RESIZE*. It should have the following informal semantics. The width and height attributes are of the shapes bounding box. The resize operation should make one corner of the bounding box be at the current mouse position (supplied as the argument *current_pos?*).

Hint: the width of a box is twice the difference between the x coordinate of the centre and the x coordinate of any corner:

$$wid = 2* \mid centre.x - corner.x \mid$$

9.3   In Section 9.2.5, we said that the specification *Algebraic – Zdraw* could be extended to say that a move, resize or unselect after a delete has no effect. The axiom for *unselect* looks like this:

(9) $unselect(delete(g)) = delete(g)$

Write two more axioms (10) and (11) which say the same about move and resize. Now use axioms (4) and (5) to show that (9) implies both your new axioms.

9.4   A two-function calculator has the following buttons 0–9, +, - and =. These would comprise the command set (C) of a PIE model of the calculator. The state (E) would consist of three components: the two current number being entered, the last number (to be operated on) and the pending operation (+ or -). The display (D) is simply a signed number. For this example, ignore the result.

Write down (semi-formally) the *doit* function updating the state for each user command and the *display* function relating the state (E) to the current display (D). To check your definitions: what does the display have on it after the user has entered '2+3+'? Most calculators would show 5, does yours?

Consider the displays after the sequences '2+2' '2+' and the effect on each of the additional user input of 3. Does the calculator satisfy the transparency property?

9.5   Imagine a calculator, normal except it displays A for 0, B for 1, up to J for 9. So the number 372 would appear as DHC. Does this affect the formal transparency of the calculator? Should it?

9.6   Can you suggest any improvements to the screen button feedback problem discussed in Section 9.4 that would distinguish at the interface between the two cases of hitting or missing the button? Is there any guarantee with your solution that the user will notice the distinction?

Recommended Reading

- M. D. Harrison and H. W. Thimbleby (eds.), *Formal Methods in Human–Computer Interaction*, Cambridge University Press, 1990.

A collected works with chapters covering a range of approaches: formal cognitive modelling, PIE-like models of interaction and formal aspects of dialogue description. Various notations are used: *TAG* (see Chapter 6), Z, functional programming and standard mathematical set theory. The chapters on dialogue description include both *eventCSP* and generative transition networks, a cross between a production system and a state transition network (see Chapter 8). There are also chapters concerning the software engineering issues of moving from formal descriptions through to running programs.

- A. J. Dix, *Formal Methods for Interactive Systems*, Academic Press, 1991.

The PIE model is described in detail, together with other, more domain-specific formal models. Issues covered in this formal framework include windowing systems, real-time response, pointing devices and direct manipulation. A chapter on models of status and events is the theoretical background for status/event analysis. In addition, the problems of refining a formal interface description into a running system are discussed.

- H. W. Thimbleby, *User Interface Design*, ACM Press, Addison-Wesley, 1990.

This is a general interface design book, but contains significant sections concerning formal aspects and models. As well as the explicitly mathematical parts, a formal approach to problems is often evident in the informal parts of the book.

- J. M. Spivey, *The Z Reference Manual*, Prentice Hall International, 1989.

This book provides the standard definition of the Z language and provides a tutorial introduction to Z specification for the interested reader. There is also a variety of other reference books and tutorials for the Z and the VDM notation.

Chapter 10

Implementation Support

Objectives

- Programming tools for interactive systems provide a means of effectively translating abstract designs and usability principles into an executable form. These tools provide different levels of services for the programmer.

- Windowing systems are a central environment for both the programmer and user of an interactive system, allowing a single workstation to support separate user–system threads of action simultaneously.

- Interaction toolkits abstract away from the physical separation of input and output devices, allowing the programmer to describe behaviours of objects at a level similar to how the user perceives them.

- User interface management systems are the final level of programming support tools, allowing the designer and programmer to control the relationship between the presentation objects of a toolkit with their functional semantics in the actual application.

10.1 Introduction

In this chapter, we will discuss the programming support which is provided for the implementation of an interactive system. We have spent much effort up to this point considering design and analysis of interactive systems from a relatively abstract perspective. We did this because it was not necessary to consider the specific details of the devices used in the interaction. Furthermore, consideration of that detail was an obstacle to understanding the interaction from the user's perspective. But we cannot forever ignore the specifics of the device. It is now time to devote some attention to understanding just how the task of coding the interactive application is structured.

The detailed specification gives the programmer instructions as to what the interactive application must do and the programmer must translate that into machine executable instructions to say how that will be achieved on the available hardware devices. The objective of the programmer then is to translate down to the level of the software that runs the hardware devices. At its crudest level, this software provides the ability to do things like read events from various input devices and write primitive graphics commands to a display. Whereas it is possible in that crude language to produce highly interactive systems, the job is very tedious and highly error-prone, amenable to computer hackers who relish the intricacy and challenge but not necessarily those whose main concern is the design of very usable interactive systems.

The programming support tools which we describe in this chapter aim to move that executable language up from the crudely expressive level to a higher level in which the programmer can code more directly in terms of the interaction objects of the application. The emphasis here is on how building levels of abstraction on top of the essential hardware and software services allows the programmer to build the system in terms of its desired *interaction techniques*, a term we use to indicate the intimate relationship between input and output. Though there is a fundamental separation between input and output devices in the hardware devices and at the lowest software level, the distinction can be removed at the programming level with the right abstractions and hiding of detail.

In the remainder of this chapter, we will address the various layers which constitute the move from the low-level hardware up to the more abstract programming concepts for interaction. We begin in Section 10.2 with the elements of a windowing system, which provide for device independence and resource sharing at the programming level. Programming in a window system frees the programmer from some of the worry about the input and output primitives of the machines the application will run on, and allows her to program the application under the assumption that it will receive a stream of event requests from the window manager. In Section 10.3 we describe the two fundamental ways this stream of events can be processed to link the interface with the application functionality—by means of a read–evaluation control loop internal to the application program or by a centralized notification based technique external to it. In Section 10.4, we describe the use of toolkits as mechanisms to link input and output at the programming level. In Section 10.5, we discuss the large class of development tools lumped under the categories of user interface management systems, or UIMS, and user interface development systems, UIDS.

10.2 Elements of Windowing Systems

In earlier chapters, we have discussed the elements of the WIMP interface but only with respect to how they enhance the interaction with the end-user. Here we will describe more details of windowing systems used to build the WIMP interface.

The first important feature of a windowing system is its ability to provide programmer independence from the specifics of the hardware devices. A typical workstation will involve some visual display screen, a keyboard and, usually, some pointing device, such as a mouse. Any variety of these hardware devices can be used in any interactive system and they are all different in terms of the data they communicate and the commands that are used to instruct them. It is imperative to be able to program an application which will run on a wide range of these devices. To do this, the programmer wants to direct commands to an *abstract terminal* which understands a more generic language and can be translated to the language of many other specific devices. Besides making the programming task easier, the abstract terminal makes portability of application programs possible. Only one translation program—or *device driver*—needs to be written for a particular hardware device and then any application program can access it.

A given windowing system will have a fixed generic language for the abstract terminal which is called its *imaging model*. Some examples of imaging models are:

Pixels The display screen is represented as a series of columns and rows of points— or pixels—which can be explicitly turned on or off, or given a colour. This is a common imaging model for personal computers and is also used by the X Windowing System.

Graphical Kernel System (GKS) An international standard which models the screen as a collection of connected segments, each of which is a macro of elementary graphics commands.

Programmer's Hierarchical Interface to Graphics (PHIGS) Another international standard, based on GKS but with an extension to model the screen as editable segments.

PostScript A programming language for developed by Adobe Corporation which models the screen as a collection of paths which serve as infinitely thin boundaries or stencils which can be filled in with various colours or textured patterns and images.

The input models are sufficient to describe very arbitrary images. For efficiency reasons, specific primitives are used to handle text images, either as specific pixel images or more generic font definitions.

Though these imaging models were initially defined to provide abstract languages for output only, they can serve at least a limited role for input as well. So, for example, the pixel model can be used to interpret input from a mouse in terms of the pixel coordinate system. It would then be the job of the application to process the input event further once it knows where in the image it occurred. The other models above can provide even more expressiveness for the input language, because they can relate the input events to structures which are identifiable by the application program. Both PHIGS and PostScript have been augmented to include a more explicit model of input.

When we discussed the WIMP interface as an interaction paradigm in Chapter 4, we pointed out its ability to support several separate user tasks simultaneously. Windowing systems provide this capability by sharing the resources of a single hardware configuration with several copies of an abstract terminal. Each abstract terminal will behave as an independent *process* and the windowing system will coordinate the control of the concurrent processes. To ease the programming task again, this coordination of simultaneously active processes can be factored out of the individual applications, so that they can be programmed as if they were to operate in isolation. The window system must also provide a means of displaying the separate applications, and this is accomplished by dedicating a region of the display screen to each active abstract terminal. The coordination task then involves resolving display conflicts when the visible screen regions of two abstract terminal overlap.

In summary, we can see the role of a windowing system, depicted in Figure 10.1, as providing:

- independence from the specifics of programming separate hardware devices;

- management of multiple, independent but simultaneously active applications.

Next, we discuss the possible architectures of a windowing system to achieve these two tasks.

10.2.1   *Architectures of windowing systems*

Bass and Coutaz [14] identify the three possible architectures for the software to implement the roles of a windowing system. All of them assume that device drivers are separate from the application programs. The first option is to implement and replicate the management of the multiple processes within each of the separate applications. This is not a very satisfactory architecture because it forces each application to consider the difficult problems of resolving synchronization conflicts with the shared hardware devices. It also reduces the portability of the separate applications. The second option is to implement the management role within the kernel of the operating system, centralizing the management task by freeing it from the individual applications. Applications must still be developed with the specifics of the particular operating system in mind. The third option provides the most portability, as the management function is written as a separate application in its own right and so can provide an interface to other application programs that is generic across all operating systems. This final option is referred to as the *client–server architecture*, and is depicted in Figure 10.2.

In practice, the divide among these proposed architectures is not so clear and any actual interactive application or set of applications operating within a window system may share features with any one of these three conceptual architectures. Therefore, it may have one component which is a separate application or process together with some built-in operating system support and hand-tuned application support to manage the shared resources. So applications built for a window system which is notionally based on the client–server model may not be as portable as one would think.

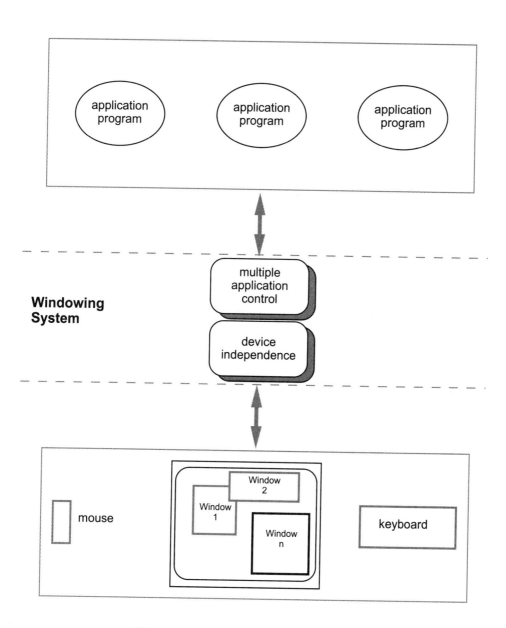

Figure 10.1　*The roles of a windowing system*

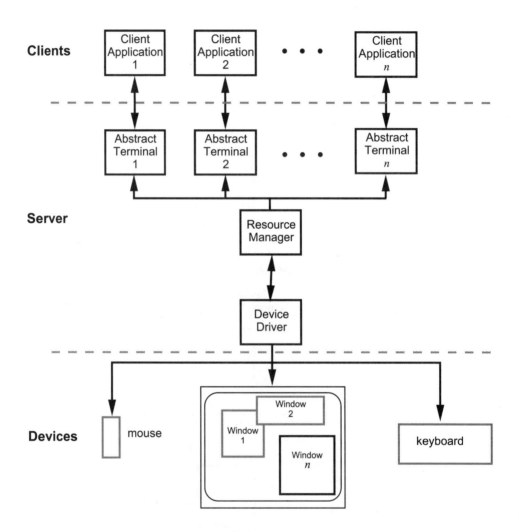

Figure 10.2   *The client–server architecture*

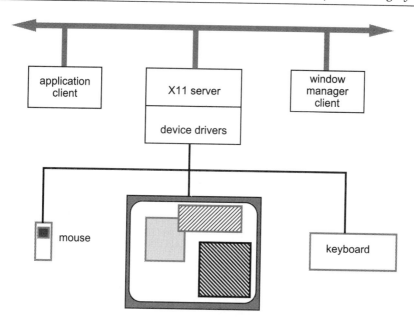

Figure 10.3   *The X Window System (Release 11) architecture*

A classic example of a window system based on the client–server architecture is the industry-standard X Window System (Release 11), developed at the Massachussetts Institute of Technology (MIT) in the mid-1980s. Figure 10.3 shows the software architecture of X. X (or X11), as we mentioned earlier, is based on a pixel-based imaging model and assumes that there is some pointing mechanism available. What distinguishes X from other window systems, and the reason it has been adopted as a standard, is that X is based on a network protocol which clearly defines the server–client communication. The X *protocol* can be implemented on different computers and operating systems, making X more device-independent. It also means that client and server need not even be on the same system in order to communicate to the server. Each client of the X11 server is associated to an abstract terminal or main window. The X server performs the following tasks:

- allows (or denies) access to the display from multiple client applications;

- interprets requests from clients to perform screen operations or provide other information;

- de-multiplexes the stream of physical input events from the user and passes them to the appropriate client; and

- minimizes the traffic along the network by relieving the clients from having to keep track of certain display information, like fonts, in complex data structures that the clients can access by ID numbers.

A separate client—the *window manager*—enforces policies to resolve conflicting input and output requests to and from the other clients. There are several different window managers which can be used in X, and they adopt different policies. For example, the window manager would decide how the user can change the focus of his input from one application to another. One option is for the user to nominate one window as the active one to which all subsequent input is directed. The other option is for the active window to be implicitly nominated by the position of the pointing device. Whenever the pointer is in the display space of a window, all input is directed to it. Once the pointer is moved to a position inside another window, that window becomes active and receives subsequent input. Another example of window manager policy is whether visible screen images of the client windows can overlap or must be non-overlapping (called tiling). As with many other windowing systems, the client applications can define their own hierarchy of sub-windows, each of which is constrained to the coordinate space of the parent window. This sub-division of the main client window allows the programmer to manage the input and output for a single application similar to the window manager.

To aid in the design of specific window managers, the X Consortium has produced a the *Inter-Client Communication Conventions Manual* (ICCCM), which provides conventions for various policy issues that are not included in the X definition. These policies include:

- rules for transferring data between clients;

- methods for selecting active client for input focus; and

- layout schemes for overlapping/tiled windows as screen regions.

10.3   Programming the Application

We now concentrate our attention on programming the actual interactive application, which would correspond to a client in the client–server architecture of Figure 10.2. Interactive applications are generally user-driven in the sense that the action the application takes is determined by the input received from the user. We describe two programming paradigms which can be used to organize the flow of control within the application. The windowing system does not necessarily determine which of these two paradigms is to be followed.

The first programming paradigm is the *read–evaluation loop*, which is internal to the application program itself (see Figure 10.4). Programming on the Macintosh follows this paradigm. The server sends user inputs as structured events to the client application. As far as the server is concerned, the only importance of the event is the client to which it must be directed. The client application is programmed to read any event passed to it and determine all of the application-specific behaviour

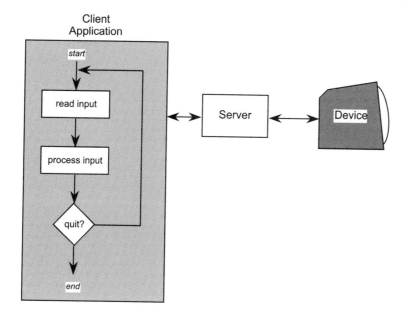

Figure 10.4   *The read–evaluate loop paradigm.*

which results as a response to it. The logical flow of the client application is indicated in the leftmost box of Figure 10.4. In pseudocode the read–evaluation loop would look like:

```
repeat
        read-event(myevent)
        case myevent.type
            type_1 :
                        do type_1 processing
            type_2 :
                        do type_2 processing

            ⋮

            type_n :
                        do type_n processing
        end case
end repeat
```

The application has complete control over the processing of events which it receives. The downside is that the programmer must execute this control over every possible event that the client will receive, which could prove a very cumbersome task. On the Macintosh, this process can be aided somewhat by programming tools, such as MacApp, which automate some of the tedium.

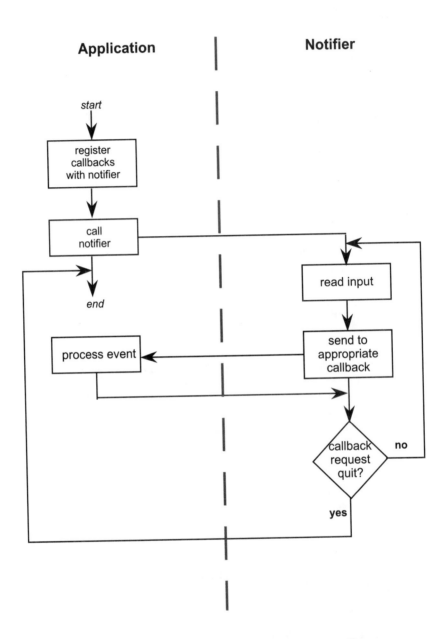

Figure 10.5   *The notification based programming paradigm.*

Figure 10.6   *Screen image produced by sample program* quit.c.

The other programming paradigm is *notification based*, in which the main control loop for the event processing does not reside within the application. Instead, a centralized *notifier* receives events from the window system and filters them to the application program in a way declared by the program (see Figure 10.5). The application program informs the notifier what events are of interest to it, and for each event declares one of its own procedures as a *callback* before turning control over to the notifier. When the notifier receives an event from the window system, it sees if that event was identified by the application program and, if so, passes the event and control over to the callback procedure that was registered for the event. After processing, the callback procedure returns control to the notifier, either telling it to continue receiving events or requesting termination.

Figure 10.7 provides an example of notification based programming in C using the XView toolkit (toolkits are described in the next section). The program produces a window, or frame, with one button, labelled Quit, which when selected by the pointer device causes the program to quit, destroying the window (see Figure 10.6 for the screen image produced by the sample program quit.c). Three objects are created in this program, the outermost frame, a panel within that frame and the button in the panel. The procedure xv_create—used on lines 17, 22 and 23 in the source code of Figure 10.7— is used by the application program to register the objects with the XView notifier. In the last instance on line 23, the application programmer informs the notifier of the callback procedure to be invoked when the object, a button, is selected. The application program then initiates the notifier by the procedure call xv_main_loop. When the notifer receives a select event for the button, control is passed to the procedure quit which destroys the outermost

```
1. /*
2.  * quit.c -- simple program to display a panel but-
ton that says "Quit".
3.  * Selecting the panel button exits the program.
4.  */
5. # include <xview/xview.h>
6. # include <xview/frame.h>
7. # include <xview/panel.h>

8. Frame frame;

9. main   (argc, argv)
10. int argc;
11. char *argv[];
12. {
13.    Panel panel;
14.    void quit();
15.
16.    xv_init(XV_INIT_ARGC_PTR_ARGV, &argc, argv, NULL);

17.    frame = (Frame) xv_create(NULL, FRAME,
18.        FRAME_LABEL,      argv[0],
19.          XV_WIDTH,         200,
20.          XV_HEIGHT,        100,
21.        NULL);

22.    panel = (Panel) xv_create(frame, PANEL, NULL);

23.    (void) xv_create(panel, PANEL_BUTTON,
24.            PANEL_LABEL_STRING,      "Quit",
25.            PANEL_NOTIFY_PROC,       quit,
26.            NULL);

27.    xv_main_loop(frame);
28.    exit(0);
29. }

30. void quit()
31. {
32.    xv_destroy_safe(frame);
33. }
```

Figure 10.7 *A simple program to demonstrate notification based programming. Example taken from the* XView **Programming Manual** *by Dan Heller* [84]

frame and requests termination.

Control flow is centralized in the notifier, which relieves the application program of much of the tedium of processing every possible event passed to it by the window system. But this freedom from control does not come without a price. Suppose, for example, that the application program wanted to produce a pre-emptive dialogue box, perhaps because it has detected an error and wants to obtain confirmation from the user before proceeding. The pre-emptive dialogue effectively discards all subsequent user actions except for ones that it requires, say selection by the user inside a certain region of the screen. To do this in the read–evaluation paradigm is fairly straightforward. Suppose the error condition occurred during the processing of an event of type type_2. Once the error condition is recognized, the application then begins another read–evaluation loop contained within that branch of the **case** statement. Within that loop, all non-relevant events can be received and discarded. The pseudocode example given earlier would be modified in the following way:

```
repeat
        read-event(myevent)
        case myevent.type
            type_1 :
                        do type_1 processing
            type_2 :
                        ...
                        if (error-condition) then
                            repeat
                                    read-event(myevent2)
                                    case myevent2.type
                                        type_1 :
                                                :
                                        type_n :
                                    end case
                            until (end-condition2)
                        end if
                        ...

                :
            type_n :
                        do type_n processing
        end case
until (end-condition)
```

In the notification based paradigm, such a pre-emptive dialogue would not be so simple, because the control flow is out of the hands of the application programmer. The callback procedures would all have to be modified to recognize the situations in which the pre-emptive dialogue is needed and in those situations disregard all events which are passed to them by the notifier. Things would be

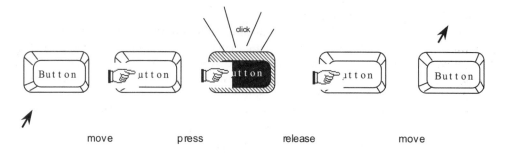

Figure 10.8   *Example of behaviour of a button interaction object*

improved, however, if the application programmer could in such situations access the notifier directly to request that previously acceptable events be ignored until further notice.

10.4   Using Toolkits

As we discussed in Chapter 4, a key feature of WIMP interfaces from the user's perspective is that input and output behaviours are intrinsically linked to independent entities on the display screen. This creates the illusion that the entities on the screen are the objects of interest—interaction objects we have called them—and that is necessary for the action world of a direct manipulation interface. A classic example is the mouse as a pointing device. The input coming from the hardware device is separate from the output of the mouse cursor on the display screen. However, since the visual movement of the screen cursor is linked with the physical movement of the mouse device, the user feels as if they are actually moving the visual cursor. Even though input and output are actually separate, the illusion causes the user to treat them as one; indeed, both the visual cursor and the physical device are referred to simply as 'the mouse'. In situations where this link is broken, it is easy to see the user's frustration.

In Figure 10.8, we show an example of how input and output are combined for interaction with a button object. As the user moves the mouse cursor over the button, it changes to a finger to suggest that the user can push it. Pressing the mouse button down causes the button to be highlighted and might even make an audible click like the keys on some keyboards, providing immediate feedback that the button has been pushed. Releasing the mouse button unhighlights the button and moving the mouse off the button changes the cursor to its initial shape, indicating that the user is no longer over the active area of the button.

From the programmer's perspective, even at the level of a windowing system, input and output are still quite separate for everything except the mouse, and it takes quite a bit of effort in the application program to create the illusion of the interaction object such as the button we have just described. To aid the programmer in fusing input and output behaviours, another level of abstraction is placed on top of the window system—the *toolkit*. A toolkit provides the programmer with a set of ready-made interaction objects—alternatively called interaction techniques, gadgets or widgets—which they can use to create their application programs. The interaction objects have a predefined behaviour, such as that described for the button, that comes for free without any further programming effort. Toolkits exist for all windowing environments (e.g. OSF/Motif and XView for the X Window system, the Macintosh Toolbox and the Software Development Toolkit for Microsoft Windows).

To provide flexibility, the interaction objects can be tailored to the specific situation in which they are invoked by the programmer. For example, the label on the button could be a parameter which the programmer can set when a particular button is created. More complex interaction objects can be built up from smaller, simpler ones. Ultimately, the entire application can be viewed as a collection of interaction objects whose combined behaviour describes the semantics of the whole application.

The sample program `quit.c` in Figure 10.7 uses the XView toolkit. Programming with toolkits is suited to the notification-based programming paradigm. As we can see in the example, the button is created as a PANEL_BUTTON object (lines 23–26) and registers the appropriate callback routine for when the notifier receives a selection event for the button object. The button interaction object in the toolkit already has defined what actual user action is classified as the selection event, so the programmer need not worry about that when creating an instance of the button. They can think of the event at a higher level of abstraction, that is, as a selection event instead of as a release of the left mouse button.

In Chapter 4 we discussed the benefits of consistency and generalizability for an interactive system. One of the advantages of programming with toolkits is that they can enforce consistency in both input form and output form by providing similar behaviour to a collection of widgets. For example, every button interaction object, within the same application program or between different ones, by default could have a behaviour like the one described in Figure 10.8. All that is required is that the developers for the different applications use the same toolkit. This consistency of behaviour for interaction objects is referred to as the *look and feel* of the toolkit. Style guides, which were described in the discussion on guidelines in Chapter 5, give additional hints to a programmer on how to preserve the look and feel of a given toolkit beyond that which is enforced by the default definition of the interaction objects.

Two features of interaction objects and toolkits make them amenable to an object-oriented approach to programming. First, they depend on being able to define a class of interaction object which can then be invoked (or instantiated)

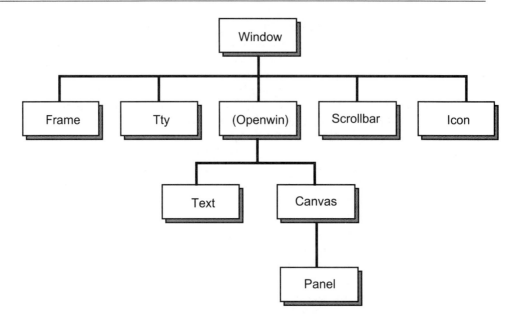

Figure 10.9   *The single inheritance class hierarchy of the XView toolkit, after Heller* [84]

many times within one application with only minor modifications to each instance. Second, building complex interaction objects is made easier by building up their definition based on existing simpler interaction objects. These notions of *instantiation* and *inheritance* are cornerstones of object-oriented programming. *Classes* are defined as templates for interaction objects. When an interaction object is created, it is declared as an instance of some predefined class. So, in the example quit.c program, frame is declared as an instance of the class FRAME (line 17), panel is declared as an instance of the class PANEL (line 22) and the button (no name) is declared as an instance of the class PANEL_BUTTON (line 23). Typically, a class template will provide default values for various attributes. Some of those attributes can be altered in any one instance; they are sometimes distinguished as *instance attributes*.

In defining the classes of interaction objects themselves, new classes can be built which inherit features of one or other classes. In the simplest case, there is a strict *class hierarchy* in which each class inherits features of only one other class, its *parent class*. This simple form of inheritance is called *single inheritance* and is exhibited in the XView toolkit standard hierarchy for the window class in Figure 10.9. A more complicated class hierarchy would permit defining new classes which inherit from more than one parent class—called *multiple inheritance*.

We should point out that though most toolkits are structured in an object-oriented manner, that does not mean that the actual application programming language is object-oriented. The example program `quit.c` was written in the C programming language, which is not an object-oriented language. It is best to think of object-orientation as yet another programming paradigm which structures the way the programmer attacks the programming task without mandating a particular syntax or semantics for the programming language.

The programmer can tailor the behaviour and appearance of an interaction object by setting the values of various instance attributes. These attributes must be set before the application program is compiled. In addition, some windowing systems allow various attributes of interaction objects to be altered without necessitating re-compilation, though they may have to be set before the actual program is run. This tailorability is achieved via *resources* which can be accessed by the application program and change the compiled value of some attributes. For efficiency reasons, this tailorability is often limited to a small set of attributes for any given class.

10.5 User Interface Management Systems

Despite the availability of toolkits and the valuable abstraction they provide programmers, there are still significant hurdles to overcome in the specification, design and implementation of interactive systems. Toolkits provide only a limited range of interaction objects, limiting the kinds of interactive behaviour allowed between user and system. Toolkits are expensive to create and are still very difficult to use by non-programmers. Even experienced programmers will have difficulty using them to produce an interface which is predictably usable. There is a need for additional support for programmers in the design and use of toolkits to overcome their deficiencies. In addition, none of the programming mechanisms we have discussed so far in this chapter is appropriate for non-expert programmers, so we still have a long way to go towards the goal of opening up interactive system implementation to those whose main concerns are with HCI and not programming.

The set of programming and design techniques which are supposed to add another level of services for interactive system design beyond the toolkit level are *user interface management systems*, or *UIMS* for short. The term UIMS is used quite widely in both industrial and academic circles and has come to represent a variety of topics. The main concerns of a UIMS, for our purposes, are:

- a conceptual architecture for the structure of an interactive system which concentrates on a separation between application semantics and presentation;

- techniques for implementing a separated application and presentation whilst preserving the intended connection between them;

- support techniques for managing, implementing and evaluating a run-time interactive enviroment.

We should acknowledge that some people feel that the term UIMS is inappropriate for all of the above tasks, preferring the term *user interface development systems*, or *UIDS* to distinguish support tools which address many of the design activities that precede the management of the run-time system.

10.5.1   *UIMS as a conceptual architecture*

A major issue in this area of research is one of *separation* between the semantics of the application and interface that is provided for the user to make use of that semantics. There are many good arguments to support this separation of concerns.

portability To allow the same application to be used on different systems it is best to consider its development separate from its device-dependent interface.

reusability Separation increases the likelihood that components can be reused in order to cut development costs.

multiple interfaces To enhance the interactive flexibility of an application, several different interfaces can be developed to access the same functionality.

customization The user interface can be customized by both the designer and the user to increase its effectiveness without having to alter the underlying application.

Once we allow for a separation between application and presentation, we must consider how those two partners communicate. This role of communication is referred to as *dialogue control*. Conceptually, this provides us with the three major components of an interactive system—the application, the presentation and the dialogue control. In terms of the actual implementation, this separation may not be so clear.

In Section 10.3, we described the two basic approaches to programming the application within an interactive system. In the read–evaluation loop, the control of the dialogue is *internal* to the application. The application calls interface procedures when input or output is required. In notification based programming, the dialogue control resides *external* to the application. When the user performs some input action, the notifier then invokes the correct application procedure to handle the event. Most UIMS fall into this class of external dialogue control systems, since they promote, to a greater extent, the separation between presentation and application. They do not, however, all use the technique of callbacks as was demonstrated in Section 10.3 for the use of toolkits.

The first acknowledged instance of a development system that supported this application–presentation separation was in 1968 with Newman's Reaction Handler. The term UIMS was coined by Kasik in 1982 after some preliminary research on how graphical input could be used to broaden the scope of HCI. The first conceptual architecture of what constituted a UIMS was formulated at a workshop in 1985 at Seeheim, Germany [137]. The logical components of a UIMS were identified as:

presentation   the component responsible for the appearance of the interface, including what output and input is available to the user;

dialogue control   the component which regulates the communication between the presentation and the application;

application interface   the view of the application semantics that is provided as the interface.

Figure 10.10 presents a graphical interpretation of the Seeheim model. We have included both application and user in Figure 10.10 to place the UIMS model more in the context of the interactive system (though you could argue that we have not provided enough of that context by mentioning only a single user and a single application). The application and the user are not explicit in the Seeheim model because it was intended only to model the components of a UIMS and not the entire interactive system. By not making the application explicit in the model, external dialogue control must have been assumed. From a programmer's perspective, the Seeheim model fits in nicely with the distinction between the classic lexical, syntactic and semantic layers of a computer system, familiar from compiler design.

One of the main problems with the Seeheim model is that, whereas it served well as a *post hoc* rationalization of how a UIMS was built up to 1985, it did not provide any real direction for how future UIMSs should be structured. A case in point can be seen in the inclusion of the lowest box in Figure 10.10, which was intended to show that for efficiency reasons it would be possible to bypass an explicit dialogue control component so that the application could provide greater application semantic feedback. There is no need for such a box in a conceptual architecture of the logical components. It is there because its creators did not separate logical concerns from implementation concerns.

Another concern not addressed by the Seeheim model is how to build large and complex interactive systems from smaller components. We have seen that object-based toolkits are amenable to such a building blocks approach, and several other conceptual architectures for interactive system development have been proposed to take advantage of this. One of the earliest was the *Model–View–Controller* paradigm—MVC for short—suggested in the *Smalltalk* programming environment [113, 99, 24]. Smalltalk was one of the earliest successful object-oriented programming systems whose main feature was the ability to build new interactive systems based on existing ones. Within Smalltalk, the link between application semantics and presentation can be built up in units by means of the MVC triad. The model represents the application semantics, the view manages the graphical and/or textual output of the application and the controller manages the input (see Figure 10.11).

The basic behaviour of models, views and controllers has been embodied in general Smalltalk object classes which can be inherited by instances and suitably modified. Smalltalk, like many other window toolkits, prescribes its own look and

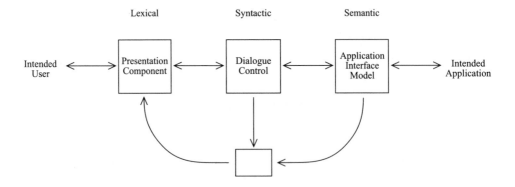

Figure 10.10   *The Seeheim model of the logical components of a UIMS*

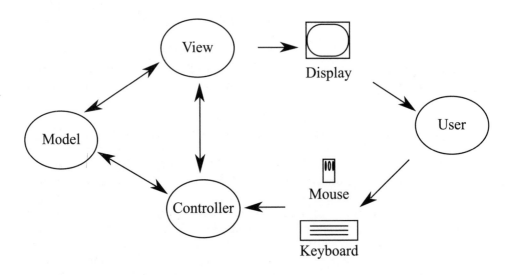

Figure 10.11   *The Model–View–Controller triad in Smalltalk*

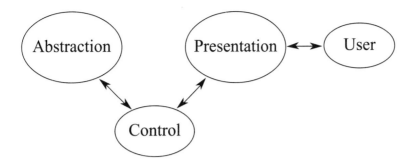

Figure 10.12   *The Presentation–Abstraction–Control model of Coutaz*

feel on input and output, so the generic view and controller classes (called `View` and `Controller`, respectively) do not need much modification after instantiation. Models, on the other hand, are very general because they must be used to portray any possible application semantics. A single model can be associated with several MVC triads, so that the same piece of application semantics can be represented by different input–output techniques. Each view–controller pair is associated to only one model.

Another so-called *multi-agent* architecture for interactive systems is the *Presentation–Abstraction–Control* — or PAC — model suggested by Coutaz [44]. PAC is based on a collection of triads also, with application semantics represented by the abstraction component, input and output combined in one presentation component and an explicit control component to manage the dialogue and correspondence between application and presentation (see Figure 10.12). There are three important differences between PAC and MVC. First, PAC groups input and output together, whereas MVC separates them. PAC provides an explicit component whose duty it is to see that abstraction and presentation are kept consistent with each other, whereas MVC does not assign this important task to any one component, leaving it to the programmer/designer to determine where that chore resides. PAC is not linked to any programming environment, though it is certainly conducive to an object-oriented approach. It is probably because of this last difference that PAC could so easily isolate the control component; PAC is more of a conceptual architecture than MVC because it is less implementation-dependent.

10.5.2   *Implementation considerations*

We have made a point of distinguishing a conceptual architecture from any implementation considerations. It is, however, important to determine how components in a conceptual architecture can be realized. Implementations based on the Seeheim model must determine how the separate components of presentation, dialogue controller and application interface are realized. Window systems and toolkits provide the separation between application and presentation. The use of callback procedures in notification based programming is one way to implement the application interface as a notifier. In the standard X Toolkit, these callbacks are directional as it is the duty of the application to register itself with the notifier. In MVC, callback procedures are also used for communication between a view or controller and its associated model, but this time it is the duty of the presentation (the view or controller) to register itself with the application (the model). Communication from the model to either view or controller, or between a view and a controller, occurs by the normal use of method-calls used in object-oriented programming. Neither of these provides a means of separately managing the dialogue.

Myers has outlined the various implementation techniques used to specify the dialogue controller separately. Many of these were discussed in Chapter 8 where we explicitly dealt with dialogue notations. Some of the techniques that have been used in dialogue modelling in UIMS are listed here.

Menu networks The communication between application and presentation is modelled as a network of menus and submenus. To control the dialogue, the programmer must simply encode the levels of menus and the connections between one menu and the next sub-menu or an action. The menu is used to embody all possible user inputs at any one point in time. Links between menu items and the next displayed menu models the application response to previous input. A menu does not have to be a linear list of textual actions. The menu can be represented as graphical items or buttons that the user can select with a pointing device. Clicking on one button moves the dialogue to the next screen of objects. In this way, a system like HyperCard can be considered a menu network.

Grammar notations The dialogue between application and presentation can be treated as a grammar of actions and responses, and, therefore, described by means of a formal context-free grammar notation, such as BNF. These are good for describing command-based interfaces, but are not so good for more graphically based interaction techniques. It is also not clear from a formal grammar what directionality is associated to each event in the grammar, that is, whether an event is initiated by the user or by the application. Therefore, it is difficult to model communication of values across the dialogue controller, and that is necessary to maintain any semantic feedback from application to presentation.

State transition diagrams State transition diagrams can be used as a graphical means of expressing dialogue. Many variants on state transition diagrams were discussed in Chapter 8. The difficulty with these notations lies in linking dialogue events with corresponding presentation or application events. Also, it is not clear how communication between application and presentation is represented.

Event languages Event languages are similar to grammar notations, except that they can be modified to express directionality and support some semantic feedback. Event languages are good for describing localized input–output behaviour in terms of production rules. A production rule is activated when input is received and it results in some output responses. This control of the input–output relationship comes at a price. It is now more difficult to model the overall flow of the dialogue.

Declarative languages All of the above techniques (except for menu networks) are poor for describing the correspondence between application and presentation because they are unable to describe effectively how information flows between the two. They only view the dialogue as a sequence of events that occur between two communicating partners. A declarative approach concentrates more on describing how presentation and application are related. This relationship can be modelled as a shared database of values that both presentation and application can access. Declarative languages, therefore, describe what should result from the communication between application and presentation, not how it should happen in terms of event sequencing.

Constraints Constraints systems are a special subset of declarative languages. *Constraints* can be used to make explicit the connection between independent information of the presentation and the application. Implicit in the control component of the PAC model is this notion of constraint between values of the application and values of the presentation. Hill has proposed the *Abstraction–Link–View*, or ALV (pronounced 'AL-vee'), which makes the same distinctions as PAC. However, Hill suggests an implementation of the communication between abstraction and view by means of the link component as a collection of two-way *constraints* between abstraction and view. Constraints embody dependencies between different values that must always be maintained. For instance, an intelligent piggy bank might display the value of its contents; there is the constraint that the value displayed to the outside observer of the piggy bank is the same as the value of money inside it. By using constraints, the link component is described separately from the abstraction and view. Hence, describing the link in terms of constraints is a way of achieving an independent description of the dialogue controller.

Graphical specification These techniques allow the dialogue specification to be programmed graphically in terms of the presentation language itself. This technique can be referred to as *programming by demonstration* since the programmer is building up the interaction dialogue directly in terms of the actual graphical interaction objects that the user will see, instead of indirectly by means of some textual specification language that must still be linked with the presentation objects. The major advantage of this graphical technique is that it opens up the dialogue specification to the non-programmer, which is a very significant contribution.

Ultimately, the programmer would want access to a variety of these techniques in any one UIMS. For example, the Myers Garnet system combines a declarative constraints language with a graphical specification technique. There is an intriguing trend we should notice as we proceed away from internal control of dialogue in the application itself to external control in an independent dialogue component to *presentation control* in the graphical specification languages. When the dialogue is specified internal to the application, then it must know about presentation issues which makes the application less generic. External control is about specifying the dialogue independent of the application or presentation. One of the problems with such an independent description is that the intended link between application and presentation is impossible to describe without some information about each, so a good deal of information of each must be represented, which may be both inefficient and cumbersome. Presentation control describes the dialogue in the language in terms of the objects the user can see at the interface. Whereas this might provide a simple means of producing a dialogue specification and be more amenable to non-programmers, it is also restrictive because the graphical language of a modern workstation is nowhere near as expressive as programming languages.

In summary, components of a UIMS which allow the description of the application separate from the presentation are advantageous from a software engineering perspective, but there has not yet been conclusive proof that they are as desirable in designing for usability. There is currently a struggle between difficult-to-use but powerful techniques for describing both the communication and the correspondence between application and presentation and simple-to-use but limited techniques. Programmers will probably always opt for powerful techniques which provide the most flexibility. Non-programmers will opt for simplicity despite the lack of expressiveness.

10.6 Summary

In this chapter, we have concentrated on describing the programming support tools which are available for implementing interactive systems. We began with a description of windowing systems, which are the foundation for modern WIMP interfaces. Window systems provide only the crudest level of abstraction for the programmer, allowing them to gain device-independence and multiple application control. They do not, however, provide a means of separating the control of presentation and application dialogue. We described two paradigms for interactive programming, and saw that these relate to two means of controlling that dialogue — either internal to the application by means of a read–evaluation loop or external to the application by means of notification based programming. Toolkits used with particular windowing systems add another level of abstraction by combining input and output behaviours to provide the programmer with access to interaction objects from which to build the components of the interactive system. Toolkits are amenable to external dialogue control by means of callback procedures within the application. Other dialogue control techniques are provided with yet another level of abstraction in interactive system development, the user interface management system. UIMS provides a conceptual architecture for dividing up the relationship between application and presentation, and various techniques were described to implement the logical components of a UIMS. An interesting additional means of dialogue control can be seen to emerge in the use of graphical specification languages which move dialogue control all the way across the spectrum to reside entirely within the presentation language. This presentation control opens up interactive programming to the non-expert programmer, but at the cost of a loss of expressiveness.

Exercises

10.1 In contrasting the read–evaluation loop and the notification based paradigm for interactive programs, construction of a pre-emptive dialogue was discussed. How would a programmer describe a pre-emptive dialoge by purely graphical means? [Hint: refer to discussion in Section 10.5 concerning the shift from external and independent dialogue management to presentation control of the dialogue]

10.2 Recall the state transition diagram for font characteristics presented in Chapter 8 (Section 8.3.3). Compare different interaction objects which could implement this kind of dialogue. Use examples from existing toolkits (pull-down menus or dialogue boxes) or create a novel interaction object.

10.3 Scrolling is an effective means of browsing through a document in a window that is too small to show the whole document. Compare the different interactive behaviour of the following two interaction objects to implement scrolling:

- A scroll bar is attached to the side of the window with arrows at the top and bottom. When the mouse is positioned over the arrow at the top of the screen (which points up), the window frame is moved upwards to reveal a part of the document above/before what is currently viewed. When the bottom arrow is selected, the frame moves down to reveal the document below/after the current view.

- The document is contained in a textual interaction object. Pressing the mouse button in the text object allows you to drag the document within the window boundaries. You drag up to browse down in the document and you drag down to browse up.

The difference between the two situations can be characterized by noticing that in the first case, the user is actually manipulating the window (moving it up or down to reveal the contents of the document), whereas in the second case, the user is manipulating the document (pushing it up or down to reveal its contents through the windows. What usability principles would you use to justify one method over the other (also consider the case when you want to scroll from side to side as well as up and down)? What implementation considerations are important?

Recommended Reading

- Len Bass and Joëlle Coutaz, *Developing Software for the User Interface*, Addison-Wesley, 1991.

  This is dedicated to the issues we discuss in this chapter, along with general issues about software engineering for interactive systems. Full of programming examples and a detailed discussion of the Serpent UIMS.

- Brad A. Myers, *Creating User Interfaces by Demonstration*, Academic Press, 1988.

  Myers' work on the Peridot system is summarized in this book. Peridot was the precursor to the Garnet system. Readers interested in learning more about Garnet should consult the November 1990 issue of the journal *IEEE Computer* for an excellent introductory overview.

- Dan Olsen, *User Interface Management Systems: Models and Algorithms*, Morgan Kaufman Publishers, 1992.

  The serious interactive system programmers who want to learn more details about the workings of a wide variety of UIMS should consult this book, written by a very respected member of the UIMS community.

- Deborah Hix, Generations of User-Interface Management Systems, *IEEE Software*, **7**:5, pp. 77–87, September, 1990.

  A good introductory overview of the advances in UIMS technology and the future possibilities.

- Brad A. Myers, User-Interface Tools: Introduction and Survey, *IEEE Software*, **6**:1, pp., 47–61, January, 1989.

  As well as providing a state-of-the-art review of user interface tools, this article provides a good set of references into the relevant literature.

- G. F. Coulouris and H. W. Thimbleby, HyperProgramming, Addison-Wesley, 1993.

  An introduction to *programming* HyperCard. Use of the programming facilities of HyperTalk allows one to prototype substantial parts of the functionality as well as the surface features of an interface.

Chapter 11

Evaluation Techniques

Overview

- Evaluation tests the usability and functionality of an interactive system.

- Evaluation may take place

  - in the laboratory
  - in the field
  - in collaboration with users

- Some approaches evaluate designs

  - analytic methods
  - review methods
  - model based methods

- Some approaches evaluate implementations

  - experimental methods
  - observational methods
  - query methods

- An evaluation method must be chosen carefully and must be suitable for the job.

11.1 What is Evaluation?

In previous chapters we have discussed methodologies and models which support the design of usable interactive systems. However, even if such techniques are employed, we still need to assess our designs and test our systems to ensure that they actually behave as we expect and meet the requirements of the user. This is the role of evaluation.

Evaluation should not be thought of as a single phase in the design process (still less as an activity tacked on the end of the process if time permits). Ideally, evaluation should occur throughout the design life cycle, with the results of the evaluation feeding back into modifications to the design. Clearly it is not usually possible to perform extensive experimental testing continuously throughout the design, but analytic and informal techniques can and should be used. In this respect there is a close link between evaluation and the modelling and prototyping techniques we have already discussed — such techniques help to ensure that the design is assessed continually. This has the advantage that problems can be ironed out before considerable effort and resources have been expended on the implementation itself: it is much easier to change a design in the early stages of development than in the later stages. We can make a broad distinction between evaluation of the design of an interactive system and evaluation of an implementation, whether full or prototype. The former tends to focus on evaluation by the designer without direct involvement by users; the latter studies actual use of the system. We will discuss evaluation techniques under these two headings. However, it should be noted that these distinctions are not fixed and some techniques can be applied at either stage. Indeed, some techniques have wider application still, being used, as we have seen in Chapter 7, to develop task analyses.

11.2 Goals of Evaluation

Evaluation has three main goals: to assess the extent of the system's functionality, to assess the effect of the interface on the user, and to identify any specific problems with the system. The system's functionality is important in that it must accord with the user's task requirements. In other words, the design of the system should enable the user to perform the required tasks more easily. This includes not only making the appropriate functionality available within the system, but making it clearly reachable by the user in terms of the actions that the user needs to take to perform the task. It also involves matching the use of the system to the user's expectations of the task. For example, if a filing clerk is used to retrieving a customer's file by the postal address, the same capability (at least) should be provided in the computerized file system. Evaluation at this level may also include measuring the user's performance with the system, to assess the effectiveness of the system in supporting the task.

In addition to evaluating the system design in terms of its functional capabilities, it is important to be able to measure the impact of the design on the user. This includes considering aspects such as how easy the system is to learn, its usability and the user's attitude to it. In addition, it is important to identify areas of the design which overload the user in some way, perhaps by requiring an excessive amount of information to be remembered, for example. A fuller classification of such usability measures is provided in Chapter 4. Much evaluation is aimed at measuring features such as these.

The final goal of evaluation is to identify specific problems with the design. These may be aspects of the design which, when used in their intended context, cause unexpected results, or confusion amongst users. This is of course related to both the functionality and usability of the design (depending on the cause of the problem). However, it is specifically concerned with the negative aspects of the design.

11.3   Styles of Evaluation

Before we consider some of the techniques that are available for evaluation we will distinguish between a number of distinct evaluation styles. There are two main styles of evaluation: those performed under laboratory conditions and those conducted in the work environment or 'in the field'. There is also a specific instance of the latter which involves the user in the design to a greater degree than simply as an experimental subject. This is known as *participatory design* and in fact has a wider scope than evaluation. However, we include it here since it employs many of the same techniques.

11.3.1   *Laboratory studies*

The first style of evaluation studies the use of the system within the laboratory. In some cases (particularly in evaluating the design) this involves the designer performing some assessment of the design without the involvement of users. However, users may also be brought into the laboratory to take part in evaluation studies. This approach has a number of benefits and disadvantages.

A well-equipped usability laboratory may contain sophisticated audio/visual recording facilities, two-way mirrors, instrumented computers and the like, which cannot be replicated in the field. In addition, the subject operates in an interruption-free environment. However, the lack of context — filing cabinets, wall calendars, books and so on — and the unnatural situation may mean that one accurately records a situation which never arises in the real world. It is especially difficult to observe several people cooperating on a task in a laboratory situation as interpersonal communication is so heavily dependent on context.

There are some situations where laboratory observation is the only option: if the system is to be located in a dangerous or remote location, for example, a space station. Also some very constrained single-user tasks may be adequately performed in a laboratory. Finally, we may deliberately want to manipulate the context in order to uncover problems or observe less used procedures, or we may want to compare alternative designs within a controlled context. For these type of applications, laboratory studies are appropriate.

11.3.2   *Field studies*

The second style of evaluation takes the designer or evaluator out into the user's work environment in order to observe the system in action. Again this approach has its pros and cons.

High levels of ambient noise, greater levels of movement and constant interruptions, such as phone-calls, all make field observation difficult. However, the very 'open' nature of the situation means that you will observe interactions between systems and between individuals which would have been missed in a laboratory study. The context is retained and you are seeing the user in his 'natural environment'. In addition, some activities, such as those taking days or months, are impossible to study in the laboratory (and difficult even in the field).

On balance, field observation is to be preferred to laboratory studies as it allows us to study the interaction as it occurs in actual use. Even interruptions are important as these will expose behaviours such as saving and restoring state during a task. However, we should remember that even in field observations, the subjects are likely to be influenced by the presence of the analyst and/or recording equipment, so we always operate slightly removed from the natural situation, a sort of Heisenberg uncertainty principle.

This is of course a generalization: there are circumstances, as we have noted, in which laboratory testing is necessary. In particular, controlled experiments can be useful for evaluation of specific interface features, and must normally be conducted under laboratory conditions. From an economic angle, we need to weigh the costs of establishing recording equipment in the field, and possibly disrupting the actual work situation, with the costs of taking one or more subjects away from their jobs into the laboratory. This balance is not at all obvious.

11.3.3   *Participatory design*

Participatory design is a philosophy which encompasses the whole design cycle, not just evaluation. However, it involves evaluation and shares a number of techniques with it so it is included here. Participatory design is design in the workplace, incorporating the user not only as an experimental subject but as a member of the design team. Users are therefore active collaborators in the design process, rather than passive participants whose involvement is entirely governed by the designer. The argument is that users are experts in the work context and a design can only be effective within that context if these experts are allowed to contribute actively to the design.

Participatory design has three specific characteristics. It aims to improve the work environment and task by the introduction of the design. This makes design and evaluation context- or work-oriented rather than system-oriented. Secondly, it is characterized by collaboration: the user is included in the design team and can contribute to every stage of the design. Finally, the approach is iterative: the design is subject to evaluation and revision at each stage.

Participatory design originated in Scandinavia, where it is now promoted in law and accepted work practices. Although principles have been adopted from the approach elsewhere, it has not been widely practised. This may be due to the time and cost involved in what is, by definition, a context-specific design, as well as the organizational implications of the shift of power and responsibility.

In addition to the specific evaluation techniques described in the next sections, the participatory design process may include a number of methods to help convey information between the user and designer. They include

brainstorming This involves all participants in the design pooling ideas. This is informal and relatively unstructured although the process tends to involve 'on-the-fly' structuring of the ideas as they materialize. All information is recorded without judgement. The session provides a range of ideas from which to work. These can be filtered using other techniques.

storyboarding This has been discussed in more detail in Chapter 5. Storyboards can be used as a means of describing the user's day-to-day activities as well as the potential designs and the impact they will have.

workshops These can be used to fill in the missing knowledge of both participants and provide a more focused view of the design. They may involve mutual enquiry in which both parties attempt to understand the context of the design from each other's point of view. The designer questions the user about the work environment in which the design is to be used, and the user can query the designer on the technology and capabilities that may be available. This establishes common ground between the user and designer and sets the foundation for the design that is to be produced. The use of role play exercises can also allow both user and designer to step briefly into one another's shoes.

pencil and paper exercises These allow designs to be talked through and evaluated with very little commitment in terms of resources. Users can 'walk through' typical tasks using paper mock-ups of the system design. This is intended to show up discrepancies between the user's requirements and the actual design as proposed. Such exercises provide a simple and cheap technique for early evaluation. In the next section we will consider a variation on this, the *cognitive walkthrough*, which attempts to introduce psychological theory into the evaluation at this stage.

These methods are obviously not exclusively used in participatory design. They can be used more widely to promote clearer understanding between designer and user. Often the design context (for example, the constraints of a particular organization) do not permit full-blown participatory design. Even if this is the case, methods such as these are useful ways of encouraging cooperation between the two parties.

11.4 Evaluating the Design

As we have noted, evaluation should occur throughout the design process. In particular, the first evaluation of a system should ideally be performed before any implementation work has started. If the design itself can be evaluated, expensive mistakes can be avoided, since the design can be altered prior to any major resource commitments. Typically, the later in the design process that an error is discovered, the more costly it is to put right. Consequently, a number of methods have been proposed to evaluate the design prior to implementation. Most of these do not involve the user directly (although there exceptions, for example the paper and pencil walkthrough described in the previous section). Instead they depend upon the designer, or a human factors expert, taking the design and assessing the impact that it will have upon a typical user. The basic intent is to identify any areas which are likely to cause difficulties because they violate known cognitive principles, or ignore accepted empirical results. The methods are therefore largely analytic.

We will consider four possible approaches to evaluating design: the *cognitive walkthrough*, *heuristic evaluation*, review based evaluation and the use of models. Again, these are not mutually exclusive methods.

11.4.1 *Cognitive walkthrough*

Cognitive walkthrough is an attempt to introduce psychological theory into the informal and subjective walkthrough technique, proposed by Polson and colleagues [141]. In particular, it aims to evaluate the design in terms of how well it supports the user as he learns how to perform the required tasks. The walkthrough is performed by the designer or an expert in cognitive psychology. The expert works through the design for a particular task, step by step, identifying potential problems against psychological criteria. It is comparable to the process by which a software engineer will work through the code under different conditions (using different data sets or error conditions, for example) in order to evaluate the performance of a piece of software.

For each task that the design is intended to support, the expert considers the following issues:

- what impact will the interaction have upon the user?

- what cognitive processes are required?

- what learning problems may occur?

The analysis is focused on the user's goals and knowledge. The cognitive walkthrough must show if, and how, the interface will guide the user to generate the correct goals to perform the required task, and to select the necessary action to fulfil each goal. Consequently, in order to perform a cognitive walkthrough, certain information is required. First, a description of the interface itself is needed. Second, a description of the task, including the correct way to perform it, and the goal structure that supports it. In addition, assumptions about the user (for example, previous knowledge) must be elaborated.

Armed with this information the evaluator is able to carry out the steps of the walkthrough: choose the task, describe the user's initial goals, work out the appropriate actions within the system to perform the task, analyze the decision process for each action. The task and user's goals should be described in terms of the work environment rather than the system environment. For example, the task of finding a reference in a database should be described in terms of the user's view of the problem. A set of initial user goals may be:

> Find reference by Dix, Finlay, Abowd and Beale in my database
>> Load my database
>> Search for reference by Dix, Finlay, Abowd and Beale
>> Save reference

It should not include goals such as 'Search for reference using :/Dix...', as these are system-specific.

Cognitive walkthrough is form based: a form is provided which guides the evaluator through a set of questions relating to the user's task and goals. This provides a structure to the method and support for the evaluator.

Cognitive walkthrough is an analytic method which can be used both in the early design phase and to evaluate extant systems. It provides information regarding the learnability of an interface. If used early in the design process it can identify design problems before the prototyping stage and direct the focus of later evaluation. It should not be viewed as a replacement for empirical evaluation but as a complementary method.

As such it is beneficial since it provides a theoretical basis for early evaluation, in which the decisions made can be justified according to cognitive constraints. However, although it is designed to be used by the designers themselves, it does require some knowledge of psychological theory and terminology to use effectively. This is eased to an extent by the use of forms. In addition, it can be time-consuming to carry out exhaustive walkthroughs of all the required tasks. However, this should be viewed in the light of the resources required to perform experimental testing, which are far greater. Evaluation is not an activity which can be rushed.

An example: programming a video by remote control

A good design will help users to generate appropriate goals and to map these goals on to the correct actions. The designer should therefore be able to show how the interface supports the user in these two activities. Cognitive walkthrough checks whether this is indeed the case. We can illustrate how it works using a simple example. Imagine we are designing a remote control for a video recorder which will

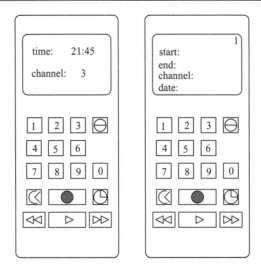

Figure 11.1   *An initial remote control design*

allow users to program the video to perform timed recording. Our initial design is shown in Figure 11.1. The first picture illustrates the hand set in normal use, the second after the timed record button has been pressed. The video allows the user to program up to three timed recordings in different 'streams'. We want to know whether our design supports the user's task. We begin by identifying the task.

Program video to time record a program starting at 18.00 and finishing 19.15 on channel 4 on the 4th.

We will assume that the user is familiar with video recorders but not with the particular design. The next step in the walkthrough is to identify the user's initial goals. We can specify this in terms of a high-level goal and a number of sub-goals:

Program video to record a timed program
        Set start time
        Set end time
        Set channel
        Set date

This is the goal as the user views it, taking into account his previous experience and knowledge. Note that it is expressed in high-level terms and does not give detail at the interface level. Having identified the user's goals, we then describe each action that is actually required to complete the task, and determine whether the interface supports the generation of the goal structure needed to complete the action. Each action is analyzed on a walkthrough form. The form presents a number of questions for the evaluator to consider. Examples of these are shown in the walkthrough illustrated here. First the action is identified and described. In our case the first action that needs to be performed is to press the 'timed recording' button (see Figure 11.1):

Action #1
Description: Press the 'timed recording' button

Next we identify the correct goal structure required to select the correct action. For illustration we show the first few sub-goals of the structure to allow comparison with the user's goal structure; the relevant goal is shown in italics:

Program video for timed recording
         Press 'timed record' button
         Set stream
                 Type stream number
                 Press 'timed recording' button
         Set start time
                 Type start time (24 hour)
                 Press 'timed recording' button
                 . . .

The next stage of the walkthrough is to compare the required goal structure with the initial user goal structure, in order to determine whether the interface supports the development of the correct goal structure. This is done with four questions:

- will the user fail to add the necessary goals?

- will the user fail to remove unwanted goals?

- will the user adopt any spurious goals based on the interface?

- will the user drop a goal that is still needed?

In the case of our design, the interface provides no indication that the user needs to press the 'timed record' button (or even which is the timed record button). Although a user familiar with videos may realize that such a key is needed, the interface does not support the generation of this goal well. The key itself is ambiguous (it may for instance be meant to set the clock). It is therefore likely that a high proportion of users would fail to add this goal to their goal structure and would therefore find it difficult to proceed.

The user's initial structure does not contain any unnecessary goals and therefore the second question does not apply in this case.

The interface has a second button for record — the filled circle. This is a standard symbol for 'record' in both audio and video systems and may be recognized as such by many users. Some users may therefore generate the spurious goal to press this button in order to perform the timed recording.

In this particular instance users are not encouraged to drop goals prematurely.

Having considered the problems users may have generating appropriate goals, we go on to consider whether they would have problems selecting the correct actions. As we have already seen, the interface does not support the selection of this action. Even if the user has the goal 'Press the timed record button' it is not easy to identify this button unambiguously. The label is open to a number of interpretations, and the presence of another possible candidate (in the record button) suggests that, as well as being unable to match the correct action with the goal, the user may in fact match the wrong action.

Finally we consider whether the interface presents any problems in terms of physical demands on the user or time constraints. Neither is a problem in this particular case.

The analysis proceeds in this fashion, with a walkthrough form completed for each action. In our case our second action is to type the stream number:

Action #2
Description: Type stream number
Goal structure:
     Set stream
       Type stream number
       Press 'timed record' button
Failure to add goal?
     Goal is not in user's initial goal structure.
     Interface indicates it by flashing the current stream number.
     Some users will not realize the significance of this.
Failure to remove goals?
     The user may attempt to complete the 'set start time' goal
     which in fact occurs later in the structure.
Add spurious goals?
     No.
Drop required goals?
     No
Identify action?
     If the goal is generated then the interface, and the user's assumed
     familiarity with numeric key pads, mean the action will be selected.
Incorrect action?
     No.
Problems with actions?
     No.

If we were to work through the rest of the task we would see that the interface provides poor support for the user's goal generation and action choice. For example, after Action #2 it is unclear as to how to proceed: no clue is given to the effect that the 'timed record' button must be pressed again. We can therefore see that our design is inadequate on a number of counts, and we can see exactly what is wrong with it. Back to the drawing board . . .

11.4.2   *Heuristic evaluation*

Heuristic evaluation, proposed by Nielsen and Molich [126], is similar to cognitive walkthrough in that it involves experts assessing the design against known usability criteria, but it is less structured and less directed. In this approach a set of usability criteria or *heuristics* is identified and the design examined for instances where these criteria are violated. The usability criteria are related to *principles* and *guidelines* (see Chapter 4), and can be selected or derived from these. For example, a set of usability criteria may include

- System behaviour is predictable

- System behaviour is consistent

- Feedback is provided

- The user's memory is not overloaded

- Dialogue is task-oriented

The goal of the heuristic evaluation is effectively to debug the design. The evaluator runs through the performance of the task set with the design, and assesses its conformance to the criteria at each stage. If a violation is detected, the design can be revised to resolve this problem, before the implementation stage.

Again, the approach is simple and relatively fast. It is not entirely subjective, in that specific criteria are used to guide the evaluation. However, it requires a certain level of knowledge in order to apply the heuristics. For example, in order to determine if a design overloads the user's memory, a designer needs to know the capabilities of human memory (see Chapter 1 for details of memory). Also, heuristic evaluation is not easy and a single evaluator is liable to miss problems in a design, even using the criteria. However, it is a useful exercise to perform, particularly if a small group of evaluators can assess the design independently and then collate results.

11.4.3   *Review based evaluation*

Experimental psychology and human–computer interaction between them possess a wealth of experimental results and empirical evidence. Some of this is specific to a particular domain, but much deals with more generic issues and applies in a variety of situations. Examples of such issues are the usability of different menu types, the recall of command names, and the choice of icons.

One approach to evaluating a design is to exploit this inheritance and scour the literature for evidence to support (or refute) aspects of the design. After all, it is wasteful to repeat experiments continually, for the sake of it, and, although a literature review is time-consuming to perform, it can probably be completed in the time that it would take to repeat just one experiment.

However, it should be noted that experimental results cannot be expected to hold arbitrarily across contexts. The reviewer must therefore select evidence carefully, noting the experimental design chosen, the population of subjects used, the analyses performed and the assumptions made. For example, an experiment testing the usability of a particular style of help system using novice subjects may not provide accurate evaluation of a help system designed for expert users. The review should therefore take account of both the similarities and the differences between the experimental context and the design under consideration.

11.4.4 *Model based evaluation*

The final approach to evaluating the design that we will note is the use of models. Certain cognitive and design models provide a means of combining design specification and evaluation into the same framework. For example, the GOMS model (see Chapter 6) predicts user performance with a particular interface and can be used to filter particular design options. Similarly, lower level modelling techniques such as the keystroke level model (Chapter 6) provide predictions of the time users will take to perform low-level physical tasks.

Design methodologies, such as design rationale (see Chapter 5), also have a role to play in evaluation at the design stage. Design rationale provides a framework in which design options can be evaluated. By examining the criteria that are associated with each option in the design, and the evidence that is provided to support these criteria, informed judgements can be made in the design.

11.5 Evaluating the Implementation

The techniques we have considered so far concentrate on evaluating the design before it exists as a runnable system. They typically involve analysis by the designer (or an expert evaluator) rather than testing with actual users. However, vital as these techniques are for filtering and refining the design, they are not a replacement for actual usability testing with the people for whom the system is intended: the users. In this section we will look at a number of different approaches to user-centred evaluation. These include empirical or experimental methods, observational methods and techniques which we will call *query techniques*, which ask the user for feedback directly.

The major difference between this type of evaluation and evaluation of design, aside from the involvement of the user, is the existence of an actual implementation of the system in some form. This may may range from a simulation of the system's interactive capabilities, without its underlying functionality (for example, the *Wizard of Oz* technique, which is discussed in Chapter 5), through a basic functional prototype to a fully implemented system. The evaluation techniques described in this section can be used to evaluate any of these.

11.5.1 *Empirical methods: experimental evaluation*

One of the most powerful methods of evaluating a design or an aspect of a design is to use a controlled experiment. This provides empirical evidence to support a particular claim or hypothesis. It can be used to study a wide range of different issues at different levels of detail.

Any experiment has the same basic form. The evaluator chooses a hypothesis to test, which can be determined by measuring some attribute of subject behaviour. A number of experimental conditions are considered which differ only in the values of certain controlled variables. Any changes in the behavioural measures are attributed to the different conditions. Within this basic form there are a number of factors that are important to the overall reliability of the experiment, which must be considered carefully in experimental design. These include the subjects chosen, the variables tested and manipulated, and the hypothesis tested.

Subjects

The choice of subjects is vital to the success of any experiment. In evaluation experiments subjects should be chosen to match the expected user population as closely as possible. Ideally this will involve experimental testing with the actual users but this is not always possible. If subjects are not actual users they should be chosen to be of a similar age and level of education as the intended user group. Their experience with computers in general, and with systems related to that being tested, should be similar as should their experience or knowledge of the task domain. It is no good testing an interface designed to be used by the general public on a subject set made up of computer science undergraduates: they are simply not representative of the intended user population.

A second issue relating to the subject set is the sample size chosen. Often this is something which is determined by pragmatic considerations: the availability of subjects is limited or resources are scarce. However, the sample size must be large enough to be considered to be representative of the population taking into account the design of the experiment and the statistical methods chosen. As a rough guide a sample size of at least ten subjects is recommended for controlled experiments.

Variables

Experiments manipulate and measure variables under controlled conditions, in order to test the hypothesis. There are two main types of variable, those that are manipulated and those that are measured. The former are known as *independent variables*, the latter as *dependent variables*.

Independent variables are those characteristics of the experiment which are manipulated to produce different conditions for comparison. Examples of independent variables in evaluation experiments are interface style, level of help, number of menu items and icon design. Each of these variables can be given a number of different values; each value that is used in an experiment is known as a *level* of the variable. So, for example, an experiment that wants to test whether search speed improves as the number of menu items decreases, may consider menus with five, seven, and ten items. Here the independent variable, number of menu items, has three levels.

More complex experiments may have more than one independent variable. For example, in the above experiment, we may suspect that the speed of the user's response depends not only on the number of menu items but also on the choice of commands used on the menu. In this case there are two independent variables. If there were two sets of command names (i.e. two levels), we would require six experimental conditions to investigate all the possibilities.

Dependent variables on the other hand are the variables which can be measured in the experiment. In the example given above, this would be the speed of menu selection. The dependent variable must be measurable in some way, it must be affected by the independent variable, and, as far as possible, unaffected by other factors. Common choices of dependent variable in evaluation experiments are the time taken to complete a task, the number of errors made, user preference and the quality of the user's performance. Obviously some of these are easier to measure objectively than others. However, the more subjective measures can be applied against predetermined scales, and can be very important factors to consider.

Hypotheses

A hypothesis is a prediction of the outcome of an experiment. It is framed in terms of the independent and dependent variables, stating that a variation in the independent variable will cause a difference in the dependent variable. The aim of the experiment is to show that this prediction is correct. This is done by disproving the *null hypothesis*, which states that there is no difference in the dependent variable between the levels of the independent variable. The statistical measures described below produce values which can be compared to various levels of significance. If a result is significant it shows, at the given level of certainty, that the differences measured would not have occurred by chance (i.e. that the null hypothesis is incorrect).

Experimental design

In order to produce reliable and generalizable results, an experiment must be carefully designed. We have already looked at a number of the factors which the experimenter must consider in the design, namely the subjects, the independent and dependent variables, and the hypothesis. The first phase in experimental design then is to choose the hypothesis: to decide exactly what it is you are trying to demonstrate. In doing this you are likely to clarify the independent and dependent variables, in that you will have identified what you are going to manipulate and what change you expect. If your hypothesis does not clearly identify these variables then you need to rethink it. At this stage you should also consider your subjects: how many are available and are they representative of the user group?

The next step is to decide on the *experimental method* which you will use. There are two main methods: *between-groups* and *within-groups*. In a between-groups (or *randomized*) design, each subject is assigned to a different condition. There are at least two conditions: the experimental condition (in which the variable has been manipulated) and the control, which is identical to the experimental condition except for this manipulation. This control serves to ensure that it is the manipulation that is responsible for any differences which are measured. There may of course be more than two groups, depending on the number of independent variables, and the number of levels which each variable can take.

The advantage of a between-groups design is that any learning effect resulting from the user performing in one condition and then the other, is controlled: each user performs under only one condition. The disadvantages are that a greater number of subjects are required, and that significant variation between the groups can negate any results. Also, individual differences between users can bias the results. These problems can be handled by a careful selection of subjects, ensuring that all are representative of the population.

The second experimental design is *within-groups*. Here each user performs under each different condition. This design can suffer from transfer of learning effects, but this can be lessened if the order in which the conditions are tackled is varied between users. Within-groups is less costly than between-groups, since fewer users are required, and it can be particularly effective where learning is involved. There is also less chance of effects from variation between subjects.

The choice of experimental method will depend on the resources available, how far learning transfer is likely or can be controlled, and how representative the subject group is considered to be. A popular compromise, in cases where there is more than one independent variable, is to devise a mixed design where one variable is placed between groups and one within groups. So, returning to our example of the menu design, the subjects would be split into two groups, one for each command set, but each group would perform in three conditions, corresponding to the three possible levels of the number of menu items.

Once we have determined the hypothesis we are trying to test, the variables we are studying, the subjects at our disposal, and the design that is most appropriate, it remains for us to decide how we are going to analyze the results we record. There are a number of statistical tests available, and the choice of test is vital to the success of the experiment. Different tests make different assumptions about the data and if an inappropriate test is chosen, the results can be invalid. The next section discusses the factors to consider in choosing a statistical test and surveys the most common statistical measures available.

Statistical measures

The first two rules of statistical analysis are to *look* at the data and to *save* the data. It is easy to carry out statistical tests blindly when a glance at a graph, histogram or table of results would have been more instructive. In particular, it can expose *outliers*, single data items which are very different from the rest. Outliers are often the result of a transcription error, or a freak event not connected to the experiment. For example, we notice that one subject took three times as long as everyone else to do a task. We investigate and discover that the subject had been suffering from flu on the day of the experiment. Clearly, if the subject's data were included it would bias the results.

Saving the data is important as we may later want to try a different analysis method. It is all too common for an experimenter to take some averages or otherwise tabulate results, and then throw away the original data. At worst, the remaining statistics can be useless for statistical purposes, and, at best, we have lost the ability to trace back odd results to the original data, as, for example, we want to do for outliers.

Our choice of statistical analysis depends on the type of data and the questions we want to answer. It is worth having important results checked by an experienced statistician, but in many situations standard tests can be used.

Variables can be classified as either *discrete variables* or *continuous variables*. A discrete variable can only take a finite number of values or *levels*, for example, a screen colour which can be: red, green or blue. A continuous variable can take any value (although may have an upper or lower limit), for example, a person's height or the time taken to complete a task. A special case of continuous data is when they are *positive*, for example, a response time cannot be negative. A continuous variable can be rendered discrete by clumping it into classes, for example, we could divide heights into short (< 5ft), medium (5ft–6ft) and tall (> 6ft). In many interface experiments we will be testing one design against another. In these cases the independent variable is usually discrete.

The dependent variable is the measured one and subject to random experimental variation. In the case when this variable is continuous, the random variation may take a special form. If the form of the data follows a known *distribution* then special and more powerful statistical tests can be used. Such tests are called *parametric tests* and the most common of these are used when the variation follows the *normal distribution*. This means that if we plot a histogram of the random errors, they will form the well-known bell-shaped graph (Figure 11.2). Happily, many of these tests are fairly *robust*, that is, they give reasonable results even when the

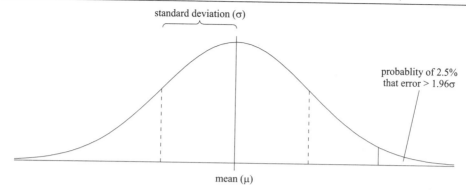

Figure 11.2   *Histogram of normally distributed errors*

data is not precisely normal. This means that you need not worry too much about checking normality during early analysis.

There are ways of checking whether data are really normal, but for these the reader should consult a statistics book, or a professional statistician. However, as a general rule, if data can be seen as the sum or average of many small *independent* effects they are likely to be normal. For example, the time taken to complete a *complex* task is the sum of the times of all the minor tasks of which it is composed. On the other hand, a subjective rating of the usability of an interface will not be normal. Occasionally data can be *transformed* to become approximately normal. The most common is the log-transformation, which is used for positive data with near-zero values. As a log-transformation has little effect when the data are clustered well away from zero, many experimenters habitually log-transform. However, this practice makes the results difficult to interpret and is not recommended.

When we cannot assume that data are normally distributed, we must often resort to *non-parametric* tests. These are statistical tests which make no assumptions about the particular distribution and are usually based purely on the ranking of the data. That is, each item of a data set (for example, 57, 32, 61, 49) is reduced to its rank (3, 1, 4, 2), before analysis begins. Because non-parametric tests make fewer assumptions about the data than parametric tests, and are more resistant to outliers, there is less danger of getting spurious results. However, they are less *powerful* than the corresponding parametric tests. This means that, given the same set of data, a parametric test might detect a difference that the non-parametric test would miss.

A third sort of test is the contingency table, where we classify data by several discrete attributes and then count the number of data items with each attribute combination.

Table 11.1 lists some of the standard tests categorized by the form of independent and dependent variables (discrete/continuous/normal). Normality is not an

Table 11.1 *Choosing a statistical technique.*

independent variable	dependent variable	
parametric		
2 valued	normal	Student's *t* test on difference of means
discrete	normal	ANOVA (ANalysis Of VARiance)
continuous	normal	linear (or non-linear) regression factor analyis
non-parametric		
2 valued	continuous	Wilcoxon (or Mann-Whitney) rank-sum test
discrete	continuous	rank-sum versions of ANOVA
continuous	continuous	Spearman's rank correlation
contingency tests		
2 valued	discrete	no special test, see next entry
discrete	discrete	contingency table and χ squared test.
continuous	discrete	(rare) group independent variable and then as above

issue for the independent variable, but a special case is when it is discrete with only two values, for example, comparing two systems. We cannot describe all the techniques here; for this the reader should use a standard statistics text. The table is intended to guide you in your choice of test.

An extensive and accurate analysis is no use if it answers the wrong question. Examples of questions one might ask about the data are:

Is there a difference? For example, is one system better than another? Techniques which address this are called *hypothesis testing*. The answers to this are not simply yes/no, but of the form – we are 99% certain selection from menus of 5 items is faster than that from menus of 7 items.

How big is the difference? For example, selection from 5 items is 260 ms faster than 7 items. This is called *point estimation*, often obtained by averages.

How accurate is the estimate? For example, selection is faster by 260 ms±30 ms. Statistical answers to this are either in the form of measures of variation such as the *standard deviation* of the estimate, or *confidence intervals*. Again, the answers one obtains are probabilistic — we are 95% certain that the difference in response time is between 230 ms and 290 ms.

The experimental design issues we have discussed have been principally addressed at the first question. However, most of the statistical techniques listed above, both parametric and non-parametric, give some answer to one or both of the other questions.

Example of non-parametric statistics

We will not see an example of the use of non-parametric statistics later, so we will go through a small example here. Imagine we had the following data for response times under two conditions:

condition A: 33, 42, 25, 79, 52
condition B: 87, 65, 92, 93, 91, 55

We gather the data together and sort them into order: 25, 33, 42, . . . , 92, 93. We then substitute for each value its rank in the list: 25 becomes 1, 33 becomes 2, etc. The transformed data are then:

condition A: 2, 3, 1, 7, 4
condition B: 8, 6, 10, 11, 9, 5

Tests are then carried out on the data. For example, to test whether there is any difference between the two conditions we can use the *Wilcoxon Test*. To do this we take each condition and calculate the sum of ranks, and subtract the smallest value it could have (i.e. $1+2+3+4+5 = 15$ for condition A, $1+2+3+4+5+6 = 21$ for condition B), giving the statistic U:

	rank sum		smallest		U
condition A:	$(2+3+1+7+4)$	$-$	15	$=$	2
condition B:	$(8+6+10+11+9+5)$	$-$	21	$=$	28

In fact, the sum of these two U statistics, $2 + 28 = 30$, is the product of the number of data values in each condition 5×6. This will always happen and so one can always get away with calculating only one of the Us. Finally, we then take the smallest statistic and compare it to a set of *critical values* in a book of statistical tables, to see if it is unusually small. The table is laid out dependent on the number of data values in each condition (5 and 6). The critical value at the 5% level turns out to be 3. As the smallest statistic is smaller than this, we can *reject the null hypothesis* and conclude that there is likely to be a difference between the conditions. To be precise it says that there is only a 1 in 20 (5%) chance that the data happened by chance. In fact the test is right — the authors constructed random data in the range 1–100 and then subtracted 10 from each of the values in condition A.

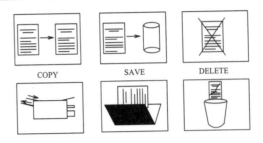

Figure 11.3   *Abstract and concrete icons for file operations*

An example: evaluating icon designs

Imagine you are designing a new word-processing package which is to use icons for presentation. You are considering two styles of icon design and you wish to know which design will be easiest for users to remember. One set of icons uses naturalistic images (based on a paper document metaphor); the other uses abstract images (see Figure 11.3). How might you design an experiment to help you decide which style to use?

The first thing you need to do is form a hypothesis: what do you consider to be the likely outcome? In this case you might expect the natural icons to be easier to recall since they are more familiar to users. We can therefore form the following hypothesis:

users will remember the natural icons more easily than the abstract ones.

The null hypothesis in this case is that there will be no difference between recall of the icon types.

This hypothesis clearly identifies the independent variable for our experiment: we are varying the style of icon. The independent variable has two levels: natural and abstract. However, when we come to consider the dependent variable, things are not so obvious. We have expressed our hypothesis in terms of users being able to remember *more easily*. How can we measure this? First we need to clarify exactly what we mean by the phrase *more easily*: are we concerned with the user's performance in terms of accurate recall or in terms of speed, for example, or are we looking at more subjective measures like user preference? In this example we will assume that the speed at which a user can accurately select an icon is an indication of how easily it is remembered. Our dependent variables are therefore the number of mistakes in selection and the time taken to select an icon.

Of course we need to control the experiment so that any differences we observe are clearly attributable to the independent variable, and so that our measurements of the dependent variables are comparable. To do this we provide an interface which is identical in every way except for the icon design, and a selection task which can be repeated for each condition. The latter could either be a naturalistic task (such as producing a document) or a more artificial task in which the user has to select the appropriate icon to a given prompt. The second task has the advantage that it is more controlled (there is little variation between users as to how they will perform the task) and it can be varied to avoid transfer of learning. Before performing the selection task the users will be allowed to learn the icons in controlled conditions, for example, they may be given a fixed amount of time to learn the icon meanings.

The next stage is to decide upon an experimental method. This may depend on the subjects that are available, but in this case we will assume that we have sufficient subjects from the intended user group. Given the fact that learning is involved in this experiment we will use a within-groups design, in which each user performs using both sets of icons.

So all that remains is to finalize the details of our experiment, given the constraints imposed by these choices. We devise two interfaces composed of blocks of icons, one for each condition. The user is presented with a task (say 'delete a document') and is required to select the appropriate icon. The selection task comprises a set of such presentations. In order to avoid learning effects from icon position, the placing of icons in the block can be randomly varied on each presentation. Each user performs the selection task under each condition. In order to avoid transfer of learning, the users are divided into two groups with each group taking a different starting condition. For each user we measure the time taken to complete the task and the number of errors made.

Finally, we must analyze our results. Table 11.2 shows a possible set of results for ten subjects[1]. The first five had the abstract icons presented first (order AN), and the last five had the natural icons presented first (order NA). Columns 1 and 2 in the table show the completion times for the task using natural and abstract icons respectively. As the times are the result of lots of presentations, we will assume that they are normally distributed. The main independent variable, the icon type, is two valued, suggesting we can use a simple difference of means with Student's *t* test (Table 11.1). In fact, because we have used a *within-groups* design, there is another independent variable we have to take into account — the subject. This means we have more than one discrete independent variable, and referring again to Table 11.1, we see that this implies we should use *analysis of variance (ANOVA)*. A full analysis of variance is quite complex, and is ideally done with the aid of a statistics package. However, this experiment is particularly simple, so we can use a simplified analysis.

Look at columns 2 and 3 of Table 11.2. The completion times range from less than 5 minutes (subject 2) to nearly 20 minutes (subject 6), showing a wide variation between individuals. This wide variation emphasizes the importance of the *within-groups* design. To see how this affects the results, we will first try to analyze them ignoring the fact that each subject performed under each condition. At the end of the table, the mean and standard deviation has been calculated for each condition. These means can then be compared using *Student's* t *test*. The

---

[1] Note these are fabricated results for the purposes of exposition.

Table 11.2   *Example experimental results — completion times.*

Subject number	Presentation order	(1) Natural (s)	(2) Abstract (s)	(3) Subject mean	(4) Natural (1)−(3)	(5) Abstract (2)−(3)
1.	AN	656	702	679	−23	23
2.	AN	259	339	299	−40	40
3.	AN	612	658	635	−23	23
4.	AN	609	645	627	−18	18
5.	AN	1049	1129	1089	−40	40
6.	NA	1135	1179	1157	−22	22
7.	NA	542	604	573	−31	31
8.	NA	495	551	523	−28	28
9.	NA	905	893	899	6	−6
10.	NA	715	803	759	−44	44
mean (μ)		698	750	724	−26	26
s.d. (σ)		265	259	262	14	14
		s.e.d. 117			s.e. 4.55	
Student's t		0.32 (n.s.)			5.78 ($p<1\%$, 2 tailed)	

difference between the means is 52 seconds, but the *standard error of the difference* (s.e.d.) is 117. This is calculated as follows:

$$s.e.d. \quad = \quad \sqrt{\frac{\sigma_N^2}{n_N} + \frac{\sigma_A^2}{n_A}} \quad = \quad \sqrt{\frac{265^2}{10} + \frac{259^2}{10}} \quad = \quad 117.2$$

where σ_N and σ_A are the standard deviations of the two conditions and n_N and n_A are the number of data items in each condition (10 in each). The s.e.d. is a measure of the expected variability of the difference between the means, and as we see the actual difference is well within this random variation. Testing the ratio 52/117 against tables of Student's t distribution indeed show that this is not significant.

However, if we glance down the table, we see that in almost every case the time taken with the abstract icons is greater than the time taken for the natural icons. That is, the data seem to support our claim that natural icons are better than abstract ones, but the wide variation between individuals has hidden the effect.

A more sophisticated analysis, a special case of ANOVA, can expose the difference. Looking back at the table, column 3 shows, for each subject, the average of the time they took under the two conditions. This subject mean is then subtracted from the data for each condition, yielding columns 4 and 5. These columns show the effect of the icon design *once the differences between subjects have been removed*. The two columns are redundant as they always add up to zero. They show that in all but one case (subject 9) the natural icons are faster than the abstract ones.

Even a non-parametric test would show this as a significant difference at the 5% level, but the use of a *t* test is more precise. We can take either column and see that the column average 26 is much greater than the standard error ($14.4/\sqrt{10}$). The ratio (mean/s.e.) is compared with the Student's t table (in statistical tables) using 9 degrees of freedom (10 values minus 1 for the mean), and is indeed far greater than the 1% level (3.250); that is, the chance of getting our results by chance is less than 1 in 100. So, we reject the *null hypothesis* that there is no difference and conclude that natural icons are more easily remembered than abstract ones.

In fact, the last statement is not quite correct. What we have shown is that in this experiment natural icons are more *rapidly* remembered. Possibly if we go on to analyze the errors, these may present a different story. If these error figures were quite large (say 15 errors or more per condition), then we may be able to assume these are normal and use ANOVA. If not, we can either use non-parametric tests, or make use of special tests based on the *binomial distribution*. We will not perform these analyses here. Possibly, looking at the errors we may find that the natural icons have *more* errors — it could well be that they are more rapidly, but less accurately, remembered. It is always worth keeping in mind the difference between the intended purpose of the experiment (to see which is better remembered) and the actual measurements (speed and accuracy).

Finally, one ought to look carefully at the experimental results to see whether there is any other effect which might confuse the results. The graphical presentation of results will help with this, possibly highlighting odd clumps in the data or other irregularities. In this experiment we may want to check to see if there has been any significant *transfer effect* between the first and second condition for each subject. The second set may be faster as the subjects are more practised, or possibly the second set may be slower as learning a second set of icons may be confusing. This will not matter if the effect is uniform — say they always are 15 seconds slower on the second test. But there may be systematic effects. For example, seeing the natural icons first might make it more difficult to learn the abstract ones, but not vice versa. If this were the case, our observed effect may be about the interference between the icon sets, rather than that one is better than the other.

11.5.2   *Observational techniques*

Think aloud

A popular way to gather information about actual use of a system is to observe users interacting with it. Usually they are asked to complete a set of pre-determined tasks, although, if observation is being carried out in the users' place of work, they may be observed going about their normal duties. The evaluator watches and records the user's actions (using a variety of techniques — see below). Simple observation is seldom sufficient to determine how well the system meets the user's requirements since it does not always give insight into the user's decision processes or attitude. Consequently users are asked to elaborate their actions by 'thinking aloud': describing what they believe is happening, why they take an action, what they are trying to do.

Think aloud has the advantage of simplicity; it requires little expertise to perform and can provide useful insight into problems with an interface. Also it may be used to observe how the system is actually used. It can be used for evaluation throughout the design process using paper or simulated mockups for the earlier stages. However, the information provided is often subjective and may be selective, depending on the tasks provided. The process of observation can alter the way that people perform tasks and so provide a biased view. The very act of describing what you are doing often changes the way you do it – like the joke about the centipede who was asked how he walked . . .

A variation on think aloud is known as *cooperative evaluation* (Monk *et al.* [115]) in which the user is encouraged to see himself as a collaborator in the evaluation and not simply as an experimental subject. As well as asking the user to think aloud at the beginning of the session the evaluator can ask the user questions (typically of the 'why?' or 'what if?' type) if the user's behaviour is unclear, and the user can ask the evaluator for clarification if a problem arises. This more relaxed view of the think aloud process has a number of advantages:

- the process is less constrained and therefore easier to learn to use by the evaluator

- the user is encouraged to criticize the system

- the evaluator can clarify points of confusion at the time they occur and so maximize the effectiveness of the approach for identifying problem areas

The usefulness of think aloud and general observation is largely dependent on the effectiveness of the recording method and subsequent analysis. The record of an evaluation session of this type is known as a *protocol*, and there are a number of methods from which to choose.

Protocol analysis

There are a number of methods for recording user actions. These include

paper and pencil This is primitive, but cheap, and allows the analyst to note interpretations and extraneous events as they occur. However, it is hard to get detailed information as it is limited to the analyst's writing speed. Coding schemes for frequent activities, developed during preliminary studies, can improve the rate of recording substantially. A variation of paper and pencil is the use of a notebook computer for direct entry, but then one is limited to the analyst's typing speed, and one loses the flexibility of paper for writing styles, quick diagrams and spatial layout.

Audio recording This is useful if the user is actively 'thinking aloud'. However, it may be difficult to record sufficient information to identify exact actions in later analysis, and difficult to match an audio recording to some other form of protocol (such as a handwritten script).

Video recording This has the advantage that we can see *what* the subject is doing, *as long* as the subject stays within the range of the camera. Choosing suitable camera positions and viewing angles so that you get sufficient detail (remember the resolution is not that good) and yet keep the subject in view is difficult. Alternatively, one has to ask the subject not to move — not conducive to normal activity. For single-user computer based tasks, one typically uses two video cameras, one looking at the computer screen and one with a wider focus including the user's face and hands. The former camera may not be necessary if the computer system is being logged.

Computer logging It is relatively easy to get a system automatically to record user actions at a keystroke level, particularly if this facility has been considered early in the design. It can be more difficult with proprietary software where source code is not available (although some software now provides built in logging and playback facilities). Obviously, computer logging only tells us what the user is doing on the system, but this may be sufficient for some purposes. Keystroke data are also 'semantics free' in that they only tell us about the lowest level actions, not why they were performed or how they are structured (although slight pauses and gaps can give clues). Direct logging has the advantage is that it is cheap (except in terms of disk storage), unobtrusive and can be used for *longitudinal studies*, where we look at one or more users over periods of weeks or months. Technical problems with it are that the sheer volume of data can become unmanageable without automatic analysis, and that one often has to be careful to restore the state of the system (file contents, etc.) before replaying the logs.

User notebooks The subjects themselves can be asked to keep logs of activity/problems. This obviously will be at a very coarse level — at most records every few minutes and more likely hourly or less. It also gives us 'interpreted' records which have advantages and problems. The technique is especially useful in longitudinal studies, and also where we want a log of unusual or infrequent tasks and problems.

In practice, one uses a mixture of recording methods as they complement one another. For instance, we may keep a paper note of special events and circumstances, even when we have more sophisticated audio/visual recording. Similarly, one may use separate audio recording, even where a video recorder is used, as the quality of specialist audio recording is better than most built in video microphones. In addition, we may use stereo audio recording which helps us to locate out-of-screen noises. If one is using a collection of different sources, say audio, video ($\times$ 2) and keystroke logging, there is considerable difficulty in synchronizing them during playback. Most video recorders can superimpose an on-screen clock, which can help, but ideally one uses specialized equipment which can automatically synchronize the different sources, possibly merging several video displays onto a single screen. Unfortunately, this sort of equipment is often only available in specialized laboratories.

With both audio and video recording, a major problem is *transcription*. Typing a transcript from a tape is not the same as taped dictation. The conversation will typically consist of part or broken sentences, mumbled words and inarticulated noises. In addition, the transcript will need annotating with the different voices (which may only be clear from context) and with non-verbal items such as pauses, emphases, equipment noises, phones ringing, etc. A good audio-typist will be used to completing mumbled words and correcting ungrammatical sentences — typing *exactly* what is recorded may prove difficult. Some practitioners say that the use of typists is not good practice anyway as the analyst will miss many nuances which are lost in the written transcript. However, if you wish to produce your own typed transcripts from tape, a course in touch typing is highly recommended.

For video transcription, professional typists are not an option; there is no standard way of annotating video recordings, and the analyst must invent notations to suit the particular circumstances. The scale of this task is not to be underestimated. It is common to talk to practitioners who have tens or hundreds of hours of video recording, but have only analyzed tiny fragments in detail. Of course, the fragments will have been chosen after more extensive perusal of the material, but it certainly removes any idea of comprehensive coverage.

Automatic protocol analysis tools

Analyzing protocols, whether video, audio or system logs, is time-consuming and tedious by hand. It is made harder if there is more than one stream of data to synchronize. A possible solution to this problem is to provide automatic analysis tools to support the task. As yet most systems of this type are experimental but they offer a means of editing and annotating video, audio and system logs and synchronizing these for detailed analysis.

EVA (Experimental Video Annotator) is a prototype system which runs on a multi-media workstation with a direct link to a video recorder [103]. The evaluator can devise a set of buttons indicating different events. These may include timestamps and snapshots, as well as notes of expected events and errors. The buttons are used within a recording session by the evaluator to annotate the video with notes. During the session the user works at a workstation and is recorded, using video, and perhaps audio and system logging as well. The evaluator uses the multi-media workstation running EVA. On the screen is the live video record and a view of the user's screen (see Figure 11.4). The evaluator can use the buttons to tag interesting events as they occur and can record additional notes using a text editor. After the session the evaluator can ask to review the tagged segments and can then use these and standard video controls to search the information. Links can be made with other types of record such as audio and system logs. A

Figure 11.4   *EVA: An automatic protocol analysis tool (courtesy Wendy Mackay)*

system such as EVA alleviates the burden of video analysis but it is not without its problems. The act of tagging and annotating events can prevent the evaluator actually concentrating on the events themselves. This may mean that events are missed or tagged late. It also requires specialist hardware to run, which may only be available in the most well equipped laboratories.

The *Workplace project* at Xerox PARC [177] is also developing a system to aid protocol analysis. The main emphasis here is to support the analysis of synchronized information from different data streams, such as video, audio, notes and diagrams. Each data stream is viewed in an aligned display so that it is possible to compare the records of each for a given point in the interaction. The alignment may be based on timestamps or on an event or action and is implemented using hypertext links.

Systems such as these, although still experimental, are extremely important as evaluation tools since they offer a means of handling the data that are collected in observational studies and allowing a more systematic approach to the analysis. The evaluator's task is facilitated and it is likely that more valuable observations will emerge as a result.

Post-task walkthroughs

Often data obtained via direct observation lack interpretation. We have the basic actions which were performed, but little knowledge as to why. Even where the subject has been encouraged to think aloud through the task, the information may be at the wrong level. For example, the subject may say 'and now I'm selecting the undo menu', but not tell us what was wrong to make undo necessary. In addition, a think aloud does not include information such as alternative, but not pursued, actions.

A walkthrough attempts to alleviate these problems, by reflecting back to the subjects their actions, after the event. The transcript, whether written or recorded, is replayed to the subject who is invited to comment, or is directly questioned by the analyst. This may be done straight away, when the subject may actually remember why certain actions were performed, or after an interval, when the answers are more likely to be the subject's post-hoc interpretation. (In fact, interpretation is likely even in the former case.) The advantage of a delayed walkthrough is that the analyst has had time to frame suitable questions and focus on specific incidents. The disadvantage is a loss of freshness.

There are some circumstances when the subject cannot be expected to talk during the actual observation, for instance, during a critical task, or when the task is too intensive. In these circumstances, the post-task walkthrough is the only way to obtain a subjective viewpoint of the user's behaviour. There is also an argument that it is preferable to minimize non-task related talk during direct observation in order to get as natural performance as possible. Again this makes the walkthrough essential.

11.5.3 *Query techniques*

Query techniques are less formal than controlled experimentation, but can be useful in eliciting detail of the user's view of a system. They embody the philosophy which states that the best way to find out how a system meets user requirements is to 'ask the user'. They can be used in evaluation and more widely to collect information about user requirements and tasks. The advantage of such methods is that they get the user's viewpoint directly and may reveal issues which have not been considered by the designer. In addition they are relatively simple and cheap to administer. However, the information gained is necessarily subjective, and may be a 'rationalized' account of events rather than a wholly accurate one. Also it may be difficult to get accurate feedback about alternative designs if the user has not experienced them, which limits the scope of the information that can be gleaned. However, the methods provide useful supplementary material to other methods. There are two main types of query technique: interviews and questionnaires.

Interviews

Interviewing users about their experience with an interactive system provides a direct and structured way of gathering information. Interviews have the advantages that the level of questioning can be varied to suit the context and that the evaluator can probe the user more deeply on interesting issues as they arise. An interview will usually follow a top-down approach, starting with a general question about a task and progressing to more leading questions (often of the form 'why...?' or 'what if ...?') to elaborate aspects of the user's response.

Interviews can be effective for high-level evaluation, particularly in eliciting information about user preferences, impressions and attitudes. They may also reveal problems which have not been anticipated by the designer or which have not occurred under observation. When used in conjunction with observation they are a useful means of clarifying an event (compare the post-task walkthrough).

In order to be as effective as possible, the interview should be planned in advance, with a set of central questions prepared. This helps to focus the purpose of the interview which may, for instance, be to probe a particular aspect of the interaction. It also helps to ensure a base of consistency between the interviews of different users. That said, the evaluator may of course choose to adapt the interview form to each user in order to get the most benefit: the interview is not intended to be a controlled experimental technique.

Questionnaires

An alternative method of querying the user is to administer a questionnaire. This is clearly less flexible than the interview technique, since questions are fixed in advance, and it is likely that the questions will be less probing. However, it can be used to reach a wider subject group, it takes less time to administer, and can be analyzed more rigorously. It can also be administered at various points in the design process, including during requirements capture, task analysis and evaluation, in order to get information on the user's needs, preferences and experience.

Given that the evaluator is not likely to be directly involved in the completion of the questionnaire, it is vital that it is well designed. The first thing that the evaluator must establish is the purpose of the questionnaire: what information is sought? It is also useful to decide at this stage how the questionnaire responses are to be analyzed. For example, do you want specific, measurable feedback on particular interface features, or do you want the user's impression of using the interface?

There are a number of styles of question which can be included in the questionnaire. These include

general These are questions which help to establish the background of the user and his place within the subject population. They include questions about age, sex, occupation, place of residence, and so on. They may also include questions on previous experience with computers which may be phrased as open-ended, multi-choice or scalar questions (see below).

open-ended These ask the user to provide his own unprompted opinion on a question, for example, 'Can you suggest any improvements to the interface?'. They are useful for gathering general subjective information but are difficult to analyze in any rigorous way, or to compare, and can only be viewed as supplementary. However, they may identify errors or make suggestions that have been missed by the designer. A special case of this type is where the user is asked for factual information, for example, how many commands were used.

scalar These ask the user to judge a specific statement on a numeric scale, usually corresponding to a measure of agreement or disagreement with the statement. For example,

> It is easy to recover from mistakes.
> Disagree   1   2   3   4   5   Agree

The granularity of the scale varies: a coarse scale (say, from 1 to 3) gives a clear indication of the meaning of the numbers (disagree, neutral and agree). However, it gives no room for varying levels of agreement, and users may therefore be tempted to give neutral responses to statements that they do not feel strongly about but with which they mildly disagree or agree. A very fine scale (say 1 to 10) suffers from the opposite problem: the numbers become difficult to interpret in a consistent way. One user will undoubtedly interpret the scale differently from another. A middle ground is therefore advisable. Scales of 1 to 5 or 1 to 7 have been used effectively. They are fine enough to allow users to differentiate adequately but still retain clarity in meaning. This can helped by providing an indication of the meaning of intermediate scalar values.

multi-choice Here the respondent is offered a choice of explicit responses, and may be asked to select only one of these, or as many as apply. For example,

> How do you most often get help with the system (tick one)?
> | | |
> |---|---|
> | On-line manual | ☐ |
> | Contextual help system | ☐ |
> | Command prompt | ☐ |
> | Ask a colleague | ☐ |
>
> Which types of software have you used (tick all that apply)?
> | | |
> |---|---|
> | Word-processor | ☐ |
> | Database | ☐ |
> | Spreadsheet | ☐ |
> | Expert system | ☐ |
> | On-line help system | ☐ |
> | Compiler | ☐ |

These are particularly useful for gathering information on a user's previous experience. A special case of this type is where the offered choices are yes or no.

ranked These place an ordering on items in a list and are useful to indicate a user's preferences. For example,

> Please rank the usefulness of these methods of
> issuing a command
> (1 most useful, 2 next, 0 if not used).
> Menu selection ☐
> Command line ☐
> Control key accelerator ☐

These question types are all useful for different purposes as we have noted. However, in order to reduce the burden of effort on the respondent, and so encourage a high response rate amongst users, it is best to use closed questions, such as scalar, ranked or multi-choice, as much as possible. These provide the user with alternative responses and so reduce the effort required. They also have the advantage of being easier to analyze. Responses can be analyzed in a number of ways, from determining simple percentages for each response, to looking at correlations and factor analysis. For more detail on available methods the reader is referred to the recommended reading list at the end of the chapter.

11.6 **Choosing an Evaluation Method**

As we have seen in this chapter, a range of techniques is available for evaluating an interactive system, at all stages in its development. So how do we decide which methods are most appropriate for our needs? There are no hard and fast rules in this — each method has its particular strengths and weaknesses and each is useful if applied appropriately. However, there are a number of factors which should be taken into account when selecting evaluation techniques. These also provide a way of categorizing the different methods so that we can compare and choose between them. In this final section we will consider these factors.

11.6.1 *Factors distinguishing evaluation techniques*

We can identify at least eight factors which distinguish different evaluation techniques and therefore help us to make an appropriate choice. These are

- the stage in the cycle at which the evaluation is carried out

- the style of evaluation

- the level of subjectivity or objectivity of the technique

- the type of measures provided

- the information provided

- the immediacy of the response

- the level of interference implied

- the resources required

Design vs. implementation

The first factor to affect our choice of evaluation method is the stage in the design process at which evaluation is required. As we saw earlier in this chapter, it is desirable to include evaluation of some sort throughout the design process. The main distinction between evaluation of a design and evaluation of an implementation is that in the latter case a physical artefact exists. This may be anything from a paper mockup to a full implementation, but it is something concrete which can be tested. Evaluation of a design on the other hand precedes this stage and seeks instead to provide information to feed the development of the physical artefact.

Roughly speaking, evaluation at the design stage tends to involve design experts only and be analytic, whereas evaluation of the implementation brings in users as subjects and is experimental. There are of course exceptions to this: participatory design involves users throughout the design process, and techniques such as cognitive walkthrough are expert based and analytic but can be used to evaluate implementations as well as designs.

Early evaluation, whether of a design or an early prototype or mockup will bring the greatest pay-off since problems can be easily resolved at this stage. As more commitment is made to a particular design in the implementation, it becomes increasingly difficult for changes to be made, no matter what the evaluation suggests. Ironically, the most resources are often ploughed into late evaluations. This is less profitable and should be avoided, although obviously some evaluation with users is required with a complete, or almost complete, system.

Laboratory vs. field studies

We have already discussed the pros and cons of these two styles of evaluation. Laboratory studies allow controlled experimentation and observation while losing something of the naturalness of the user's environment. Field studies retain the latter but do not allow control over user activity. Ideally the design process should include both styles of evaluation, probably with laboratory studies dominating the early stages and field studies conducted with the new implementation.

Subjective vs. objective

Evaluation techniques also vary according to their objectivity — some techniques rely heavily on the interpretation of the evaluator, others would provide the same information more or less regardless of who is performing the evaluation. The more subjective techniques, such as cognitive walkthrough or think aloud, rely to a large extent on the knowledge and expertise of the evaluator, who must recognize problems and understand what the user is doing. They can be powerful if used correctly and will provide information that may not be available from more objective methods. However, the problem of evaluator bias should be recognized and avoided. One way to decrease the possibility of bias is to use more than one evaluator. Objective techniques, on the other hand, should produce repeatable results which are not dependent on the persuasion of the particular evaluator. Controlled experiments are an example of an objective measure. These avoid bias and provide comparable results but may not reveal the unexpected problem or give detailed feedback on user experience. Ideally, both objective and subjective measures should be used.

Qualitative vs. quantitative measures

The type of measurement provided by the evaluation technique is also an important consideration. There are two main types: *quantitative measurement* and *qualitative measurement*. The former is usually numeric and can be easily analyzed using statistical techniques. The latter is non-numeric and is therefore more difficult to analyze, but can provide important detail which cannot be determined from numbers. The type of measure is related to the subjectivity or objectivity of the technique, with subjective techniques tending to provide qualitative measures and objective techniques, quantitative measures. This is not a hard and fast rule, however. It is sometimes possible to quantify what is in fact qualitative information by mapping it on to a scale or similar measure. An common example of this is in questionnaires where qualitative information is being sought (for example, user preferences) but a quantitative scale is used. This is also common in experimental design where factors such as the quality of the user's performance are used as dependent variables, and measured on a quantitative scale.

Information provided

The level of information required from an evaluation may also vary. The information required by an evaluator at any stage of the design process may range from low-level information to enable a design decision to be made (for example, which font is most readable) to higher level information, such as 'Is the system usable?'. Some evaluation techniques, such as controlled experiments, are excellent at providing low-level information — an experiment can be designed to measure a particular aspect of the interface. Higher level information can be gathered using questionnaire and interview techniques which provide a more general impression of the user's view of the system.

Immediacy of response

Another factor distinguishing evaluation techniques is the immediacy of the response they provide. Some methods, such as think aloud, record the user's behaviour at the time of the interaction itself. Others, such as post task walkthrough, rely on the user's recollection of events. Such recollection is liable to suffer from bias in recall and reconstruction, with users interpreting events according to their preconceptions. Recall may also be incomplete. However, immediate techniques can also be problematic, since the process of measurement can actually alter the way the user works.

Intrusiveness

Related to the immediacy of the response is the intrusiveness of the technique itself. Certain techniques, particularly those which produce immediate measurements, are obvious to the user during the interaction and therefore run the risk of influencing the way the user behaves. Sensitive activity on the part of the evaluator can help to reduce this but cannot remove it altogether. Most immediate evaluation techniques are intrusive, with the exception of automatic system logging. Unfortunately this is limited in the information that it can provide and is difficult to interpret.

Resources

The final consideration when selecting an evaluation technique is the availability of resources. Resources to consider include equipment, time, money, subjects, expertise of evaluator and context. Some decisions are forced by resource limitations: it is not possible to produce a video protocol without access to a video camera (and probably editing facilities to boot). However, other decisions are not so clear cut. For example, time and money may be limited forcing a choice between two possible evaluations. In these circumstances, the evaluator must decide which evaluation tactic will produce the most effective and useful information for the system under consideration. It may be possible to use results from other people's experiments to avoid having to conduct new experiments.

Some techniques are more reliant on evaluator expertise than others, for example, the more formal analytic techniques. If evaluator expertise is limited it may be more practical to use heuristic methods than analytic methods which require understanding of user goal structures and so on.

Table 11.3   *Classification of analytic evaluation techniques*

	Cognitive Walkthrough	Heuristic Evaluation	Review Based	Model Based
Stage	Throughout	Throughout	Design	Design
Style	Laboratory	Laboratory	Laboratory	Laboratory
Objective?	No	No	As source	No
Measure	Qualitative	Qualitative	As source	Qualitative
Information	Low level	High level	As source	Low level
Immediacy	N/A	N/A	As source	N/A
Intrusive?	No	No	No	No
Time	Medium	Low	Low-medium	Medium
Equipment	Low	Low	Low	Low
Expertise	High	Medium	Low	High

Finally the context in which evaluation can occur will influence what can be done. For practical reasons it may not be possible to gain access to the intended users of a system (if it is a general system for example) or it may not be feasible to test the system in its intended environment (for example, a system for a space station or a defence system). In these circumstances simulations must be used.

11.6.2 *A classification of evaluation techniques*

Using the factors discussed in the previous section we can classify the evaluation techniques we have considered in this chapter. This allows us to identify the techniques which most closely fit our requirements. Table 11.3 shows the classification for analytic techniques, Table 11.4 for experimental and query techniques and Table 11.5 for observational techniques.

The classification is intended as a rough guide only — some of the techniques do not fit easily into such a classification since their use can vary considerably.

11.7 Summary

Evaluation is an integral part of the design process and should take place throughout the design life cycle. Its aim is to test the functionality and usability of the design and to identify and rectify any problems. It can take place in the laboratory or in the user's workplace, and may involve active participation on the part of the user.

A design can be evaluated before any implementation work has started, to minimize the cost of early design errors. Most techniques for evaluation at this

Table 11.4   *Classification of experimental and query evaluation techniques*

	Experiment	Interviews	Questionnaire
Stage	Throughout	Throughout	Throughout
Style	Laboratory	Lab/Field	Lab/Field
Objective?	Yes	No	No
Measure	Quantitative	Qualitative/ Quantitative	Qualitative/ Quantitative
Information	Low/High level	High level	High level
Immediacy	Yes	No	No
Intrusive?	Yes	No	No
Time	High	Low	Low
Equipment	Medium	Low	Low
Expertise	Medium	Low	Low

Table 11.5   *Classification of observational evaluation techniques*

	Think-aloud[a]	Protocol analysis[b]	Post-task WT[c]
Stage	Implementation	Implementation	Implementation
Style	Lab/Field	Lab/Field	Lab/Field
Objective?	No	No	No
Measure	Qualitative	Qualitative	Qualitative
Information	High/Low level	High/Low level	High/Low level
Immediacy	Yes	Yes	No
Intrusive?	Yes	Yes[d]	No
Time	High	High	Medium
Equipment	Low	High	Low
Expertise	Medium	High	Medium

[a] Assuming a simple paper and pencil record
[b] Including video, audio, and system recording
[c] WT=walkthrough
[d] Except system logs

stage are analytic and involve using an expert to assess the design against cognitive and usability principles. Previous experimental results and modelling approaches can also provide insight at this stage. Once an artefact has been developed (whether a prototype or full system), experimental and observational techniques can be used to get both quantitative and qualitative results. Query techniques provide subjective information from the user.

The choice of evaluation method is largely dependent on what is required of the evaluation. They vary in the stage at which they are commonly used and where they can be used. Some are more subjective than others and provide qualitative rather than quantitative measures. Some provide immediate information while others get feedback after the event. However, the more immediate methods also tend to intrude most seriously on the interaction. Finally some require more resources in terms of time, equipment and expertise than others.

Exercises

11.1 In groups or pairs, use the cognitive walkthrough example, and what you know about user psychology (see Chapter 1), to discuss the design of a computer application of your choice (for example, a word-processor or a drawing package). Hint: focus your discussion on one or two specific tasks within the application.

11.2 Design an experiment to test whether adding colour coding to an interface will improve accuracy.

11.3 You have been asked to compare user performance and preferences with two different learning systems, one using hypermedia (see Chapter 15), the other sequential lessons. Design a questionnaire to find out what the users think of the system. How would you go about comparing user performance with these two systems?

11.4 What are the benefits and problems of using video in experimentation? If you have access to a video recorder, attempt to transcribe a piece of action and conversation (it does not have to be an experiment — a soap opera will do!). What problems did you encounter?

11.5 In Section 11.5.1, we saw that the observed results could be the result of interference. Can you think of alternative designs that may make this less likely. Remember that individual variation was very high, so you *must* retain a within-groups design, but you may perform more tests on each subject.

Recommended Reading

- Colin Robson, *Experiment, Design and Statistics in Psychology* (2nd ed.), Penguin, 1985.

  An accessible introduction to statistics and experimental design and analysis for the uninitiated, using worked examples throughout.

- A. Monk, P. Wright, J. Haber and L. Davenport, *Improving your human computer interface: a practical approach*, Prentice Hall, 1992.

  An evaluator's guide to using the cooperative evaluation approach successfully.

- M. Helander (ed.), *Handbook of Human–Computer Interaction*, North-Holland, 1988, Part V: Tools for Design and Evaluation.

  Reviews the major evaluation techniques.

- P. Polson, C. Lewis, J. Rieman and C. Wharton, 'Cognitive Walkthroughs: A Method for Theory-Based Evaluation of User Interfaces', in *International Journal of Man-Machine Studies*, 1992.

  Describes the cognitive walkthrough method of evaluation.

- J. Nielsen and R. Molich, 'Heuristic evaluation of user interfaces', in *Proceedings of ACM CHI'90*, pp. 249-256, ACM Press, 1990.

  Introduces the heuristic evaluation approach.

- *SIGCHI Bulletin*, Special Issue on video as a research and design tool, Vol 21, 2, October 1989.

  A collection of papers dealing with recent advances in video analysis technology, including EVA and the Workplace project.

Chapter 12

Help and Documentation

Overview

- Users have different requirements for support at different times.

- User support should be

  - available but unobtrusive

  - accurate and robust

  - consistent and flexible

- User support comes in a number of styles:

  - command based methods

  - context-sensitive help

  - tutorial help

  - on-line documentation

  - intelligent help

- Design of user support must take account of

  - presentation

  - implementation

12.1 Introduction

There is often an implicit assumption that if an interactive system is properly designed it will be completely intuitive to use and the user will require no help or training. This may be a grand ideal but it is far from true with even the best designed systems currently available. It is even perhaps an unhelpful ideal: a computer is a complex piece of equipment — what other such equipment do we expect people to use without instruction or help? A more helpful approach is to assume that the user will require assistance at various times and design this help into the system.

The type of assistance users require varies and is dependent on many factors: their familiarity with the system, the job they are trying to do and so on. There are four main types of assistance that users require:

- quick reference
- task-specific help
- full explanation
- tutorial

Quick reference is used primarily as a reminder to the user of the details of tools he is basically familiar with and has used before. It may, for example, be used to find a particular command option, or to remind the user of the syntax of the command. Task-specific help is required when the user has encountered a problem in performing a particular task or when he is uncertain how to apply the tool to his particular problem. The help that is offered is directly related to what is being done. The more experienced or inquisitive user may require a full explanation of a tool or command to enable him to understand it more fully. This explanation will almost certainly include information which the user does not need at that time. The fourth type of support required by users is tutorial help. This is particularly aimed at new users of a tool and provides step by step instruction (perhaps by working through examples) of how to use the tool.

Each of these types of user support is complementary — they are required at different points in the user's experience with the system and fulfil distinct needs. Within these types of required support there will be numerous pieces of information which the user wants — definitions, examples, known errors and error recovery information, command options and accelerators to name but a few. Some of these may be provided within the design of the interface itself but others must be included within the help or support system. We will look at appropriate ways of supporting these requirements. The different types of help required also imply the need for provision of different types of help system. In this chapter we will look at a number of different types of user support system and will try to determine how to design a good user support system.

A distinction is often made between help systems and documentation. Help systems are problem-oriented and specific, whereas documentation is system-oriented and generic. This is an artificial distinction when considering the design of such systems since the same principles apply to both, and indeed there is a lot of overlap between the two. Instead of drawing a fixed line between the two we will consider all types of user support in terms of the requirements they fulfil. We will also concentrate on on-line support, although much of what is said will be helpful in designing paper documentation and tutorials. Before we look in more detail at the different approaches to providing user support, we will think for a while about the general requirements that the ideal help system should have.

12.2 Requirements of User Support

If we were to design the ideal help system, what would it look like? This is a difficult question to answer, but we can point to some features which we might like our help system to have. Not every help system will have all of these features, sometimes for good reason, but they are helpful as benchmarks against which we can test the support tools we design. Then, if our system does not have these features, it will be by design and not by accident! Some if these terms have also been used in Chapter 4 in discussing requirements for usability. The use of the terms here is more constrained but related.

12.2.1 *Availability*

The user needs to be able to access help at any time during his interaction with the system. In particular, he should not have to quit the application he is working on in order to open the help application. Ideally, it should run concurrently with any other application. This is obviously a problem for non-windowed systems if the help system is independent of the application that is running. However, in windowed systems there is no reason why a help facility should not be available constantly, at the press of a button.

12.2.2 *Accuracy and completeness*

It may seem obvious to state that the assistance provided should be accurate and complete. However, in an age where applications are frequently updated, and different versions may be active at the same time, it is not such a trivial problem. However, if the assistance provided proves not to match the actual behaviour of the system the user will, at best, become disillusioned with the help facilities, and, at worst, get into difficulties. As well as providing an accurate reflection of the current state of the system, help should cover the *whole* system. This completeness is very important if the help provided is to be used effectively. The designer cannot predict which parts of the system the user is going to require assistance with and must therefore assume that all parts must be supported. Finding no help available on a topic of interest is guaranteed to frustrate the user.

12.2.3 *Consistency*

As we have noted, users require different types of help for different purposes. This implies that a help system may incorporate a number of parts. The help provided by each of these must be consistent with all the others and within itself. On-line help should also be consistent with paper documentation. It should be consistent in terms of content, terminology and style of presentation. This is also an issue where applications have internal user support — these should be consistent across the system. It is unhelpful if a command is described in one way here and in another there, or if the way in which help is accessed varies across applications. In fact, consistency itself can be thought of as a means of supporting the user since it reinforces learning of system usage.

12.2.4   *Robustness*

Help systems are often used by people who are in difficulty, perhaps because the system is behaving unexpectedly or has failed altogether. It is important then that the help system itself should be robust, both by correct error handling and predictable behaviour. The user should be able to rely on being able to get assistance when required. In fact, robustness is even more important for help systems than for any other part of the system for these reasons.

12.2.5   *Flexibility*

Many help systems are rigid in that they will produce the same help message regardless of the expertise of the person seeking help or the context in which they are working. A flexible help system will allow each user to interact with it in a way appropriate to his needs. This will range from designing a modularized interactive help system, through context-sensitive help, to a full blown adaptive or intelligent help system, which will infer the user's expertise and task. We will look at context-sensitive and intelligent help in more detail later in the chapter. However, any help system can be designed to allow greater interactivity and flexibility in the level of help presented. For example, help systems built using hypertext principles allow the user to browse through the help, expanding topics as required. The top level provides a map of the subjects covered by the help and the user can get back to this level at any point. Although hypertext may not be appropriate for all help systems, the principle of flexible access is a useful one.

12.2.6   *Unobtrusiveness*

The final principle for help system design is unobtrusiveness. The help system should not prevent the user from continuing with normal work, nor should it interfere with the user's application. This is a problem at both ends of the spectrum. At one end the textual help system on a non-windowed interface may interrupt the user's work. A possible solution to this if no alternative is available is to use a split-screen presentation. At the other end of the spectrum, an intelligent help system which can provide help actively on its own initiative, rather than at the request of the user, can intrude on the user and so become a hindrance rather than a help. It is important with these types of system that the 'suggest' option can be overridden by the user and switched off!

12.3   Approaches to User Support

As we noted in the last section there are a number of different approaches to providing help, each of which meets a particular need. These vary from simple prompts to full intelligent help and tutoring systems. In this section we will concentrate on the styles of help provided rather than any particular help system (although we will use real help systems for illustration). We will then go on to look at intelligent help in more detail.

12.3.1   *Command assistance*

Perhaps the most common approach to user support is to provide assistance at the command level — the user requests help on a particular command and is presented with a help screen or manual page describing it. This is the approach used in the UNIX *man* help system and the DOS *help* command.

This type of help is simple and efficient if the user knows what he wants to know about and is seeking either a reminder or more detailed information. However, it assumes that the user does know what he is looking for which is often not the case. In any complex computer system there will be some commands which the user knows well and can use and some of which he is aware but which he uses rarely. Command assistance deals well with these. However, there will also be commands which the user does not know about but needs, and even commands which the user thinks exist but which do not. Command assistance cannot provide the user with help for these two groups of command. Facilities such as the UNIX command *apropos* aim to resolve this problem to an extent by allowing the user to use synonyms to the command or related commands. However, this is limited in practice since the user may not know about the command at all.

12.3.2   *Command prompts*

Command prompts provide help when the user encounters an error, usually in the form of correct usage prompts. Such prompts are useful if the error is a simple one, such as incorrect syntax, but again they assume knowledge of the command.

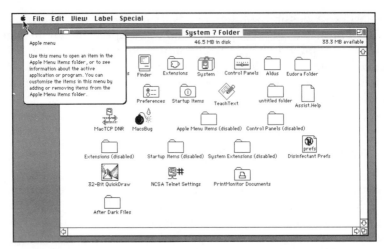

Figure 12.1 *Macintosh Balloon help. ©1983-1991, Apple Computer, Inc. Used with permission of Apple Computer U.K. Ltd.*

Another form of command prompting, which is not specifically intended to provide help but which supports the user to a limited degree, is the use of menus and selectable icons. These provide an aid to memory as well as making explicit what commands are available at a given time. However, they still assume a certain amount of knowledge about what the commands are for, so additional support is still required.

12.3.3 *Context-sensitive help*

Some help systems are context-sensitive. These range from those that have specific knowledge of the particular user (which we will consider under intelligent help) to those that provide a simple help key or function which is interpreted according to the context in which it is called and will present help accordingly. Such systems are not necessarily particularly sophisticated. However, they do move away from placing the onus on the user to remember the command. They are often used in menu based systems to provide help on menu options. The *Spy* editor help command and the Macintosh *Balloons* help are examples of this. In Spy, the third mouse button is dedicated to help. The user positions the cursor over the menu option of interests and presses this button. Help on that topic is presented in a new window. Balloons help is an option in Macintosh System 7 which can be enabled or disabled. When enabled, an explanatory balloon is displayed when the cursor is over a screen widget (see Figure 12.1). In both cases, the invocation of help is interpreted in terms of the context in which it is made.

12.3.4   *On-line tutorials*

On-line tutorials allow the user to work through the basics of an application within a test environment. The user can progress at his own speed and can repeat parts of the tutorial if needed. He will also get a feel for how the application works by experimenting with examples, albeit small ones. Most on-line tutorials have no intelligence: they know nothing about the user and his previous experience, nor about the domain nor even about teaching style. Intelligent tutoring systems, which use similar techniques to intelligent help systems (see Section 12.4), attempt to address this issue but, apart from tutoring programming applications, are impractical as tutorials for most applications. On-line tutorials are therefore inflexible and often unforgiving. Some will fail to recognize the correct answer to a problem, simply because it is not formatted as expected.

An alternative to the traditional on-line tutorial is to allow the user to learn the system by exploring and experimenting with a version with limited functionality. This is the idea behind the *Training Wheels* interface proposed by Carroll and his colleagues at IBM [30]. The user is presented with a version of the full interface in which some of the functionality has been disabled. He can explore the rest of the system freely but if he attempts to use the blocked functionality he is told that it is unavailable. This approach allows the user freedom to investigate the system as he pleases but without risk. It was found that new users spent more time using this system than they did the full version, spent less time recovering from errors and gained a better understanding of the operation of the system.

12.3.5   *On-line documentation*

On-line documentation effectively makes the existing paper documentation available on computer. This makes the material available continually (assuming the machine is running!) in the same medium as the user's work and, potentially, to a large number of users concurrently. However, it can be argued that the type of (usually large) manuals that are appropriate as paper reference systems, are less appropriate on line. Paper is a familiar medium to most of us, and it is still the case that people prefer reading text on paper than on a computer screen. We have developed quite sophisticated browsing skills with a paper medium and books are designed to provide cues to aid this, such as indexing, contents and page numbering, as well as having physical cues such as position in the book. These features are not reproduced in most documentation systems. However, paper manuals get lost easily, are constrained to one physical location, and are invariably somewhere else when you want them. On-line documentation is one way of avoiding these problems.

Documentation is designed to provide a full description of the system's functionality and behaviour in a systematic manner. It provides generic information

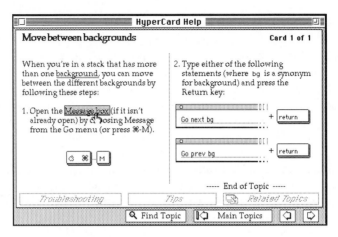

Figure 12.2   *HyperCard help system.* ©*1983-1991, Apple Computer, Inc. Used with permission of Apple Computer U.K. Ltd.*

which is not directed at any particular problem. The amount of information contained in manual pages is usually high, which can in itself create problems for the user — there is too much detail and this effectively 'masks' the information the user wants to find. Perhaps for this reason, on-line documentation is often used by more expert users as a resource or reference, often to enable them to advise less experienced users. The experts may not know the information but they know where to find it and how to extract the details which are relevant to a given problem.

Attempts to make on-line documentation more accessible to the inexperienced user include the use of hypertext techniques (see Chapter 15 for more details of hypertext). Hypertext stores text in a network and connects related sections of text using selectable links. By clicking on a link, the user can go to a related subject instantly. Most hypertext systems can include pictures as well as text. Documentation structured using hypertext supports browsing and allows different media to be included in the documentation (for example, diagrams). An example is the HyperCard help system shown in Figure 12.2.

However, it does suffer from a problem common to hypertext systems, navigation. The user can get lost within the hypertext and lose track of where he is and where he has been. A facility to return 'home' (to the top level) is usually provided but this may mean that the user wastes considerable time restarting his search.

An alternative approach which attempts to simplify on-line documentation and make it more accessible to novice and casual users, is the *minimal manual* [29]. This simplifies the documentation by stripping out all but the bare essentials. The documentation that remains is focused towards the user's tasks and emphasizes error recovery. Experiments with this manual showed that users learned to use the system 40% faster than with the full manual.

12.4 Intelligent Help Systems

In any large or complex computer system, users will be familiar with a sub-set of the available functionality, demonstrating expertise in some applications and having no experience with others, even to the point of being unaware of their existence. In addition, different users will have different needs and levels of understanding. Intelligent help systems attempt to address these problems by adapting the help that they provide to the individual user who is making the request and by actively suggesting alternative courses of action of which the user may not be aware.

Intelligent help is a special case of a general class of interactive systems, known as intelligent systems. These include domain-specific expert systems, intelligent tutoring systems and general adaptive interfaces. We will concentrate in this discussion on intelligent help systems, since they are most relevant here, and incorporate aspects of the others, but it should be noted that many of the techniques we will look at can be applied in these other systems. Since these represent a significant class of interactive system we will cover the techniques in some detail.

Intelligent help systems operate by monitoring the activity of the user and constructing a model of him. This may include a model of his experience, preferences, mistakes, or a combination of some or all of these. Using this knowledge, together with knowledge of the domain in which the user is working, and, sometimes, general advisory or tutorial strategies, the intelligent help system will present help relevant to the user's current task and suited to his experience. That at least is the theory. In practice it is not as simple as it sounds. Firstly, the knowledge requirements of such a system are considerable, and data on interaction are particularly difficult to interpret. Secondly, there is the issue of control and initiative within the interaction. Should the help system take an active role, removing some control from the user, and will the adaptivity confuse the user, if he perceives it as 'shifting ground'? Thirdly, what exactly should be adapted and what will be the result of the adaptivity? Finally, what is the scope of the modelling and adaptivity: does it extend beyond the application level and, if so, how does it deal with the variation in expertise of a single user across an entire system? Some of these issues are still the subject of research, but we will look at some of the developments and solutions, concentrating, in particular, on the knowledge requirements.

12.4.1 *Knowledge representation: user modelling*

Every interactive system that is built incorporates some model of the user for whom it is intended. In many systems this model is the designer's view of the user and is implicit within the design. The designer has in mind a 'typical' user, and builds the interface accordingly. If the designer has done her homework this model can be quite effective. However, it does assume that all users are essentially the same and have the same requirements.

Other systems allow the user to provide a model of himself around which the system will be configured. A simple example of this is the UNIX *.profile*, which is executed when the user logs into the system and sets system and environment variables according to the user's preference. Such systems are called *adaptable*, since the user is able to adapt his own environment to suit his preferences. This increases the flexibility of the system but places the onus of the customization on the user. The result of this is that users have access only to the default system when they most need flexibility: when they first start out. It is only later that they have the know-how to construct the necessary model.

The third approach to providing the system with a model of the user, and the one used in intelligent help systems, is to have the system construct and maintain a model of the user based on data gleaned from monitoring the user's interaction. This model can then be consulted when required. This automatic approach to user modelling also has the problem of the set-up time required, during which time the user has a default system, but the onus to build the model is taken away from the user. Various suggestions have been made as to how to deal with the set-up time, including getting the user to choose an initial default model, and building a model based on pre-use activity, such as game playing. The former is problematic in that again it makes the user decide on a model at a time when he may not have sufficient experience to do so effectively. The latter may not produce a model which is transferable to the actual domain. The most common approach is still to provide a basic start-up default model and concentrate on rapidly updating this for the actual user. The default model may be based on experimental or observational results gleaned in evaluation.

So how are user models constructed and maintained? There are a number of approaches. Some quantify user experience or classify users into stereotypes; some compare the user's behaviour with some norm; others maintain a catalogue of known errors and compare user actions to these.

Quantification

This is one of the most simple approaches to user modelling. The system recognizes a number of levels of expertise, which it will respond to in different ways. The user is placed on one of these levels, and moves between them, based on a quantitative measure of his expertise at that time. Different activities are given weightings, and the user is scored according to the weightings of the activities he takes part in. If the score exceeds a certain threshold, the user is moved to a different expertise level and the system adapts accordingly.

This approach is simple and measures the user at a coarse level of granularity. However, it is effective for simple adaptivity. For example, this method was used by Mason to adapt the presentation of command prompts to the user's level of experience [109]. The system used a set of rules which dictated when a user's level of expertise changed. For example,

Move from Level 1 to Level 2

If

> the system has been used more than twice (0.25)
> commands x and y have been used effectively (0.20)
> help has not been accessed this session (0.25)
> the system has been used in the last 5 days

Such a model can only give a rough approximation of the user's expertise, but at the same time requires little analysis to extract the required information from the system logs.

Stereotypes

Another approach to automatic user modelling is to work with stereotypes. Rather than attempting to build a truly individual model of the user, the system classifies the user as a member of a known category of users or stereotype. Stereotypes are based on user characteristics and may be simple, such as making a distinction between novice and expert users, or more complex, for example building a compound stereotype based on more than one piece of information. There are several ways of building stereotypes. One is to use information such as command use and errors to categorize different types of user and then to use rules to identify the stereotype to which the user belongs. An alternative approach is to use a machine learning approach, such as neural networks, to learn examples of different types of user behaviour (from actual logs) and then to classify users according to their closeness to the examples previously learned. Stereotypes are useful in that they represent the user at the level of granularity at which most intelligent help systems work, and do not attempt to produce a sophisticated model which will not be fully utilized. After all, if the only information that is available about the user at any time is how he is interacting with the system, it is not possible to infer very much about the user himself. However, what can be inferred may be exactly what is required to provide the necessary level of help.

Overlay models

One of the most common techniques used is the overlay model. Here an idealized model, often of an expert user, is constructed and the individual user's behaviour compared to it. The resulting user profile may represent either the commonality between the two models or the differences. An advantage of this style of modelling is that it allows a certain degree of diagnostic activity on the part of the system. Not only is the system aware of what the user is doing, but it also has a representation of optimal behaviour. This provides a benchmark against which to measure the user's performance, and, if the user does not take the optimal course of action, gives an indication of the type of help or hint that is required.

A similar approach is used in error based models where the system holds a record of known user errors and the user's actual behaviour is compared to these. If this behaviour matches an error in the catalogue, then remedial action can be taken. Potential errors may be matched when partially executed and help given to enable the user to avoid the error, or recover more quickly. These types of modelling are also useful in intelligent tutoring systems where diagnostic information is required in order to decide how to proceed with the tutorial.

12.4.2   *Knowledge representation: domain and task modelling*

All intelligent help systems must have some knowledge of the system itself, in order to provide relevant and appropriate advice. This knowledge may include command use, common errors and common tasks. However, some help systems also attempt to build a model of the user's current task or plan. The motivation behind this is that the user is engaged in a particular problem-solving task and requires help at that level. Generic help, even adapted to the expertise and preference of the user, is not enough.

A common approach to this problem is to represent user tasks in terms of the command sequences which are required to execute them. As the user works, the commands used are compared to the stored task sequences and matched sequences are recovered. If the user's command sequence does not match a recognized task, help is offered. This approach is used in the PRIAM system [46].

Although an attractive idea, task recognition is problematic. In large domains it is unlikely that every possible method for reaching every possible user goal could be represented. Users may reasonably approach a task in a non-standard way, and inferring the user's intention from command usage is not a trivial problem. As we saw in Chapter 11, system logs do not always contain sufficient information for a human expert to ascertain what the user was trying to do. The problem is far greater for a computer.

12.4.3   *Knowledge representation: modelling advisory strategy*

A third area of knowledge representation which is sometimes included in intelligent help is modelling advisory or tutorial strategies. Providing a help system with this type of information allows it not only to select appropriate advice for the user but also to use an appropriate method of advice giving.

As we have already seen, people require different types of help depending on their knowledge and circumstances. These include reminders, task-specific help and tutorial help. There is evidence to indicate that human experts follow different strategies when advising colleagues [140]. These include inferring the intention of the person seeking help and advising at that level or providing a number of solutions to the person's problem. Alternatively they may attempt to place the problem in a context and provide a 'sample solution' in that context.

Few intelligent help systems have attempted to model advisory strategy, and those that do provide a limited choice. Ideally, it would be useful if the help system had access to a number of alternative strategies and was able to choose an appropriate style of guidance in each case. However, this is very ambitious — too little is known about what makes a guidance strategy appropriate in which contexts. However, it is important that designers of intelligent help systems give some thought to advisory strategies, if only to make an informed choice about the strategy that is to be used.

The EuroHelp intelligent help system adopts a model of teacher–pupil, in which the system is envisaged as a teacher watching the user (pupil) work and offering advice and suggestions in an 'over-the-shoulder' fashion [61]. In this case instruction may be high to begin with but will become less obtrusive as the user finds his feet. The user is able to question the system at any point and responses are given in terms of the current context.

This mixed initiative dialogue is also used in the Activist/Passivist help system, which will accept requests from the user and actively offer suggestions and hints, particularly about areas of functionality which it infers the user is unfamiliar with [64].

12.4.4 *Techniques for knowledge representation*

All of the modelling approaches described rely heavily on techniques for knowledge representation from artificial intelligence. This is a whole subject in its own right and there is only room to outline the methods here (although some of the techniques are elaborated further in Chapter 1). The interested reader is also referred to the text on artificial intelligence in the recommended reading list.

There are four main groups of techniques used in knowledge representation for intelligent help systems: rule based, frame based, network based and example based.

Rule based techniques

Knowledge is represented as a set of rules and facts, which are interpreted using some inference mechanism. Predicate logic provides a powerful mechanism for representing declarative information, while production rules (see Chapter 1) represent procedural information. Rule based techniques can be used in relatively large domains and can represent actions to perform as well as knowledge for inference. A user model implemented using rule based methods may include rules of the form:

```
IF
    command is EDIT file1
AND
    last command is COMPILE file1
THEN
    task is DEBUG
    action is describe automatic debugger
```

Frame based techniques

Frame based systems are used to represent commonly occurring situations and default knowledge (see Chapter 1). A frame is a structure which contains labelled slots, representing related features. Each slot can be assigned a value or alternatively be given a default value. User input is matched against the frame values and a successful match may cause some action to be taken. They are useful in small domains. In user modelling the frame may represent the current profile of the user:

```
User
        Expertise level: novice
        Command: EDIT file1
        Last command: COMPILE file1
        Errors this session: 6
        Action: describe automatic debugger
```

Network based techniques

Networks represent knowledge about the user and system in terms of relationships between facts. One of the most common examples is the semantic network (see Chapter 1). The network is a hierarchy and children can inherit properties associated with their parents. This makes it a relatively efficient representation scheme and is useful for linking information clearly. Networks can also be used to link frame based representations.

The compile example could be expanded within a semantic network:

```
CC is an instance of COMPILE
COMPILE is a command
COMPILE is related to DEBUG
COMPILE is related to EDIT
Automatic debugger facilitates DEBUG
```

Example based techniques

Example based techniques represent knowledge implicitly within a decision structure of a classification system. This may be a decision tree, in the case of an inductive learning approach such as ID3 [145], or links in a network in the case of neural networks. The decision structure is constructed automatically based on examples presented to the classifier. The classifiers effectively detect recurrent features within the examples and are able to use these to classify other input. An example may be a trace of user activity:

EDIT file1
COMPILE file1

This would be trained as an example of a particular task, for example, DEBUG.

12.4.5 *Problems with knowledge representation and modelling*

Knowledge representation is the central issue in intelligent help systems, but it is not without its problems. Knowledge is often difficult to elicit, particularly if a domain expert is not available. This is particularly true of knowledge of user behaviour, due to its variability. It is particularly difficult to ensure completeness and correctness of the knowledge base in these circumstances. Even if knowledge is available, the amount of knowledge required is substantial, making intelligent help an expensive option.

A second problem is interpreting the information appropriately. Although the knowledge base can be provided with detailed knowledge of the expected contexts and the domain in advance, during the interaction the only information that is available is the system log of the user's actions. As we saw in Chapter 11, interpreting system logs is very difficult because it is stripped of much context and there is no access to the user's intention or goal (except by inference). However, these data are not arbitrary and do contain recurrent patterns of activity which can be used with care to infer task sequences and the like. However, it should be realized that these represent approximations only.

12.4.6 *Other issues*

Other issues that should be considered in designing an intelligent help system are initiative, effect and scope.

Initiative A major issue in intelligent help system design is that of initiative and control: should the user retain complete control over the system, should the system direct the interaction, or should a mixed dialogue be supported? System activity can be intrusive to the user, particularly if badly handled. No user wants to be constantly told he is not performing a task in the most efficient manner! However, we know that there are normally large sections of system functionality of which the user is simply not aware. Without some form of system activity this problem will not be addressed. The solution seems to be to encourage mixed initiative in the interaction. The user should be able to question the system at any time, and the system can offer hints to the user. However, the latter should be offered sensitively and the user always allowed to continue as before if he wishes.

Effect Another issue which the designer should consider is the effect of the modelling and adaptivity: what exactly is going to be adapted and what information is needed to do this? All too often modelling systems use vast resources producing a detailed profile of the user, the bulk of which is never used. Modelling, whether of the user, the domain or strategies, should be directed towards the requirements of the help system. For example, if it is simply to offer different help to novices and experts, the system does not need details of task execution. Such considerations may reduce the overheads of intelligent help systems and make them more viable.

Scope Finally, the designer must consider the scope of the help: is it to be offered at an application level or system wide? The latter may be the ideal but is much more complex. If users are to be modelled at a system level the model should take into account the levels of activity in which they are engaged and be able to distinguish actions at an application level. In many systems it would also have to cope with interleaving of activities and concurrent execution. Each of these makes the modelling activity more complex.

12.5   Designing User Support Systems

There are many ways of providing user support and it is up to the designer to decide which is most appropriate for any given system. However, there are a number of things which the designer should take into account. Firstly, the design of user support should not be seen as an 'add-on' to system design. Ideally the help system should be designed integrally with the rest of the system. If this is done, the help system will be relevant and consistent with the rest of the system. The same modelling and analytic techniques (for example, task analysis) used to design the system can guide the design of support material as well. Secondly, the designer should consider the content of the help and the context in which it will be used before the technology that will be required. Obviously, available technology is an important issue. However, concentrating on the task and the user will help to clarify the type of help required within the constraints of technical resources. Viewing the process in reverse may prevent the designer seeing beyond the technology she is familiar with. Bearing in mind the expected user requirements, the designer of help also needs to make decisions about how the help will be presented to the user and how this will be affected by implementation issues.

12.5.1   *Presentation issues*

How is help requested?

The first decision the designer must make is how help will be accessed by the user. There are a number of choices. Help may be a command, a button, a function which can be switched on or off, or a separate application. A command (usually) requires the user to specify a topic, and therefore assumes some knowledge, but may fit most consistently within the rest of the interface. A help button is readily accessible and does not interfere with existing applications, but may not always provide information specific to the user's needs. However, if the help button is a keyboard or mouse button, it can support context sensitivity as we saw earlier. The help function is flexible since it can be activated when required and disabled when not. The separate application allows flexibility and multiple help styles but may interfere with the user's current application.

How is help displayed?

The second major decision that the designer must make is how the help will be viewed by the user. In a windowed system it may be presented in a new window. In other systems it may use the whole screen or part of the screen. Alternatively, help hints and prompts can be given in pop-up boxes or at the command line level. The presentation style that is appropriate depends largely on the level of help being offered and the space that it requires. Obviously, opening a manual page line by line is unhelpful, as is taking over the whole screen to give the user a hint. Some active help systems provide visual cues when they have a suggestion to make (for example, a icon may be highlighted) — this gives the user the option of taking the suggestion without forcing him to abandon or interrupt his work. Again this decision should take account of the rest of the design, and aim to provide consistency.

Effective presentation of help

Help screens and documentation should be designed in much the same way as an interface should be designed, taking into account the capabilities and task requirements of the user. No matter what technology is used to provide support there are some principles for writing and presenting it effectively.   Help and tutorial material should be written in clear, familiar language, avoiding jargon as much as possible. If paper manuals and tutorials exist, the terminology should be consistent between these and the on-line support material. Instructional material requires instructional language and a help system should tell the user how to use the system rather than simply describing the system. It should not make assumptions about what the user knows in advance. For example, a help message on the use of windows might read

> To close the window, place the mouse cursor on the box in the top left hand corner of the window and click the mouse button.

rather than

> Windows can be closed by moving the mouse cursor to the box in the top left hand corner of the window and clicking the mouse button.

An exception to this is in documentation where the intention is not only to instruct the user in how to use the system but to record a full description of the system's functionality. However, documentation should be presented so that information is readily accessible, and should present both instructional and descriptive information clearly. The physical layout of documentation can make a difference to its usability. Large blocks of text are difficult to read on screen, for example. This can be alleviated by breaking the documentation into clear logical sections, or by using technology such as hypertext to organize it. A useful style is to provide a summary of the key information prominently, with further information available if required. This can be done either by devising a hierarchical help system where each layer in the hierarchy provides increasing detail, or simply by using layout carefully. An index can be used as a summary of available topics but should be organized to reflect the functional relationships between the subjects rather than their alphabetic ordering. Consistency is also important here — each topic in the documentation should be described using the same format so that the user knows where to look for a particular type of information. Documentation and help may contain definitions, descriptions, examples, details of error messages, options and instructions. These should be clearly recognizable.

12.5.2   *Implementation issues*

Alongside the presentation issues the designer must make implementation decisions. Some of these may be forced by physical constraints, others by the choices made regarding the user's requirements for help. We have already considered how help may be requested and how it appears to the user. Obviously each of these decisions involves implementation questions: will help be an operating system command, a meta-command or an application? What physical constraints does the machine impose in terms of screen space, memory capacity and speed? Speed is a very important consideration, since an unacceptably slow response time is liable to make the system unusable no matter how well it has been designed. It is better to provide a simple help facility which responds quickly than a sophisticated one which takes minutes to provide a solution.

Another issue the designer must decide is how the help data are to be structured: in a single file, a file hierarchy, a database? Again this will depend on the type of help that is required, but any structure should be flexible and extensible — systems are not static and new topics will inevitably need to be added to the help system. The data structure used will, to an extent, determine the type of search or navigation strategy that is provided. Will users be able to browse through the system or only request help on one topic at a time? The user may also want to make a hard copy of part of the help system to study later (this is particularly true of manuals and documentation). Will this facility be provided as part of the support system?

Finally the designer should consider the authors of help material as well as its users. It is likely that, even if the designer writes the initial help texts, these will be extended by other authors at different times. Clear conventions and constraints on the presentation and implementation of help facilitate the addition of new material.

12.6 **Summary**

This chapter has been concerned with user support in the form of help and documentation. No interactive system of any complexity is so intuitive that the user never requires help. Help should therefore be an integral part of the design. Users require different types of help, depending on the context and circumstances, and the user support facilities should support these. Different styles of help support different requirements and different types of user. We have considered several types of help system, including intelligent user support. It is important to select a support style and design user support with the user in mind, just as the design of the system is user-centred. In particular, the presentation of help should take into account usability principles, and the language should be clear and instructional.

Exercises

12.1 Write a manual page for making a cup of coffee. Assume your user has no experience but will recognize a cup, a kettle, a spoon, etc. Swap your manual with a partner. Does your partner's manual give you sufficient instruction to make the cup of coffee? Discuss improvements with your partner and agree on a final version of the manual.

12.2 Find a computer application that you have never used before. Attempt to learn to use it using only the on-line support. Is there enough information to allow you to use the application effectively? Is the information easy to find? What improvements (if any) would you suggest?

12.3 What knowledge is needed to build an intelligent help system? Which do you think is most difficult to provide and why?

12.4 Look at as many on-line support systems as you can. Which do you find most useful and why? Try to assess them using the requirements discussed in Section 12.2.

Recommended Reading

- R. C. Houghton, 'On-line help systems: a conspectus', *Communications of the ACM*, Vol. 27, 2, February 1984.

  A good review of non-intelligent help systems, most of which is still relevant today.

- C. Turk and J. Kirkham, *Effective Writing (2nd Edition)*, E. and F.N. Spon, 1989.

  An excellent introduction to technical writing, including writing instructional material.

- E. Rich and K. Knight, *Artificial Intelligence*, 2nd Edition, McGraw-Hill, 1991.

  A detailed text on artificial intelligence techniques. Readers should select appropriate sections on knowledge representation.

Part III

Advanced Topics

In this Part, we extend the scope of detailed discussion by presenting work that goes beyond the implicit view of a single user with a desk-based computer. The issues of groupware and CSCW are presented and discussed in Chapter 13 and Chapter 14. The first of these shows what groupware can support, how it can be classified, as well as highlighting the implementation problems that exist. The second shows that before we can understand computer-supported cooperative work, we need an understanding of human–human interaction and cooperation. This can then be applied to develop theory that supports the development of CSCW applications, but the problems of group working and organizational characteristics are not easy to overcome.

Chapter 15 looks at systems that offer a multi-channel approach to interaction, with information simultaneously presented to more than one sense. Such multi-modal, multi-media systems offer great potential for producing more involving, realistic interactive experiences. The technology required is described, and a number of different applications are examined in the context of understanding the principles on which they operate.

Chapter 13

<hr>

Groupware

<hr>

Overview

Groupware is a term for applications written to support the collaboration of several users.

- Groupware can support different activities:
    - direct interpersonal communication
    - ideas generation and decision-making
    - sharing computer objects
- It can be classified in several ways:
    - by where and when it happens
    - by the sort of information shared
    - by the aspects of cooperations supported
- Implementing groupware is more difficult than single-user applications:
    - because of network delays
    - because there are so many components to go wrong
    - because graphical toolkits assume a single user

13.1 Introduction

Most of the discussion in this book concerns a single user with a computer. Computer-supported cooperative work (*CSCW*) is about groups of users — how to design systems to support their work *as a group* and how to understand the effect of technology on their work patterns. Both HCI and CSCW draw on knowledge from a wide range of disciplines, but whereas the principal axis in HCI is psychology–computing, the equivalent axis in CSCW is sociology–computing. If we allow the *human* in HCI to be plural, we can regard CSCW to be within the general sphere of HCI, which is why it is present in this book and in conferences and journals on HCI. However, CSCW is now a field in itself, and would require a book of its own to do it justice. We hope that this chapter and the next will give a flavour of this relatively new and exciting field.

One major area within CSCW is the provision of computer systems to support group working. These products are often called *groupware*. As the reader is unlikely to have come across any but the most common such systems, this chapter describes the range of such groupware systems and the associated architectural and implementation issues. In addition, we shall discuss frameworks which classify groupware systems and which describe how they fit into the wider area of cooperative working. Many of these applications are at present research systems; however, the number of commercial systems with a groupware component will rise significantly during the coming years.

Any computer system, whether or not it is specifically groupware, will have an effect on the work groups within an organization and upon the organization as a whole. It is not possible to cover the full sociological and anthropological background that is being brought to bear on these issues, but it is important that the reader is aware of these knock on effects of even individual computer systems. In Chapter 14, we will describe some of the theory of human communication and the group and organizational factors which influence the design of groupware.

13.2   Groupware Systems

In this chapter, Sections 13.3–13.5 describe a range of groupware systems, from email and video conferencing to shared editors and co-authoring systems. Section 13.6 uses several frameworks which help us to analyze groupware systems, and which will give some structure to the issues which arise during the previous three sections. Section 13.7 discusses some of the implementation problems facing a groupware developer.

Groupware can be classified in several ways. One of these is by *where* and *when* the participants are performing the cooperative work. This is summarized in a *time/space matrix*. Another classification is by the *function* of the system, for example, meeting support or group authoring. The sub-sections on specific areas of groupware follow this functional classification. However, there at least ten such categories here and the list could extend as fast as one could think up new application areas. To give a broader categorization for the sections, we follow a framework which classifies groupware by the aspect of cooperative work which it supports.

The rest of this section describes briefly the time/space matrix and cooperative work framework, both in terms of non-computerized 'real-world' examples. We will return to these and other frameworks in Section 13.6, once the reader is familiar

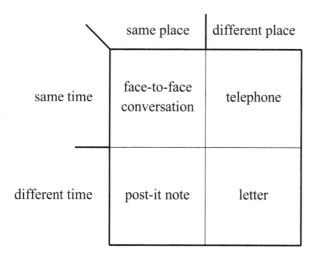

Figure 13.1   *Time/space matrix*

with range of groupware systems currently available. As with analysis techniques for single-user systems, these frameworks can help to structure the design of new systems, or to suggest possible application areas.

The time/space matrix is a very useful shorthand to refer to the particular circumstances a groupware system aims to address. Basically, we look at the participants and ask whether they are in the same place or not, and whether they are operating at the same time or not. Figure 13.1 shows how various non-computer communication technologies fit into the time/space matrix.

The axes are given different names by different authors. The space dimension is also called the geographical dimension and is divided into *co-located* (same place) and *remote* (different place). Many of the earliest groupware systems were aimed at overcoming the barriers of distance, for example, email and video conferencing. More recently, systems have arisen which aim to augment face-to-face meetings and other co-located cooperation.

The time axis is often divided into *synchronous* and *asynchronous* systems; so we would refer to telephone as a synchronous remote communication mechanism, whereas post-it notes are asynchronous co-located. These terms are used heavily in the CSCW literature; often the intended geographical location is obvious from context, or the application domain and thus synchronous/asynchronous becomes the principal distinction. However, there are some problems with this simple distinction which we will return to in Section 13.6.1. As we discuss each groupware system, it will be placed in its appropriate time/space category.

The framework used to organize Sections 13.3–13.5 is based on the entities

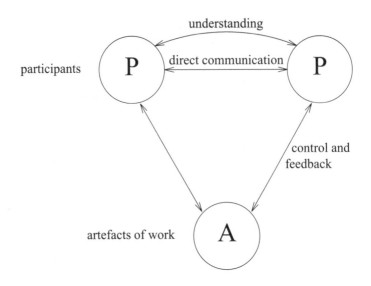

Figure 13.2   *Cooperative work framework*

involved in cooperative work, that is, the participants themselves and the things upon which they work. Figure 13.2 summarizes these relationships.

Implicit in the term 'cooperative work' is that there are two or more participants. These are denoted by the circles labelled 'P'. They are engaged in some common work, and to do so interact with various tools and products. Some of these are physically shared (e.g. two builders holding the ends of a measuring tape), but all are shared in the sense that they contribute to the cooperative purpose. These tools and other objects are denoted by the circle labelled 'A' — the *artefacts of work*.

The participants communicate with one another as they work, denoted by the arrow between the participants. In real life this may be by speech (the builders with the tape), or letter (a lawyer and client); in fact, this *direct communication* may be in any of the categories of the time/space matrix. Part of the purpose of communication is to establish a common understanding of the task they are engaged in. This understanding may be implicit in the conversation, or may be made explicit in diagrams or text.

For some jobs, such as research and aspects of management, the development of understanding and ideas constitutes the primary task. Where this is not the case, the participants will interact with the tools and work objects to perform their job. This is shown by the arrows between the participants and the artefacts of work. This arrow represents a two way flow of information: of *control* from the participants to the artefacts, and *feedback* from the artefacts to the participants. In real-world tasks, these two hardly seem distinct: as you wield a hammer, you feel the weight of it. However, as should be evident from previous discussion of single-user interfaces this will not necessarily be the case for computer systems.

We will classify groupware systems by the function in this framework, which they primarily support:

Computer-mediated communication supporting the direct communication between participants

Meeting and decision support systems capturing common understanding

Shared applications and artefacts supporting the participants' interaction with shared work objects — the *artefacts of work*.

Of course, many systems may support more than one of these functions, and indeed this can be seen as a sign of good groupware. Furthermore, there are some further relationships between these functions. Both these aspects will be developed in Section 13.6.3.

13.3 Computer-mediated Communication

Implicit in the terms groupware and CSCW is that we have two or more participants and that they are communicating with one another. We begin by looking at systems which support this direct communication. This is called *computer-mediated communication (CMC)*, and is an important part of CSCW. However, good communication is not sufficient — they must be able to cooperate about their work. Improving communications may help this, but not necessarily.

Under the heading of computer-mediated communication we will look at email and bulletin boards, well-established, largely text based means of *asynchronous remote* communication, structured message systems, developed from simple email, and various video based systems, which support *synchronous remote* communication.

13.3.1 Email and bulletin boards

Most readers of this book will have used some form of email system. Many will also have used some form of bulletin board or electronic conferencing system such as Usenet news or one of the dial-up services. Although among the simplest groupware systems, they are most certainly the most popular and successful.

Consider the stages during the sending of a simple email message:

preparation You type a message at your computer, possibly adding a subject header.

despatch You then instruct the email program to send it to the recipient.

delivery At some time later, anything from a few seconds (for *LAN* based email), to hours or days (for some international email via slow gateways) it will arrive at the recipient's computer.

notification If the recipient is using the computer a message may be displayed, saying that mail has arrived, or the terminal may beep.

receipt The recipient reads the message using an email program, possibly different from that of the sender.

These stages differ slightly from tool to tool, but are essentially similar. For example, preparation may take place within the mail tool itself, or the tool may import an externally prepared document. Although email systems are so well known and simple, they have been the springboard for several more advanced groupware applications.

In theory, from the user's perspective we need not worry about the exact delivery mechanism — it should be hidden — just as we do not worry about the details of telephone exchanges. However, with email these mechanisms become only too apparent, most obviously in the varying delays we may experience and in the reliability of different channels. These factors are not always predictable as they may depend on faults and loadings of computers used to relay the message. Furthermore, error messages and even the forms of addressing relate directly to the path from computer to computer which the message takes. As international email standards take effect, these problems of reliability should reduce, but they are still a major barrier to the effective use of email over long distances.

In the simple email example, there was just one recipient. However, most email systems also allow a set of recipients to be named, all of whom receive the message (see Figure 13.3). Like letters, these recipients may be divided into the direct recipients (often denoted by a To: field) and those who receive copies (Cc:). These two types of recipient are treated *no differently* by the computer systems — the distinction serves a social purpose for the participants. This is a frequent observation about any groupware system — the system should support *people* in their cooperation.

Often users will be able to set up *distribution lists*, named groups of other users to whom mail is often sent. There is only a small difference between the use of such lists and fully fledged bulletin boards or electronic conferencing systems. In these systems you address your message (or contribution) to a particular conference or newsgroup, then anyone who has subscribed to that newsgroup receives the message.

It is to be expected that the differences between email and electronic conferencing, especially within the interface, will blur over time. However, there are important differences for the participants. Firstly, they vary in terms of who controls the distribution list. Some email distribution lists are private to the sender,

```
To: janet, abowd
From: alan
Subject: HCI book
Cc: R.Beale@cs.brum.ac.uk

How are your chapters getting on?
Could one of you meet me over lunch?
I'm having trouble using the minipage
environment doing illustrations of email messages.
```

Figure 13.3   *Simple email message*

that is, the *sender* can vary the list at will, and knows exactly who is on it. Altern-atively, a distribution list may be shared, in which case it is often added to and updated by the *system administrator*. Finally, in a bulletin board or news systems, it is the *recipient* who decides which news groups to subscribe to. For example, Usenet news sends *all* news items to *all* connected computers. Users may well read contributions posted before they subscribed, and certainly the sender will have no idea as to who will read the contribution. We can see this progression in two ways. One is control which moves from the sender, to the administrator and then to the recipient. The second is the nature of the recipient, from specific individuals in email, through organizational or social groups, to topic areas. Again these different emphases have important social implications — communication is about people, not systems.

Although email between sites takes from several minutes to days to arrive, LAN based email within a single site will often arrive within seconds. It is thus possible to have email 'conversations'. Typically email interfaces are not designed to deal with this form of exchange, but it is relatively easy to have a sequence of exchanges, say every minute or so. Many computer systems also allow a form of *synchronous* text based communication, whereby two (or more) participants can instantly see each other's contributions. Examples of this are the UNIX 'talk' program or VAX's 'phone'. In these, the participants' screens are divided into two and while your typing goes to the bottom half, your colleague's goes into the top. The typing is usually echoed character by character, so you can see your colleague's half typed phrases, deletions, etc. A variant of this concept, used as part of several groupware systems, is to have a single transcript. The participants have a separate composition area and when they hit the return key (or click on a special button), their contribution is added to the end of the transcript. Notice the difference in *granularity*, the 'talk' program works with a grain size of characters, whereas the transcript acts on contributions (often a single line, or at most a short paragraph).

The granularity of standard email and bulletin boards tends to be greater again, as people may send quite large messages (although some interfaces discourage this).

13.3.2 *Structured message systems*

A common problem with email and electronic conferencing systems is *overload* for the recipient. As distribution lists become longer, the number of email messages received begins to explode. This is obvious: if each message you send goes to, on average, ten people, then everyone will receive, on average, ten messages for each one sent. The problem is similar to that caused for paper mail by photocopiers and mail merge programs. If we consider that newsgroups may have hundreds of subscribers, the problem becomes extreme. Happily, most newsgroups have only a few active contributers and many passive readers, but still the piles of unread electronic mail grow. Various forms of *structured message system* have been developed to help deal with this overload, perhaps the most well known being the *Information Lens* [107]. They adopt some form of *filtering* in order to sort items into different categories, either by importance or by subject matter. As well as a text message, normal email has several named fields: To, From, Subject. Structured message systems have far more, domain-specific, fields. The sender of the message chooses the appropriate message type, say a notification of a seminar. The system then presents a *template* which includes blank fields pertinent to the message type, e.g. Time, Place, Speaker and Title. Figure 13.4 shows a typical structured message similar to those in Lens.

The named fields make the message more like a typical database record than a normal email message. Thus the recipient can filter incoming mail using database-like queries. This can be used during normal reading — 'show me all messages From "abowd" or with Status "urgent"'. Alternatively, users may set up filtering agents to act on their behalf. Such an agent is a sort of electronic secretary; it is programmed with rules based on the field contents and can perform actions such as moving the message into a specific mailbox, deleting the message or informing the user.

The problem with such systems is that they put a great burden on the sender to fill in the fields accurately, but it is the recipient who benefits. This problem of disproportionate benefit recurs throughout CSCW. In order to make the job of the sender as easy as possible, message types will often be created with easy defaults for fields, and perhaps menus of alternatives. Also, in order to make finding appropriate message templates easier, they may be arranged in a type hierarchy.

Until recently these structured message systems were only found in academic and research centres, but simpler forms are now available in commercial PC based email products.

More complex structured message systems are based on models of conversation. So, for example, if I am sent a message of type 'request for information', I am obliged to return either a message of type 'informative reply' or of type 'don't

```
Type: Seminar announcement
To: all
From: Alan Dix
Subject: departmental seminar

Time: 2:15 Wednesday
Place: D014
Speaker: W.T. Pooh
Title: The Honey Pot
Text: Recent research on socially constructed
      meaning has focused on the image of the
      Honey Pot and its dialectic interpretation
      within an encultured hermeneutic.
      This talk . . .
```

Figure 13.4   *Structured message*

know'. There is a variety of such systems differing in the models used and the rigidity with which they are applied. In the most rigid, you are only allowed one of the pre-programmed replys, whereas more flexible systems merely suggest possibilities. We will discuss one such system, *Coordinator*, in Chapter 14 (Section 14.3.6), in the context of models of conversation.

There is in fact considerable debate between those who feel that a messaging system should impose conversational structures and constraints, and those who believe they should supply systems within which the participants can develop their own structures. It is argued that such user-defined structures are more likely to meet their needs, and the systems will be more flexible to accommodate changes in group working. The message systems based upon conversational models are the most constrained. Those offering structured messages, as we have described above, are towards the middle of the spectrum. The original email and bulletin board systems were at the other, unstructured, extreme, but lack sufficient features for the users to define their own structure. More modern systems from the 'user structured' arena are developed from the bulletin board concept, but are more like a shared hypertext. The structure allowed by links and cross references allows users to have sub-conferences and digressions, to annotate each other's messages and to post follow on messages. An example of such a system is the *Amsterdam Conversation Environment* [52].

This conflict between *global structuring* by the designers and *local structuring* by the participants in their own situation, arises within many areas of CSCW and has similarities to issues of user control in HCI in general (see Chapter 4).

13.3.3 *Video conferences and communication*

The idea of *video-phones* has been around for a long time, from Flash Gordon's days onwards, and early video-phones have been available for at least 15 years. Until recently pervasive person-to-person video has been impossible without special and very expensive cabling. However, the introduction of *ISDN* is likely to change this dramatically. ISDN is a form of moderately high bandwidth (64 kbaud) digital telephone connection. It is available in major cities across the world and enables, amongst other things, LAN-type connections between computers and real-time video connections. The need for this becomes apparent if you calculate the bandwidth required for a typical video image. If we consider an 8-bit 600 × 400 pixel image being sent at 25 frames a second, this amounts to 24 million bits per second. This is not high video quality and yet requires a vast bandwidth far in excess of a normal telephone line. It is also far greater than the capacity of ISDN lines. However, recent (and expensive) *video compression* techniques can reduce the required capacity to a level within the range of ISDN. Pervasive video communication is clearly a technology coming of age.

As these hardware developments are quite recent, most experimental and commercial video systems use existing technology and *lots* of wire. There are three broad uses of video: *video conferences*, pervasive video for enhancing social communication and video integrated with another shared application. These are all *synchronous remote* facilities.

Video conferences sit rather oddly in CSCW in that they typically do not use computers at all! However, computers and telecommunications are becoming so interlinked that it is widely considered an appropriate area of CSCW. Video conference facilities are readily available commercially using dedicated telecommunications lines and satellites for trans-continental conferences. The quality of a video conference compared to a face-to-face meeting is appalling, but, when faced with the costs of, say, flying executives across an ocean or even across the American continent, the inconveniences are often accepted.

One set of problems is connected with the small field of view of a television camera, and the size and quality of the resulting images. Even with a one-to-one video conversation, we need to decide whether to take a simple head and shoulders shot, the whole torso, or head to foot. If there is a group at either end, even just two or three people, the problems magnify enormously. If you view all three people at once, then the image of the speaker may become so small that it is hard to see the body gestures. These gestures are one of the big advantages of video conferences over the much cheaper telephone conference. However, you need a skilled camera technician to follow the speaker, zooming in and out as necessary. Furthermore, zooming in to the speaker runs the risk of losing the sense of presence. The participants at the far end do not know whether the speaker's colleagues are nodding in agreement or falling asleep!

Video conferences support specific planned meetings. However, one of the losses of working in a different site from a colleague is the chance meetings whilst walking down a corridor or drinking tea. Several experimental systems aim to counter this, giving a sense of *social presence* at a distance. One solution is the *video-window* or *video-wall*, a very large television screen set into the wall of common rooms at different sites [65]. The idea is that as people wander about the common room at one site they can see and talk to people at the other site — the video-wall is almost like a window or doorway between the sites.

The problems of camera positioning and focusing are if anything worse for the video-wall than for the simple video-conference. At least in a video-conference the participants stay relatively still, probably seated at a table, whereas in a common room, the participants are likely to wander about. It is quite easy to move out of the range of the camera, whilst still being able to see your colleague. That is, there is a lack of *reciprocity* compared to normal face-to-face conversation. In addition, positioning the camera is a nightmare. To give the 'window' illusion the camera must be positioned very close to the video-wall and must be focused to get a full depth shot of the conversants. Even then, because of the camera's restricted field of view, you must not stand too close or your colleague will get a six foot high view of your navel.

A stereo audio channel for the video-wall, and indeed for any video connection, can help the participants orient to the speaker and also filter out unwanted noises (see Chapter 1 for a discussion of selective attention to sound). However, a problem with communicating using loud speakers in a common room is a lack of privacy. Normally, people just move closer and lower their voice, but this is not effective with the video-wall.

Similar facilities have been made available within individual offices at several research sites. For example, at Xerox EuroParc in Cambridge U.K. every office is wired up with video cameras and monitors. Typically, one has a camera strapped to the top of one's monitor, or on an angle-poise-like arm, and an image on a separate monitor, or even in a window on the computer screen. Participants may have two-way or multi-way video conversations, or set up virtual rooms — a constant video connection.

Even with the camera strapped just above a monitor, it is very difficult for the participants to get *eye contact*. In normal face-to-face conversation participants periodically look one another straight in the eye. If the camera is just above the monitor, your partner will always see you looking slightly downwards, and vice versa. For strictly one-to-one conversation, a technique called the *video-tunnel* can be used (Figure 13.5). A half-silvered mirror is used so that the camera can view the user as if it were in the middle of the screen. The feeling of engagement between the participants is reported to be far greater than more standard video arrangements [162]. Unfortunately, the shear bulk of the video-tunnel means that it is not really practical for large scale use. However, frequent users of less optimal camera/monitor configurations eventually get used to the rather odd visual angles involved.

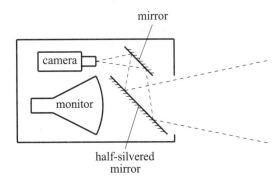

mirror

camera

monitor

half-silvered
mirror

Figure 13.5   *Video tunnel*

13.4   Meeting and Decision Support Systems

In any conversation the participants must establish a common understanding about the task they are to perform, and generate ideas. In some areas this is a secondary activity: you are discussing the job you are doing, the ideas support that job. However, there is a class of activities where the job is itself generating ideas and understanding. This is typically the case in a research environment, in design tasks, in management meetings and brainstorming sessions.

We will discuss three types of system where the generation and recording of ideas and decisions is the primary focus.

Argumentation tools which record the arguments used to arrive at a decision and support principally *asynchronous co-located* design teams.

Meeting rooms which support face-to-face groups (*synchronous co-located*) in brainstorming and management meetings.

Shared drawing surfaces which can be used for *synchronous remote* design meetings.

13.4.1   *Argumentation tools*

In Chapter 5, we discussed *design rationale*, methods of recording decisions and the arguments that lead to those decisions. We saw that design rationale could fulfil two roles: recording design decisions for future references and clarifying the available options during design. Both of these have a potential CSCW impact. One reason to record your design decisions is so that a future designer can understand why you made the decisions you did and hence be in a better position to modify or learn from your design. That is, you are communicating with someone possibly years in advance. However, the one-way nature of the communication makes it information passing rather than collaboration.

More important from a CSCW viewpoint is when the design argument is used to communicate decisions between a group of designers. Here the communication is two-way — the designers may both add to the design argument and look at each other's contributions. Argumentation support tools often have a hypertext-like structure, and may easily be used to support design teams as well as individuals. At the simplest level the designers can use the tool one at a time, rather like writing a co-authored document by taking turns to use the word-processor. As the detailed design of, say, a piece of software may take many months it is unlikely that two people will want to use the tool at exactly the same moment, and if they do . . . well it is a chance for an impromptu design meeting!

Sophisticated tools also have facilities to allow several designers to use the system simultaneously. To allow this, the tool must have mechanisms to stop the different designers' work interfering with that of another. This problem is called *concurrency control*. Happily, this is particularly easy with hypertext — so long as people work on different nodes, there is no conflict. To ensure this a node must be *locked*, that is, when one participant starts to edit the node, no other participant is allowed to edit or update the same node. Given that there are typically hundreds of nodes in a design rationale, with only a short text description in each, the chances of two participants wanting to work on the same node is small. However, if they do, the system will refuse permission to one or other. In addition to these locking mechanisms, the systems have *notification mechanisms* to let the participants know which nodes have been edited. For example, changed nodes may be highlighted until the participant has examined them or marked them as read. This highlighting must of course be on a per user basis — if Jane edits a node and Sam marks it as read, then when Mary comes to the system she should still see the node highlighted.

A good example of argumentation tools is the family of tools developed to support the argumentation model called *issue based information system* (IBIS), the best known being gIBIS [40] (see Chapter 5 for a fuller description of gIBIS). The gIBIS system has node types including 'issues', 'positions' and 'arguments', and these are linked together by relationships such as 'argument *supports* position'.

Notice that argumentation tools may allow a range of interaction styles from asynchronous, when the designers use it one at a time, to fully synchronous, when several use it at once. Although there is no reason why the systems should not be used for distant collaboration they are typically used by groups within the same office, and in the case of one-at-a-time use, on one machine. They are thus largely, but not solely, *asynchronous co-located* groupware systems.

Figure 13.6   *A computer supported meeting (courtesy Douglas Engelbart)*

13.4.2   *Meeting rooms*

The advantages of email, bulletin boards and video conferences are obvious — if you are a long way apart, you cannot have a face-to-face meeting. Similarly, it is obvious why one should want to record decisions during a long-lived design process. The need for *meeting rooms* is less obvious. These are specially constructed rooms, with extensive computer equipment designed to support face-to-face meetings. Given face-to-face meetings work reasonably well to start with, such rooms must be very well designed if the equipment is to enhance rather than disrupt the meeting.

There are about half a dozen such rooms at present catering for groups of between 4 and 30 participants. These include Xerox Parc's *CoLab* [166], Project Nick [17] and Capture Lab [108]. The general layout consists of a large screen, regarded as an electronic whiteboard, at one end of the room, with chairs and tables arranged so that all the participants can see the screen. This leads to a U or C shaped arrangement around the screen, and in the biggest room even several tiers of seating. In addition, all the participants have their own terminals, which may be recessed into the tabletop to reduce their visual effect. Figure 13.6 shows a computer supported meeting using NLS, a very early groupware system [59]. Obviously changes in display technology have made the displays less obtrusive, but the basic principle remains.

Such systems will support various forms of working including private use of the terminals and sub-group working on a tele-conferencing or email basis. However, the characteristic mode of operation is where all the participants' screens and the central screen show the same image. This is termed *WYSIWIS* ('*what you see is what I see*'). The screen then takes the form of an electronic whiteboard, similar to a simple graphics drawing package, on which the participants can all write. One advantage of such an arrangement over a normal whiteboard is the ease with which data can be moved to and from the participants' normal computer files. As more work is prepared on-line this will increase in importance. Also the electronic whiteboard has some advantages over the real thing. Whereas on a real whiteboard, you can only write and rub out, on the electronic version you can move items around just as you would with a drawing tool, and, of course, you can get a print-out of the results rather than just hoping the cleaners do not wipe it all off.

There are potential problems if several participants decide to write at the same time, so different systems adopt different *floor control policies* to determine which participant can write at any moment.

The simplest policy to implement is to use *locking*, similar to that described previously. When a participant, say Jane, wants to write to the screen she presses a key, or clicks on an on-screen button to request the floor. If no one else has the floor, she may go ahead and type on the screen, or if it supports graphics draw a diagram. When she has finished, she relinquishes the floor, using some other key or mouse selection. However, if some other participant, say Sam, already has the floor when Jane requests it, she must wait until Sam relinquishes the floor. There will be some sort of status indicator to say who has the floor at any moment, so Jane can ask Sam to relinquish, just as you might ask for the pen to write on a whiteboard.

In practice, such meetings tend to be punctuated with far too many requests such as 'Sam have you finished yet?', as often a participant will forget to relinquish the floor after writing. Also, it can be a pain to explicitly request the floor from the system — with a whiteboard you simply pick up your pen and write. Various more lenient locking mechanisms are used to reduce these problems. A lock may be *implicitly* requested when you begin to type or draw. If no one else has the floor, then the floor is implicitly granted. If someone else has the floor, then your writing will be blocked. There is also implicit relinquishing, the lock may be automatically released after several seconds of inactivity. This may of course happen during a pause, rather than when the floor holder has finished, but the ease with which the floor can be regained does not make it a nuisance.

A conceptually simpler idea is to let everyone write to the screen at the same time — just as people may use several pens to write on a whiteboard at the same time. This sounds like a recipe for chaos, with people forever writing on top of one another. However, with reasonably small groups there is little problem. Try going to the whiteboard as someone is writing on it, and writing on top of what they write. It is possible, but it does not make you many friends. Similarly in the electronic version, as soon as two people begin to write on the same part of the screen they say 'oops!' and start to write elsewhere.

The various forms of locking constitute a software protocol for floor control. The way that people negotiate for screen space in the free-for-all situation is a *social protocol*. The reason that this is possible is because the participants are in the same room and are able to talk to one another.

If there is only one floor holder, then the screens can all show the floor holder's cursor. However, as soon as several participants are active at once, it is less clear what to do. One option is to display all the users' cursors. These may be accompanied by the user's name so that you can tell who is entering what. With large numbers of participants this can become distracting, also it is costly in terms of network traffic. The alternative is to show none of the cursors. If the participants are talking as they write, it is usually obvious who is writing what. In addition, during brainstorming phases, anonymity is an advantage — people are more likely to put up an 'off the wall' suggestion, thus stimulating more ideas and discussion.

If you are using a real whiteboard, you may go up to a diagram on the board and say 'I think *that* should go *there*'. As you say the words '*that*' and '*there*', you point at the relevant parts of the diagram. This is called *deictic reference* or simply *deixis*. If the participants' cursors are invisible to one another, then this form of pointing is impossible. Indeed, in such a meeting, even where the cursors are visible, the participants may momentarily forget and point at their own screen. Obviously the participant can get up and point at the shared screen as you would at a whiteboard, but that is rather intrusive and precludes writing at the same time. To allow this deictic reference a *group pointer* may be supplied. This is an icon visible on all the screens, perhaps in the form of a pointing finger. Any participant can pick it up with his own mouse and use it to gesture on the screen. The control of the group pointer poses similar problems to those of floor control. However, the most lenient locking policies work well since the use of the pointer is usually synchronized with speaking, and thus it is easy to avoid and resolve conflicts.

The design and building of meeting rooms is both expensive and time-consuming, but less sophisticated facilities are more widely available. The simplest is the hard-copy whiteboard, which has some of the advantages of an electronic whiteboard (and with greater resolution). If these were more closely coupled to a computer system, they would have even more scope. Transparent LCD screens for putting on top of an overhead projector can give any computer a vast screen image. In the simplest case this can just be manipulated by one person, but if several computers are networked together and use commercial shared screen software (see below in Section 13.5.1), one can obtain a similar effect to that of the more expensive conferencing facilities. However, experience of the various meeting room projects has shown that the social dynamics are very fragile and the difference between a successful meeting environment and a complete disaster is narrow.

13.4.3   *Shared work surfaces*

The idea of a shared screen forming an electronic whiteboard is not confined to face-to-face meetings. One can easily imagine using the same software which runs in a meeting room, working between several sites. That is, we can take the *synchronous co-located* meeting room software and use it for *synchronous remote* meetings. As before, each participant's screen shows the same image, and the participants can write on the screen with the same sort of floor control policies as discussed earlier. There are additional problems. First, the participants will also require at least an audio link to one another and quite likely video as well. Remember that the social protocols used during lenient floor control, not to mention the discussion one has during a meeting, are difficult or impossible without additional channels of communication. As well as the person-to-person communications, the computer networks may have trouble handling the information. If there are delays between one person writing something on the board and another seeing it, the second participant may write to the same location. A situation which is easily avoided in the co-located meeting could become a major problem when remote. Many researchers in the area blithely assume that such problems will be solved by cheaper high-bandwidth telecommunications, such as ISDN.

In order to make the whiteboard effect more realistic, several systems are arranged so that participants write by hand directly onto large screens. The writing is either filmed by camera (using complex arrangements of mirrors), or captured digitally using a sensitive screen. The image of one participant's writing is then displayed on the other's screens. The effect is very like all being able to write at once on the same screen, except that the other participants' writing will be slightly less distinct than your own because of the resolution of the TV image. You may also experience problems of *parallax* as your own writing is on the outer surface of the screen and the projected image on the inside.

One system, VideoWhiteboard [172], arranges its lighting and cameras such that you can see not only the other participants' writing, but also shadowy images of their hands and bodies, getting gradually dimmer and more out of focus as they move away from the screen. For two participants, it is rather as if your colleague is writing on the other side of a smoked glass panel. When used by more than two participants, your ghostly colleagues can appear to occupy the same space and move through one another! This sounds rather disconcerting, but the users soon got used to the effect and are able to interpret one another's body language, even as a soft focus shadow.

A third variation of the shared worksurface is where the participants write on a sheet of paper on their desktop, which is then filmed from above. The images from each participant are then mixed and displayed on a screen in each participant's work area. By looking at the screen while they point and write, the participants can refer to one another's work. The advantage of such a system is that the participants' individual paper work is easily integrated into their shared environment. The desktop images can also be mixed with a shared computer screen, so that paper and computer work can be mixed. One such system, the *TeamWorkStation* [91], has been used for the remote teaching of Japanese calligraphy. The student is able to paint letters on paper or on the computer screen, and see these strokes overlaid with the teacher's strokes. In this system, the participants also have a face-to-face video link.

13.5   Shared Applications and Artefacts

The things that were being shared in the last section were ephemera; they were there to support the meeting or design process, but were not the end purpose. In this section we will look at systems where the focus of sharing is the participants' work domain itself. These include the computers people are using, applications on those computers, and the documents they are working with. Some of these systems are similar in technology to the various shared work surfaces above, but the focus in this section is on *work*.

13.5.1   *Shared PCs and shared window systems*

Most of the groupware tools we have discussed require special *collaboration aware* applications to be written. However, *shared PCs* and *shared window systems* allow ordinary applications to be the focus of cooperative work. Of course, you can cooperate simply by sitting together at the same computer, passing the keyboard and mouse between you and your colleague. The idea of a shared PC is that you have two (or more) computers which function as if they were one. What is typed on one appears on all the rest. This sounds at first just like a meeting room without the large shared screen. The difference is that the meeting rooms have special shared drawing tools, but the shared PC is just running your ordinary program. The sharing software monitors your keystrokes and mouse movements and sends them to all the other computers, so that their systems behave exactly like yours. Their keystrokes and movements are similarly relayed to you. As far as the application is concerned there is one keyboard and one mouse.

Imagine two users type at once. As the application does not know about the multiple users it will merely interleave the keystrokes, or should we say 'inkeyterslt reaokeve tshe'. Interleaved mouse movements are, if anything, more meaningless. The sharing software therefore imposes some form of lenient locking. For the mouse, this will be an automatic lock while the mouse is being moved, with the lock being relinquished after a very short period of inactivity. The keyboard lock will have a longer period as natural gaps in typing are greater than gaps in mousing. Alternatively, the keyboard may have no lock, the users being left to sort out the control with their own *social protocol*.

A shared window system is similar except, rather than the whole screen, it is individual windows which are shared. While the user works with unshared windows, the system behaves as normal, but when the user selects a shared window the shared windowing system intervenes. As with the shared PC all the user's keystrokes and mouse movements within the window are broadcast to the other computers sharing the window.

These facilities may be used within the same room, as originally suggested, in which case we have a *synchronous co-located* system. Alternatively, they may be used in conjunction with telephone or video connections at a distance, that is, *synchronous remote*. The extra audio or video channel is necessary when used remotely as the systems in themselves offer no direct communication. It is just possible to use such systems, without additional channels, by writing messages in the application's workspace (document, drawing surface, etc.). However, the social protocols needed to mediate the mouse and keyboard cannot be achieved by this channel.

Shared PCs and window systems have two main uses. One is where the focus is on the documents being processed, for example, if the participants are using a spreadsheet together to solve a financial problem. The other is technical support: if you have a problem with an application, you can ring up your local (or even remote) technical guru, who will connect to your computer, examine where you are and offer advice. Compare this scenario with trying to explain over the phone why your column is not formatting as you want.

13.5.2 *Shared editors*

A *shared editor* is an editor (for text or graphics) which is *collaboration aware*, that is, it knows that it is being shared. It can thus provide several insertion points, or locking protocols more tuned to the editor's behaviour. The software used in meeting rooms can be thought of as a form of shared editor and many of the issues are the same, but the purpose of a shared editor is to collaborate over normal documents. Just as with shared PCs and windows, the users are expected to have some additional means of communication, either face-to-face (co-located), audio or video channels, or at very least textual communications.

Shared editors may be text based or include graphics. For simplicity, we shall just consider text. Even so, there are a wide range of design options. Should you have a single insertion point with some form of *floor control* to avoid interleaving, or should you have one insertion point per participant? Assuming you have several insertion points, do you just see your own, or do you see your colleagues' insertion points as well, and if you can see them should they be identified by the user's name or be anonymous? In addition to the insertion point options, there is the issue about what you should see. Do all the participants see the same part of the screen, so if one participant scrolls, so do all the rest? Or do we allow different views on the document so that one participant can edit the beginning of the document while another edits the end?

There is not a right answer to these questions, different policies are useful for different purposes: close cooperation on a single sentence, or writing separate sections. Even within a single editing session the appropriate policy will vary. Unfortunately, in the past, these policy decisions were usually enshrined in the various shared editors, rather than being configured by the users. However, there is a growing recognition that more adaptable systems are needed to allow for the wide variation between groups, and within the same group over time. We will look at some of the options and how they affect the style of cooperation.

Thinking about the shared view vs. different view options, it at first seems obvious that we should allow people to edit different parts of a document. This is certainly true while they are working effectively independently. However, as soon as they begin to discuss the text together — that is really *collaborate* synchronously — problems arise: 'I don't really like that line at the top' you say, 'I just wrote that, I think it's really good' your colleague replies. Possibly the end of your good working relationship, and, sadly, unnecessary. Your screens show different parts of the document and so the line at the top of your screen (which you disliked) is not the one your colleague has just written (Figure 13.7). Of course, the participants know they do not necessarily see the same screen, but you naturally use terms which relate to the context you can see, called *indexical expressions*. One reason given for the Charge of the Light Brigade is that the commander gave the order 'take the position on the hill'. Unfortunately the hill the commander could see was not the one in front of the Light Brigade. Paradoxically, the better the impression of a shared environment, the more likely it is that participants will accidently use indexical expressions.

These problems are precisely why the principle of *WYSIWIS* ('what you see is what I see') is used in meeting rooms. Even minor differences between displays, such as lags between the appearance of one participant's typing appearing on the other's screens, can cause severe problems — no wonder different views cause trouble. Of course, WYSIWIS is not always appropriate, for example if we want to edit different parts of a document. Neither is it a solution to all problems. For example, if two people try to scroll the shared view at the same time, we have scroll wars. People find this conflict harder to resolve than typing clashes. This is probably because scrolling is a less direct and less predictable action anyway, and thus it is more difficult to diagnose what is going wrong. This suggests that better locking of scroll bars and visual clues are required. As we will discuss later (Section 13.7) graphics toolkits do not make such modifications easy.

Separate views of course demand separate insertion points. Even with shared views, it is not obvious why one should want a single insertion point with the attendant floor control problems. However, a shared cursor offers a point of focus for close cooperation, and should perhaps be an option. Of course, a shared view with shared cursor is almost identical to a single user editor in a shared window. Where there is no shared cursor, a *group pointer* can be used to focus discussion.

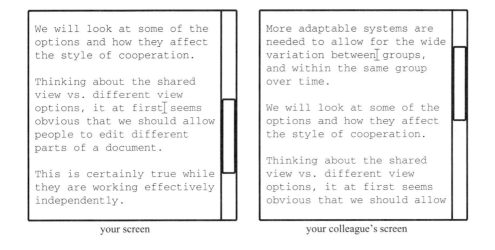

Figure 13.7 *Shared editor with separate insertion points and different views*

Indeed, one could imagine using a group pointer with different views, but there are no extant systems which allow this.

As we have indicated, the differences between groups mean that some configuration by the group is essential. That is, shared editors require some form of *local structuring*. However, that does not mean that there will be no problems. Participants will point at the screen with their fingers when in different rooms, and use indexical expressions when they are in separate screen mode. The more their sense of *engagement*, that is, the more they feel as if they are working together, the more likely they are to revert to natural forms of expression. We cannot prevent this entirely; as we saw, mistakes can happen in 'real life' too.

13.5.3 Co-authoring systems

Shared text editing is a short-term activity, occurring over a time-scale of, at most, a few hours. Co-authoring is much longer term, taking weeks or months. Whereas shared editing is synchronous, co-authoring is largely *asynchronous*, with occasional periods of synchronous work. This may involve shared editing, but even if it does this is only one of the activities. Authors may work out some sort of plan together, apportion work between them, then exchange drafts commenting on one another's work. In fact, this is only one scenario and if there is one consistent result from numerous studies of individual and collaborative writing, it is this: everyone and every group is different.

Fortunately, even though the details of writing differ, especially in the process, there are enough similarities to produce systems which support co-authoring. The majority of these are built around a hypertext model. The text itself is the basis and comments and discussion of these comments are linked into this basic structure. Although a general-purpose shared hypertext can be used, specific co-authoring systems are tuned to the writing task. The shape of the hypertext may be limited to a tree rather than the arbitrary graph of a hypertext. The document itself may be flat, a linear list of sections or may be grouped into a hierarchical section–sub-section tree. Comment nodes are then attached to the document nodes, and other follow-on remarks attached to the comments. These are intended to emulate the scribblings on paper drafts during normal collaborative writing. Special facilities may be added to inform one writer of another's comments or additions.

As in previous systems, co-authoring systems must have some sort of *concurrency control* to cater for times when two participants attempt to edit the same text at the same time. This may take the form of locking, as described previously, or the system may allow the users to enter into periods of synchronous activity. That is, the node editor acts as a shared editor. However, this is not the dominant form of working and most often co-authors will have divided up the work amongst themselves, so that a section will have only one principal author, and thus *social protocols* ensure that writing clashes do not occur.

These social protocols may be supported or enforced by the co-authoring system. For example, in one system *Quilt* [102], users are assigned *roles*, such as author, commentator, reader, with respect to each document node. An author is allowed to edit the text and add comments, a commentator is only allowed to add comments, and a reader cannot alter it at all. These roles resemble access rights in a normal filestore or database. However, both their naming and their particular semantics are aimed at supporting the types of role which occur in co-authoring situation. Of course, we are again into the territory of local vs. global structuring. Who decides on the roles and the associated access rights, and can they be changed during use? These questions are not too much of a problem for Quilt, where the roles are on a per node basis, but some systems have roles which apply to the whole document. It is often the case that a person who gives extensive constructive comments is asked to co-author a paper, or someone who originally was to be an author cannot find sufficient time. Roles in real life have a degree of flexibility; those in groupware must try to keep suit.

13.5.4   Shared diaries

We want to find a time for a meeting to discuss the book we are writing: when should it be? Four diaries come out and we search for a mutually acceptable slot. We eventually find a free slot, but decide we had better double check with our desk diaries and the departmental seminar programme. This sort of scenario is repeated time and again in offices across the world. The idea of a *shared diary* or *shared calendar* is simple. Each person uses a shared electronic diary, similar to that often found on personal computers and pocket organizers. When you want to arrange a meeting, the system searches everyone's diaries for one or more free slots.

There are technical problems, such as what to do if no slots are free (often the norm). The system can return a set of slots with the least other arrangements, which can then form a basis for negotiation. Alternatively, the participants can mark their appointments with levels of importance. The system can then assign costs to breaking the appointments, and find slots with least cost. Mind you, someone may regard all their appointments as critical.

This reminds us that whatever the technical sophistication, it is people who use these systems and people who must cooperate. There are varying reports of success and failure with shared diaries. Where they have failed it is invariably because they have ignored the social needs and behaviour of their users.

One such area is privacy. Are people allowed to look at your diary to find free slots? If so, do they just see 'busy' or can they see exactly what you are doing? You would be extremely annoyed if someone looked in your personal paper diary; is the electronic one any different? There is a trade-off between privacy and cooperation. In an office situation, one has a succession of diaries and calendars for specific purposes: a private diary with personal information, a desk diary and possibly a parallel desk diary with your secretary, and various forms of wall calendar showing periods on holiday and similar major meetings. These vary in their visibility to other members of the organization: your secretary can consult her copy of your diary but not your personal diary, anyone can look at the wall calendar. You choose your level of privacy by where you put information. Of course, the problems of keeping such diaries up to date with one another is one reason why electronic diaries are produced, but they must supply similar forms of privacy control or people will simply not use them. This is precisely what happens.

There are similar problems with the update of diaries. If someone wants to book a meeting with you, can they fill in a slot, or must they ask you? Again you may want to vary these rights according to who it is and the sort of appointment. Many systems allow other users to 'pencil in' appointments, but require them to be confirmed by the diary's owner.

Many people use private electronic diaries and time management software. It is reasonable to expect that groupware versions of these will become commonly available in the near future. The extent to which they work will be largely the extent to which the design takes note of personal and social factors.

13.5.5 *Communication through the artefact*

In each of last four systems — shared PCs and windows, shared editors, co-authoring systems and shared diaries — the focus has been upon the artefacts on which the participants are working. They act *upon* the artefacts and communicate with one another *about* the artefacts. However, as well as observing their own actions on the artefacts, the participants are aware of one another's actions. This awareness of one another's actions is a form of communication *through* the artefact.

This can happen even where the shared artefact is not 'real' groupware. For instance, shared files and databases can be a locus for cooperation. Sales figures may be entered into the company database by a person in one department and then used as part of a query by another employee. At a loose level, the two are cooperating in jobs, but the database, and the information in it, may be their only means of communication. Such communication is one way, and is thus a weak form of collaboration, but often important. For example, casework files are a central mechanism for communication and cooperation in many areas from taxation to social work. However, the facilities for cooperation in a typical shared filestore or database are limited to locking, and even that may be rudimentary.

People may also explicitly pass documents, produced by single-user systems, between themselves. For example, the cooperative use of spreadsheets has been studied. Some of this involves close working between the participants, but some users simply pass the spreadsheet data itself between them with little, if any, comment. If you change a formula, then the intent is obvious — you thought it was wrong.

Of course, in most situations, direct communication is necessary as well, especially where there is some conflict (your colleague thinks the original formula was right). The lesson from these more extreme examples is that cooperation does not necessarily involve direct communication and, even where it does, the indirect channel through the artefact may be central to effective working.

One shared database which is explicitly designed to promote cooperation is *Liveware* [187]. This is a card index type database implemented over HyperCard, designed to be updated by users at many sites, and spreading the information by floppy disk as people meet during normal social contact. When different versions of the Liveware database 'meet', they choose the newest version of each record. Each record has a single owner, so problems of conflicting updates are avoided.

13.6   Frameworks for Groupware

In this section we will discuss several frameworks for understanding the role of groupware. One use for these is as a classification mechanism, which can help us discuss groupware issues. In addition, they both suggest new application areas and can help structure the design of new systems.

13.6.1   *Time/space matrix and asynchronous working*

First of all we will look again at the time/space matrix. At the beginning of Section 13.2, we placed familiar technologies in the matrix. Figure 13.8 shows the

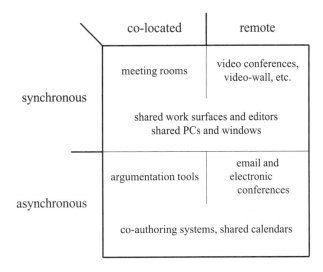

Figure 13.8 *Groupware in the time/space matrix*

same matrix, but populated with the groupware systems we have discussed.

This matrix has become a common language amongst the CSCW community. It can also be useful during design as one of the earliest decisions is what sort of interaction you are planning. The design space for *synchronous* interaction is entirely different from that for *asynchronous*.

However, the synchronous/asynchronous distinction is not as simple as it at first seems. In Section 13.2 we simply said 'whether (the participants) are operating at the same time or not'. However, for an email system, it makes no difference whether or not people are operating at the same time. Indeed, even in Figure 13.1, when we classified letter writing as different time/different place, a similar objection could be brought.

The difference between email systems and (most) co-authoring systems is that the latter have a single shared database. Thus when people work together, they know they are working together, and, depending on the locking regime used, can see each other's changes. An email system, on the other hand may take some time to propagate changes. Perhaps, a better distinction is to look at the data store and classify systems as *synchronized*, when there is a real-time computer connection, or *unsynchronized*, when there is none.

For unsynchronized systems it makes little difference whether or not the participants are operating at the same time. Also location is not very significant. (A co-located unsynchronized system is possible; imagine two computers in the same room with no network, which are periodically brought up-to-date with one

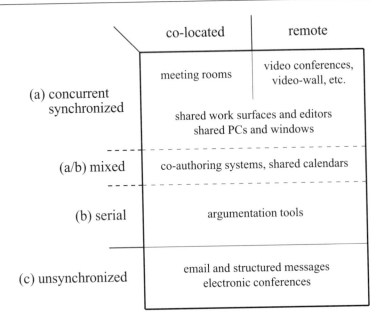

Figure 13.9 *Refined time/space matrix*

another by floppy disk transfer.)

If we consider synchronized systems, then the actual time of use becomes more important. If the participants are operating at the same time (*concurrent access*), we have real-time interaction as seen in meeting rooms (co-located) or video conferences (remote).

Alternatively, the system may prevent users working at the same time, by large scale locks, leading to non-concurrent synchronized working. Earlier argumentation tools fall into this category. Because the participants are forced to use the system one after another, we can call this *serial access*.

Finally, co-authoring systems like *Quilt* [102] allow fine grained locking so that participants can use the system at the same time or not. Therefore, they allow both serial and concurrent synchronized access.

Figure 13.9 places the groupware systems into this refined matrix. This matrix is not widely used, but is far more accurate for placing a prospective design. This is particularly obvious when one considers systems designed for users of mobile computers or home computers. These may be totally unconnected to central computers, except by occasional direct connection, floppy disk transfer or dial-up modem. The only existing groupware systems which could support such users are email and message systems, and *Liveware*. However, even email systems are rarely available except when connected via a modem. Liveware is the only groupware system *designed* for unsynchronized cooperation.

Systems, principally co-authoring tools, which describe themselves as operating in both synchronous and asynchronous modes are normally in class (b/c) in the diagram. That is, they have centralized data and allow users to operate in closely coupled modes like a group editor, or one at a time. No current system allows fluid access across the synchronized/unsynchronized divide. The authors of this book are operating from different sites and all often work at home. So we can vouch for the need for such systems.

13.6.2 *Shared information*

Electronic conferences and shared workspaces share information primarily for communication, whereas a document is shared for the purpose of working. Both raise similar issues concerning the degree of sharing required.

Granularity

The groupware systems we have seen differ as to the *granularity* of sharing they allow, in terms of both object chunk size and frequency of update.

Looking first at object chunk size. Some systems operate at a very fine grain, allowing participants to edit the same sentence, or even the same word in a sentence. At the other extreme shared file systems may often have locks so that only one user can edit a file at the same time. The granularity here is the document. The majority of groupware systems, in particular argumentation and co-authoring tools, operate somewhere between these extremes. They have some idea of a node or a section, which only one person can update at once, but which is significantly smaller than a whole document.

In the time dimension, systems may show participants' updates to one another immediately, within seconds, or when the user has finished editing the chunk. It is usually the case that a fine grained chunk size requires fine grained updates. For example, if you are allowed to edit the same word, it is not helpful if it takes a minute to see your colleague's typing! However, the converse is not necessarily true. Some systems operate locks on largish chunks but show other participants the updates immediately. Examples of this are some meeting rooms which have long-lived floor holders. This means that groupware systems all reside in the hatched region of Figure 13.10.

In the figure four points are plotted representing different grain size choices, as typified by the examples we have discussed:

(a) shared editors

(b) co-authoring systems like Quilt

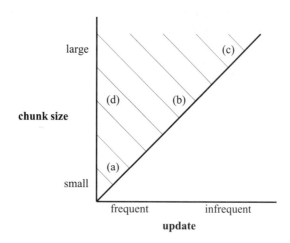

Figure 13.10   *Granularity of sharing*

(c) network file systems with locking

(d) meeting system with floor holder

Levels of sharing

As well as varying in terms of how much is shared, systems vary as to what is shared. At one extreme are *WYSIWIS* systems, such as shared window systems and many meeting rooms. In these, the participants all see exactly the same presentation of the data. However, in other shared editors, such as *Grove* [57, 58], the participants can edit different parts of the document at once. That is, they share the object, but not the presentation.

There is an interesting middle ground which is rare in explicit groupware, but common in the use of shared databases. That is sharing a view, but not the presentation of that view. For example, two people may be viewing the same part of a database, but one person sees it presented as a graph, and the other in tabular form. We thus have three levels, as depicted in Figure 13.11.

In addition to this output-oriented sharing, we can also look at input. On the one hand there are those systems which have a single shared virtual keyboard, for example, the shared window systems. On the other, we have the majority where the participants can input at different places. This can be characterized as single vs. multiple insertion points. There is no real middle ground here, but for those with separate insertion points we have the issue of visibility, whether or not the participants can see each other's insertion points or mouse pointers. Furthermore,

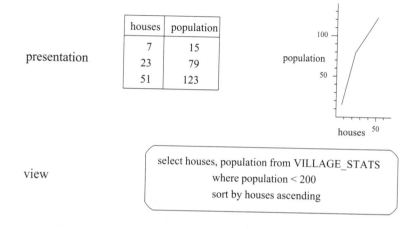

presentation

view

object

VILLAGE_STATS

Figure 13.11 *Levels of sharing*

if the other participants' cursors are not visible, we may have a *group pointer*, as discussed in Section 13.4.2. This gives us four levels of input sharing:

single insertion point
multiple insertion points

- shared virtual keyboard
- other participants visible
- group pointer
- no visibility

Again, there are loose connections between the two levels of sharing. For example, it makes little sense to have a single insertion point but different views. However, one document annotation system has separate insertion points but a shared view. Any user can choose to scroll the view of the document, but it then scrolls for all users. To make matters worse, the other users' insertion points stay at the same point on the *screen* as the document moves. So if they are typing when the screen is scrolled, their characters appear all over the document! It is a testimony to the power of *social protocols* that this system is not only used successfully, but is also enjoyed.

Types of object

The kind of object or data we are cooperating over obviously affects the way we share it. This is particularly important in the *unsynchronized* case or where there is a danger of *race conditions*. That is, where two participants perform updates simultaneously and there is confusion as to which comes first.

Consider first the text of a shared editor. Participants can add, edit or delete text anywhere in the document. We thus have to worry about them interfering with one another, for example, one participant deleting the text that another participant is in the middle of editing. Contrast this with a linear text transcript, as produced by some electronic conferencing systems. The transcript is *monotonic*, that is one can only add to it, never take away, and *appending* contributions are always added to the end. This makes the job of handling updates much easier. Every time a participant completes a contribution, it is simply added to the end.

However, the text transcript is inherently *sequenced*. This makes it best suited to *synchronized* groupware. If we imagine two distant sites, with no fast communications, it is difficult to keep the transcripts similar. If each site adds any new items to the end, the sites will show different transcripts. Imagine we have a user, Alison, at site A, and a user, Brian, at site B. The transcript has two contributions 'a1 b1'. Alison and Brian both make a contribution at the same time, say 'a2' and 'b2' respectively. So site A sees 'a2' first and site B sees 'b2' first. After a while the contributions are transmitted from site to site, leaving at site A the transcript 'a1 b1 a2 b2' and at site B the transcript 'a1 b1 b2 a2'. The alternative is for the contributions to be time-stamped, and to be ordered by time. However, this would mean that when a site received a contribution before the current time, it would have to *insert* it into the conversation. That is the transcript ceases to be appending. We will see in Chapter 14 some of the effects this has on the participants' conversation.

Now, consider a shared hypertext, with no editing and deleting, just adding new nodes. It is not only monotonic, but it is also *unsequenced*: the order in which contributions are added does not matter. They are structured explicitly by the links between nodes, not by the order in which they occurred. It has a weaker appending property in that all new contributions are towards the leaves of the hypertext, but there are of course many leaves. A monotonic unsequenced data structure is ideally suited to unsynchronized groupware; indeed several electronic conferencing systems adopt just such a structure.

A shared whiteboard, again without an eraser, is also monotonic and un-sequenced, but the limited size of the display does not make it feasible for large scale conferencing. However, the properties are useful when implementing such a system. Basically, one only needs to worry about synchronizing the participant's systems when one of them is using an eraser. Another advantage of such spatially organized data is that the participants can use proximity to denote relationships and set aside areas for different purposes. The participants can create their own structure, rather than use predefined structures.

Finally, imagine a complex structured object, such as a hypertext, or a shared file system. What happens if someone moves a portion of the hypertext tree while I am editing a node in it? This is similar to the problems of shared text, but the nature of text makes it easier for social protocols to operate. Furthermore, it is even harder to make sense of multiple structural updates than textual ones.

13.6.3 *Integrating communication and work*

In Section 13.2, we described the framework for cooperative work used to structure Sections 13.3–13.5. Figure 13.12 shows the framework diagram, but with two extra arcs added. Recall first the arcs that were in the original diagram in Section 13.2. Each of the sections dealt with the computer support of one of these arcs:

direct communication supported by email, electronic conferences and video connections.

common understanding supported by argumentation tools, meeting rooms and shared worksurfaces.

control and feedback from shared artefacts supported by shared PCs and windows, shared editors, co-authoring systems and shared diaries.

The first new arc represents *deixis*. Recall that we first encountered deictic reference in the context of meeting room software (Section 13.4.2). The participants needed to refer to items on the shared screen, but could not use their fingers to point. In general, direct communication about a task will refer to the artefacts used as part of that task.

The other new arc runs between the participants, but through the artefact. This reflects the *feedthrough* where one participant's manipulation of shared objects can be observed by the other participants. As we discussed in Section 13.5.5, this *communication through the artefact*, can be as important as direct communication between the participants.

Although systems have been classified by the arc which they most directly support, many support several of these aspects of cooperative work. In particular, if the participants are not co-located, many systems will supply some alternative means of direct communication. For example, shared window systems are often used in conjunction with audio or video communications. However, these channels are very obviously separate, compared with, say, the *TeamWorkStation* where the shared worksurface video images of hands are overlaid (see Section 13.4.3). In particular, this close association of direct communication with the artefacts makes deixis more fluid — the participants can simply point and gesture as normal.

In general, a test of a groupware product is how well it supports the whole of cooperative work. Another example of a system which does closely integrate direct communication and shared artefacts is the co-authoring system *Quilt*. In Section 13.5.3, we emphasized the structure of the artefact, but this is integrated

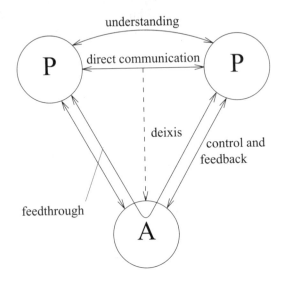

Figure 13.12   *Cooperative work framework*

with communication in two ways. First of all (and common to many similar systems), the comments which are attached to the text are themselves a form of direct communication — *embedded* within the *context* of work. This embedding makes deixis particularly easy. The comment itself may be attached to a particular point in the text, and also indexical terms like 'the last sentence', are easily interpreted. In addition, directed messages can contain references to Quilt objects, aiding deictic reference in that medium also.

Finally, note that a groupware system need not automate every aspect of communication and shared work, but it should be open to supporting cooperative work as a whole. As an example of this consider *bar-codes*. A can of beans may be baked in Boston and sold in a supermarket in Solihull, but the bar-code printed on the tin and its packaging can be read by the staff at the supermarket. The bar-code can be used for stocktaking and can be read by laser at the checkout, both pricing the item and keeping track of sales. These sales figures can then be used as part of stock-control and for marketing. This is possible because of international standards of bar-coding. The code identifies the manufacturer, factory, product and package size, and can thus be used to identify the product at many stages in its journey from production to consumption. That is, the bar-code is a computerized form of deixis. However, even though it only automates one aspect it aids very diffuse but large scale cooperative work, crossing national and organizational boundaries.

13.7 **Implementing Synchronous Groupware**

We have discussed a wide range of groupware systems, but there are formidable problems with implementing such systems, particularly *synchronous* groupware. Groupware systems are intrinsically more complicated than single-user systems. Issues like handling updates from several users whilst not getting internal data structures or the users' screens in a mess are just plain difficult. These are made more complicated by the limited bandwidth and delays of the networks used to connect the computers, and by the single-user assumptions built into graphics toolkits.

13.7.1 *Feedback and network delays*

When editing text, a delay of more than a fraction of a second between typing and the appearance of characters is unacceptable. For text entry a slightly greater delay is acceptable as you are able to type ahead without feedback from the screen. Drawing, on the other hand, demands even faster feedback then text editing. Groupware systems usually involve several computers connected by a network. If the feedback loop includes transmission over the network, it may be hard to achieve acceptable response times. To see why, consider what happens when the user types a character:

1 The user's application gets an event from the window manager

2 It calls the operating system ...

3 which sends a message over the network, often through several levels of protocol.

4 The message is received by the operating system at the remote machine,

5 which gives it to the remote application to process.

6–8 the reply returns (as steps 2–4)

9 and the feedback is given on the user's screen.

This process requires two network messages and four context switches between operating system and application programs in addition to the normal communication between window manager and application. However, even this is just a minimum time and other factors can make the eventual figure far worse. Network protocols with handshaking can increase the number of network messages to at least four (two messages plus handshakes). If the application is running on a multi-tasking machine, it may need to wait for a time slice or even be swapped out! Furthermore, the network traffic is unlikely to be just between two computers: in meeting rooms we may have dozens of workstations. Clearly any architectural

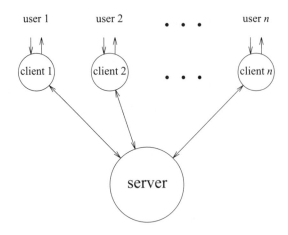

Figure 13.13   *Client-server architecture*

design for cooperative systems must take the potential for network delays very seriously.

13.7.2   *Architectures for groupware*

There are two major architectural alternatives for groupware, *centralized* and *replicated*, with variations upon them both. In a centralized or *client–server architecture* each participant's workstation has a minimal program (the client) which handles the screen and accepts the participant's inputs. The real work of the application is performed by the server, which runs on a central computer and holds all the application's data (Figure 13.13). Client–server architectures are probably the simplest to implement as we have essentially one program, with several front ends. Furthermore, if you use X windows then there are standard facilities for one program to access several screens[1] (see also Chapter 10).

As a special case, the server may run on one of the user's workstations and subsume the client there. Typically this would be the user who first invoked the shared application. This arrangement is a *master–slave architecture*, the master being the merged server–client and the slaves the remainder of the clients. The user of the master will have a particularly fast response compared to the other users.

The second major architecture is *replicated*. Each user's workstation runs its

---

[1]But beware, X uses the terms client and server in the opposite sense. The X server is on the workstation and the X client is the application program.

own copy of the application. These copies communicate with one another and attempt to keep their data structures consistent with one another. Each replicate handles its own user's feedback, and must also update the screen in response to messages from other replicates. The intention is often to give the impression of a centralized application, but to obtain the performance advantages of distribution.

Compared to a client–server architecture, the replicated architecture is difficult to program. In the last paragraph we deliberately wrote '*attempt* to keep their data structures consistent' as this is a major problem. If two users, say Jane and Sam, hit a key almost simultaneously, then Jane's workstation will process Jane's keystroke first, and Sam's second, but Sam's workstation will process them the other way round — and yet they must give the same result — help!

This race condition is a common problem in distributed computing. A standard solution there is to *rollback* one or other replica and re-execute the commands. However, if the results have already been displayed on the user's screen this is not acceptable — standard computing algorithms often fail for groupware. Happily, many of the *concurrency control* mechanisms, such as locking or floor holders, mean that such races do not occur, or at worst occur only when users obtain locks or other large scale events. So, when rapid feedback is not required, standard mechanisms may be applied, but, for real synchronous update, special-purpose algorithms are required.

The main advantage of a replicated architecture over the client–server is in the local feedback. However, the clients are often not completely dumb and are able to handle a certain amount of feedback themselves. Indeed, the server often becomes merely a central repository for shared data with the clients having most of the application's functionality. On the other hand a replicated architecture will rarely treat all the replicas identically. If a user tries to load or save a document, that action does not want to be replicated. Either one of the replicas is special, or there is a minimal server handling movement of data in and out of the system. So we see that there is a continuum between the client-server and the replicated architecture.

13.7.3   *Shared window architectures*

Shared window systems have some similarities with general groupware architectures, but also some special features. Recall that there is a single-user application which is being shared by several participants on different workstations. The single-user application normally interacts with the user via a window manager, say X (Figure 13.14). The shared window manager works by intercepting the calls between the application and X.

Where the application would normally send graphics calls to X, these are instead routed to a special application stub. This then passes the graphics calls on to a user stub on each participant's workstation. A copy of X is running on each workstation and the user stub passes the graphics calls to the local copy

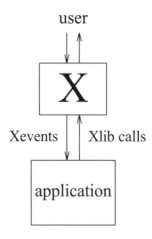

Figure 13.14   *Single-user application*

of X. Similarly the users' keystrokes and other actions cause X events which are passed to the user stub and thence through the application stub to the application (Figure 13.15). In fact, the nature of X's own client-server approach can make the user stub unnecessary, the application stub talking directly to an X 'server' on each workstation.

The input side has to include some form of floor control, especially for the mouse. This can be handled by the application stub which determines how the users' separate event streams are merged. For example, it can ignore any events other than those of the floor holder, or can simply allow users' keystrokes to intermingle. If key combinations are used to request and relinquish the floor, then the application stub can simply monitor the event streams for the appropriate sequences. Alternatively, the user stub may add its own elements to the interface: a floor request button and an indication of other participants' activities, including the current floor holder.

The problem with a client–server based shared window system is that graphics calls may involve very large data structures, and corresponding network delays. One can have replicated versions where a copy of the application sits on each work-station and stubs communicate between one another. But, because the application is not *collaboration aware*, problems such as race conditions and reading and saving files become virtually intractable. For this reason, most shared window systems take a master–slave approach where the application runs on the first user's work-station and subsequent users get slave processes. The delays for other users are most noticeable when starting up the application.

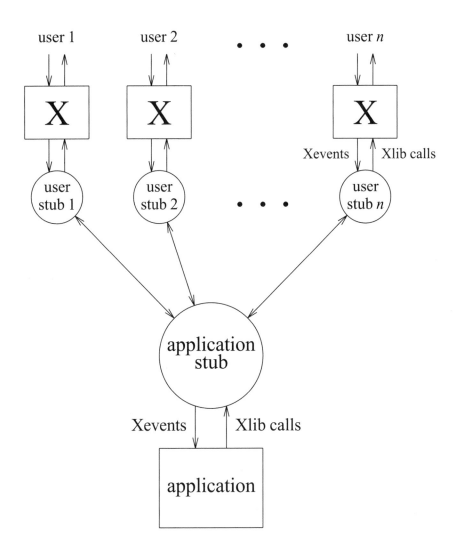

Figure 13.15   *Shared window architecture*

13.7.4   *Feedthrough and network traffic*

We have discussed the necessity of rapid *feedback* to the user who performs an action, and we have seen how replication or partial replication can solve this. However, we must also worry about *feedthrough*, the reflection of one user's actions on the other users' screens. The requirements for feedthrough are not quite so stringent as for feedback, and this can be used to reduce the amount of network traffic. There is little difference in this respect between client–server and replicated architectures, so, for the sake of argument, we will assume a client–server architecture.

Imagine a user has just typed a character. The character appears on the user's screen, either through local feedback or after an exchange with the server. However, all the other clients need to be informed also. That is, with n participants, each user action causes a minimum of $n - 1$ network messages. If this is repeated for each character, the network will grind to a halt with the number of messages. Just think of the effect if we wanted to send out updates for each mouse movement!

There are several ways out of this, the common thread being to reduce the number of messages. In principle, one could send a single *broadcast message* to all the other clients, as the information is the same for all of them. Unfortunately, in practice, many network protocols only support point-to-point messages. A more successful approach is to increase the *granularity* of the messages. The rapid feedback to the user who initiated an action is necessary, but the feedthrough to other users may be able to cope with less frequent update. The server can save up several characters worth of updates and send a single message. We thus only need to send the $n - 1$ messages to the clients on each chunk.

The choice of this chunk size can be crucial to the success of the system. If the participants can talk to each other (either co-located or with audio/video channels) they will refer to the contents of their screens. In such cases, lags of more than a few seconds can be disastrous. However, even if the computer is the only communications medium, the chunk size has an effect as the gradual appearance of text is an indication of other people's activity.

13.7.5   *Graphical toolkits*

We discussed in Chapter 10 some of the *widgets* one finds in a typical graphics toolkit or window manager, such as menus, buttons, dialogue boxes and text and graphics regions. These are useful for creating single-user interfaces, and one would like to use the same components to build a groupware system. Unfortunately, the single-user assumptions built into such toolkits can make this very difficult.

Some widgets may take control away from the application. For instance, a pop-up menu may be invoked by a call such as:

```
sel  =  do_pop_up("new","open","save","exit",0);
```

The call to do_pop_up_menu constructs the pop-up menu, waits for the user to enter a selection, and then returns a code indicating which choice the user made (1 for 'new', 2 for 'open', etc.). Of course, during this time the application cannot monitor the network. This can be got round, by careful programming, but is awkward.

More fundamentally, the functionality of toolkit widgets may be insufficient for groupware. This is particularly obvious for text areas. The toolkit often takes over a lot of the tedium of handling an editable text region: the user can type and delete, do cursor movement and even cut and paste, all without the application's intervention. However, the groupware developer may want to have multiple cursors, or to ensure that all the participants can see the same portion of a document. Unfortunately, even information such as what portion of the document is in view, or where a particular logical character is displayed on the screen is difficult to come by, as is control over a scrollbar if this is to be shared. One is often forced to design the application round the limited capabilities of the text widget, or to use bitmap operations to paint the text oneself.

Despite the difficulties of toolkits, some have facilities which are a positive help. For example, the SunView toolkit and its X version, XView, are both *notification based* (see Chapter 10). As well as notifications of user events, they can be asked to tell you when a network channel is ready for reading or writing. Thus, the interface and the network can be programmed in a similar style.

13.7.6 *Robustness and scaleability*

If you are producing a shared application to test an idea, or for use in an experiment, then you can make a wide range of assumptions, for instance, a fixed number of participants. Also, the occasional crash, although annoying, is not disastrous. However, if you expect a system to be used for protracted tests or for commercial production then the standards of engineering must be correspondingly higher. Four potential sources of problems are:

- failures in the network, workstations or operating systems

- errors in programming the shared application

- unforeseen sequences of events, such as *race conditions*

- the system does not scale as the number of users or rate of activity increases

A full description of these problems and their solutions is, of course, beyond this book. For this, the reader should turn to texts on software engineering, real-time and distributed programming. Furthermore, the details will differ between networking software, operating systems and other software support. However, there are a few general remarks and specific issues which we will discuss.

To some extent the above problems are common to single-user systems: hardware problems, bad programming and the like. Indeed, most commercial software the authors have used suffers the occasional (or frequent) crash. However, there are factors which make multi-user systems more fragile. The large number of different hardware and software components of a multi-user system means that a fault of type 1 is more likely to occur. Also, the complexity of the algorithms used in groupware makes a fault of type 2 more likely. In both cases there is a danger that the consequences of the failure will propagate throughout the system. If a single failure crashes the whole system, it probably will not be used twice! Interleaving of different users' actions and the unpredictable effects of network delays increases the chance of errors of type 3. Finally, system development and testing may involve only two or three people, and thus hidden assumptions about the number and activity of users may not become apparent until the system 'goes live'. So, faults are more likely and the effects are far worse — instead of losing one user's document or datafile (sad though that might be), a groupware crash can destroy the work of a whole team of people.

Server faults

The most obviously disastrous problem in a client–server based system is a server crash, whether hardware or software. Fortunately, this is most amenable to standard solutions. Most large commercial databases have facilities (such as transaction logging) to recover all but the most recent changes. If the groupware system is not built using such a system then similar solutions can be applied, for example, you can periodically save the current state using two or three files in rotation. The *last* entry[2] in each file is the date of writing and the system uses the most recent file when it restarts, ignoring any partially written file. Remember, though, that this might mean your server going 'silent' for a few seconds each time it saves the file — can your clients handle this? In really critical situations one can have multiple servers and copies of the data, so that a backup server can take over after a crash of the primary server.

Workstation faults

More often, individual workstations, or the programs running on them, will crash. This is partly because there are more of them, and partly because their code is more complex. In particular, these programs are handling all the user's interactions and are built upon complex (and frequently flaky) graphical toolkits. Of course, one tries to program carefully and avoid these errors, but experience shows that they will continue to occur. The aim is to confine the fault to the particular user concerned and to recover from the fault as quickly as possible. When thinking about a client–server architecture, there are three 'R's for the server:

---

[2]A crash might happen in the middle of the save.

robust a client failure should not destroy or 'hang' the server. In particular, *never* have the server wait for a response from the client — it may never come. The server should either be *event-driven* or *poll* the clients using non-blocking network operations.

reconfigure the server must detect that the client has failed and reconfigure the rest of the system accordingly. The client's failure can be detected by standard network failure codes, or by timing out the client if it is silent for too long. Reconfiguring will involve resetting internal data structures, and informing other participants that one of them is unavailable and why. Do not let them think their colleague is just being rude and not replying!

resynchronize when the workstation/client recovers, the server must send sufficient information for it to catch up. A server may normally broadcast incremental information (new messages, etc.), so make sure that the server keeps track of all the information needed to send to the recovered client. This is very similar to the case of a new participant joining the groupware session.

Replicated architectures have similar issues. Imagine we have three replicates A, B and C. Replicate A has crashed, so both B and C must detect this and correct their internal data structures accordingly. An additional problem is that one replica, say B, may detect the failure before the other. So, C may send B a message which refers to A in some way — B must deal with this situation gracefully.

Algorithm faults

Some application failures do not crash the application and may therefore be more difficult to detect. For instance, data structures between replicates or between client and server may become inconsistent. Obviously this *should not* happen, if the algorithms are correct. Indeed, such critical algorithms should be given the closest scrutiny and perhaps proved correct using formal methods (see Chapter 9). However, one should be prepared for errors and, where possible, include sufficient redundancy and sanity checks in the code so that inconsistencies are at least detected and, ideally, corrected.

Such defensive programming mechanisms, against hardware and software errors, may be very expensive in programming effort and execution time. For experimental systems they may be excessive. A minimum requirement for all but toy systems is some form of reset, which forces the system to resynchronize all its data structures between clients and server or between replicates; hopefully, losing none but the most recent updates in the process.

Unforeseen sequences of events

Distributed programming has many problems of which possibly the most well known is *deadlock*. This is when two (or more) processes are each waiting for the other to do something. A common scenario is where process A is trying to send a message to B and B is trying to send one to A. Because A is busy trying to send, it does not want to receive a message from B, and vice versa. The possibility of deadlock can often go undetected during testing because of operating system and network buffers. A's message to B is stored in the operating system's buffer, so A can then read B's message. Unfortunately, as load increases, one day the buffer is full and deadlock can no longer be avoided — this may only happen *after* the system has been released.

The first rule to avoid deadlock is *never* to use blocking input or output. That is, always use network calls which time out, or return immediately if the operation cannot continue. Use of an event-driven programming style can also help, as does the use of constructs such as the UNIX 'select' system call, which monitors several communication channels simultaneously.

At a higher level, one should also avoid making assumptions about the ordering of incoming events. This is also important to avoid problems with race conditions. For example, if a client process has sent a message to a server requesting information, it should *not* assume that the next message from the server will answer the query.

A common assumption in groupware programs is that messages sent from one computer arrive in the same form at another. This depends very much on the particular protocols used. Consider UNIX stream based sockets, commonly used in experimental groupware applications. The communication paradigm is not packet based, but of a character stream. Imagine a client sends two messages to the server. The first is 26 characters long, 'abcd...xyz', the second is 10 characters long, '0123456789'. When testing such a system it is very likely that the server will read two messages of 26 and 10 characters, exactly as sent, but this is not guaranteed. It is perfectly possible to get one message of 36 characters, 'abc...xyz01...89', or even one of 10 and one of 26, 'abcdefghij' and 'klm...xyz01...89'. The solution is easy, one always uses fixed length messages, or alternatively codes the message length into the message header. The recipient can then reconstruct the messages from the byte stream. The difficulty is that the problem can go undetected for a long time and then cause a major disaster. Read your network manual *very* carefully and assume nothing.

Scaling up

In general, the most certain way to avoid algorithmic errors is to use simple algorithms: tables rather than complicated data structures, fixed length fields for names and messages. These all go towards reducing the likelihood of some of the faults described earlier, and are the recommended techniques for prototyping an application. Unfortunately, these are precisely the programming techniques which frustrate the scaling up of the system to larger numbers of users, or greater loads.

As the system develops the initial algorithms and data structures will need to evolve. This will be easier if the future scaling of the system is taken into account at the beginning. Good software engineering practice helps. For example, if the message passing is in a separate module then an initial design can use fixed length and textually coded messages (for ease of debugging). But, when the throughput of the system increases, the message passing can be easily changed to variable length messages perhaps buffering several messages together (to reduce network traffic) and binary coding of the messages (for efficiency).

Where fixed size assumptions are made in early versions, these should be documented: 'the present design only caters for up to six users'. Even more important, the system ought to detect when these bounds are broken and behave sensibly. In programming terms, this tends to mean checking array bounds, rather than scribbling randomly over memory! Sometimes these bounds are known in advance, but always try to encapsulate these decisions so that if the bounds do need to change you know where in the code to find them.

A particular problem for the server is that the operating system may limit the number of open files/network connections at any time. For example, let us suppose the limit is 16 files and suppose the server is using one for the application data file and one for logging. This means that at most 14 clients can be connected at once. Even worse, say the server periodically opens the data file to save data, but closes it between times. Unless the server itself keeps the number of clients below 14, it may be that 15 clients get connected, which including the logging file, saturates the server's allowable files. Now, when the server comes to save the data, it cannot open the data file. Obviously, the groupware writer must at least be aware of these limits in order to prevent such a disaster.

There are a few solutions to this problem. The operating system limit can be altered; for example, in MSDOS this involves changing the 'FILES=' line in the file 'config.sys'. However, this is more difficult under UNIX, and in general the limits and how to alter them are very system-dependent. The server can avoid the use of permanent network connections and instead use *datagram protocols*, where the client and the server are only connected while a message is being exchanged. Finally, there may be more system-dependent 'tricks', for example, forking extra servers under UNIX.

Testing for robustness

Often the functionality of an application is tested by having several windows on the same workstation, each acting as a different 'user'. Unfortunately this is unlikely to catch the sort of problems discussed above as it is impossible to type simultaneously into two windows. A more violent approach is required, in fact, the general rule is ... mistreat it.

Crashes and major faults can be simulated. Try rebooting a workstation or pulling out a network connector[3]. To be slightly more gentle, you could simply

---

[3]But beware, check with other users and your system administrator first — this may crash some operating systems.

kill a client process and see the effect on the server (or on replicates).

Similarly, you can simulate race conditions and odd sequences by running the system between two workstations and then hitting keys on them simultaneously. A little bit of knowledge of the system will suggest the best combination.

Random input may crash your system. Push it hard at several levels. Have a group of colleagues on different workstations type and hit mouse buttons as fast as they can — but log the keystrokes as you may want to recreate the resulting situations for later debugging. Create a rogue client/replicate, which sends random, but correctly formed, messages to the server or other replicates. Alternatively, this can be arranged without network communications by building a test harness round a single process. A similar, possibly less fair, approach is to send random data down the network at a process.

Finally, the real acid test. Offer a group of computer science undergraduates a drink each if they can break the system — you will lose your money, of course.

Unfortunately, discovering you have a fault is only the first step — correcting it is more difficult still. Modular and defensive programming and logging of communications so that errors can be recreated are a good beginning, but experience and hard work are the final answer.

13.8 **Summary**

We discussed groupware under three headings: computer-mediated communication, meeting and decision support systems, and shared applications and artefacts. Computer-mediated communication supports direct interpersonal contact. Some of these were asynchronous systems, including traditional email and structured messaging systems. Various forms of video communication support synchronous communication, either video conferences, direct person-to-person video or social contact.

Meeting and decision support systems are aimed at helping users to generate and record new ideas and reach decisions. Meeting rooms use large shared screens to support synchronous co-located collaboration. Participants' own terminals are often WYSIWIS and they may use group pointers to support deictic reference. When the participants are remote, various forms of work surface can be used instead. Finally, for asynchronous working, systems like gIBIS help designers to record their decisions and why they came by them.

Shared window systems and PCs allow non-collaboration aware applications to be used by a group. However, collaboration aware applications such as shared editors, diaries and co-authoring systems can better support the use of shared objects. Shared objects may even be the sole means of communication. Whether or not there is additional direct communication, we must always recall the importance of communication through the artefact.

Several frameworks for classifying groupware were discussed. The time/space matrix classifies systems by where and when the participants are working.

However, we saw that the term 'asynchronous' is rather ambiguous. Shared information may be shared at different granularities, and at different levels of detail. Also different data structures are better suited to different situations. Finally, we discussed the framework used to structure the discussion in this chapter. This looks at the different paths of communication between the participants and the artefacts of work and at which aspects are automated: direct communication, shared understanding, deictic reference, control of and feedback from the object. A good groupware system will not just automate one path, but do so in a way which supports the whole process of cooperation. As an example, bar-codes merely automate deixis, but are important in facilitating trans-national collaboration.

Groupware systems are more complex than single-user ones. We considered architectures for synchronous groupware, client–server and replicated, and for shared windowed systems. The choice of architecture combined with network delays influences the sort of feedback participants receive of their own actions. As important, it also influences the feedthrough they experience of other participants' actions. The widgets supplied by graphical toolkits are designed with single-user applications in mind, and so the groupware designer must either fit around these limitations or program group widgets from scratch. Finally, it is very important that groupware is robust. Problems are more likely to occur due to the increased complexity, but are more damaging, due to the large number of people affected.

Exercises

13.1 We discussed the use of a group pointer in a shared editor with a shared view. Consider the advantages and problems of using a group pointer when participants have different views. How do you show the pointer if it is outside part of the document you are working on? Think also about the issues when the system is a hypertext based co-authoring system. Is there any use for a group pointer in this case?

13.2 Find out how many different forms of direct computer-mediated communication are available on your system (start with email). Are they heavily used, and if so, where do they fit in the time/space matrix (Figure 13.8) and its refinement (Figure 13.9).

13.3 Repeat the previous exercise, but this time look for shared data on your system. Is the data updated by one person and viewed by many, or have you files or databases which are updated by several people? If the latter, find out what methods are used to prevent two users changing the same data at the same time. There may be no mechanism at all, a computerised one (e.g., locking) or a social protocol (e.g., a floppy disk is passed around).

Recommended Reading

- Tom Rodden, A survey of CSCW systems. *Interacting with Computers*, Vol. 3, No. 3 , 1991.

- J. S. Olson, L. A. Mack and P. Wellner, Concurrent editing: the group's interface. In *Human-Computer Interaction – INTERACT'90*, pages 835-839, North-Holland, 1990.

- C. Ellis, S. J. Gibbs and G. L. Rein, Groupware: Some issues and experience, *Communications of the ACM*, 34(1):38–58, January 1991.

  Overview and survey articles on groupware systems. The last article also includes a description of the Grove system.

- A. Wexelblat, *Building Collaborative Interfaces*, CHI'91 Tutorial No. 28, 1991.

  This CHI tutorial describes some of the implementation issues that are omitted from research papers, but it is difficult to obtain. In particular, it includes code for a shared drawing application under X windows. If you are going to write groupware applications, a tutorial of this kind, at CHI or one of the CSCW conferences is recommended as there are many potential pitfalls.

- ACM CSCW conference proceedings: CSCW'86, CSCW'88, CSCW'90, CSCW'92, all ACM publications, but it is now hard to get hold of earlier proceedings.

- European CSCW conference proceedings: ECSCW'89, ECSCW'91. The former proceedings have also been produced as a book (below). The latter can be obtained from Sageforce, Surrey, UK.

- J. M. Bowers and S. D. Benford (eds.), *Studies in Computer-supported Cooperative Work: Theory, practice and design*, North-Holland, Amsterdam, 1991.

  Selected papers from ECSCW'89.

- See also references in the text to papers describing particular groupware systems.

Chapter 14

CSCW Issues and Theory

Overview

All computer systems, single user or multi-user, interact with the work groups and organizations in which they are used.

- We need to understand normal human–human communication:

    - face-to-face communication involves eyes, face and body
    - conversation can be analyzed to establish its detailed structure

- This can then be applied to text based conversation, which has

    - reduced feedback for confirmation
    - less context to disambiguate utterances
    - slower pace of interaction
    - but is more easily reviewed

- Group working is more complex than that of a single person

    - it is influenced by the physical environment
    - experiments are more difficult to control and record
    - field studies must take into account the social situation

- Organizational factors can make or break groupware (or single-user) systems:

    - those who benefit may not do the work
    - not everyone may use systems
    - systems may not take into account conflict and power relationships
    - it is difficult to measure the benefits of groupware to the organization

14.1 Introduction

'No man is an *Iland*, intire of it selfe; every man is a peece of the *Continent*,
a part of the *maine*'   John Donne[1]

It is clear that the groupware systems described in the last chapter involve more
than one person. However, to some extent all systems influence and are influenced
by the groups and social situations in which they are placed. The field of computer-
supported cooperative work encompasses both specific groupware systems and
the effects of computers on cooperative working in general. We have already seen
this larger picture in the CSCW framework in the last chapter, which talked about
rather diffuse examples such as bar-codes, but we shall see further examples in
this chapter, especially towards the end in Sections 14.5 and 14.6.

We begin the chapter by looking at human communication. Effective communication clearly underlies much collaborative work and many systems aim to support
communication at a distance. Face-to-face communication is often seen as the ideal
to which computer-mediated communication should aim. Section 14.2 describes
some of its features, and shows how even video based communications lose many
of the subtle cues. Body language, tone of voice and eye contact are all crucial
in enabling smooth conversation. We then look at a slightly higher level in Section 14.3, at the structure of conversation. In particular, we will see that typical
utterances are ambiguous and dependent on the context in which they are spoken.
This section concludes by looking at speech act theory and the Coordinator system
which has been both influential and controversial in CSCW. Understanding spoken
conversation gives some clues as to the effective design of text based communication such as email systems or electronic conferencing. Section 14.4 discusses text
based communication in this context, including a discussion of the relative merits
and features of linear text and hypertext systems.

In Section 14.5 we move away from computer-mediated communication and look
at the wider issues of group working. Groups are dynamic both in composition and
behaviour, and effective group working is dependent on the work environment.
Because of these and other factors, the study of group behaviour, and therefore
evaluating groupware, is far more complex than that of single-user systems.

Finally, Section 14.6 looks at the organizational and social setting of group work.
Installing any new technology, but especially computer systems, may have unexpected consequences on the organization, causing conflicts of interest and power
struggles. Balancing the costs and benefits in such a complex social setting is no
easy task, but is often the final determinant of the success of a system.

14.2 Face-to-face Communication

Face-to-face contact is the most primitive form of communication — primitive,
that is, in terms of technology. If, on the other hand, we consider the style of

---

[1]Devotions upon Emergent Occasions, XVII, 1624.

communication, the interplay between different channels and productivity, we instead find that face-to-face is the most sophisticated communication mechanism available.

The first thing to note is that face-to-face communication involves not just speech and hearing, but also the subtle use of body language and eye gaze. We will discuss a range of these phenomena, and how they influence our use of computer-mediated communications. We will concentrate on two-person conversations as group dynamics are discussed later in Section 14.5. Also we will principally compare face-to-face with video and audio channels as we will address the special problems of text based communications in Section 14.4.

14.2.1 *Transfer effects and personal space*

When we come to use computer-mediated forms of communication, we carry forward all our expectations and social norms from face-to-face. People are very adaptable and can learn new norms to go with new media (for example, the use of 'over' for turn-taking when using a walkie-talkie). However, success with a new media is often dependent on whether the participants can use their existing norms. Furthermore, the rules of face-to-face conversation are not conscious, so, when they are broken, we do not always recognize the true problem. We may just have a feeling of unease, or we may feel that our colleague has been rude.

An example of these problems concerns personal space. When we converse with one another we tend to stand with our heads a fairly constant distance apart. If people start to converse at opposite ends of a room, they will quickly move towards one another until they are a few feet apart. The exact distance depends somewhat on context, a high level of noise may make people come closer just to be heard. However, even in crowded rooms, conversants will dip their heads towards one another whilst speaking and then straighten up to restore their personal distance. Direction is also important. We can accept people closer to us if they are at our sides or behind than if we are facing them. Because of this, passengers on tube trains, forced to be close, will incline their faces at an angle to one another whilst talking.

Personal space also differs across cultures, North Americans get closer than Britons and southern Europeans and Arabs closer still. This can cause considerable problems during cross-cultural meetings. Imagine a Briton, Eustace Warbuck-Smyth, and an American, Bud Sterton, conversing. After a few minutes Eustace is bent backwards over a table, trying to maintain his personal distance, whilst Bud stands almost knee to knee trying to get close enough. Eustace feels Bud is either rather aggressive, or possibly over-friendly. Bud on the other hand feels Eustace is rather distant and uninterested. Unless the situation gets extreme, or the participants are trained in non-verbal skills, they will be unaware of why they feel uncomfortable.

A similar problem can occur in a video conference. Imagine Eustace and Bud have monitors with cameras mounted above, so that their offices are connected. The zoom on each camera is adjustable and Bud's camera is set with a wide focus, whilst Eustace's is set with a high level of zoom. So, if Bud and Eustace are the same distance from their cameras and monitors, then Bud sees Eustace's whole face filling the screen, whereas Eustace sees Bud sat on his chair in the middle of his office. Eustace moves closer to the monitor to see Bud more clearly, while Bud pushed his chair back to get away from Eustace's two foot high face — *touché*. Of course, the problem gets worse if the cameras are positioned in different places relative to the monitors, or if the monitors are different sizes. Ideally, Bud ought to be able to adjust the zoom on Eustace's camera and vice versa. In fact there is some evidence that the 'glass wall' afforded by the video screen makes the precise distance less important, which could have a positive effect during cross-cultural meetings. However, gross distortions, as described above, need to be avoided.

14.2.2   *Eye contact and gaze*

Long term gazing in to one another's eyes is usually reserved for lovers. However, normal conversation uses eye contact extensively, if not as intently. Our eyes tell us whether our colleague is listening or not, they can convey interest, confusion or boredom. Sporadic direct eye contact (both looking at one another's eyes) is important in establishing a sense of engagement and social presence. People who look away when you look at them may seem shifty and appear to be hiding something. Furthermore relative frequency of eye contact and who 'gives way' from direct eye contact is closely linked to authority and power.

   Naturally, all these clues are lost if we have no visual contact. However, the misleading clues via a video connection can be worse. In Chapter 13 (Section 13.3.3) we discussed the problems of obtaining effective eye contact with standard video equipment. If the camera is strapped to the top of the monitor (a common arrangement) both participants will look as if their eyes are slightly dropped. Recall that a *video-tunnel* can allow true eye contact (although may suffer from other problems).

   Despite these problems with direct eye contact, many signals can be easily read through a video-channel. You can see whether your colleague looks quizzical or bored, confused or excited. This involves not just the eyes, but the whole facial expression, and these are apparent even on poor quality video or very small (pocket TV sized) monitors. Experiments have shown that remotely working participants experience a greater sense of social presence if video is used in addition to an audio link.

   As well as having a role in establishing rapport between the participants, eye gaze is useful in establishing the focus of the conversation. If you say 'now where does this screw go?', there may be many screws, but your colleague can see which one you are looking at. Video connections are unlikely to show enough of your office for your colleague to be able to interpret such clues, but a focus that just catches the corner of the monitor and desk can help.

14.2.3   *Gestures and body language*

In a similar but more direct way, we use our hands to indicate items of interest. This may be conscious and deliberate as we point to the item, or may be a slight wave of the hand or alignment of the body. Again a video connection may not be sufficient to allow our colleagues to read our movements. This can be a serious problem since our conversation is full of expressions such as 'let's move this one there', where the 'this' and 'there' are indicated by gestures (or eye gaze). Recall that this is called *deictic reference* (see Chapter 13, Sections 13.4 and 13.6).

We have seen several groupware systems which attempt to compensate for these losses. In Section 13.4.2, we discussed the idea of a group pointer, a mouse controlled icon which can be used to point to things on a shared screen. Somewhat more esoteric, but more immediate, are the shared work surfaces (Section 13.4.3) which mix an image of the participants' hands with the electronic screen. The participants can then simply point at the relevant item on the screen, as they would face-to-face.

Of course, the group pointer, although used in remote groupware, is also used in synchronous co-located groupware such as meeting rooms. That is, even though the participants can converse face-to-face, they still need deictic aids. One reason for this is that their electronic screens, although logically shared (they can all see the same thing) are not physically shared (they are in different places). So, if Jemima points to her own screen, her colleagues do not know what she is pointing at.

Even when the participants are in the same room, the existence of electronic equipment can interfere with the body language used in normal face-to-face communication. The fact that attention is focused on keyboard and screen can reduce the opportunities for eye contact. Also large monitors may block participants' views of one another's bodies, reducing their ability to interpret gestures and body position. Most computer-supported meeting rooms recess monitors into the desks to reduce these problems.

14.2.4   *Back channels, confirmation and interruption*

It is easy to think of conversation as a sequence of utterances: A says something, then B says something, then back to A. This process is called *turn-taking* and is one of the fundamental structures of conversation. However, each utterance is itself the result of intricate negotiation and interaction. Consider the following transcript:

> **Alison:** Do you fancy that film . . . *err* . . . 'The Green' *um* . . .
> it starts at eight.
> **Brian:**   Great!

Alison has asked Brian whether he wants to go to the cinema (or possibly to watch the television at home). She is a bit vague about the film, but Brian obviously does not mind! However, if we had listened to the conversation more closely and watched Alison and Brian we would have seen more exchanges. As Alison says 'that film *err* . . .', she looks at Brian. From the quizzical look on his face he obviously does not know which film she is talking about. She begins to expand 'The Green *um* . . .', and light dawns; she can see it in his eyes and he probably makes a small affirmative sound 'uh huh'.

The nods, grimaces, shrugs of the shoulder and small noises are called *back channels*. They feed information back from the listener to the speaker at a level below the turn-taking of the conversation. The existence of back channels means that the speaker can afford to be slightly vague, adding details until it is obvious that the listener understands. Imagine making no response as someone talks to you, no little 'yes'es, no nods or raised eyebrows. You could answer questions and speak in turn, but not use back channels. It is likely that your colleague would soon become very uncomfortable, possibly rambling on with ever more detailed explanations, looking for some sign of understanding[2]:

> Do you fancy that film . . . *err* . . . 'The Green' *um* . . . the one with Charles Dermot in . . . you know with that song, *err* and the black cat on the poster . . . *uhh*

These back channel responses use a range of sensory channels. So, as we restrict the forms of communication we lose the back channels. Even video communications tend to use, at most, head and shoulder shots, so we lose some body movement and gestures. On the other hand, a larger view means reduced detail, so we lose information whatever focus we choose. Audio only links (such as the telephone) have to rely on purely verbal back channel responses – the little 'yes'es. Surprisingly, despite the loss of many back channels, people still cope well with these restricted media, and communication is still reasonably effective. However, you may have had the experience, when speaking to someone on the telephone, of suddenly getting the feeling that they have gone away, or the line has gone dead. This is likely to be when you have received insufficient back channel responses (and perhaps you have been going on a bit). Trans-continental telephones are especially problematic as they are often only half duplex, that is, the sound only goes in one direction at a time. So, while you are speaking, you can hear none of your partner's back channel responses.

Text based communication, in electronic conferencing, usually has no back channels whatsoever. Any confirmation must be given explicitly in the listener's next utterance. This may confuse an analysis of text based conversation as the utterances do not correspond simply to utterances in speech.

---

[2]Don't try this as an experiment on your friends, you may end up without any! Instead try it with a colleague who knows what is going on. Even when you both know not to expect back channel responses the experience can be disconcerting. Furthermore, you will both find it very difficult to refrain from back channel responses.

14.2.5   *Turn-taking*

As well as giving confirmation to the speaker that you understand and indications when you do not, back channels can be used to interrupt politely. Starting to speak in the middle of someone's utterance can be rude, but one can say something like 'well uh' accompanied by a slight raising of the hands and a general tensing of the body and screwing of the eyes. This tells the speaker that you would like to interrupt, allowing a graceful transition. In this case, the listener *requested* the floor. *Turn-taking* is the process by which the roles of speaker and listener are exchanged. Back channels are often a crucial part of this process.

In other cases, the speaker may explicitly offer the floor to the other participant. This may be in the form of a direct question, 'what do you think?', or simply a very strong change of tone.

More often the speaker will *offer* the floor to the listener by leaving a small gap in speech. These gaps are typically no more than a fraction of a second, indeed gaps of even a few seconds give completely different signals and interrupt the flow of conversation. The gap is often at some point which may require clarification, or where the listener may want to comment. So, Alison may well have waited for half a second after saying 'Do you fancy that film', in case Brian were to respond 'Oh you mean the one with the black cat on the poster'. As he did not say anything, she continued with her turn.

The role of '*um*'s and '*ah*'s is very important. They can be used by either participant during the gap to *claim* the turn. So, if Brian wanted to respond in the middle of the utterance, but had not yet framed his utterance, he might begin '*ummm* the one . . .'. As it was, Brian did not respond, so Alison starts '*err*' which says to Brian 'I'm going to continue, but I'm thinking'. Alternatively, Alison could have started to '*err*' as soon as she had said the word 'film'. This would have told Brian *not* to interrupt.

These turn-offering gaps are just the places where the speaker expects some back channel response even if no turn exchange takes place. A total lack of response will be taken, depending on the circumstances, as assent to the speaker, or perhaps as lack of understanding.

As we can see, turn-offering gaps form a central part in the eliciting of back channel responses and in negotiating turn-taking. They are obviously connected principally with the audio channel (although some gestures may be used to maintain or claim the floor). Half-duplex channels (such as inter-continental phone calls) are volume sensitive in order to track the speaker. Unfortunately, some of the '*um*'s and '*err*'s used to maintain or claim the floor may fall below the volume threshold and thus not be transmitted. This may lead to apparent rude interruptions or snubbing of one party by the other.

An even more serious problem is encountered during long distance, satellite based communications due to the time lags. To transmit a signal, it must go up to the satellite and then back down to the earth. A geostationary satellite is at a height of approximately 100, 000 km above the earth — a quarter of the distance to the moon. Radio waves will take about 700 milliseconds to go up to the satellite and back down again. This time together with the processing delays on the ground and in the satellite add up to about a two second lag. There is thus a four second gap between when one participant does or says something and when the effects of that upon the other participant become evident.

We now imagine Alison and Brian talking via satellite. Alison pauses for half a second after the words 'that film', two seconds later Brian hears the end of the word 'film', after a few hundred milliseconds he notices the gap and begins to say 'Oh', by this time Alison has waited two and a half seconds, the gap is getting embarrassing, so she continues 'The Green *um* . . . the one with Charles Dermot in'. Two seconds into this, that is over four seconds since she began to pause, she hears Brian try to cut in (how rude!), but he shuts up again when he hears her continuing.

The above scenario is *not* contrived. Tapes of video conferences show just this behaviour, with a single speaker going on and on as all her attempts to pass on the floor fail. There is no obvious solution to this problem, except the technological one of using high bandwidth land or sub-ocean lines, when these become available, rather than satellite.

14.3 Conversation

We have looked at the low-level issues of speech and gesture during face-to-face conversation. We now turn to the structure of the conversation itself. Most analysis of conversation focuses on two-person conversations, but this ranges from informal 'social chat' over the telephone to formal courtroom cross examination. As well as the discipline of *conversational analysis*, there are other sociological and psychological understandings of conversation. However, the techniques as 'borrowed' and used to study computer-mediated conversation would not always find favour with the purist from the discipline from which they originated!

There are three uses for theories of conversation in CSCW. Firstly, they can be used to analyze transcripts, for example, from an electronic conference. This can help us to understand how well the participants are coping with electronic communication. Secondly, they can be used as a guide for design decisions — an understanding of normal human–human conversation can help avoid blunders in the design of electronic media. Thirdly, and most controversially, they can be used to drive design — structuring the system around the theory.

We will concentrate mainly on the first goal, although this will have implications throughout for design. Only when we consider *speech act theory* and *Coordinator* in Section 14.3.6 will we see an example of a theory-driven system.

14.3.1   *Basic conversational structure*

Imagine we have a transcript of a conversation, recalling from Chapter 11 that the production of such a transcript is not a simple task. For example, a slightly different version of Alison and Brian's conversation may look like this:

Alison: Do you fancy that film
Brian: the *uh* (*500 ms*) with the black cat — 'The Green whatsit'
Alison: yeah, go at *uh* . . . (*looks at watch* — *1.2 s*). . . 20 to?
Brian: sure

This transcript is quite heavily annotated with the lengths of pauses and even Alison's action of looking at her watch. However, it certainly lacks the wealth of gesture and back channel activity that were present during the actual conversation. Transcripts may be less well documented, perhaps dropping the pause timings, or more detailed, adding more actions, where people were looking and some back channelling. Whilst thinking about the structure of conversation, the transcript above is sufficient.

As we have noted previously, the most basic conversational structure is *turn-taking*. On the whole we have an alternating pattern: Alison says something, then Brian, then Alison again. The speech within each turn is called an *utterance*. There can be exceptions to this turn-taking structure even within two-party conversation. For example, if there is a gap in the conversation, the same party may pick up the thread, even if she were the last speaker. However, such gaps are normally of short duration, enough to allow turn claiming if required, but short enough to consider the speech a single utterance.

Often we can group the utterances of the conversation into pairs: a question and an answer, a statement and an agreement. The answer or response will normally follow directly after the question or statement and so these are called *adjacency pairs*. We can look at Alison and Brian's conversation above as two adjacency pairs, one after the other. First, Alison asks Brian whether he knows about the film and he responds. Second, she suggests a time to go and he agrees. We can codify this structure as: A-x, B-x, A-y, B-y, where the first letter denotes the speaker (Alison or Brian) and the second letter labels the adjacency pair.

The requirement of adjacency can be broken if the pair is interposed with other pairs for clarification, etc.:

Brian: Do you want some gateau?
Alison: is it very fattening?
Brian: yes, very
Alison: and lots of chocolate?
Brian: masses
Alison: I'll have a big slice then.

This conversation can be denoted: A-x, B-y, A-y, B-z, A-z, B-x. Adjacency pair 'x' ('Do you want some gateau?'– 'I'll have a big slice then') is split by two other pairs 'y' and 'z'. One would normally expect the interposed pairs to be relevant to the outer pair, seeking clarification or determining information needed for the response.

Some would say that the adjacency pair is not just a basic structure of conversation but *the* fundamental structure. It is clearly true that we normally respond to the most recent utterance. However, it is less clear whether a simple pairing up of utterances is always possible or useful.

For an example of this difficulty, let us look back to the transcript at the beginning of the section. We see that the pair structure is not completely clear. Alison's second utterance begins a new pair, 'go at 20 to?', but it began with 'yeah' responding to Brian's previous utterance. Indeed, Brian's first response 'the *uh* . . . with the black cat . . .' could be seen as a request for clarification. That is we are now looking at the conversation as having a structure of: A-x, B-y, A-yz, B-z, where Alison's second utterance serves as both a response to Brian's request for clarification ('y') and starts a new pair concerning the time ('z'). But in this case, what happens to the second half of the original 'x' pair? We are forced to regard it as implicit in one of Brian's utterances. Alison's 'go at 20 to?' clearly suggests that Brian has committed himself, so we assume that the tone of Brian's description of the film suggested acceptance. So, Brian's first utterance, like Alison's second, serves a dual purpose: A-x, B-xy, A-yz, B-z.

Despite these difficulties, we see that the search for adjacency pairs forces us to examine closely the structure of the conversation. Whether such structures are really part of the conversation, or imposed by us upon it, is less clear. Later we shall see far more complex conversational structures.

14.3.2 *Context*

Take a single utterance from a conversation, and it will usually be highly ambiguous if not meaningless: 'the *uh* with the black cat — "The Green whatsit"'. Each utterance and each fragment of conversation is heavily dependent on *context*, which must be used to *disambiguate* the utterance. We can identify two types of context within conversation:

internal context dependence on earlier utterances. For example, when Brian says 'masses' in the last transcript, this is meaningful in the light of Alison's question 'and lots of chocolate?'. This in turn is interpreted in the context of Brian's original offer of gateau.

external context dependence on the environment. For example, if Brian had said simply 'do you want one?', this could have meant a slice of gateau, or, if he had been holding a bottle, a glass of wine, or, if accompanied by a clenched fist, a punch on the nose.

Arguably, even a complete conversation is heavily context-dependent — without knowing the situation and the social relations between the participants, how can we understand their words? Taking a more pragmatic approach, the importance of external context has implications for system design and for data collection. From a design perspective, we will look for groupware which both maximizes shared context and which makes the level of sharing clear.

Turning to data collection, we can see the importance of annotating transcripts with gestures, eye gaze and details of the environment. However, if one noted everything down, 90% would be irrelevant to the conversational level of analysis. Recording the interesting details without flooding the transcript is clearly a skilled job. If one has rich recordings, say from several video sources, then a simple verbal transcript may be sufficient as it will be possible to refer back to the video when interesting incidents are found in the written transcript.

When collecting data from groupware systems, it is also very important to have synchronized records of the participants' conversation (whether audio, video or text based) and their electronic workspaces. We need to know what the participants can see on their screens in order to interpret their remarks to one another. In the case where participants may have different views at the same time, we are likely to see *breakdowns* in the conversation, where one participant makes an utterance depending on his screen, whereas his colleague sees something different on her screen.

A specific form of context dependence is *deictic reference*. When accompanied by a pointed finger, an expression like 'that post is leaning a bit' is clearly dependent on external context. However, there are very similar uses of internal context:

Brian: (*points*) that post is leaning a bit
Alison: that's the one you put in

Brian's utterance uses external context, whereas Alison's very similar utterance uses internal context. Her 'that' refers to the post Brian was talking about, not the one he is pointing at. To see this, consider the similar fragment:

Brian: the corner post is leaning a bit
Alison: that's the one you put in

Real speech, probably more than the written word, is full of *indexicals*, words like 'that', 'this', 'he', 'she' and 'it'. Obviously when used in written text, like *this*, words such as *these* make use of purely internal context. In spoken speech any of the above words can be accompanied by gestures or eye gaze for external context, or simply used, as Alison did, to refer to previous things in the conversation. Some of the words tend to be more likely to be external ('that', 'this') than others ('he', 'she'), but you can easily think of cases of both forms of use. Furthermore, the attachment of pronouns and other indexicals to the things they denote may depend on the semantics of a sentence: 'Oh no! Eustace's hit Bud. He'll kill him, I know he will.' Does the speaker mean that Eustace will kill Bud, or vice versa? The answer depends on the speaker's knowledge of Eustace and Bud. If Bud is a 22 stone trucker and Eustace has trouble lifting cans of beans then we interpret the sentence one way. If, on the other hand, Eustace has a black belt in karate...

One consequence of the use of context in speech is the fragmentary nature of utterances. The example transcripts are, if anything, atypically grammatical. Although there is evidence of rules of grammar for the spoken word, these are very different, and much more relaxed, than the written equivalent.

14.3.3 *Topics, focus and forms of utterance*

Given that conversation is so dependent on context, it is important that the participants have a shared focus. We have addressed this in terms of the external focus — the objects that are visible to the participants, but it is also true of the internal focus of the conversation.

> **Alison:** Oh, look at your roses ...
> **Brian:** mmm, but I've had trouble with greenfly.
> **Alison:** they're the symbol of the English summer.
> **Brian:** greenfly?
> **Alison:** no roses silly!

Alison began the conversation with the *topic* of roses. Brian shifts to the related, but distinct, topic of greenfly. However, for some reason Alison has missed this shift in focus, so when she makes her second utterance, her focus and Brian's differ, leading to the *breakdown* in communication. The last two utterances are a recovery which re-establishes a shared *dialogue focus*.

In general, we can go through a transcript annotating the utterances by the topics to which they refer. The identification of topics and assigning utterances to them is a somewhat subjective affair, and one may want to use several levels of topic categorization. Of course, those points where such a labelling is difficult are interesting in themselves. They may either represent potential points of breakdown (as above), or may show where external context is needed to disambiguate the conversation. Also of interest is the way that the participants negotiate changes in dialogue focus, either because they recognize a divergence, or because one party wants to shift the focus of the conversation.

This sort of analysis can be pursued for its own sake, but has a more pragmatic interest in the analysis of computer-mediated conversation and design of groupware. We want to know where breakdowns occur in order to see whether these are due to the electronic medium. We also want to understand the shifts in focus and the reliance on external context and compare these with the shared objects available through the computer system.

Another way of classifying utterances is by their relation to the task in hand. At one extreme the utterance may have no direct relevance at all, either a digression or purely social. Looking at the task-related conversation, the utterances can be classified into three kinds [168]:

substantive directly relevant to the development of the topic

annotative points of clarification, elaborations, etc.

procedural talking about the process of collaboration itself

In addition, the procedural utterances may be related to the structure of collaboration itself, or may be about the technology supporting the collaboration. The latter is usually in response to a breakdown where the technology has intruded into the communication.

Alison and Brian are now discussing the best way to get to the cinema. Alison is using a whiteboard to draw a map.

1. **Alison:** you go along this road until you get to the river,
2. **Brian:** do you stop before the river or after you cross it?
3. **Alison:** before.
4. **Brian:** draw the river in blue and the roads black . . .
5. **Alison:** so, you turn right beside the river.
6. **Brian:** past the pub.
7. **Alison:** yeah . . . Is there another black pen, this one's gone dry?

Alison's first utterance, turn 1, is substantive. Brian then interrupts with an annotative utterance, asking a question of clarification, which is answered by Alison at 3. Brian then makes a procedural point (perhaps prompted by his confusion at 2). In turns 5 and 6, the conversation again becomes substantive, but then the pen runs out, and utterance 7 is a procedural remark concerning the communication technology (pen and whiteboard).

The last form of utterance (procedural technological) is most interesting when analyzing transcripts of computer-mediated conversation as it represents points where the system became apparent to the participants. However, it is also interesting to compare the forms of conversation used in, say, an electronic conference with those in normal speech. For example, a hypertext-oriented conference will allow digressions without any danger of losing the flow of the conference, thus encouraging annotative and procedural utterances.

14.3.4   *Breakdown and repair*

We have already seen an example of *breakdown* in conversation. When Alison and Brian were talking about Brian's roses, they failed to maintain a shared focus. Brian tried to interpret Alison's utterance in terms of his focus and failed, or rather the meaning in that focus was unusual — greenfly are the symbol of the English summer? He then questioned Alison and the confusion was cleared. This correction after breakdown is called *repair*.

If we look at transcripts of computer-mediated conversations, and see many breakdowns, we should not be surprised: face-to-face and spoken conversations are full of it. We may see breakdowns at many levels. The divergence of topic focus is a quite high level of breakdown. It often becomes apparent when we find failures to identify the referent of an indexical or deictic reference. Alternatively, such a failure may be due to the speaker using an ambiguous indexical: 'Eustace's just hit Bud ...he's bleeding' — that is, Eustace is bleeding, Bud was wearing a crash helmet.

At a lower level, we may see breakdown due to incorrectly read gestures or eye gaze, and through missed or inappropriate back channel responses. For instance, in Section 14.2.5, we described the problems in turn-taking during satellite based video conferences. It may be difficult to interpret just where a breakdown occurred, as the breakdown may take some time to come to light, and be apparent at a different level from which it began. Alison and Brian are enjoying a day out at a country park:

> **Alison:** Isn't that beautiful
> *she points at a stag standing beside a large tree, Brian sees the tree*
> **Brian:** the symmetry of the branches
> **Alison:** how some people can dislike them I can't understand
> **Brian:** yes, the rangers ought to cull those deer,
>   they strip the bark terribly in winter
> **Alison:** (*silence*)

The breakdown began with a confused gesture, but lead to a divergence of dialogue focus. Unfortunately, Brian's remark about the branching (of the tree) could be interpreted in terms of Alison's focus (the stag's antlers) and thus the breakdown did not become apparent until Brian had well and truly put his foot in it. Happily, most breakdowns are detected more quickly, but the deeper the breakdown, and the longer it lasts, the more difficult it is to recover.

Despite the frequency of breakdowns in normal speech, our communication is not usually significantly affected because we are so efficient at *repair*. (Although Brian may have some difficulty.) Redundancy, frequency of turn-taking, back channels, all contribute to the detection of breakdown and its rapid repair. Electronic communications often reduce redundancy (a single channel), reduce the frequency of turn-taking and reduce back channels. The problem is thus not so much breakdowns in communication, but a reduced ability to recover from them.

14.3.5 *Constructing a shared understanding*

We have seen that human conversation is in itself inherently ambiguous, relying on context and shared understanding between the parties to disambiguate the utterances. In some spheres, such as legal contracts, the precise meaning out of context becomes very important and thus highly stylized language is used to reduce ambiguity[3]. However, even the legal profession depends on a large body of

---

[3]Or left deliberately ambiguous.

shared knowledge and understanding about legal terms, case law, etc. Similarly, a book, such as this, attempts to use less ambiguous language, and only commonly available knowledge.

The major difference between a book and conversation is that the latter is interactive. The shared knowledge used in a book is static, whereas that used during a conversation is dynamic, as the participants increase their understanding of one another and as they shift their focus from topic to topic.

When participants come to a conversation, they may come from different backgrounds and bring different knowledge. Even close colleagues will have different recent experiences, and as we have seen in previous examples, have different foci. The participants do not try to unify their knowledge and background — indeed, they could not fully do so without living one another's lives. Instead, they seek to obtain a *common ground*, a shared understanding sufficient for the task in hand. Establishing this common ground will involve negotiating the meanings of words and constructing shared interpretations of the world. Clark and Schaefer [37] refer to this process as *grounding*.

A consequence of this model of conversation is that the participants are, at various levels both conscious and subconscious, aware that their common ground is incomplete. Their conversation is not then just an exchange of information about their task, but involves continual testing and cross checking of the other party's understanding. Consider again a fragment from Alison's conversation about the way to the cinema:

Alison: So, you turn right beside the river.
Brian: past the pub.
Alison: yeah . . .

Alison makes an utterance concerning the way to the cinema. Brian interprets this utterance given his current understanding of the conversation and the world. However, in order to check this understanding he makes the statement 'past the pub'. Now this is not a question of clarification like his earlier question about the bridge, instead it merely echoes back some evidence that he has correctly interpreted Alison's utterance. Alison is happy with this and so confirms it 'yeah'.

Such exchanges can be more protracted, for instance, if Brian's reply does not satisfy Alison she may reflect Brian's evidence back to him: 'you mean the Black Bull', or attempt to re-present her original utterance: 'along the road on this side of the river'. Alternatively, the exchange may be much shorter: rather than explicitly presenting evidence, Brian could have simply continued the conversation, making his understanding implicit in his future utterances. If these utterances were not compatible with Alison's original utterance, she could then initiate repair. This was the course adopted in their conversation in the country park, although, in that case, with unfortunate results. Finally, the evidence of understanding may often be presented via back channels, little 'yes'es, or simply a continued look of comprehension.

Common ground is always partial, and thus any utterance will have a different meaning for the speaker and the listener. The aim of grounding is to construct a meaning *in the conversation* which is sufficient for the task. For example, Brian's understanding of the Black Bull may be of pleasant evenings sitting on its river terrace. Alison may never have visited the pub, but has seen its distinctive sign hanging over the road. These different understandings are not important: for the purpose of finding directions the pub is merely a way of identifying the road they are to follow.

In a conversation, we know that our partner does not share our knowledge of the world. In addition, we know that our partner will attempt to interpret our utterances. We thus frame our utterances based on this knowledge. Two guiding principles for our utterances is that they should be *relevant* and *helpful*.

To be *relevant* an utterance should further the current topic. This is because our partner is expecting an utterance in this context and any sudden shift in our topic focus will make it more difficult for our partner to make sense of the utterance. Such shifts happen in a conversation, but require less ambiguous utterances (as the common ground for that particular utterance is lower).

To be *helpful*, an utterance should be understandable to the listener and be sufficiently unambiguous given the listener's understanding. This requires the speaker to have a model of the listener's understanding and vice versa. So assuming he is being helpful, in saying 'past the pub', Brian implicitly assumes that there is a particular pub, which Alison will recognize as being significant. It is no good the pub being significant to Brian alone, he must know that it will carry its intended significance to Alison.

The ability to build such models is part of our social maturing. One of the key developmental steps for a child is from an egocentric world view, where things are interpreted in relation to the child, to a social one where the child recognizes other's viewpoints. At the age of two and a half, one of the author's children was interviewed by a linguistics researcher. At one stage the conversation proceeded:

Child: we went to the doctor
Researcher: where was the doctor?
Child: up the steps

The researcher was clearly (in the context and to an adult) wanting to know whether the doctor was in a hospital or not. The child's answer would have been instantly meaningful to any local parent as the steps to the local doctor were a constant problem for people with prams. However, the child was at that stage unable to phrase the utterance in a way suited to her listener's understanding. At a certain age children assume you know everything they know[4].

So, we see that conversation is an inherently social activity, based on a constructed shared understanding, and relying on the participant's models of one another. In addition, it depends on continuous interaction to correct misinterpretations and to confirm understanding.

---

[4]To be fair adults often make the same assumption of children!

14.3.6   *Speech act theory*

A particular form of conversational analysis, *speech act theory*, has been both influential and controversial in CSCW. Not only is it an analytic technique, but it has been used as the guiding force behind the design of a commercial system, Coordinator. Speech act theory has origins going back over 20 years, but was popularized by Winograd and Flores in the design of Coordinator [185].

The basic premise of speech act theory is that utterances can be characterized by what they *do*. If you say 'I'm hungry', this has a certain *propositional meaning* — that you are feeling hungry. However, depending on who is talking and to whom, this may also carry the meaning 'get me some food' — the intent of the statement is to evoke an action on the part of the hearer. Speech act theory concerns itself with the way utterances interact with the actions of the participants.

Some speech acts actually cause a significant effect by the act of being said. The classic example is when a minister says 'I pronounce you husband and wife'. This is not simply a statement that the minister is making about the couple. The act of saying the words changes the state of the couple. Other acts include promises by the speaker to do something and requests that the hearer do something. These basic acts are called *illocutionary points*.

Individual speech acts can contribute to a conversation. The basic structure of conversations can be then seen as instances of generic conversations. One example of such a generic structure is a *conversation for action* (CfA). This is shown as a state diagram in Figure 14.1. It represents the stages two participants go through in initiating an external action that one of them should perform. There are two variants, the one shown represents a conversation where the first speaker (A) is requesting that the other participant (B) does something. The other, similar, variant is where the first speaker begins with an offer.

The numbered circles in Figure 14.1 are 'states' of the conversation, and the labelled arcs represent the speech acts which move the conversation from state to state. Note that the speech acts are named slightly differently in different sources (by the same author even!), but the structure of a CfA is the same. The simplest route through the diagram is through states 1–5.

> **Alison:** have you got the market survey on chocolate mousse?
> **Brian:** sure
> *rummages in filing cabinet and hands it to Alison*
> **Brian:** there you are
> **Alison:** thanks

Alison makes a *request* for the survey (although it is phrased as a question). Brian *promises* to fulfil the request ('sure'). After he feels he has done so (by handing it to Alison), Brian *asserts* that the request has been fulfilled ('there you are') and Alison *declares* her satisfaction that Brian has completed her request.

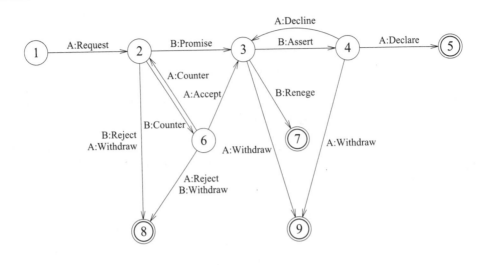

Figure 14.1   *Conversation for action (from Winograd and Flores [185])*

More complex routes may involve some negotiating between the parties. For example, the conversation might have begun:

Alison: have you got the market survey on chocolate mousse?
Brian: I've only got the summary figures
Alison: that'll do

In this Alison's *request* is met by a *counter* from Brian, that is, Brian attempts to modify Alison's request. This brings us to state 6 in the diagram. Alison then *accepts* Brian's counter, bringing the conversation back to state 3.

The network has some nodes marked with a double circle. These are the completion nodes, and at these points neither party expects any more acts by the other as part of this conversation. So the fragment above which left Alison and Brian in state 3 must continue. Of these completion nodes only state 5 represents conclusions where the request has been satisfied. For example, Alison's initial request could have been answered with 'it's confidential' (meaning 'you can't have it'). This is the action of Brian *rejecting* Alison's request, leaving the conversation in state 8 and complete.

Not all speech acts need be spoken! Often a silence or an unspoken action forms a speech act. For example, let us imagine that the market survey had not been handy and so Brian answers Alison's request with 'sure, I'll get it later'. Later in the day he finds an electronic copy of the report and then emails it to Alison. His action will be interpreted as *asserting* completion. If Alison does not respond within a short time, her silence will be read as *declaring* satisfaction and the conversation will be completed.

There are other generic conversation forms as well as CfA. These include:

conversation for clarification usually embedded within a CfA to clarify the required action. (Different from countering a request).

conversation for possibilities looking towards future actions.

conversation for orientation building up a shared understanding.

In addition, the participants may indulge in meta-conversation, discussing the acts themselves, perhaps questioning the legitimacy of an act: 'I'm hungry' . . . 'well I'm not your skivvy, get your own food'. Also CfA is the most extensive and well developed of the conversational forms. For example, the 'creative' conversation for possibilities will have a much less structured form.

The importance of CfA is that actions are central to organizational administration. In the words of Terry Winograd:

> Conversations for action are the central coordinating structure for human organizations. Winograd [186]

This belief in the importance of CfA, together with the assumption that making speech acts explicit will aid communication, prompted the design of the tool *Coordinator*. Coordinator is a form of structured email system. When sending a message, the participants must say what kind of illocutionary act they are performing and what part it plays in a conversation. The tool knows about CfA and a few other conversational forms. In addition, it allows time limits to be put on messages. Together these facilities allow the participants to keep track of their own commitments and those of others.

As an example, imagine Alison wishes to use Coordinator to request the market survey from Brian. She selects a menu option saying that she wants to initiate a CfA. The system then offers her two possibilities, a request or an offer. She chooses to make a request and from now on, the system knows that a CfA is in progress. She then types 'have you got the market survey on chocolate mousse' into the text area of the message. Note that the system does not try to structure or interpret the natural language *content* of the utterance, but only demands that the sender declares the illocutionary point of it. Brian receives Alison's message and is told by the system that it is a request. He is then offered the various conversational moves that can follow: promise, counter-offer or decline (*reject*), plus a few more not on Figure 14.1. If he chooses promise, the system fills the message area with the default words 'I promise to do as you request', which can be altered (to 'sure') if Brian desires, or sent as it is. The intention is that many simple acts can be completed by the defaults.

Coordinator, being one of the earlier CSCW systems, has had plenty of criticism. Indeed, 'Coordinator bashing' has become so common in CSCW circles that it (the bashing) is coming under criticism itself. There are three main problems: reservations about speech act theory itself and CfA in particular, that people dislike using Coordinator, and whether the whole concept of making intentions explicit is a good idea.

The first criticism is that speech acts do not adequately describe conversations. For example, Alison walks into Brian's office while he is on the phone, he picks a report from the table and gives it to her, she walks out. Speech act theory would regard this as a conversation for action. The request is implicit, presumably Brian knows what Alison wants from some previous context. Then when Brian hands over the report, he is, by complying with her request, both implicitly *promising* to fulfill and *asserting* completion of the request. Finally, by going out of the office Alison implicitly declares completion. There seems to be an awful lot of squeezing to get the interchange to fit the CfA! Indeed, this is recognized in part within Coordinator as a valid response to a request is a report of completion (*assert*), that is, taking the *promise* as read.

There have been mixed responses as to the usefulness of Coordinator, but most (certainly the most vocal) have been negative. The conversational forms basically do not do what people want. Those users who continued to use it ended up using 'free-form' messages — a non-interpreted action. Effectively, they used Coordinator as a standard email. It has been claimed that the only organizations that have used Coordinator successfully are those with strong authoritarian managerial structures where the employees have been ordered to use it. Coordinator has even been dubbed 'the world's first fascist computer system'[5] — which was certainly *not* the intention of the designers. As you can see, emotions tend to run high when discussing Coordinator!

The fundamental approach of Coordinator is different from any previous system, and from most since. Rather than starting with technology — build it and play with it — Coordinator started with a theory of communication and then used this to drive design. Such theory-led design is a thoroughly proper design approach. The debatable issue is the way in which the theory was incorporated into the tool.

Coordinator expects its users to make explicit what is normally implicit in our utterances. We hope the reader will have realized by now just how rich human conversation is, and how effective people are at communication. However, one of the fundamental lessons learnt by the expert systems' community is that experts *do* things, they do not know *how* they do them. Forcing expert communicators (people) to think about their communication is rather like asking a centipede to think about walking. This all suggests that theory should be used to guide the design, but should not be embedded explicitly within it.

There is a counter argument however. First of all there is some evidence to suggest that teaching managers to recognize their speech acts improved their communication. The extrapolation is that making the acts explicit improves communication, but that is a major extrapolation. A more measured claim would be that explicit representation is *at least* a good tool for training communication skills. The second argument concerns the nature of electronic communication. Although we are all experts at face-to-face communication with all its subtleties, our expertise

---

[5]Even if one agreed with the sentiment, it would certainly not be the first.

is sorely challenged when faced with a blank screen. We lack the facilities to make our intentions implicit in our communications and thus explicit means will help.

Whatever the rights and wrongs of Coordinator's design, the evidence is that its users have largely voted with their feet. More recent systems have included a much greater level of user control, allowing users to build conversational structures of their own. Possibly, the structures they build are merely special cases of CfA and other speech act structures, but users clearly prefer to feel that they have the power over the system.

14.4 **Text Based Communication**

For *asynchronous* groupware (and even some synchronous systems), the major form of direct communication is text based. There are exceptions to this, for instance, voice messaging systems and answerphones, and other media may be used in addition to text such as graphics, voice annotation or even video clips. But despite these, text is still the dominant medium.

Text based communication is familiar to most people, in that they will have written and received letters. However, the style of letter writing and that of face-to-face communication are very different. The text based communication in groupware systems is acting as a speech substitute, and, thus, there are some problems adapting between the two media.

There are four types of textual communication in current groupware:

discrete directed message as in email. There is no explicit connection between different messages, except insofar as the text of the message refers to a previous one.

linear participants' messages are added in (usually temporal) order to the end of a single transcript.

non-linear when messages are linked to one another in a hypertext fashion.

spatial where messages are arranged on a two dimensional surface.

In addition, the communication may be connected to other shared computer artefacts as described in Chapter 13 (Section 13.6). In the case where the communication is an annotation, the annotation itself may be structured in any of the ways listed above.

A special case of a linear transcript is structured message systems such as Coordinator, where not only the order but also the function of each message is determined. The other extreme is where the transcript is presented as a single stream, with no special fields except the name of the contributor. Figure 14.2 shows a screenshot of the York Conferencer system showing such a transcript on the left of the screen. On the right is an electronic pin-board, an example of spatially organized text.

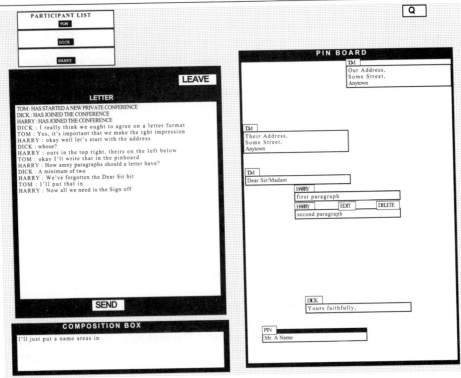

Figure 14.2   *Conferencer screenshot: showing text transcript and pin-board*

In this section, we will discuss some of the differences between face-to-face conversation and text based communications. We will use several of the concepts introduced during our discussion of face-to-face communication and conversational structure in Sections 14.2 and 14.3.

14.4.1   Back channels and affective state

One of the most profound differences between face-to-face and text based communication is the lack of fine grained channels. So much of the coordination of face-to-face conversation depends on back channels and interpretation of the listener's expressions. Text based communication loses these back channels completely. Consider the effect of this on even a two-party conversation. Where the speaker would pause to seek back channel confirmation or to offer the floor, the text 'speaker' must either continue regardless, or finish the message, effectively passing the turn. One consequence of the lack of interruptions and more measured pace of interaction is that the utterances are more grammatical than speech — but still *not* Queen's English!

In addition to this loss of back channels, the speaker's tone of voice and body language are of course absent. These normally convey the *affective state* of the speaker (happy, sad, angry, humorous) and the *illocutionary force* of the message (an important and urgent demand or a deferential request). Email users have taken to including explicit tokens of their affective state by the use of 'flamming' and 'smilies':

> : -) – smiling face, happy
> : - (– sad face, upset or angry
> ; -) – winking face, humorous

People tend to use stronger language in email than in face-to-face conversation, for example, they are more likely to be highly and emotively critical. On the other hand, they are less likely to get emotionally charged themselves. These apparently contradictory findings make sense when you take into account the lack of implicit affective communication. The participants have to put this explicitly into their messages — thus accounting for their stronger language. On the other hand, they are emotionally 'distanced' by the text from their conversants and have the conversation spread out over time. In addition, they do not have to express their affective state by *acting* emotionally. Together these factors contribute to a more heated conversation by calmer conversants!

14.4.2   *Grounding constraints*

In Section 14.3.5, we discussed the process by which conversants obtain common ground. This grounding process is linked strongly with the types of channels through which the conversants communicate. Clark and Brennan [36] describe the properties of these channels in terms of *grounding constraints*. These include:

cotemporality an utterance is heard as a soon as it is said (or typed).

simultaneity the participants can send and receive at the same time.

sequence the utterances are ordered.

These are all constraints which are weaker in text based compared with face-to-face interaction. For example, simultaneity in face-to-face conversation allows back channel responses. Even where, say, two participants can see each other's typed messages as they are produced, the nature of typing makes it all but impossible to type your message whilst looking for your colleague's 'back channel' response.

In a text based system, different participants can compose simultaneously, but they lack cotemporality. As we saw, even if the messages appear as they are produced, they will not be read in real time. In addition, the messages may only be delivered when complete and even then may be delayed by slow communications networks.

Linear transcripts obviously have some idea of sequence, but this is confused by the overlap and interleaving caused by the lack of cotemporality and simultaneity. Consider this typical interchange during the use of the York Conferencer system:

1. **Bethan:** how many should be in the group?
2. **Rowena:** maybe this could be one of the 4 strongest reasons
3. **Rowena:** please clarify what you mean
4. **Bethan:** I agree
5. **Rowena:** hang on
6. **Rowena:** Bethan what did you mean?

Rowena and Bethan composed their first utterances simultaneously. When Rowena looks up to the transcript area, she sees Bethan's message and does not understand it, so she enters the canned phrase 'Please clarify what you mean' which is generated by a button marked 'Clarify'. Simultaneously, Bethan reads Rowena's message (2) and hits her canned phrase button 'Agree'. Rowena is then confused about what Bethan means by 'I agree' as the preceding message was her request for clarification.

In a spoken conversation, Rowena and Bethan would have quickly corrected themselves if they began to speak at once, and the linearity would have reflected a *common* experience. The trouble is that the participants in the text based conference each experienced the messages in a different order

    Rowena: 2 1 3 4 5 6
    Bethan: 1 2 4 3 5 6

We will discuss these problems of interleaving and overlapped messages further in the following sections.

Altogether, the lack of grounding constraints in text based communication make it more difficult to obtain a common ground. It has also been found that email and text based meetings are less effective at resolving conflicts than a face-to-face meeting.

14.4.3   *Turn-taking*

We saw that one of the fundamental structures of conversation was *turn-taking* (Section 14.2.5). The last transcript was an example of a breakdown in turn-taking. In fact, such breakdowns are quite rare in two-party electronic conversations and are quickly corrected. What is more surprising is that such breakdowns so rarely occur during letter writing, which is in some ways similar. However, when conversing by letter, one has an objective time-scale with which to work out whether your fellow conversant ought to have replied. One therefore does not send a second letter unless your conversant is very remiss in replying to your first missive. However, in synchronous text based conversation, the time taken to compose a message (from 30 seconds to several minutes) is far greater than the few seconds which feels 'immediate' on a computer system, but is too short to be able to reason about rationally. The replies always seem a long time coming and hence one is tempted to send a 'follow on' message.

Despite the occasional breakdown, most observers of two-party text based interaction report an overall turn-taking protocol, which exhibits many of the structures of normal conversation including *adjacency pairs*. However, when we look at three or more participants, turn-taking and adjacency pair structure begin to break down completely.

In a pair of participants, turn-taking is simple; first one person says something, then the other. The only problem is deciding exactly *when* the exchange should happen. With three or more participants, turn-taking is more complex. They must decide *who* should have the next turn. This is resolved by face-to-face groups in a number of ways. First, the conversation may, for a period, be focused on two of the parties, in which case normal two-party turn-taking holds. Second, the speaker may specifically address another participant as the utterance is finished, either implicitly by body position, or explicitly 'what do you think Alison?'. Finally, the next speaker may be left open, but the cotemporality of the audio channel allows the other participants to negotiate the turn. Basically, whoever speaks first, or most strongly, gets in.

These mechanisms are aided by back channels, as one of the listeners may make it clear that she wants to speak. In this case either the speaker will explicitly pass the turn (the second option above), or at least the other listeners are expecting her to speak. In addition, the movement between effective two-party conversation (the first option) and open discussion will be mediated by back channel messages from the other participants.

In an unstructured text based conversation the third option is not available, nor, of course, are the back channels. Paired conversation is quite common and the second option, explicitly naming the next speaker, is possible, However, this naming is not particularly natural unless a direct question is being asked. In both options, the absence of back channels makes it difficult for another listener to interrupt the conversation. Some systems use more structured mechanisms to get round these problems, perhaps having a round-robin protocol (each participant 'speaks' in turn) or having a queue of turn-requests. Whether the strictures of such mechanisms are worse than the problems of occasional breakdown depends very much on the context and is a matter of opinion.

14.4.4 *Context and deixis*

We have seen how important context is in ordinary speech. Utterances are highly ambiguous and are only meaningful with respect to *external context*, the state of the world, and *internal context*, the state of the conversation. Both of these are problems in text based communication.

The very fact that the participants are not co-present makes it more difficult to use external context to disambiguate utterances. This is why many groupware system strive so hard to make the participants' views the same; that is, to maintain *WYSIWIS* ('what you see is what I see'). As we saw in Chapter 13, this is an issue even when the participants have audio–video communications or are even in the same room!

Whatever the means of direct communication, remote participants have difficulty in using deictic reference. They cannot simply say 'that one', but must usually describe the referrant: 'the big circle in the corner'. If their displays are not WYSIWIS then they must also ensure that their colleague's display includes the object referred to and that the description is unambiguous. Asynchronous participants have even more problems with deixis as there is no opportunity for their colleagues to clarify a reference (without extremely lengthy exchanges). Furthermore, the objects referred to by a message may have changed by the time someone comes to read it! Similarly, group pointers are not really an option, but one can use methods of linking the conversation to its context, either by embedding it within the objects as annotations or by having hypertext links between the conversation and the object.

The trouble does not end with external context; there are also problems with deictic reference to internal context. In speech the context is intimately connected to linear sequence and adjacency. As we have seen, even in linear text transcripts, overlap breaks the strict sequentiality of the conversation, and thus causes problems with indexicals and with context in general.

1. **Alison:** Brian's got some lovely roses
2. **Brian:** I'm afraid they're covered in greenfly
3. **Clarise:** I've seen them, they're beautiful

Brian and Clarise both reply to Alison's message at the same time. However, in the transcript, where Clarise says 'they' it appears, at first, to refer to the greenfly. Brian is expecting a consoling reply like 'I've seen them. Have you tried companion planting?'. Of course, the breakdown quickly becomes apparent in this case. The problem is not so much that people cannot recover from such breakdowns, as in the extra burden the recovery puts on the participants. If these messages are being sent, say, between continents, network delays and time differences may limit exchanges to once a day. Even one or two messages recovering from breakdown is then a major disaster.

Most email systems and some bulletin boards lack any implied sequentiality and thus any context to the messages. The users (ever inventive) get round this by including copies of previous messages in their replies. This is only partially effective and of course incredibly clumsy.

Hypertext based systems avoid the implied sequentiality of a linear transcript. In the above example, both Brain and Clarise replied to Alison's message at the

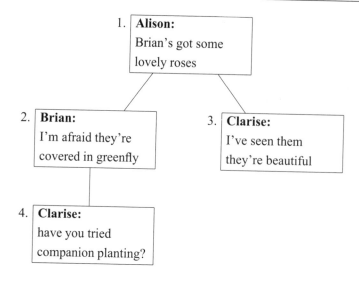

Figure 14.3   *Hypertext conversation structure*

same time. In a hypertext these would form parallel conversations. This is shown in Figure 14.3 where in addition Clarise has sent a second message offering advice on Brian's greenfly. The use of 'they' in Clarise's message (3) is now perfectly clear.

14.4.5   *Pace and granularity*

In a spoken conversation, the turns are often only a few tens of seconds long. If we take into account minor confirmations and back channels, the pace is still faster, perhaps a turn or back channel response every few seconds. Compared with this the pace of email is very slow: messages can take from a few minutes to several hours to deliver. Even synchronous text based conversations are limited by the participants' typing speed and have a pace of at most one turn every minute or so.

The term *pace* is being used in a precise sense above. Imagine a message being composed and sent, the recipient reading (or hearing) the message and then composing and sending a reply. The pace of the conversation is the rate of such a sequence of connected messages and replies. Clearly as the pace of a conversation reduces, there is a tendency for the *granularity* to increase. To get the same information across, you must send more per message. However, it is not as easy as that. We have seen the importance of feedback from listener to speaker in clarifying meaning and negotiating common ground. Even most

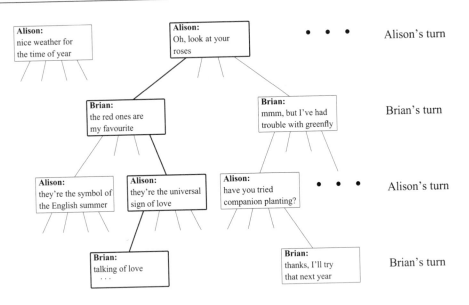

Figure 14.4   *The conversation 'game'*

monologues are interactive in the sense that the speaker is constantly looking for cues of comprehension in the listener. Reducing the pace of a conversation reduces its *interactivity*.

As well as at the small scale of clarifying individual utterances, interactivity is important in determining the direction of a conversation. Imagine that the conversation is a little like a game, where the participants can make moves. In Figure 14.4, we can see some of the moves Alison and Brian can make whilst talking in the garden (Clarise has gone home). At each turn of the conversation, Alison or Brian can choose to say one thing which continues the discussion. That is, they gradually work out a path from the top of the tree downwards. A particularly promising conversation is shown in bold.

In a hypertext based system one can expand several branches of a conversation tree, but in speech or in a linear text transcript the conversation follows one branch. Whatever medium is used, you cannot normally progress down the tree faster than the pace of the conversation. To overcome these limitations, people adopt several *coping strategies*.

The simplest strategy is just to avoid conversation. This can be done by delegating parts of a task to the different participants. Each participant can then perform much of the task without communication. They must still communicate for large scale strategic decisions, but have significantly reduced the normal communications. Of course, this approach reduces *communication* by reducing *collaboration*.

More interesting in a cooperative work setting are two coping strategies which

E: I don't like the other three being in
cahoots — shall I form an alliance with
one to stitch them up? I'll move to
Holland first.

Figure 14.5   *Excerpt of transcript from Hewitt* et al. [85]

increase the chunk size of messages in order to reduce the number of interactions
required to complete a task. These strategies are frequently seen in both text based
conferences and in letter writing.

The first of these coping strategies is *multiplexing*. Basically, the conversants
hold several conversations in parallel, each message referring to several topics. In
terms of the conversation tree, this corresponds to going down several branches
at once. For an example, consider the transcript in Figure 14.5 taken during a
computer-mediated game of Diplomacy as part of the TMPI project [85]. The turn
by England (E) introduces two topics: the forming of an alliance (for subversive
purposes), and a particular line of attack (through Holland).

The second coping strategy for increasing the size of message chunks is *eagerness*. The participants can foresee the possible course of the interaction and frame
communications which encompass many of the possibilities: e.g. 'If you don't
pay within 7 days we will take you to court'. Thinking of the conversation tree,
eagerness is a sort of depth first strategy. The participant explores a branch of the
tree guessing the other participant's responses.

If we compare spoken with written communication we find that letters are
far more eager than speech. When writing a letter one takes more care that the
points are stated clearly, and one may even consider alternative responses of the
recipient and state your position on each. For instance, a letter may say 'if you
marry me I will be happy for ever, but if not, life will lie like bitter herbs upon
my tongue' (lovers have a tradition of being over eager). In extremis one frames a
communication which describes one's reaction in all possible situations.

One can find similar incidents of eagerness in electronic conversations, for
example, the messages in Figure 14.6 from Severinson Eklundh's corpus [153],
quoted by Bowers and Churcher [22], both exhibit eagerness, the contingent part
of each message being introduced by the key phrase 'In that case'.

Eagerness is less likely to lead to breakdown, except where the message tries
to foresee too great a breadth of possibilities and becomes confusing. However,
there are various circumstances, for instance, in many process control tasks, where
the number of possibilities at each stage of the tree is large. In this case eagerness
cannot solve the communication problems.

A potential problem of eagerness is that by following a particular branch of the
conversation, other branches, which your colleague would have liked to explore,
are missed. In spoken conversations it is quite difficult to return to a previous point.
It is possible to say 'going back to…', but this can form a potentially rude break in

A: Subject: Report C 123660
      The above mentioned report is out of stock. The
      remaining ones are C 12366 + C 123660. What
      to do? Reprint? In that case, do you have any
      changes to suggest?

           . . .   . . .

A: Subject: SIGSIM meeting
      Are you going to Linkoping tomorrow?
      In that case when are you leaving?
      Does SIGSIM pay for the trip or what?

Figure 14.6   *Excerpt from Severinson Eklundh's corpus* [153]

the conversation. In text based communications, the *reviewability* of the medium reduces this effect. It is easier to return to a missed point as both participants can refer to the conversation up to that point. In addition, the break in the line of conversation is less rude as both participants know that the current topic can itself be picked up again. Finally, there is even the option of multiplexing the current topic with the lost point.

Reviewability is another grounding constraint of communication, but this time one where text based communication has the advantage over speech. You can of course tape speech, but it is far from easy to use this as a review mechanism.

14.4.6   Linear text vs. hypertext

Considerations of potential overlap suggest that hypertext based communications may be better suited as a text based communication medium. Similarly, the problems of pace may be partially solved in a hypertext. Multiplexed messages can be represented as updates to several parts of the hypertext, thus reducing the likelihood of breakdown and lost topics. In addition, if the messages themselves can be mini-hypertexts, then eager messages listing several possible courses of action can be explicitly represented by the message.

On the other hand, hypertext has its disadvantages. Even static hypertexts, which have been carefully crafted by their authors, can be difficult to navigate. A hypertext that is created 'on the fly' is unlikely to be comprehensible to any but those involved in its creation. Conklin and Begeman, themselves associated with the hypertext based argumentation tool gIBIS, conclude that '. . . traditional linear text provides a continuous, unwinding thread of context as ideas are proposed and discussed' [41]. For the asynchronous reader trying to catch up with a conversation, a linear transcript is clearly easier, but it is precisely in more asynchronous settings where overlap in linear text is most likely to cause confusion.

We can see that there is no best solution, with possibly the best course in many situations being linear transcripts arranged by topic, with some automatically generated indication of overlap.

14.5 Group Working

So far we have been principally looking at the properties of direct communication, and largely two party conversations. Group behaviour is more complex still as we have to take into account the dynamic social relationships during group working. We will begin by looking at several factors which affect group working, and then discuss the problems of studying group working. This section deals with groups which are actively working together, whereas the next, on organizational issues, is primarily concerned with the long term structures within which people work.

14.5.1 *Group dynamics*

Whereas organizational relationships such as supervisor/supervisee are relatively stable, the roles and relationships within a group may change dramatically within the lifetime of a task and even within a single work session. For example, studies of joint authoring have found that roles such as author, co-author and commentator, change throughout the lifetime of a document [122, 142]. This means that systems, such as co-authoring systems, which use a formal concept of *role*, must allow these roles to change together with the socially defined roles.

Even the naming of roles can cause problems. A person may be an author of a book or paper, but never write the words in it, acting instead as a source of ideas and comments. A particular case of this is the biographical story where the individual concerned and a professional writer co-author the book, but only the professional author writes. A co-authoring system such as Quilt would call the non-writing author a 'commentator' or a 'reviewer', but *not* an 'author'. One can imagine some of the social friction such naming will cause.

Within the microcosm of group interaction, authority roles can be entirely inverted. For example, if the Managing Director of a coal mining company visited the coal face, he should act under the authority of the foreman at the face, for his own safety and that of the mine. These inversions can cause problems even in computer-free situations — it is hard for the foreman to say 'No' to the MD. But, if a system demands an explicit controlling role, it is even harder for the manager to relinquish this explicit role, even if in the context the subordinate should be in control.

Not only do the social relationships *within* the group change, but the group membership and structure can change in time. The leaving of a member or introduction of a new member can cause dramatic changes in the behaviour of the group. For example, if a very dominant member leaves, the group may change from a leader–follower to a democratic structure. New members have special problems adapting to the particular group sub-culture, which can develop very quickly among close colleagues. In addition to this social adaptation, the new member must 'catch up' with the substantive work of the group. Groupware systems, for example *argumentation tools*, can help in that they record the history of the group. Groupware designers should in general be aware that new members can enter the group and design their software accordingly. For example, a late comer to a synchronous conference should be able to review all past contributions, not just the new ones.

The group may also divide into sub-groups for detailed discussion and then reform. Tools must be able to support this. For example, early versions of *CoLab*'s software *only* catered for a single WYSIWIS screen — that is, it only supported a single group. In later versions they were forced to allow sub-groups to work independently and then share results. Note that the CoLab meeting room only has room for six persons, in larger meeting rooms sub-group working is the norm.

14.5.2   *Physical layout*

In Section 14.2, we discussed the importance of eye gaze and gesture in face-to-face communication and how these help to mediate turn-taking. In particular, we noted in Section 14.2.3, that we must ensure that monitors do not block the participants' views of one another. In general, the physical layout of a room has a profound effect upon the working relationship of those in it. This is particularly obvious for meeting rooms, but should be considered in any group working environment.

As well as being unobtrusive, the orientation of computing equipment can affect group working. If we wish to encourage conversation, as we do in a meeting room, the participants must be encouraged to look towards one another. Meeting rooms have a natural focus towards the screen at the front of the room, but inward facing terminals can counteract this focus and thus encourage eye contact [108].

The designers of Capture Lab, an eight-person meeting room, considered all these features and many other subtle effects. However, the users still had some difficulty in adapting to the *power positions* in the electronic meeting room. At first sight, the electronic meeting room is not unlike a normal conference room. If the shared screen were a whiteboard or an overhead projector, then the most powerful position would be towards the front of the room (seat 1 or 6 in Figure 14.7). Managers would normally take this seat as they can then easily move to the whiteboard or overhead projector to point out some item and draw the group's attention.

Unless primed beforehand, managers of groups using Capture Lab took one of these seats, but quickly became uncomfortable and moved. In the electronic meeting room, there is no advantage to being at the front, the screen can be controlled from any terminal. Instead, the power seat is at the back of the room

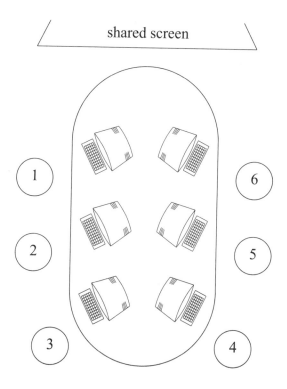

Figure 14.7   *Meeting room layout*

(seat 3 or 4), as from here the manager can observe other people whilst still seeing the screen. Also the other participants have to turn round when the manager speaks, again adding to the manager's authority over the meeting.

14.5.3 *Distributed cognition*

In Chapter 1, we discussed human cognition, but the emphasis was, as in all traditional psychology, upon the activity *within* the person's head. A school of thinking has recently developed which regards thinking as happening not just within the head, but in the external relationships with things in the world and with other people. This viewpoint is called *distributed cognition*.

In fact, this viewpoint is not as radical as it first appears. Traditional views talk about the movement of information between *working memory* and *long-term memory*: it is not so difficult then to regard bits of paper, books and computer systems as extensions to these internal memory systems. Similarly, many models of human cognition regard the mind a set of interacting sub-systems: the step to regarding several people as involved in joint thinking is not difficult. Remember that this is a view of cognition, that is, thinking; it says nothing about awareness, personality or individuality.

Distributed cognition has profound effects on the way we look at group working and even individual work. It emphasizes the importance of *mediating representations*, for example, the drawings on a whiteboard. These are no longer just a means of communicating between the parties, but can be a concrete embodiment of group knowledge. Furthermore, it constantly reminds us that communication is not just about getting knowledge from one person's head to another, but is about the creation of new group knowledge, not necessarily grasped in totality by any single member.

The emphasis on external forms is encouraging for a designer. It is not necessary to completely understand the individual's cognitive processing in order to design effective groupware. That is an impossible task. Instead, we can focus our analysis of existing group situations and design of groupware on the external representations used by the participants.

14.5.4 Experimental studies

Given the complexities of human–human communication and group working, it is hardly surprising that experimental studies of groups and of groupware are more difficult than the corresponding single-user experiments (see Chapter 11 for basic experimental issues). For the purpose of discussion, let us assume that we are evaluating a shared application with video connections between the participants and consider some of the problems we will encounter.

The subject groups

To organize, say, ten experiments of a single-user system requires ten subjects. For an experiment involving groups of three, we will of course need 30 subjects for the same number of experiments. In addition, experiments in group working are often longer then the single-user equivalents as we must allow time for the group to 'settle down' and some rapport to develop. This all means more disruption for subjects and possibly more expense payments.

Arranging a mutually convenient slot when both subjects and the equipment are available is no mean feat. Often the workstations being used in the experiment will be colleagues' personal systems, so we are trying to accommodate at least six people, not to mention the experimenters themselves (perhaps if we had a shared calendar system . . .).

Not surprisingly, many reports of group working involve only three or four groups. This is obviously a problem for statistical purposes, but not the primary obstacle.

The experimental task

Choosing a suitable task is also difficult. We may want to test a variety of different task types: creative, structured, information passing, and so on. Also, the tasks must encourage active cooperation, either because the task requires consensus, or because information and control is distributed among the participants. Obviously, the task also depends on the nature of the groupware system: if it has several available channels, we want to encourage broad use. For example, in the case of shared application with video, it should not be possible (or at least not easy) to perform the task without using the application, otherwise we are simply investigating video conferencing.

Creative tasks such as 'write a short report on . . .' or 'write a research proposal' are often effective, in that the participants must reach agreement, and can be asked to produce their final report using the shared application. Design tasks are also used, for instance, in one experiment users of the York Conferencer system (see Figure 14.2 in Section 14.4) were asked to redesign a bank layout. A picture of the current layout was used as a background for the spatially arranged electronic pinboard, and the participants made use of this to arrange comments and suggestions close to the features they referred to.

Decision games, as used in management courses, are designed as to test and train cooperative activity. They often rely for their success on group coordination, not individual ability. An example of this is the desert survival task, where the participants are told that they have crashed in the desert. They are given a list of items to rank in order of importance for their survival: knife, plastic sheet, etc. The participants must produce *one* list between them, a single knowledgeable participant cannot 'go it alone'. A computerized version of the game of Diplomacy has also been used (see Figure 14.5 in Section 14.4) as it includes aspects of conflict as well as cooperation.

Finally, time-critical simulated process control tasks force a higher pace of interaction as the participants control different parts of the model. An example of this is ARKola [71], a simulated bottling plant, which was used at Xerox Parc to investigate the importance of background noise in complex cooperative control tasks.

Often the chosen task will require extra implementation effort, and, in the case of games this may be extensive. This is obviously a strong factor in the choice of a suitable task.

Data gathering

Even in a single-user experiment we may well use several video cameras as well as direct logging of the application (see Chapter 11). In a group setting this is replicated for each participant. So for a three-person group, we are trying to synchronize the recording of six or more video sources and three keystroke logs. To compound matters these may be spread over different offices, or even different sites. The technical problems are clearly enormous. Four-into-one video recording is possible, storing a different image in each quadrant of the screen, but even this is insufficient for the number of channels we would like.

One way round this is to focus on the participants individually, recording for each one the video images that are being relayed as part of the system (assuming there is a video connection), recording the sounds that participant hears, and synchronizing these with the particular participant's keystrokes and additional video observations. Thus, we can recreate the situation as it appeared *to the participant*. From this recording, we may not be able to interpret the other participants' actions, but at least we have a complete record for one.

Given sufficient recording equipment, this can be repeated for each participant. Happily, the level of synchronization required between participants is not as great as that required for each one individually. One can simply start the recorders' clocks at the same time, but not worry about sub-second accuracy between participants. The important thing is that we can, as it were, relive the experience for each individual.

Analysis

In true experimental tradition, we would like to see statistical differences between experimental conditions. We saw in Chapter 11 that individual differences made this difficult in single-user experiments. If anything, group variation is more extreme. Given randomly mixed groups, one group will act in a democratic fashion, in another a particular pair will dominate discussion, in a third one of the participants will act as coordinator, filtering the other's contributions. The level of variation is such that even catastrophic failures under one condition and fabulous successes in another may not always lead to statistically significant results.

As an example of this, imagine we have some quantitative measure of quality of output. We will almost certainly have to use non-parametric tests, so imagine we are have found that all the groups under one condition obtained higher scores than any group under the other condition. We would need at least four in each group to obtain even 5% significance (one tailed). If our results were only slightly less good, say one of the generally better groups performed poorly, we would then require at least five in each group.

Now this example only considered one condition, and assumed the best possible results. In general, we would expect that the spread between groups within conditions would be greater, and we may want to test more conditions at once.

Our ten groups will have to increase rapidly to stand any chance of statistically significant results. However, we saw above that even gathering ten experimental groups is a significant problem.

There are three possible solutions to this problem. First, one can use within-group experiments, having each group work under several conditions. We have of course the normal problems of such analysis, transfer effects and the like, but have more chance of cancelling out the group effect. Second, we can look to a micro-analysis of features like gaps between utterances. Such measures are more likely to fit a standard distribution, and thus one can use more powerful parametric tests. In addition, they may be more robust to the large scale social differences between groups.

The third solution is to opt for a more anecdotal analysis, looking for critical incidents in the data (such as the real and simulated transcripts in this chapter). The concepts and methods throughout this chapter can be used to drive such an analysis. The advantage of this approach is that instead of regarding group differences as a 'problem', they can be included in the analysis. That is, we can begin to look for the systematic ways in which different group structures interact with the communications media and applications they use.

Of course, experiments can be analyzed using both quantitative and qualitative methods. Indeed, any detailed anecdotal analysis of the logs will indicate fruitful measures for statistical analysis. However, if the number of experimental groups is limited, attempts at controlled experiments may not be productive, and may effectively 'waste' the groups used in the control. Given the high costs of group working experiments, one must choose conditions which are likely to give interesting results even if statistical analysis proves impossible.

14.5.5 *Field studies*

There are problems with taking groups and putting them in an experimental situation. If the groups are randomly mixed, then we are effectively examining the process of group formation, rather than that of a normal working group. Even where a pre-existent group is used, excluding people from their normal working environment can completely alter their working patterns. For a new system, there may be no 'normal' workplace and all we can do is produce an artificial environment. However, even with a new system we have the choice of producing a 'good' experiment or a naturalistic setting. The traditions of experimental psychology are at odds with those of more qualitative sociological analysis.

Indeed, it is argued that work can only be studied in context. This is consonant with the ideas of distributed cognition. Taking a worker away from the workplace changes the very nature of the worker's actions. Real action is *situated action*, it occurs in interaction the materials and people of the workplace. In extremis, it is claimed that an action can only be understood in the place, in the social situation, and at the *time* at which it occurred. Such a level of contextualization is obviously useless for design, and its advocates will in practice generalize from their theory, even if they eschew such generalization in theory.

Even if one does not wish to take such an extreme view, it is clear that studying workers in their own situations is extremely worthwhile.

Many branches of sociology and anthropology have long recognized that one cannot study people divorced from their social and cultural context. In particular *ethnography* has become very influential in CSCW. It is based on very detailed recording of the interactions between people and between people and their environment. It has a special focus on social relationships and how they affect the nature of work. The ethnographer does not enter actively into the situation, and does not see things from a particular person's viewpoint. However, an aim is to be encultured, to understand the situation from within its own cultural framework. Culture here means that of the particular work group or organization, rather than that of society as a whole. Ethnographers try to take an unbiased and open ended view of the situation. They report and do not like to speculate. So, it is not yet clear how well their approach can contribute to the design of new systems.

The ethnographic approach differs markedly from the *Scandinavian approach* of *participatory design* (see Chapter 11). In participatory design the workers come *out* of their work situation, either physically or mentally, and share the design task with the professional designers — effectively the workers become designers. The participatory designer enters into the subjective experience of the workplace. Ethnographic and other situated approaches take the analyst *into* the workplace, while retaining a level of objectivity. The advantage is that the analyst can see the whole groups' perspective, rather than that of a single individual, but, the analyst, however much in tune with the workers, is still 'out there'. On the other hand, involving the workers in the design process in itself increases their motivation and acceptance whether or not the resulting design is 'optimal'.

14.6 Organizational Issues

In this section, we shall look at some of the organizational issues which affect the acceptance and relevance of groupware systems in particular, and information technology in general. These factors often sit 'outside' the system as such, and may involve individuals who never use it. Yet it is these factors more than any other which determine the success or failure of computer systems.

Frequently the examples in this section will refer to email as this is the greatest extant groupware application. It is inevitable that other applications will encounter similar problems.

14.6.1   *Who benefits?*

One frequent reason for the failure of groupware systems is that the people who get the benefits from the system are not the same as those who do the work. We encountered one example of *disproportionate effort* in Chapter 13, when we discussed structured message systems such as Lens. In these systems the sender has to do work in appropriately putting information into fields, but it is the recipient who benefits. Another frequently cited example is with shared calendars. The beneficiary of the system is a manager who uses the system to arrange meeting times, but whose personal secretary does the work of keeping the calendar up to date. The subordinates are less likely to have secretarial support and yet must keep up the calendar with little perceived benefit. Of course, chaos results when a meeting is automatically arranged and the subordinates may have to rearrange commitments which have not been recorded on the system. The manager may force use by edict or the system may simply fall into disuse. Many groupware systems are introduced on a 'see if it works' basis, and so the latter option is most likely.

The lesson is that groupware systems should aim for some level of *symmetry*. If you have to do work for the system, you should obtain some benefit from it. For the shared calendar, this might involve improving the personal user interface, so that there are definite advantages in using the on-line system to plan one's time rather than using paper (it could even print out File-o-Fax pages). In addition, if people use electronic organizers, one could consider integrating these into the system.

14.6.2   *Free rider problem*

Even where the groupware has no bias towards any particular persons, it may still not function symmetrically. One reason for this is the *free rider problem*. Take an electronic conferencing system. If there is plenty of discussion of relevant topics then there are obvious advantages to subscribing and reading the contributions. However, when considering writing a contribution, the effort of doing so may outweigh any benefits. The total benefit of the system for each user outweighs the costs, but for any particular decision the balance is overturned.

To see this situation in a different context imagine an eccentric philanthropist who has gathered three strangers into a room. They are invited to throw money into a pot in the centre. When they have done so, the philanthropist will double the money in the pot and then divide it up between them and send them on their way. Each stranger reasons 'If I put in three pennies, then our benefactor will double this to six. These will be distributed between three of us, so I will have only two returned to me.' Clearly, unless the strangers can come to some understanding none of them will put any money in the pot, and none will benefit.

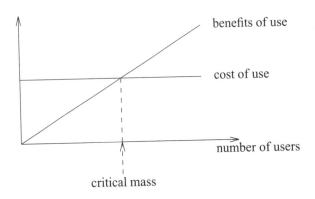

Figure 14.8 *Cost/benefit of system use*

A few free riders in a conference system are often not a problem, as the danger is more likely from too much activity. In addition, in electronic conferences the patterns of activity and silence may reflect other factors such as expertise. However, it is easy for the number of free riders gradually to increase and the system slide into disuse. It is hard to enforce equal use, except by restrictive schemes such as round robin contributions (everyone contributes something however short). In the real world, such problems are often solved by social pressure, and the free rider reacts to the collective censure of the group. Increasing the *visibility* of participants' contributions might help these social mechanisms. For example, one could display an activity meter showing the number of contributions from each subscriber. Of course, people may then choose not to subscribe in the first place!

14.6.3   *Critical mass*

A linked issue to free riders is the need to develop a *critical mass*. When telephones were only in public places, their use as a form of pervasive inter-personal communication was limited. However, once a large number of people have telephones in their homes it becomes worthwhile paying to have a telephone to be installed. In cost/benefit terms, the early subscribers probably have a smaller benefit than the cost. Only when the number of subscribers increases beyond the critical mass does the benefit *for all* dominate the cost (see Figure 14.8). The situation for conferencing systems and email is, of course, very similar.

We can learn something from the lessons of the telephone system and other successful technologies (but remember telephones took the best part of a hundred years to become pervasive in affluent countries). The telephone was useful for sub-groups before it became beneficial for all. Even when only a small proportion of the population had personal telephones, they still formed a significant proportion of their social group, so these cliques of use could grow gradually over time. One would hope that the growth of groupware systems need not be so class biased, but we can make use of a similar mechanism. If an organization consists of widening circles of highly connected sub-groups, then take up can grow from the core to the wider group. This is possibly one reason for the popularity of email. Even a group of two or three people in an organization can use email effectively between themselves. Of course, the benefits increase as it becomes pervasive, but even a tiny user group ensures that the benefits outweigh the costs.

Clearly, we must design any new groupware systems so that it has benefits even when its user population is small.

14.6.4   *Cooperation or conflict?*

The term 'computer-supported *cooperative* work' seems to assume that groups will be acting in a cooperative manner. This is obviously true to some extent; even opposing football teams cooperate to the extent that they keep (largely) within the rules of the game, but their cooperation only goes so far. People in organizations and groups have conflicting goals, and systems which ignore this are likely to fail spectacularly. Meeting rooms obviously expect conflict between individuals or between departments; part of the purpose of the meeting may be to resolve these conflicts. However, there are likely to be many more, less explicit, conflicts with which a system must cope.

Imagine an organization is already highly computerized, the different departments all have their own systems and the board decides that an integrated information system is needed. The production manager can now look directly at stocks when planning the week's work, and the marketing department can consult the sales department's contact list to send out marketing questionnaires. All is rosy and the company will clearly run more efficiently, or will it?

The storekeeper always used to understate stock levels slightly in order to keep an emergency supply, or sometimes inflate the quoted levels when a delivery was due from a reliable supplier. Also requests for stock information allowed the storekeeper to keep track of future demands and hence plan future orders. The storekeeper has now lost a sense of control and important sources of information. The sales department are also unhappy: their contacts are their livelihood. The last thing they want is someone from marketing blundering in and spoiling a relationship with a customer built up over many years. Some of these people may resort to subverting the system, keeping 'sanitized' information on-line, but the real information in personal files. The system gradually loses respect as the data it holds are incorrect, the morale in the organization suffers and productivity drops. The board gets worried and meets to consider upgrading the computer system!

Before installing a new computer system, whether explicitly 'cooperative' or not, one must identify the *stakeholders* who will be affected by it. These are not just the immediate users, but anyone whose jobs will be altered, who supplies or gains information from it, or whose power or influence within the organization will increase or decrease. It will frequently be the case that the formal 'client' who orders the system falls very low on the list of those affected. Be very wary of changes which take power, influence or control from some stakeholders without returning something tangible in its place.

14.6.5   Changing power structures

The identification of stakeholders will uncover information transfer and power relationships which cut across the organizational structure. Indeed, all organizations have these informal networks which support both social and functional contacts. However, the official lines of authority and information tend to flow up and down through line management. New communications media may challenge and disrupt these formal managerial structures.

The physical layout of an organization often reflects the formal hierarchy: each department is on a different floor, with sections working in the same area of an office. If someone from sales wants to talk to someone from marketing then one of them must walk to the other's office. The contact can be monitored by their respective supervisors. Furthermore, the physical proximity of colleagues can foster a sense of departmental loyalty. An email system has no such barriers, it is as easy to 'chat' to someone in another department as in your own. This challenges the mediating and controlling role of the line managers.

Furthermore, in face-to-face conversation, the manager can easily exert influence over a subordinate: both know their relative positions and this is reflected in the patterns of conversation and in other non-verbal cues. Email messages lose much of this sense of presence and it is more difficult for a manager to exercise authority. The 'levelling' effect even makes it possible for a subordinate to direct messages 'diagonally' across the hierarchy, to one's manager's peers, or, even worse, to one's manager's manager!

Many organizations are moving towards flatter management structures anyway, so from a strategic viewpoint, these effects may be acceptable. But, can the organization cope with a disaffected junior management during the transition? For other organizations the effects may be less welcome and the system dropped or heavily regulated. In one case, an email system was introduced and was agreed to be functioning well, but the management, feeling a loss of control and suspicion over their subordinates' communications, introduced logging so that all email messages could be monitored by management. The system quickly fell into disuse.

Technology can be an important vector of social change, but if violent reaction is to be avoided, the impact of the technology must be assessed before it is introduced.

In the short term, solutions must be carefully matched to the existing social and organizational structures.

14.6.6 *The invisible worker*

The ability to collaborate whilst at a distance can allow functional groups to be distributed over different sites. This can take the form of cross-functional neighbourhood centres, where workers from different departments do their jobs in electronic contact with their functional colleagues. Alternatively, distributed groupware can allow the true home-based tele-worker to operate on similar terms to an office-based equivalent. The ecological and economic advantages of such working practices are now becoming well established, and it seems that communications and CSCW technology can overcome many of the traditional barriers.

In fact, a closer examination reveals that the barriers to such working are not technological but managerial. First of all, management style may make remote working all but impossible. If the approach is 'management by presence', that is, you know someone is working because they are in the office, then there is no way a remote worker is going to be trusted. If, on the other hand, the style is 'management by objectives', you know your subordinates are working because they are doing their jobs, then remote working is not so problematical. Even where remote working is accepted, the lack of physical presence can be a problem. When the time comes for promotion the present employee may seem more worthy than the distant one — not because of any objective criteria, but because presence increases perceived worth.

Again we see that social and managerial relationships completely dominate technological considerations. Many video based groupware systems are intended to create a sense of engagement, of active participation and social presence. Whether this will be sufficient to overcome ingrained attitudes remains to be seen.

14.6.7 *Evaluating the benefits*

We have seen several problems which can arise due to the mismatch between collaborative systems and organizational and social factors. Let us assume that we have a groupware system in place — and it has not fallen apart at the seams. Everyone seems happy with it and there are no secret resentments. Now it is time to count the cost — it was an expensive system to buy and install, but was it worth it?

This is an almost impossible question to answer. The benefits from groupware, especially organization-wide systems such as email or electronic conferencing, are in terms of job satisfaction or more fluid information flow. Some, such as the *video-wall*, are expected primarily to help social contact within the organization. It may be possible to measure contentment and job satisfaction using attitude questionnaires (see Chapter 11), but any hard economic benefit will be so diffuse as to be unquantifiable.

However, a similar argument could be (and has been) framed for computer use in general. The benefits are difficult to quantify, but over time, it has become clear that the competitive edge of information technology is necessary for survival in the modern world. Perhaps the same will be said of cooperative systems in a few years.

14.7 Summary

Face-to-face communication is extremely complex. People maintain precise distances, which can be disrupted through video links. Each utterance is mediated by subtle back channel responses signifying agreement, or on attempting to interrupt. Body movement, facial expression, eye contact and gaze are all used for these back channels and also to establish context.

At a higher level, the structure of conversation can be seen as a sequence of turns, usually alternating between the participants. Context is important in disambiguating utterances, especially when deictic reference is also used. This also depends on the participants establishing a common understanding during the conversation. Breakdowns do occur in conversation, but conversational repair is very effective. Speech act theory, a detailed analysis of conversational structure, has been used to drive the design of Coordinator, a highly controversial, commercial structured messaging system.

Text based communication loses most of the low-level feedback of face-to-face conversation. This, and the possibility of overlapping turns, makes it more difficult to establish the context of a textual utterance, and therefore to disambiguate deixis. The reduced pace of text-based conversation means that participants are forced to increase the granularity of their messages. They may achieve this by multiplexing messages or by being eager, predicting their colleagues' responses.

Group dynamics make it very difficult to predict how a particular group will behave. In particular, small things, such as the layout of chairs in a room, can have a major effect. We can see the thinking in a group as being distributed, not locked in any individual, but being within the whole group and the physical representations they use. Group variability and synchronization of recordings makes experiments difficult, but many assert that group working can only be studied in the work situation. One such approach is ethnographics, whereby the analyst seeks to become encultured, interpreting individuals' actions within the social context.

Organizational factors can make or break groupware (or single-user) systems. There may be a mismatch between those who benefit, and those who do the work. Even where there is no inbuilt bias, the free-rider may put in little personal effort, benefitting from the work of the rest of the group. Any computer system may interfere with the existing authority and social relationships within an organization. One needs to identify stakeholders who will be affected directly or indirectly.

In particular, junior and middle management may feel they lose control and authority by the introduction of electronic communications. Another example is tele-working, which is made easier by advances in telecommunications, but which makes the worker less visible to management. Even where a groupware system is perceived to be useful, it is hard to quantify its benefits as they are diffused throughout the organization.

Exercises

14.1 In Section 14.3.2, we discussed the highly contextual nature of the spoken word, including the use of deictic reference and indexicals, and the (officially) ungrammatical and fragmentary use of sentences. Try listening to social chat over cups of tea — collect examples of different forms of contextual utterance.

14.2 Go into an office or other place where several people are working together. Try to note down in as much detail as possible what they are doing and when. Do this with different foci: focus on the direct interpersonal communications, focus on the shared objects such as a calendar or document, or focus on one worker at a time. Whilst collecting data and when ordering your notes, look for breakdowns and misunderstandings, and for implicit communication through objects. Look also at a particular task over a period of time, and note the number of interruptions as a worker performs the task, or the way a single task is contributed to by several workers.

Recommended Reading

- Lucy A. Suchman. *Plans and Situated Actions: The Problem of Human–Machine Communication*. Cambridge University Press, 1987.

  This book popularized *ethnography* within HCI. It puts forward the viewpoint that most actions are not pre-planned, but situated within the context in which they occur. The principal domain of the book is the design of help for a photocopier. This is itself a single-user task, but the methodology applied is based on both ethnographic and conversational analysis. The book includes several chapters discussing the contextual nature of language and analysis of conversation transcripts.

- T. Winograd, and F. Flores. *Understanding Computers and Cognition: a new foundation for design*. Addison-Wesley, New York, 1986.

  Like Suchman, this book emphasizes the contextual nature of language and the weakness of traditional artificial intelligence research. It includes an account of *speech act theory* as applied to *Coordinator*. Many people disagree with their use of speech act theory, but, whether by application or reaction, this work has been highly influential.

- Jonathon Grudin. Why CSCW applications fail: Problems in the design and evaluation of organizational interfaces. In *CSCW'88, Proceedings of th Conference on Computer Supported Cooperative Work*, pages 85–94, ACM, New York, 1988.

  Discusses further, and with case studies, the sorts of social and organizational problems introduced in Section 14.6.

- Saul Greenberg, editor. *Computer-supported Cooperative Work and Groupware*, Academic Press, 1991.

  The contents of this collection originally made up two special issues of the *International Journal of Man–Machine Studies*. In addition, the book contains Greenberg's extensive annotated bibliography of CSCW, a major entry point for any research into the field. Updated versions of the bibliography can be obtained from the Department of Computer Science, University of Calgary, Calgary, Alberta, Canada.

- *Communications of the ACM*, Vol. 34, No. 12, December 1991.

  Special issue on 'collaborative computing'.

- Several issues of the journal *Interacting with Computers* from late 1992 through early 1993 have a special emphasis on CSCW.

- *Computer-Supported Cooperative Work*, a new journal dedicated to CSCW.

- See also the reading list for Chapter 13, especially the conference proceedings.

Chapter 15

Multi-sensory Systems

Overview

- Multi-sensory systems are those that use more than one sensory channel in the interaction.

- These systems may use:
  - non-speech sound
  - text and hypertext
  - animation and video
  - speech
  - handwriting
  - gestures
  - computer vision

- Multi-sensory systems have a range of applications, including:
  - providing interfaces for users with special needs
  - virtual reality

15.1 Introduction

As we saw in Chapter 1, there are five senses: sight, sound, touch, taste and smell. Of these, sight is used predominantly, but this is backed up in everyday life by the others. Some of us are without one or more of these senses, and are considered to be disabled, less able to perform well in some activities. There are many social effects and attitudes suffered by those with a lack of one or more of these senses, which are more disabling than any actual reduced ability. However, many things are inherently harder if we have only limited sensory input.

Consider an onion and an apple: both very different foods. They have different uses in cooking because of their different natures, and most people would think they look, smell, taste and feel very different. However, when eaten, their texture is remarkably similar. Moreover, if you are blindfolded and cannot use sight to disambiguate them, you are left with taste and smell to tell them apart. The interesting thing is that if you have a cold, and thus your sense of smell is also removed, there is no way of distinguishing between them. It is only the smell of an onion that is different from that of an apple, not its taste, and so people who are blindfolded, with a cold, will happily eat an onion in just the same way as an apple. Thus our senses cannot always be relied upon on their own; indeed, we have seen in Chapter 1 that the visual system is easily fooled by optical illusions. However, together the senses represent a much more potent force. We utilize sound to keep us aware of our surroundings, subconsciously monitoring the movement of people around us, the conversations going on that we are not consciously listening to, reacting to sudden noises, providing clues and cues that switch our attention from one thing to another. Such reactions were probably honed over thousands of years as being useful for survival, but our existence in the world of today is just as active and reactive as it ever was in the age of the dinosaurs; only the problems have altered and we have swapped predators — cars for dinosaurs, gunfire for stealthy assault with clubs, mugging for tribal warfare.

Sound is not only useful for providing us with information about our environment. It can also have a profound effect upon us which is not well understood, particularly in the form of music. Music is almost completely an auditory experience, and yet it is exceptionally emotive, able to alter moods, conjure up visual images, evoke whole atmospheres or scenes in the mind of the listener.

Smell provides us with other useful information in daily life; checking if food is off, detecting early signs of fire, noticing that manure has been spread in a field. Touch too is a vital sense for us: tactile feedback forms an intrinsic part of the operation of many common tools; cars, typewriters, pens, anything that requires holding or moving. It can form a sensuous bond between individuals, communicating a wealth of non-verbal information. Examples of the use of sensory information are easy to come by (we looked at some in Chapter 1), but a vital feature is that our everyday interaction with each other and the world around us is a multi-sensory one, each sense providing different information that is built up into a whole. Since our interaction with the world is improved by multi-sensory input, it makes sense to ask whether multi-sensory information would benefit human–computer interaction. As we consider ourselves to be disabled if we are without one or more of our senses, why should we handicap our users by insisting that they use only their visual sense? The majority of interactive computer systems are almost completely visual in their interactive properties; often WIMP-based, they offer only the most rudimentary sounds whilst adding more and more information on to the screen. As systems become more complex, the visual channel may be overloaded if too much information for the user to comprehend is presented all at once. This may lead to frustration or errors in use. By utilizing the other sensory channels, the visual channel can be relieved of the pressure of providing all the information required and so interaction should improve. The use of multiple sensory channels increases the *bandwidth* of the interaction between the human and the computer, and it also makes human–computer interaction more like the interaction between humans and their everyday environment, perhaps making the use of such systems more natural.

15.2 Usable Sensory Inputs

The visual channel is used as the predominant channel for communication, but if we are to use the other senses we have to consider their suitability and the nature of the information that they can convey.

The use of sound is an obvious area for further exploitation. There is little doubt that we use hearing a great deal in daily life, and so extending its application to the interface may be beneficial. Sound is already used, in a limited manner, in some interfaces: beeps are used as warnings and synthesized speech is also used. Tactile feedback, as we have already seen, is also important in improving interactivity and so this represents another sense that we can utilize more effectively. However, taste and smell pose more serious problems for us. They are the least used of our senses, and are used more for receiving information than for communicating it. There is currently very little way of implementing devices that can generate tastes and smells, and so these two areas are not supported. Whether this is a serious omission remains to be seen, but the tertiary nature of those senses tends to suggest that their incorporation, if it were possible, would lead to only a marginal improvement.

15.3 Multi-modal and Multi-media Systems

We have to distinguish what we mean when we talk about multi-modal and multi-media systems. Multi-modal systems have been developed to take advantage of the multi-sensory nature of humans. Utilizing more than one sense, or *mode* of communication, these systems make much fuller use of the auditory channel, and to a lesser extent, the tactile channel, to improve the interactive nature of the system. Thus multi-modal systems increase the bandwidth of human–computer interaction. Multi-media systems, on the other hand, use a number of different media to communicate supplementary, additional or redundant information. Often this may take the form of using multiple sensory channels, but it may also take the form of different types of visual input — textual, graphical, iconic, animation, video and CD-i. Thus multi-media systems are often multi-modal, but not always.

The next sections of this chapter will concentrate on advances to 'standard' modes of human–computer communication, looking particularly at the use of sound in the interface, and different media, including hypertext, video and so on.

We will look at some of the multi-modal and multi-media systems currently being developed, which integrate a number of these modes and media into a higher-bandwidth communication interface. Applications include interfaces for users with special needs and virtual reality.

15.4   Speech in the Interface

As human beings, the ability to speak to each other has been instrumental in our rapid development and mastery of our environment. Endemic to all peoples in the world today, language is one of the major factors that sets us apart from the rest of the animal kingdom. The languages that we have developed are rich and complex, but so great is our mastery that we take them very much for granted. It is only when attempting to learn a new one, or to quantify the rules of our native one, that we begin to realize the structure and difficulty inherent in language, and the considerable skills we have to have in order to use it effectively. It is this great mastery of such a complex area that makes speech recognition and synthesis on computers so difficult, since we are unaware of the inherent difficulties in the task we are asking the system to perform. However, since speech is such an effective and natural means of communication between humans, it seems appropriate that its use in the interface should be investigated. Offering in principle a very natural mode of communication at rapid speeds, it may present an ideal way of extending and enhancing human–computer interaction. It is estimated that speech recognition and synthesis will become a multi-million pound industry by the year 2000.

15.4.1   *Structure of speech*

If we are fully to appreciate the problems involved with the computer-based recognition and generation of speech, we need first to understand the basic structure of speech. The English language is made up of 40 *phonemes*, which are the atomic elements of speech. Each phoneme represents a distinct sound, there being 24 consonants and 16 vowel sounds. Language is more than simple sounds, however. Emphasis, stress, pauses and pitch can all be used to alter the meaning and nature of an utterance, a common example being the rise in pitch at the end of a sentence to indicate a question in English. This alteration in tone and quality of the phonemes is termed *prosody* and is used to convey a great deal of meaning and emotion within a sentence, in addition to the actual words used. Prosodic information gives language its richness and texture, but is very difficult to quantify. Due to the manner in which sound is produced in the vocal tract, mouth and nose of the speaker, the limitation in response speed means that phonemes sound differently when preceded by different phonemes. This is termed *co-articulation*, and the resulting differences in sound can be used to construct a set of *allophones*, which represent all the different sounds within the language. Ignoring prosodic information, the concatenation of allophones together should produce intelligible, articulate speech. However, depending on the analysis of language used, and the regional accent studied, there are between 120 and 130 allophones. These in turn can be formed into *morphemes*, which represent the smallest unit of language that has meaning. They are the basic building blocks of language rather than of speech. Morphemes can be either parts of words or whole words, and they are built into sentences using the rules of grammar of the language.

Even being able to decompose sentences into their basic parts does not mean that we can then understand them; the syntax (structure) only serves as a standard base upon which the semantics (meaning) is based. We are rarely aware of the complex structure of speech, and concentrate on extracting the meaning from the sentences we hear, rather than decomposing the sounds into their constituent parts.

15.4.2 *Speech recognition*

There have been many attempts at developing speech recognition systems, but they have met only limited success. The complexity of language is one barrier to success, but there are other, more practical, problems also associated with the automatic recognition of the spoken word. Background noise can interfere with the input, masking or distorting the information, whilst speakers can introduce redundant or meaningless noises into the information stream by repeating themselves, pausing, or using 'continuation' noises such as 'Ummm' and 'Errr' to fill in gaps in their usual speech. Variations between individuals also cause problems; people have unique voices and systems that are successful are tuned to be sensitive to minute variations in tone and frequency of the speaker's voice — new speakers present different inflections to the system which fails to perform as well. A more serious problem is caused by regional accents, which vary considerably, to the extent that we can often place people in the county of their upbringing by their accent. This strong variation upsets the trained response of the recognition system. More serious still is the problem posed by different languages; everything from phonemes up can be different.

There are some systems that have found acceptance, however. One of these, the 'Phonetic Typewriter', uses a neural network which clusters similar sounds together (see Figure 15.1).

Trained to produce typed output from speech input in Finnish (a phonetic language, that is one which is spelt as it sounds), it is trained on one particular speaker, and then generalizes to others. However, its performance with speakers other than the one on which it was trained is noticeably poorer, and it relies on a large dictionary of minute variations to supplement its general transcription mechanism. Without the dictionary, it achieves a significantly lower recognition rate.

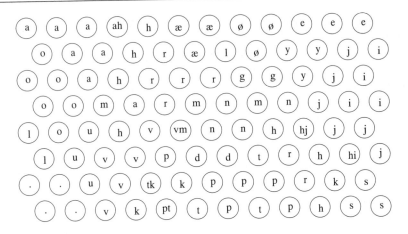

Figure 15.1   *The phonetic typewriter*

Considering speech recognition from the point of view of multi-modal inter-action, there is no doubt that it offers another mode of communication that may in some contexts be used to supplement existing channels or become the primary one. When a user's hands are already occupied, such as in a factory, speech may prove to be the ideal input medium. Speech input does not require the use of a cumbersome keyboard and so in lightweight mobile situations there is a potential role for such systems. It also provides an alternative means of input for users with visual impairment, physical disabilities and learning disabilities, such as dyslexia. Single-user, limited vocabulary systems can work satisfactorily, but the current success rate of recognition for general users and unconstrained language is sufficiently low for there to be no astounding commercial successes as yet.

15.4.3   *Speech synthesis*

Complementary to speech recognition is speech synthesis. The notion of being able to converse naturally with a computer is an appealing one for many users, especially those who do not regard themselves as computer literate, since it re-flects their natural, daily medium of expression and communication with their colleagues. However, there are as many problems in speech synthesis as there are in recognition. The most difficult problem is that we are highly sensitive to variations and intonation in speech, and are therefore intolerant of imperfections in synthesized speech. We are so used to hearing natural speech that we find it difficult to adjust to the monotonic, non-prosodic tones that are presented to us by speech synthesizers. No-one would pretend that speech like that of the Daleks was human-like: indeed, it was so effective precisely because of the machine-like impartiality and emotionless presentation. Other problems exist in using synthesized speech. Existing as a transient phenomena, spoken output cannot be reviewed or browsed easily. It is intrusive, requiring either an increase in noise in the office environment, or the wearing of headphones by the user, either of which may be too large a price to pay for whatever benefits the system may offer. There are a few application areas in which speech synthesis has been successful. Particularly for blind users, speech offers a medium of communication to which they have unrestricted access, and they are highly motivated to overcome the inherent limitations within current systems. Screen readers, which read the textual display back to the user, and systems that speak menu selections and such like, are available, and within a restricted domain they are highly utilized. As a supplementary channel, they are occasionally used in applications where the user's visual and haptic skills are focused elsewhere, such as for warning signals in aircraft cockpits. However, their success is difficult to determine, since often a visual warning is at least as effective.

15.5 Non-speech Sound

Non-speech sound has traditionally been used in the interface to provide warnings and alarms, or status information. For example, there is experimental evidence to suggest that the addition of audio confirmation of modes, in the form of changes in key clicks, reduces errors [116]. Video games offer further evidence, since experts tend to score less when the sound is turned off than when it is on; they pick up vital clues and information from the sound whilst concentrating their visual attention on different things. Dual mode displays are, in general, thought to be better since the presentation of similar information along different channels allows the brain to search along two paths, with the best path finishing first and therefore maximizing response time. The presentation of redundant information in this way may increase a user's performance since, for example, he may be able to remember the sound associated with a particular icon but not its visual representation. Ambiguity in one mode can also be resolved by using the information presented in the other. One such example is of a speech recognition system that also uses a camera to video the lip movements of the speaker. Indistinct words or phrases can be resolved more accurately by using the visual information as well as analyzing the sound.

However, in spite of this, the auditory channel is comparatively little used in standard interfaces. Information is almost entirely provided visually. There is a danger that this will overload the visual channel, demanding that the user attend to too many things at once and select appropriate information from a mass of detail on the display. Reliance on visual information forces attention to remain focused on the screen, and the persistence of visual information means that even detail which is quickly out of date may remain on display after it is required, cluttering the screen further. Careful use of sound in the interface would alleviate these problems. Hearing is our second most used sense and provides us with a range of information in everyday life, as we saw in Chapter 1. Humans can differentiate a wide range of sounds and can react faster to auditory stimuli than to visual. So how can we exploit this capability in interface design?

We have previously discussed the role of speech in the interface, but non-speech sounds offer a number of inherent advantages. Speech is serial and we have to listen to most of a sentence before we can extract the meaning; since many words make up a message this can take a reasonably long period of time. On the other hand, non-speech sounds can be associated with a particular action and assimilated in a much shorter period. Non-speech sounds can also be universal; in much the same way as visual icons have the same meaning in many different countries, so can non-speech sounds. The same is not true of speech, which requires that we understand and interpret it and so have to know the language used. Non-speech sound is also able to make use of the phenomena of auditory adaptation, in which sounds that are unchanging can fade into the background, only becoming evident when they alter or cease. One problem is that non-speech sounds have to be learnt, whereas the meaning of a spoken message is obvious (at least to a user conversant in the language used). However, since users are able to learn the visual icons associated with things, this should not be seen as too great a disadvantage.

There have been a number of suggestions for applications of sound in inter-active systems. Since sound is short-lived it can be used successfully to provide transitory information, such as indications of network or system changes, or of errors. It can also be used to provide status information on background processes, since we are able to ignore continuous sounds but still respond to changes in those sounds. Users of early home computers with their noisy power supplies, and computer operators listening to the chatter of the printer and the spinning of disks and tape drives both report that they are able to tell at what stage a process is at by the characteristic sounds that are made.

Sound can be used to present a second representation of actions and objects in the interface to support the visual mode and provide confirmation for the user. It can be used for navigation round a system, either giving redundant supporting information to the sighted user or providing the primary source of information for the visually impaired. Experiments on auditory navigation [138] have demon-strated that purely auditory clues are adequate for a user to locate up to eight targets on a screen with reasonable speed and accuracy, so there is no excuse for ignoring the role of sound in interfaces on the grounds that it may be too vague or inaccurate.

15.5.1   *Soundtrack*

A word-processor with an auditory interface, designed for visually disabled users, has been developed by Edwards [54], and is called *Soundtrack*. The visual items in the display have been given auditory analogs, made up of tones, with synthesized

File Menu	Edit Menu	Sound Menu	Format Menu
Alert	Dialog	Document1	Document2

Figure 15.2   *The screen division in Soundtrack (used by permission)*

speech also being used. A two-row grid of four columns is Soundtrack's main screen (see Figure 15.2); each cell makes a different tone when the cursor is in it, and by using these tones the user can navigate around the system. The tones increase in pitch from left to right, whilst the two rows have different timbres. Clicking on a cell makes it speak its name, giving precise information that can reorient a user who is lost or confused. Double clicking on a cell reveals a sub-menu of items associated with the main screen item. Items in the sub-menu also have tones; moving down the menu causes the tone to fall whilst moving up it rises. A single click causes the cell to speak its name, as before, whilst double clicking executes the associated action. Soundtrack allows text entry by speaking the words or characters as they are entered, with the user having control over the degree of feedback provided. It was found that users tended to count the different tones in order to locate their position on the screen rather than just listen to the tones themselves, though one user with musical training did use the pitch. Soundtrack provides an auditory solution to representing a visually based word-processor, though the results are not extensible to visual interfaces in general. However, it does show that the human auditory system is capable of coping with the demands of highly interactive systems, and that the notion of auditory interfaces is a reasonable one.

15.5.2   *Auditory icons*

Auditory icons [68] use natural sounds to represent different types of objects and actions in the interface. The SonicFinder [69] for the Macintosh was developed from these ideas. It is intended as an aid for sighted users, providing support through redundancy. Natural sounds are used since people recognize, not timbre and pitch, but the source of a sound and its behaviour [181]. They will recognize a particular noise as glass breaking or a hollow pipe being tapped; a solid pipe will give a different noise indicating not only the source but also the behaviour of the sound under different conditions. In the SonicFinder, auditory icons are used to represent desktop objects and actions. So, for example, a folder is represented by a papery noise, and throwing something in the wastebasket by the sound of smashing. This helps the user to learn the sounds since they suggest familiar actions from everyday life. However, this advantage also creates a problem for auditory icons. Some objects and actions do not have obvious, naturally occurring sounds that identify them. In these cases a sound effect can be created to suggest the action or object but this moves away from the ideal of using familiar everyday sounds which require little learning. Copying has no immediate analogous sound; in the SonicFinder it is indicated by the sound of pouring a liquid into a receptacle, with the pitch rising to indicate the progress of the copying. These non-speech sounds can convey vast amounts of meaning very economically; a file arrives in a mailbox, and being a large file it makes a weighty sound. If it is a text file it makes a rustling noise, whereas a compiled program may make a metallic clang. The sound could be muffled or clear, indicating whether the mailbox was hidden by other windows or not, whilst the direction of the sound would indicate the position on the screen. If the sound then echoed, as it would in a large, empty room, the system load is low. All this information can be presented in a second or so.

These ideas have been used to model environments such as a physics laboratory [70], called *SharedARK* (Shared Alternate Reality Kit) and a manufacturing plant [72], *ARKola*. In SharedARK, multiple users could perform physics experiments in a virtual laboratory. Sound was used in three different ways: as confirmation of actions, for status information and as aids to navigation. Confirmatory sounds use similar principles to the SonicFinder, providing redundant information that increase feedback. Process and state information sounds exist on two levels, global and local. Global sounds represent the state of the whole system, and can be heard anywhere, whilst local sounds are specific to particular experiments and alter when the user changes from one experiment to another. Navigational information is provided by soundholders which are auditory landmarks. They can be placed anywhere in the system and get louder as the user moves towards them, decreasing in volume when moving away. This allows the user to wander through an arena much greater than the size of the screen without getting lost and lets him return to specific areas very easily by returning to the soundholder.

In ARKola, a soft drinks factory was modelled, with two users working remotely from each other and using an audio/video link attempting to optimize the factory's output. Input machines supplied raw materials whilst the output ones capped the bottles and shipped them out. Each machine had an on/off switch and a rate control, with a sound that indicated its status; for example the bottle dispenser made the sound of clinking glass, with a rhythm that indicated its operating speed. Splashing sounds indicated spilled liquids, whilst breaking glass showed that bottles were being lost. The users monitored the status of the plant by listening to the auditory clues, and were able to help each other more effectively, since they found it easier to monitor their own machines without having to spend time looking at them, and could hear when something had gone wrong with their partner's part of the system.

15.5.3   *Earcons*

An alternative to using natural sounds is to devise synthetic sounds. *Earcons* [18] use structured combinations of notes, called *motives*, to represent actions and objects (see Figure 15.3). These vary according to rhythm, pitch, timbre, scale and volume. There are two types of combination of earcon. *Compound earcons* combine different motives to build up a specific action, for example combining the motives for 'create' and 'file'. *Family earcons* represent compound earcons of similar types. As an example, operating system errors and syntax errors would be in the 'error' family. In this way earcons can be hierarchically structured to represent menus. Earcons are easily grouped and refined due to their compositional and hierarchical nature, but they may be harder to associate with a specific task in the interface since there is an arbitrary mapping. Conversely, auditory icons have a semantic relationship with the function that they represent, but can suffer from there being no appropriate sound for some actions.

15.6   Handwriting Recognition

Like speech, we consider handwriting to be a very natural form of communication. The idea of being able to interpret handwritten input is very appealing, and handwriting appears to offer both textual and graphical input using the same tools. There are problems associated with the use of handwriting as an input medium, however, and in this section we shall consider these. We will firstly look at the mechanisms for capturing handwritten information, and then look at the problems of interpreting it.

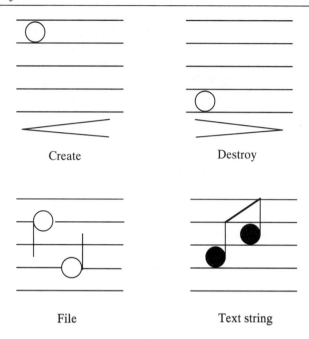

Create

Destroy

File

Text string

Figure 15.3   *Earcons (after Blattner* [18]*)*

15.6.1   *The technology*

The major piece of technology used to capture handwriting is the digitizing tablet, explained in more detail in Chapter 2. Free-flowing strokes made with a pen are transformed into a series of coordinates, approximately one every 1/50th second (or at the sampling rate of the digitizer). Rapid movements produce dots widely spaced in comparison to slow movements: this introduces immediate errors into the information, since the details of the stroke between dots is lost, as is the pressure information.

Digitizing tablets have been refined by incorporating a thin screen on top to display the information, producing *electronic paper*. Recent advances in screen technology means that such devices are becoming small and portable enough to be realistically useful, and Apple is bringing out a hand-held personal organizer that uses pen input, writing recognition and electronic paper. Information written on to the digitizer can simply be redisplayed, or stored and redisplayed for further reference. However, whilst this has limited use in itself, systems will only become useful if they are able to interpret the strokes received and produce text. It is this recognition that we will look at next.

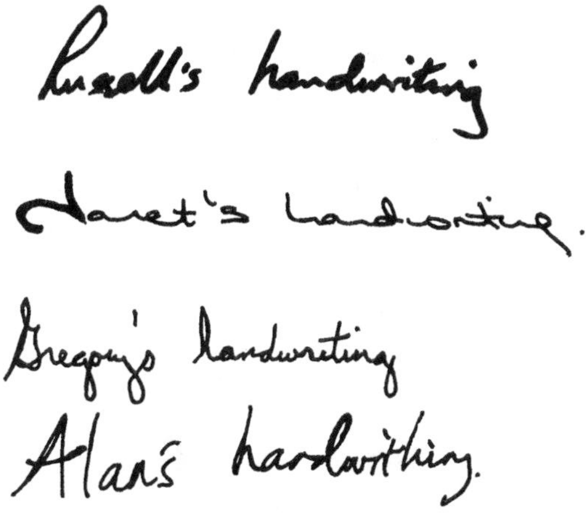

Figure 15.4 *Handwriting varies considerably*

15.6.2 *Recognizing handwriting*

The variation between the handwriting of individuals is large (see Figure 15.4); moreover, the handwriting of a single person varies from day to day, and evolves over the years.

These problems are reminiscent of those already discussed in speech recognition, and indeed the recognition problem is not dissimilar. The equivalent of co-articulation is also prevalent in handwriting, since different letters are written differently according to the preceding and successive ones. This causes problems for recognition systems, which work by trying to identify the lines that contain text, then to segment the digitized image into separate characters. This is so difficult to achieve reliably that there are no good systems in use today that are good at general cursive script recognition. However, when letters are individually written, with a small separation, the success of systems becomes more respectable, although they have to be trained to recognize the characteristics of the different users. If tested on an untrained person, success is limited again. Many of the solutions that are being attempted in speech recognition are also being tried in handwriting recognition systems, and vice versa, such as whole word recognition, the use of context to disambiguate characters, and neural networks, which learn by example.

15.7 **Text, Hypertext and Hypermedia**

Textual output is a common form of communication: information is presented as

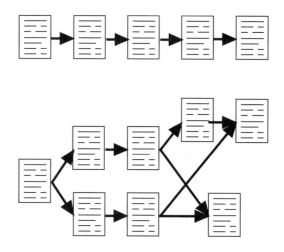

Figure 15.5   *Typical structures of linear text and hypertext*

blocks of text, or as a series of pages that have to be read. This is often the case for on-line help systems, or on-line manuals, as we saw in Chapter 12. However, presenting text in a linear fashion, one page after another, is highly unsuitable for browsing, since it forces the reader to follow the author's idea of which things should come in which order.

If the user is following one particular line of interest, he may wish to skip from one part of a discussion to another, which can be difficult. More serious problems may be encountered when using manuals, since the user may not understand all the terms used in the text, and will have to keep going back to a different series of pages to look up the definitions, returning to the original pages and trying to pick up the thread of discussion afterwards. Hypertext attempts to get around these limitations of text by structuring the text into a mesh rather than a line. This allows a number of different pages to be accessed from the current one, and, if well designed, the user should find it easier to follow his own particular idea through the mesh rather than being forced down one route. Typically, hypertext systems incorporate diagrams, photographs and other media as well as text. Such systems are often known as *hypermedia* systems, although the terms are used interchangeably.

A hypertext system comprises a number of pages, and a set of *links* that are used to connect pages together. The links can join any page to any other page, and there can be more than one link per page. Thus a hypertext document does not simply start and follow a linear progression to an end, but goes in lots of different directions, some of which terminate, while others link back into different parts of the document (see Figure 15.5 which illustrates the difference betwen linear text and hypertext).

There are many different ways of traversing the network, and so there are many different ways of reading a hypertext document — the intention is that the user is able to read it in the way that suits him best. Links can exist at the end of pages, with the user choosing which one to follow, or can be embedded within the document itself. For example, in an on-line manual, links may be attached to all the technical words, linking them directly to their definitions in the glossary. Simply clicking on an unknown word takes the user to the relevant place in the glossary. Another unknown word encountered there can also be traced back to its definition, and then the user can easily return to his original place in the manual. The positions of these links are known as *hot-spots* since they respond to mouse clicks. Hot-spots can also be embedded within diagrams, pictures or maps, allowing the user to focus his attention on aspects that interest him.

15.7.1   *Applications of hypermedia*

There are many applications of hypermedia, too many to describe in detail here. However, it is worth noting the type of domains in which hypermedia systems have proved successful, looking briefly at some example systems. Perhaps the most well-known commercial hypermedia system is HyperCard, which uses the metaphor of a card index, around which the user can navigate. Each card can hold text, diagrams, photographs, bitmaps and so on, and hot spots on the cards allow movement between cards. Cards may also contain forward and backward buttons and a home icon, to allow the user to move sequentially and start from scratch respectively. HyperCard can be used for a range of applications including information management, teaching and the like. It is most commonly used as a rapid prototyping tool for generating interactive systems. This application is discussed in more detail in Chapter 5.

Hypermedia are ideally suited to on-line manuals and other help system applications (see Chapter 12). They allow user-oriented access to the information, and support browsing. In addition the information can be organized hierarchically, with successive selections providing more detailed information. This supports the varying needs that users have, such as quick reference, usage information, full details and so on. Many commercial help systems now use hypermedia style help. Good examples are the Sun Guide system and HyperCard help.

Another common application is educational systems. Hypermedia provide an environment for the learner to explore, in his own time and at his own pace. The inclusion of animation and graphics can allow the user to see things happen as well as read about them. So, for example, animation can be used to simulate an experiment. Hypermedia also allow different subject matter to be related in numerous ways so that the learner can investigate the links between different subjects. An example of a hypermedia learning environment is Intermedia [188]. This is an hypermedia system built and used at Brown University to support teaching in subjects as varied as English Literature and Biology. The system includes text, diagrams, photos and so on. Both learners and teachers can add information

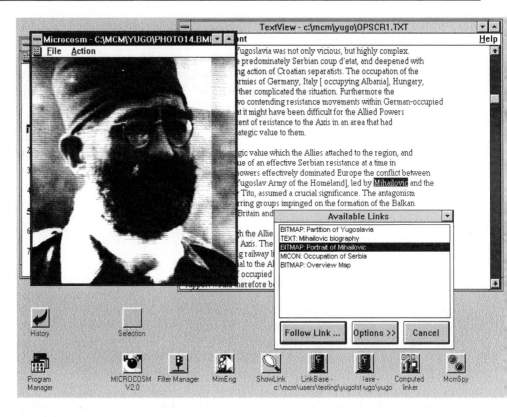

Figure 15.6   *Microcosm: an open hypermedia environment shown running a teaching application entitled 'The civil war in Yugoslavia 1941-45' (developed by the Departments of Electronics and Computer Science and History at the University of Southampton and used by permission)*

and links, giving students access to each other's opinions as well as those of their tutors. A map provides an overall view of the information for direct access and navigation, with links providing browsing facilities in the normal way. Intermedia has been successfully used for university level teaching.

Microcosm is an open hypermedia system, developed in the Electronics and Computer Science department at the University of Southampton and shown in Figure 15.6, which allows users to browse through large amounts of multi-media information by following links. Microcosm does not contain links explicitly hard-wired into its structure, but instead holds a database of link sources and destinations. Not only does this allow processes to examine the links divorced from their surrounding information, but allows links to be made to read-only media such as CD-ROM and video disks. Microcosm is able to integrate many different types of media, including other applications, and provides a set of viewing tools to look at text, bitmaps, video, audio and other component information media.

15.7.2   Problems with hypermedia

There are a number of problems with hypermedia, however, and these have reduced the range of applications. One problem is navigating the hypertext web. It
can be very difficult to determine exactly where one is in the hypertext web, and,
more worrying for a user, it can be difficult to work out how to return to home
base, or get to the end. This is a natural consequence of giving the user control
of his progress through the hypertext document, but the feeling of being lost in
hypertextual space is a daunting one that puts off many potential users. One solution to this is to provide a map of the hypertext document identifying the current
position of the reader within it. Links to home or end points can then be identified
and the user is less likely to get lost. There are still difficulties with the system:
each hypertext page may have been accessed from one of many different routes,
and so it provides no contextual information as to where it is. Large hypertext
documents will have either very complex, crowded maps, or will choose to show
only part of it, and the context presented to the user may not be enough for him to
feel confident in knowing where he is located.

Another problem is that since the information is presented in a more complex
structure, it is possible to miss out certain pages or items of information by moving
along routes that avoid them. This leads to uncertainty in the mind of a user,
who can find it difficult to determine if he has actually visited all the pages in
the hypertext system. This identifies a further problem: once information has
been retrieved, a paper version is often needed. Printing a document requires the
pages to be in a particular order, but hypertext does not support the concepts of
one single order. It can therefore be a difficult problem to get a hard copy of the
information that is required, since the user is responsible for structuring the way
in which it is presented. This is against the ethos of hypertext, which intends the
user to structure the information in the way which suits him best.

Both of these problems have been addressed by providing the user with 'recommended routes' through hypertext documents, but this somewhat defeats the
objectives of the system, and has not proved too popular. Another form of hypertext takes the form of 'levels of access' to a document. Different levels of access
privilege 'see' different amounts of information. A document structured in this
way may provide one level of access that only provides a brief overview of the
topic. The next level of access presents a fuller description of the system, whilst
the next level may also include information regarding the precise meaning of technical terms used in the system. The final level of access may also add historical
information and such like. The user can choose at which level he wants to read
the document, cutting out irrelevant information whilst obtaining all the necessary
details. Such a document only tends to be linear in nature, which makes navigating and printing it easier but removes the user choice in structuring his progress
through it.

15.8 **Animation and Video**

Improvements to the graphical presentation of information have taken a number of forms, most notably involving the use of animation, interactive compact disc video and real-time video. We will consider each of these in turn.

15.8.1 *Animation*

The advent of ever-faster processors has meant that the graphical capabilities of computer systems have become much better over the past few years, allowing more complex displays to be drawn. The ability to draw thousands of lines on the screen every second has meant that the range of possibilities for presenting information has been extended. One effect of this is that animation has become a more common element in systems. Animation is the term given to the addition of motion to images, making them move, alter and change in time. A simple example of animation in an interface is in the form of a clock. Digital clocks can flick by the seconds, whilst others imitate Salvador Dali and bend and warp one numeral into the next. Analog clocks have moving hour and minute hands, with an optional second hand sweeping round the clock face. Such a desktop accessory is quite common in a lot of interface setups, and the additional processing time required to produce such effects is no longer a major factor. Another common use for animation in current windowing systems is that of animating the cursor. Instead of simply having a basic pointer always on the screen, many interfaces now use the typical 16x16 bitmap that the cursor is made up of to indicate more complex information. We have seen in Chapter 3 that there are a number of different static cursors that are used, but animation takes this one stage further by adding motion to the images. This is usually done to indicate that some process is in progress, to confirm to the user that something is actually happening. By animating the cursor, messages do not need to be printed out to a window, making it a neat and concise way of presenting the desired information. On the Macintosh, work in progress is indicated by a watch icon, with the hands moving round and round, or by a spinning disk. One system uses a stick person apparently doing weight lifting, to show that heavy work is in progress, whilst another has an hour glass trickling down. Non-cursor process indicators usually take the form of a pop-up box with a moving slider in, or a stick person walking backwards and forwards.

Animation can be used to great effect to show the changes in data sets, where slowly fluctuating changes can be visualized with the help of rippling three-dimensional coloured surfaces, or abrupt changes shown by the sudden discontinuities in an otherwise regular motion. Data visualization makes great use of the computational power of modern computers and their high-quality graphics by producing accurate renderings of objects, real or virtual, and then altering and moving them in real time. New ways of representing data, especially changing data, allow users to gain new insights into the behaviour of systems they are trying to understand and makes the computer into an invaluable tool for understanding and discovery as well as for interpretation and mundane calculation.

Animation is also used in a manner similar to that in cartoons, where animated objects are used to perform particular functions for the user. For example, in an animated help system, a character can appear on the screen and interact with the user, guiding him through a number of stages of help before being dismissed. Such a guide can be endowed with a certain character, making the interaction less impersonal and more interesting for the user, who becomes more involved with the system and is happy to learn more about it.

15.8.2   *Video and digital video*

The idea of being able to store reasonable quantities of video, text, graphics and sound on one medium is fast being realized with the introduction of compact disc technologies. Indeed this medium is partially responsible for the burgeoning interest in multi-media, since it offers an affordable way for users to incorporate many different presentation and visualization styles into their work. The use of video extends the potential of the interface and gives the designer yet another tool and approach to displaying information. Compact discs store information digitally in a series of pits on a metal disc that is then protected by a clear laquer coating. This disc is read by a small laser beam reflected off the surface of the disc that picks up the presence or absence of the pits and therefore provides a binary signal. Compact discs have become the dominant form of storage medium in the domestic music market, replacing the vinyl record and cassette tape. Both the latter technologies are analog, and in the video field their equivalent is the videodisc. Previously the principal medium in the multi-media field, interactive videodiscs could store about half an hour of video on two sides of a 12-inch disc. One of their drawbacks was the limited nature of the interactivity that they allowed, whereas the promise of digital systems lies in the high degree of flexibility that ought to be possible.

There are a number of different CD approaches which are primarily distinguished by the different forms of compression that they use to get more on to less. *CD-I* has limited video and still image capability, and is targetted more at the domestic market. It is excellent for full screen animation rather than for video work, whilst *CD-XA* (Extended Architecture) represents a development of CD-I that better supports digital audio and still images. Full motion video is being served by *DVI* (Digital Video Interactive), competing with *UVC* (Universal Video Communications). DVI can place more than an hour of full motion video onto a single CD and technology is improving the compression and storage capabilities all the time. *Palenque* is an example of a DVI application. It is a prototype system, in which a user can learn by exploration and discovery. The user is allowed to wander around all the paths in a Mayan site, and is presented with video, still images, sounds and text that present information about many different aspects of the site. The system offers a variety of interaction modes and media to allow the user to access the database of information, ranging from video overviews to guided tours with an animated character, allowing the user to explore and interact with the system in many different ways. CD systems have found a niche market in the video games industry, since the interactive nature of the system and the high quality of graphics are both necessary components of the ever-refined video games. However, a number of computer manufacturers have recently brought out machines with integrated CD drives that are designed to be used as multimedia workstations, and so their use in education and training is likely to increase dramatically in the near future.

One example of the incorporation of video into the interface is QuickTime from Apple. QuickTime represents a standard format for the compression, storage and general format of images, and provides synchronization facilities to ensure constant playback speed and sound timing. Video clips can be loaded, viewed, edited and saved, and then incorporated into applications. Being such a new technology, the number of applications that use these techniques are limited, but are increasing all the time. It is difficult to assess the impact that these technologies will have, but it seems likely that they will be highly significant. Moving pictures are excellent at conveying information, and exert a fairly hypnotic hold over us; note the success of television. It is fair to say that many design practices will have to be updated to make the most of the possibilities that these techniques offer; moreover, it is also the case that people are unsure how to get the most out of such technology. The techniques required to gain maximum benefit from moving images are very different from those that are used for static or minimal motion displays, and designers do not have enough experience to start applying the relevant technology at the relevant time. It may well be that computer interface designers will have to study the techniques of the film makers and cartoonists before they start to discover the real benefits that these techniques can provide.

15.9   Gesture Recognition

Gesture is a component of human–computer interaction that has become the subject of attention in multi-modal systems. Being able to control the computer with certain movements of the hand would be advantageous in many situations where there is no possibility of typing, or when other senses are fully occupied. For some disabled users, such as the deaf, it offers a mode of communication that is familiar. But like speech and handwriting, gesture is user-dependent, subject to variation and co-articulation. The technology for capturing gestures is expensive; either a vision system (see below) or a dataglove (see Chapter 2) is needed. The dataglove provides easier access to highly accurate information, but is a relatively intrusive technology, requiring the user to wear the special Lycra glove. The interpretation of the sampled data is very difficult, since segmenting the gestures causes problems. A team from Toronto [63] has produced a gesture recognition system that translates hand movements into synthesized speech, using five neural networks working in parallel to learn and then interpret different parts of the inputs.

The Media Room at MIT uses a different approach in order to incorporate gestures into the interaction. The Media Room has one wall that acts as a large screen, with smaller touchscreens on either side of the user who sits in a central chair. The user can navigate through information using the touchscreens, or by joystick, or by voice. Gestures are incorporated by using a position-sensing cube attached to a wristband worn by the user. The *put that there* system uses this gestural information coupled with speech recognition to allow the user to indicate what should be moved where by pointing at it. This is a much more natural form of interaction than having to specify verbally what it is that has to be moved and describing where it has to go to, as well has having the advantage of conciseness. Such a short simple verbal statement is much more easily interpreted by the speech recognition system than a long and complex one, with the resolution of ambiguity done by interpreting the other mode of interaction, the gesture. Each modality supports the other. An extension to this has used the eyegaze system (see Chapter 2) instead of gesture recognition to control the display.

15.10 Computer Vision

Computer vision is a vast subject, and we are not attempting to summarize the achievements and problems in computer vision in a few paragraphs. However, in this chapter on multi-media systems, there is a role for discussing computer vision, since it represents an additional input channel for the computer. Video cameras can be relatively easily interfaced to many computers, and there are many algorithms available to process the resultant images. This provides rudimentary vision for the computer, and opens up a whole wealth of interaction possibilities.

With decent vision systems, it would be possible for computers to recognize their users and tailor the system to their perceived requirements. Computer vision may have a more profound effect on interaction, however, as it may allow the computer to perform its tasks independently of the user, and so make continuous interaction unnecessary.

Computer vision systems tend to be based on a 'bottom-up' approach, in which images are treated as a set of pixels which are progressively analyzed to extract meaning. A typical set of processing operations would be to take an input image and process it to remove noise and adjust the light levels. Edges would then be detected, and then reduced to one pixel wide, a process called thinning. These sets of disjoint lines would then be joined to produce shapes, and then higher level 3D information may be used to extract shape descriptions from the edges in the scene. Texture and colour can be used here to aid the process, until at the highest level a description of the scene in terms of objects and their relative positions is produced. However, the problems of computer vision are much greater than either speech or handwriting, and progress towards the goal of high-quality, human-like visual systems for machines is very slow. It is difficult to assess the impact that computer vision will have on interactive computer systems, but its importance should not be underrated.

15.11   Applications of Multi-media Systems

We have already considered a number of applications of multi-media systems, but there are two areas which deserve special mention. Designing interfaces which are accessible for all users, and which support those with special needs, is a continuing and important problem, attracting growing research interest. Virtual reality is catching the imagination not only of researchers but of the public and media and is liable to become a huge industry in time. We conclude this chapter by looking briefly at these two areas.

15.11.1   *Interfaces for users with special needs*

We noted in Chapter 1 that, although we can make general observations about human capabilities, users in fact have different needs and limitations. Interfaces are usually designed to cater for the 'average' user, but unfortunately this may exclude other user groups. Research on interfaces for users with special needs focuses on providing effective interactive systems for users whose needs are not met by standard computing approaches, usually because the standard interface uses an input or output channel which the user cannot use effectively.

The rise in the use of graphical interfaces reduces the possibilities for visually impaired users. In text based interaction, screen readers using synthesized speech or Braille output devices meant that such users had complete access to computers: input relied on touch typing, with these mechanisms providing the output. However, today the standard interface is graphical. Since it is not possible to use a screen reader or Braille output to represent pictures, access to computers, and therefore work involving computers, for visually impaired users has been reduced rather than expanded. A number of systems attempt to provide access to graphical interfaces for this user group, by adding sound to the interface — we have previously discussed Soundtrack which uses tones to represent menus. Outspoken is a Macintosh application which uses synthetic speech to make Macintosh applications available to visually impaired users. This has had some success but (in common with Soundtrack) suffers from the problem of the sheer amount of information that needs to be represented.

For users with speech and hearing impairments, multi-media systems provide a number of tools for communication, including synthetic speech and text-based communication and conferencing systems (see Chapter 13). Textual communication is slow which can lower the effectiveness of the communication. Predictive algorithms have been used to anticipate the words used and fill them in, to reduce the amount of typing required. Conventions can help to provide context, which is lost from face-to-face communication, for example, the 'smilie' (:-)) to indicate a joke. Facilities to allow turn-taking protocols to be established also help natural communication [125].

Users with physical disabilities vary in the amount of control and movement that they have over their hands, but many find the precision required in mouse control difficult. Speech input and output is an option for those without speech difficulties. An alternative is the Eyegaze system (Chapter 2) which tracks eye movements to control the cursor, or a keyboard driver which can be attached to the user's head. If the user is unable to control head movement, gesture and movement tracking can be used to allow the user control. If the user has limited use of a keyboard, a predictive system, such as the Reactive keyboard [154] can help, by anticipating the commands that are being typed and offering them for execution. This can cut the typing requirement considerably. Predictions are based on what the user has typed in this session or a previous one. The predictions therefore anticipate within the context in which the user is currently working (for example, operating system commands, programming text or free text). Figure 15.7 shows an interaction using the Reactive keyboard.

Finally, users with learning disabilities such as dyslexia can find textual information difficult. In severe cases speech input and output can alleviate the need to read and write and allow more accurate input and output. In cases where the problem is less severe, spelling correction facilities can help users. However, these need to be designed carefully: often conventional spelling correction programs are useless for dyslexic users since the programs do not recognize the word construction of such users. As well as simple transpositions of characters, dyslexic users may spell phonetically, and correction programs must be able to deal with these errors.

15.11.2   *Virtual reality*

Virtual reality (VR) refers to the computer-generated simulation of a world, or a sub-set of it, in which the user is immersed. It represents the state of the art in multi-media systems, but concentrates on the visual senses. The technology involved in virtual reality is quite elaborate, and is discussed briefly, followed by some of examples of virtual reality systems.

Since the user has to 'see' a new environment, a headset is usually used in a VR set up. With independent screens for each eye, in order to give a 3D image, the headset is a large, relatively cumbersome piece of head-mounted gear. Powering the headset are a couple of very fast graphics computers, one for each eye. Having to produce and render realistic images in real-time requires vast amount of computing power, and the resources for full realism are rarely available; they may not even exist as yet. This means that the world inhabited by the user tends to be 'blocky', with little variation in texture, and flat lighting. This makes the

```
$ mail                                        ↑ N
  cd news                                     ↑ W
cd news                                       ↑ N
cd rk/papers/ieee.computer                    ↑ L
cd rk/papers/ieee.computer

$ emacs paper.tex                             ↑ L
  emacs paper.tex

$ rm paper.tex.CKP paper.tex.BAK              ↑ L
  rm paper.tex.CKP paper.tex.BAK

$ wc -w paper.tex                             ↑ L
  wc -w paper.tex

$ readnews -n comp.sources.unix               ↑ N
  mail                                        ↑ W
mail                                          ↑ N
mail bdarragh%uncamult.bitnet@ucnet.ucalgary.c ↑ L
mail bdarragh%uncamult.bitnet@ucnet.ucalgary.c
```

User's dialogue with the reactive keyboard.
Only the last line in each group is actually executed.

Key	Description
↑ C (control-C)	Accept the next predicted character
↑ W	Accept the next predicted word
↑ L	Accept the whole predicted line
↑ N	Show the next alternative prediction
↑ P	Show the previous alternative prediction

reactive keyboard commands

Figure 15.7 *An interaction using the Reactive Keyboard (used by permission)*

calculations much simpler and achievable. As far as input to VR systems is concerned, a dataglove which captures gestural information is often used. Feedback can be incorporated into the glove, so that resistance is felt when grasping a virtual object. Speech recognition systems can also be incorporated, and, in general, audio feedback is utilized in some for or another. Stereo headphones are a simpler piece of VR kit, but at the other extreme a full body version of the dataglove is available too!

Being a new area, only made possible by the advent of very fast, high-performance computers, virtual reality has yet to see mass market applications, and most systems are primarily research projects. One such application is a game in 3D space, in which a user has to capture and manipulate blocks that materialize and float through space, using a disembodied hand controlled by a dataglove. If one manipulates the blocks correctly, one can capture the opponent's blocks, being careful to avoid hazards such as exploding cubes or similar. A more serious application is a medical one, in which a virtual operation can be carried out on the actual patient: the patient's scans provide data for a computer model of the body, which can then be operated on by a surgeon until she perfects the technique for that particular person. Once correct, the actual operation can be performed.

Another application of virtual reality is that of data visualization, particularly in the field of protein chemistry. Proteins are complex chemicals, made up of convoluted folded chains of simpler components known as amino acids. The particular acids involved, their order in the chain and the nature of the folding all contribute to the particular behaviour and function of the protein. In trying to understand the behaviour of particular proteins, scientists have turned to VR techniques to help them probe the secrets of these vital components of life. Work by Hubbard [88] has produced a virtual reality system using a headset and dataglove. The user dons the headset, and is immersed in a three-dimensional world where atomic dimensions become tangible distances and the protein exists like a ball of hairy twine. Using the dataglove the user can reach out into the space and grab hold of the molecule, twisting it this way and that to appreciate its complex structure better. The chain of amino acids can be followed from one end to the other, winding around and almost back on itself as the complex chemistry is created. A better knowledge of the structure has allowed the scientists to understand how some very complex proteins work; one particular protein reacts with specific enzymes but the reactive site is hidden deep inside the coiled structure. Data obtained during reactions and used in the system have showed that the protein opens up what is effectively a molecular trapdoor when the enzyme approaches, allowing it to dock with the reactive site. Once seen in animated form the nature of the reaction is obvious, but without this technique to visualize things, the situation is much less clear. In the VR setup, colour and shading are used in a primitive form to give dimension and depth to the images, but work is continuing on developing efficient algorithms on dedicated machines to allow more detailed imaging.

One interactive virtual reality application in widespread use is the flight simulator. A full cockpit system is placed in a hydraulically supported container, with large screens replacing the cockpit windows. Images are generated and projected onto the screens, whilst the box can be moved rapidly in any direction by the hydraulic rams. The visual information and physical motion simulate accurately the conditions encountered by aircraft, and flight simulators are used extensively in pilot training programmes. Landings can be practised, with the system responding to the commands of the pilot; perhaps descending too fast and off to one side, the pilot will have to correct the situation if he wishes to avoid a crash. Emergency situations can also be created, in which aircraft system malfunctions can be artificially created in order to train the pilot to take the correct course of corrective or life-preserving action.

The military is heavily involved in virtual reality, and the U.S. army has a full virtual reality set up in which war scenarios can be fought out with great realism, or training given about particular territories that are to be infiltrated. The increased realism at this stage is designed to save lives later on, when by being better prepared people are more able to cope with whatever arises. It is in such application areas that VR has been most used since the cost of the necessary equipment is negligible compared to the savings that can be made in terms of human life and expensive military hardware. More esoteric and less violent uses of VR have been proposed; the imagination is the limit! Since worlds with arbitrary physics and behaviours can be created, anything is possible within VR. One appealing suggestion is the idea of VR holidays — by walking into a VR environment, you can go on holiday to the tropical rain forest, go on safari, walk on the moon, fly over the cities of the world, sunbathe on a beach or ski in the mountains, all without moving from the room!

15.12   Summary

Multi-media and multi-modal systems offer a number of tools and techniques with which to enhance the interface. However, there is very little theory or even consensus about how and when to use such systems, and the facilities provided must be used with caution. Consider colour: even now, many years after it became widely available, there are many instances when it has been used very badly in interface design so that it influences interaction for the worse. The situation is much exaggerated with multi-media, multi-modal systems, and we may find that interface designers have to rely as much on the skills of cinematographers, animators and musicians as they do on graphic designers, psychologists and computer scientists. Disabled users may find systems that take full advantage of their capabilities so that their disability is minimized and not highlighted, whereas able-bodied people might find that interaction becomes natural, fun, efficient and effortless. We may all benefit from these newer interaction styles that utilize more of our senses in an involving interactive experience, but only if this is wisely done.

Exercises

15.1 What factors are likely to delay the widespread use of video in interfaces? What applications could benefit most from its use?

15.2 In Section 15.11.1, we look at alternative interfaces for users with special needs. How could standard interface design be improved to provide better access to these users?

15.3 Think of a set of naturally occurring sounds to represent the operations in a standard drawing package (for example, draw, move, copy, delete, rotate).

15.4 Experiment with HyperCard or another hypertext system if you have access to one. As you work through the system, draw a map of the links and connections. Is it clear where you are and where you can get to at any point? If not, how could this be improved?

15.5 Data visualization techniques have often increased our comprehension of phenomena: consider the effect that 3-D graphics has had on looking at complex models such as those of the atmosphere or the ocean, or in understanding the structure of molecules. What do you consider to be the areas that may benefit most from virtual reality visualization techniques?

15.6 Virtual reality has found a number of applications in the games market. Is this a suitable use of such technology? Discuss the possible benefits and disadvantages of exploiting leading edge technology in a leisure market.

15.7 What are the major achievements of computer vision? What are the major problems that still remain to be solved?

Recommended Reading

- E.J. Conklin, Hypertext: An Introduction and Survey, *IEEE Computer*, 20(9):17-41, September 1987.

  Review of hypertext.

- Alistair D.N. Edwards, editor. *Extra-ordinary Human–Computer Interaction*. Cambridge University Press, 1993.

  A collection of papers representing research on interfaces for users with special needs. The first of its kind.

- Alistair D.N. Edwards and Simon Holland, editors. *Multimedia Interface Design in Education*. Springer Verlag, 1993.

  The proceedings of a NATO Workshop in the topic — contains a range of articles on different applications of multi-media to education.

- Randy Pausch, Virtual Reality on Five Dollars a Day. In *Proceedings of ACM CHI'91*, pages 265–270, ACM Press, 1991.

  A paper describing how virtual reality systems can be built on a low budget.

- R. Beale and J. Finlay, editors. *Neural Networks and Pattern Recognition in Human–Computer Interaction*. Ellis Horwood, 1992.

  A collection containing several papers on multi-modal interaction, including gesture, speech and handwriting.

References

[1] G. Abowd. Agents: recognition and interaction models. In D. Diaper, D. Gilmore, G. Cockton, and B. Shackel, editors, *Human–Computer Interaction—Proceedings INTERACT'90*, pages 143–146. North-Holland, Amsterdam, 1990.

[2] G.D. Abowd and R. Beale. Users, systems and interfaces: A unifying framework for interaction. In D. Diaper and N. Hammond, editors, *HCI'91: People and Computers VI*, pages 73–87. Cambridge University Press, Cambridge, 1991.

[3] ACM Special Interest Group on Computer–Human Interaction Curriculum Development Group. ACM SIGCHI curricula for human–computer interaction. Technical report, ACM, New York, 1992.

[4] H. Alexander. *Formally-based Tools and Techniques for Human-Computer Dialogues*. Ellis Horwood, Chichester, UK, 1987.

[5] J.R. Anderson. *The architecture of cognition*. Harvard University Press, Cambridge, Massachusetts, 1983.

[6] J. Annett and K. D. Duncan. Task analysis and training design. *Occupational Psychology*, 41:211–221, 1967.

[7] A.D. Baddeley. *Human Memory: Theory and Practice*. Lawrence Erlbaum Associates, Hove, 1990. p.68ff.

[8] A.D. Baddeley and D.J.A. Longman. The influence of length and frequency of training sessions on rate of learning to type. *Ergonomics*, 21:627–635, 1978.

[9] Robert W. Bailey. *Human Performance Engineering: A Guide for System Designers*. Prentice Hall, Englewood Cliffs, New Jersey, 1982.

[10] P. Barnard. Cognitive resources and the learning of human-computer dialogs. In J.M. Carroll, editor, *Interfacing Thought: Cognitive Aspects of Human-Computer Interaction*, pages 112–158. MIT Press, Cambridge, Massachusetts, 1987.

[11] P. Barnard, M. Wilson, and A. MacLean. Approximate modelling of cognitive activity with an expert system: A theory-based strategy for developing an interactive design tool. *The Computer Journal*, 31(5):445–456, 1988.

[12] Philip Barnard. Interacting cognitive subsystems: A psycholinguistic approach to short-term memory. In A. Ellis, editor, *Progress in the psychology of language*, volume 2, chapter 6. Lawrence Erlbaum Associates, Hove, 1985.

[13] F.C. Bartlett. *Remembering*. Cambridge University Press, Cambridge, 1932.

[14] Len Bass and Joëlle Coutaz. *Developing Software for the User Interface*. Addison Wesley, New York, 1991.

[15] D. Bauer and C. R. Cavonius. Improving the legibility of visual display units through contrast reversal. In E. Grandjean and E. Vigliani, editors, *Ergonomic Aspects of Visual Display Units*. Taylor and Francis, 1980.

[16] Russell Beale and Janet Finlay, editors. *Neural Networks and Pattern Recognition in Human–Computer Interaction*. Ellis Horwood, Chichester, UK, 1992.

[17] M. Begeman, P. Cook, C. Ellis, M. Graf, G. Rein, and T. Smith. Project Nick: meetings augmentation and analysis. In D. Peterson, editor, *CSCW'86: Conference on Computer Supported Cooperative Work*, MCC Software Technology Program, Austin, Texas, 1986. ACM Press, New York.

[18] M. Blattner, D. Sumikawa, and R. Greenberg. Earcons and icons: their structure and common design principles. *Human Computer Interaction*, 4,1:11–44, 1989.

[19] W.A. Bousfield. The occurrence of clustering in recall of randomly arranged associates. *Journal of General Psychology*, 49:229–240, 1953.

[20] Susan Bovair, David E. Kieras, and Peter G. Polson. The acquisition and performance of text-editing skill: A cognitive complexity analysis. *Human-Computer Interaction*, 5(1):1–48, 1990.

[21] J. M. Bowers and S. D. Benford, editors. *Studies in Computer Supported Co-operative Work*. North-Holland, Amsterdam, 1991.

[22] John Bowers and John Churcher. Local and global structuring of computer mediated communication: developing linguistic perspectives on CSCW in COSMOS. In *CSCW'88: Proceedings of the Conference on Computer-Supported Cooperative Work*, pages 125–139, Portland, Oregon, September 26-28 1988. ACM SIGCHI and SIGOIS, ACM, New York.

[23] S. Brewster. Providing a model for the use of sound in usr interfaces. Technical Report YCS 169, University of York, Department of Computer Science, 1992.

[24] S. Burbeck. *Applications Programming in Smalltalk-80: How to Use Model-View-Controller (MVC)*. Softsmarts Inc., 1987.

[25] W. Buxton. A three-state model of graphical input. In D. Diaper, D. Gilmore, G. Cockton, and B. Shackel, editors, *Human–Computer Interaction—INTERACT'90*, pages 449–456. North-Holland, Amsterdam, 1990.

[26] William Buxton. There's more to interaction than meets the eye: Some issues in manual input. In Ronald M. Baecker and William A. S. Buxton, editors, *Readings in Human-Computer Interaction: A Multidisciplinary Approach*. Morgan Kaufmann, 1987.

[27] S.K. Card, T.P. Moran, and A. Newell. The keystroke-level model for user performance with interactive systems. *Communications of the ACM*, 23:396–410, 1980.

[28] S.K. Card, T.P. Moran, and A. Newell. *The Psychology of Human Computer Interaction*. Lawrence Erlbaum Associates, New Jersey, 1983.

[29] J.M. Carroll. Minimalist design for active users. In B. Shackel, editor, *Proceedings of IFIP conference, Interact'84*, pages 39–45. North-Holland, Amsterdam, 1984.

[30] J.M. Carroll and C. Carrithers. Blocking learner errors in a training wheels system. *Human Factors*, 26:377–389, 1984.

[31] John M. Carroll. Infinite detail and emulation in an ontologically minimized HCI. In Jane Carrasco Chew and John Whiteside, editors, *Empowering People — CHI'90 conference proceedings*, pages 321–327. ACM Press, New York, 1990.

[32] John M. Carroll and Mary Beth Rosson. Deliberated evolution: stalking the view matcher in design space. *Human-Computer Interaction*, 6(3 & 4):281–318, 1991.

[33] Human–computer interaction, 1991. 6(3 & 4), special journal double issue on Design Rationale.

[34] W.G. Chase and H. A. Simon. The mind's eye in chess. In W.G. Chase, editor, *Visual Information Processing*. Academic Press, New York, 1973.

[35] W.G. Chase and H. A. Simon. Perception in chess. *Cognitive Psychology*, 4:55–81, 1973.

[36] H.H. Clark and S.E. Brennan. Grounding in communication. In L.B. Resnick, J. Levine, and S.D. Behreno, editors, *Socially Shared Cognition*. American Psychological Association, Washington, 1991.

[37] H.H. Clark and E.F. Schaefer. Contributing to discourse. *Cognitive Science*, 13:259–294, 1989.

[38] Gilbert Cockton. Designing abstractions for communication control. In M. Harrison and H. Thimbleby, editors, *Formal Methods in Human–Computer Interaction*, chapter 10. Cambridge University Press, Cambridge, 1990.

[39] A.M. Collins and M.R Quillian. Retrieval time from semantic memory. *Journal of Verbal Learning and Verbal Behaviour*, 8:240–247, 1969.

[40] J. Conklin. Hypertext: an introduction and survey. *Computer*, pages 17–41, Sept 1987.

[41] J. Conklin and M.L. Begeman. gIBIS: A tool for all reasons. *Journal of the American Society for Information Science*, March 1989.

[42] Jeffrey E. Conklin and KC Burgess Yakemovic. A process-oriented approach to design rationale. *Human-Computer Interaction*, 6(3 & 4):357–391, 1991.

[43] G. F. Coulouris and H. W. Thimbleby. *HyperProgramming*. Addison-Wesley, Wokingham, 1993.

[44] J. Coutaz. Pac, an object oriented model for dialog design. In H. J. Bullinger and B. Shackel, editors, *Human–Computer Interaction—INTERACT'87*, pages 431–436. North-Holland, Amsterdam, 1987.

[45] Joëlle Coutaz. Architectural design for user interfaces. In *Proceedings of the 3rd European Conference of Software Engineering, ESEC'91*, 1991.

[46] C. Davenport and G. Weir. Plan recognition for intelligent advice and monitoring. In M.D. Harrison and A. F. Monk, editors, *HCI'86: People and Computers II*, pages 296–315. Cambridge University Press, Cambridge, 1986.

[47] A.D. DeGroot. *Thought and Choice in Chess*. Mouton, The Hague, 1965.

[48] A.D. DeGroot. Perception and memory versus thought. In B. Kleinmuntz, editor, *Problem Solving*. John Wiley and Sons, New York, 1966.

[49] Dan Diaper, editor. *Task Analysis for Human–Computer Interaction*. Ellis Horwood, Chichester, 1989.

[50] Dan Diaper. Task Analysis for Knowledge Descriptions (TAKD); the method and an example. In Dan Diaper, editor, *Task Analysis for Human–Computer Interaction*, chapter 4, pages 108–159. Ellis Horwood, Chichester, 1989.

[51] A.J. Dix. *Formal methods for interactive systems*, chapter 10. Academic Press, London, 1991.

[52] E.A. Dykstra and R.P. Carasik. Structure and support in cooperative environments: the amsterdam conversation environment. *International Journal of Man-Machine Studies*, 34:419–434, 1991.

[53] H. Ebbinghaus. *Uber das Gedactnis*. Dunker, 1885. Translated by H. Ruyer and C.E. Bussenius, 1913, Memory, Teacher's College, Columbia University.

[54] A. Edwards. Soundtrack: an auditory interface for blind users. *Human Computer Interaction*, 4,1:45–66, 1989.

[55] Alistair D.N. Edwards, editor. *Extra-ordinary Human–Computer Interaction*. Cambridge University Press, Cambridge, 1993.

[56] Alistair D.N. Edwards and Simon Holland, editors. *Multimedia Interface Design in Education*. Springer-Verlag, Berlin, 1993.

[57] C.A. Ellis, S.J. Gibbs, and G.L. Rein. Design and use of a group editor. In G. Cockton, editor, *Proceedings of the IFIP Engineering for Human Computer Interaction Conference*, pages 13–25. North-Holland, Amsterdam, 1990.

[58] C.A. Ellis, S.J. Gibbs, and G.L. Rein. Groupware: Some issues and experiences. *Communications of the ACM*, 34(1):38–58, January 1991.

[59] D. C. Engelbart and W. K. English. A research centre for augmenting human intellect. In *Proceedings Fall Joint Computing Conference*, pages 395–410. Thompson Book Co., Washington, D.C., Dec. 1968.

[60] Douglas C. Engelbart. A conceptual framework for the augmentation of man's intellect. In Paul William Howerton and David C. Weeks, editors, *Vistas in Information Handling*, volume 1, pages 1–29. Spartan Books, Washington, 1963.

[61] J. Erlandson and J. Holm. Intelligent help systems. *Information and Software Technology*, 29,3:115–121, 1987.

[62] Michael W. Eysenck and Mark T. Keane. *Cognitive Psychology: A Student's Handbook*. Lawrence Erlbaum Associates, New Jersey, 1990.

[63] S.S. Fels and G. E. Hinton. Building adaptive interfaces with neural networks: the glove-talk pilot study. In D. Diaper, D. Gilmore, G. Cockton, and B. Shackel, editors, *Proceedings of Interact'90*, pages 683–687. North-Holland, Amsterdam, 1990.

[64] G. Fischer, A. Lemke, and T. Schwab. Knowledge-based help systems. In *Human Factors in Computing Systems CHI'85 Proceedings*, pages 161–167, 1985.

[65] Robert S. Fish, Robert E. Kraut, and Barbara L. Chalfonte. The VideoWindow system in informal communications. In *CSCW'90: Proceedings of the Conference on Computer-Supported Cooperative Work*, pages 1–11, Los Angeles, CA, October 1990. ACM SIGCHI and SIGOIS, ACM Press, New York.

[66] P.M. Fitts and M.I. Posner. *Human Performance*. Wadsworth Publishing, 1967.

[67] Margaret M. Gardiner and Bruce Christie, editors. *Applying Cognitive Psychology to User–Interface Design.* John Wiley and Sons, Chichester, 1987.

[68] W. Gaver. Auditory icons: using sound in computer interfaces. *Human Computer Interaction,* 2,2:167–177, 1986.

[69] W. Gaver. The sonicfinder: an interface that uses auditory icons. *Human Computer Interaction,* 4,1:67–94, 1989.

[70] W. Gaver and R. Smith. Auditory icons in large-scale collaborative environments. In D. Diaper, D. Gilmore, G. Cockton, and B. Shackel, editors, *Proceedings of Interact'90,* pages 735–740. North-Holland, Amsterdam, 1990.

[71] William W. Gaver, Randall B. Smith, and Tim O'Shea. Effective sounds in complex situations: The ARKola simulation. In S.P Robertson, G.M. Olson, and J.S. Olson, editors, *Reaching through technology — CHI'91 conference proceedings,* pages 85–90. Human Factors in Computing Systems, ACM Press, New York, April 1991.

[72] William W. Gaver, Randall B. Smith, and Tim O'Shea. Effective sounds in complex situations: The ARKola simulation. In S.P Robertson, G.M. Olson, and J.S. Olson, editors, *Reaching through technology — CHI'91 conference proceedings,* pages 85–90. Human Factors in Computing Systems, ACM Press, New York, April 1991.

[73] M.L. Gick and K.J. Holyoak. Analogical problem solving. *Cognitive Psychology,* 12:306–355, 1980.

[74] E.B. Goldstein. *Sensation and Perception, 3rd Edition.* Wadsworth, 1989.

[75] John D. Gould, Stephen J. Boies, Stephen Levy, John T. Richards, and Jim Schoonard. The 1984 Olympic message system: A test of behavioural principles of system design. In Jenny Preece and Laurie Keller, editors, *Human-Computer Interaction,* chapter 12. Prentice-Hall, Hemel Hempstead, 1990.

[76] Saul Greenberg, editor. *Computer-Supported Cooperative Work and Groupware.* Academic Press, New York, 1991.

[77] J. Grudin. Why CSCW application fail: Problems in the design and evaluation of organizational interfaces. In *CSCW'88: Proceedings of the Conference on Computer Supported Cooperative Work,* pages 85–94, Portland, Oregon, September 26-28 1988. ACM SIGCHI and SIGOIS, ACM, New York.

[78] J. Grudin. The case against user interface consistency. *Communications of the ACM,* 4(3):245–264, 1989.

[79] M. Harrison and H. Thimbleby, editors. *Formal Methods in Human–Computer Interaction.* Cambridge University Press, Cambridge, 1990.

[80] H. Rex. Hartson, Antonio C. Siochi, and Deborah Hix. The UAN: A user-oriented representation for direct manipulation. *ACM Transactions on Information Systems*, 8(3):181–203, July 1990.

[81] The HCI Service, Department of Trade and Industry, UK. *HCI Tools & Methods Handbook*, 1991.

[82] M. Helander, editor. *Handbook of Human–Computer Interaction*. North-Holland, Amsterdam, 1988. Part II: User interface design.

[83] M. Helander, editor. *Handbook of Human–Computer Interaction*. North-Holland, Amsterdam, 1988. Part V: Tools for Design and Evaluation.

[84] Dan Heller. *XView Programming Manual*, volume Seven of *The X Window System*. O'Reilly and Associates, Inc., 1990.

[85] B. Hewitt, N. Gilbert, M. Jirotka, and S. Wilbur. Theories of multi-party interaction. Technical report, Social and Computer Sciences Research Group, University of Surrey and Queen Mary and Westfield Colleges, University of London, 1990.

[86] Deborah Hix. Generations of user-interface management systems. *IEEE Software*, 7(5):77–87, September 1990.

[87] R. C. Houghton. On-line help systems: a conspectus. *Communications of the ACM*, 27, 2, 1984.

[88] R. E. Hubbard. Molecular graphics: From pen plotter to virtual reality. In A. Monk, D. Diaper, and M. D. Harrison, editors, *HCI'92: People and Computers VII*, pages 21–27. Cambridge University Press, Cambridge, 1992.

[89] D. A. Huffman. A method for the construction of minimum-redundancy codes. *Proceedings of the IRE*, 40, 1952.

[90] E. L. Hutchins, J. D. Hollan, and D. A. Norman. Direct manipulation interfaces. In D. A. Norman and S. W. Draper, editors, *User Centered System Design*, pages 87–124. Lawrence Erlbaum Associates, New Jersey, January 1986.

[91] Hiroshi Ishii and Naomi Miyake. Towards an open shared workspace: computer and video fusion approach of TeamWorkStation. *Communications of the ACM*, 34(12):37–50, December 1991.

[92] R.J.K. Jacob. Survey and examples of specification techniques for user-computer interfaces. Technical report, Naval Research Laboratory, Washington, D.C., 1983.

[93] Peter Johnson. *Human–Computer Interaction: psychology, task analysis and software engineering*. McGraw Hill, London, 1992.

[94] Patrick W. Jordan, Stephen W. Draper, Kirsteen K. MacFarlane, and Shirley-Anne McNulty. Guessability, learnability and experienced user performance. In D. Diaper and N. Hammond, editors, *HCI'91: People and Computers VI*, pages 237–245. British Computer Society Special Interest Group on Human-Computer Interaction, Cambridge University Press, Cambridge, 1991.

[95] Alan Kay and Adele Goldberg. Personal dynamic media. *IEEE Computer*, 10(3):31–42, March 1977.

[96] D.E. Kieras and P.G. Polson. An approach to the formal analysis of user complexity. *International Journal of Man-Machine Studies*, 22:365–394, 1985.

[97] C. Knowles. Can cognitive complexity thoery (CCT) produce an adequate measure of system usability? In Jones and Winder, editors, *HCI'88: People and Computers IV*, pages 291–307. Cambridge University Press, Cambridge, 1988.

[98] W. Kohler. *The mentality of apes (2nd edition)*. Harcourt Brace, New York, 1927.

[99] Glenn E. Krasner and Stephen T. Pope. A cookbook for using the model-view-controller user interface paradigm in Smalltalk-80. *JOOP*, 1(3), August 1988.

[100] J.E. Laird, A. Newell, and P. Rosenbloom. Soar: an architecture for general intelligence. *Artificial Intelligence*, 33:1–64, 1987.

[101] Jintai Lee and Kum-Yew Lai. What's in a design rationale. *Human-Computer Interaction*, 6(3 & 4):251–280, 1991.

[102] M.D.P. Leland, R.S. Fish, and R.E. Kraut. Collaborative document production using quilt. In *CSCW'88: Proceedings of the Conference on Computer Supported Cooperative Work*, pages 206–215, Portland, Oregon, September 26-28 1988. ACM SIGCHI and SIGOIS, ACM, New York.

[103] W. E. Mackay. EVA: An experimental video annotator for symbolic analysis of video data. *SIGCHI Bulletin: Special issue on video as a research and design tool*, 21, 1:68–71, 1989.

[104] I. Scott MacKenzie, Abigail Sellen, and William Buxton. A comparison of input devices in elemental pointing and dragging tasks. In S.P. Robertson, G.M. Olson, and J.S. Olson, editors, *Reaching through technology — CHI'91 conference proceedings*, pages 161–166. Human Factors in Computing Systems, ACM Press, New York, April 1991.

[105] Allan MacLean, Richard M. Young, Victoria M.E. Bellotti, and Thomas P. Moran. Questions, options, and criteria: elements of design space analysis. *Human-Computer Interaction*, 6(3 & 4):201–250, 1991.

[106] N.R.F. Maier. Reasoning in humans II: The solution of a problem and its appearance in consciousness. *Journal of Comparative Psychology*, 12:181–194, 1931.

[107] T.W. Malone, K.R. Grant, K. Lai, R. Rao, and D. Rosenblitt. Semistructured messages are surprisingly useful for computer supported coordination. *ACM Transactions on Office Information Systems*, 5(2):115–131, 1987.

[108] Marilyn Mantei. Capturing the capture lab concepts: a case study in the design of computer supported meeting environments. In *CSCW'88: Proceedings of the Conference on Computer-Supported Cooperative Work*, pages 257–270, Portland, Oregon, September 26-28 1988. ACM SIGCHI and SIGOIS, ACM, New York.

[109] M.V. Mason. Adaptive command prompting in an on-line documentation system. *International Journal of Man-Machine Studies*, 25,1:33–51, 1986.

[110] Deborah J. Mayhew. *Principles and guidelines in software and user interface design*. Prentice-Hall, Englewood Cliffs, New Jersey, 1992.

[111] R. J. McCall. PHI: A conceptual foundation for design hypermedia. *Design Studies*, 12(1):30–41, 1991.

[112] John A. McDermid, editor. *The Software Engineer's Reference Book*. Butterworth-Heinemann, 1991.

[113] A. Mével and T. Guéguen. *Smalltalk-80*. Macmillan Education, Basingstoke, 1987.

[114] G.A. Miller. The magical number seven, plus or minus two: some limits on our capacity to process information. *Psychological Review*, 63,2:81–97, 1956.

[115] A. Monk, P. Wright, J. Haber, and L. Davenport. *Improving your human computer interface: a practical approach*. Prentice Hall International UK, Hemel Hempstead, 1993.

[116] A.F. Monk. Mode errors: a user-centred analysis and some preventative measures using keying contingent sound. *International Journal of Man-Machine Studies*, 24, 1986.

[117] Andrew Monk, editor. *Fundamentals of Human Computer Interaction*. Academic Press, London, 1985.

[118] P. Muter, S.A. Latremouille, W.C. Treurniet, and P. Beam. Extended reading of continuous text on television screens. *Human Factors*, 24:501–508, 1982.

[119] Brad A. Myers. *Creating User Interfaces by Demonstration*. Academic Press, New York, 1988.

[120] Brad A. Myers. User-interface tools: Introduction and survey. *IEEE Software*, 6(1):47–61, January 1989.

[121] Brad A. Myers and Mary Beth Rosson. Survey on user interface programming. In Penny Bauersfeld, John Bennett, and Gene Lynch, editors, *CHI'92 Conference Proceedings on Human Factors in Computing Systems*, pages 195–202. ACM Press, New York, 1992.

[122] C.M. Neuwirth, D.S. Kaufer, R. Chandhok, and J.H. Morris. Issues in the design of computer support for co-authoring and commenting. In *CSCW'90: Proceedings of the Conference on Computer-Supported Cooperative Work*, pages 183–195, Los Angeles, CA, October 1990. ACM SIGCHI and SIGOIS, ACM, New York.

[123] A. Newell and H. Simon. *Human Problem Solving*. Prentice Hall, Englewood Cliffs, New Jersey, 1972.

[124] A. Newell, G. Yost, J. E. Laird, P. S. Rosenbloom, and E. Altmann. Formulating the problem-space computational model. In R. F. Rashid, editor, *CMU Computer Science: a 25th Anniversary Commemorative*, chapter 11. ACM Press, New York, 1991.

[125] A.F. Newell, J. L. Arnott, A. Y. Cairns, I.W. Ricketts, and P. Gregor. Intelligent systems for speech and language impaired people: a portfolio of research. In Alistair D.N. Edwards, editor, *Extra-ordinary Human–Computer Interaction*. Cambridge University Press, Cambridge, 1993 (In press).

[126] J. Nielsen and R. Molich. Heuristic evaluation of user interfaces. In *Empowering people — CHI'90 conference proceedings*. ACM Press, New York, 1990.

[127] Jakob Nielsen. *Usability Engineering*. Academic Press, New York, 1992.

[128] Jakob Nielsen. The usability engineering life cycle. *IEEE Computer*, 25(3):12–22, March 1992.

[129] D.A. Norman. *The Psychology of Everyday Things*. Basic Books, 1988.

[130] Donald A. Norman and Stephen W. Draper, editors. *User-Centred System Design: New Perspectives on Human-Computer Interaction*. Lawrence Erlbaum Associates, New Jersey, 1986.

[131] Dan Olsen. *User Interface Management Systems: Models and Algorithms*. Morgan Kaufmann Publishers, 1991.

[132] Dan R. Olsen. Propositional Production Systems for dialogue description. In J.C. Chew and J. Whiteside, editors, *Empowering People — CHI'90 Conference Proceedings*, pages 57–63. Human Factors in Computing Systems, ACM Press, New York, 1990.

[133] Judith S. Olson, Gary M. Olson, Lisbeth A. Mack, and Pierre Wellner. Concurrent editing: the group's interface. In D Diaper, D Gilmore, G Cockton, and B Shackel, editors, *Human–Computer Interaction—INTERACT'90*, pages 835–840. North-Holland, Amsterdam, 1990.

[134] Open Software Foundation. *OSF/Motif Style Guide*. Prentice Hall, 1991.

[135] Randy Pausch. Virtual reality on five dollars a day. In *Reaching through technology — CHI'91 conference proceedings*, pages 265–270. ACM Press, New York, 1991.

[136] S.J. Payne and T.R.G. Green. Task-action grammars: a model of mental representation of task languages. *Human-Computer Interaction*, 2(2):93–133, 1986.

[137] G. Pfaff and P.J.W. ten Hagen, editors. *Seeheim Workshop on User Interface Management Systems*. Springer-Verlag, Berlin, 1985.

[138] I. Pitt and A. Edwards. Navigating the interface by sound for blind users. In D. Diaper and N. Hammond, editors, *HCI'91: People and Computers VI*, pages 373–383. British Computer Society Special Interest Group on Human-Computer Interaction, Cambridge University Press, Cambridge, 1991.

[139] M.J. Plasmeijer. Input tools - a language model for interaction and process communication. Technical report, de Katholieke Universiteit to Nijmegen, 1981.

[140] M. E. Pollack. Information sought and information provided: an empirical study of user/expert dialogues. In L. Borman and B. Curtis, editors, *Proceedings of CHI'85*, pages 155–160. ACM Press, New York, 1985.

[141] P. Polson, C. Lewis, J. Rieman, and C. Wharton. Cognitive walkthroughs: A method for theory-based evaluation of user interfaces. *International Journal of Man-Machine Studies*, 1992.

[142] L.R. Posner, R.M. Baecker, and M.M. Mantei. How people write together. Technical report, Computer Systems Research Institute and Department of Computer Science, University of Toronto, 6 Kings College Road, Toronto, Ontario, M5S 1A1, Canada., 1991.

[143] L. Postman and L.W. Phillips. Short-term temporal changes in free recall. *Quarterly Journal of Experimental Psychology*, 17:132–138, 1965.

[144] C. Potts and G. Bruns. Recording the reasons for design decisions. In *Proceedings of 10th International Conference on Software Engineering*, pages 418–427, 1988.

[145] J.R. Quinlan. Discovering rules by induction from large collections of data. In D. Michie, editor, *Expert systems in the Micro-Electronic Age*. Edinburgh University Press, Edinburgh, 1979.

[146] P. Reisner. Formal grammar and human factors design of an interactive graphics system. *IEEE Transactions on Software Engineering*, SE-7(2):229–240, 1981.

[147] Howard Rheingold. *Tools for Thought*. Prentice Hall, Englewood Cliffs, New Jersey, 1985.

[148] E. Rich and K. Knight. *Artificial Intelligence, 2nd Edition*. McGraw Hill, New York, 1991.

[149] H. Rittel and W. Kunz. Issues as elements of information systems. Working paper #131, Institut fur Grundlagen der Planung I.A., University of Stuttgart, 1970.

[150] C. Robson. *Experiment, Design and Statistics in Psychology (2nd ed.)*. Penguin, Harmondsworth, 1985.

[151] Tom Rodden. A survey of CSCW systems. *Interacting with Computers*, 3(3):319–353, 1991.

[152] Franz Schiele and Thomas Green. HCI formalisms and cognitive psychology: the case of task-action grammars. In M. Harrison and H. Thimbleby, editors, *Formal Methods in Human–Computer Interaction*, chapter 2. Cambridge University Press, Cambridge, 1990.

[153] K. Severinson Eklundh. Dialogue processes in computer-mediated communication: A study of letters in the com system. Technical report, Linkoping Studies in Arts and Science, 1986.

[154] S.Greenberg, J. Darragh, D. Maulsby, and I. H. Witten. Predictive interfaces: What will they think of next? In Alistair D.N. Edwards, editor, *Extra-ordinary Human–Computer Interaction*. Cambridge University Press, Cambridge, 1993 (In press).

[155] Andrew Shepherd. Analysis and training in information technology tasks. In Dan Diaper, editor, *Task Analysis for Human–Computer Interaction*, chapter 1, pages 15–55. Ellis Horwood, Chichester, 1989.

[156] B. Shneiderman. The future of interactive systems and the emergence of direct manipulation. *Behaviour and Information Technology*, 1(3):237–256, 1982.

[157] B. Shneiderman. *Designing the User Interface: Strategies for Effective Human–Computer Interaction*. Addison-Wesley, New York, 1987.

[158] Simon Shum. *A Cognitive Analysis of Design Rationale Representation*. D.Phil. thesis, University of York, Department of Psychology, 1991.

[159] SIGCHI Bulletin Special issue on video as a research and design tool, 1989. 21(2).

[160] T. Simon. Analysing the scope of cognitive models in human-computer interaction: A trade-off approach. In Jones and Winder, editors, *HCI'88: People and Computers IV*, pages 79–93. Cambridge University Press, Cambridge, 1988.

[161] R. B. Smith. The alternate reality kit - an animated environment for creating interactive simulations. In *Proceedings of Workshop on Visual Languages*, pages 99–106, Dallas, Texas, June 1986. IEEE.

[162] Randall B. Smith, Tom O'Shea, Claire O'Malley, Eileen Scanlon, and Josie Taylor. Preliminary experiments with a distributed, multimedia, problem solving environment. In J. M. Bowers and S. D. Benford, editors, *Studies in Computer Supported Cooperative Work*, pages 31–48. North-Holland, Amsterdam, 1991.

[163] S. L. Smith and J. N. Mosier. Guidelines for designing user interface software. Mitre Corporation Report MTR–9420, Mitre Corporation, 1986.

[164] Ian Sommerville. *Software Engineering*. Addison-Wesley, Wokingham, fourth edition, 1992.

[165] J. M. Spivey. *The Z Notation: A Reference Manual*. Prentice-Hall International, Hemel Hempstead, 1988.

[166] M. Stefik, D.G. Bobrow, G. Foster, S. Lanning, and D. Tatar. WYSIWIS revisited: early experiences with multiuser interfaces. *ACM Transactions on Office Information Systems*, 5(2):147–167, 1987.

[167] L. Suchman. *Plans and Situated Actions: The Problem of Human Machine Interaction*. Cambridge University Press, Cambridge, 1987.

[168] Lucy A. Suchman and Randall H. Trigg. A framework for studying research collaboration. In D. Peterson, editor, *CSCW'86: Conference on Computer Supported Cooperative Work*, pages 221–228, MCC Software Technology Program, Austin, Texas, December 1986. ACM Press, New York.

[169] B. Sufrin. Formal specification of a display editor. *Science of Computer Programming*, 1:157–202, 1982.

[170] Sun Microsystems, Inc. OPEN LOOK *Graphical User Interface Application Style Guidelines*. Addison-Wesley, 1990.

[171] Jimmy A. Sutton and Ralph H. Sprague Jr. A study of display generation and management in interactive business applications. Technical Report RJ2392, IBM, 1978.

[172] John C. Tang and Scott L. Minneman. VideoWhiteboard: video shadows to support remote collaboration. In S.P Robertson, G.M. Olson, and J.S. Olson, editors, *Reaching through technology — CHI'91 conference proceedings*, pages

315–322. Human Factors in Computing Systems, ACM Press, New York, April 1991.

[173] Harold Thimbleby. Design of interactive systems. In John A. McDermid, editor, *The Software Engineer's Reference Book*, chapter chapter 57. Butterworth-Heinemann, 1991.

[174] Harold W. Thimbleby. *User Interface Design*. ACM Press, Addison-Wesley, New York, 1990.

[175] M.A. Tinker. *Bases for Effective Reading*. University of Minesota Press, 1965.

[176] Roger Took. Surface interaction: a paradigm and model for separating application and interface. In J.C. Chew and J. Whiteside, editors, *Empowering People — CHI'90 Conference Proceedings*, pages 35–42. Human Factors in Computing Systems, ACM Press, New York, 1990.

[177] R. H. Trigg. Computer support for transcribing recorded activity. *SIGCHI Bulletin: Special issue on video as a research and design tool*, 21, 1:72–74, 1989.

[178] C. Turk and J. Kirkham. *Effective Writing (2nd ed.)*. E. and F.N. Spon, 1989.

[179] J. van de Bos and R. Plasmeijer. Input-output tools: a language facility for interactive and real time systems. *IEEE Transactions on Software Engineering*, SE-9(3):247–259, 1983.

[180] Paul Walsh. Analysis for task object modelling (ATOM): towards a method of integrating task analysis with Jackson system development for user interface software design. In Dan Diaper, editor, *Task Analysis for Human–Computer Interaction*, pages 186–209. Ellis Horwood, Chichester, 1989.

[181] W. H. Warren and R. R. Verbrugge. Auditory perception of breaking and bouncing events: a case study in ecological acoustics. *Journal of Experimental Psychology: Human Perception and Performance*, 10:704–712, 1984.

[182] P.C. Wason. Reasoning. In B.M. Foss, editor, *New Horizons in Psychology*. Penguin, Harmondsworth, 1966.

[183] A. Wexelblat. Building collaborative interfaces. CHI'91 Tutorial No. 28, 1991.

[184] John Whiteside, John Bennett, and Karen Holtzblatt. Usability engineering: Our experience and evolution. In Martin Helander, editor, *Handbook of Human-Computer Interaction*. North-Holland, Amsterdam, 1988.

[185] T. Winograd and F. Flores. *Understanding computers and cognition : a new foundation for design*. Addison-Wesley, New York, 1986.

[186] Terry Winograd. A language/action perspective on the design of cooperative work. In Irene Greif, editor, *Computer–Supported Cooperative Work: A Book of Readings*, pages 623–651. Kaufmann, 1988.

[187] Ian H. Witten, Harold W. Thimbleby, George Coulouris, and Saul Greenberg. Liveware: a new approach to sharing data in social networks. *International Journal of Man-Machine Studies*, 34:337–348, 1991.

[188] N. Yankelovich, B.J. Haan, N. K. Meyrowitz, and S. M. Drucker. Intermedia: the concept and construction of a seamless information environment. *IEEE Computer*, pages 81–96, January 1988.

[189] Richard M. Young and Thomas R. G. Green. Programmable user models for predictive evaluation of interface designs. In K. Bice and C. Lewis, editors, *Proceedings of CHI'89: Human Factors in Computing Systems*, pages 15–19. ACM Press, New York, 1989.

Index